NEPALIS INSIDE AND OUTSIDE NEPAL

The Japanese Association for South Asian Studies
Established in 1988

- **Office Bearers as of 1 November 2006**

President
Hiroshi Ishii, Professor Emeritus, Tokyo University of Foreign Studies

General Secretary
Shingo Einoo, University of Tokyo

Members of the Board of Executive Directors
Norio Kondo, Institute of Developing Economies
Yoshifumi Mizuno, Tokyo University of Foreign Studies
Tsukasa Mizushima, University of Tokyo
Fumiko Oshikawa, Kyoto University
Masahiro Shimoda, University of Tokyo
Akio Tanabe, Kyoto University
Shinkichi Taniguchi, Hitotsubashi University
Kohei Wakimura, Osaka City University

- **Head Office** (until September 2008)

c/o Institute of Oriental Culture, University of Tokyo
7-3-1 Hongo, Bunkyo-ku, Tokyo, 113-0033, Japan
Fax. +81-3-5841-5898
Email. jasas@ioc.u-tokyo.ac.jp
http://wwwsoc.nii.ac.jp/jasas/index-e.html

- **Publications in English**

1 *JJASAS (Journal of the Japanese Association for South Asian Studies)*, (annual publication in Japanese and English, the current issue: No. 18)

2 Japanese Studies on South Asia Series

No. 1 H. Kotani ed., *Caste System, Untouchability and the Depressed*, Manohar, New Delhi, 1997.

No. 2 N. Karashima ed., *Kingship in Indian History*, Manohar, New Delhi, 1999.

No. 3 S. Maeda ed., *The Way to Liberation*, Manohar, New Delhi, 2000.

No. 4 S. Einoo and J. Takashima eds., *From Material to Deity*, Manohar, New Delhi, 2005.

No. 5 H. Okahasi ed., *Emerging New Industrial Spaces and Regional Developments in India*, Manohar, New Delhi, 2007.

No. 6 H. Ishii, D.N. Gellner, and K. Nawa eds., *Social Dynamics in Northern South Asia*, Vol. 1: *Nepalis Inside and Outside Nepal*, Manohar, New Delhi, 2007.

No. 7 H. Ishii, D.N. Gellner, and K. Nawa eds., *Social Dynamics in Northern South Asia*, Vol. 2: *Political and Social Transformations in North India and Nepal*, Manohar, New Delhi, 2007.

Japanese Studies on South Asia No. 6

Social Dynamics in Northern South Asia

Volume 1

Nepalis Inside and Outside Nepal

Edited by

HIROSHI ISHII
DAVID N. GELLNER
KATSUO NAWA

MANOHAR
2020

First published 2007
First paperback edition 2020

ISBN 978-93-90035-23-6

Published by
Ajay Kumar Jain *for*
Manohar Publishers & Distributors
4753/23 Ansari Road, Daryaganj
New Delhi 110 002

Printed at
Replika Press Pvt. Ltd.

Contents

Tables and Figures

Preface

In 1997 the Japanese Association for South Asian Studies initiated an academic series entitled 'Japanese Studies on South Asia' under an agreement with Manohar Publishers & Distributors. The initial purpose of the series was (and remains) to introduce the work of Japanese scholars of South Asia to the international academic community. So far, five volumes have been published in this series and the contributors are Japanese authors (previous volumes in the series are listed on the fly leaf). Unlike these previous volumes, the present set, consisting of two volumes, contains articles by scholars from various countries and Japanese scholars make up just half of the authors.

The present volumes (i.e. *Social Dynamics in Northern South Asia*, Vol. 1: *Nepalis Inside and Outside Nepal* and Vol. 2: *Political and Social Transformations in North India and Nepal*) are the outcome of two international workshops held in February and June 2004 at the Research Institute for Languages and Cultures of Asia and Africa (ILCAA or AA-ken), Tokyo University of Foreign Studies, Tokyo. The workshops were entitled 'The Dynamics of Social and Political Change in Nepal' and 'Social Dynamics in Northern South Asia' and included ten and twenty-one papers respectively.

This collaborative study began with two institutional research projects, each with around twenty members (all Japanese except for one Nepali scholar based in Japan). In its preparatory stage, seminars were held as part of a regular research project of the Institute of Oriental Culture, the University of Tokyo 'Reconsidering Anthropological Studies in the Northern Part of South Asia' organized by Katsuo Nawa in 2002. In 2003, an ILCAA research project entitled 'Comparative Study of Sociocultural Changes: On Changes in Northern South Asia' was organized by Hiroshi Ishii. David Gellner joined ILCAA as a visiting research scholar in September 2003. The idea of the international workshops emerged during occasional discussions between them. The main aim of the projects was to achieve a better understanding of the societies and cultures of northern South Asia focusing on various aspects of change in the region.

Revised versions of all but two of the papers from the two conferences have been incorporated in the present volumes. However, in order to group the papers thematically, and in view of the preponderance of papers on Nepal, we considered it appropriate in producing two edited volumes to reorganize the order in which the papers had been originally presented. Thus in the first volume (*Nepalis Inside and Outside Nepal*) we have the following four parts:

1. Urbanization, Ethnicity, and Occupation
2. Marriage, Kinship, and Transformation of Intimacy
3. Transnational Links Inside and Outside Nepal
4. Nepal as Viewed from the Indian Himalayas

In the second volume (*Political and Social Transformations in North India and Nepal*) the subdivisions are as follows:

1. Local Political and Social Change
2. Transformations of Religious Identities and Practices
3. Forms of 'Secular' Activism: Resistance, Negotiation, and Violence and 'Afterword'.

Although the first volume contains chapters on Nepal only (except for the last one), it is impossible, as the book's title implies, to treat modern Nepal in isolation. It is very much a part of the wider region – northern South Asia – indicated by the umbrella title of the set. And at the same time, Nepalis, as described in several chapters in the volume, have forged substantial transnational links with many countries further afield, not least Japan. The final chapter in *Nepalis Inside and Outside Nepal*, by Gerald Berreman, puts forward explicit comparisons with the Indian Himalayas to the west of Nepal in a form which deserves to stimulate debate and further research from Nepal and Himalayan specialists.

It is necessary here to mention what we mean by 'northern South Asia' and why we find it meaningful to see it as one area. We use the term to include north and central India (i.e. India excluding the Dravidian-speaking areas), Pakistan, Bangladesh, Nepal, and Bhutan. As can immediately be seen, it is an area of great cultural diversity. For example, as regards religion, it is characterized by Hinduism, Islam, and Buddhism (all incorporating, of course, numerous forms of local belief and practice). There is conflict between these various traditions, certainly, but also considerable evidence of deep-rooted patterns of coexistence as well. Despite this diversity, there are important cultural and linguistic continuities right across the region, for all that fifty years of nation-building processes have driven neighbours apart from each other and set them on different trajectories.

Northern South Asia is a very rich field for comparison. Take, for example, Nepal and (north and central) India. We can immediately notice many cultural and historical links and similarities in the fields of religious relationships, ideologies of kingship and government, caste system(s), popular culture, clothes and food, and these days even practices of violence and revolution. But at the same time, we can easily point out that similar institutions have different manifestations. Though Islam is not absent in Nepal, communal struggle is much less harsh there than in India. Contemporary castes in Nepal have much less of a history of caste associations, reservations (as affirmative action is known in South Asia) have only just begun to be introduced there, and the way in which the Nepalese state has incorporated subordinate groups differs considerably from similar processes in India. As general historical background, the difference in the experiences of colonialism (direct in India and indirect in Nepal) should be kept in mind.

Comparison between Nepal and Bhutan, though not included in the present volumes, would also produce interesting results. Despite the first obvious similarities of location and mountainous environment, the two countries are contrastive in many aspects: Hinduism *vs.* Tibetan Buddhism, rapid *vs.* slow population increase, and their respective policies towards cultural diversity and nature conservation, are but a few examples of the ways in which the two countries would appear to have taken diametrically opposed paths.

It was one of our initial aims to encourage the comparative study of social change. It is true that only a few of the papers in these volumes take up the challenge to compare explicitly. It is also true that, geographically, the areas dealt with are limited to Nepal and India. Nonetheless, we are glad that some authors are keen on comparison and that the other papers in combination convey detailed and analytical pictures of the many diverse but comparable ways in which local societies of the area are changing. We hope that the present collections will encourage further and deeper comparative studies of the region in future.

Hiroshi ISHII
David N. GELLNER
Katsuo NAWA

Contributors

Jagannath ADHIKARI works in Nepal as an independent researcher and development consultant. He obtained his Ph.D. from the Australian National University in 1996, and since then has carried out several research projects on labour migration and the remittance economy, food security, conflict, poverty, and social issues in natural resources management. He is the author of *Beginnings of Agrarian Change: A Case Study in Central Nepal* (TM Publication, 1996) and *Decisions for Survival: Farm Management Strategies in Middle Hills, Nepal* (Adroit Publication, 2001), and a co-author of *Food Crisis in Nepal: How Mountain Farmers Cope* (Adroit Publication, 1999), *New Lahures: Labour Migration and Remittances Economy of Nepal* (NIDS, 2001), *Pokhara: Biography of a Town* (Mandala Book Point, 2002), and *Conflict and Food Security: A Preliminary Analysis* (RRN, 2004). He has also authored and edited several books on various aspects of development in Nepal in Nepali, of which *Debate on Poverty in Nepal* (Martin Chautari, 2004) is the most recent. At present, he is also the convener of Martin Chautari, a discussion forum in Kathmandu.

Gerald D. BERREMAN is Professor Emeritus in the Department of Anthropology, University of California, Berkeley. He has also taught as visiting professor in the Universities of Stockholm, Uppsala, and Delhi, and in Tribhuvan University. He is the author of *Hindus of the Himalayas: Ethnography and Change*; *The Politics of Truth: Essays in Critical Anthropology*; *Caste and Other Inequities: Essays on Inequality*, and articles on these and other topics relating to India, Nepal, 'race', and racism in America, the Aleuts of Alaska, the 'Tasaday' hoax in the Philippines, ethnographic methods, and research ethics.

Ram Bahadur CHHETRI (Ph.D. 1990, University of Hawaii) is Reader in Anthropology at Tribhuvan University, Kathmandu. Currently he is the Head of the Central Department of Sociology/Anthropology. He has been a visiting faculty/scholar at the University of Georgia, USA (on Fulbright Award 1997-8 and 2002), the University of Bergen, Norway (1995), Chr. Michelsen Institute, Norway, and the Institute of Social Studies, The Hague (2005). He has co-authored several books including *User Group Forestry in Far-Western Nepal* (ICIMOD, Kathmandu, 1992), *Nepal-Australia Community Forestry Project: Socio-Economic Study* (ANUTECH, Canberra, 1996), *Dispute Resolution in Nepal: A Socio-Cultural Perspective* (CVICT, Kathmandu, 2004), and co-edited *Anthropology and Sociology of Nepal* (SASON, 1999), *Occasional Papers in Sociology and Anthropology 9* (Tribhuvan University, 2005). He has conducted ethnographic research among the Loba of upper Mustang (1983-4) and studied Tibetan refugees in Nepal for his doctoral dissertation.

David N. GELLNER is Professor of Social Anthropology and a Fellow of All Souls College in the University of Oxford. From 2003 to 2004 he was a Visiting Professor at the Research Institute for Cultures and Languages of Asia and Africa, Tokyo University of Foreign Studies. He is the author or editor of many books on Nepal and Northern South Asia, including *Borderland Lives in Northern South Asia* (Duke, 2013), *Religion, Secularism, and Ethnicity in Contemporary Nepal* (OUP, 2016), *Global Nepalis: Religion, Culture, and Community in a New and Old Diaspora* (OUP, 2018), *Vernacular Religion: Cultural Politics, Community Belonging, and Personal Practice in the UK's Nepali Diaspora* (Vajra, 2019), and a special issue of *Contributions to Nepalese Studies 46.1: Nepali Dalits in Transition* (CNAS, TU, 2019)

Makiko HABAZAKI is a Ph.D. candidate in cultural anthropology at Hokkaido University, Sapporo. She is currently doing research on family conflict, conjugal relationships and the changing family order in Nepal and Japan. Her publications include 'Regional Development by Tourism in Aomori, Japan' (2002, in Japanese).

Hiroshi ISHII is Professor Emeritus at the Research Institute for Languages and Cultures of Asia and Africa (ILCAA), Tokyo University of Foreign Studies. He has conducted anthropological research among the Newars, the Parbate Hindus, and the Maithils in Nepal since 1970. He has published *Nepal: A Himalayan Kingdom in Transition* (UNU Press, 1996, with P.P. Karan et al.), as well as other books and articles in both Japanese and English.

Sarah LEVINE is an Associate of the Department of Sanskrit & Indian Studies, Harvard University. Her books include *Mothers and Wives: Gusii Women of East Africa* (University of Chicago Press, 1979), *Dolor y Alegria: Women & Social Change in Urban Mexico* (University of Wisconsin Press, 1993), and, with David N. Gellner, *Rebuilding Buddhism: The Theravada Movement in Twentieth-Century Nepal* (Harvard University Press, 2005).

Makito MINAMI is Associate Professor in the Department of Social Research, National Museum of Ethnology (NME), Osaka. He has published 'Technological and Social Changes among Coppersmith Castes and Typology of Copper Water Jugs (*gagri*): A Case Study in Western Nepal' (*Bulletin of the NME*, 2003) and 'Socio-Ecology of Poison Fishing: A Case Study of the Magars in the Middle Hills of Nepal' (*Bulletin of the NME*, 1993), both in Japanese. Recently he has been studying transnational Nepali communities in Japan, Hong Kong, India, and Bhutan, and read a paper titled 'Seeking for Ideal Social Spaces: Transnational Nepalese Labour Migrants in Japan' at the seminar of NEFIN, in Oct. 2003.

Izumi MORIMOTO is Associate Professor in the Faculty of International Studies, Meijigakuin University, Japan. Her recent publications include 'Kokusai Tourism wo Meguru Nepal Chiikizo (International tourism and geographical images of Nepal)', Ph.D. dissertation, Ochanomizu University, Tokyo, 2001, and 'Adaptation of the Gandharbas to Growing International Tourism in Nepal', *Journal of the Japanese Association for South Asian Studies* 14, 2002. From April 2005 to March 2006 she was a visiting scholar in the Department of South Asia, the School of Oriental and African Studies, University of London.

Katsuo NAWA is Associate Professor of Cultural Anthropology, Institute of Oriental Culture, the University of Tokyo. He is the author of *Nepal, Byans oyobi Shuhen Chiiki ni okeru Girei to Shakaihanchu ni kansuru Minzokushiteki Kenkyu: Mo Hitotsu no 'Kindai' no Fuchi* (*An Ethnographic Study on Rituals and Social Categories of Byans, Nepal, and Adjacent Regions: Another Constellation of 'Modernity'*) (Sangensha, 2002), which was awarded the 30th Shibusawa Prize. His publications in English include 'Ethnic Categories and their Usages in Byans, Far Western Nepal' (*European Bulletin of Himalayan Research* 18, 2000).

Biswo Kallyan PARAJULI is Lecturer in Sociology, Tribhuvan University, Prithvi Narayan Campus, Pokhara. He is Head of the Department of Sociology and Anthropology, Prithvi Narayan Campus, Pokhara, Nepal. He is the editor of the *Himalayan Journal of Sociology & Anthropology*.

Judith PETTIGREW is a social anthropologist and Senior Lecturer at the University of Central Lancashire. She started her professional career as an occupational therapist, has extensive clinical experience in mental health, and is also trained as a psychotherapist. Her recent publications include 'Living between the Maoists and the Army in Rural Nepal' in *Himalayan 'People's War': Nepal's Maoist Rebellion* (ed. Michael Hutt, Indiana University Press, 2004), 'Relationships, Complicity and Representation: Conducting Research in Nepal during the Maoist Insurgency' (with Sara Shneiderman and Ian Harper, 2004) in *Anthropology Today,* and 'Guns, Kinship and Fear: Maoists among the Tamu-mai (Gurungs)' in *Resistance and the State: Nepalese Experiences* (ed. David N. Gellner, Social Science Press, 2003). She is currently writing a book on the impact of the Maoist insurgency on rural civilians.

Seika SATO is Lecturer in Cultural Anthropology, Teikyo University (Tokyo). She recently received her Ph.D. for a thesis entitled 'The Modern State of Community: Yolmos of Nepal in the Age of Ethnic Activism' (University of Tokyo, 2004, in Japanese).

Khusiyali SUBBA passed her MA in sociology and anthropology from Tribhuvan University in 1999 with a thesis on indigenous knowledge of seed conservation. She has worked in development and has taught anthropology and sociology at Mahendra Multiple Campus, Dharan. Currently she works for the National Foundation for Development of Indigenous Nationalities (NFDIN) in Kathmandu.

Taeko UESUGI teaches Cultural Anthropology at Senshu University, Tokyo. She is the author of *Ihai-wake: Nagano-ken Saku-Chiho ni okeru Sosen-saishi no Hendo (Dividing up the Ancestral Tablets: Changing Ancestor Worship in the Nagano Region, Japan)* (Daiichi-shobo, in Japanese). Her current interest includes the transnationalism of military workers, and she has been conducting research on Gurkha soldiers in Brunei, the UK, and Nepal.

Yuji YAMAMOTO is Professor and Dean of Faculty of Politics, Economics, and Law, Osaka International University, Japan. He is the author of 'Inter-caste Marriages in Pokhara' (*Journal of Asian and African Studies*, 1983), 'Rethinking Matwali Chhetris' (ILCAA, 1985, in Japanese), and 'Ideological Conflicts between Hinduism and Communism in Nepal' (Ritsumeikan Daigaku Jinmonkagaku Kenkyusho, 2004, in Japanese).

Keiko YAMANAKA is a sociologist, Lecturer in the Department of Ethnic Studies, and Research Associate in the Institute for the Study of Social Change, University of California, Berkeley. Since 1993, she has studied transnational migration and social transformation in Japan, focusing on two immigrant populations: 250,000 authorized Brazilians of Japanese descent and 3,000 unauthorized Nepalis. She has published journal articles and book chapters on these topics. She is co-editor of and contributor to 'Gender, Migration and Governance in Asia', a special issue of *Asian and Pacific Migration Journal* (2003). Most recently, she co-authored *Feminized Migration in East and*

Southeast Asia: Policies, Actions and Empowerment, Occasional Paper 11 (2006), United Nations Research Institute for Social Development, Geneva.

Hayami YASUNO is an anthropologist, Professor and Dean of the Faculty of International Studies, Yamaguchi Prefectural University. She is the author of *Spirit Possession Cult of Western Nepal: Resolution of Misfortune and Conflicts in Popular Hinduism* (Tokyo: Keiso Shobo, 2000, in Japanese) She is co-editor of *Creation of International Studies* (Tokyo: Akashi Shoten, 2002, in Japanese).

Introduction

H. ISHII, D.N. GELLNER, AND K. NAWA

When colonial officers and early anthropologists made the first ethnographic observations of the South Asian peoples it was natural for them to think in terms of fixed and long-lasting social units. Today, by contrast, the salient social fact is change – in a variety of forms and directions, both within and beyond the boundaries of the nation-state. Hence the umbrella title of the pair of volumes of which this forms a part is social dynamics. The focus here is on the dynamics of social categories, groups, or identities. The contributors to both volumes analyse recent changes in the context of study by focusing on one or other concept such as caste, ethnic group (less often tribe), gender, nationality (from the aspect of transnational links), or religious identity. The changing nature of such identities is no less present when various aspects of secular activism are analysed. Even when new forms of identity emerge – such as that of squatter or entrepreneur – older identities, based on caste or ethnicity, continue to play an important role in influencing the way they develop, as chapters 4 and 11 below demonstrate.

Since caste and ethnicity are important in all the contexts dealt with in these two books, since we aim to encourage comparison, and since Nepal and north India differ significantly – despite profound cultural and historical continuities – in the ways in which caste and ethnic group (or 'tribe') are institutionalized, a detailed, if introductory, explanation of these differences is in order and will help to set the scene for the detailed studies that follow.

It may be possible to distinguish between 'caste' and 'ethnic group' (or 'tribe') analytically (though inevitably different scholars will prefer different definitions[1]). In actual situations, however, it is often difficult to make a clear demarcation between the two. Scholars and bureaucrats in colonial India faced just this problem when carrying out censuses and proceeded by trial and error in their classification of castes and tribes (and sometimes 'races'), a process of governmental classification which continued for more than a hundred years (Cohn 1987: ch. 10; Bayly 1999; Dirks 2001: ch. 10;

---

[1] See Höfer (1979: 46-7) for a discussion of some of the difficulties.

Mise 2004: 203-30). After independence the category of Scheduled Tribes was added as part of the reservation system along with the Scheduled Castes, an official status which had existed before 1947. This had the effect of making the demarcation between castes and tribes clearer than before, or at least it meant that there was a clear official marker. Various groups had to decide whether to campaign for recognition as a Scheduled Caste or Scheduled Tribe in order to win the advantages of reservations. Census reports include Scheduled Castes and Scheduled Tribes but do not list castes other than Scheduled Castes (Mise 2004: 222).

As far as the day-to-day use of indigenous terms meaning 'caste' in contemporary north India is concerned, scholars agree that in recent years there has been a conscious attempt to avoid using the word *jat* or *jati*:

> The alternative use of the neutral and morally inoffensive word *samaj* (association) in place of the more loaded term *jat* (species) when referring to caste may be an indication that caste distinction and discrimination are seen as values which should not be publicly supported). ... the shying away from the use of the word *jat* implies a change in the value given to inequality ... (Mayer 1996: 59, 63)
>
> Castes are no longer referred to as *jatis* ('breeds' or 'species') ... (Parry 2007: 484, drawing on this same article; Mayer 1996)

To sum up the argument so far:

1. Castes and tribes have to be kept separate bureaucratically in relation to the reservation system in India, and this has political consequences.
2. The words *jat* and *jati* are much less used than before in north India.
3. There is no distinction between the meaning of *jat* and *jati* as seen in Mayer's and Parry's usage.

On all these points, Nepal is quite different from north India. Historically in Nepal the word *jat* has been used more commonly than *jati*. A well-known early example is the oft-quoted description of Nepal by King Prithvi Narayan Shah (1723-75): *sabai jatko phulbari* (a flower garden of all the *jats*). This phrase was used by D.B. Bista (2030 v.s./1973) for the title of the revised Nepali version of his book *People of Nepal*, which contains descriptions of both castes and ethnic groups; he uses the term *jat* to cover both.

At the time when the British colonial government was attempting to grasp the complexities of Indian society by means of censuses and surveys, and thereby inducing a new and unprecedented degree of fixity to social boundaries (Cohn 1987: ch. 10; Dirks 2001), the Nepalese Rana regime (1845-1951) was deliberately and consciously setting out to mould its subject peoples by means of Hindu law: "a caste society was conceptualized by its members in the legal code Muluki Ain (henceforth MA) of 1854" (Höfer 1979: 37). As for the use of the term *jat*, Höfer remarks:

> It must be emphasized that the terminology of MA does not distinguish between caste and ethnic group (tribe): the term *jat* is used for both. (Höfer 1979: 46)

Thus we see that the term *jat* was commonly used to refer to castes and ethnic groups indiscriminately from the eighteenth to the twentieth century. Briefly stated, the Shah (Gorkha) dynasty of Nepal led by Parbatiya high castes tried to establish a uniform rule based on the caste system and incorporated many ethnic groups mainly into the middle ranks of their caste hierarchy. The instrumental term utilized for covering every group was *jat* ('caste' from the government point of view). This was reinforced and formalized under the Rana regime and continued up to the middle of the twentieth century and the situation still prevails today in which ordinary people use *jat* for both castes and ethnic groups (for the last point see also Morimoto Ch. 11, n.13, this volume).

However, a different usage has emerged in legal and official spheres, and recently among ethnic groups themselves. For example, we find the following sentence in Pt. 3-10-(2) of the Constitution of Nepal 1962:

> Samanya kanunko prayogma kunai pani nagarikmathi dharma, varna, linga, jat, jati va timadhye kunai kurako adharma bhedbhav garine chaina.
> (Official English translation: No discrimination shall be made against any citizen in the application of general laws on grounds of religion, race, sex, caste, tribe or any of them.)

The corresponding sentence in the Constitution of Nepal 1990, Pt. 3-11-(2) is not very different except for the addition of the phrase 'ideological conviction':

> Samanya kanunko prayogma kunai pani nagarikmathi dharma, varna, linga, jat, jati va vaicarik astha va ti madhye kunai kurako adharma bhedbhav garine chaina.
> (Official English translation: No discrimination shall be made against any citizen in the application of general laws on grounds of religion, race, sex, caste, tribe or ideological conviction or any of these.)

In both of the above, *jat* is translated as 'caste', and *jati* as 'tribe'. (It is interesting that *varna* is translated as 'race', but to discuss this here would take us too far afield.) If we take 'tribe' as equivalent to 'ethnic group', we can say that the Nepalese government, at least after the Constitution of 1962, acknowledged the existence of ethnic groups as distinct from castes. This is a considerable change from the policy of the Shah-Rana rulers who tried to integrate Nepal by incorporating all their subjects on the model of castes.

It should also be noted here that the word 'tribe' is used in the official

English translation even of the 1990 constitution, while virtually no scholar dealing with Nepal in the present volumes, be they Nepali or otherwise, makes use of it. However, official usage is not uniform, as we will see in the terminology used in the censuses.

The Nepalese National Census, officially said to have started from 1911,[2] began to include data on caste and ethnic groups from 1991. The questionnaire forms in the censuses of 1991 and 2001 (or even those of previous censuses) are written in Nepali, and the pertinent columns have the wording *jat/jati* in both years. On the other hand, census reports of both years are written in English and *jat/jati* is translated as 'caste/ethnic group' (CBS 1993, 2002).[3] The term 'tribe' is nowhere to be found in the census reports. Thus one might well conclude that *jat* corresponds to 'caste' and *jati* to 'ethnic group', but the distinction is not at all clear as far as the census reports are concerned; various groups are listed according to three geographical regions with no systematic internal order in the report for 1991, and according to their population size in that for 2001, in either case making no distinction between 'castes' and 'ethnic groups'.

Manuals for census enumerators, on the other hand, show an interesting change in the meanings of *jat* and *jati*. They were not differentiated in 1991 but were conferred different meanings in 2001:

> [For the 1991 census:]
> The specific (social) category demarcated according to a person's genealogy, rites of passage, religion and beliefs, etc. is called *jat/jati*.[4]
>
> (Kendriya Tathyank Bibhag [CBS] 2047 v.s. [1990]: 35)

> [For the 2001 census:]
> Generally what is called *jat* are – groups of various classes under Hindu *varnashram* [*varna* and *ashram* or classical four 'castes' and four stages of life in Hinduism]. Among these are cord-wearers, non-cord-wearers, and Dalit *jats*. ...
>
> What is called *jati* are – Janajati [ethnic groups] who have their distinct mother tongues and rites of passage.
>
> For example, Brahman, Kshatri, Kami, Rajput, Kayastha, Marwari are *jats* and Bhote, Limbu, Tamang, Thami, etc. are *jatis*.
>
> (Kendriya Tathyank Bibhag [CBS] 2057? [2000?]: 20)

---

[2] Kendriya Tathyank Bibhag (CBS) 2047 v.s. (1990): 3. Ishii would like to thank the late Dr Harka Gurung for kindly providing the materials on the various censuses.

[3] English has been used for the reports since the 1971 census.

[4] These are translations by Ishii of the original Nepali.

It is interesting to note that the manual for the 1991 census not only treats *jat/jati* synonymously but also gives no connotation that the terms are related to the English word 'caste'. The definition is closer to that of *jati* ('ethnic group') in the manual for the 2001 census. As seen above, the constitution of 1990 (and of 1962 also) shuns discrimination as far as the application of general laws is concerned. And the treatment of the term *jat/jati* in 1991 coincided well with this policy. At the same time, as amply shown in this volume and elsewhere, castes in Nepal have been losing their inter-caste connections and becoming more like ethnic groups. The definition of *jat* in 1991, which gave it a meaning close to 'ethnic group', can be interpreted as a reflection of this reality.

Since the democratization of 1990, ethnic activism and to some extent low-caste movements have grown in intensity in Nepal. Many ethnic groups have come to define themselves as non-caste, non-Hindu ethnic groups (Gellner 1997: 20-3; Minami, this volume). The terms Janajati and Dalit have become popular, though these terms were hardly known and rarely recognized before the democratization. After 1990, representative organizations joined together to form the Nepal Federation of Nationalities, now renamed the Nepal Federation of Indigenous Nationalities. On the Chinese model, 'nationality' was the translation that they preferred for *janajati.* Successive Nepalese governments have given greater and greater recognition to them. In 2000 it published an official list of sixty-one Janajatis, which was subsequently revised to fifty-nine.[5] Fourteen of these fifty-nine groups, most of them from the high mountain region, were not listed in the 2001 census and so their exact population numbers were not recorded, but no doubt they will be included in the next census. A government-funded National Foundation of Indigenous Nationalities, charged with directing resources towards Janajatis, especially the disadvantaged, was set up in 2003.

In the 2001 census manual the terms *jat* and *jati* were clearly distinguished so that *jat* was used to mean 'caste' and *jati* 'ethnic group'. The definitions here have come close to the usage in the constitution in that they distinguish between the two words. The main intention here was certainly to make the definitions fit the current trend of democratization and ethnic awareness by delineating a word corresponding to 'ethnic group'. But in order to do this, they had to attach the conventional meaning of 'caste' to *jat* at the same time. Thus, the obligation to acknowledge the existence of ethnic groups (by equating *jati* with Janajati) has entailed the recognition of 'caste' (probably unintentionally), which had been avoided in 1991. This corre-

[5] For details, see the paper by Gellner & Karki 'The Sociology of Activism in Nepal' in *Political and Social Transformations in North India and Nepal* (next volume). On ethnicity in Nepal up till the mid 1990s, see Höfer (1979) and Gellner et al. (1997). For more recent perspectives, see Lecomte-Tilouine (2004) and Whelpton (2005).

sponds to the above-cited efforts of ethnic activists: by defining themselves as non-caste and non-Hindu, they separated out Hindu caste groups.

To sum up: compared to north India, in Nepal:

a. Until recently 'castes' and 'ethnic groups' were not clearly distinguished from each other, either bureaucratically or popularly. (There was no reservation system until 2003 in Nepal.)
b. The word *jat* has been in widespread common usage to mean both 'caste' and 'ethnic group'.
c. The terms *jat* and *jati* began to be differentiated in the latter half of the twentieth century, i.e. after the collapse of the Rana regime; in recent years this has become more widely accepted and gained official recognition.

Though in Nepal the single word *jat* has covered both 'caste' and 'ethnic group' from the Shah period up until the present day, its core meaning has been swinging within the caste-ethnic group continuum. We can distinguish three stages in this regard:

1. Shah-Rana period (late eighteenth century to mid twentieth century):
   With the caste system backed by government policy as a means to integrate the kingdom, the term *jat* was heavily loaded with the meaning 'caste'.
2. The latter half of the twentieth century:
   i. The fall of the Rana regime, the weakening of inter-caste relationships, and the rise of egalitarian notions, all meant that the term *jat* lost its integrative role. In some spheres (e.g. in the census manual of 1991) its meaning came closer to 'ethnic group';
   ii. The term *jati* was used in legal documents, such as the various constitutions, to mean 'ethnic group (tribe)' but it did not gain acceptance in popular usage.
3. After the democratization of 1990:
   The term *jat* seems to have been deprived of its 'ethnic group' connotation as the term *janajati* began to be widely used in political and academic circles and started to gain recognition more widely as equivalent to 'ethnic group(s)'.

In this way, the tendency to separate out ethnic groups from the caste-ethnic group continuum has paradoxically led to the solidification of the term *jat* as equivalent to 'caste' in recent years.

As a reflection of these changing usages, many of the following chapters contain expressions such as 'caste/ethnic group(s)', 'ethnic/caste group(s)', 'caste(s) and ethnic group(s)', etc., as well as Janajati and Dalit. The terminology adopted in any particular case partly reflects the usages of the respective places and times and is also partly dependent on the perspective and questions raised by the respective authors.

With these distinctions in mind, it is now possible to consider the individual chapters of this volume.

As indicated by its title, this book deals mainly with Nepal. Change in the various societies and cultures of Nepal is dealt with by focusing on urbanization, marriage and intimacy, transnational links, and a comparison between India and Nepal.

All four of the articles in Part 1 deal with Pokhara, a town in the hill area 200 km. to the west of Kathmandu. Three of the authors were born and/or work(ed) in Pokhara and one (Yamamoto) is Japanese. All of them have been observing and experiencing changes of/in Pokhara for a long time.

This part begins with Jagannath Adhikari's chapter which provides an overall view of the urbanization of Pokhara. Taking Pokhara's strategic position and government policies as the principal causative factors, the author draws out some important consequences. Notable among them are the increase of the number of ethnic and caste groups, increasing political participation of minority groups, widening economic disparity, and decline of untouchability. As for the relationships between ethnic groups and castes, Adhikari is able to present evidence of an increase of inter-caste/ethnic marriages and he points out that they have come closer despite the increased self-awareness on the part of ethnic groups and their reconstruction of identity based on non-Sanskritic cultural elements. This interesting point shows that the processes of changes of castes and ethnic groups and their relations are multifaceted and not so unilinear. It also indicates the need for more studies of the relationship between kinship and politico-economic structures.

Among the Gaine (Minstrel) caste studied by Biswo Kallyan Parajuli, their traditional occupation has been replaced by modern occupations to a considerable extent, which, however, are mostly limited to low-income positions because of their socio-economic background. He also notes that the traditional occupations of occupational castes have in some cases been interchanged and swapped. However, he does not broach the question whether this leads to the emergence of wider alliances and new identities among Dalit castes. Perhaps a different picture might have emerged had the analysis looked at the Gaines from the perspective of kinship or political practice.

Ram Chhetri's analysis shows that Dalits (including Newari-speaking Jalaris or Podes) and Kumals used to have mutual exchange relationships with farmers, but have been losing them with the consequence that Dalit youths face great difficulties in competing with other groups in the job market. He comments that this phenomenon is common to many places in

Nepal. Here, groups of very different ethnic and caste backgrounds had built up social relations on the basis of caste principles and are now having to adapt to their disintegration. As pointed out earlier, the integration of disparate groups, be they castes or ethnic groups, has always been an important theme in Nepal, both on the state and the local levels. And this chapter (together with others in this section) shows that Pokhara is a good example to illustrate the process of integration as well as its metamorphosis.

The *sukumbasi* (squatter) settlements analysed by Yuji Yamamoto give us one example of new sites of caste and ethnic mixture. But unlike the societies dealt with by the above authors, *sukumbasi* settlements have no inter-caste structure of mutual dependence. Rather, Yamamoto analyses them by resorting to the notions 'communitas' and 'proto-charisma'. In order to make their position secure and their living conditions better, *sukumbasi*s depend on leaders who have the appropriate characteristics. If successful in gaining legal titles to their plots, according to Yamamoto, a settlement will be furnished with facilities and may become a community. It is a question for future research what kind of identity is formed in such settlements, but Yamamoto's analysis indicates that this is likely to be easier to achieve when there are pre-existing ties and relationships.

Part 2, 'Marriage, Kinship, and Transformation of Intimacy', deals mainly with life, social relations, and problems of women and children in various local areas in Nepal. Studies of kinship and marriage, once a central topic in sociocultural anthropology, are now reviving after several decades of relative neglect, with concepts like gender, sexuality, and agency (Carsten 2000; Stone 2001; Parkin & Stone 2004). Since Bennett's now classic study of high-caste Parbatiya women (Bennett 1983), many fascinating contributions have been made in the field of kinship, marriage, and family in Nepal (Ahearn 2001; Cameron 1998; March 2002; Skinner et al. 1998; and Watkins 1996 among many others), demonstrating the diverse, changing, and often contested nature of the phenomena, thus also undermining the cliché – now a politically significant discourse – that would posit a simple and straightforward contrast between 'egalitarian' 'Tibeto-Burman' ethnic groups in Nepal on the one side, and hierarchical Parbatiya Hindu society on the other, not only in terms of caste but in terms of gender. All six chapters of this part contribute to this ongoing debate by focusing on particular incidents and concrete processes in contemporary Nepal.

The section starts with Hayami Yasuno's chapter, which deals with three types of extramarital relation in the Khas Brahman society of western Nepal. In this society, like many other Hindu societies in northern South Asia, *kanyadan* (the gift of the virgin) is regarded as the most fundamental and most prestigious form of marriage, while other types of conjugal union are socially permitted. For various reasons some villagers look for a chance to have such permitted unions (and at times even strictly prohibited ones), though these attempts cause serious tension and rupture within the society. Using minutely detailed case studies based on tape-recorded dialogues of the villagers as well as her participant observation, Yasuno describes the process of negotiation and settlement of *tipne* (abduction), *jari* (adultery), and *had nata* (incest), thus vividly evoking the social reality that is so often neglected in the mainstream discourse of both anthropologists and villagers who adopt the canonical 'dangerous wives and sacred sisters' scheme. This chapter can also be read as a pioneering legal anthropological account of pluralism in processes of dispute resolution in rural Nepal.

The main question of Seika Sato's analysis is why Yolmo women (Yolmo being a Tibeto-Burman-speaking ethnic group in Nepal) do not mind being born as women even though women are considered socioculturally inferior to men. Based on the scrutiny of two domains in everyday practice in Yolmo, namely the organization of labour in the household and space arrangements inside the house, Sato finds first that Yolmo daily life is clearly gendered, though it lacks overt gender separation and segregation, and that gender inequality in Yolmo has been reproduced through everyday practices that are not overtly gendered. She then presents a detailed account of the stubborn 'resistance' of a Yolmo woman who repeatedly tried to escape from her marriage. Sato thus represents the relation between structural constraints and the (restricted) agency of Yolmo women ethnographically, to contribute to the ongoing debate on women's status, resistance, and agency in Nepal. Her answer to the question above, i.e. it is partly because their very wishes, longings, or dreams are *made out of their being a woman,* invites readers to further thought and discussion.

Like Yasuno, Sarah LeVine tries to relativize the prevailing view of Hindu women and marriage, though from a totally different viewpoint. The rising age of marriage for women as well as the spread of education and urbanization has increased significantly the chances for adolescents and young adults in the Kathmandu Valley to nurture 'romantic attachments', some of which are inter-class, inter-caste, and/or inter-ethnic. Comparing urban Newars of Patan and rural Bahun-Chetris of Godavari, LeVine examines recent trends in marriage practices mainly from the female perspective: the required conditions (sociocultural as well as personal) for the would-be husband/son-in-law, the actual process of selection of spouses and engagement, and the options when organizing the wedding. Several cases are presented to show how the parents managed to domesticate the romantic love of their daughters. Her paper also suggests that a single female conception of marriage does not exist in Hindu Nepal, not only because Nepali women are divided by ethnic, caste, economic, as well as on many other lines, but also because a woman may evaluate 'love marriage' very differently depending on whether the marriage is her own or her daughter's.

The topic of Makiko Habazaki's chapter is domestic violence, a largely hidden but serious problem in contemporary Nepal. After quickly reviewing the status quo of domestic violence, its social and legal background, and activities currently being undertaken in an attempt to eradicate it in Nepal, she presents detailed narratives by the victims of domestic violence who are in a shelter in Kathmandu run by an NGO called Saathi. These interviews show that the victims and NGO staff manipulate the concept of domestic violence itself in desperate situations. What they call domestic violence includes not only physical violence, neglect, and verbal abuse, but also the husband's disappearance. Habazaki's analysis of the cultural factors behind domestic violence, though it may be considered rather seminal in an anthropological context, contains reference to many of the topics discussed in the first three papers of this section. This very fact suggests the necessity of rethinking marriage and the transformation of intimacy in contemporary Nepal as a whole. What is needed is a comprehensive reconsideration of the sociocultural processes that produce such persecution of women (bearing in mind that there are evidently many who suffer from domestic violence but have no access to any shelter or NGO).

Khusiyali Subba focuses on another serious and sensitive social problem, drug abuse. It is noteworthy that her field is not Kathmandu or Pokhara but Dharan, a town in eastern Nepal with a population of about 95,000. More than 4 per cent of the population of this town is estimated to be drug users, a high rate compared to other towns of this size in Nepal. A native of Dharan herself, Subba tries to trace several causes of this phenomenon, mainly based on her detailed interviews with many drug users, their parents, social workers, and other inhabitants of the town. The transformation of intimacy, mainly due to the absence of fathers who are abroad as Gurkha soldiers or migrant workers, the shrinking local economy, the peculiar political history of Dharan, the social status and cultural background of the Janajati population, as well as modernization and globalization produce several ironic twists. This chapter is not only a significant contribution to understanding the mechanism of drug abuse in Nepal, but also a fascinating account from a native anthropologist engaged in tackling a social problem of her own community.

Judith Pettigrew tackles probably the largest, most recent, most serious, and still ongoing process of the transformation of intimacy in Nepal: that which is caused by the 'People's War'. There is a growing body of literature revealing the grave impact, both direct and indirect, of the war on daily life in rural Nepal, writien by academics (including many anthropologists), as well as journalists, NGO workers, and human rights activists. Pettigrew's contribution to this volume is unique in that she focuses on children under fire. Adopting a critical stance on the concept of 'culture of terror' and combining interviews (mainly to caregivers) with her own observations, she reconstructs the experience of the 'People's War' for the children of a Gurung village and its complicated psychological impacts on them. A curious amalgam of continuity and change can be observed: not only their way of expressing intimacy but also their personal roles within a family have changed, while they conceptualize the very danger their children are facing by using their own Gurung terminology. The points she discusses are crucial in order to understand what those who cannot get away from living between Maoists and security forces experience. The next generation will have to cope with the consequences of these experiences.

The six chapters in Part 2 may appear at first glance to be diverse and unintegrated. Yet all the cases treated in them were occurring almost simultaneously in post-1990 Nepal. Ranging from rather 'traditional' rural social customs to contemporary worldwide problems, they combine to give an illuminating picture of the changes women, men, and children in Nepal have been facing in their everyday life.

In Part 3 of the book transnational links inside and outside Nepal are analysed from perspectives illustrative of contemporary Nepal. One chapter focuses on a tourist area within Nepal, the other three on what happens when Nepalis go to work outside. Two of these touch on Nepalis in Japan.

Izumi Morimoto analyses the tourism business in Thamel, Kathmandu, the one Kathmandu locality which, above all others, is identified with services for tourism. She looks at the historical development of the area, and the factors that enabled it to emerge in this way. She examines the rise of Tibetan and Gurung entrepreneurs (alongside the predominance of local Newars) and relates this to the transposition (by foreigners) of the image of Tibet on to Nepal and the entrepreneurs' response to these foreign perceptions. At the same time she points out that local hoteliers and businessmen also maintain and value a non-ethnic, professional identity as tourism entrepreneurs.

Taeko Uesugi, studying the British Gurkhas' life strategies and the Brigade of Gurkhas' employment policies, examines the policies that were designed to secure the allegiance of Gurkha soldiers to the British Army while maintaining their links to their mother country. Uesugi looks closely at interactions and negotiations between the policies and Gurkha soldiers' actual practices, transnational ties, and life strategies. She shows how Gurkha soldiers have adapted to the new transnational order, how they negotiate and conceptualize the complex discourses on Hinduism that they confront at home and at work, and how they have used emerging multiculturalist ideas to strategic advantage.

In her chapter, which presents a very different context of labour migration, Keiko Yamanaka analyses Nepali migrant workers in Japan some of whom are without official permits. Facing hostile policies as visa-overstayers on the one hand, Nepali migrants are highly sensitive to the internal political situation in Nepal on the other hand, and have been facing an erosion of group solidarity. This reflects the rise of ethnic and political movements within Nepal after 1990. Despite this, and despite the insecurity within Japan – perhaps precisely because of this insecurity – the Nepali workers demonstrate high levels of cooperation and solidarity.

Global connections within an ethnic group are also the subject of Makito Minami's study in which he analyses the Magars among refugees of Nepali ethnicity from Bhutan to Nepal, the Magars in Darjeeling and Hong Kong, and the Magars in Japan. All these different groups have been strongly influenced by the trend towards an assertive ethnic identity back in Nepal itself. At the same time, he shows how developments within Nepal are stimulated by the support, both moral and financial, which the expatriate communities are able to bring. The question of adopting Buddhism and rejecting Hinduism is crucial for Magar activists, but its significance varies with context, each set of expatriates or refugees facing different political constraints and contextual incentives. Meanwhile, as Minami's exemplary set of comparisons shows, for many Magar villagers within Nepal, the issue of rejecting Hinduism remains remote.

Part 4 consists of a single very substantial chapter, 'Issues, Activism, and Responses to Research in the Indian and Nepalese Himalayas: A Comparison', by Gerald Berreman. He makes a series of direct comparisons between the two Himalayan areas, with reference to the Maoist insurgency (in Nepal), a grassroots anti-deforestation movement (in India), big dams which evoked grassroots opposition in both countries, Dalits (in both), and the question, "What have been the responses by social scientists, the media and publics of India and Nepal, to social science research conducted in their Himalayan regions?". As the outcome of one of his comparisons he concludes that Nepalis, although riven by the Hindu-Janajati divide, and by caste, ethnicity, and class, are culturally, psychologically, and geographically located at the centre of their Himalayan society and culture; and by contrast, Paharis (in India) are culturally, psychologically, and geographically on the periphery of the larger society of which they are a part. This is an interesting piece of work by a fieldworker of unparalleled experience, which deserves to be widely read and to stimulate further explicit comparison of the areas, both with regard to the important questions raised by Berreman himself and others as well.

Further aspects of social and political change of and within Nepal are dealt with in the second volume, *Political and Social Transformations in North India and Nepal*. It also contains many studies of India dealing with similar subjects, thus bringing to the fore the comparative regional angle.

REFERENCES

Ahearn, L.M. 2001. *Invitations to Love: Literacy, Love Letters, and Social Change in Nepal*. Ann Arbor: The University of Michigan Press.

Bayly, S. 1999. *The New Cambridge History of India*, IV. 3: *Caste, Society and Politics in India from the Eighteenth Century to the Modern Age*. Cambridge: Cambridge University Press.

Bennett, L. 1983. *Dangerous Wives and Sacred Sisters: Social and Symbolic Roles of High-Caste Women in Nepal*. New York: Columbia University Press.

Bista, D.B. 2030 v.s. (1973). *Sabai Jatko Phulbari (A Flower Garden of All the Jats)*. Kathmandu: Sajha Prakashan (in Nepali).

Cameron, M.M. 1998. *On the Edge of the Auspicious: Gender and Caste in Nepal*. Urbana and Chicago: University of Illinois Press.

Carsten, J. (ed.). 2000. *Cultures of Relatedness: New Approaches to the Study of Kinship*. Cambridge: Cambridge University Press.

CBS (Central Bureau of Statistics) 1993. Population Census 1991: *Social Characteristic Tables*, Vol. I, Pt. VII. Kathmandu: HMG (His Majesty's Government of Nepal), NPC (National Planning Commission) Secretariat.

CBS 2002. Population Census 2001: *National Report*. Kathmandu: HMG, NPC Secretariat, CBS in collaboration with UNFPA Nepal.

Cohn, B.S. 1987. *An Anthropologist among the Historians and Other Essays*. Delhi: OUP.

Dirks, N. 2001. *Castes of Mind: Colonialism and the Making of Modern India*. Princeton and Oxford: Princeton University Press.

Gellner, D.N. 1997. 'Introduction: Ethnicity and Nationalism in the World's Only Hindu State', in D.N. Gellner, J. Pfaff-Czarnecka, and J. Whelpton (eds.), *Nationalism and Ethnicity in a Hindu Kingdom: The Politics of Culture in Contemporary Nepal*, pp. 3-31. Amsterdam: Harwood.

Gellner, D.N., J. Pfaff-Czarnecka, and J. Whelpton (eds.). 1997. *Nationalism and Ethnicity in a Hindu Kingdom: The Politics of Culture in Contemporary Nepal*. Amsterdam: Harwood.

Höfer, A. 1979. *The Caste Hierarchy and the State in Nepal*. Innsbruck: Universitätsverlag Wagner. (Reissued 2004 by Himal Books, Lalitpur, Nepal.)

Kanun Kitab Vyavastha Samiti (Law Books Management Commitee). 2033 v.s. (1976). *Nepalko Samvidhan 2019 (The Constitution of Nepal 1962)*. Kanun tatha Nyay Mantralaya (Kathmandu: Ministry of Law and Justice) (in Nepali).

Kanun Kitab Vyavastha Samiti (Law Books Management Board). 2051 v.s. (1994). *Nepal Adhirajyako Samvidhan 2047 (The Constitution of the Kingdom of Nepal 1990)*. Sri 5-ko Sarkar: Kanun, Nyay tatha Samsadiya Vyavastha Mantralaya (Kathmandu: HMG, Ministry of Law, Justice, and Parliamentary Affairs) (in Nepali).

Kendriya Tathyank Bibhag (CBS). 2047 v.s. (1990). *Rashtriya Janaganana 2048, Ganak Nirdesika (National Census 1991: Directions to Enumerators)*. Kathmandu: HMG, NPC (in Nepali).

Kendriya Tathyank Bibhag (CBS). 2057? (2000?). *Rashtriya Janaganana 2058, Prasnavali Nirdesika (National Census 2001: Questionnaire Directions).* Kathmandu: HMG, NPC (in Nepali). [no publication year listed]

Law Books Management Board. 1992. *The Constitution of the Kingdom of Nepal 2047 (1990).* HMG, Ministry of Law, Justice, and Parliamentary Affairs.

Law Books Management Committee. 1976. *The Constitution of Nepal* [1962]. Kathmandu: HMG, Ministry of Law and Justice (reprint).

Lecomte-Tilouine, M. 2004. 'Ethnic Demands within Maoism: Questions of Magar Territorial Autonomy, Nationality and Class', in M. Hutt (ed.), *Himalayan 'People's War': Nepal's Maoist Rebellion*, pp. 112-35. London: Hurst & Co.

March, K.S. 2002. *"If Each Comes Halfway": Meeting Tamang Women in Nepal.* Ithaca and London: Cornell University Press.

Mayer, A. 1996. 'Caste in an Indian Village: Change and Continuity 1954-1992', in C.J. Fuller (ed.) *Caste Today*, pp. 32-64. Delhi: OUP.

Mise, T. 2004. 'Indo: Caste no Shuhen-gainen toshite no Tribe, Race (Tribe and Race as Peripheral Concepts of Caste)', in M. Aoyagi (ed.), *Kokusei-chosa no Bunka-jinruigaku (Cultural Anthropology of National Censuses)*, pp. 203-30. Tokyo: Kokon Shoin (in Japanese).

Parkin, R. and L. Stone (eds.) 2004. *Kinship and Family: An Anthropological Reader.* Oxford: Blackwell.

Parry, J. 2007. 'Afterword', in H. Ishii, D.N. Gellner, and K. Nawa (eds.), *Social Dynamics in Northern South Asia*, Vol. 2: *Political and Social Transformations in North India and Nepal*, pp. 479-95. Delhi: Manohar.

Skinner, D., A. Pach III, and D. Holland (eds.) 1998. *Selves in Time and Place: Identities, Experience, and History in Nepal.* Lanham: Rowman and Littlefield Publishers.

Stone, L. 2000. *Kinship and Gender: An Introduction* (2nd edn.). Boulder: Westview.

Watkins, J.C. 1996. *Spirited Women: Gender, Religion, and Cultural Identity in the Nepal Himalaya.* New York: Columbia University Press.

Whelpton, J. 2005. *A History of Nepal.* Cambridge: Cambridge University Press.

PART 1

URBANIZATION, ETHNICITY, AND OCCUPATION

1

Urbanization and Change in Pokhara, Nepal

JAGANNATH ADHIKARI

INTRODUCTION

This chapter analyses the historical, social, economic, and political factors that have shaped or directed the process of urbanization in Pokhara.[1] The impacts and changes brought by this urbanization process to the society, polity, and lives of Pokhara's inhabitants are then examined. The main focus of the chapter is on the changes in Pokhara since the 1950s, which is also a period of rapid urbanization.

Pokhara is now regarded as an important city and a growth centre for the Western Development Region. Accordingly, it has been receiving increasing attention from both government and external agencies; their interventions here are mainly for the development of the whole region through regional interrelationships. The government also considers it an important centre for foreign tourism on which the future of the country, after its membership of WTO, is seen to rest. Tourism, especially trekking tourism, is one sector in which Nepal is said to have a comparative advantage, and Pokhara, being the main entry point for trekking tourism, earns much-needed foreign exchange. During the 1970s and 1980s Pokhara was also seen to have industrial development potential. To promote industry, the government established an industrial estate and several financial institutions. These interventions have also led to changes in the pace of urbanization and in the socio-economic sphere. In the light of these recent developments, this paper focuses on the following questions:

---

[1]I would like to thank David Gellner for his comments and suggestions at various stages of this chapter, and for his editorial help. Thanks are also due to the participants of the conference where the paper was originally presented.

- What is the scale and rapidity of urban growth in Pokhara?
- What are the reasons for the development of Pokhara as an urban centre?
- What are the socio-economic, cultural, and political changes that have occurred as urbanization has proceeded?
- What are the consequences of urbanization on the development of Pokhara and its region in general?

Most of the data and information presented here have been collected by the author and his study team at different times. I am a native of Pokhara, growing up there and living there until 2001. I visit the town frequently for personal reasons, for study, and for public interest advocacy (activism) mainly in areas of preserving public properties, safeguarding the environment and reducing river pollution, providing basic needs (drinking water and electricity) to poorer neighbourhoods, particularly squatter settlements, and reducing environmental injustices. Creating awareness through seminars, media briefings, and legal actions are some of the forms taken by such public interest activism. In this paper I also make use of information obtained from secondary sources, mainly the 2001 census reports, studies conducted by development agencies in Pokhara, and theses written by students.

POKHARA'S URBANIZATION IN COMPARATIVE PERSPECTIVE

In the study of urban phenomena, sociologists/anthropologists and development experts are particularly interested in changes in human behaviour and ties in family, kin-groups, and community, and in the impact of economic and political change upon well-being, stratification, and the general development of the society. From this perspective urbanization is understood, very broadly, as a change from community life to a more individualistic style of life in which people are enabled to make more independent decisions. From the study of Pokhara, even though it is seen that individuals are somewhat independent in making decisions – partly because of independence in economic matters due to the availability of jobs – new types of community and social organization have also been formed to cope with the changing urban environment or to improve the urban livability (Evans 2001).[2] This is particularly noticeable among recent immigrants

[2]By 'livability', Evans (2001) means livelihood and sustainability. Urban communities and individuals struggle through their networks and communities to cope with the problems related to these twin problems. This can also be seen in Pokhara, where poor communities and environmentalists have increased their voice for a better urban life.

into a metropolis, but in the case of Pokhara it is more noticeable than in other urban areas in Nepal. This is especially so among the wealthier immigrants. This is one of the reasons for a large number of residents of Pokhara leaving their joint families without much adverse impact on the family and the dominance of the newly immigrated people on the sociocultural, economic, and political life of the town. Poorer immigrants have also formed their own communities and social organizations but this can be seen more as a survival strategy in the face of constant threat of eviction and to obtain cooperation in the absence of state support.

In Nepal, as in other developing countries, planners and policy makers have seen urbanization mainly as a demographic feature. They have considered urban areas as those areas that exceed a specified population size and/or density threshold. For example, in all regulations related to municipalities, urban areas are defined as those having a certain minimum threshold of population. In the latest Municipal Act (Municipal Act 1992), urban centres were defined as settlements with a population exceeding 20,000. Further, this Act defines three categories of urban centre: Metropolitan City (with a minimum population of 300,000, annual revenue of Rs.70 million, and with urban facilities), Sub-Metropolitan City (with a minimum population of 100,000, annual revenue of Rs.20 million, and with urban facilities) and Municipalities (with a minimum population of 20,000, annual revenue of Rs.1 million, and with some basic urban facilities). In the earlier Municipal Acts also population density was the main criterion used to designate towns, although rules were relaxed to consider some other areas as urban centres under political and administrative pressure.[3] Using the criteria of the recent Act, the government has declared fifty-eight urban areas in Nepal, and Pokhara is considered a Sub-Metropolitan City.

Economic development and industrialization are other reasons for the urbanization process. This is also based on the model of urbanization in Western developed economies. The case of Pokhara illustrates, as is demonstrated in this study, that urban development may not necessarily be linked with the process of industrialization. Rather, it represents a city/town rapidly developed thanks to its access to capital, goods, and services in the global market and to a globalization process facilitated by increased transport and communication facilities.

Pokhara is not a historic centre of any particular religious prominence, like Kathmandu or towns in India such as Varanasi and Madurai, which were planned and urbanized according to religious values and customs. On

---

[3]In 1961 the government set a criterion of declaring a settlement as an urban area if it exceeded the 5,000 population mark. This threshold was later increased to 10,000 by the Town Panchayat Act of 1962.

the other hand, Pokhara had some locational advantages in the sense that it facilitated north-south trading activity. The main impetus for its early urbanization, however, came from the 'political-military' interests of early rulers (Blaikie et al. 1980: 124). The rulers, after unification of the country in 1769, developed Pokhara as an administrative centre of West No. 3 district, which comprised three of the present seventy-five districts (Kaski, Lamjung, and Parbat). Similarly, it was also developed as a military centre for the western region, which led to the establishment of military camps and other related offices. The process of reducing the economic and political power of village-based government institutions and their establishment in Pokhara in the recent past, and its recognition as a centre for the western region, has increased the inflow of people from rural areas. Therefore, the impetus for urbanization has not come from economic necessity, but from administrative and political interests.

In Nepal, the study of cities and towns, and of policies concerning their development, has been greatly influenced by geographical thought. Therefore, changes in discourses in urban geography have also influenced urban development. The approach of regional geography (like growth poles, central place theory, growth corridors, rural-urban linkages) in particular has influenced development interventions in urban areas. This approach pays attention to the regional relations of towns and cities with surrounding areas (for examples relating to Nepal, see Johnston et al. 1986: 506; Gurung 1989: 14). In addition, the concept of rural-urban linkages and its possible impact on development of rural and urban areas has been given priority in Nepal in the last three five-year plans (NPC 1998: 259, NPC 2003; Rondinelli 1985, Rondinelli & Evans 1983). Even though only about 16 per cent of population of Nepal is said to live in urban areas now, the growth rate of the urban population is extremely high (7 per cent per year as compared to 2.1 per cent per year in rural areas), which increasingly turns urban areas into major centres of human habitation. Pokhara has been seen as a place which is likely to become an even bigger town in future, which could trigger economic growth for the surrounding rural areas.

Towns and cities in Nepal have not been much studied from the point of view of social and political change. Most of the few studies that have been conducted in this regard are limited to the Kathmandu Valley cities. Outside of the Kathmandu Valley there are only studies by Caplan (1975) and Mikesell (1988). But given the fact that the urban population is growing exponentially, mainly because of rural to urban migration, and that rapid social, economic, and political changes are occurring in the towns and cities, one cannot comprehensively understand the future of the country without proper attention to such changes. With respect to Pokhara, there are numerous studies on migration, land-use changes, and demographic changes (see Adhikari & Seddon 2002 for details of these studies).

This town has not been much studied from the perspective of social and political changes, except for a few studies of inter-caste marriage (Yamamoto 1983), squatter settlements (K.C. et al. 1992), environmental problems (Parajuli 1999), and cultural change in a group of immigrants (Gurungs or Tamu) in the process of resettlement in Pokhara (Pettigrew 2000; Tamblyn 2002).

THE NEPALESE CONTEXT OF URBANIZATION IN POKHARA

Towns and cities in Nepal show diverse trends in terms of urban growth. There are some towns (bazaars) and cities that have been experiencing rapid urbanization; some are growing moderately, some are stagnant, and some have in fact declined (see Map 1.1 for the location of urban areas in Nepal). This is a worldwide phenomenon. Even though there has not been actual decline in the population (except in the case of bazaars like Bandipur for a period) in urban centres, the relative growth of population and urban indicators differ widely. A study of Pokhara in the context of the overall urbanization process of the country can shed light on why towns grow or decline and what consequences this has for the overall development of the country. But, given the arbitrary and changing nature of definition of urban areas in Nepal, this type of study and analysis is extremely difficult. For example, in the 1952/4 census, there was no mention of *sahar* (town), even though it identified ten prominent settlements. The 1961 census for the first time defined *sahar* as those areas with a population over 5,000 and having an urban environment. The Nagar Panchayat Act of 1962 redefined urban areas (*nagars*) as those having "not less than 10,000 population". But it was also considered as an insufficient condition. But P. Sharma (1989) argues that this criterion was not followed in declaring Nagar Panchayats, and that even some areas with less than 10,000 population were declared as *nagars*. The Municipal Act of 1992 and the Local Self Governance Act of 1999 redefined and classified municipal areas into different categories. But again universally accepted criteria (like population size, density, contiguity, and occupational structure) are given scant attention (Sharma 2003).

Nepal is still considered as the least urbanized country in the world and also in South Asia. Only about 16.2 per cent of its 23 million people in 2001 lived in the fifty-eight government-declared urban areas (CBS 2003). The urban population of Nepal was 3.0 per cent of the total population in the 1952/4 census, 3.7 per cent in 1961, 4.2 per cent in 1971, 6.8 per cent in 1981, and 10.1 per cent in 1991. Historically, only the Kathmandu Valley had urban areas before the unification of Nepal in 1769. After the unification of the country, settlements located at strategic places for the collection of agricultural surplus and distribution or marketing of goods, centres for

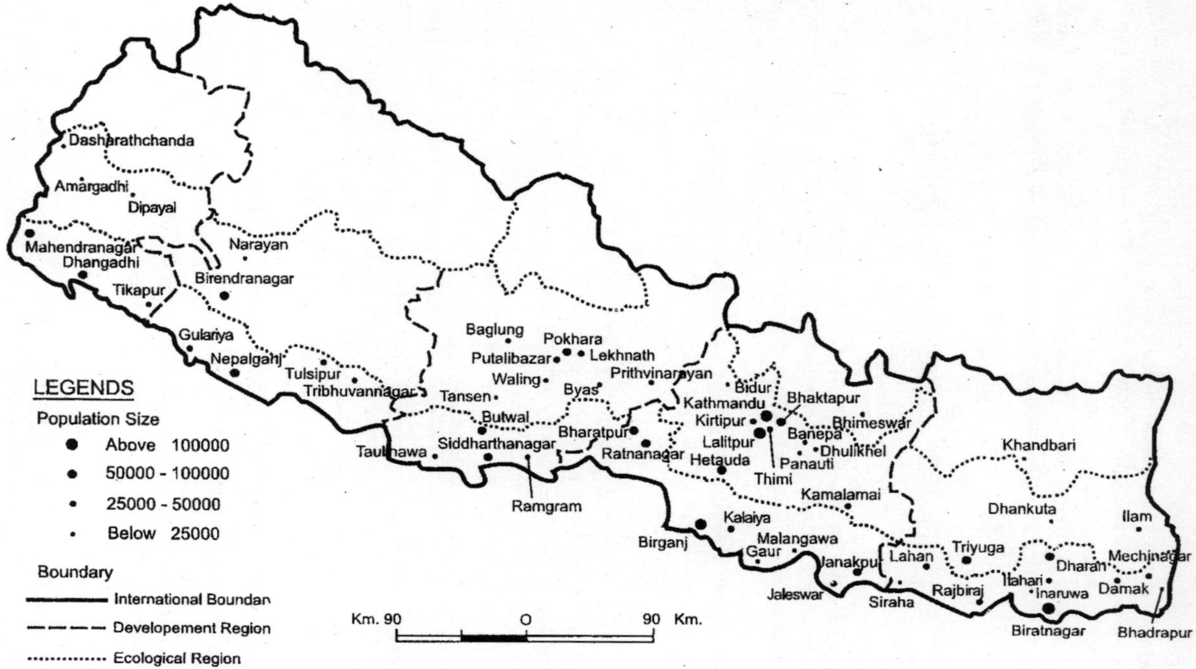

Map 1.1: Location of Pokhara in Relation to Other 58 Government-Declared Urban Centres in Nepal.

the location of offices for the collection of revenues and for stationing of armies, began to grow and later on became important bazaars, towns, and cities (Blaikie et al. 1980; Caplan 1975). In the absence of transportation facilities, strategically located areas on trade routes developed as important bazaars and densely settled areas. Examples of such places are Pokhara, Bandipur, and Tansen in central Nepal.

The strategic locations or importance of areas also changed as the government introduced new policies in urban and economic development, developed infrastructure like roads, and established offices in new and politically and economically important places. This led to changes or shift in the population resulting in the decline of some old bazaars and centres and the emergence and rapid development of others. The regional planning concept introduced in 1972, which aimed to create new development and growth centres, and the development of infrastructure were also instrumental in changing the pace of urbanization of different urban centres. Pokhara was considered as a growth centre for central Nepal (Western Development Region of the four, later five, Development Regions created for the regionally balanced development of the country). The completion of the Siddhartha highway in 1969 linking Pokhara with the Tarai towns (Butwal and Bhairahawa) and the Prithivi highway in 1971 linking Pokhara with Kathmandu led to the changes in the centrality and accessibility of different places. For example, Bandipur, which was an important bazaar until the construction of the Prithivi highway, became relatively inaccessible, but locations like Dumre and Damauli, which are now located along the road, became more accessible. These places grew in importance. Damauli replaced Bandipur as the district headquarters of Tanahu and eventually became a municipality in 1992. The linking of the Prithivi highway with the east-west Mahendra highway in the Tarai region in the early 1980s caused Bandipur to decline still further as a market centre. But this led to the rapid growth of centrally located towns like Bharatpur and Narayangarh. Bharatpur was declared urban only in 1978, but its population increased rapidly in the 1980s and 1990s and reached about 90,000 in 2001 (CBS 2003). Narayangarh was the place where the businessmen of Bandipur would stop for the night on their trading journeys to India. Realizing the strategic location of this place, they had already invested money in purchasing land here. It was through this route that ideas about democracy entered Nepal from India. These traders, who used to visit India regularly, had contacts with Nepali and Indian leaders based there and used to bring booklets and information about political change back to Nepal. It was also through this route that information would pass to Pokhara. Once Bandipur's importance declined, its businessmen moved to Narayangarh. Now the market of Narayangarh is largely controlled by these Bandipur Newar business families.

As in Bandipur, the opening of the Siddhartha highway in 1969 led to the decline of traditional market centres like Tansen to the south of Pokhara. Other places, such as Butwal and Waling located along the highway, became more accessible and centrally located for marketing and other official functions. Tansen was declared an urban area in 1957 but its population grew only very slowly and reached about 20,000 in 2001. Butwal, on the other hand, was declared as a municipal area in 1959 (two years later), but its population increased rapidly to about 75,000 in 2001 (CBS 2003).

The importance or centrality of Pokhara further increased with the opening of these two highways and after the increase in the number of government offices. The opportunities for business and industry, including tourism enterprises and social facilities like health and education, led to a rapid increase in population and urban activities. This is discussed in detail below.

As we have seen, the process of urbanization is not uniform in Nepal. It differs ecologically and according to development regions. Categorization based solely on the ecological belt, however, masks the wide variation that exists between the Kathmandu Valley, the traditional hub of urbanization, and other hill areas. There is also a wide variation in the urbanization in Tarai and Inner Tarai or *bhitri madesh*. So it is important to have a categorization that distinguishes hills/mountains, the Kathmandu Valley, Inner Tarai, and Tarai, as in Table 1.1. If the Kathmandu Valley and the hills are taken together, the hills have a major share in urban population in the last five decades, although the share has declined from 82.4 per cent

Table 1.1: Percentage Distribution of Urban Population and Places by Geographical Region, 1952/4-2001

Regions	1952/4	1961	1971	1981	1991	2001
Hills/ Mountains*	-	4.8 (3)	7.4 (3)	8.7 (4)	11.4 (8)	17.8 (20)
Kathmandu Valley	82.6 (5)	64.9 (5)	54.0 (3)	38.0 (3)	35.3 (3)	30.9 (5)
Inner Tarai	-	-	3.5 (1)	10.1 (4)	9.5 (4)	12.1 (8)
Tarai	17.4 (5)	30.3 (8)	35.0 (9)	43.2 (12)	43.9 (18)	39.2 (25)
Total	100 (10)	100 (16)	100 (16)	100 (23)	100 (33)	100 (58)

Sources: Adhikari & Seddon 2002; CBS 1991, 1994, 2003.

Notes: Figures in parentheses are the number of urban places.

*The Mountain region had no urban population until 2001 by which time two places, Khandbari and Bhimeswar, had received municipal status. The Inner Tarai includes six districts: Sindhuli, Udaypur, Makwanpur, Surkhet, Chitwan, and Dang. In the more usual classification of Hill and Tarai, the first four are included in the Hill region and the last two are included in the Tarai region.

in 1952/4 to 48.7 per cent in 2001. But if the Kathmandu Valley is separated from the hills, the latter contributes only about 17.8 per cent to the total urban population. The Tarai and Inner Tarai share of the total urban population has been increasing. In other words, the Tarai and Inner Tarai towns have been growing faster than the hill towns.

P. Sharma (2003) analyses the changes in rank hierarchy of urban places since 1952/4. This is also reproduced here (see Appendix Table 1A.1) because it shows the relative position of urban areas in different census periods and the overall relative changes between them. For example, in this table, Pokhara did not have any place in the 1952/4 census because it was not yet declared as an urban centre then. In 1961, it was in 13th position, but it moved to 6th position in 1971, 5th position in 1981, and 4th position in the 1991 and 2001 censuses. Tansen occupied the 15th position in 1961, it was 16th in 1971, 21st in 1981, 29th in 1991, and by 2001 it had fallen to the 49th position. This means that relative to other urban centres Tansen has been on the decline. In contrast to Tansen, the positions of Butwal and Bharatpur have increased consistently and they became the 9th and 7th most important towns, respectively, in the 2001 census.

The above discussion shows the fluctuations in the relative growth in urbanization in the country as a whole. The same pattern is also seen among different spatial units within a town. Some areas within the town experience decline (called urban decay) and others experience growth. Urban development within Pokhara also illustrates this. The traditionally important bazaar area in Pokhara has experienced decline, but new emerging places are booming.

THE BEGINNINGS OF URBANIZATION IN POKHARA

As in the case of other towns in west-central Nepal, Pokhara's growth as a market centre can be traced to the spread of Newars westwards from Kathmandu during the latter half of the nineteenth century. Before that the centre of human activity was Kaskikot on the top of a hillock where there was a fort and a palace. This was so when Pokhara was under the jurisdiction of a Ghale (Gurung) king before the invasion of the Shah kings. Kulmandan Shah, who conquered Kaski, which was under the Gurung king in the fourteenth century, also maintained his capital in the same place. But afterwards he made his winter palace at Batulechaur in Pokhara. This led to the development of some settlements there (cf. Parajuli, this volume). Bahuns settled first near Bindyabasini temple when it was built here.[4]

[4]See Shrestha (2000) for the expansion of different types of settlements. He argues that

During the period of unification of the country, Pokhara had become an important military centre in terms of communication and supply of arms. Unification of the country led to an increased movement of people within the country, and helped the development of towns, including Pokhara.

Much of the commercial activity that occurred in Pokhara was the result of its location. It was a gateway to Tibet, and people going to Thak Khola to fetch salt had their stopover here. Tibetan goods, mostly spices and medicinal herbs, were also brought here for trading. As a result, the number of shops began to increase. Goods were brought from as far away as Kathmandu and Bhairahawa. The main products that the merchants of Pokhara supplied to India through trading in Butwal (then Batauli) were *ghee,* honey, wax, oilseeds, and woollen blankets of various types made by hill ethnic groups like Gurungs and Magars who also reared sheep. These products were first collected in Pokhara from the producers in west-central Nepal and then transported to Butwal by porters. Sugar, tea, spices, medicine, and clothes were brought from Butwal on the return trip. Historical sources reveal that Nepali merchants used to travel to Indian cities like Lucknow and Patna for marketing (Regmi 1971: 171). The town and hinterland were self-sufficient in food, and so food items were not imported from outside. Later on, the market also facilitated the distribution of goods produced by rural households and required for farming: spades, axes, sickles, bamboo baskets of various types, tobacco, and ropes. Rural households themselves produced these goods, but traders acted as middlemen. Mobile trading was also very common. Shop owners established mobile camps in the important centres to sell clothes, sugar, spices, and tobacco to rural households and to purchase rural produce like grains and ghee. These mobile trading centres later became second- and third-order market centres.

The Newars of Pokhara still maintain links with their ancestral town in the Kathmandu Valley, Bhaktapur, and invite priests from there to perform various rituals. They maintain many cultural festivals, but they have also modified them in Pokhara to suit the new social-cultural environment. Some festivals, like the Bagh dance, are entirely new developments in Pokhara. The Bhairav dance, Lakhe dance, Krishna Lila, and Gai Jatra are other festivals *(jatra)* that are performed with suitable modifications. These festivals used to attract large crowds from the hinterland and facilitated the exchange or marketing of goods. Temporary markets used to be set up at religious places like Dungesangu, Baidam, and Satmuhane, on auspicious days in the past. As a result, the cultural richness of the Newars was maintained while also serving the important function of market exchange.

---

changes are in the order of "fort settlement", "castle settlement", "temple settlement", and "bazaar settlement".

The early immigrants were not only traders but also small manufacturers who developed metal and weaving industries. Although the weaving industry was well established in Bandipur, the production of cotton clothes was also common in Pokhara. Older residents recall that open spaces, which were abundant at that time, used to be fully occupied with weaving activities like bundling of thread, drying of clothes, and dyeing. Similarly all the metal utensils were produced locally by the Newars. Occupational castes, chiefly Kami (blacksmiths), used to collect ores from scattered small mines and refine them locally. These metals were brought to Pokhara where Newar craftsmen made various artistic utensils.

With the stability of political organization in the mid-eighteenth century, after the unification of the country, permanent commercial bazaars replaced the periodic fairs and further accelerated the migration of people from the hills into the Valley. This trend quickened after malaria eradication programmes commenced in the late 1950s. The expansion in irrigation facilities, location of governmental offices, and initiation of developmental activities were other reasons for migration into the Valley. Transport facilities led to a further concentration of population and the urbanization process commenced after Pokhara was linked by road to the border town of Bhairahawa in 1969 and with Kathmandu in 1971. These roads facilitated the quick movement of goods and people, thus integrating Pokhara and its hinterland with the world economy.

Until the early 1950s, the city area was confined to the areas along the length of a footpath which linked the three temples established by the earlier generations of Newar immigrants. The market area was limited to a row of houses from Ram Krishna Tol to Bagar and to a branch starting from Nalamukh and ending at Ranipauwa.

The opening of the country to the outside world in 1950 led to an increase in commercial activities in Nepal, even though this also wiped out indigenous industries because of the import of cheaper mass-produced goods and commodities from India. Pokhara then started to become a market centre for commodities brought from towns in the Tarai and India for consumption within the town and for supply to the hinterland. The Town Panchayat census in 1965 revealed that there were only about 450 business establishments in Pokhara, of which 56 per cent were *kirana* shops (general stores). From the growth pattern of these *kirana* shops, Blaikie et al. (1980: 128) argue that commercial expansion is a recent phenomenon. By the end of the century (1999), there were altogether 4,047 shops, 1,084 hospitality service units (hotels, restaurants, lodges), 1,740 service units (nursing homes, clinics, repairing, and the like), 39 banks and financial service institutions, and 492 industries.

EXPANSION OF THE TOWN AND ITS URBAN FUNCTIONS

With Pokhara continuing to expand rapidly, the government recognized it as a town in 1965, as regional headquarters of the Western Development Region in 1972, and as a submetropolis in 1995. Even though the supply of goods from distant markets in the Tarai, India, or overseas is still the main function of the town, it has grown to provide many other urban services like education, transportation, communication, administration, hospitality, and health. Population too has been growing rapidly, by about 5.9 per cent per year in the 1990s as compared to the national average of 2.1 per cent (CBS 2003). The population growth rate of the city was even higher in earlier times, and was the highest (about 14.3 per cent per year) during the 1960s (Table 1.2), a period which coincides with the eradication of malaria and the initiation of development activities.

This growth in population is mainly due to inward migration from the hill villages. The expansion of the physical boundary of the municipality, which was mainly due to various political vested interests, has also led to the increase in the population of Pokhara. Gurung (1989) estimates that about 20 per cent of the increase in population is due to the expansion in the territory of Pokhara municipality, but since 1981 this has not been the case. Because of the in-migration of people from rural areas to Pokhara, population growth rates in the environs (rural hinterlands) of Pokhara have remained low, less than 1.2 per cent per annum in the 1980s and 1990s (nationally the growth rate has remained about 2.1 per cent to 2.7 per cent per annum in the last three decades) (Adhikari & Seddon 2002: 253 – Annex Table 34). Some villages have also faced stagnation in population size. For example, in Thak, there were 491 persons in 1969 and 494 in 1992 (Pettigrew 2000: 8). A similar situation exists in most Gurung villages, where remittance income from abroad is instrumental in recent times in instigating out-migration and resettlement in Pokhara. Previously, until approximately the 1970s, remittance income was invested in the village itself, in land, animals, ornaments, and housing. But now there is a high rate of capital flight to Pokhara.

Table 1.2: Population Size and Growth Rate in Pokhara Town

Year	Population size	Population growth rate (annual)
1952/4	3,755	-
1961	5,413	*c.* 5.0% (1952/4-61)
1971	20,611	14.3% (1961-71)
1981	46,642	8.5% (1971-81)
1991	95,268	7.4% (1981-91)
2001	169,160	5.9% (1991-2001)

Sources: Gurung et al. 2048 v.s. (1992); CBS 1998; CBS 2003.
Growth rate calculated by the author.

A major factor which has brought more people from the hills to settle permanently in Pokhara is education, which is seen as essential for job opportunities in the future, and also because of the social prestige that is given to education in modern life. The wealthier people in particular have been attracted to the town because of its education facilities for their children who find it unsatisfying and physically exhausting to commute every day from the villages. Macfarlane (1989: 186) has noted from his study area (Thak) that scarcely any of those who went off to Pokhara to school in the 1970s returned to the village. Other researchers (Pettigrew 2000; McHugh 2001) have also stressed that one of the main reasons for out-migration of Gurung men, and also women even though to a lesser extent, to foreign countries, is to enable their children to get a good education. This is why Pokhara has a large number of private English schools (popularly known as boarding schools) and it is usually the *lahure* Gurungs and Magars who keep their children as boarders in these schools. The permanent settlement of retired army personnel (mainly Gurungs and Magars) in Pokhara has also helped to increase the pace of urbanization. Table 1.3 illustrates the number of Gurung households in Pokhara at various periods. It shows that while there were only 33 Gurung households in Pokhara in 1957, this number had increased to 8,046 households by 2001, an increase of 250 times in three and half decades.

The migration of Gurungs from various hill villages has also resulted in separate enclaves of people hailing from the same region. For example, the Matepani area of Pokhara town has a predominance of Gurungs from the eastern part of Kaski district. Similarly, the Deep area is settled by Gurungs from districts to the west of Pokhara, and the Pardi area has Gurungs and Magars from Syangjya district. The Rambazar area has more people from Syangjya. Even the names of new neighbourhoods reflect the settlers' places of origin. This happens primarily because a person buying land in Pokhara utilizes his social network of people who have already migrated here. As these former migrants tend to have a good knowledge of their locality, they convince the prospective buyer to buy land in their

Table 1.3: Total Gurung Households in Pokhara from 1957 to 2001

Period (Year)	Number of households	Main wards settled, largest first
1957	33	1,7,12
1958-78	632	1,7,10,12,16,13
1978-98	5,500	1,10,12,13,7,16
1998-2001	2,546	1,10,12,13,7,16
Total	8,046	1,10,12,13,7,16

Sources: Gurung (1979) for data up to 1978; other data are my estimates based on population data collected by the Office of Pokhara Sub-Metropolitan City. The estimate for 2001 was based on census data on population which was divided by 4.2, the average family size for Pokhara for that year. Pettigrew also writes that the family size of Tamu (Gurungs) in Pokhara is small (2000: 12).

neighbourhood. Moreover, for reasons of security, people from the same origin and having a kinship network tend to cluster together. Because of this clustering of village-folk or kin-groups, immigrants do not hesitate to leave their family behind when they go abroad for a prolonged period. Mary Des Chene (1992) reports a similar situation in Bhairahawa, another town in the Tarai where retired army personnel have settled. She comments that "when relocating within Nepal, Gurungs have created enclaves that reproduce, in an attenuated form, the communities of the hills" (1992: 7). In other words, it is the reproduction of the social geography of the hills. Pettigrew (2000: 12) also writes that Gurung urban settlements bear a strong resemblance to their rural settlement patterns, which is considered as a reason for the Gurungs' preference to live in densely nucleated clusters. This finding also lends support to the theory that community life can continue to exist within an urban space. As a result of this process of clustering, one can find in Pokhara a little Ghandrung, a little Siklis, a little Syangja, and the like. The Gurungs of Pokhara also organize various cultural activities, derived mainly from their rural roots. Pettigrew (2000: 13) argues that they remain connected to, and to an extent, dependent on their villages. As a result, she refers to them as "urban villagers". They have also established their religious institutions, which have helped them maintain solidarity and assert their cultural symbols in this urban landscape. For example, they have built their monasteries and cremation places in a distinctive way.[5] The revival of this culture, especially the healing culture using a shaman, is also attributed to growing social and psychological stress that Gurungs face in an alien, stressful, and competitive urban society (Pettigrew 2000). This solidarity coupled with the increase in the number of Gurung households (discussed above) has resulted in an increased participation of Gurungs in the public sphere in recent times.

The enhanced awareness of cultural identity is also seen in other minor ethnic groups, like the Tibetans in Pokhara. About 3,000 Tibetan refugees, sheltered in three camps, regularly organize various cultural and religious activities. This increased ethnic and religious assertiveness on the part of new immigrants has also led to increased freedom of movement for the early settlers of Pokhara, i.e. Bahuns and Chetris. This was seen mainly in the 1990s. The new-found freedom in 1990 is one of the main reasons for

---

[5] A Gurung (Tamu) organization called Tamu Pye Lhu Sangh has built a *kul* (lineage) temple called *Kairibo* in Ramghat, Pokhara. This *Kairibo* or *Failu Kairibo* (ancestral *Kairibo*) has four pointed towers at the four corners and a pillar in the middle in accordance with Gurung shamanic cosmology. These towers and pillar represent the five basic elements of life. As the Gurungs are nature worshippers, these five elements play an important role in their religion. Gurungs have also set up a Buddhist monastery in Ramghat, and other smaller ones in many of the neighbourhoods in which they have settled (Tamblyn 2002).

the increased sensitivity towards religious and cultural values. Various Hindu Pandits are now seen in Pokhara organizing rituals and ceremonies more frequently than before. Pandit Narayan Pokharel, who was also president of the Bishwa Hindu Parishad (Nepal Chapter), was very popular in Pokhara, frequently organizing Hindu ceremonies to generate funds for religious and social purposes (e.g. school buildings). (He was assassinated, presumably by Maoists, in early May 2005.) Pokhara has also been seen as a place where more funds can be generated from such ceremonies. For example, a Shrimad Bhagavat Saptahik Puran ceremony was organized in Lekhnath-1, from 19 to 24 February 2004, to raise funds to build a community hospital. In this Hindu religious ceremony, Gurungs, particularly Gurung women, were also conspicuous participants. The ceremony was able to raise Rs.15 million. At least seven such ceremonies have been organized in Pokhara in the last seven years. More and more temples have also been built in Pokhara through such fund-raising ceremonies. The growing number of 'Ama Tolis' (women's groups) in Pokhara has also been instrumental in the increase in the number of temples.

As Pokhara was a main stopover on the trade route between India and Tibet, it received traders from both north and south. The Thakalis and Lobas of the Mustang area came, especially in winter, to trade their goods for food grains. The Thakalis, who acted as middlemen between the hill people and the Tibetans, controlled the salt trade. Until the 1960s, one could see several makeshift tea shops and restaurants in Pokhara during winter catering to traders coming mainly from the north. The Thakalis maintained warehouses in Pokhara where they stored food grains and commodities to be supplied to the north. Since mule trains were the main means of transportation in the hills, pack animals were a common sight in the town. After the annexation of Tibet by China in 1959, trade suffered and the Thakalis began to spread across the country. Many settled permanently in Pokhara, where they helped develop the hospitality industry. The local populace adopted some of their social mechanisms (such as the *dhukuti*, or rotating credit association) to raise capital for the establishment of business and industry (Fisher 2001). Today, *dhukuti* is 'played' in almost all neighbourhoods in Pokhara, and this also seems to have increased the interaction among different caste and ethnic groups. Generally, however, *dhukutis* are set up by members of the same social group. The migration of Thakalis into Pokhara continues to this day, and the process of immigration to Pokhara takes the same form as with Gurungs and Magars, i.e. first migrating to a foreign country, and then slowly developing a platform in Pokhara by buying land, developing networks and building a house, and finally moving there.

SOCIO-ECONOMIC CHANGES IN POKHARA

Changes in the Ethnic Composition of Pokhara

The migration of hill people to Pokhara Valley has also changed the social structure of Pokhara town. Until the mid 1960s, Bahuns, Chetris, and other Hindu castes dominated the population of the town. Gurungs and Magars were very few in number. But the migration of Gurungs and Magars since the 1960s, especially those employed in the British and Indian armies, has changed the ethnic composition of the town. Since the 1990s there has been a slight reduction in the proportion of Chetris and Newars and an increase in Magars, Tamangs, other hill groups, and Tarai people. In other words, the numbers of minor groups has been on the increase in Pokhara. Altogether eighty-one ethnic and caste groups were recorded in Pokhara according to the census report of 2001 (CBS 2003). But in the past, in the early 1950s, there were at most ten to fifteen, mainly caste groups. Thus urbanization has brought increasing ethnic diversity to Pokhara (Table 1.4).

Table 1.4: Changes in the Ethnic Composition of Pokhara's Population

Ethnic Groups	1978		1991		2001	
	Population	%age	Population	%age	Population	%age
Bahun	17,489*	8.30*	20,494	21.51	35,679	22.82
Chetri/Thakuri			17,007	17.85	26,379	16.88
Newar	6,356	17.60	12,009	12.60	15,710	10.05
Gurung	4,320	11.30	20,482	21.49	33,795	21.25
Dalits	3,184	8.80	8,289	8.70	13,216	8.45
Magar	1,507	4.20	6,358	6.67	12,829	8.21
Thakali	606	1.70	1,462	1.53	1,696	1.08
Muslims	426	1.20	1,289	1.36	1,896	1.21
Tamang			1,611	1.69	4,153	2.65
Sanyasi			1,456	1.53	1,514	0.97
Tarai people			1,785	1.87	4,678	3.00
Other hill people			2,112	2.22	3,576	2.29
Others	2,301	5.80	932	0.98	1,191	0.76
Total	36,189	100.00	95,286	100.00	156,312	100.00

Sources: CBS (2003) and Adhikari & Seddon (2002).
Note: *This includes both Bahun and Chetri populations as they were not disaggregated in the 1978 survey.

Changes in Occupational Patterns and Income Sources

Moving away from the agriculture sector is one of the main characteristics of urbanization (cf. Parajuli, Chhetri, this volume). Pokhara has also seen this change. In 1971, 63 per cent of households depended mainly on farming as a source of income. This declined to 27 per cent in 1991 and to 9.8 per cent in 2001 (Parajuli 1999: 3; CBS 2003). This means that about 90 per cent of Pokhara's population now depends mainly on non-farm sources of income. The decline in farming as an occupation is the result not only of a lack of land, but also because people are reluctant to do it because of the hard work involved (Parajuli 1999).

One of the main non-farm sources of income for the Pokhara citizens has been foreign labour migration. A recent study conducted by Pokhara Municipality revealed that about 3,500 people held jobs in foreign countries and their remittances contributed 23 per cent of the income of Pokhara. Similarly, 2,500 people from Pokhara are reported to receive pensions, mainly from their employment in British and Indian armies. Their income contributes 3.3 per cent to the total income of the town. Adding what flows directly into Pokhara to the flow of savings from villages and income from tourism (about 9.6 per cent of the income of the town),[6] Pokhara can be considered a town dependent on outside income. The number of Pokhara citizens working in foreign countries is reported to be higher in the census report of 2001 (CBS 2003: 15-25) than in the study conducted by the Pokhara Metropolis Office (mentioned above). This report reveals that 7,579 people (5.83 per cent of the total population) from Pokhara are living in more than 25 foreign countries, most of them in Hong Kong (23 per cent), followed by India (20 per cent), Saudi Arabia (11.8 per cent), UK (9.2 per cent), and Japan (5.9 per cent). Again previous work in the British Gurkhas is also linked with the present patterns of out-migration. Many Pokhara youths got the chance to work and reside in Hong Kong because they were born there while their fathers were working in the British Army. Previously, in the 1970s and 1980s, Pokhara was known as a crime-prone town. The recent migration is also said to have increased crime rates as the children of the migrant parents are also considered to be involved in crime and drugs. Because of the heavy dependence of Pokhara on external income and its unproductive use, local popular poet, Tirtha Shrestha, calls the town a "*lahure* town" (*Kantipur*, 10 January 2004, Saturday supplementary). He has also written a popular poem "Lahure (dahlia) flower I want to change your name", which was written when he saw a young woman enduring the death of her *lahure* husband in a conflict in India.

Immigration and Inflow of Capital into Pokhara

Income brought in by these new rural migrants (mainly Gurung and Magar), and its investment in housing, industry, and business, has accelerated the pace of urbanization in Pokhara. The main source of savings for people in

---

[6]The other sources of income of households in Pokhara are trade and commerce (14.2 per cent of income), industry (15.5 per cent), services (15 per cent), transportation (8.3 per cent), and agriculture (10.4 per cent) (PSMC 2000, based on a comparatively larger field study conducted in 1998 by the Tourism Infrastructure Development Project, financed by the Asian Development Bank).

rural central Nepal is remittances[7] and some ethnic groups, such as Gurungs, Magars, and Tamangs, have relatively greater access to them (Adhikari 1996). Outside income (mainly remittances) contributes as much as 40 per cent to the household income in Kaski district; among the Gurungs this rises to as much as 60 per cent (Adhikari 1996). The savings thus generated flow into Pokhara where they are used for developing small business or industrial enterprises, hotels, and real estate. These investments also attract labourers from central Nepal as well as from other regions. As reported in *Himal* (Dahal 1999: 30), Pokhara is the main centre where remittances have played a major role in transforming the economy and urban structure. Yet, a large part of the remittance money has not been utilized in productive sectors which would create job opportunities and initiate multiplier impacts in the economy. The same article reports that a substantial amount of remittance money has gone as 'bad debt' and much is spent on the conspicuous consumption of foreign commodities which make little contribution to the local economy. This is also reflected in an article by Pettigrew (2000), who writes that a large amount of remittance money has been lost without producing successful businesses or industries. She also indicates that the Gurungs have lost out in businesses to longer-established business families of other groups and are always hard-pressed for money. However, other people, especially Pokhara Brahmans and Chetris, feel that *lahure* Gurungs are indeed very wealthy as they have access to remunerative outside employment. Middle-class Brahmans and Chetris often decry the expensive lifestyle of the *lahure*s and bemoan the adverse impact this has on their children and on their traditional frugal household economy.

Although the exact amount of remittance money coming into Pokhara has still not been accurately calculated, it is substantial. The Indian Pension Camp alone disburses about Rs.4 billion per year to 60,000 retired personnel of the Indian Army residing in the Western Development Region. A large part of this income also flows into Pokhara. Similarly, there are several thousand retired British Army personnel in Pokhara who receive slightly higher pensions.

The foregoing discussion raises the question: which are the places from where people migrate and what are the reasons for their migration? A study conducted in 1986 among a sample of immigrants (192 households) in Pokhara revealed that a majority of them came from Kaski district, followed by Syangjya, Parbat, and Tanahu districts, and the Kathmandu

[7]This has largely been so in other parts of the country too and is now seen as a main factor for the reduction of poverty by 11 per cent in the last eight years (1995/6 to 2003/4). This was revealed by a Living Standard Survey Conducted by CBS in 2003/4, and made public on 12 May 2005 through a press release.

Valley (Sharma 1986: 22-6). Other districts from which Pokhara receives a smaller proportion of immigrants include Baglung, Mustang, Lamjung, Gorkha, and Dhading. A majority (37 per cent) of the immigrants said they came for employment (service). Others said they came there for business opportunities (29 per cent), education of children (19 per cent), urban facilities (8 per cent), and to establish industry (7 per cent). Apart from those who have settled permanently, this study also identified seasonal migrants who come mainly from Kaski, Tanahu, and Mustang districts. Other districts of lesser importance in terms of seasonal migration are, in descending order, Parbat, Syangjya, Gorkha, Baglung, Rupandehi, Dhading, Lamjung, and the Kathmandu Valley. A large proportion of these seasonal migrants were involved in construction-related work and in jobs like portering. The hotel industry attracts a significant number of these seasonal migrants. They are also involved in selling farm produce, tailoring, knitting, and the manufacture of utensils, bangles, shoes, and jewellery (Sharma 1986: 27-8). The census of 2001 revealed that 33.6 per cent of the population (156,312) was born outside Kaski district in which Pokhara is located, and 3.8 per cent were foreign-born.

Changes in Business and Service Structures

Bazaar areas or shopping centres have also expanded significantly in Pokhara over the past two to three decades. For example, Mahendrapul, Bagar, Ranipauwa, Chipledhunga - New Road, Prithvichok - Srijanachok, Pardi - Birauta, and Rambazar (pension camp) have emerged as the main trading centres. On the other hand, the importance of the old bazaar – Ramkrishna Tol to Bagar – has declined. Some of the shops there are still of a traditional nature, catering to the needs of rural people. This change, resulting from the development of new infrastructure and communication systems, has also altered the population density of various places within the town. The new marketing centres no longer resemble the old bazaar in that the former do not incorporate religious and cultural symbols in the physical planning of the space or in the construction of shop buildings.

Besides Newars, who are traditionally business-oriented, members of other cultural groups have turned to business in increasing numbers. A survey conducted in 1974-5 revealed that of the 127 businesspersons surveyed randomly in Pokhara, 48 per cent were Newar. Other major businesspersons were from the Chetri, Bahun, and Thakali groups. None were from the Gurung or Magar group (Blaikie et al. 1980: 154). Although Newars may still be in a dominant position in terms of numbers, partly due also to the inheritance of business enterprises, other groups, including today Gurungs and Magars, are now increasing their presence in business and industries by investing remittance money. Because of the decline of some old market centres, Newars have also been moving to new nodal points (e.g. Mahendrapul, Prithivichok, Zero-Kilometer, and the like) to start new businesses. Accordingly, Newars are also spreading throughout the town. Traditional cooperation among the Newars is still helping them remain successful in business. This cooperation is even stronger among the Thakalis. Although the system of *dhukuti* (rotating credit) began among the Thakalis and helped them succeed in business, it has been widely adopted by others involved in businesses. These changes in the structure of ownership of commercial activities and access to different types of business, and the expression of immigrant identities in an urban context, have not yet been studied in detail, with a few exceptions (e.g. Doherty 1975, and Pettigrew 2000, which focused on the Gurung case).

As with the growth of population and the expansion of marketing facilities, other urban facilities too have expanded in the town. There are now 14 university campuses and 143 schools of various types, about 600 hospital beds, and 8,500 telephone lines (PSMC 1999). Since Pokhara is the administrative centre for the Western Development Region, the number of government and quasi-government offices has also increased significantly. The industrial base of the town has also been strengthened with the establishment of thirty-three medium- to large-scale industries each employing more than fifty people. The number of small and cottage industries is well over 1,442 and employed 10,988 people in 1999 (DHPP 1999). Traditional industries like brass, bronze, and other metal industries still provide employment opportunities for a large number: 80 such industries provide employment to 1,280 persons. Other industries providing employment include construction services (1,163 persons) and rice and oil mills (991 persons). Carpet industries provide employment to about 779 persons and hotels, lodges, and restaurants employ 1,248 persons (ibid.).

Tourism also has great potential in Pokhara mainly because of the area's natural beauty. It is estimated that 103,895 tourists visited Pokhara in 1998 (PSMC 1999). But since then their numbers have reduced almost by half because of political and military conflict. The total investment in the hotel industry in Pokhara has been estimated at some Rs.15 billion (mainly coming from remittances), but now the industry is running at a loss. As a result, an important source of local income has gone into steep decline.

The rapidity of urbanization and in-migration is also reflected in increased land values in Pokhara. Even in smaller towns, such as Baglung, Beni, Syangjya, and the like, land prices are extremely high, and the main reason that local people cite for this is remittances, which are not invested in rural areas but are invested in urban centres. A huge increase occurred during 1960-70, when in-migration was high. Land per *ropani* in 1960 was estimated at Rs.1,000, but by 1970 the same fetched Rs.18,000, an eighteen-fold increase in ten years (Pandit 1989: 40). As poor rural migrants who enter Pokhara for employment cannot afford to buy land, they end up as squatters (see Yamamoto, this volume). On the other hand, land prices in villages seem to be declining, as suggested by, for example, Macfarlane (2001) for the village of Thak. Even though it may not be correct to generalize this finding (because in some places the price of paddy land has increased considerably, even in villages), the rate of increase is certainly far less than that in Pokhara.

Changes in Inter-Caste Relations

Urbanization in Pokhara has led to greater closeness between the diverse ethnic groups now living in Pokhara. This is despite the fact that there is a simultaneous increase in self-awareness among ethnic groups like Gurungs, Magars, and Tamangs and among the caste groups in terms of their religious identity. This tendency is not largely motivated by religious values. As a result, marriages and interactions are not restricted within the caste or ethnic groups. Therefore, more and more people are mixing and merging together than before. Greater independence, because of the availability of jobs and influence of foreign culture, has led to independence of thought, which has also facilitated inter-caste marriage (compare LeVine on Kathmandu, this volume). Urbanization in Pokhara also means that traditional values regarding marriage have been declining. For example, Brahmans are no longer concerned about the distinction between the Upadhyaya and Jaisi categories when selecting marriage partners. Among the new immigrants, such as the Gurungs, traditional cross-cousin marriages have been declining. On the other hand, the practice of 'love marriage' is growing (Pettigrew 2000; McHugh 2001). In arranged marriages, a *lahure* groom is generally preferred by parents for their daughters.[8] In the past, there have been cases of a Gurung girl entering into a love marriage with man of another caste, and being taken back by her parents even after some years of marriage so that she could be remarried to a man they judged proper. But nowadays this practice is not seen.

Y. Yamamoto (1983) has found some interesting patterns in inter-caste marriages in Pokhara. His study revealed that there are more cases (in relation to population size) of inter-caste marriage in Pokhara than in other urban areas in Nepal. The most common type of inter-caste marriage was hypogamous, i.e. women marrying men from a lower position in the caste

---

[8]In one case a prominent Gurung occupying a high political position and high social status in Pokhara (who had married two of his daughters to British *lahures*) did not marry his last daughter to an educated Gurung man who had claimed her in marriage because he was related as a cross cousin. Frustrated, the prospective groom tried hard to enter the army, in which he was successful. He later asked for the same girl in marriage and this time his proposal was accepted. This prominent Gurung, who was also a university teacher, always told his students that they should not go to foreign countries for work.

hierarchy. As this type of marriage is disadvantageous to women in Hindu society, Yamamoto considers this to be the result of urbanization.

To make some comparison with Yamamoto's study, I collected information in December 2003 on the types and extent of inter-caste marriage based on the marriage register at the Pokhara Municipality office. In principle, everyone from Pokhara should register their marriage at this office, and with the requirement to show one's marriage certificate in most official processes, more and more marriages are now being registered. In the year from mid July 2002 to mid July 2003, 845 marriages were registered, of which 154 were inter-caste marriages. Even though questions may be raised on how many, or what proportion, of marriages in Pokhara are registered in a year, the registering of 845 marriages is quite high considering the fact that one third of Pokhara's population of 156,000 are children below the age of fourteen. Another third consists of the age group of fifteen to thirty years. This means that traditional as well as inter-caste marriages are increasingly registered in the office, but it is likely that more of the inter-caste marriages are registered than the traditional arranged marriages. Of the total marriages registered in the year studied, 18 per cent were inter-caste. But when Yamamoto conducted his study in the early 1980s, only 1.8 per cent were inter-caste. In the present study 51 per cent of the inter-caste marriages were hypogamous, i.e. women marrying men of 'lower' caste status. It was also interesting to find that women from Bahun, Gurung, Magar, and Newar groups showed a higher tendency to opt for inter-caste marriages than the men of these groups. The opposite tendency was found among the Chetris and Dalits, where men were seen to choose inter-caste marriages, and it is difficult to ascertain the reasons for this pattern. Three Japanese citizens had also registered their inter-ethnic group marriages: greater availability of jobs (discussed earlier) leading to independence from family and loss of social pressure, the outcome of the urbanization process, could be the main reason prompting women to take the bold step of entering into an inter-caste marriage, as the parents in most cases still seem traditional. Marriages with foreign citizens also occur in Pokhara, and this tendency seems to have increased in recent times. A small neighbourhood has been developed on the upstream of Phewa Lake (Sedi Bagar, at the foot of Sarangkot hill) where these couples (locals marrying foreigners) have built their houses. This neighbourhood is popularly known as Jwain Tol ('son-in-law' or 'brother-in-law' neighbourhood).

The higher incidence of inter-caste marriage among Dalit males (18 out of 154 cases) may convey some message with regard to the caste hierarchy.[9] It raises the question whether urbanization is slowly blurring

[9]Many Dalits have the same 'surnames' (clan names) as higher castes, e.g. Gautam, Kafle, and

caste distinctions and untouchability. There were eight cases of marriage of Dalits with high-caste groups (Bahun, Chetri, and Newar), six cases with Janajatis (Gurung and 'Lama'), and four cases between different Dalit groups in 2002-3. Unfortunately such a small number of cases do not permit any conclusions about the blurring of untouchability, but there is other evidence which suggests that Pokhara's urban society has been favourable for such inter-caste marriages and for the reduction of untouchability. In most hotels and restaurants one no longer sees Dalits washing their own glasses or plates, nor can people be observed sprinkling water on their bodies after touching a Dalit. Only in some interior parts of the town do some local people try to impose on local Dalits such caste-based behaviour. Dalits and non-Dalits can often be seen eating together, and Dalits serve food in public functions. This shows that traditional exclusions towards Dalits are on the decline. However, this does not mean that caste boundaries have all disappeared, but that their open expression is much rarer.[10] Changes in attitudes have not yet favoured Dalit candidates in the political process. As discussed below, Dalit candidates do not attract voters. However, urbanization in Pokhara has enabled greater social and political activism from Dalits and given a higher profile to the campaign to abolish untouchability.

The higher incidence (41 in 154) of marriage between caste groups (Bahun, Chetri, and Newar) and Janajatis may also lead one to think that ethnic boundaries are being diluted.[11] But, as discussed below, in other political and cultural areas, the boundaries among the caste groups and Janajatis seem to be solidifying.[12] The other 95 cases of inter-caste mar-

---

so on. This is especially so in the far west and mid-west of Nepal. How far this has given an erroneous impression of a high rate of Dalit-high-caste marriage cannot be ascertained without checking with the persons themselves. It is also equally likely that because of this practice some relevant cases were omitted.

[10]The difficulty Dalits face in finding a place to rent is also occasionally reported in the newspapers.

[11]The analysis of inter-caste marriage should also be done at the class level, but this was not possible at this stage. The list of names of people registering their marriage collected from the office was not sufficient for such an analysis. Moreover, it would be interesting to examine the geographical boundary of rural (VDC) and urban areas in an inter-caste marriage.

[12]It is a well-known fact that there are controversies in defining Janajatis. This is especially so about the inclusion of Newars in the Janajati fold. Among the sixty-one Janajatis initially recognized by the government, the Newars were also included. After some time, some Newars asked for the Newars to be withdrawn from the list. But the pro-Janajati lobby was stronger. At present, the government has reserved a certain number of government jobs and educational seats for Janajatis, women, and Dalits. For example, 15 per cent, 20 per cent and 10 per cent, respectively of the educational seats are reserved for them. In government jobs, this is 5 per cent, 10 per cent and 20 per cent, respectively. It has been mainly the Newars who have been successful in obtaining the seats reserved for Janajatis. Therefore, they may now be more

riage were between caste groups, mainly Bahun, Chetri, and Newar. Nowadays, in Pokhara, it is also seen that arranged inter-caste/ethnic group marriages are held, but they seem to be limited to within a certain class.

The increased flexibility for marriage between caste and Janajatis, which has been brought about mainly by urbanization and independence, also leads to another question for future investigation whether the children born from such marriages will act to dismantle the boundaries among the people in terms of languages, caste/ethnic identity, and political organization.

The decline in farming practices in Pokhara (discussed earlier) has also some repercussions on the Dalits and higher caste relationships. Their patron-client relationship has almost been wiped out by the loss of farming traditions and increased incorporation within the market economy (cf. Chhetri, this volume). The services earlier provided by Dalits are now cheaply available in the market and provided by non-Dalit households. At present Dalits are not able to find jobs (they often work as sweepers, waste collectors, tailors, or shoemakers in shoemaking shops owned mostly by non-Dalits). They face difficult livelihood problems and their economic position seems to have deteriorated. The increased land value had helped to sustain them for some time, but selling off their land pushed them to the fringes of the town. With the exception of a few who are well off Dalits, the Dalits seem to be alienated from society and are not able to unite politically or to participate in the political process.

Traditionally Pokhara's population consisted of a significant proportion of Dalit households. They were not concentrated in any location but were distributed all over Pokhara. But in each village or ward, Dalit houses were built at a place which was known by the name of the subgroup residing there. Therefore, Dalits were physically segregated because of their perceived untouchability. Damai (traditionally tailors), Kami (blacksmiths), Sarki (cobblers), Sunar (goldsmiths), Gaine (Gandharva, singers), and Pode (fishermen) were the prominent Dalit groups in Pokhara. Though all other Dalit groups speak Nepali, the Pode or traditional fishermen speak Newari as their mother tongue; however lately, they have begun to speak more Nepali than Newari.

Because of the decline in the demand from traditional patrons, Dalits in general have also turned towards tourism-related activities in Pokhara. For example, Gaines now see more opportunities in selling their musical

motivated to retain that title. As far as Pokhara is concerned, my observation is that Newars feel closer to the caste groups than to the Janajatis in terms of social and cultural perspectives. Therefore, Janajatis here refers mainly to the so-called hill tribes, and in this chapter Newars are considered as a separate group. Because of various adjustments and amalgamations, there are now fifty-nine officially recognized Janajati groups.

instruments and providing singing and dancing service to tourists (Parajuli, this volume; Morimoto 2002). The same is also true of the Damais, who work making clothes for tourists or in clothing-repair shops. They also work as trekking guides and porters. Dalits, especially Gaines, are also employed as cleaners. They have taken the responsibility of managing the solid waste in Pokhara, whether as employees of the Municipality office or of private companies.

The large-scale selling off of their land by Pokhara Dalits means that they have mostly shifted from their original places or given their space to outside immigrants. This has led to the inclusion of non-Dalits in the previously solely Dalit settlements.

Diverse Responses to Sanskritization

Recent sociocultural features in Pokhara lead one to the conclusion that people, especially the Janajatis, are moving against Sanskritization, i.e. against the adoption of the sociocultural and religious practices of so-called higher castes like Bahuns and Chetris, or of the Hindu religion. A revivalist trend can be clearly observed in Pokhara, especially among the wealthier Janajatis and after 1990, i.e. after the institutionalization of the open democratic political system. Among some of these revivalists, shamanistic death rituals (involving animal sacrifice) are also followed. At present there are two main Gurung monasteries in Pokhara and several smaller monasteries in various neighbourhoods. It is said that the one at the Ramghat (near the hospital) is more frequented by *charjat* Gurungs, whereas the one on the northern side of Ramghat is frequented by *sorajat* Gurungs. Some Gurungs now blame the Bahuns for dividing their society into castes (*sorajat* and *charjat*), and for writing their history in a distorted way. Such activists also argue that the use of lamas as priests is a relatively newly introduced practice (Macfarlane 1997). In Pokhara the celebration of the Gurungs' festivals, such as Loshar and Tote, is prominent and draws considerable public attention. They have opened shops that sell traditional Gurung dress for both men and women. On the Loshar day, various activities are organized as in a traditional Gurung community. In addition, competitions in fluency in the Gurung language, the screening of Gurung films, and so forth, are also organized by Gurung associations like the Tamu Choja Dhi and Tamu Pya Hlu. Pokhara has also become a centre for the promotion of the Gurung language. Similar revivalist activities are also to be seen among other prominent ethnic groups such as the Thakalis, Tamangs, and Magars. The greater economic independence and freedom provided by political changes are also responsible for the search for identity in an otherwise alien world.

The consequence of these attempts to reconstruct one's identity in a changed urban culture is the existence of diversity and plurality in the sociocultural life of the town. Pokhara has become more vibrant than before. I feel that the impact of this change is also seen in the preservation of the language. In Pokhara now, as the census report of 2001 shows, about 69 per cent of the people speak Nepali, and 31 per cent speak their own language/dialect. Considering the fact that 37 per cent of the population of Pokhara are Janajatis, one would assume that 63 per cent would speak Nepali if every group spoke its own language. Gurungs represent 22 per cent of the population in Pokhara and 17 per cent speak Gurung. Newars make up 10 per cent but only 6 per cent speak Newari. With the thirty years of effort that the government has put in, during the Panchayat era, to make people speak Nepali, it could be assumed that there would be an even more severe decline in the percentage of people speaking their own languages and dialects. This suggests the question: why there has not been a drastic decline in the population speaking non-Nepali languages in Pokhara? Is it due to the continuous immigration of non-Nepali-speaking people or due to the social activism that seeks to preserve minority languages? At this stage it is difficult to answer these questions as both processes are operating simultaneously.

Among the Janajatis as well there is controversy as to whether they should abandon Hindu traditions which have already been incorporated into their religious and cultural practices. For example, among the Gurungs there are some who advocate a complete boycott of the main Hindu festival, Dasain Tika. But there are some Gurung scholars who claim that Dasain Tika is in fact their own indigenous festival later adopted by the Hindus. They also argue for its continuation as it is politically desirable to secure army jobs in India, largely a Hindu country. This has been the argument forwarded by Jagman Gurung (2000). It was interesting to note that when a Hindu ceremony (Bhagavat) was organized recently with Narayan Pokharel as the main speaker to raise funds for a school (the Multipurpose School in Bagar), Gurungs made the largest donations. Gurung women are generally present in significant numbers at such speeches. I was surprised, when visiting a friend who is adamantly opposed to Gurungs following Hindu practices, to see photos of Hindus gods and goddesses at the altar where his wife performs her daily worship. Gurung women follow the same female rituals as Bahun-Chetri women, such as worshipping the holy basil plant (*tulsi*), fasting on the eleventh day of the lunar month, and so on. It can be seen that men are generally more vocal in resisting the so-called Sanskritization than women. Pettigrew (2000) argues that apparent Sanskritization by Gurungs may in fact be relatively superficial. Despite rhetoric about the language politics, Gurungs do not encourage their children to speak the Gurung language or open a Gurung school. But the growing competition, higher expenses involved in maintaining urban life, and the compulsion to show others that they are 'modern', means that many Gurungs are also deliberately avoiding their traditional practices. In order to take up a public position, Gurungs advocate one thing, but adopt a different practice in the domestic sphere (see also fn. 8). Moreover, Pettigrew argues that the stress of urban life means that they continue to sponsor traditional practices like shamanistic healing. She argues that this whole paradox of loss of culture (language) and revival of some threatened 'village practices' springs from the transformations and adaptations required in an urban environment.

The case of the Thakalis is even more complex. Thakalis celebrate their minor festivals in Pokhara, but often return to their Thak Khola homeland for the major ones. In most houses of the Thakalis in Pokhara, it is common to see photos of Hindu gods and goddesses. They also give the impression that they celebrate more Hindu than Buddhist practices. Nowadays, however, they also keep Buddhist images in their homes. As Thakalis are generally wealthy and clean, they are considered by most people in Pokhara to be of high status. Even Bahuns, Newars, and Chetris would accept Thakalis in marriage. Thakalis have developed a welfare organization called the Thakali Sewa Samiti in Pokhara, under which there are various facilities, one of which is a hall for holding parties. This place is much sought after in Pokhara, especially by Bahuns and Chetris. The Thakalis' "fluid boundaries", as Fisher (2001) calls them, have helped them adapt in a society dominated by Bahuns, Chetris, and Newars. They too have experienced internal controversies over their own history and identity. Thakalis have also taken a prominent role in the political development of Pokhara. As for the Newars of Pokhara, they seem to be more concerned with promoting their festivities and language than with resisting Sanskritization.

Growing Religious Pluralism

Urbanization and immigration by diverse people of different cultures and religions have also increased the degree of religious pluralism among Pokhara's inhabitants. This can be seen particularly as between Buddhism, shamanism, and Hinduism. In an interesting article, Ben Tamblyn (2002) shows how the revival of the shamanistic path followed by the Gurungs shows their faith towards both Buddhism and shamanism, even though in the early phase of urbanization and due to the influence of Tibetan lamas they were slowly abandoning shamanism (sacrificing animals) and converting towards formal Buddhism. Nowadays in Pokhara even Hindus' attachment to Buddhism is intensifying. Tamblyn (2002) listed nine Buddhist monasteries of different sects in 2000. But there are numerous other smaller monasteries in Pokhara as well. It is a common experience in Pokhara that even Hindus visit Buddhist monasteries and respect Buddhism.

Even the old Hindu priests increased their attachment towards Buddhism when a prominent local Brahman (Jagannath Lamsal) became a Buddhist monk at the age of seventy-five in 1979. Among the Gurungs religious pluralism is demonstrated by the fact that they were found to use five types of priests: two types of shamans, plus priests from Buddhism, Hinduism, and even Christianity (Tamblyn 2002). Among lower-caste households also, it can be observed that they follow the religions of those to whom they provide their services. As more of them now work in Gurung families (because of their dominance in the local population and in the economy), some lower-caste households also attend Buddhist monasteries. Their easy acceptance in Buddhist milieu as compared to Hindu temples may also have been a factor in this development.

Growing Economic Disparities and Marginalized Groups

As discussed above, urbanization has also attracted poor people from near and far who have migrated here to take advantage of employment opportunities created by the expansion of businesses and industries. They are usually uneducated and displaced from their villages due to a shortage of land for cultivation or because of natural calamities. Their permanent migration has caused the development of squatter settlements, a noticeable feature of public spaces in Pokhara today. Some of the squatter settlements were also developed and maintained because of political vested interests. To win elections and to gain more votes during the referendum in 1979 in favour of the then Panchayat political system, a large number of people (usually of lower economic position) were also settled in Pokhara as squatters. As of September 1989, there were 2,060 people living in 427 squatter households in the town, making up 3.05 per cent of the population (K.C. et al. 1992). Although squatter settlements are scattered all over, they are concentrated in the Rato-Pahiro, Ghari-Patan, Ghari-Kulo, Rambazar, Ramghat, and Bagar areas. By 2002, according to our study, there were 2,300 families living in 42 squatter settlements (i.e. having more than 5 families). Considering that 7 people live in a household, there are about 16,000 slum dwellers in Pokhara. This is 15 per cent of the population. It is often difficult to estimate the number of the population. If they think that the administration is weak, they come in hordes to occupy the public land. If the administration is strong, they disappear into the larger main society. But considering the present growth rate of the squatter population, it is estimated by the planners that by 2021, 55-60 per cent of Pokhara's population will consist of squatters (*sukumbasi*), i.e. those who do not own any property and live illegally on public land (see Adhikari 2003a for details and Yamamoto, this volume). But in reality, not all squatters are totally landless. Although most of them are poor, some are not without any property-like land. A few of the squatters also seem to be in good economic condition and are known locally as *hukumbasi* (Yamamoto, this volume). In 1992, 75 per cent of the squatter population was reported to be living below the poverty line as against an average of 6 per cent for the town and 49 per cent for Nepal. The literacy rate among squatters was about 40 per cent whereas it was about 70 per cent among town dwellers in general. In terms of the ethnic composition of the squatters, our sample survey in 2002 showed that 36 per cent were Gurungs, 16 per cent each of Magars and Dalits, 12 per cent each of Chetris and Bahuns, and 8 per cent Newars. Here, it is interesting to note that Gurungs, considered wealthier generally, represent a greater proportion of the squatters. These Gurungs were mainly those who did not have the opportunity to receive foreign remittances. But as they too were motivated to settle in Pokhara (this drive also comes from the fact that wealthier Gurungs have tended to move to Pokhara) but did not have sufficient income, they ended up being squatters. It is also a common practice for non-Gurung people from the so-called 'Tibeto-Burman' fold to use 'Gurung' as a surname. These include mainly the Himalayan tribal people. This is another reason why the proportion of Gurungs in the squatter population appears so high. Most of these squatters find employment in the informal sector as wage labourers, retailers, and drivers. It is because of their presence in Pokhara that informal services are cheap. On the other hand, because of poverty, the squatter settlements represent places with higher levels of crime, and prevalence of the flesh trade, alcoholism, and domestic violence. It is also reported that a large proportion of street children come from squatter settlements. There are also social organizations formed by squatters. They have squatters' organizations, women's groups, neighbourhood improvement committees, and the like. These organizations were formed to develop mutual help and to resist possible eviction by the government.

These marginalized people face the brunt of 'boom and burst' business cycles. After the slowdown in the tourism industry in the late 1990s, their 'livelihood security' has been eroding gradually. Women and children of such households have generally been affected adversely. Weaving carpets, selling vegetables in shops, and working in hotels are some of the jobs undertaken by the women of poorer households. But with the decline in business generally, their hardships have been growing. Because of these economic problems, the number of street children has been growing rapidly in recent times in Pokhara. This is the general observation of the citizens of Pokhara. A local newspaper (*Annapurna Post*, 25 March 2003, p. 4) reported that the number of street children had increased by 25 per cent in the previous year (2058-9 V.S. or 2002-3). It reported that there were about 500 street children in Pokhara.

Apart from the growth in the squatter population, growing inequalities in the economic status of households are beginning to appear. Even though no study has been conducted in this respect, it is now felt that differentiation is growing among the households with access to remittances (having a *lahure* in the family) and those without such access (having no *lahure* in the family). On the other hand, within the middle class, social problems are more frequent within *lahure* families. These problems include growing family disintegration and excesses like gambling, drug abuse, and alcoholism. Most spoilt children also belong to *lahure* families. No specific study has been conducted in this regard in Pokhara (but see Subba, this volume, on Dharan).

A study from 1998 documents the growing economic polarization in Pokhara (PSMC 2000). The study reveals that 52 per cent of Pokhara's households belong to the 'poorer group' (earning less than Rs.4,000 a month per household), 34 per cent to the 'middle group' (earning Rs.4,000 to 8,000 a month per household), 12 per cent to the 'higher class' (income Rs.8,000 to 20,000 a month per household), and 2 per cent to the 'top income group' (more than Rs.20,000 a month per household). Among the total population, 8 per cent were 'destitute' (income less than Rs.1,500 a month per household), 12 per cent very poor (income Rs.1,500 to 2,500 a month per household), and the remaining 32 per cent were poor (income Rs.2,500 to 4,000 a month per household). Squatters and low-caste households belonged mainly to the 'destitute' and 'poor' groups. The position of the poor group constituting 52 per cent of the population is worrisome. As most of these people are new immigrants, they are worst hit by poverty and low incomes. Even though it is a common practice among these people to find their previous village acquaintances and patrons in Pokhara when they come here for work or for settlement and seek help from them, they face problems in earning a livelihood. They are also hit hard by environmental problems like the dumping of solid waste.[13] However, squatters are not without any political agency. As mentioned earlier, they have often organized themselves and protested. They have developed organizations and networks. They also often change their political alignment to gain benefits from politicians. But still their position is precarious.

The process of marginalization discussed above seems to have broad negative effects both at the personal level and at the social level. It is mainly seen in rises in crime. As a result, more expenditure goes into policing work and in imprisoning the culprits. This unproductive expenditure will have adverse impacts on the development of the whole municipality. The squatter settlements are constantly in fear of the police and the government. As the Maoist insurgency grew, squatters in Pokhara (at least

---

[13]For detail on various kinds of environmental injustices, their causation, and the impact on marginalized groups, see Adhikari (2003a).

some of them) increasingly became involved. Some of the local leaders of these poorer communities faced great harassment during the emergency rule. When a ceasefire was declared for a short time in 2003, many prominent leaders of these settlements were killed. In the past seven years, it has become difficult for welfare agencies to work in poorer communities because of the Maoist problem. Police also look with suspicion on anyone trying to interact with, or provide some help to, poorer groups settled in squatter communities.

Individualization and the Loss of Public Properties

With the loss of community values and social control mechanisms, more and more public properties have been lost in Pokhara. A study conducted in 2002 on the loss of public properties (mainly *chautaras* – platforms with huge shade trees – public land, and water ponds) showed that in a period of twenty-three years from 1978 to 2001, 56 per cent of the chautaras, 92 per cent of water ponds, 66 per cent of public land plots, and 72 per cent of public land area have been lost (Adhikari 2003a, 2004). It is surprising that there has been no reduction in the number of temples. Rather their numbers have increased. It was seen that common property trees were destroyed and public land was registered under private ownership. Similarly, there has been tremendous encroachment on Guthi (religious) land and on community orchards. In the past, there were at least two to three mango groves in each community, but now they seem to be almost extinct. As the land value increased, people with power and influence increasingly used loopholes in the legal system to convert common property into private property (ibid.).

Economic Impacts at the Regional Level

The government's policy of developing Pokhara as an urban centre has been aimed at the economic development of the whole region. Has this been realized? A study conducted by the author on the growth of enterprises and production in hinterlands shows that Pokhara has not been able to bring about economic growth in the region (Adhikari 2000). The hinterland does not seem to be able to capitalize on the opportunities presented by the demand created in Pokhara. The region as a whole suffers from a food deficit (Adhikari & Bohle 1999) and Pokhara acts as a supply centre for goods and commodities (mainly clothes, rice, tea, sugar, kerosene, medicine, cigarettes, and stationery) that are not produced locally. Even rice is supplied to the hinterland from Pokhara, while the reverse is true in the case of towns in the Tarai. The size of the inflow of goods and commodities is very low compared to the outflow. Milk, vegetables, and fruits are the main products supplied to Pokhara from places in the hinterland, some located at a four hours' walking distance. These commodities supplied from the hinterland are consumed within the town. The high demand for some commodities has also caused changes in the land use patterns of areas located in the immediate periphery of the town. Dairying and vegetable farming have become popular in the immediate periphery, although the scale of operation is still small and is aimed just at meeting the demands of the town. Despite these new developments, Pokhara continues to receive a large part of its vegetables, rice, fruits, and other consumables from India, and to a lesser extent from the Tarai.

The study conducted in Pokhara reveals that a large quantity of fruits come from India, and only a small fraction from the Tarai, and the contribution of neighbouring VDCs is almost negligible in comparison (RUP-Pokhara 1997). Because of the rising income of town dwellers in recent times, due mainly to remittances and income from tourism, the habit of consuming fruits has increased. The increasing demand is met primarily by imports from India. The only common fruits supplied from the hinterland are oranges (available only in winter) and a small part of the bananas consumed. As for vegetables, neighbouring villages meet only a part of the demand. The bulk of the vegetables come from the Tarai and other parts of the country. The dependence on Indian markets for vegetables is considerably lower. Most of the fruits and vegetables are consumed within the town. The town also does not get its food grains like rice, maize, millet, and pulses from the hinterland, except for a small amount of high-quality rice from neighbouring villages which is consumed by the elite class. Villagers who sell this fine rice in turn purchase low quality rice from the Tarai for their own consumption. This analysis clearly indicates that Pokhara, while not serving the function of value addition, has remained a break-of-the-bulk nodal point to supply products received from the Tarai and distant markets. This broad conclusion is also seen in the study of long-term changes conducted in the environs of Pokhara in the late 1990s by Seddon, Blaikie, and others (see Bagchi et al. 1998; Cameron et al. 1998). They point out that what they had earlier predicted (the collapse of the economy and ecosystem of the hill region) has not come about. But this is not due to the positive impact of development; rather, it is the result of remittances and migration in balancing livelihood. Migration has been transnational as well as 'rural to urban' and 'hill to Tarai'. It may be partly because of the inability of Pokhara to develop enterprises and agricultural production that poorer people from rural areas are migrating to Pokhara at exceptionally high rates.[14]

---

[14]Urbanization in Pokhara has also had manifold repercussions on the environment. The dumping of pollution and solid waste into the river in Pokhara is affecting the rural areas downstream (Adhikari 2003a).

THE DYNAMICS OF PARTICIPATION IN THE POLITICAL PROCESS

Political participation in Pokhara seems to have changed distinctly in the recent past. A study conducted over the past twenty years has shown that socio-economic changes brought about mainly by the urbanization process have had a great impact on the ability of different groups to take part in political decision-making. It is well known that Pokhara's politics was dominated mainly by the Bahuns, Chetris, and Newars in the past. These groups were also responsible for the increase of political consciousness and organized movements which brought democracy and overthrew the Ranas in 1950. At that time, as demonstrated above, there were few Janajatis in the Valley. Dalits were economically weak and socially disadvantaged. Therefore, their participation in the political process was not significant.

In recent times, by contrast, the access of new immigrants like Gurungs and Magars to political power has increased significantly (as compared to their proportion in the population). After the democratic movement of 1990, new immigrants have likewise been gaining more of a voice in politics. Their income from foreign lands is mainly responsible for their ascendancy to political power. Their urban-based organizations and institutions (e.g. Tamu Dhi among Gurungs, and other cultural and social organizations) developed as a way to adapt in a city environment. They have been instrumental in developing loose networks among these groups, which in turn have been helpful in winning elections. Even though at the national level it is mainly the higher castes (Bahuns and Chetris) who occupy the major political positions, a study of Pokhara (Adhikari 2003b) reveals that a new dynamic has been developing which is giving opportunities to the new but wealthy residents. This finding contradicts the general observation of Pettigrew (2000: 34) that the Gurungs' transnational experience and wealth has not been translated into political power because urban bureaucracies remain monopolized by Brahmans, Chetris, and Newars. My empirical study (2003b) shows that 'economic and social assets' have been instrumental in helping the Gurungs to increase their share of political positions in Pokhara. They now hold a greater share of positions than their proportion in the demographic structure. Regarding their involvement in the bureaucracy, this has not changed much because of their tradition of looking down upon such meagrely paid jobs in preference to jobs in the British and Indian armies.

In the local elections of 1993 and 1998, Gurungs occupied about 30 per cent of the political positions in Pokhara Municipality, even though they constitute about 22 per cent of the population. But in the election in 1983 (during the Panchayat period), they occupied only a few positions (10-13 per cent), even though their proportion in the population was about 16 per cent. The proportion of political participation among the Newars and other caste groups now seems to be declining. The marginalized groups' participation is almost negligible. Dalits did not win elections at all, but were members of the municipality councils because of the quotas fixed for them in 1993 and 1998 elections (for details, see Adhikari 2003b). Participation by women is also insignificant except for those filling quotas. It seems that Dalits and women did not attract more votes in the elections. Dalit candidates received fewer votes than they would have on ideological grounds (i.e. affiliation to a certain political party). On the other hand, Gurungs were seen to bring more votes because of their strong social/ cultural organizations and networks and because of their higher economic positions.

CONCLUSION

Recent socio-economic and political changes in Pokhara are the result of growing urbanization for which the initial impetus came from its locational advantage for north-south trade, and then from the administrative and military policies of the government. The increased interventions by the government in terms of urban facilities, business opportunities, and transportation led to high immigration from rural areas to Pokhara. This immigration also meant a greater flow of savings and income from rural areas to Pokhara, which has been used for real estate development, land speculation, businesses, and industries. This seems to be the main reason for the rapid urbanization of Pokhara in recent times.

Various social and political changes seem to have taken place in Pokhara as it went through a process of urbanization. There has been a significant change in social structures with a rapid increase in the proportion of new immigrants like Gurungs and Magars. Because of the presence of various ethnic and caste groups in 2001, it appears that Pokhara has become more diverse than in the early 1950s, when there were only the caste groups. But now the proportion of Janajatis in the population is about 37 per cent and there are about eighty-one different ethnic and caste groups represented in the city. The inter-caste and caste-Janajati relationships also seem to have been affected by the urbanization process. Socially, there seems to be greater closeness among different castes and Janajatis. The high incidence and increasing trend of inter-caste and inter-ethnic group (and caste) marriages is a case in point. The observance of untouchability also seems to be on the decline. A sense of reviving and adhering to one's cultural and traditional practices and resisting Sanskritization is apparent among the Janajatis in Pokhara. But, again, there are controversies over how this should be done. Some have even proposed that culture is developed according to political needs and thus argue that resisting the component of alien culture incorporated into their own is not necessary. But the growing awareness of one's history, culture, and traditional practices seems to have some impact in restricting the decline in minority languages and increasing the cultural diversity and plurality. It may be because of this that Pokhara today has a more vibrant 'feel' than before. There have also been significant changes in occupational patterns and in the adoption of traditional occupations. Trade and business are no longer solely controlled by Newars, but also by new immigrants and other groups. Dependence on farming has been drastically reduced as a source of income.

Urbanization in Pokhara also seems to show a new direction in political change. Over the past twenty years (1983-2002) elections reveal a slow shift of political power towards new immigrants in Pokhara. For example, Gurungs and Magars in Pokhara have been increasing their ascendancy in political power, especially after 1990 (i.e. in democratic set up), and have now become dominant. As compared to their population size, their occupancy in political positions (as measured by elections) seems to be high. One of the reasons for this is certainly economic. Since a large section of the immigrants, particularly Gurungs and Magars, is wealthier, it has a comparative advantage in elections. The cultural and social factors are equally important. The social organizations they have developed to reproduce the cultural geography of their village and community life with modifications to suit the urban context have been helping them to take advantage of political opportunities. But the political participation of Dalits and women is low, and they are also not able to attract voters. They have many candidates in the elections, but political parties put them up in places where they are weak.

Economic stratification and growth in squatter settlements are other changes associated with the urbanization of Pokhara. We have seen that about 52 per cent of the households in Pokhara belong to 'poorer groups' earning less than Rs.4,000 a month. A large proportion of this income is spent on food. Therefore, the decline in employment opportunities and income has been affecting these households. As they have lost many livelihood opportunities (like those depending on forests, uncultivated foods, and on common property) that are available in village communities, their position has become vulnerable. Following or developing violent politics is an expression of this marginalization. In Pokhara, supporters of the Maoist movement are usually from these marginalized groups who have settled mainly in squatter settlements. Because of the increase in poorer groups in Pokhara and generally in the region, squatter settlements have been growing rapidly. At present the squatter population in Pokhara is increasing at an annual rate of 26 per cent, and if this persists, about 55-60 per cent of the total population will be living in squatter settlements by 2021.

Even though Pokhara has been developed by the government as a growth centre which could trigger economic growth in hinterlands of the region, the studies conducted show that this has not been happening. Pokhara depends for its capital on rural areas, but depends on Indian markets and Tarai for food and other products necessary for the inhabitants. The town has not been able to add value to the products of its hinterlands or to increase production. Peace is essential in order to stimulate growth in tourism, thus providing employment opportunities for poorer families and reducing their chances of becoming involved in violence and crime. Apart from these livelihood opportunities, a political process in which every section of society is included – whether through civil society, NGOs, or formal political processes (i.e. elections and political parties) – is an essential precondition for sustainable livelihood opportunities, for reducing environmental injustices, and for improving the 'urban livability' of Pokhara.

REFERENCES

Adhikari, J. 1996. *The Beginnings of Agrarian Change: A Case Study in Central Nepal*. Kathmandu: TM Publications.

——. 2000. 'Mobility and Agrarian Change in Central Nepal'. *Contributions to Nepalese Studies* 28 (2): 247-67.

——. 2003a. *Urban Context of Environmental Justice: A Study of Pokhara*. Kathmandu: Martin Chautari and Centre for Social Research and Development.

——. 2003b. 'Exclusion and Access to Economic Opportunities: Implications for Political Participation and Conflicts'. Paper presented at the conference 'The Agenda of Transformation: Inclusion in Nepali Democracy' organized by Social Science Baha in Kathmandu, 24-26 April 2003.

——. 2004. 'A Socio-ecological Analysis of Loss of Public Properties in an Urban Environment: A Case Study of Pokhara, Nepal'. *Contributions to Nepalese Studies* 31 (1): 85-114.

Adhikari, J. and H.-G. Bohle. 1999. *Food Crisis in Nepal: How Farmers Cope*. Delhi: Adroit Publications.

Adhikari, J. and D. Seddon. 2002. *Pokhara: Biography of a Town*. Kathmandu: Mandala Book Point.

Blaikie, P., D. Seddon, and J. Cameron. 1980. *Nepal in Crisis: Growth and Stagnation at the Periphery*. Oxford: Clarendon Press.

Bagchi, D.K., P. Blaikie, J. Cameron, M. Chattopadhyay, N. Gyawali, and D. Seddon. 1998. 'Conceptual and Methodological Challenges in the Study of Livelihood Trajectories: Case Studies in Eastern India and Western Nepal'. *Journal of International Development* 10: 453-68.

Cameron, J., P. Blaikie, N. Gyawali, and D. Seddon. 1998. 'Patterns of Change in Western Nepal: Rural Households of the 1970s and 1980s Compared'. *Himalayan Research Bulletin* 18 (2): 15-27.

Caplan, L. 1975. *Administration and Politics in a Nepalese Town*. London: Oxford University Press.

CBS. 1991. *Statistical Pocket Book, 1990*. Kathmandu: HMG, NPC Secretariat.

——. 1994. *Census Reports, 1991*. Kathmandu: HMG, NPC Secretariat.

——. 1995. *Statistical Pocket Book*. Kathmandu: HMG, NPC Secretariat.

——. 1998. *Statistical Year Book*. Kathmandu: HMG, NPC Secretariat.

——. 2003. *Population Census 2001 (Selected Urban Tables)*. Kathmandu: HMG, NPC Secretariat.

Dahal, R. 1999. 'Dhani (Rich) Gorkhali'. *Himal Khabar Patrika* 9 (10): 30-3.

Des Chene, M. 1992. 'Traversing Social Space'. *Himalayan Research Bulletin* 12 (1-2): 1-10.

DHPP (Department of Housing and Physical Planning). 1999. *Integrated Action Plan of Pokhara, 1999*. Pokhara: DHPP, Nepal.

Doherty, V.S. 1975. 'Kinship and Economic Choice: Modern Adaptation in West Central Nepal'. Unpublished Ph.D. thesis, University of Wisconsin - Madison.

Evans, P.B. (ed.). 2001. *Livable Cities? Urban Struggles for Livelihood and Sustainability*. Berkeley, CA: University of California Press.

Fisher, W.F. 2001. *Fluid Boundaries: Forming and Transforming Identity in Nepal*. New York: Colombia University Press.

Gurung, B., K.B. Gurung, and M. Thapa. 2048 v.s. (1992). 'Development of Urban Function and Municipal Management, Pokhara'. A study report submitted to The Local and Urban Development Training Centre, Pokhara.

Gurung, H. 1965. 'Pokhara Valley: A Field Study in Regional Geography'. Unpublished Ph.D. thesis, University of Edinburgh.

——. 1989. *Nepal: Dimensions of Development*. Kathmandu: Sahayogi Prakashan.

Gurung, J. 2000 (2057 v.s.). 'Discarding or Necessity of Dashain in Gurung Society: An Analysis'. *Historia* 4 and 5: 55-69.

Gurung, T.B. 1979. 'Pattern of Gurungs' Migration in Pokhara'. MA thesis (Geography), Tribhuvan University, Pokhara.

Johnston, R., D. Gregory, and D.M. Smith. 1986. *The Dictionary of Human Geography*. Oxford: Basil Blackwell Ltd.

K.C., Krishna et al. 1992. 'A Study of Squatter Settlement in Pokhara Town, Nepal', in R.B. Singh and M. Singh (eds.), *Perspective on Urbanisation and Urban System*, pp. 254-66. Varanasi: Shakti Publishing House.

Khatiwada, S.K. Sharma. 1998. 'Employment Structure in Tourism: A Case of Hotel Industries in Pokhara'. Unpublished MA thesis (Economics), PN Campus, Tribhuvan University, Pokhara.

Klein, C. 1996. 'Tourism in Pokhara'. A report on a survey of tourism in Pokhara in November, 1995. Mainz, Germany.

Macfarlane, A. 1989. 'Some Background Notes on Gurung Identity in a Period of Rapid Change'. *Kailash* 15 (3-4): 179-90.

——. 1997. 'Identity and Change among the Gurung (Tamu-mai) of Central Nepal', in D.N. Gellner, J. Pfaff-Czarnecka, and J. Whelpton (eds.), *Nationalism and Ethnicity in a Hindu Kingdom: The Politics of Culture in Contemporary Nepal*, pp. 185-204. Amsterdam: Harwood Press.

——. 2001. 'Sliding Down Hill: Some Reflections on Thirty Years of Change in a Himalayan Village'. *European Bulletin of Himalayan Research* 20-1: 105-10.

McHugh, E. 2001. 'Sliding, Shifting and Re-drawing Boundaries'. *European Bulletin of Himalayan Research* 20-1: 113-17.

Mikesell, S.L. 1988. 'Cotton on the Silk Road: Subjection of Labour to the Global Economy in the Shadow of Empire (or The Dialectics of Merchant Community in Nepal)'. Unpublished Ph.D. thesis, University of Wisconsin - Madison.

MTCA (Ministry of Tourism and Civil Aviation). 1997. *Tourism Statistics of Nepal, 1997*. Kathmandu: HMG.

Morimoto, I. 2002. 'Adaptation of Gandharbas to Growing International Tourism in Nepal'. *Journal of the Japanese Association for South Asian Studies* 14: 69-91.

NPC. 1998. *The Ninth Plan, 1997-2002*. Kathmandu: HMG.

——. 2003. *The Tenth Plan, 2002-2007*. Kathmandu: HMG.

Nepal South Asia Centre. 1998. *Nepal: Human Development Report 1998*. Kathmandu.

Pandit, D.L. 1989. 'Urban Growth and Land Value Pattern: A Case Study of Pokhara Town Panchayat'. Unpublished MA thesis, P.N. Campus, Tribhuvan University, Pokhara.

Parajuli, B.K. 1999. 'Mobility and Change in Occupational Structure of Pokhara City'. *Journal of Political Science* 2 (1): 1-23. Pokhara: P.N. Campus, Tribhuvan University.

Pettigrew, J. 2000. 'Gurkhas in the Town: Migration, Language, and Healing'. *European Bulletin of Himalayan Research* 19: 7-40.

Pokharel, B. 2004. 'Urban Development in Nepal'. *Economic Journal of Development Studies* 4 (2) and 5 (1): 30-43. Kathmandu: Tribhuvan University, Department of Economics, Patan Campus.

PSMC (Pokhara Sub-Metropolitan City). 1999. *Pokhara Sub-Metropolitan City: An Introduction*. (A pamphlet of the Pokhara Sub-Metropolitan City.) Pokhara: New Road.

——. 2000. 'Estimations of Income of Pokhara'. A draft research paper, PSMC, Rural-Urban Partnership Programme, Pokhara.

Regmi, M.C. 1971. *A Study in Nepali Economic History*. Delhi: Adroit Publishers.

Rondinelli, D. and H. Evans. 1983. 'Integrated Regional Development Planning: Linking Urban Centres and Rural Areas in Bolivia'. *World Development* 11 (1): 31-53.

Rondinelli, D.A. 1985. *Applied Methods of Regional Planning. The Spatial Dimensions of Development Policy*. Boulder: Westview Press.

RUP (Rural Urban Project)-Pokhara. 1997. 'Flow of Goods and Commodities to Pokhara'. Pokhara: RUP (unpublished data analysed by the author).

Sharma, B. 1986. 'In-migration in Pokhara'. A research report submitted to Tribhuvan University, Kathmandu.

Sharma, P. 1989. *Urbanisation in Nepal.* Papers of the East-West Population Institute. No. 110. Honolulu: East-West Centre.

——. 2003. 'Urbanisation and Development', in *Population Monograph of Nepal*, Vol. I, pp. 375-412. Kathmandu: CBS, HMG.

Shrestha, H. 2000. 'Evolution and Growth Process of Urban Pokhara: A Historical Appraisal'. *Historia* 4 and 5. Pokhara: P.N. Campus, Tribhuvan University.

Tamblyn, B. 2002. 'Ancient Dialogue amidst a Modern Cacophony: Gurung Religious Pluralism and the Founding of Tibetan Buddhist Monasteries in the Pokhara Valley'. *European Bulletin of Himalayan Research* 22 (Spring 2002): 81-100.

Whelpton, J. 1997. 'Political Identity in Nepal: State, Nation and Community', in D.N. Gellner, J. Pfaff-Czarnecka, and J. Whelpton (eds.), *Nationalism and Ethnicity in a Hindu Kingdom: The Politics of Culture in Contemporary Nepal*, pp. 39-78. Amsterdam: Hardwood.

Yamamoto, Y. 1983. 'Inter-Caste Marriage in Pokhara: Sanskritization and Urbanization'. *Journal of Asian and African Studies* 25: 1-38.

APPENDIX

Table 1A.1: Rank Order of Municipalities in Nepal 1952/4-2001

Ranks	1952/4	1961	1971	1981	1991	2001
1	Kathmandu	Kathmandu	Kathmandu	Kathmandu	Kathmandu	Kathmandu
2	Lalitpur	Lalitpur	Lalitpur	Biratnagar	Biratnagar	Biratnagar
3	Bhaktapur	Biratnagar	Biratnagar	Lalitpur	Lalitpur	Lalitpur
4	Nepalgunj	Bhaktapur	Bhaktapur	Bhaktapur	Pokhara	Pokhara
5	Birgunj	Nepalgunj	Nepalgunj	Pokhara	Birgunj	Birgunj
6	Thimi	Dharan	Pokhara	Mahendra-nagar	Dharan	Dharan
7	Biratnagar	Birgunj	Dharan	Birgunj	Mahendra-nagar	Bharatpur
8	Kirtipur	Thimi	Siddhartha-nagar	Dharan	Bhaktapur	Mahendra-nagar
9	Janakpur	Janakpur	Hetauda	Janakpur	Janakpur	Butwal
10	Malangwa	Malangwa	Janakpur	Hetauda	Bharatpur	Janakpur
11		Kirtipur	Birgunj	Nepalgunj	Hetauda	Bhaktapur
12		Banepa	Butwal	Siddhartha-nagar	Nepalgunj	Hetauda
13		Pokhara	Rajbiraj	Bharatpur	Dhangadhi	Dhangadhi
14		Rajbiraj	Bhadrapur	Dhangadhi	Butwal	Nepalgunj
15		Tansen	Ilam	Butwal	Damak	Trijuga
16		Matihani	Tansen	Tribhuvan-nagar	Siddhartha-nagar	Siddhartha-nagar
17				Rajbiraj	Tribhuvan-nagar	Mechinagar
18				Birendra-nagar	Rajbiraj	Madhyapur Thimi
19				Dhankuta	Birendra nagar	Gulariya
20				Lahan	Lahan	Tribhuvan-nagar
21				Tansen	Bidur	Lekhnath
22				Ilam	Inaruwa	Itahari
23				Bhadrapur	Kalaiya	Kirtipur
24					Jaleshwar	Tikapur
25					Kapilbastu	Ratnanagar
26					Dhankuta	Damak
27					Bhadrapur	Tulsipur
28					Malangwa	Kamalamai
29					Tansen	Kalaiya
30					Ilam	Birendra-nagar
31					Banepa	Rajbiraj
32					Dipayal	Putalibazar
33					Dhulikhel	Byas

(contd.)

Table 1A.1 (contd.)

Ranks	1952/4	1961	1971	1981	1991	2001
34						Lahan
35						Kapilbastu
36						Prithvi-narayan
37						Panauti
38						Gaur
39						Siraha
40						Inaruwa
41						Ramgram
42						Dipayal
43						Jaleshwar
44						Bhimeshwar
45						Khandbari
46						Bidur
47						Baglung
48						Dhankuta
49						Tansen
50						Waling
51						Narayan
52						Malangwa
53						Amargadhi
54						Dashrath-chand
55						Bhadrapur
56						Ilam
57						Banepa
58						Dhulikhel

Source: Pokharel 2004: 42-3.

2

Occupational Change among the Gaines of Pokhara City

BISWO KALLYAN PARAJULI

INTRODUCTION

Nepal has frequently been characterized as exhibiting 'unity in diversity', as being an ethnic and cultural mosaic, and as exemplifying cultural plurality.[1] This was expressed by King Prithvi Narayan Shah, the founder of modern Nepal, when he said "Nepal is a garden of the four *varna* and thirty-six *jat*", a phrase which has been endlessly repeated in the modern period. For thousands of years the Nepalese hills have served as a kind of refuge for various religions, cultures, and ethnic groups (Sharma 1989: 139-68). Toni Hagen (1971) justly remarked, "Few countries exhibit such social, ethnical, linguistic and cultural diversity within such a small compass as Nepal so that the country may rightly be called the ethnic turn-table of Asia." Thus today Nepal is a cultural mosaic, undoubtedly a pluralistic and multicultural society, even if the terms on which different groups coexist are having to be renegotiated (Gellner et al. 1997). In the census of 1991, sixty different ethnic groups and castes were recorded, in addition to the category of 'others'; in 2001 this was increased to 101. The Gaines are one of these distinct groups of people. They are scattered mainly in the mid-hill region from Mechi to Mahakali (i.e. from the east to the west of the country). However the Gaines are more concentrated in the Western Development Region (Pokhara Region) of Nepal. Gayak Tol of Batulechaur is one of the most famous and largest Gaine settlements of Nepal. Approximately 300 people within 45 households are living there and sharing the Gaine culture. Traditionally the sources of livelihood of

[1]The author wishes to thank David Gellner for his constructive suggestions, comments, and language editing.

Gaines were singing, fishing, and begging. But nowadays, owing to the growth in economic activities and urbanization, they are shifting their primary source of livelihood to service, business, and skilled labour. Various scholars, such as Morimoto (2002), Bhattarai (2002), Sharma et al. (1994); Bhandari (2053 V.S. [1996-7]), Gautam & Thapa-Magar (1994), and Macdonald (1975) have written about the music, society, culture, history, and ethnography of the Gaines. But so far there has been no study of occupational mobility, or of occupational preferences and satisfaction, among them. This chapter, therefore, aims to analyse the occupational mobility and change among the Gaines of Pokhara City.

OBJECTIVES AND METHODOLOGY

The site of the present study is the Gaine settlement located in Batulechaur, a suburb of about 6,000 inhabitants in northern Pokhara. As noted, there are forty-five households of Gaines. I generated most of the data and information presented in this chapter by holding a Focus Group Discussion (FGD)[2] in the Gaine community of Batulechaur in May 2004. The participants of the FGD were twenty-five in number and varied in age from thirteen to sixty-nine years. As I myself was born and brought up in Pokhara, I have made several observations in and around the Gaine settlement of Batulechaur. I have also worked as a Social Development Specialist in the Pokhara Sub-Metropolis office; hence I have had ample opportunities to work with the cleaning labourers and helpers of Pokhara Sub-Metropolis, who are mostly from the Gaine community. Thus, the observational method was also used as a source of information. In addition to the direct collection of information through the FGD and observation, secondary sources of information such as books, monographs, theses, journals, and official reports were also used for the purposes of the present study. The main objective was to explore the occupational preferences, change, and mobility among the Gaines in Pokhara.

Pokhara is growing as a Sub-Metropolitan City (as it is classified in Nepal) of the Western Development Region of Nepal. Owing to governmental, non-governmental, and spontaneous efforts (planned and unplanned development) various changes have been experienced in Pokhara. One of the major consequences of such change is occupational shift among the city dwellers (see also Chhetri and Yamamoto, this volume). Before undertaking the study the author made the following assumptions, which were indeed fully borne out by the field observations:

---

[2]The FGD was organized in Gayak Tol of Batulechaur with the help of the Nepal Gandharva Community Development Centre, Pokhara, on 7 and 12 May 2004.

- Modern types of occupations are replacing the traditional occupational pattern among the Gaines.
- The socio-economic background of the people determines the change of occupation.
- The selection of occupation is governed by modern rather than by traditional values.

This chapter is divided into three parts. The first deals with the people and culture of Pokhara City, the second part is devoted to a brief ethnography of the Gaines of Pokhara, and the third part is about occupational change and mobility among the Gaines of Pokhara. The study is limited to the context of the Gaine settlement of Pokhara city only.

POKHARA CITY: PEOPLE AND CULTURE

The picturesque town of Pokhara is located immediately to the south of the Annapurna Himal and Machapuchare (the famous 'fish-tail' peak) with an average height of 855 metres above sea level. Pokhara city covers only a 52.5 sq. km. area of Pokhara Valley. Geographically it is surrounded by a number of hills and riverine areas with varying heights and capacities. However, Pokhara, the largest urban nucleus of western Nepal, is not a historical town like those of the Kathmandu Valley. Historical documents and information are still rare concerning the existence of Pokhara town before the unification of the kingdom by the rulers of Gorkha in the late eighteenth century. The history of the *Kaski Rajya* or kingdom of Kaski encompasses the history of Pokhara. Recorded history begins with the Malla dynasty: when the great Malla king, Prithvi Malla, was on the throne in the twelfth century, Kaski was under the Mallas. Up to this period no historical reference was made about Pokhara (B.S. Gurung 1985). Later, in the sixteenth century, when Kaski was ruled by Kulmandan Shah, Batulechaur, the northern part of Pokhara town (presently ward 16 of the municipality), was the site of the winter palace of the king (Kirkpatrick 1969). Though Pokhara is quite new and has no ancient and medieval history, prehistoric evidence from the Mustang region and fossils of Ramapithecus found in Butwal demonstrate that there has been human settlement in this part of the Himalayas for thousands of years.

Pokhara acquired an important administrative role only after the eighteenth century when Newar people migrated and settled in Pokhara bazaar to promote their trade and business (Gurung 1965). The art and architecture of the temples in Pokhara, which indicate the origin of the town, are thus not very old (Tucci 1977). The Japanese citizen, Kawaguchi, was the first recorded foreigner to visit Pokhara in 1899. He described it as "like a town of villas at home" and wrote that "in all my travels in the Himalayas I saw no scenery so enchanting as that which enraptured me at Pokhara" (Kawaguchi 2003; cited Gurung 1985: 147). From the early twentieth century onwards, Pokhara grew as a trade centre. The city was declared an urban centre with an estimated population of 4,000 in 1959. Thus, passing through the different historical, social, and cultural stages in different periods of history, the town of Pokhara has grown to the present stage (i.e. a population of 156,312) with abundant urban resources to its credit.

The history of Pokhara city shows that settlement was initiated from Bindyabasini (presently ward 2) and Batulechaur (presently ward 16). At that time the settlers were ruling-class people (Thakuri), Brahman, Chetri, and occupational caste groups such as Kami, Damai, Sarki, and Gaine. The Newars, mostly traders, followed later on. It was only after the eradication of malaria from the valley in the mid 1960s and the subsequent urbanization process, including the development of transport, health, education, trade, commerce, industries, etc., that there was enormous immigration of people from the surrounding hills, who gravitated towards this heterogeneous settlement. Settlers converged on the town from different parts of the country as well as from abroad. Gradually the town became even more heterogeneous than before.

The people of Nepal are the outcome of successive waves of migration of Mongoloids and Caucasoids from the two major Asiatic civilizations. In many ways and contexts there have been intermarriages between the two 'stocks'; in particular the largest group in Nepal, the Chetri caste with over 3.5 million members has absorbed many people from the Mongoloid side (and not only because in the past many Brahman and Chetri men took Janajati/Mongoloid wives). Representatives of both these 'stocks' are found equally in Pokhara. Approximately 95 per cent of the city's population has its origin in the Hills, while people of the Tarai and mountain regions are 3 per cent and 2 per cent, respectively. The 1991 census recognized sixty ethnic and caste groups. Of these twenty-nine are from the Hills, twenty-nine from the Tarai, and two from the Mountain region. In 2001 almost 70 of the 101 different ethnic groups and castes found in Nepal were represented in Pokhara city (see Appendix Table 2A.2). Thus Pokhara well represents the ethnic and linguistic heterogeneity of Nepal. Most people are either Hindu or Buddhist but there are also followers of Christianity, Jainism, Islam, and Sikhism. In the 1960s there was only one church, but now there are more than two dozen in Pokhara. The popularity of Christianity is growing among backward and low-income groups. Mostly it is Hindus who convert to Christianity because of the social evil of untouchability, but so far no instance of conversion from the Gaine community has been noticed. Tolerance and coexistence are generally characteristic of the local cultural milieu. The linguistic and religious breakdowns of the city are given in Tables 2.1 and 2.2 respectively.

Table 2.1: Linguistic Structure of Pokhara City (Population by Mother Tongue in Pokhara, 2001)

Sr. No.	Linguistic Group	Population	Percentage
1.	Nepali	107,930	69.05
2.	Gurung	25,512	16.32
3.	Newar	9,768	6.25
4.	Magar	3,633	2.32
5.	Tamang	2,379	1.52
6.	Hindi	1,772	1.13
7.	Thakali	1,049	0.67
8.	Maithali	863	0.55
9.	Other small groups*	2,589	1.66
10.	Others	817	0.52
	Total	156,312	100.00

Source: CBS 2003.
*Note:**Bhojpuri, Bantawa, Tharu, Sherpa, Urdu, Bangla, Dura, Limbu, Chantyal, Oriya, English, Byanshi, Rajbanshi, Tibetan, Awadhi, Sunuwar, Ghale, Bahing, Punjabi, Marwari.

Nepali is the language of the majority as well as the lingua franca. Newari, Gurung, Magar, Churaute, Maithali (Maithili), Thakali, Tamang, Bhojpuri, etc., are other local languages of Pokhara. Out of a population of 156,312 the Brahmans (Bahun) form the biggest single group followed by Gurung, Chetri, Newar, and Magar. The Kami, Tamang, Sarki, Damai, Thakali, Muslims, and many of the Tarai people, are minority groups. Not surprisingly, with such cultural and religious diversity, a wide variety of festivals are observed in Pokhara. More than 90 per cent of local cultural ceremonies and activities have a religious origin (Deep 1992). Of these, Buddha Jayanti, Shravan Sankranti, Nag Panchami, Janai Purnima, Tij, Bada Dasain, Tihar, Shri Panchami, Shivaratri, Chaite Dasain, etc., may be said to be primarily religious. During celebrations such as Lakhe Nach, Gai Jatra, Bhairab Jatra, and Lohsar, cultural activities such as dancing and singing, repeating lores and legends are performed. In addition, Muslims observe Id and Ramzan, and Christians Easter, Good Friday, and so on.

The oldest, originally rural, settlement sites – Batulechaur, Bindyabasini, Baidam, Simalchaur, Kundhar, Chinedanda, and so on – are occupied by high-caste Brahman and Chetri people. The bazaar (market) areas of Singhanath Tol, Moharia Tol, Bhairab Tol, Ganesh Tol, Terchapatti Tol, and Sangu Ko Mukh are inhabited by Newars. The newly developed settlements such as Bagar, Deep, Rambazaar, Chorepatan, Bajhapatan, etc., are dominated by Gurungs. The Gaine people are settled only in Batulechaur (near the then winter palace of the Raja of Kaski), which is indicative of the fact that they have been in Pokhara for a long time. The total population of Gaines was 202 in the year 1991, which increased to 245 in 2001, making them the twenty-second largest group in Pokhara. Other diverse

Table 2.2: Religious Structure of Pokhara City (Population by Religion in Pokhara 1978-2001)

Sr. No.	Population in 1978			Population in 2001		
	Religion	Population	Percentage	Religion	Population	Percentage
1	Hindu	32,382	89.50	Hindu	119,668	76.56
2	Buddhist	3,103	8.58	Buddhist	30,738	19.66
3	Muslim	386	1.07	Muslim	1,889	1.21
4	Christian	311	0.86	Christian	2,481	1.58
5	Kirat	-	-	Kirat	143	0.09
6	Jain	-	-	Jain	19	0.02
7	Sikh	-	-	Sikh	62	0.04
8	Bahai	-	-	Bahai	4	0.00
9	Not stated	-	-	Not stated	1,308	0.84
	Total	36,182	100.00	Total	156,312	100.00

Sources: Population 1978; CBS 2002b.

groups of people are scattered all over the town (on squatter settlements, see Yamamoto, this volume). This is the cultural morphology of Pokhara as reflected in its residential patterns.

Though Pokhara is evidently multi-religious, it is Hinduism and Buddhism that have been mainly responsible for its religious and cultural development. There are a number of temples, shrines, monasteries, mosques, churches, etc. Most of the temples and shrines are along the market area running from Bindyabasini to Ramkrishna Tol and Terchapati. Among the major sacred sites of Pokhara are the Bindyabasini Temple, Bhadrakali Temple, Barahi Temple, Sobha Bhagavati Temple, Shitala Devi, Jalpa Devi, Bhairab Mandir, Bhimsen Mandir, Ganesh Mandir, Ramkrishna Mandir, Saraswati Mandir, Narayan Mandir, Gaseling Gumba, Manang Gumba, Dharmashila Bihar, Boudha Arghu Sadan, Tamu Pe Lhu Museum, and the Jame Mosque. The Buddha Bihar of Bindyabasini was built by Buddhist Newar settlers long ago, but the Theravadin Dharmashila Buddha Bihar is a more recent addition. The Tibetan Buddhist monasteries of Pokhara are even more recent, one being founded in the 1960s, one in the 1970s, and the rest from the 1980s onwards (Tamblyn 2002). The temple of Bindyabasini is said to be the oldest Hindu shrine in the city. Of the Christian churches, Bagar Church is the oldest; it was erected only after 1970. The Churaute (Hill Muslims) are concentrated in the eastern part of Pokhara and there is a mosque which was built in the 1960s.

The river Seti (Gandaki) has great importance in the religious life of both Hindus and Buddhists. Both banks of Seti Gandaki are considered sacred. The Gaighat in the north, the Tulsighat and Narayanthan in the north-east, and Ramghat in the south-east are the main holy bathing sites and cremation grounds. These Ghats are regarded as gateways to heaven.

A BRIEF SKETCH OF THE GAINES

Origin and History

The Gaines are also known as Gandharva, Gayak, and Gandhar. The etymological meaning of all these names is 'singer', but as regards the origin of the Gaine people there are interesting stories. According to a Hindu mythological story Brahma, the supreme creator of the world, created four *rishis* (sage). One of them was called Gandharva and it is supposed that the Gaines are the descendants of Gandharva Rishi. Some argue that Gandharva was a well-known musician in the palace of Indra, the King of Heaven. Being the descendants of Gandharva these people were supposed to earn their living by singing songs and playing the *sarangi* and the *arbajo.*[3] Some of the Gaines argue that when there was division of labour Gandharva was sitting by the side of an *apsara* (nymph) and watching her performance, hence he was given the task of singing a song to accompany her. It is believed that just the Badi caste of today are supposed to be descended from the nymph, the Gaines are descended from Gandharva Rishi, and that both groups by fulfilling these roles for society, are maintaining tradition.

As for their more immediate historical provenance, both D.R. Thapa (2030 V.S.) and Bhandari (2053 V.S.) argue that the Gaines migrated from Chitaurgarh of India to Nepal as the porters of the ancestors of Kulmandan Shah. In the time of Kulmandan Shah, whose winter palace was near the Batulechaur settlement, the Gaines were granted *guthi* land in remuneration for their services.[4] They were supposed to sing various types of ritual and religious songs, success stories, patriotic songs, songs of loyalty to the kings as well as to the *jamindars* and *mukhiyas* of the village who were the king's representatives. They were to sing the songs in temples, palaces, and households of the villages as well. Thus the origin of the Gaines as explained in various sources is a blend of myth and history (Morimoto 2002). The recorded history of Nepal shows that at the time of the unification of Nepal, the Gaines used to travel around villages and the countryside disseminating messages of patriotism and loyalty to the house of Gurkha through their songs.

Population and Habitat

Exact ethnic and caste data was not released for any census before that of 1991. According to the census of 1991, the total Gaine population was

---

[3]These are the two major musical instruments of the Gaine. Sometimes the words *sarangi* and 'Gaine' are used as synonyms of each other.

[4]*Guthi* land used to be provided by the state to support the performance of regular work or rituals in temples and public places.

4,484. It increased to 5,887 by the year 2001. P. Nepali (2003: 26) guesses that the real Gaine population could actually be around 9,500 to 10,000, because some of the Gaines do not write their surnames as *Gayak*, *Gaine*, or *Gandharva* in order to hide their caste. The Gaines reside mainly in the mid-Hill and inner-Tarai regions of Nepal. More of their population is concentrated in Gandaki Zone and fewer of them are dispersed in Jhapa, Bhojpur, Chitwan, Dhading, Kathmandu Valley, Lamjung, Tanahun, Gorkha, Baglung, Dang, Dailekh, Surkhet, and so on. The major habitat of the Gaines in Gandaki Zone is Batulechaur of Pokhara. According to the census of 2001, the population of the Gaines in Kaski district is around 500, of whom 245 live in Pokhara. The figures in Table 2A.2 show that the Gaines were the tenth largest group in Pokhara in 1977, the nineteenth largest group in the year 1991, dropping to twenty second today. According to Khim Bahadur Gayak (aged sixty-nine) the population of the Gaines was almost equal to that of the Muslims (Churaute) of Pokhara during the 1960s. Thus, the previous figure of the Gaines' population shows that the population growth rate is slow among them. Data from the last two censuses also shows that it is less in Pokhara than among the Gaines generally (Table 2.3). Nowadays the majority of the Gaines of Batulechaur have undergone sterilization to control their family size.

According to a study carried out in 2002 (Bhattarai 2002), the Gaine population in Kaski district was about 518. Batulechaur is the largest settlement in Kaski, where more than half of them are living together. Altogether there are eight places where Gaines live in Kaski district. The recent population and household distribution of the Gaines in Kaski district is given in Table 2.4.

At present there are forty-five Gaine households in Batulechaur. The average household size is 5.4. They still follow the joint family system. Compared to the high castes the Gaines appear to be relatively egalitarian in their gender relations. Nonetheless, they do follow the general Nepalese patriarchal practice regarding family leadership. Owing to increasing inter-ethnic/inter-caste marriages among the younger generation, some Gaines are worried about the possible extinction of the Gaine identity. Yamamoto (1983) revealed that there are many cases of inter-caste marriages in Pokhara. According to his research, the hypogamous type (women from a

Table 2.3: Gaine Population in Nepal and in Pokhara, 1991-2001

Census Year	Population in Nepal	Population in Pokhara
1991	4484	202
2001	5887	245
Change in 10 years	+1403	+43
Percentage increase	31.29	21.29

Sources: CBS 1993, 2002.

Table 2.4: Gaine Population and Household Distribution in Kaski, 2002

Sr. No.	Name of the Settlements	Number of Households in Each Settlements	Population of Corresponding Settlements
1.	Batulechaur (Pokhara - 16)	57 (52.29)	271 (52.32)
2.	Hemja	12 (11.00)	58 (11.20)
3.	Arghaun	19 (17.43)	85 (16.41)
4.	Gagangaunda	12 (11.00)	62 (11.97)
5.	Rithepani	2 (1.83)	10 (1.93)
6.	Bharatpokhari	3 (2.76)	14 (2.70)
7.	Kaskikot	1 (0.92)	3 (0.58)
8.	Begnas	3 (2.77)	15 (2.89)
	Total	109 (100.00)	518 (100.00)

Source: Bhattarai 2002: 35.
Note: Out of fifty-seven households listed for Batulechaur, two of them are abandoned and some households situated in Simalkhorea and Kholakhet are not considered as part of study area. Therefore the present article covers only the information obtained from Gayak Tol of Batulechaur, which consists of forty-five households.

higher caste status marrying men from a lower status) was the predominant type of inter-caste marriage in Pokhara. However, in the context of the Gaines, several inter-caste marriages are recorded in Batulechaur. Gaine women are married to men from castes such as Thapa (Chetri), Rai, Biswakarma (Kami), Nepali (Sarki), which are supposed to be superior to Gaine in the caste hierarchy. Only very rarely has a Gaine male married a woman of higher caste. According to information from the Gaines themselves, only one person was married to a Sarki woman. It is believed in the Gaine community that the Pode, Damai, and Wadi are inferior to them and the rest are superior. Thus, where inter-caste marriage occurs among the Gaines, it is predominantly hypergamous.

The Present Status of Gaines

Constitutionally speaking there is supposed to be no discrimination of any kind in terms of race, ethnicity/caste, sex, and so on in Nepalese society. But, in practice there exist different types of disparity, of which caste is a major one. According to the caste structure of Nepalese society, the Gaines are considered as one of the lower, inferior, and oppressed people. As indicated by the rites, rituals, beliefs, culture, and even the documented sources recorded by a few 'Gandharva', they claim and believe themselves to be Hindu. And, in terms of deities worshipped, rituals performed, and festivals observed, the Gaines are indeed Hindus. But in the Hindu social hierarchy Gaines are placed at the bottom of society. Traditionally they were considered as untouchable. Today, younger Gaines feel uncomfortable being considered untouchable, because it hinders them from getting a job and because they feel ashamed to be labelled *magne* (beggar). Because of such inferiority and social oppression in the past, Gaines are rarely found in esteemed public positions. During the meeting of the FGD one of the participants revealed that ten years earlier he had been a candidate for the post of peon in a school near their settlement. He was young (twenty), energetic, handsome, and literate but the committee did not select him because one of the job requirements was to serve tea and water to the teachers and staff of the school. Instead, another 'relatively weak' candidate from a 'touchable' background was appointed. Now, however, a Gaine woman is working as a peon in that very school, and she serves food and drink to the teachers and staff. Thus, over the years people have changed their attitude towards the Gaines due to the various efforts made by NGOs and governmental policies.

The Gaines' family names (*thar*), such as Adhikari, Budathoki, Kayastha, Kalo Gopal, Thakuri, Bista, Brahma Baikar, Jogi Baikar, Parbat, Bogete, Kalichan, Maheshor, Sahi, etc., also reveal that they are very close to Hindu groups such as the Brahmans and Chetris. Gaines were almost semi-nomadic beggars in earlier times; they were illiterate and landless. To some extent they show that they are susceptible to the Sanskritization process because some of them use upper-caste surnames such as Nepali, Kayastha, Thapa, etc. On the other hand, this trend does not appear to ruin the Gaines' pride in the least. They consider themselves on a high level among untouchables because they take the front spotlight (at the front of the procession) in all the rituals and festivals in which they perform (Yezbick 2001). Their major source of livelihood is begging, singing, fishing, and daily wage labour. Their living conditions and lifestyle reflect their economic life, which is not better in relation to others. Most of the forty-five families own no land other than the plot on which their tiny cottages stand. Unlike many other residents of Pokhara, they do not have any domestic animals or kitchen garden whose produce they could consume. Singing and begging in and around Pokhara was their major occupation. Besides singing they do a lot of manual labour on the farmland of neighbouring Chetri and Brahman people. Some of the participants of the FGD were afraid of losing the basis of 'Gaine culture', especially the folk songs and the ability to play the *sarangi*. As expressed by the participants of the FGD, most young people have no knowledge about traditional culture, folk songs, fishing techniques, or how to make the *sarangi* and *arbajo*. Fishing has vanished from Pokhara due to the excessive use of pesticides in Kalikhola and other sources. According to the participants of the FGD, fewer than a dozen youths (aged between 18 and 25) are unemployed among the Gaines of Gayak Tol. Whatever work is available, it is hard, unpleasant, and not well paid. However, almost all the economically active people of Gayak Tol are employed as sweepers (cleaners), cab and tractor drivers, municipal policemen, teachers, and so on. Around a dozen families still depend upon singing for their livelihood. Some are in esteemed positions such as teachers, musicians, engineers, agricultural technicians, office bearers, etc. Democracy was restored in 1990 but to date no Gaine has been elected as a local representative in Pokhara Municipality. The reason is that the population of Gaine is only 0.03 per cent of the total population of Pokhara. According to P. Nepali (2003), Durga Bahadur, the father of renowned folk singer Jhalak Man Gandharva, was at one time *Mijhar*, a local revenue collector for the government, in the period before 1951.

In the past, owing to their ignorance and poverty, the Gaine school enrollment ratio was negligible. But today a degree of social awakening and community consciousness can be observed in the Gaine community of Pokhara. In terms of educational attainment a few of them are graduates. Some of them, namely Jhalak Man Gandharva, Khim Bahadur Gayak, and Purna Nepali, have become so popular that they have become nationally famous in the field of music and folk singing. Out of the total national Gaine population, fewer than 100 are matriculated and fewer than 50 have graduated (Nepali 2003). Of these, more than a dozen are from Pokhara, particularly from Batulechaur. This figure illustrates that the Gaines of Pokhara are more advanced, conscious, and educated than Gaines from other parts of Nepal. In Gayak Tol of Batulechaur around 25-30 per cent of their children have been enrolled in private 'boarding' schools.[5] The remaining children are enrolled in government schools. Recently, at the instigation of the Nepal Cultural Protection Centre, twenty-two Gaine students were admitted to the Galaxy Boarding School of Kathmandu in different grades; fourteen of the twenty-two are from Batulechaur. All of the foregoing discussion shows that the present generation of the Gaines in Pokhara is relatively forward-looking and keen to see that their children are educated.

CHANGE AND MOBILITY

Occupations in Pokhara

Any form of paid employment in which an individual works in a regular way is an occupation (Giddens 2001). In other words, an activity of expenditure of energy, which produces services and products of value to

[5]In Nepal private so-called boarding schools are run by trustees and private individuals, and they are much more expensive than the government schools. Presently, as the government is not supposed to charge a single penny at the school level, some of the students from under-privileged backgrounds receive government scholarships for their schooling.

other people, is an occupation or work (Fox & Hesse-Biber 1984). Furthermore, it may be considered as the effort of activity of an individual that is undertaken for the purpose of providing goods or services of value to others (Hall & Buttran 1994). The division of labour is an important indicator of society in the analysis of occupational mobility. In the traditional social structure, occupations were followed ascriptively on the basis of caste identity, whereas in modern times the majority of the population in the urban areas depends upon non-agricultural sources of income that in principle they are free to adopt as individuals. Even in the past some castes in Nepal depended upon non-farm activities. In spite of the overwhelmingly agrarian nature of Nepalese society, the majority of the Kami, Sarki, Damai, Kumal, Gaine, and similar groups do not usually practise agriculture.

Before 1950 spinning, weaving, grinding, metallurgy, service occupations, trade, business, administration, and army service were the major non-farm activities. Most high-grade occupations, i.e. teaching, administrative service, army service, and business, were captured by high-caste people, namely, Brahmans, Thakuris, Chetris, and Newars. Apart from the Newars, most other ethnic people who would generally be classified as Vaishyas were involved in agricultural production. The lower castes or Shudras were involved in service occupations such as barbers, washermen, sweepers, tailors, cobblers, and blacksmiths, according to caste. Because of this, up to the present, high-caste people predominate in the better occupations in Nepalese society (Bista 1990). It was only after the dawn of democracy in 1950 that the aforesaid pattern started gradually to change. As a result, diversification of the occupational structure is now taking place in Nepalese society.

Occupationally speaking, Nepal is basically an agricultural country, where the population dependent on agriculture for its livelihood constituted 94 per cent, 91 per cent, and 81 per cent in the years 1971, 1981, and 1991 respectively (CBS 1995, Parajuli 2001). Farming and animal husbandry are, and were, the most prevalent and important occupations for the people of Nepal. The majority of the population was more or less dependent upon agriculture either as a primary or secondary source of income. But the Gaines hardly keep domestic animals because they are almost landless and in order to keep animals some land is necessary. This explains why not even a fowl can be seen around their settlement. Even when Gaines do possess a small piece of land on which they could grow vegetables, usually they are not keen to do so.

As Table 2.5 shows, the share of non-farm occupations has shown a substantial increase in Pokhara city over the last three decades. In 1977, 62.9 per cent of the population was engaged in the agricultural sector whereas in 2001 the percentage of this population was reduced to 9.8 per

Table 2.5: Percentage of the Population Dependent upon Agricultural and Non-Agricultural Sources of Income in Pokhara, 1977-2001

Year	Source of income		Differences
	Agricultural Sector	Non-Agricultural Sector	
1977*	62.9	37.1	-25.8
1991**	27.3	72.7	+45.4
1998***	16.7	83.3	+66.6
2001**	9.8	90.2	+80.4

Sources: * Population 1978;
** Parajuli 1998; CBS 2002c;
*** Parajuli 1998.

cent. The population engaged in non-agricultural activities in 1977 was 37.1 per cent; by 2001 it had gone up to 90.2 per cent. The table also shows that the proportion of non-agricultural sources of income is increasing in Pokhara, which is a strong reflection of a growing trend of urbanization, and the difference between agriculture and the non-agricultural sector is increasing rapidly simultaneously. On the other hand, traditional urban occupations have been replaced by the newer occupations available in the city. Today business, hotels and restaurants, tourism, transportation, administrative services, recreation, communication, teaching, etc., are rapidly becoming sources of income for a majority of the population. In addition, shifting from farm-based into non-farm activities, traditional occupations are being abandoned or downgraded due to the industrialization and urbanization of society.

Occupational Structure and Diversity among the Gaines

According to an earlier study (Parajuli 1998) the majority of people in Pokhara earn their livelihood from business (42 per cent), followed by service (25 per cent), agriculture (17 per cent), labour (12 per cent), and miscellaneous (4 per cent). But in relation to the Gaines, the proportions are very different. Traditionally, as we have seen, the Gaines were itinerant singers so they do not have agricultural land. They were considered untouchable, therefore they practise neither agriculture nor business. According to Chhetri (1989), in 1984 there were thirty-four Gaine households in Batulechaur. At that time there were twenty-four households which were engaged only in singing as the major source of their livelihood. In addition to this, fishing was another traditional occupation for Gaines; some of them were engaged as manual labourers in various construction work throughout the city. Traditionally, Gaine men were the main earners. Females were supposed to support their family by wandering from door to door and collecting different types of food grains, cereals, vegetable, rice, etc., especially from the households of high castes. Usually they did not go

Table 2.6: Households Dependent upon Traditional Occupations among the Batulechaur Gaines, 1984-2004

Year	Number of Households
1984	24
2001	20
2004	11

Sources: Field Survey 2004; Chhetri 1989; and Karki 2001.

to unknown people's houses to beg; it was rather a part of the *bista* (*jajmani*) system. When the present author was young, he frequently heard the words at his door: *Panditni Baraju! kehi magna ayako* ('Venerable priestly lady! We are here to beg something'). In response his grandmother would provide grain, cereals, vegetables, etc., to the Gaine women. These days Gaine women no longer come to beg. They are rather to be seen in the market of Pokhara with bamboo baskets selling fruits and vegetables.

Table 2.6 shows that the number of traditional occupation holders is decreasing. This clearly reflects the rapid occupational shift among the Gaines of Pokhara. Within the last twenty years the households dependent upon traditional occupations have decreased tremendously, from 70 per cent in 1984 to 19 per cent in 2004. On the basis of the FGD the traditional and modern types of occupations found among the Gaines are listed in Table 2.7.

From Table 2.7 it is evident that there were fewer opportunities to explore new jobs in the past. There are more than twenty different fields of opportunity now undertaken, out of which sixteen are non-traditional. Instead of their traditional occupation some of the new generation are studying computer engineering, a few others are working as lab technicians and junior technical assistants. A remarkable number of youths are engaged as cab drivers, some, both male and female, are running petty businesses (tea, vegetable, and grocery shops) in their own community. Almost seventy persons from this single settlement of Batulechaur are working as sweepers and cleaners in municipal offices and other institutions in Pokhara city. One elderly man (sixty-nine) is working as a music teacher, teaching *sarangi* at the Sangit Prashikshan Kendra (Music Training Centre) near the Bindyabasini Temple. Purna Nepali, one of the members of this community from Pokhara, is a music teacher at the royal palace in Kathmandu. The discussion above proves that the occupations among the Gaines are more diverse at present than they were in the past. Hence a large number of people are engaged in different fields as their major source of livelihood. So far there are no professionals, namely, experts, civil servants, university teachers, lawyers, physicians, parliamentarians, representatives in local government, etc., from this community. The occupational structure of the Gaines of Pokhara is distinct from that of other parts of Nepal.

Table 2.7: Traditional and Modern Occupations in Batulechaur, 2004

	Previous Occupation	Present-day Occupation
Traditional Occupations	Itinerant singer Performing *sarangi* Manufacturing musical instruments (*sarangi*) Fishing Agricultural Labour	Itinerant singer (some) Playing *sarangi* (some) Manufacturing *sarangi* (a handful) Fishing (very rare)
Non-Traditional Occupations	Non Agricultural Labour (some) (specially in construction, building and mending of traditional Nepali house, hut/cow-house etc.)	Construction/Factory Workers School Teacher Office Clerk Music Teacher Sweeper Municipal Police Cab Driver Tractor Driver/Helper Lab Technician/Assistant Shopkeeper Professional Singer Police & Army Personnel Factory Worker Junior Technical Assistant (Agriculture) Computer Engineer (studying) Working Abroad Hawker & Vendor

Source: FGD, 2004.

Gaines from rural parts of Nepal are still migrating towards the city areas to perform their *sarangi* in the hope of a better livelihood.

On the basis of information provided by the participants of the FGD, an attempt has been made to illustrate the occupational structure of the Gaines of Batulechaur and this is shown in Table 2.8. The table shows that a majority of the households are engaged in service (54.38 per cent), followed by traditional occupations (19.29) and manual labour (15.78). The remaining 8.77 per cent are running businesses and 1.75 per cent are in other occupations. The study by Chhetri (1989), as mentioned earlier, showed that just two decades earlier almost 70 per cent of them were engaged in traditional occupations. This demonstrates that the abandonment of traditional occupations is not just a nostalgic discourse about the past. Often some of them are working as farm labourers but they do not possess agricultural land. Therefore they do not consider agriculture as their primary source of income. Most of the Gaines are service-oriented;

Table 2.8: Occupational Structure of the Gaines at Batulechaur, 2004

Major Occupation	Occupational Structure among the Gaine (%)
Agriculture	-
Business	8.77
Service	54.38
Labour	15.78
Traditional Occupation	19.29
Others	1.75
Total	100.00

Source: Field Survey 2004.

and in fact one can easily observe that almost one person from each household is a service-holder. According to the participants in the FGD, only two households in Gayak Tol have no service-holder at all. Those who are practising traditional occupations are carrying it on in a non-traditional way by singing and playing *sarangi* in restaurants, and a few of them have recorded their songs as music albums as another way to earn money.

According to Harka and Bhoj Bahadur Gayak, both employees of Pokhara Sub-Metropolitan City, two Gaines were employed in the municipality office as sweepers some fifteen years ago, each with a salary of Rs.600 per month. Looking at their regular income and routine life, other Gaines were inspired to get similar jobs in the same municipal office. Consequently, their lifestyles changed such that now they enjoy better living conditions. This has encouraged others to involve themselves in service-oriented jobs. Following this tradition, approximately thirty-seven Gaines are working in the Pokhara Sub-Metropolis office as junior employees, i.e. clerks, drivers, helpers, peons, sweepers. Out of a total of eighty employees working in the environment and sanitation section of Pokhara Sub-Metropolis, almost half are from the Gaine community of Batulechaur. On the basis of the above analysis and discussion, it is clear that there has been a growing trend among the Gaines to take up service occupations and leave off their traditional occupations. If this trend continues for two or three decades, the *sarangi*-related occupation may disappear as part of their livelihood entirely.

The change in occupation has given impetus to their economic prosperity. No one is homeless and very few persons are jobless. Their housing conditions have also improved along with their occupational shift. However, the fact still remains that 19.29 per cent of Batulechaur Gaines have not changed their previous traditional occupation. The reasons behind it as derived from the Focus Group Discussion with respondents are:

- There is no risk, it is easy to take up, and there is no need of further training and investment. They learn to play the *sarangi* and sing as part of normal socialization in the Gaine community (or rather, used to do so).

- Some of them are still earning a handsome amount of money through traditional occupations. Singing songs and playing the *sarangi* has been a free job to earn an income at hotels and restaurants at Pokhara. So some are not willing to change their traditional occupation.
- Giving up the traditional occupations is considered as a loss of social prestige in their traditional surroundings. Some of them are worried about the loss of their traditional occupation by the younger generation of Pokhara.
- Occupations other than their traditional one require necessary training and skill, knowledge and capital too, which they lack.

These are the reasons that some individuals of the older generation both desire and feel compelled to continue their traditional occupation. But, by and large, despite the above considerations, there is a rapid occupational shift from traditional to non-traditional sources of livelihood.

The majority of Pokhara Gaines have shifted their hereditary traditional occupation in successive generations and given up their previous occupations. An attempt was made in the FGD to explore the reasons for leaving previous occupations. Various reasons were given by the participants. The push factors for leaving the previous occupations were the low status of begging, low income, and public apathy towards traditional culture. The pull factors of more modern occupations were the availability of new sources of income, growing awareness, and the regular and handsome income on offer. The growth of urbanization in Pokhara has also altered people's way of life in respect of food, dress, education, health, entertainment, and so on (cf. Parajuli 1998). A new kind of lifestyle required adequate expenditure, which reinforced the economic reasons for giving up their previous occupation. It is to be noted that owing to the increased consciousness and literacy rate among the Gaines and urbanization of Pokhara, profitable, pleasant, and respectable occupations are like a much awaited 'dream occupation' for them. Some of the Gaines have entered into such new occupations and realized their dream. As an example: according to Maya Gayak, she took a loan from a commercial bank to run a petty shop in the Gaine neighbourhood of Batulechaur.

Occupational Aspirations

Though the Gaines are traditionally a nomadic/itinerant singer group because of the place of their birth, their upbringing, educational attainments, skill, and training are all undergoing a change. The modern environment is making a difference. Aspirations for a new type of occupation are growing within the Gaine people of urban areas like Kathmandu and Pokhara. The occupational attitude of urban dwellers under the process of urbanization is distinct from rural dwellers. In order to examine the occupational aspirations and preferences of the Gaines of Pokhara City, they were asked a set of questions: (i) If you could choose your own occupation which one would you prefer? (ii) What type of occupation do the young boys prefer today and why? (iii) What type of occupation do the young ladies prefer and why? In response to these questions most of the participants of the FGD put forward service as their preferred occupation for earning their livelihood. Secondly, the majority of them expressed their preference for business, while a few of them preferred their traditional occupations with some modification. Service occupations such as office clerk, schoolteacher, municipal police, lab technician, peon, and sweeper were the most preferred occupations. Service occupations like professional singer in restaurants, music teacher, cab driver, factory worker were also in their second preference. Even today, females do not express a preference for learning to play the *sarangi* because of the traditional belief that a woman who does so threatens her husband's life. Young men expressed preferences for working abroad, but no women did so. Preferences were not expressed for professional and technical service occupations because such positions require special training and education, which is beyond their access. Only a few of the younger generation are studying and getting ready to compete for such occupations. It is clear from the above discussion that most of the participants in the FGD expressed a preference for service and business activities.

Tourism is another big industry in Pokhara, which has attracted a significant number of Gaines. Owing to its growing importance, a number of Gaines are engaged in their traditional but modified occupation of singing and performing the *sarangi* in and around the lakeside of Pokhara. The growth and development of Pokhara has generated some new types of occupation, which along with the steady development of tourism as a leisure industry, have attracted a significant number of people. Due to the growing opportunities in the leisure industry a participant of the FGD reported that he could earn much more through musical performances than at his regular service in the Pokhara municipal office. Regardless of the discomfort they feel about being singers and *magne*s (beggars), a few of them are proud of their *sarangi*. Once, when the author was accompanied by his students in the Gaine community, one of the young Gaines shouted out in English, "My *sarangi*, my pride!" One participant in the FGD was more serious and influenced by the cultural heritage of the *sarangi* and was thinking of sending his son to music school for his academic career, specializing in the field of *sarangi*. He added that he would like his son to obtain a doctoral degree like the author, not in urban sociology but specializing in the *sarangi*.

The most important reasons cited for occupational preferences were high income, status, personal interest, ease of acquisition, and so on. A good number of the participants mentioned that regular income, social status, and personal interest were the dominant reasons for guiding them in their choice of occupations.

CONCLUSION

Nepal is a pluralistic and multicultural society with more than a hundred of diverse groups of people. The census of 2001 has recorded 101 caste and ethnic groups in Nepalese society. The Gaines are one of these groups and are found scattered throughout the country, mainly in the mid hill region. Their population is more concentrated in Pokhara region, and Gayak Tol of Batulechaur is one of the famous Gaine settlements in Nepal with the largest Gaine population. Singing, playing with their handmade *sarangi*, fishing, manufacturing of *sarangi*, and begging were their traditional means of livelihood. To explore occupational preferences, change, and mobility, I generated primary data through observation and focus group discussions, combining them with secondary sources for comparison and background information. Pokhara city was declared as an urban unit with an estimated population of 4,000 in 1959. Within the last forty years the city has experienced a number of distinct changes and grown to its present size. One of the major consequences of such change is occupational change among the city-dwellers. Owing to the growth in economic activities and the urbanization of Pokhara, the traditional occupations of city dwellers are being replaced by modern types of occupations.

It is supposed that the Gaines migrated to Nepal from India as porters to the Shah dynasty. According to the census of 2001, their population in the whole of Nepal is 5,887, of whom 245 (4.16 per cent) live in Pokhara. Traditionally they were considered as untouchable, so most of them are engaged in low-paid and difficult occupations in the public sphere. Various efforts have been made by NGOs and by government agencies to uplift their economic and social status. Community consciousness is relatively high among the Gaine community of Pokhara compared to other Gaines. They are relatively advanced, conscious, and educated.

Nepal is basically an agrarian country but the Gaines do not practise any sort of agriculture. On the other hand, traditional urban occupations have been replaced by the newer occupations. Nowadays business, tourism, hotel and restaurant, transportation, administrative service, recreation, communication, and teaching are rapidly becoming sources of earning for the majority of the population of Pokhara. In addition to shifting from farm-based activities to non-farm-based activities, the traditional occupations of occupational castes (i.e. Kami, Damai, Sarki, Gaine, Kumal, Kasai, and so on) are interchanged and switched due to the industrialization and urbanization of Pokhara.

As we have seen, the Gaines have taken up a variety of modern occupations. A good number of youths are engaged as cab drivers, some run petty businesses like tea stalls, or vegetable and grocery shops in their own community. Almost seventy persons from a single settlement of Batulechaur are working as sweepers and cleaners in municipal offices and other institutions in Pokhara City. Because of the regular income from their service, job benefits such as pensions, Dasain allowances, leave, training, etc., such jobs are highly attractive. Thus most Gaines have abandoned their traditional occupations like singing, performing the *sarangi*, manufacturing of *sarangi*, fishing, etc. Due to the improvement in their economic condition, they are improving their social status as well. At least in their place of work they are no longer treated as untouchable.

This study suggests that a majority of Gaine households are engaged in service at different institutions in and around Pokhara City. Almost one person per household is engaged in the service sector and only a few of them are still continuing in their traditional occupations. The most interesting finding is that no one is homeless and only a handful are jobless in this community. The switch from singing, *sarangi* performance, manufacturing, and fishing to office jobs, technical work, teaching, service as municipal policemen, cab drivers, shopkeepers, service abroad, or as factory workers, and so on, has been dramatic. By and large the occupational shift has been rapid from traditional to non-traditional sources of livelihood among the Gaine community of Pokhara City. This is, of course, similar to many other groups with specialized occupational niches in the traditional caste system, but the change has probably gone even further and faster among the Gaines than among other such groups.

REFERENCES

Adhikari, J. 2007. 'Urbanization and Change in Pokhara, Nepal', in this volume.

Arthur, B. et al. (eds.) 1989. *Handbook of Career Theory.* Cambridge: Cambridge University Press.

Bhandari, R. 2053 v.s. (1996-7). 'Gaine Jatiko Samajik Avastha: Ek Singhabalokan (An overview of Social Condition of Gaine)', *Historia* (Journal of History and Culture, Department of History and Culture) I: 82-8. Pokhara: Prithvi Narayan Campus, Tribhuvan University (T.U.) (in Nepali).

Bhattarai, P. 2002. 'Kaski Jillaka Gaine Jatiko Samajik, Sanskritik tatha Arthik

Abastha Ek Adhyayan (A Study of Social, Cultural, and Economic Conditions of the Gaine Caste in Kaski District)'. Unpublished MA thesis, Prithvi Narayan Campus, T.U., Pokhara (in Nepali).

Bista, D.B. 1990 (1967). *People of Nepal.* Kathmandu: Ratna Pustak Bhandar.

Boskoff, A. 1970. *The Sociology of Urban Regions.* NY: Application-Century-Crofts, Educational Division Meredith Corporation.

CBS. 1993. *Population Census 1991: Social Characteristic Tables* Vol. I, Pt. VII. Kathmandu: HMG, NPC Secretariat.

——. 1995. *Statistical Year Book of Nepal 1995.* Kathmandu: HMG, NPC Secretariat.

——. 2002a. *Population Census 2001: National Report.* Kathmandu: HMG, NPC Secretariat, CBS in collaboration with UNFPA.

——. 2002b. *Population of Nepal, Population Census 2001–Selected Tables on Caste/Ethnicity, Mother Tongue and Religion.* Kathmandu: HMG, NPC Secretariat, CBS in collaboration with UNFPA.

——. 2002c. *Population of Nepal: Village Development Committees/Municipalities, Population Census 2001 – Selected Tables (Western Development Region).* Kathmandu: HMG, NPC Secretariat, CBS in collaboration with UNFPA.

——. 2003. *Population Monograph of Nepal,* Vol. I. Kathmandu: HMG, NPC Secretariat, CBS in collaboration with UNFPA.

Chhetri, G. 1989. 'Gaineko Sarangi Euta Magne Bhado ki Nepali Samskritiko Anga?: Ek Samajsastriya Dristikon (Is the Gaines' Sarangi a Tool for Begging or a Part of Nepalese Culture?: A Sociological Perspective)', *Contributions to Nepalese Studies* 16 (1): 55-69 (in Nepali).

Deep, D.K. 1992. *The Nepal Festivals* (2nd edn.). Kathmandu: Ratna Pustak Bhandar.

Elliot, P. 1972. *The Sociology of the Professions.* London: Macmillan Press Limited.

Fox, M.F. and S. Hesse-Biber. 1984. *Women at Work.* Palo Alto, CA: Mayfield.

Gautam, R. and A.K. Thapa-Magar. 1994. *Tribal Ethnography of Nepal,* Vol. II. Delhi: Book Faith India.

Gellner, D.N., J. Pfaff-Czarnecka, and J. Whelpton (eds.). 1997. *Nationalism and Ethnicity in a Hindu Kingdom: The Politics of Culture in Contemporary Nepal.* Amsterdam: Harwood.

Giddens, A. 2001. *Sociology.* Cambridge: Polity Press.

Gurung, B.S. 1985. 'Pokhara: A Study in Urban Geography'. Ph.D. thesis, Department of Geography, Ranchi University.

Gurung, H.B. 1965. 'Pokhara Valley: A Study in Regional Geography'. Ph.D. thesis, University of Edinburgh.

——. 1985. *Vignettes of Nepal.* Kathmandu: Sajha Prakashan.

Hagen, T. 1971. *Nepal: The Kingdom in Himalaya.* New Delhi: Oxford and IBH.

Hall, R.H. and R.T. Buttran. 1994. *Sociology of Work.* Thousand Oaks: Pine Forge Press.

Karki, M.B. 2001. 'Gaine Jatiko Samajik tatha Arthik Paribartan (Social and Economic Changes of the Gaine Caste)'. Unpublished MA thesis, Department of Sociology and Anthropology, Patan Campus, T.U. (in Nepali).

Kawaguchi, E. 2003 (1909). *Three Years in Tibet.* Bangkok: Orchid Press.

Kirkpatrick. 1969 (1811). *An Account of the Kingdom of Nepaul.* New Delhi: Manjushri Publishing House.

Macdonald, A.W. 1975. *Essays on the Ethnology of Nepal and South Asia.* Kathmandu: Ratna Pustak Bhandar.

Morimoto, I. 2002. 'Adaptation of the Gandharbas to Growing International Tourism in Nepal'. *Journal of the Japanese Association for South Asian Studies* 14: 68-91.

Nepali, P. 2003. *Gandharva Sangit ra Sanskriti (Gandharva Songs and Culture).* Kathmandu: UNESCO Office (in Nepali).

Parajuli, B.K. 1997. *Occupational Aspect of Urbanization of Pokhara City.* Kathmandu: University Grant Commission.

——. 1998. 'Selected Aspects of Urbanization: A Sociological Study of Pokhara Town, Nepal'. Ph.D. thesis, Department of Sociology, Banaras Hindu University.

——. 1999. 'Mobility and Change in Occupational Structure of Pokhara City'. *Journal of Political Science* II (1): 1-23. Pokhara: Department of Political Science and Sociology, Prithvi Narayan Campus, T.U.

——. 2001. 'Trend of Urban Growth in Nepal: A Case Study of Demographic Dimension of Urbanization of Pokhara City', *Journal of Political Science* III and IV (1): 33-50. Pokhara: Department of Political Science and Sociology, Prithvi Narayan Campus, T.U.

Population 1978. 'Population Study of Pokhara Nagar Panchayat (Janasankhya Adhyayan)'. Study report prepared by Pokhara Nagar Panchayat and Institute of Humanities and Social Science, Pokhara.

Pradhan, R. 2002. 'Ethnicity, Caste and a Pluralist Society', in K.M. Dixit and S. Ramachandran (eds.). *State of Nepal*, pp. 1-21. Lalitpur: Himal Books.

Sharma, K., G. Chhetri, and S. Rana. 1994. *A Modest Study of the Current Socio-Economic Situation of the Lowest Status Caste and Tribal Communities in Nepal.* Kathmandu: Save the Children US.

Sharma, P.R. 1989. 'Nepali Culture and Society: Reflection on Some Historical Currents', in K.P. Malla (ed.), *Nepal: Perspectives on Continuity and Change*, pp. 139-68. Kirtipur: Centre for Nepal and Asian Studies, T.U.

Tamblyn, B. 2002. 'Ancient Dialogue amidst a Modern Cacophony: Gurung Religious Pluralism and the Founding of Tibetan Buddhist Monasteries in the Pokhara Valley'. *European Bulletin of Himalayan Research* 22: 81-100.

Thapa, D.R. 2030 v.s. (1973-4). *Gandaki ko Suseli (Whistling of the Gandaki River).* Kathmandu: Sajha Prakashan (in Nepali).

Tucci, G. 1977 (1953). *Journey to Mustang. 1952,* tr. D. Fussell from Italian. Kathmandu: Ratna Pustak Bhandar.

Yamamoto, Y. 1983. 'Inter-Caste Marriages in Pokhara: Sanskritization and Urbanization'. *Journal of Asian and African Studies* 25: 1-38.

Yezbick, J. 2001. 'Modernization vs. Marginalization: The Gaine People of Pokhara, Nepal'. ANP 490 Independent Study Paper, Study Abroad Program of Michigan State University.

APPENDIX 1

Table 2A.1: Participants of Focus Group Discussion

Date of FGD : 7 and 12 May 2004

Venue: Maya's Tea shop
Gayak Tol (Batulechaur) Pokhara Sub-Metropolis - 16

Supported by: Nepal Gandharva Community Development Center Pokhara

1.	Balaram Gayak	14.	Lakshu Gayak
2.	Khagda Bahadur Gayak	15.	Belman Gayak
3.	Hom Bahadur Gayak	16.	Meena Gayak
4.	Bayan Bahadur Gayak	17.	Bir Bahadur Gayak
5.	Raj Kumar Thapa	18.	Suman Gayak
6.	Kishan Gayak	19.	Dinesh Gayak
7.	Maya Gayak	20.	Binod Gayak
8.	Bhoj Bahadur Gayak	21.	Bikendra Nepali
9.	Karna Bahadur Gayak	22.	Dhurva Gayak
10.	Khim Bahadur Gayak	23.	Sunil Gayak
11.	Bhim Bahadur Gayak	24.	Pradeep Gayak
12.	Hark Bahadur Gayak	25.	Deepak Gayak
13.	Bhagawati Gayak		

APPENDIX 2

Table 2A.2: Ethnic/Caste Structure of Pokhara City (Population by Caste/Ethnicity at Pokhara 1977/8-2001)

Sr. No.	In the Year 1978*			In the Year 1991			In the Year 2001		
	Caste/Ethnicity	Population	Per cent	Caste/Ethnicity	Population	Per cent	Caste/Ethnicity	Population	Per cent
1.	Brahman/			Gurung	20482	21.4952	Brahman (Hill)	35679	22.8255
2.	Chetri	17489	48.3268	Brahman (Hill)	20350	21.3567	Gurung	33795	21.6202
3.	Newar	6356	17.5633	Chetri	15726	16.5039	Chetri	23985	15.3443
4.	Gurung	4320	11.9373	Newar	12009	12.6031	Newar	15710	10.0504
5.	Dalit**	3184	8.7982	Magar	6358	6.6725	Magar	12829	8.2073
6.	Magar	1507	4.1642	Kami	3250	3.4107	Damai/Dholi	4746	3.0362
7.	Thakali	606	1.6745	Damai	2913	3.0571	Kami	4601	2.9434
8.	Muslim	426	1.1771	Sarki	1804	1.8932	Tamang	4153	2.6568
9.	Bhote	325	0.8980	Tamang	1611	1.6906	Thakuri	2394	1.5315
10.	Other	1767	4.8826	Thakali	1462	1.5343	Sarki	2307	1.4758
11.				Sanyasi	1456	1.5280	Muslim	1896	1.2129
12.				Thakuri	1281	1.3443	Sonar	1700	1.0875
13.				Muslim	998	1.0473	Thakali	1696	1.0850
14.				no caste /foreign	939	0.9854	Sanyasi	1514	0.9685
15.				Bania	426	0.4470	Rai	1327	0.8489
16.				Rai	338	0.3547	unidentified Dalit	1247	0.7977
17.				Sherpa	320	0.3358	unidentified caste	1191	0.7619
18.				Churaute	219	0.2298	Gharti/Bhujel	1049	0.6710
19.				**Gaine**	**202**	**0.2119**	Tharu	702	0.4491
20.				Kumhar	197	0.2067	Baniya	460	0.2942
21.				Yadav/Ahir	156	0.1637	Sherpa	383	0.2450
22.				Brahman (Tarai)	144	0.1511	**Gaine**	**245**	**0.1567**
23.				Tharu	140	0.1469	Kalwar	235	0.1503
24.				Sudhi/Kalwar	123	0.1290	Teli	219	0.1401
25.				Kayastha	107	0.1122	Majhi	213	0.1362
26.				Majhi	101	0.1059	Limbu	199	0.1273

27.	Teli	92	0.0965	Yadav	190	0.1215
28.	Not Stated	90	0.0944	Kumal	184	0.1177
29.	Bhote	85	0.0892	Hajam/Thakur	169	0.1081
30.	Limbu	76	0.0797	Brahman (Tarai)	143	0.0914
31.	Kushwha	69	0.0724	Dura	131	0.0838
32.	Kumal	67	0.0703	Chantel	124	0.0793
33.	Dhobi	58	0.0608	Sunuwar	70	0.0447
34.	Lepcha	51	0.0535	Koiri	69	0.0441
35.	Rajput	48	0.0503	Kayastha	67	0.0428
36.	Kanu	48	0.0503	Marwadi	62	0.0396
37.	Sunuwar	45	0.0472	Bhote	55	0.0351
38.	Raute	39	0.0409	Nurang	45	0.0287
39.	Rajbhar	39	0.0409	Rajput	43	0.0275
40.	Thami	30	0.0314	Gangai	43	0.0275
41.	Kurmi	29	0.0304	Bangali	42	0.0268
42.	Danuwar	17	0.0178	Kanu	40	0.0255
43.	Bengali	14	0.0146	Chamar/Harijan	35	0.0223
44.	Kewat	14	0.0146	Dhobi	25	0.0159
45.	Chamar	12	0.0125	Sudhi	23	0.0147
46.	Darai	11	0.0115	Kewat	20	0.0127
47.	Khatway	11	0.0115	Praja	16	0.0102
48.	Raji	9	0.0094	Bote	16	0.0102
49.	Marwadi	9	0.0094	Kurmi	15	0.0095
50.	Haluwai	8	0.0083	Kumhar	14	0.0089
51.	Bote	7	0.0073	Darai	14	0.0089
52.	Wadi	6	0.0062	Mallah	13	0.0083
53.	Dusadh	5	0.0052	Lohar	12	0.0076
54.	Musahar	5	0.0052	Kahar	12	0.0076
55.	Gangain	3	0.0031	Rajbansi	11	0.0070

(contd.)

Table 2A.2 (contd.)

Sr. No.	In the Year 1978			In the Year 1991			In the Year 2001		
	Caste/Ethnicity	Population	Per cent	Caste/Ethnicity	Population	Per cent	Caste/Ethnicity	Population	Per cent
56.				Dhanuk	3	0.0031	Haluwai	11	0.0070
57.				Jirel	2	0.0020	Jirel	11	0.0070
58.				Chepang	2	0.0020	Badhae	10	0.0063
59.				Mallah	2	0.0020	Rajbhar	10	0.0063
60.				Sikh	2	0.0020	Kamar	10	0.0063
61.				Rajbanshi	1	0.0010	Danuwar	8	0.0051
62.				Dhimal	1	0.0010	Gaderi	8	0.0051
63.				other (Hill)	862	0.9046	Dhanuk	7	0.0044
64.				other (Tarai)	185	0.1941	Chidimar	7	0.0044
65.				other/(mountain)	45	0.0472	Dhimal	6	0.0038
66.							Dusadh/Paswan	5	0.0031
67.							Adibasi/Janajati	5	0.0031
68.							Lepcha	5	0.0031
69.							Sikh	5	0.0031
70.							Other	26	0.0166
	Total	36,189	100.00	Total	95,286	100.00	Total	156,312	100.00

Sources: CBS 1993, 2002b; Pokhara Town Panchayat (Population 1978).

Note: *Population study carried out by Pokhara Town Panchayat and Institute of Humanities and Social Science in 1978.

**Includes all those now classed as Dalit (Damai, Kami, Sarki, and Gaine).

3

Changing Environments, Society, and Culture: Case Studies of Some Dalits and Kumals in Pokhara Valley

RAM B. CHHETRI

INTRODUCTION

This chapter focuses on the changing environments and lifeways of some marginalized groups in Pokhara Valley.[1] No society or culture has ever been static: change has been ubiquitous everywhere all the time, although the pace of change may have varied across time within one society or among groups of people living in different places at the same time.[2] In line with the spirit of Karl Popper's point that "knowledge is always a modification of earlier knowledge" (quoted in Barth 1987: 84), I believe that cultural norms, values, and practices prevailing today in any society are the

---

[1]I would like to express my gratitude to the Norwegian Research Council and the Chr. Michelsen Institute for the research funds given to the project, *Livelihoods and Environmental Change in the Hills of Nepal,* and for recognizing me as Co-Principal Investigator. I am also grateful to my friend and colleague, Tone Bleie (who was the other Principal Investigator of this project), for all her intellectual inputs and cooperation from time to time. Assistant Researchers Krishna Adhikari, Lok Bhattarai, Parmeswor Khati, Lok Raj Pandey, and Ganga Sen deserve thanks for helping me with the field survey. I would also like to mention that Bidya Bhurtel and Sanjeeb Pokharel agreed to do their MA thesis work as part of the above-mentioned project and they collected information on the Kumal and Damai/Kami/Sarki presented in this paper. I also thank David Gellner and Hiroshi Ishii who read an earlier draft of this paper and provided constructive comments. Comments from Seika Sato and other participants of the AA-ken conference were also useful in preparing this revised version. Of course, I am responsible for any weaknesses still remaining in the paper.

[2]Geertz's conceptualization of culture (1973) would see it as a text – to be interpreted by the ethnographer. Such a notion relegates culture to being something 'fixed' even if it were for a short while thereby de-emphasizing the ever transforming potential of culture (see also Maskarinec 2000).

adapted forms of earlier times. This could very well be true for most of today's cultural practices, rituals, the ways of celebrating festivals or life-cycle events, and so on, in Nepal. That is, whatever lifeways any groups of people follow today should be seen as the results of continual adaptation of what they practised at an earlier period.

But some of the plain questions with regard to the process of change have continued to intrigue scholars, including anthropologists, for quite some time now. What makes people change their lifeways? What triggers social and cultural change? Why do different groups of people respond (therefore change) in different ways to similar dynamics in the total environment? An attempt is made to address these questions in this chapter. I will argue on the basis of empirical evidence that the adoption of new occupations by individuals or a group of people could also result in cultural change at the wider societal level. The experiences of the Kumals and some Dalits (i.e. Jalaris, Damai, Kami, and Sarkis) in Begnas of Pokhara Valley provide apt illustrations to respond to the above questions.

In analysing the ecologic relationships of ethnic groups in Swat, Barth makes the point that in plural sociocultural contexts, "ethnic segmentation" and "economic dependence" remain as fundamental features. He further argues that the environment of any one ethnic group is defined by natural conditions in the locality as well as "by the presence and activities of other ethnic groups on which it depends. Each group exploits only a section of the total environment, and leaves large parts of it open for other groups to exploit" (Barth 1987: 3). It is in this context that Barth borrows the concept of a niche from animal ecology and defines it as "the place of a group in the total environment, its relations to resources and competitors" (1981: 3).

The concept of niche and Barth's ideas on the 'total environment' are relevant for the discussion of change in the lifeways of the groups of people selected for analysis in this chapter. Barth has rightly pointed out that any single group of people cannot exploit the total environment and that parts of it (niches) are left open for others to exploit. Perhaps one example of this is the division of occupations or types of services among caste/ethnic groups in Nepal and elsewhere. I bring up the issue of caste-based occupations (or vice versa) because some exceptions to Barth's generalizing statement seem to crop up here. On the basis of the case studies presented in this chapter I will show that some of the existing niches (i.e. livelihood options) could disappear for certain groups of people as the "total environment" gradually transforms over time. Furthermore, in the process of change in the total environment, two or more groups of people could also compete for a given niche previously occupied by one particular caste/ethnic group.

Pokhara Valley has been known for its sociocultural plurality. In the total environment of the Valley, different caste/ethnic groups have tended to maintain cultural and ethnic boundaries as distinct from others, but economic interdependence becomes inevitable or unavoidable and thus they are bound to live as part of one economic environment (Chhetri 1986, 1990). However, they may become parts of different social and cultural environments, and inter-group relations could be either close or distant depending on the ideas of similarity or difference of ethnicity from each other (see Chhetri 1990 on the Tibetans in Pokhara).

In places like Begnas and Pokhara, people belonging to many different caste/ethnic groups occupy the same geographical and socio-economic space. But each of these groups may have their own 'pre-dominant' form of interaction with the biophysical, socio-economic, political, and cultural environment of the area. Given such a situation, Barth's concept of niche allows us to imagine the multicultural nature of the field-level reality. Since a number of groups are to be found interspersed with others, it becomes difficult to hold on to the ideas of isolated groups or populations and cultures untouched by external influences. Physical boundaries cannot be drawn. But a number of other boundaries (occupation, cultural, etc.) can be easily discovered (see Chhetri 1990). Vayda's concept of "progressive contextualization" is equally useful because it allows analysis of the issues or activities of groups under study in any given locality by placing them within wider contexts (Vayda 1983).

In Nepal, we hear and read about a general improvement in the living conditions – because of 'developments' in infrastructure, schools, health facilities, roads, communications, etc. – for most of the places in the country during the post-1950 years. While I agree with the assertions that there have been additions or improvements in the amenities of the kind mentioned earlier, I contest the idea that their impacts have always been positive for everyone. I am sceptical of the utility of the concept of 'development' with a positive connotation as an appropriate heuristic tool to anchor the discussion of sociocultural processes in countries like Nepal. Unconditional acceptance of such an idea of 'development' to depict the empirical reality in various parts of the country and among its many caste/ethnic groups would only commit oneself to misreading the socio-economic realities in the country.

Escobar comments on the emergence and dominance of the concept of development in recent decades and argues,

> Wherever one looked, one found the repetitive and omnipresent reality of development: governments designing and implementing ambitious development plans, institutions carrying out development programs ... experts of all kinds studying underdevelopment and producing theories ad nauseam. The fact that most people's conditions not only did not improve but deteriorate with the passing of time did not seem to bother most experts. (Escobar 1995: 5)

The worsening situation of poverty in some parts of Nepal over the years, in spite of the claims of governments or the donor agencies, projects, and NGOs to have done things to treat the malady, provides a good illustration in support of Escobar's argument quoted above. It is because of this conviction that I have chosen to place 'development' within single quotation marks throughout the following text. Because of the limited and lopsided connotation attached to the concept of 'development' I have opted to use concepts like change, transition, and adaptation while talking about the social and cultural processes in Nepal (see Chhetri 1986, 1990).

Research Site, Approach, and Data

In this chapter, I draw upon ethnographic information and survey data collected between 1998 and 2000 in the Begnas area of Pokhara Valley. As I come from Pokhara, I have visited the Begnas area many times since the 1970s and witnessed the physical changes (so-called 'development') as well as the changes in the social, economic, and cultural practices occurring in Pokhara Valley over the years. Begnas was a small farming village in those days. But after the construction of a motorable road linking it to the Prithvi highway (in the late 1970s) and the construction of the dam on the Begnas lake (in the late 1980s), Begnas has quickly grown into a bazaar.

In recent years, ethnographic studies have departed from what used to be the conventional approach of focusing on one group of people and of seeking out as isolated a field site as possible. The context of ethnographic discourse has changed. When scholars have studied their own peoples, they have striven to go beyond the tradition of regarding only one group of people – 'them' – as the subjects of discourse. The focus on village studies in India by scholars like Srinivas towards the middle of the last century is a good example: his approach acknowledged the difficulty of isolating one group in any village for ethnographic study. The unit of ethnographic study thus became the whole village (see also Berreman 1972).

In Nepal, however, many ethnographers have continued to limit themselves to the study of one or the other of the many ethnic groups of people (e.g. Gurung, Newar, Sherpa, Tamang, Thakali). Some ethnographic studies in recent years may have departed from the tradition of limiting research to fieldwork conducted within a given locality (e.g. Guneratne 2002; Fisher 2001). Such practices are indeed indications that the concept of 'field' or the space of ethnographic study has been redefined in the anthropology of Nepal. The study presented in this chapter also contributes to that endeavour.

The narratives of change presented here are likely to resemble the experiences of similar groups of people in other parts of Nepal. The emerging arguments and questions may therefore have a wider significance for understanding or reading the general processes of social, cultural, and economic change in the region.

The research project in Begnas was characterized by an attempt to understand changes in environments and livelihood strategies among several groups of people living in the area. That is, studies were carried out on several groups of people. Initially I began my research on the Jalaris and then included other groups of people in the study. This was done because of my conviction that in a study of social and cultural change, a focus on one group only would not allow us to know whether the processes of change being discussed were similar or different for other groups sharing the same total environment. Moreover, social and cultural change observed in any group of people comes about as a result of that group's changing interactions with other groups around it. And, the changes in the nature of the interactions may be the result of changes in the wider context or the total environment. Each of the groups of people living within a given area like Pokhara Valley may have their own reasons or contexts for the way they modify their interactions with other groups over time. Given this, a focus on only one such group (if understanding change is the focus) would allow us only a partial understanding of the contexts of change; the pattern of change described for one group might not be true for other groups around them. Thus I chose to diverge from the conventional approach and talk about more than one group of people. I believe, this will enable us to understand more profoundly the pattern of overall change in environment, society, and culture. The experiences of the Kumals and Dalits (all of them living in Begnas area today) in the context of the changes in the environments and social and cultural change in Pokhara Valley have been presented as case studies in order to make the point that similar sets of 'developments' could bring different things for different groups of people living together. Seeing the process of change from the point of view of each of the groups in question saves us from making generalizations that sound attractive but fail to account for the complex nature and actual dynamics of sociocultural processes.

The groups dealt with in this chapter – Kumal, DKS (Damai-Kami-Sarki), and Podes – might be considered similar to other larger, local groups of people in terms of culture, language, religious persuasions, etc. Such a consideration confounds the reality. Groups such as these possess their own special 'cultural specificities', like pottery, *panchai baja* musical ensembles, etc. The historical events and processes that relegated the Damai, Kami, Sarkis, Pode, etc., to their current social positions remain intriguing issues but are beyond the scope of this chapter. The changing social interactions between and among these and other people in Nepali society, however, will be my primary concern.

In order to talk about adaptation and change in the life ways of Kumals and Dalits in the Valley today, it will be necessary (as a way of contextualizing) to refer to some of the changes that have been observed in and around Pokhara. I have chosen to talk about changes in Pokhara Valley – my hometown – because I have myself been a witness to a number of factors which may have brought about change in the lives of the people here. I admit that the way in which I look at the changing society and culture in Nepal, and thereby form a particular outlook towards such processes, may be coloured also by my personal experience of living in Pokhara as a member of a lower-middle-class family (for previously published accounts of change in Pokhara, see Mierow 1997; Adhikari & Seddon 2002). I tend to believe that the pace of change in the overall lifeways, cultural norms, and values in Pokhara was much slower up until the 1950s. The people of Pokhara, as elsewhere in Nepal, were perhaps trying to maintain distance as well as a less permeable boundary (of interaction) between themselves and the exotic/outer world that was little known to them. But life within the villages was characterized by close interactions between households and individuals from a cross section of caste/ethnic groups as well as the rich and the poor. In fact, people relied mainly on their relatives and fellow villagers in order to move on with the seasonal as well as life-cycle events from year to year. Such a support system was highly valued as revealed in a popular expression: *dhungako bhara mato, matoko bhara dhunga* implying that rocks/stones and soil have to rely on each other in order to keep themselves in places.

POKHARA VALLEY: CHANGES IN THE TOTAL ENVIRONMENT

Pokhara was still following a seasonal or annual rhythm of activities until the late 1950s, which was perhaps a setup that had emerged or been put in place over many generations of limited or no contact with the outer exotic world. When I look back in time, I see that changes in the various facets of life for the locals began slowly in the early 1960s and accelerated over the years and decades that followed.

Up until the mid 1960s, there were no cars or buses (except some government-owned vehicles) in Pokhara. People had to travel on foot to reach the market centres in order to buy their supplies of salt, clothes, spices, kerosene, etc. In fact, until the 1950s salt was obtained from the northern districts of Manang and Mustang (referred to by locals in those days as Bhot or 'Tibet'). Normally villagers organized into groups for the trips to go to Bhot in order to fetch salt (it was commonly bartered with cereals carried on their backs for several days from home).

Farm activities were carried out by means of labour exchange arrangements (*parma*). Even the construction of dwellings and periodic repair of thatch roofing were accomplished through mutual support from fellow villagers. These exchanges of services or labour and also materials were obligatory and were in nature similar to what Mauss calls 'total prestations' (Mauss 1967). Money was not a common medium of exchange as it is today and paper money in particular was still rare. Barter prevailed (alongside the mutual give and take of goods and services) as a means of exchange of goods including cereals, spices, salt, etc., among people not falling in the circle of obligatory exchange relations. The Kumals and the Jalaris in Pokhara bartered (besides being engaged in *parma* relations with their neighbours). The Damai, Kami, and Sarkis mostly had their regular clients called *jajman* or *bista*[3] with whom they were involved in exchange relations termed as *bali* and *majuri* – an arrangement in which the artisans were compensated for their regular services in kind at the time of harvests, major celebrations, and rituals (see also Prindle 1977).

The pace of urbanization and other changes in Pokhara accelerated from the 1970s onwards (see Adhikari, this volume). Looking back at the 1960s and 1970s, a number of external inputs and achievements can be identified that may be responsible for this. Secondary schools were already there by the 1950s, but the first college in Pokhara was started only in 1960 (Mierow 1997). A successful malaria eradication campaign was also launched in the early 1960s. Moreover, the introduction of high-yielding varieties of crops like maize and wheat began in the mid 1960s (locally called *amrikane* maize or wheat) and the same period saw the entry of chemical fertilizers and factory-made farm implements (e.g. ploughs and spades) in the Valley. The population of Pokhara also began to increase faster when hill migrants (mostly *lahure*s and ex-*lahure*s) chose to settle in Pokhara perhaps in order to remain closer to the roads, markets, schools, and health facilities.[4] This contributed to the expansion of the urban settlement and the urbanization in Pokhara Valley (see also Gurung 2002: 22-3).

[3]In Nepali *bista* (not to be confused with the surname of a group of Bahuns and Chetris) refers to the people who employ service castes for sewing clothes, making and mending farm implements, etc., by paying an annual share of the harvest of principal crops like paddy, maize, millet, etc. The payment itself is called *bali*, which also means standing crops. The artisans so engaged by the *bista*s were referred to as *Baliko Damai*, *~Kami* or *~Sarki*. Quite a few of my neighbours in Pokhara (mainly Bahun and Chetri landlords) employed even their ploughmen on *bali* arrangements until about the beginning of the 1980s. In the Nepalese context, it is only priests or Bahuns who refer to their clients as *jajman*. Here, the priests receive *dan/dakshina* (gifts) from their *jajman*s in return for their religious and ritual services. The gifts are generally given at the conclusion of the priestly services. The amount or the nature of the gifts could vary depending on the economic status of the *jajman* and the type of ritual service in question. These and other types of obligations and rewards relationships among various groups or individuals and households could be the subject of a separate study.

[4]What such migrations have done to village social organization, the farming economy, etc., would be an interesting research topic in itself.

The opening of the Siddhartha highway in 1969 (the Sunauli-Pokhara Road) and the Prithvi highway in 1971 (Blaikie et al. 1980) had far-reaching consequences for Pokhara and its people. Along with the farm implements mentioned above, many necessary commodities (like pots and pans, shoes, ready-made clothes, etc.) came in from India and China thereby replacing many items manufactured or crafted by local artisans. For instance, most households adopted the more durable metal pots and pans as well as factory-made shoes, clothes, and farm implements that were readily available in the mushrooming shops in the town. This could be considered to mark the beginning of the severing of exchange relations between the Damai, Kami, and Sarkis and their *bista* farmer households. Most farming households began to purchase their occasional needs of clothing and farm implements from the shops instead of having them made by the village artisans (i.e. Damai, Kami, and Sarkis). Many people also sold their lands and made investments in businesses (e.g. shops selling daily consumables, clothes, etc.). The case studies presented in this chapter make it evident that giving up of agriculture by many besides the changes in the modes of production, affected the traditional *parma* relations as well as other traditional arrangements for sharing or distribution of farm products.

Pokhara, just as any urban centre, has been undergoing changes in terms of its population size and amenities in recent years. Landon wrote about Pokhara in the early 1920s: "Pokhara is a second city in Nepal. ... It contains perhaps ten thousand inhabitants and lies in a wide flat plain encircled by hills" (1993: 18). Landon and other early visitors were impressed by the lakes (there are a total of seven within the Valley) in and around Pokhara).[5] Development projects of various types including those on power generation, irrigation, watershed management, soil conservation, fisheries, community forestry have been investing resources in and around the Phewa, Begnas, and Rupa lakes in the Valley for more than four decades now.

The Pokhara visited by Landon and Kirkpatrick, however, seems to have been less important in terms of its wealth and political status at that time. This may have made Landon remark that because of its size, its fertile soil, and its geographical location in the central part of the country, it was "destined to play no small part in the future industrial development of

[5] See Landon (1993), Kirkpatrick (1986). In his section on 'Routes and Distances' where Kirkpatrick gives the travel routes used in those days between a number of important places (to and from Kathmandu as well) with interesting remarks. The seven lakes in the Valley are known today as Phewa Tal, Begnas Tal, Rupa Tal, Maidi Tal, Dipang Tal, Khaste Tal, and Mandre Tal. Of these, the Fisheries Development Project in Pokhara covers the first three, which are larger in size than the rest.

Nepal" (1993: 18). Landon's prediction made in the 1920s has come true and Pokhara today not only has some industries (although of small scale) but is one of the fastest-growing urban centres and is also one of the most important urban and administrative centres outside the Kathmandu Valley.

Today one can travel by car or bus or fly into Pokhara from Kathmandu and a number of other urban centres. The first aeroplane must have landed in Pokhara towards the end of 1952 since Toni Hagen who had come to Nepal in the early 1950s writes that in April 1952, when he went to Pokhara on his way to Mustang, he "had to go the entire way on foot (10 days)" (Hagen 1994). Similarly, the Italian visitor Giuseppe Tucci walked to Pokhara from Kathmandu in September 1952 but took a Himalayan Airways plane to get back to Kathmandu from Pokhara in December of the same year (see Tucci 1977). Tucci wrote, "after the rains have finished, Himalayan Air Ways run an irregular service between Pokhara and the capital, using the deserted plain around the city as an unofficial landing field" (Tucci 1977: 76).

Historical accounts also reveal that the people of Pokhara were not quite ready to welcome foreigners when the country had been closed to outsiders by the then governments in the country. Landon alludes that there prevailed "the traditional hatred of the presence of foreigners" (1993: 19) in the country and he notes that such a feeling among the people had inhibited the Rana rulers from undertaking development projects which required the presence of European technical experts. Things are very different today.[6] In fact, within fifty years of Landon's visit to Nepal, the country and its people saw foreigners and foreign aid go through a process characterized by some scholars as "a trickle turning into a torrent" (Mishra & Sharma 1983). Pokhara Valley and its environs has been a scene where a number of projects have been implemented during the past four decades or so which are mostly fuelled by foreign aid, donor supports, or bank loans. Such interventions have had far-reaching consequences for the life and culture of the people as well as their environments and resources. The case study of Dalits and Kumals in Pokhara presented below will illustrate this point.

Apparently Pokhara was not on the list of urban places until the 1952/4 census information was published (e.g. see Karan & Ishii 1996, Table 20, p. 328; Sharma 1989). But though it had a population of only 5,413 in 1961, it had grown to 95,286 in 1991, and today it has a total population of 156,313 (see CBS 1995, 2002). The increase in Pokhara's population size can be attributed to at least two factors. One is the in-migration of people

[6]Places like Kathmandu, Pokhara, etc., today have a fairly large number of resident expatriate staff employed by the various projects or international organizations – directly hired and sent to Nepal from the countries of the origin of aid as part of the package.

from rural areas in the adjoining hills and the other is the process of annexation or inclusion of additional suburban areas into the town area in recent years (Adhikari, this volume; see also Adhikari & Seddon 2002; Gurung 2002; Sharma 1989).

After his visit to Pokhara in 1952, Tucci wrote: "Pokhara is on the western side of a broad and fertile valley which used to be more intensively cultivated than it does [*sic*] today; we come across more and more abandoned fields" (1977: 39). After more than fifty years things have certainly changed much; today, most of the rice fields Tucci may have seen are under settlements, roads, or under other public uses. Tucci had commented that Pokhara was "said to be the largest town after Kathmandu, but it is not really a town at all, it is an enormous bazaar winding along one endless street. Because of its position it is bound to see a great expansion" (1977: 39). The expansion did happen as Tucci predicted, and that process seems to have activated the centrifugal and centripetal forces for the people in and around Pokhara Valley.[7]

CHANGING ENVIRONMENTS, PEOPLES AND CULTURES: CASE STUDIES

In this section I present case studies of three different groups of people in order to show that the course of their respective life ways have indeed been different in spite of their having lived in the same Pokhara Valley for generations.

The Jalaris in Begnas: Movements and Competition in Fishing

There is no detailed ethnography on the Pode people who are called Jalaris in Pokhara now. They are an endogamous group although some intermarriage with the Majhi people is also to be observed. Most of the reference to the Jalaris and their way of life is to be found in the research works on the Newars or the low castes of the Kathmandu Valley (e.g. Gellner 1995; Levy 1992; Nepali 1965; but see Toffin et al. 1991). In the available literature several terms are used to refer to them, such as Po(n) thar, Podhya, Pore,[8] Poriya, Dyahla, and Deopala. I will use the term Jalari, the name

[7]See Yamamoto, Adhikari, this volume. Along with the expansion of urban settlement, some people from the surrounding suburban areas or villages have been drawn towards the urban areas while some long-time residents of the urban areas have moved away from there. These are the processes I am labelling as centripetal (moving in towards the urban centre) and centrifugal (moving away from the urban centre).

[8]Levy writes that the word Po(n) used ordinarily to refer to the Podes, "has a pejorative quality" and therefore they "use a relatively neutral term 'Pore' (in Kathmandu Newari, 'Poriya'; in Nepali, 'Pode') to refer to themselves" (Levy 1992: 368-9). However, we see that

preferred by those living in Pokhara today.[9] However, I will also use the term Pode when referring to them in other contexts.

The Pokhara Jalaris give two different explanations for adopting this new name. First, they make a living from *jal* (Sanskrit *jal* = water; *ahara* = meal or food). That is, they eke a living out of a special 'field' which consists of a stretch of water and thus they are called Jalari. Second, they use a *jal* (a net) in order to survive and hence the name Jalari. The Jalaris of Pokhara are known as fishermen, while their fellow Podes in Kathmandu are described as sweepers or Dyalas (see Levy 1990; Nepali 1965). The Jalaris of Pokhara believe that their ancestors came from Kathmandu, as indeed is indicated by the fact that they still speak Newari, and argue that they are a sub-caste group within the Newar community.

There were a total of 34 Jalari households in Begnas in 1998. The total population in these households at the time of the field survey (June-August 1998) was 174 with an average household size of 5.1. The smallest household consisted of a couple while the largest one had 11 members in it. There was no single-person household among Jalaris in the study area. The overall sex ratio was 100 (male) : 97.7 (female). There was no female who had survived to the age of sixty-five or more and in fact, except for one female in her early sixties, there were no female survivors above fifty-five. Life expectancy seems to be very low for females (no data to calculate life expectancy was collected) and did not seem to be much higher for the males either.

Podes in general have had limited access to agricultural land. As a socially and economically marginal people within a strictly hierarchical Nepali society, which subscribed to the idea of people being 'pure or impure', clean or unclean, etc., Podes normally lived in the marginal lands on the outskirts of the urban or administrative centres (see Nepali 1965; Levy 1992). The Pode Tol in Pokhara was also at the southern end of the municipality until the town itself expanded (starting with the construction of the airport in the early 1950s, and accelerating after the completion of the Siddhartha and Prithvi highways) and encompassed it.

Until the mid 1970s, I remember seeing the Pode Tol on a rocky site about two kilometres north of the Pokhara airport with its small huts by the roadside in what is known today as Naya Bazaar. Thus the Pode houses

---

the Podes are still in the process of adopting more neutral and honourable surnames to refer to themselves, such as Dyala (temple caretakers).

[9] A number of caste/ethnic groups have, in the recent decades, started using new honorific surnames to avoid the derogatory overtones of older names. The new surnames often invoke the occupation of the caste/ethnic group in question. Does this process indicate the genesis of new caste/ethnic identities – starting with a new label? Is this process adequate and strong enough to generate a 'seamless' society – one devoid of social or ritual hierarchies? These are questions for future research.

were clustered together at the southern end of Pokhara.[10] The Pode Tol, with fishing nets (and of course, the smell of fish) hanging outside their huts, which were surrounded by maize or millet during the agricultural season, has disappeared from Pokhara town. Urbanization and urban growth in Pokhara have attracted many people but apparently the same processes have also pushed some people out – and the Jalaris seem to be one such group (see also Mierow 1997).[11]

The pace of change in Pokhara accelerated in the mid to late 1970s and created 'new opportunities' for many. However, elderly Jalaris in Begnas recall that they did not see anything coming their way. For instance, they could not start a tea shop nor could they run a restaurant or a *pasal* (shop) since they were both untouchable and poor. At that time the caste-based society would not patronize such endeavours by the Jalaris or similar people. Therefore, an option for the Jalaris was to sell their property at whatever prices offered by the hill migrants and settle elsewhere where they felt comfortable and could find cheap or free public land to build living quarters. It is evident that accelerated urbanization in Pokhara resulted in the transfer of land ownership from poor and subsistence farming people like the Jalaris (and, as discussed later, the Kumals, Damai, Kami, and Sarkis too) to the new migrants who not only had money but were also willing to make investments.[12]

A survey conducted recently (Chhetri forthcoming) revealed that the Jalaris began to sell their land to the new settlers and leave the Pode Tol by the late 1960s. Most of the Jalari households in the Begnas area today moved out from the Pode Tol and settled here during the 1970s and 1980s.[13] They left their place in Pode Tol as *bikas* or 'development' had begun to speed up in Pokhara and they could not keep pace with it. The Pode Tol of Pokhara has totally disappeared from the municipality.

Most of the studies that talk about Podes mention that they have been a community of fishermen, sweepers, temple guards, etc. (Gellner 1995;

---

[10]As a child in the late 1950s, I remember going with my grandmother to visit a match factory in Nagdhunga, which was way outside the town in those days and the only thing close by the then Pode Tol.

[11]Vinding writes: "Pokhara was established in 1752 by Newar of Kathmandu at the invitation of the rulers of the petty state of Kaski" (1998: 362). He of course goes on to cite Blaikie, Cameron, and Seddon (1980: 124) in the footnote to support his statement. I hope these authors mean the establishment of Pokhara as a market and not as a settlement as such because the settlement in this Valley is reported to be at least 600 years old.

[12]The extent of land transfers and changes in land use in Pokhara within the last twenty to thirty years deserves further research.

[13]Begnas is the name of a lake. The settlement around it is now called Begnas Bazaar. This place, located to the east of Pokhara municipality, is about 14 km. away from the site of the earlier settlement of the Jalaris. Many Jalaris from Pode Tol have also settled in a cluster at the north-western end of Phewa Lake.

Levy 1992; Nepali 1965; Toffin et al. 1991). Toffin writes that Podes in Panauti "derive the major part of their resources from fishing. They fish in rivers, ponds, irrigation canals, and even rice fields when they are flooded" (Toffin et al. 1991: 117). It is also reported that Podes would "beg for grain or money at the time of certain festivals", and from their Newar patrons "receive the clothes of the dead and the rice dishes offered to the spirit of the departed soul seven days after cremation" (ibid.). Elderly informants in Pokhara concurred that the Jalaris in Pokhara also used to receive alms from the so-called clean castes during special rituals including the purifying bath people take in a nearby river or stream soon after the end of eclipse.

In the past, it was possible to see Jalaris throwing fishing nets along the streams in Pokhara Valley while carrying a little *pyarungo* (a bamboo basket to carry the catch) on their backs. Their fishing activities were mostly carried out in the shallow points of the rushing streams or in what Kirkpatrick refers to (describing fishing activities in the Rapti river near Hetauda) as "some depths and pits in which great plenty of fish are found" (1986: 35). This (and the mode of fishing described by Kirkpatrick 1986: 35-6) was also common among the Jalaris in Pokhara until the 1970s but is much rarer today.

The Jalaris in Pokhara have not given up their traditional occupations as yet. But in order to continue to follow them, they have already left their earlier places of settlement (their dwellings and land property passed on to them by their parents and grandparents). Today, the majority of the Jalaris who moved to the Begnas area have settled in a hamlet called Piple Tundo. Twenty-one families live in this cluster, while the remaining households have settled not very far away in smaller hamlets around the Begnas or Rupa lakes.

The Jalaris in Begnas were asked to list the 'developments' in the area in recent decades and describe the perceived influences of such 'developments' on the life and livelihood strategies of the people in the area. Most of the Jalari informants listed changes to their fishing and fish-farming activities. The major 'developments' they listed included:

- The construction of a dam on Begnas Lake (completed in the late 1980s);
- The construction of a motorable road linking Begnas to the Prithvi highway two decades ago;
- The improved market for fish and the setting up of a fish collection centre at Begnas;
- The emergence of pleasure-boating in Begnas Lake during the past decade; and
- The opening up of hotels and restaurants in response to the increasing number of daytime visitors and tourists in recent years.

The Jalaris believe that these 'developments' have had a positive influence on their fishing and fish-farming activities. Most of them see the construction of the dam on the Begnas lake and the road connecting Begnas to the Prithvi highway as major 'development' interventions which have had a tremendous influence on people's ways of life in the area. Many concur that if it were not for these interventions, the Begnas Bazaar would have remained a small village.[14]

In recent years economic opportunities for the Jalaris seem to have improved in Pokhara Valley because of the Fisheries Development Projects in the Phewa, Begnas, and Rupa lakes. In my informal discussions with some Jalari people in Piple (1998-2000), it was revealed that most of them had savings deposited in banks.[15] Harka, an elderly man, estimated that each Jalari household in Begnas today should be earning between Rs.5,000 to 30,000 per month during the fishing season.[16] He noted that the investments of each household in fishing nets and other equipment (including wooden boats) have also been quite substantial.

The Jalaris had to leave their homes in Pode Tol of Pokhara municipality. But economically they seem to be doing fine so far. They are happy that they now have a better fishing business, because the traditional fishing in the rivers and streams did not always guarantee a catch, while the fish in the lakes and the cages therein are there for them to harvest. For the Jalaris, lacking agricultural land and with no resources other than their fishing skills, this is considered as a positive trend for now.

It should be mentioned here that quite a few non-Jalaris in the Begnas area (including the Bahun-Chetri households) have also made investments in fish farming. They own enclosures and cages and employ the Jalaris or others with fishing skills to help them harvest the fish. The Bahuns and Chetris in Pokhara would not have adopted fishing as a way of making income, let alone taking it up as a livelihood strategy, fifteen to twenty years ago. I recall that fishing was considered a lowly occupation by the orthodox Bahun-Chetris up until the mid 1970s. But today things seem to have changed. Raising pigs and poultry and fishing business (in cages or enclosures) are not considered lowly any more. The stigma of the past is

---

[14] I recall that in 1973 I went for a picnic with my college mates to Begnas. We had to get off the bus on Prithvi highway (near Begnas) and then walk about 3 km. to reach there. Begnas did not even have tea shops then. But at the time of the field survey in 1998-9, there were fourteen hotels/restaurants, and forty-one shops of various types in Begnas Bazaar. Today public buses depart every fifteen minutes from Mahendra Pul in Pokhara for Begnas Bazaar and from Begnas to Pokhara.

[15] It was mentioned that some households might have bank deposits of Rs.200,000 to 300,000. This is an indication that accumulation of wealth is gradually occurring among Jalaris now.

[16] The appropriate season for harvesting fish is nowadays considered to be from October to February. The traditional fishing season was mainly during the wet months of June to September when flooding in the streams was supposed to yield a larger catch.

not sufficient to deter Bahuns and Chetris (who previously would have seen such activity as a threat to their ritual status). The handsome income potential from these businesses has been a strong incentive for them to adopt fish farming also. Obviously this means the beginning of competition for the Jalaris in the fish-farming business.

The younger generation of Jalaris is becoming more literate and educated in comparison to their elders. The field survey revealed that about fifty Jalari children were enrolled in schools. Fourteen Jalaris had either completed the School Leaving Certificate (SLC) or were about to complete secondary school education. One Jalari male was also attending college in Pokhara. In the future this could change and more Jalari children could go on to receive college-level education. These should be considered as significant achievements when one considers the fact that some older Jalaris, like Juthe, reported how difficult it had been for them to continue school beyond the primary level until the 1960s, because of the discrimination and harassment that prevailed in the school system.[17]

The Kumals of Kumal Gaun: Pottery, Farming, and Migrant Labour

In the traditional form of prescriptive (ascribed) social organization based on occupational pursuits of various caste/ethnic groups in Nepal, Kumals have been associated with the craft of making clay pots. The Muluki Ain (Civil Code) of 1854 encoded the concepts of caste society, and according to the caste hierarchy set up then, Kumals are placed in the category of "enslavable alcohol drinkers" (see Höfer 2004: 9). As a community of potters, the Kumals are distributed across various parts of the country. In fact, three different groups of potters are to be found in Nepal, viz., the Pahade Kumals who call themselves Jatkumals, the Newar Kumals, and the Tarai Kumals who are recognized as Kumhars in the census reports (see also Kattel 2000). According to the census report for 2001, the total population of Pahade Kumals in Nepal stands at 99,389 or 0.44 per cent, and the Tarai Kumals or Kumhars at 54,413 or 0.24 per cent (see CBS 2002). The census report lists only the Kumhars (the Tarai Kumals) and the Kumals (Hill Kumals) as separate groups but does not do the same for the Newar Kumals (even though they too are a community of potters).[18]

In Pokhara Valley the Kumals are found in several villages within the Lekhnath municipality (Bhurtel 2000). These people are Pahade Kumals

[17] Apparently the situation has not changed much in favour of the Podes and most of the 'untouchable' community throughout the country. Talking about the Podes in Panauti, Toffin and others (1991: 115-17) write that the younger generation is waging a social battle against the status quo-minded local dignitaries. It is disheartening to find that "Pode children are not allowed to attend the public schools."

[18] It may be presumed that the Newar Kumals like the Podes were registered/counted as Newars in the census.

and at the time of field survey in 2000, there were a total of 406 people (206 male and 200 female) in 73 households in Kumal Gaun. The Kumals normally follow the rules of caste endogamy and clan exogamy.[19]

Most of the Kumal households in Pokhara Valley live in clusters around a central village which is known as Kumal Gaun (i.e. the village of the Kumals) located about 12 km. east of downtown Pokhara. The clustered settlement has allowed them to form close-knit groups among themselves for carrying out various economic activities including securing raw materials (clay or firewood) for pottery work. Until the 1960s, the main trail from Pokhara to Kathmandu (via Lamjung) passed through Kumal Gaun. Traders, travellers, and caravans of mules carrying merchandise used this trail. This is not so any more. The Prithvi highway now goes through an area about 1.5 km. north of Kumal Gaun.

Traditionally, the Kumal households in the study area were engaged in making clay pots which were in great demand among the people in Pokhara Valley and beyond. Most of the Kumal informants today report that their parents or grandparents were engaged in making the clay pots and selling them in the village as well as in the surrounding areas. They argue that the clay pots made here were much better in quality than those made by the Kumals elsewhere. Furthermore, the various types of clay pots that were made here were in line with the needs of different groups of people. The most common types of pots included pitchers (of various sizes) to carry and store drinking water, the *handi* (a round pot used to roast corn or other cereals), smaller containers for storing or carrying milk products such as curd, as well as pots required for brewing *jand* (beer made from fermented cooked rice, millet, or other cereals) or distilling the alcoholic drink called *raksi*.

The source of clay for the Kumals was on the other side of the Seti River, which flows from west to east a few kilometres to the south of Kumal Gaun. (Local people often refer to this river as the Gandaki.) Elderly Kumals recall that a decision was made through informal consultations in the village as to when it would be a good time to go and fetch the clay. Generally several able-bodied men and women would travel together across the Seti river in order to dig out the clay and carry it back home after the rainy season was over every year. At the 'clay mine' men took turns in digging while the women scooped the best-quality clay to fill their *doko*s (bamboo baskets) as quickly as possible. Kumal informants also point out that this work of digging clay was risky. Therefore cooperation and teamwork among fellow Kumals was essential.[20]

---

[19]The Kumals in the study area belong to six clans, viz., Khattri, Gotanye, Rana, Chittaure, Rajput, and Kumbhakarna Shiladevi.

[20]A couple of elderly Kumals recalled a sad accident from about twenty-five years ago. On a normal day at the beginning of winter that year, some ten to twelve people went to fetch clay.

Local seasonal markets, or the *melas* (fairs), such as the Maghe Sankranti Jatra held at Dhungesangu to this day on the first of the Nepali month of Magh (mid January), were the occasions when the Kumals could sell their clay pots in large numbers. I remember seeing the fields of Dhungesangu filled with clay pots among other items for sale during the Jatra every year until the early 1970s. But in January 1999 when I visited the Jatra there was not a single clay pot stall in the market. In the past, Kumals were also seen going around with loads of clay pots at the rapidly growing bazaars of Pokhara, Khudikomuhan, Syangkhudi, Talbesi (around the Begnas-Rupa lakes), and the surrounding villages. Those Kumals who could sell the pots in the neighbouring villages and had a deficit of food productions at home also bought or took maize and millet in exchange for their pots.

The traditional pottery work with which they were identified is being given up completely. It was revealed during the field survey that young Kumals have not acquired the pot-making skills from their parents. They are now in school and learning to read and write. Our field survey also revealed that 46 Kumals (31 males and 15 females) had either completed or were about to complete secondary school education, while 8 others (4 males and 4 females) had acquired or were about to acquire college degrees. This should be considered a significant change among the Kumals, since education was not accessible to everyone in the past (as pointed out earlier). However, education has not helped the Kumal youths to compete with non-Kumals in the country's job market. As a result, many have either gone or are in the process of going abroad to the Gulf countries (locally known as 'going to Arab' or *Arab jane*). The field survey revealed that a total of 19 Kumal youths were in *Arab* and were reported to be engaged in unskilled or semi-skilled jobs.

Remittances are considered important for the family members remaining behind in Nepal. But sending a family member to *Arab* in the first place does not happen easily and also constitutes a high-risk investment. The Kumals reported that the total cost for sending one person to the Gulf comes to about Rs.85,000 to 100,000 (US $1=Rs.74). A number of households had to sell private land in order to accumulate the required cash for this purpose. Those who do not possess land end up taking loans from local moneylenders at interest rates of up to 60 per cent per annum.

When the youths finally get their paperwork completed to go to the Gulf countries, they get a visa which is valid for two years only. Informants reported that the jobs there pay about 500 Riyals a month (1 Riyal was equal to about Rs.18 at the time of the field survey). If they had to return home in two years, their savings would therefore not be adequate to cover

While digging in the burrows that they had used in the past the ceilings of the tunnels collapsed on them. Only two survivors returned home in the evening to recount this tragedy.

the expenses involved in sending them away from home. Therefore, unless they are able to extend their visas or continue to stay there illegally for longer periods they cannot send or bring back much money. If this is the case, the only people benefiting from this recent practice of labour export are either the local moneylenders or the real estate agents who buy land at cheaper prices from the households that are in need of quick cash.

The Kumals here were also engaged in farming. They used to cultivate maize, millet, and rice, besides growing some vegetables in the home gardens mainly for household consumption. Mutual exchange of labour called *parma* was a common practice in carrying out farming work. *Parma* among Kumals was not limited to agriculture and this is similar to the practice called *pareli* reported for people in other parts of Nepal (Caplan 1970; Messerschmidt 1981; Ishii 1982). As a part of the *parma* the host among the Kumals treated the *khetala*s (the workers) to a large meal including a drink of *raksi* or *jand* at the end of the day. They were also given light food during the day. Everyone was obliged to participate in this exchange of labour and food.

Elderly Kumal informants claim that they owned more land per household in the past than they do now. It was revealed that a number of Kumals had migrated to Bardia district (in western Tarai) during the past two to three decades after selling their property to new settlers from the hills. Many other Kumals concur that they too had sold most of their land to *lahures*[21] and others within the past decade, and this process still continues. As a result, the relatively homogeneous and small settlement of Kumal Gaun is now surrounded by new hamlets comprised of settlers belonging to such ethnic/caste groups as Gurungs, Magars, Bahuns, and Chetris.

The Kumal households who owned smaller or less productive farms were engaged in sharecropping arrangements called *adhiyan. Adhiyan* ensured that no farms were left fallow while it was also a local method of sharing of food and other farm resources between those who had surplus and those who had little.

As a seasonal activity, Kumal men were also engaged in fishing (using nets, hooks, or by placing an entrapment called *dhadiya*, an elongated basket made out of fine bamboo-sticks) in the streams and lakes during the rainy season as well as in winter. The catch was sold in most cases to the owners of the roadside inns known as *bhatti*. Fishing is not a regular activity for the Kumals now. The formation of fish-farming groups in recent years around the major lakes like Phewa, Begnas, and Rupa has

---

[21]The word *lahure* denoted anyone who was visiting home from a job or employment of any kind in another country. It was, of course, more commonly used to refer to those employed in the Indian or British armies. The second usage of the term is more popular among people in Pokhara Valley.

meant no fishing rights for the Kumals since they do not live in the proximity of these lakes.[22]

Pottery, which provided a secure source of income for Kumals in the past, has now been given up and the skills related to this work are not being passed down to the younger generation. Kumal informants give several reasons for this. First, the youths are not interested in obtaining the skills. Second, the raw materials (clay and firewood) are not as easily available. Finally, the most important fact is that factory-made metal pots, pans, and utensils have displaced most of Kumal's clay pots from the market. Kumal informants agree that they could have adapted by making other types of clay products that are still in demand (e.g. flowerpots and other items used in internal decorations by hotels and middle-class households). However, the difficult access to the raw materials needed (clay as well as the firewood for firing the kilns) for pottery seems to have discouraged the Kumals from practising the craft as a source of regular income. The Kumals in the study area claim that their access to forest resources has decreased after the local forests were handed over as community forests to forest users groups.

Elderly Kumal informants also point out that some of their traditional practices related to marriages have been replaced by non-Kumal customs now. For instance, in a traditional arranged marriage, a custom known as *vundko khuwaune* was practised. This custom involved the prospective bridegroom's parents visiting the prospective bride's parents' home with a good-sized earthen jug (known as *vundko*) filled with home-brewed *raksi* and giving a small feast to the bride's parents as a token of the confirmation of the relationship (i.e. a betrothal). The bride's parents accepted the homemade *raksi* if they approved of the proposed relationship. But today, the Kumals have adopted the practice of *janai-supari*, an engagement ceremony common principally among the Bahun-Chetris in which the bridegroom and his close relatives visit the bride's house so that he and the bride can exchange engagement garlands and rings. These are further examples of how the Kumals are giving up their own traditional cultural practices and adopting new ones.

Dalits in Pachbhaiya: New Livelihood Options and Challenges

The Kami, Damai, and Sarki together constituted 7.06 per cent of the total population of Nepal in 2001 (CBS 2002). Of the 101 caste/ethnic groups (plus the categories of unidentified Dalit and unidentified caste/ethnic

---

[22] A programme funded by JICA, Japan, has made significant investments in the conservation and management of watersheds and the resources therein, in and around these three major lakes in Pokhara Valley. The Fisheries Development Project under the same programme has benefited those living closer to the lakes including the Jalaris.

groups), the Kami, Damai, and Sarki rank as the eighth, twelfth, and fifteenth largest groups, respectively, in terms of population size. Of the total population of 22,736,934 in 2001 in Nepal, there were 895,954 (3.94 per cent) Kamis, 390,305 (1.72 per cent) Damais, and 318,989 (1.40 per cent) Sarkis (CBS 2002, Table 16, pp. 72-3). These groups of people are Hindus and follow the rules of caste endogamy. In the traditional caste hierarchy of Nepal, these three groups of people were placed towards the bottom of the social hierarchy and classified as 'untouchables': *pani nachalnya choi chito halnuparnya*, which literally means 'water unacceptable' (i.e. water from them was not to be accepted by 'clean' castes), and 'if touched, requiring purification' (i.e. if a member of the 'clean' caste should touch them, purificatory water needed to be sprinkled on them) (Höfer 2004: 9). Such historical placements have had far-reaching consequences for the current status of Dalit peoples like the Kami, Damai, and Sarki. To put it bluntly, they are among the most discriminated against people in the country in the social, economic, political, and educational spheres.

Traditionally Kamis have been known as blacksmiths, Damais as tailors and musicians, and Sarkis as tanners and shoemakers. The Muluki Ain of 1854 declared the Kami and Sarki as equal in status, which would be challenged by the orthodox Kamis and Sarkis themselves, each claiming superiority over the other. All three groups of Dalits under discussion in this section are distributed throughout the country often living in hamlets at the edges of the villages of other caste/ethnic groups of people.

The Kami, Damai, and Sarki people of Pachbhaiya may not be different in terms of the overall social and economic position of Dalits living in other parts of the country. There were 45 households of these three Dalits together at the study site at the time of the field survey in 2000, of which 21 were Kami, 11 Damai, and 13 Sarki. The total population in these 45 households was 236 (125 male and 111 female; Kami total 101, Damai 70, and Sarki 65).

The youths in all three groups are now acquiring education. There were 24 people (21 male and 3 female) who had completed or were about to complete SLC while 2 males who had gone to college (1 each from Kami and Sarki castes). It is interesting to note that of the 21 males who had SLC level education, 9 each were Damais and Kamis while only 3 were Sarkis. Besides, among the Sarkis no females had been educated beyond the primary level. That is, Sarkis are noticeably behind the other two groups in terms of educational attainment.

The survey also revealed an interesting landownership pattern among these three groups. Proportionately the largest number of landless households occurred among the Damais. Of the total of 11 Damai households, 10 did not possess any *khet* (wetland), and 5 did not own any *bari* (non-irrigated farm) land either. The Kami and Sarki households were better off in this regard. Two-thirds (14 out of the 21 households) of the Kamis owned *bari* lands (ranging from 1 to 9 *ropani*[23]) while 4 households also possessed *khet* lands (ranging from 1 to 5 *ropani*). In terms of landownership, the Sarki households seemed even better off since all of them owned *bari* lands (ranging from 2 to 5 *ropani*) while 3 households also owned 3 to 5 *ropani* of *khet*.

Until about the 1970s, most of the Dalit households in Pokhara Valley were involved in some kind of exchange of services and goods with the farming households of Bahuns, Chetris, and other caste/ethnic groups. Each of the artisan (Dalit) households would have a number of farming families as their regular clients or *bista*. The payments for the services would be on an annual basis as *bali* or *majuri* (labour cost or wages) at the time of the harvest of cereal crops. These types of relations have prevailed in other parts of Nepal as well even though the names given to them may vary from place to place. For instance, M.M. Cameron (1998) talks of the prevalence of the *riti bhagya* practice in western Nepal which ties the local artisans and farmers in similar exchange relations. Prindle (1977), on the other hand calls it the Jajmani system.[24] In a study in east Nepal he looked at how the annual *jajmani* payments were determined and discovered that there were fixed rates of exchange – of labour and payments in kind. While the system provided some sort of economic security for the lower castes, Prindle argued that this system also served to reinforce traditional hierarchical relations among castes.

In Pokhara Valley, the Baliko Damai used to be obliged to stitch and repair clothes for their clients throughout the year. People of course normally had new pairs of clothes made for family members once or twice a year at the time of Dasain or other important festivals. The other regular service provided by the Baliko Damai (and often the tailor's wife used to do most of the work) was annual repair of clothes including bedding

---

[23] 1 *ropani* of land = 0.05 ha. That is, 1 ha is approximately 20 *ropani*.

[24] W.H. Wiser (1936, cited in Kolenda 1967) was the first scholar to give a full description of a multi-caste village exchange relationship known as the Jajmani system and "to recognize that the occupational division of labour in an Indian village with distribution of services and products was a system of network of role relationships" (Kolenda 1967: 290). Subsequently, the Jajmani system has been discussed in village studies in India by many social anthropologists (see an extensive review of the Jajmani models in India by Kolenda 1967). In Nepal, the *jajmani*-type relationship was reported in a full-scale article in 1977 (Prindle 1977: 288-301). The *bali-majuri* relations and other patron-client relations must be common in many parts of Nepal, particularly in multi-caste village settings (see Ishii 2007 for the Newar case, which also argues against seeing *jajmani*-type relations as any kind of system). In my own observations as a member of Nepali society, I feel that there were or have been several types of such exchange relations but not all of them necessarily predicated upon one-way hierarchical relations between castes. Since very few ethnographic studies on Nepal have taken multi-caste/ethnic relations as their focus so far, these types of exchange relations are yet to be fully understood.

materials. They were also expected to stitch additional clothes/dresses at the time of life-cycle rituals in the *bista*'s family, or make school uniforms for the children. However, for such additional services the Baliko Damai was adequately compensated in cash or in kind. The Damai also played music on the traditional musical instruments called *panchai baja* (see Tingey 1994 for more details on Damai musicians) during marriage ceremonies, festivals, and religious celebrations or rituals, and would be paid separately for this service as well.

The Kami and Sarki households too used to have a clientele comprising the farmers in the locality. The Baliko Kami (or the blacksmith) was mainly responsible for the manufacture and repair of farm implements. New farm implements were actually sold by the blacksmith to the farmers. His obligation in return for the *bali* was to repair all farm and household implements for the *bista* households. The Baliko Sarki, on the other hand, manufactured and repaired leather items (by locally processing the skins of dead cattle and buffaloes) such as *hallundo* (a leather strap used in tying the plough to the yoke), traditional musical instruments, shoes, etc.

Dalit informants in Pachbhaiya reported that they do not work on *bali* arrangements any more with the local farmers. In recent years, the farmers have been buying factory-made farm implements in the market and have started paying the Kamis with cash whenever such implements need to be repaired. Due to changes in the farming system the Dalits cannot depend on the traditional systems of *bali* and *majuri* in order to obtain cereal grains on a regular basis to meet most of their food requirements during the year. This has forced them to look for other ways of earning a living. Very few of them still depend on their traditional crafts such as metalworking, cobbling, tanning, tailoring, and playing music as options for earning a reasonable income.

A change in the forest management policy and practice in the country also seems to have had an impact on the livelihood options of the Dalits. The Community Forestry (CF) Programme that began in 1978 can be cited as an example. Under this programme, local forest users groups can take over the responsibilities of forest protection and management under an agreement between the District Forest Office and the Community Forest Users Groups (CFUG). Once the CFUGs take over the responsibility of local forest protection and management, they generally tend to make and implement their own rules and regulations for access and use of forest products from their community's forest. The Dalits in Begnas area reported that they have been affected by the CF programme's implementation since they seem to have been excluded from the CFUG membership in their locality. As non-members of a CFUG, they cannot obtain the forest products that are the raw materials for their traditional craft works. The blacksmiths, for instance, require firewood to make charcoal but were not given the amount they required for this purpose. Similarly, the Sarkis require the leaves and bark of *Woodfordia fruticosa* (*dhairo*), *Castanopsis Indica* (*katus*), *Schima wallichii* (*chilaune*), and *Myrica esculenta* (*kaphal*) in order to process raw leather. They too were not allowed to enter the local forest when they needed these products. Such restrictions have also made it difficult for the local artisans to continue their traditional occupations or craft work.

One of the options chosen by Dalit youths for earning income in recent years has been to work as wage labourers. Some Dalits have migrated to the Gulf countries just like the Kumal youths discussed earlier. Our field survey (2000) revealed that thirteen young Dalit men were away working in these countries as watchmen, carpenters, factory labourers, and domestic servants. Besides, twenty Dalit youths had already returned from the Gulf countries after having worked there for an average period of two years. Some had also taken to locally available wage labouring such as working as porters in the local bus stations. A few young Dalits were working as helpers/conductors in the public buses plying between Pokhara and Begnas Bazaar.

UNDERSTANDING SOCIAL AND CULTURAL CHANGE: SOME OBSERVATIONS

Changes in the total environment in Pokhara Valley during the last few decades have prompted different responses and resulted in diverse livelihood outcomes. Continuity and change in the pursuit of traditional occupations by the communities under study appear to have been influenced by changes in the total environment in Pokhara. For instance, natural resource management policies and practices have changed, Dalits and Kumals are able to send their children to school, farmers have opted to use factory made utensils and farm implements, etc.

It is evident that the Dalit households in Begnas, just as the Kumals (and this could be true for people from other caste/ethnic groups as well), have adopted diverse economic activities in order to make a living today. The pattern whereby most households belonging to a given caste/ethnic group and co-residing in a locality or village adopt similar economic activities has become a thing of the past. This trend of diversification in livelihood options at the household level among various groups of people is likely to continue in the days to come and in the face of changes in the total environment for the people discussed in this chapter. As a consequence of this, it is likely that the association of particular occupations with certain caste/ethnic groups in Nepal will become weaker.

Of the three groups whose lifeways have been discussed above, the

Jalaris seem to be doing well so far. Of course, they were somehow pushed out of their homes in Pode Tol by the urbanization process that has occurred in Pokhara during the past few decades. But now that they are settled around Begnas Lake, they report that the fish farming there plus other 'developments' have been in their favour. Impending competition in the fish-farming business does not seem to concern them yet. The Kumals, on the other hand, have given up pottery making, their traditional occupation. In this case, the traditional skills passed down from generations are about to be lost. In recent years, Kumal youths are not learning the skills related to pottery. In order to make a living, the Kumals have been able to adopt vegetable farming since they possessed some land and already possessed the necessary skills. The Damai, Kami, and Sarki seem to be the worst hit by 'development' or changes in the total environment. Their traditional *bista* ties with farming households in the locality have been severed since many of the latter either adopted factory-made farm implements or sold their farmlands and made investments elsewhere.

The traditional skills of Kumal, Damai, Kami, and Sarki artisans were passed down from parents to children through apprenticeship. But now the younger generation is either in school or is not interested in learning these traditional skills (which would neither allow them to earn a living easily nor bring them any social prestige). This is also one reason why the traditional knowledge and skills of the Kami, Damai, Sarki, and Kumal are on the verge of being lost.

Various groups of people in Pokhara have for long interacted with each other and lived in a symbiotic relationship. However, within the past four to five decades, the changes in the environments here have come about in such a way that the sets of people interacting with each other and mutually depending on each other are not the same as they were in the past. In the process of change in the environments, some people are finding that new niches have opened up for them (e.g. vegetable farming for landowning Kumals) while others are finding that their traditional niches have been rendered less dependable for survival. This clearly demonstrates how dynamic society and socio-economic processes can be. Jalaris must have certainly depended upon other groups of people around them while others too must have depended upon them in the past when they used to live in Pode Tol in Pokhara. But the traditional two-way linkage seems to have shifted and today the groups of people Jalaris depend on and interact with are different from those in the past. Similar things have happened to the Damai, Kami, Sarki, Kumal, and many other communities like them in Nepal. The factors and processes that have been responsible for such changes, and the consequent changes in livelihoods of the people involved have been noted on the basis of empirical evidence.

For instance, village societies (i.e. the many caste/ethnic groups) in

Nepal today are no more 'close-knit' ones as they were believed to be in the past. They not only knew each other well (which they still do) but were part of a social network, with frequent and intimate interactions through exchange of labour, services, and supports (materials, morale, etc.) in times of need. Today, all such relations are less important as suggested by the case studies here. For instance, the Kumal vegetable farmers today do not find it necessary to work closely with each other whereas collective work was an imperative when working as potters in the past.

Individuals and households in a community also differ in their engagements in economic activities in general. The primary economic activities of people within a community of Kumals or Damais, Kamis, and Sarkis are less common to each other today. In the past, they mostly followed the same 'traditional' occupations. But today these are being given up and the new occupations differ according to the individual: personal choices, skills, qualifications, connections, and a host of factors seem to be at work. What is valued by society has changed too. For instance, among the Kumals in Begnas, earning higher income is valued more now than being recognized in the community for making the best-quality clay pots. The same is true for the Dalits who were very proud of their ability to earn a reputation as the best Kamis/blacksmiths, or the best Damais/musicians in the locality until not long ago.

It is also evident that in the new economic activities that are being adopted to earn a livelihood by the communities under study, there is going to be competition. Whether they will be able to withstand such competition remains an open question for now. For instance, will the Jalaris in Pokhara be able to remain in the fishing and fish-farming business when others with larger investments and more elaborate business networks enter the field? People have also been further marginalized in their own homelands. The Jalaris have been displaced from the Pode Tol while the Kumals and other Dalits have been selling their farmlands, which could result in their displacement from their current settlements eventually. These are not isolated cases. Similar things are happening for other groups of people too. The case of the Tharus in the Tarai stands out as the best example of this (see Chhetri 2005), while the Kumals of Tumlingtar in east Nepal present another case clearly exemplifying the same trend (see Kattel 2000).

CONCLUSION

The term 'development' is impregnated with the assumption of progress. It also seems to endorse the technocratic approach to solving social and economic problems in societies. Thus the construction of roads, hydro-power plants, schools, hospitals, etc., is assumed to bring benefits to everyone equally. 'Development' as a term tends to be used with reference to a state's movement towards a stage that the West has reached or passed through (see Escobar 1995). The concept, therefore, is not really useful when talking about individuals or the small groups of people generally chosen for study by ethnographers.

In the past, as discussed in the foregoing case studies, there were mutual exchange relations between the artisans and the farmers. But such relations seem to have been in the favour of the farmers, the recipients of the services and goods, and not those who were receiving payments in kind. As soon as alternative sources of services and goods appeared, the age-old exchange relations between the artisans and the *bista*s were broken by the *bista*s. While the *bista*s had nothing to lose, the artisans dependent on *bali* were in trouble. Some informants described this troubled conditions of theirs by means of a Nepali saying: '*Na tekne hango, na samaune laharo*' ('Neither a branch to stand on nor vines to cling on to'). The unequal exchange relations (like the *bali* system of annual payments noted above) may have seemed like cooperation, sharing, or the redistribution of resources and thereby exhibiting a sense of self-reliant and interdependent local communities. Such exchange relations provided only limited economic security to Dalits, because once the *bista*s had an alternative they abandoned their artisans without sentiment.

The exchange of goods and services between different communities within the locality is no longer a dominant pattern. Thus, traditional mutual interdependence and relations/ties are attenuating or disappearing. This means that societies and social relations in Nepal will continue to change and evolve in future. Given this, we can only speculate now as to the nature of social relations in Nepal in the days to come.

The system or chain of exchange relationships between the Dalit artisans and the farmer was apparently broken due to changes in a number of facets of the total environment in the Valley. First, access to education for the Dalits has been easier, as already indicated. This positive aspect of change too had a negative impact on the continuation of the traditional skills of the artisans since the school educated youths are no longer interested in learning traditional skills and following in the footsteps of their parents. Second, the Kumal and Dalit youths who have acquired some education recently have given up their family's traditional occupations without having acquired the skills required to compete successfully with others in the job market. Third, the inflow of factory-made tools, ready-made clothes, pots and pans, etc., has displaced the items manufactured locally by the artisans. Fourth, access to raw materials for the continuation of such traditional craft works has become difficult due to recent changes in the policies related to the management of natural resources in the country. As we have discussed earlier, many youths are finding it very hard to cope with the situations at present, and thus seem desperate to adopt any sort of income-earning work.

To conclude, I would argue that the narratives of change presented in this chapter are likely to resemble the experiences of similar groups of people in other parts of Nepal. The emerging arguments and questions may therefore have a wider significance for understanding or reading the process of social, cultural, and economic change among similar groups of people living in other parts of Nepal as well.

REFERENCES

Adhikari, J. and D. Seddon. 2002. *Pokhara: Biography of a Town*. Kathmandu: Mandala Book Point.

Barth, F. 1981. *Features of Person and Society in Swat: Collected Essays on Pathans*. London: Routledge & Kegan Paul.

——. 1987. *Cosmologies in the Making: A Generative Approach to Cultural Variation in Inner New Guinea*. New York: Cambridge University Press.

Berreman, G.D. 1972. *Hindus of the Himalayas: Ethnography and Change*. Berkeley: University of California Press (2nd edn).

Bhurtel, B. 2000. 'Changing Livelihood Strategies of the Kumals Living in Pokhara Valley of Western Nepal'. Unpublished MA thesis, Tribhuvan University, Kathmandu.

Blaikie, P., J. Cameron, and D. Seddon. 1980. *Nepal in Crisis: Growth and Stagnation at the Periphery*. Delhi: Oxford University Press.

Cameron, M.M. 1998. *On the Edge of the Auspicious: Gender and Caste in Nepal*. Urbana: University of Illinois Press.

Caplan, L. 1970. *Land and Social Change in East Nepal*. Berkeley: University of California Press.

CBS. 1995. *Statistical Year Book of Nepal*. Kathmandu: HMG, NPC Secretariat.

——. 2002. *Population Census 2001: National Report*. Kathmandu: HMG, NPC Secretariat, CBS in Collaboration with UNFPA, Nepal.

Chhetri, R.B. 1986. 'Migration, Adaptation and Socio-Cultural Change: The Case of Thakalis in Pokhara, Nepal'. *Contributions to Nepalese Studies* 13 (3): 241-59.

——. 1990. 'Adaptation of Tibetan Refugees in Pokhara, Nepal: A Study on Persistence and Change'. Unpublished Ph.D. thesis, University of Hawaii.

——. 2005. 'The Plight of the Tharu Kamaiyas in Nepal: A Review of the Social, Economic and Political Facets', in R.B. Chhetri, K.B. Bhattachan and B. Pokharel (eds.), *Occasional Papers in Sociology and Anthropology: Caste/Ethnic Issues, Water Resource Management, Trends in Local Development*, Vol. 9, pp. 22-46. Kathmandu: CDSA, Tribhuvan University.

——. n.d. forthcoming. 'Changing Environments and Livelihoods in the Hills of Nepal: Adaptation of the Jalari People in Pokhara Valley', in R.B. Chhetri (ed.), *Changing Environments and Livelihoods in Nepal.*

Escobar, A. 1995. *Encountering Development: The Making and Unmaking of the Third World.* Princeton, New Jersey: Princeton University Press.

Fisher, W.F. 2001. *Fluid Boundaries: Forming and Transforming Identity in Nepal.* New York: Columbia University Press.

Geertz, C. 1973. *The Interpretation of Cultures.* New York: Basic Books.

Gellner, D.N. 1995. 'Low Castes in Lalitpur', in D.N. Gellner and D. Quigley (eds.), *Contested Hierarchies: A Collaborative Ethnography of Caste among the Newars of the Kathmandu Valley, Nepal*, pp. 264-94. Oxford: Clarendon Press.

Guneratne, A. 2002. *Many Tongues, One People: The Making of Tharu Identity in Nepal.* Ithaca: Cornell University Press.

Gurung, H. 2002. *Pokhara Valley: A Geographical Survey.* Kathmandu: Nepal Geographical Society (original mimeograph edition by Department of Geography, SOAS, December 1965).

Hagen, T. 1994. *Building Bridges to the Third World*, tr. P. Pierce. Delhi: Book Faith India.

Höfer, A. 2004 (1979). *The Caste Hierarchy and the State in Nepal: A Study of the Muluki Ain of Nepal 1854.* Kathmandu: Himal Books.

Ishii, H. 1982. 'Agricultural Labour Recruitment in a Parbate Village in Nepal', in D.B. Bista et al. (eds.), *Anthropological and Linguistic Studies of the Gandaki Area in Nepal.* Monumenta Serindica 10, pp. 40-80. Tokyo, ICLAA: Tokyo University of Foreign Studies.

——. 2007. 'The Transformation of Caste Relationships in Nepal', in H. Ishii, D.N. Gellner, and K. Nawa (eds.), *Social Dynamics in Northern South Asia*, Vol. 2: *Social and Political Transformations in North India and Nepal*, pp. 91-129. Delhi: Manohar.

Karan, P.P. and H. Ishii. 1996. *Nepal: A Himalayan Kingdom in Transition.* Tokyo: United Nations University Press.

Kattel, S.P. 2000. 'Development and Its Victims: From Pottery Makers to Porters: The Changing Life-World of the Kumals of the Arun Valley, Eastern Nepal'. Unpublished M.Phil. thesis, University of Bergen, Norway.

Kirkpatrick, Col. 1986 (1811). *An Account of the Kingdom of Nepaul: Being the Substance of Observations Made during a Mission to That Country in the Year 1793.* New Delhi: Asian Educational Services.

Kolenda, P.M. 1967. 'Toward a Model of the Hindu Jajmani System', in G. Dalton (ed.), *Tribal and Peasant Economies: Readings in Economic Anthropology*, pp. 285-332. Austin: University of Texas Press.

Landon, P. 1993 (1928). *Nepal.* New Delhi and Madras: Asian Educational Services.

Levy, R.I. 1992 (1990). *Mesocosm: Hinduism and the Organization of a Traditional Newar City in Nepal.* Delhi: Motilal Banarsidass.

Maskarinec, G.G. 2000 (1995). *The Rulings of the Night: An Ethnography of Nepalese Shaman Oral Texts.* Kathmandu: Mandala Book Point.

Mauss, M. 1967 (1925). *The Gift: Forms and Functions of Exchange in Archaic Society.* New York: W.W. Norton and Company.

Messerschmidt, D.A. 1981. 'Nogar and Other Traditional Forms of Cooperation in Nepal: Significance for Development'. *Human Organization* 40 (1): 40-7.

Mierow, D. 1997. *Thirty Years in Pokhara.* Kathmandu: Pilgrims Book House.

Mishra, C. and P. Sharma. 1983. 'Foreign Aid and Social Structure: Notes on Intra-State Relationships'. Proceedings of a Sèminar, 4-5 October 1983. Kathmandu: Integrated Development Systems.

Nepali, G.S. 1965. *The Newars: An Ethno-Sociological Study of a Himalayan Community.* Bombay: United Asia Publications.

Prindle, P.H. 1977. 'The Jajmani System: A Nepalese Example'. *Journal of Anthropological Research* 33: 288-301.

Sharma, P. 1989. *Urbanization in Nepal* (Papers of the East-West Population Institute, Number 110). Honolulu: East-West Center.

Tingey, C. 1994. *Auspicious Music in a Changing Society: The Damai Musicians of Nepal* (SOAS Musicology Series, Vol. 2). London: School of Oriental and African Studies, University of London.

Toffin, G., V. Barré, L. Berger, and P. Berger 1991 [1981]. 'The Pode House: A Caste of Newar Fishermen', in G.Toffin (ed.), *Man and His House in the Himalayas: Ecology of Nepal*, pp. 115-26. Delhi: Sterling.

Tucci, G. 1977 (1953). *Journey to Mustang, 1952,* tr. Diana Fussel from Italian. Kathmandu: Ratna Pustak Bhandar (originally published in Rome).

Vayda, A.P. 1983. 'Progressive Contextualization: Methods for Research in Human Ecology'. *Human Ecology* 11 (3): 265-81.

Vinding, M. 1998. *The Thakali: A Himalayan Ethnography.* London: Serindia Publications.

4

The *Sukumbasi* Transformation from Communitas to Community: The Birth and Death of 'Proto-Charisma' among Squatters in Pokhara, Nepal

YUJI YAMAMOTO

INTRODUCTION

Despite its rich cultural heritage, in tables of economic performance the kingdom of Nepal ranks among the lowest countries in Asia. According to Karan and Ishii (1994: 9), its per capita annual income increased by an average of only 0.9 per cent per year in the twenty-five years from 1964 to 1990. Such a low economic growth rate can be ascribed partly to the geographical reason of being a landlocked mountainous country and partly to particular historical causes. Among the latter, the fact that before 1951 the feudal Rana regime made few attempts to found modern industries must surely be significant.

Sukumbasi (usually translated as 'squatter(s)' in English) have been increasing these days and have become one of the symbols of Nepalese low development and poverty. Going into details, we find that two key factors have fuelled the increase in the number of *sukumbasi*: (1) nationwide urbanization and participation in the monetary market, which has resulted in economic polarization; and (2) the gap in the living standards between mountain villagers and urban dwellers which has opened up. Hence poor villagers in the mountain areas, attracted by job opportunities, have started rushing to the cities in the valleys. However, they cannot afford to buy land in the city and are obliged to occupy some vacant or public land within the city.

This chapter aims to provide a comprehensive view of *sukumbasi* settlements in Pokhara, a city in the western hills whose population is

156,312 (2001). It presents a typology of *sukumbasi* settlements and a sociological and historical reconstruction of their process of formation based on detailed field surveys carried out between 1998 and 2004. A *sukumbasi* settlement begins with the building of tens of *bhakari*s (shanties, shacks) on vacant land without water supply, drainage, or toilet facilities. Over time the settlement develops and the shanties are remodelled into small cottages made of concrete breeze-blocks or wood. The Nepalese term *lal purja* (red card) can be translated as 'land register title'. After occupying the land for a couple of months, and encouraged by the fact that their land does not appear to be subject to public claim, the squatters apply to the Sukumbasi Ayog (an ad hoc government office that issues *lal purja* to *sukumbasi*s) for a *lal purja* for their land. After close examination of their application, if everything is in order, the *lal purja* will be provided to them. In order to conceptualize the distinct character of this early phase of *sukumbasi* settlement, I make use of Victor Turner's concept of 'communitas'. Further, I highlight the role of the leaders of *sukumbasi* settlements, who play a vital role in the process of transformation from communitas to community.

RESEARCH PERIODS AND RESEARCH METHODS

In March 1998 I undertook a one-week preliminary survey in Pokhara. I decided to take the *sukumbasi*s as the research theme of my fieldwork during the summer of 1998-9 to be supported by the Japanese Ministry of Education. My initial *sukumbasi* research in Pokhara was conducted from 5 August through 16 September 1998. With the help of three Nepali research assistants, Min Bahadur Giri, Rajendra Giri, and Ananda Thapa, and thanks to the use of motorcycles, we surveyed Pokhara's *sukumbasi* settlements using both quantitative and qualitative methods. After dark the four of us would return to my hotel room and all the data for the day was reviewed and stored in my computer. We found a total of thirty-nine *sukumbasi* and ex-*sukumbasi* settlements (shown in Map 4.1 and numbered from #1 to #39) within Pokhara municipality.

We used a standard questionnaire sheet on which the answers could be recorded directly. All the questions were listed on the sheet:

(1) a serial number per area,
(2) area (settlement) names,
(3) shanty (or house) number,
(4) the full name of the family head,
(5) acquisition of *lal purja* (yes or no),
(6) relation to the family head, sex, age, education, occupation of each family member,

(7) original home before coming to Pokhara,
(8) year of arrival in Pokhara,
(9) previous residence within Pokhara,
(10) when they started living in the present settlement,
(11) the occupation of each adult family member,
(12) the monthly income of each adult member, and
(13) the reason(s) why they became a *sukumbasi*.

The following year, 1999, I returned to Pokhara for a second period of fieldwork, between 2 August and 19 September. The same research assistants helped with my research again. There were two main goals in the second period of research: (1) to locate all the newly arrived families as well as all those who had left each settlement between the two research periods, and (2) to conduct detailed interviews with as many *sukumbasi* leaders in as many different settlements as possible. Around the middle of our second research we discovered two additional ex-*sukumbasi* settlements, Belbot (#40) and Phirke (#41), near the south-east border of Pokhara. We immediately carried out intensive research in them. Needless to say, whenever ambiguous or missing points were raised, we returned to see the person in question, and collected or verified those points immediately. Data on all 2,087 *sukumbasi* and ex-*sukumbasi* households living in the forty-one settlements was stored in my computer before my departure from Pokhara.

Research funding from Ritsumeikan University made it possible for me to conduct a further two-week period of fieldwork in Pokhara in August 2001 after two years' absence. To my surprise I found five newly established *sukumbasi* settlements: Yandi (#42), Behind Hospital II (#43), Ram Ghat II (#43), Gai Kharka (#45), and Bacche Buduwa (#46). All these five were set up in 2000 and all of them were evacuated before 2003. I visited and took a look at each of these new settlements, but I could not conduct the same kind of research as before on my own. Nonetheless I include all forty-six settlements in Map 4.1. Some of the results of my 1998-9 researches have already been presented in Japanese (Yamamoto 2001a, 2001b, 2002). Though the present chapter repeats some of that material, it has been reworked to include new material as well.

THE HISTORY OF *SUKUMBASI* DEVELOPMENT IN POKHARA

In 1952 Pokhara opened its airport at its present site, which enabled foreign visitors to come to Pokhara by air from Kathmandu or even from India. It was the dawn of the tourist industry in Pokhara. In the early 1960s the WHO declared the eradication of malaria from Pokhara Valley which

Map 4.1: *Sukumbasi* Settlements in 2003.

Legends

☼	Campus	✈	Airport
⌂	Temple	⊃–	Drainage
8	Baudha Monastery	═	Metalled Road
⊞	Hospital	:::::	Unmetalled Road
⇧	Tower	-----	Foot Trail

① Pani Tanki
② Simal Bote
③ Sim Pani
④ Sarangkot
⑤ Bager
⑥ Tundako Patan
⑦ Male Patan
⑧ Mahendra Pul
⑨ Sita Paila
⑩ Naya Bazar

⑪ Behind Hospital
⑫ Mate Pani
⑬ Prithvi Chok
⑭ Shanti Ban
⑮ Ram Ghat
⑯ Front of Hospital
⑰ Bus Stop (old)
⑱ Airport
⑲ Shiva Tol
⑳ Miya Patan

㉑ Pragati Tol
㉒ Amar Singh Chok
㉓ Janapriya Tol
*㉔ Gai Ghat
㉕ Kulako Dil (Dam Side)
㉖ Kaji Pokhari
㉗ Bijayapur
㉘ Simal Tunda
㉙ Rato Pairo
㉚ Hanuman Tol (Eye Hospital Area)

㉛ Thanti Patan
㉜ Amintara
㉝ Kranti Tol
㉞ Shanti Tol
㉟ Dobilla
㊱ Masina
㊲ Khalte
㊳ Samintara
㊴ Mate

㊵ Belbot
㊶ Phirke
*㊷ Yandi
*㊸ Behind Hospital II
*㊹ Ram Ghat II
*㊺ Gai Kharka
*㊻ Bacche Buduwa

(* Expired in 2001~02)

encouraged people to move to Pokhara in search of jobs. In 1969 the Siddhartha highway and in 1973 the Prithvi highway were constructed. These highways have made it possible for backpacker tourists to come to Pokhara by cheap long-distance bus from Kathmandu and from India. It was in the first half of the 1970s that a growing number of foreign tourists began to appear in Pokhara, and this coincided with the full-scale urbanization in the town. I have summarized the developmental histories of each of the forty-six settlements in Pokhara in Table 4.1.

First Period: Sukumbasi *Explorers*

Our research revealed three major trajectories or reasons for becoming a *sukumbasi*: these can be conveyed by the labels natural refugee, social refugee, and economic refugee. 'Natural refugee' refers to those who have lost their houses and lands because of landslides or other natural disasters, and so have moved to Pokhara. Social refugees are those who have run away from their home villages because of inter-caste marriages, family disputes, or similar social problems. Economic refugees are those who have come to Pokhara looking for jobs or better economic opportunities. The last category includes more than 90 per cent of all the *sukumbasis*. The initial *sukumbasi* explorers were also economic refugees.

As shown in Map 4.1 and Table 4.2, there is a *sukumbasi* settlement named Old Bus Stop (#17), which was established in 1973 just after the completion of the Prithvi highway. There are now around 150 shops, such as *bhatti* (inns), *dokan* (general stores), and automobile workshops, surrounding the bus terminal in Pokhara. None of the shopowners in this area have *lal purja* for their lands; instead they have to pay monthly rental to a few magnates of the city (such as Mr M, a well-known local bank owner) who have lodged a public claim that they own these lands.

Two years later another flow of people arrived in Pokhara and established a series of *sukumbasi* settlements (#3, #10, #11, #19, #29) almost simultaneously. These *sukumbasi* settlements were stimulated by the first comers to the Old Bus Stop settlement.

Second Period: Rehabilitation of Landslide Victims

In late August 1976, heavy rainfall afflicted the north-eastern outskirts of Pokhara causing landslides in three villages, Paire, Mijure, and Thumako Danda. Many people died and many of the survivors lost members of their family as well as houses and fields. The government asked the mayor of Pokhara to provide some public land in the city to these refugees. In 1977 the government-supported *sukumbasi* settlements, Masina (#36) and Khalte (#37), were established in the south-east of Pokhara. In the following year, 1978, another *sukumbasi* settlement, Mate (#39), was added by later arrivals from the three landslide-affected villages.

Table 4.1: The Historical Development of *Sukumbasi* Areas in Pokhara

Year	Historical Events	Year of *Sukumbasi* Settlements
1950	Nepal opens to foreign tourists	
1952	Pokhara opens its airport	
1969	Siddhartha highway opens to Bhairahawa	
1973	Prithvi highway opens to Kathmandu	#17
1975		#3, #10, #11, #19, #29
1976	Landslides in three villages to the north-east of Pokhara	
1977	Refugees move into the south of Pokhara	#36, #37
1978		#39
1979	Anti-government movements rise	#5, #13, #20, #23
1980	Referendum	#8, #9, #12, #24, #25A, #40, #41
1981		#1
1982		#28
1985		#6
1988		#35
1989	Anti-government movements revive	#15, #34
1990	A multi-party constitution and democratization in Nepal	#2, #16, #21, #22, #26, #27, #31, #33
1991		#14
1992		#32
1995		#7, #38
1997		#4, #18, #25B, #30
1998		#25B is privately removed by force.
2000	Maoists encourage *sukumbasi*s in Pokhara	#42, #43, #44, #45, #46
2001	Police bans Maoist inducement in Pokhara	#42, #24 are removed by police.
2002		#43, #44, #45, #46 are removed by police.

Source: Author's own fieldwork.

Note: Each number of the *sukumbasi* settlement corresponds to the numbers and areas shown in Map 4.1.

Table 4.2: *Sukumbasi* Areas in Pokhara, Nepal (1998-99)

(f. = family)

Area No.	Area Names	Ward No.	Geography	Since	No. of f., '98	No. of f., '99	new f.	f. left
1	Pani Tanki	16	hill slope	1981	9	9	1	1
2	Simal Bote	16	river-side	1990	5	4	-	1
3	Sim Pani	1	river bed	1975	79	79	2	2
4	Sarangkot	19	hill slope	1997	80	134	82	28
5	Bagar	1	plain area	1979	12	12	-	-
6	Tundako Patan	4	plain area	1985	12	15	3	-
7	Male Patan	5	plain area	1995	12	18	6	-
8	Mahendra Pul	9	plain area	1980	21	45	24	-
9	Sita Paila	9	river-side	1980	29	29	1	1
10	Naya Bazar	9	plain area	1975	24	24	-	-
11	Behind Hospital	11	plain area	1975	25	26	1	-
12	Mate Pani	12	plain area	1980	14	14	-	-
13	Prithvi Chok	9	plain area	1979	31	33	2	-
14	Shanti Ban	9	river-side	1991	37	37	-	-
15	Ram Ghat	10&11	plain area	1989	31	35	4	-
16	Front of Hospital	12	plain area	1990	12	12	-	-
17	Old Bus Stop	9	plain area	1973	122	149	27	-
18	Airport	9	plain area	1997	128	186	58	-
19	Shiva Tol	13	plain area	1975	209	194	-	15
20	Miya Patan	7	plain area	1979	34	34	-	-
21	Pragati Tol	7	plain area	1990	97	116	19	-
22	Amar Singh Chok	10	plain area	1990	48	48	-	-
23	Janapriya Tol	10	plain area	1979	77	77	-	-
24	Gai Ghat	6	lake-side	1980	23	23	-	-
25	Kulako Dil A	17	lake-side	1980	13	13	-	-
26	Kaji Pokhari	18	plain area	1990	30	41	11	-
27	Bijayapur	14	river-side	1990	5	5	-	-
28	Simal Tunda	17	hill peak	1982	28	28	-	-
29	Rato Pairo	17	river-side	1975	69	69	-	-
30	Hanuman Tol	17	plain area	1997	120	117	2	5
31	Thanti Patan	15	plain area	1990	30	30	-	-
32	Amintara	15	river-side	1992	8	8	-	-
33	Kranti Tol	18	plain area	1990	112	112	-	-
34	Shanti Tol	18	plain area	1989	76	86	10	-
35	Dobilla	17	river-side	1988	25	30	5	-
36	Masina	18	plain area	1977	61	61	-	-
37	Khalte	18	plain area	1977	51	51	-	-
38	Samintara	18	river-side	1995	11	15	4	-
39	Mate	14	plain area	1978	18	18	-	-
40	Belbot	14	river-side	1980	30	33	3	-
41	Phirke	8	on stream	1980	17	17	-	-

Source: Author's own fieldwork.

Table 4.2 (contd.)

Toilet	Water Pipe	Electri-city	Temple	Shop	School	*Lal Purja*	Conflict	Pro-cess	Leader's name
△	○	○	×	○	○	No	–	○	
×	×	×	×	×	×	No	○	–	
◎△	○	○	○	○	○	1981	–	–	
△	×	×	×	○	○	No	○	–	
◎△	○	○	○	○	○	1981	–	–	P. G.
△	○	○	×	○	○	1998	–	–	
◎△	○	○	×	○	○	1995	–	–	
◎△	○	○	○	○	○	1998	–	–	
◎	○	○	○	○	○	1998	–	–	
◎△	○	○	○	○	○	1998	–	–	K. B. S.
○	○	○	×	○	×	No	○	–	
×△	○	○	×	○	○	No	○	–	
○	×	○	×	○	×	No	○	–	
△○	○	○	○	○	×	No	○	–	S. P.
△	×	×	○	○	×	1998	–	–	
○	×	○	×	○	×	No	○	–	
○	○	○	×	○	×	No	○	–	
△○	○	×	×	○	×	No	○	–	L. B. T.
△○	○	○	○	○	○	No	–	○	J. L. P.
○	○	○	○	○	○	1998	–	–	
△○	○	○	×	×	×	No	–	○	
△○	×	○	×	○	×	No	○	–	M. G.
○	○	○	○	○	×	1998	–	–	D. R. G.
△	○	○	×	○	×	No	○	–	M.B.B.K.
◎	○	○	×	○	×	1998	–	–	B. B. P.
△	×	×	×	×	×	No	○	–	K. G.
△	×	×	×	×	×	No	○	–	
△	○	○	×	×	×	1998	-	–	
○△	○	○	○	○	×	No	-	-	
△	×	×	×	×	×	No	○	-	B. R. R
◎	×	○	×	×	×	1998	-	-	B. G
△	×	×	×	×	×	No	-	○	S. B. P.
△○	○	○	○	○	◎	1995	-	-	
△	×	×	×	×	×	1995?	-	-	B. R. P.
△	○	○	○	×	×	1995	-	-	
△○	○	○	○	○	◎	1977	-	-	B. R. S.
△○	○	○	○	○	◎	1977	-	-	P. B. G
△	×	×	○	×	×	No	○	-	
△	○	×	×	×	×	No	-	-	
△	○	○	×	×	×	1996	-	-	C.L.B.K.
△	○	○	×	○	×	1998	-	-	

Third Period: Anti-Panchayat Revolt and Referendum

In 1979, influenced by the Islamic Revolution in Iran, Nepali students started their anti-Panchayat movement. This student revolt won a nation-wide following; criticism spread from Panchayat officials up to the King himself. Prime Minister Surya Bahadur Thapa succeeded in putting an end to the revolt by announcing a referendum in 1980. During the period of political instability many people rushed into Pokhara and established new *sukumbasi* settlements. In 1979, four settlements (#5, #13, #20, #23) and in 1980 another seven settlements (#8, #9, #12, #24, #25A, #40, #41) were built. After the referendum, settlements #1 in 1981, #28 in 1982, and #6 in 1985 were also added.

Fourth Period: Democratization

In 1988, anti-government movements broke out again and spread throughout the country. Eventually there were violent confrontations between the anti-government demonstration and the police force in Kathmandu in February 1990. The late King Birendra promised to bring the Panchayat regime to an end and to promulgate a new and more democratic constitution. An interim government was established and the anti-government movement calmed down. In November 1990 a new constitution was proclaimed and the first national elections under the multi-party system were held in May 1991.

As had happened ten years previously, *sukumbasi* settlements increased rapidly in this period of instability. In 1988 #35 and in 1989 #15 and #34 were built. On the wave of the democratization movement, in 1990 eight new *sukumbasi* settlements (#2, #16, #21, #22, #26, #27, #31, #33) were also established almost simultaneously. Thereafter, in 1991 #14 and in 1992 #32 followed.

Fifth Period: Over-Heated Democratization

After 1990 many new private enterprises – including banks, airlines, and many others – sprang up and the entire population of Nepal seemed to have become very active. However, from the mid 1990s parliamentary politics became more and more unstable and corrupt, because of competition between and within political parties. Such political instability did not help the level of Nepali civil servants' public morality and most ordinary Nepalis tended to misunderstand democratization to mean freedom from any government restrictions. In this easy-going mood of liberalization, *sukumbasi* movements became much bolder and began to expand into illegal and larger settlements in Pokhara at a more rapid rate than before. In 1997, four large *sukumbasi* settlements were built simultaneously and in a great hurry: #4, #18, #25B (Kulako Dil B), and #30. Each of these settlements exceeds more than 200 shanties.

The annual population growth rate of Pokhara between 1961 and 2001 has been over 8 per cent. In the 1960s Pokhara was expanding at 14.3 per cent per year. Such a high rate of population growth has resulted in a clear shortage of residential land and land prices have soared. In some cases the ownership of the land is ambiguous, and even private land has been targeted by *sukumbasi* settlers. For example, the areas of Sarangkot (#4), Airport (#18), Kulako Dil B (#25B), and Hanuman Tol (#30) lie relatively close to the central area of Pokhara, and the price of land in those areas is very high. The presence of *sukumbasis* on those lands has led to confrontations between them and those who claim ownership of the land.

As soon as *sukumbasis* started living in Airport (#18), the Pokhara City Office informed them that the settlement was illegal and warned them to move. This is because it lies just below the course of airplanes landing and taking off and it is too dangerous to live there. But the *sukumbasis* of the area did not listen to the warnings and have continued to live there. In April 1997 a violent clash took place in Sarangkot (#4) between the *sukumbasis* and the police who moved in at the request of those who claimed to own the land. But the Sarangkot *sukumbasis* drove the police back. In May of the same year, another violent clash occurred in Hanuman Tol (#30) between the *sukumbasis* and the police. In this area also the *sukumbasis* managed to protect their land against the law enforcers.

In May 1998 a violent eviction occurred in Kulako Dil B (#25B). According to Mr D, a hotel owner in Dam Side and a friend of the Thakali big man who claimed ownership of the land of Kulako Dil B (#25B), the 'owner' attempted to pay a little compensation money to each *sukumbasi* family to move away. A few tens of *sukumbasi* families accepted, but the majority refused to accept the money. Finally, it is said that a group of young people showed up suddenly at this settlement and expelled all the occupants from the land. Mr D justified the action by saying, "Nowadays the Pokhara Police takes a very weak attitude toward the *sukumbasis* ... We have to protect our property even if it means using violence."

Sixth Period: The Influence of the Maoist Movement

I revisited Pokhara after a two-year absence on 24 August 2001 and found five newly built *sukumbasi* settlements. The number of 'tents' in Yandi (#42) was 15, in Behind Hospital II (#43) there were 30, in Ram Ghat II (#44) 310, in Gai Kharka (#45) 550, and in Bacche Buduwa (#46) countless, but they probably amounted to around 3,000. On 27 August I made my first visit to the largest Bacche Buduwa Sukumbasi Settlement which was in the 2,000 *ropani* (=252 acres)-wide riverbed along the river Seti. Anyone visiting this place will immediately catch sight of a high-power cable tower in the middle of the huge riverbed and a large red banner hanging from the middle point of the tower: it reads 'All-Kaski district

Sukumbasi Association' and is a public announcement of a Maoist-aligned organization. During my first visit to Bacche Buduwa, I came across Mr DM and his wife. He had been on the committee of Shanti Tol Sukumbasi Committee (#34) when I met him two years earlier. According to him, he became a member of the All-Kaski Sukumbasi Association (Revolutionary) recently and he was here to get a plot although he already had one in Shanti Tol settlement.

These five new *sukumbasi* settlements had some shared characteristics when contrasted with the forty-one earlier settlements. First, all the blue vinyl tents in the new settlements were much smaller than the shanties in the old settlements. The new tents were not furnished with any living utensils, and most of them barely enabled one or two men to stay overnight. By contrast, the older shanties were equipped with some living utensils and other necessities. Second, the number of gathering tents (and shanties) showed a big difference between the new and old *sukumbasi* settlements. The average number of shanties in the old settlements was less than 100, whereas the average number of blue tents in the new settlements was over 1,000.

It was said that the Bacche Buduwa Sukumbasi Committee had already announced that mere occupation of the land by setting up a tent, without actually living in it, would not entitle one to be provided with a *lal purja* for the land. On the other hand, occupation by someone else while the main claimant was absent was allowed. A single and poor *sukumbasi* could not win such a competitive race for land acquisition as occurred in Bacche Buduwa. A man with a large family would be able to send some family members to be on guard by turn in his installed tent over a long period of time, or a man with plenty of money could pay men to guard his tent by turns, so long as his capital lasted. Indeed a poor man or woman without money has to do two things simultaneously by him/herself: watch his/her tent all day long, and work for money to survive. Furthermore, Bacche Buduwa is too far on foot from the town area where labouring work can be found.

TWO GEOGRAPHICAL TYPES OF *SUKUMBASI* SETTLEMENTS

There are two geographical types of *sukumbasi* settlements: rural and urban. Table 4.3 provides a list of approximate land prices of the settlement areas in 1999. (Land prices of the five newly built *sukumbasi* settlements are not included.) People use two units to measure land in Pokhara: the *hat* or 'hand' and the *ropani* (equivalent to 0.0509 hectare, mainly used for agricultural land). *Hat* is ordinarily a unit of length equivalent to one half arm's length. However, one *hat* of land here is conceived as a long strip of

Table 4.3: Market Price of Land in 1999 for Each *Sukumbasi* Settlement Location

Area No. & Name	Land Price (NRs.)	Area No. & Name	Land Price (NRs.)
1. Pani Tanki	0.2 lakh/*hat*	22.Amar Singh Chok	15-20 lakh/*ropani*
2. Simal Bot	0.2-0.25 lakh/*hat*	23. Jana Priya Tol	10 lakh/*ropani*
3. Sim Pani	0.3 lakh/*hat*	24. Gai Ghat	3 lakh/*ropani*
4. Sarangkot	1.5 lakh/*ropani*	25. Kulako Dil A	10 lakh/*ropani*
5. Bagar	0.5 lakh/*hat*	26. Kaji Pokhari	5 lakh/*ropani*
6. Tundako Patan	3 lakh/*ropani*	27. Bijayapur	3 lakh/*ropani*
7. Male Patan	0.5 lakh/*hat*	28. Simal Tunda	0.5-0.7 lakh/*ropani*
8. Mahendra Pul	0.6-0.7 lakh/*hat*	29. Rato Pairo	5 lakh/*ropani*
9. Sita Paila	1 lakh/*ropani*	30. Hanuman Tol	7 lakh/*ropani*
10. Naya Bazar	0.3 lakh/*hat*	31. Thanti Patan	0.3 lakh/*hat*
11. Behind Hospital	0.2-0.25 lakh/*hat*	32. Amintara	1 lakh/*ropani*
12. Mate Pani	0.3-0.4 lakh/*hat*	33. Kranti Tol	2 lakh/*ropani*
13. Prithvi Chok	1 lakh/*hat*	34. Shanti Tol	1 lakh/*ropani*
14. Shanti Ban	1.5 lakh/*ropani*	35. Dobilla	0.5 lakh/*ropani*
15. Ram Ghat	0.1-0.2 lakh/*hat*	36. Masina	2 lakh/*ropani*
16. Front of Hospital	0.3-0.4 lakh/*hat*	37. Khalte	1 lakh/*ropani*
17. Old Bus Stop	15 lakh/*ropani*	38. Samintara	1 lakh/*ropani*
18. Airport	15 lakh/*ropani*	39. Mate	1 lakh/*ropani*
19. Shiva Tol	15 lakh/*ropani*	40. Belbot	?
20. Miya Patan	4-5 lakh/*ropani*	41. Phirke	?
21. Pragati Tol	5-6 lakh/*ropani*	--------------	--------------

Source: Author's own fieldwork.
Note: 1 lakh is 100,000.

land having one *hat* length of road frontage and one hundred *hat* depth (which corresponds to one twenty-fifth of a *ropani*). People tend to use *hat* for measuring (or estimating) urban land which is generally much more expensive than its rural counterpart.

Rural Sukumbasi *Settlements*

Thirteen of the settlements (#2, #3, #9, #14, #15, #25, #27, #29, #32, #35, #38, #40, and #41) are regarded as rural in type. The rural settlements usually stand on the riverside or river bed and face the potential danger of floods or river-bank slides at times of heavy rainfall. This is why those areas had been left unclaimed as private land until the land shortage became so severe in Pokhara.

From the *sukumbasi*'s viewpoint, however, such land is still worth living on for the following reasons. First, they have learned that nobody will claim to be the legitimate owner of the land. Second, since the river is within a few minutes' walking distance of their shanties, it is convenient for them to get water which is essential for bathing, laundry, and excretion. Third, they can make a very stout shanty at no expense by collecting and piling up tens of natural stones, cementing them with mud, and roofing them with the reeds that grow at the riverside. Fourth, it is possible for them to find some labouring work in the vicinity of their shanty. They can collect driftwood from the river and sell it in the market area. They can also collect river sand and gravel, put them in a cement or rice bag (usually second hand), and sell them in the market. Labour of this sort is referred to as *majdur.* An adult man or woman who is capable of filling seven to ten bags a day can earn Rs.70 to 100 per day. The job of cutting stones into pieces to make ballast is called *gitti kutne* (stone chopping). If neighbours cooperate with one another, they can collect their bagged products together in one place. Then a truck will come to pick them up and buy all the bags once or twice a week. Legally speaking, they have to get a municipal licence to collect natural resources for commercial purposes. However most *sukumbasi*s do not bother about such regulations. Fifth, the *sukumbasi* people living in the riverbed can still farm plenty of uncultivated land. They can thus continue an agrarian life as in their mountain villages. In addition, some of them can get work as agricultural labourers (*khetala, khetali*) in the nearby large farms owned by non-*sukumbasi* people.

Urban Sukumbasi *Settlements*

Pokhara City consists of eighteen wards, and Ward 9 lies in the centre of Pokhara. Ward 9 includes Pokhara Airport, the long-distance bus terminal, various offices and shopping areas, and the most densely inhabited areas. In Ward 9 there are eight *sukumbasi* settlements (#8, #9, #10, #13, #14, #17, #18, #19). Old Bus Stop (#17), Airport (#18), and Shiva Tol (#19) are the largest of all the forty-one settlements in Pokhara. The 1999 price of land in these areas was Rs.1.5 million per *ropani*, making it the most expensive area in Pokhara. In these areas each *sukumbasi* holds a tiny parcel of land of 1 or 2 *annas*. (An *anna* is a sixteenth of a *ropani*, nearly equal to 10 Japanese *tsubo*.)

The concentration of *sukumbasi*s in Ward 9 is partly the result of the politics of a certain Congress party politician who was the Ward 9 Chairman until recently. He supported *sukumbasi*s in Ward 9, helping them to obtain water pipes, electricity lines, and *lal purja* (certificates), in return for voting for the Congress. However, he did not give any aid to Communist-inclined leaders of the *sukumbasi*s unless they promised to support the Congress. His vote-buying activities had become so obvious as to become a liability and the NC did not give him a party ticket in the 1997 local election.

There are several convenient aspects to living in these urban settlements. First, it is quite easy to find some labouring work within walking distance of the settlement, which is surrounded by crowded offices, shops, and residential areas. Second, infrastructure such as water pipes and electricity is already set up in the vicinity and can be accessed with time and/or money. Third, medical, educational, and recreational facilities are available within walking distance. Hence even *sukumbasis* are able to enjoy modern conveniences.

Jobs available for urban *sukumbasis* can be categorized as: (1) simple muscle labour (*jyami*), (2) skilled labour (*dakarmi*), and (3) pedlary/market stall (*byapari*). Coolie (*kulli*), roadman (*majdur*), and general servant (*nokar, nokarni*) are types of simple labouring work. The daily wage (*jyala*) for such simple labouring is around Rs.100. But labourers are not guaranteed that they will find such a job every day. Most of them do not like working outside on rainy days, even if they have no food. On average they work 15 to 20 days per month.

Skilled labour, carpentry (*sikarmi*), plasterer/brick-masonry (*mistri*), work as mechanics (*mistri*), woolmaking (*un katne*) are popular among *sukumbasis* in urban settlements. Generally the daily wage for such skilled labour is Rs.200. Woolmaking is the most popular female job in Pokhara. There are two Tibetan refugee camps in Pokhara, and they enjoy a monopoly of Tibetan carpet production in west Nepal. The Tibetan refugee camps have a constant demand for wool which is their raw material. Woolmakers are able to earn money at home even while taking care of small children. This explains the popularity of wool-making among females in Pokhara not only in all *sukumbasi* settlements but also in lower-class non-*sukumbasi* milieus.

Commercial sexual work (*beshya-britti, randi*) appears to be increasing for women particularly in such settlements as #17, #18, and #19. A female commercial sexual worker in these areas earns an average of Rs.200 per customer. Compared to the average daily wage for male skilled labour, a female commercial sexual worker is able to make much better money much more quickly. However, female commercial sexual workers in the *sukumbasi* settlements usually bring their male clients back to their own shanty, and this usually makes the neighbours very hostile. Sometimes they are driven out of the settlement by other female *sukumbasi* dwellers acting collectively.

SUKUMBASI AND EX-*SUKUMBASI* SETTLEMENTS IN 1998 AND 1999

Table 4.2 is a summary of our 1998-9 *sukumbasi* researches. Forty-six *sukumbasi* or ex-*sukumbasi* settlements are shown on Map 4.1, but the last five settlements (from #42 to #46) are not included in Table 4.2 because detailed research was not carried out there.

We conducted checks on the continued residence of all the *sukumbasi/ hukumbasi* families we recorded in our 1998 summer research during our 1999 summer research (for *hukumbasi* see the discussion later in this chapter). Looking at items (6) through (9) in Table 4.2, the pattern of fluctuations in family size is easily visible. We are led to the conclusion that at least five major *sukumbasi* settlements located in the centre of the city have experienced a flood of newcomers between 1998 and 1999.

Acquiring a Lal Purja

Our research revealed that there are twenty *sukumbasi* and twenty-one ex-*sukumbasi* settlements in Pokhara. Shiva Tol settlement (#19) is uniquely divided into two zones: the old zone in which people were provided with *lal purja* in 1975, and the new zone in which people do not yet have a *lal purja*. As far as the locals are concerned, the new *sukumbasi* area is much more heavily populated than the old ex-*sukumbasi* area, so we decided to categorize Shiva Tol as a whole as a *sukumbasi* settlement. Out of the twenty *sukumbasi* settlements, four (#1, #19, #21, and #32) are waiting for *lal purjas* to be issued. Where there are conflicts over the ownership of the land occupied by *sukumbasis* they have never been provided with a *lal purja*. According to our research, there are fifteen *sukumbasi* settlements with such conflicts.

One has to go through a complex procedure when applying to the Sukumbasi Ayog for a *lal purja*. Applicants have to prepare various kinds of official certificates. A fifty-year-old Damai man who had been living in Gai Ghat Sukumbasi Settlement (#24) in Ward 6 since 1980, and could read and write in Nepali, was chair of the Gai Ghat *sukumbasis*. As a *sukumbasi* committee chairman, he had been working seriously to get a *lal purja* for the previous nine years. On my third visit he allowed me to take a close look at all the necessary papers that had already been submitted to Pokhara City Office.

His documents were as follows: (1) birth certificate (*janma darta*) issued in May 1989 by Kaski District Office; (2) *sukumbasi* certificate issued in March 1994 by Ward 6 Office; (3) non-landownership certificate (*praman-patra*) issued in May 1994 by Syangja VDC Office; (4) non-landownership certificate issued in May 1994 by Kaski District Land Revenue Office; (5) a special certificate to prove that the 5 *ropani* land in Gai Ghat Sukumbasi Settlement is public and not private land issued in July 1998 by Kaski District Land Revenue Office (with a map). Despite having all these documents his application was rejected on the grounds that the land had already been purchased by the City Planning Office of Pokhara to preserve the natural environment around Phewa Lake. The police came and forcefully evacuated all the shanties in 2001. When I came back to Pokhara in the summer of 2003, a public park designed with tourists in mind had been constructed on the evacuated land.

Another case is that of T.N. Adhikari (a thirty-five-year-old Brahman) who owns a small general shop (*dokan*) in Male Patan ex-*sukumbasi* settlements (#7) in Ward 5. He let me see his *lal purja*, which was transferred from his father. His father had been chairman of the Male Patan Sukumbasi Committee, and made a great contribution in helping most of his committee members to obtain *lal purja*s. (Most, though not necessarily all the residents of the settlement, will be members of the committee, which costs between Rs.20 and 30 per month.) His father retired from the Committee after obtaining his *lal purja* and the committee itself gradually disintegrated. This happens to the committees in many ex-*sukumbasi* settlements. The reason is that, once all the members of the *sukumbasi* committee have achieved their basic need (obtaining a *lal purja*), they no longer need or want the leader or other dominant neighbours.

On the reverse of the *lal purja* paper, which T.N. Adhikari showed me, six conditions for the endorsement of the validity of the *lal purja* were written. The first four are particularly significant:

1. The original person who is offered the right of *lal purja* shall not sell or give it to anyone within 25 years from the date of its issue. In the case of the original owner's death, the right to the *lal purja* can be inherited by one's close relatives.
2. The person offered a *lal purja* should build a house and start living in it within a year of its being issued. Otherwise, the government shall terminate the right of *lal purja*.
3. If it should become clear that any non-landownership certificate issued by any Ward or VDC Offices is a false certificate, HMG will be able to cancel the *lal purja*.
4. If one needs to apply for a bank loan to build one's house on the present land ensured by this *lal purja*, one can use this *lal purja* as a mortgage for the loan.

However, the fourth condition logically contradicts the first one. No bank would accept such a *lal purja* as security for a loan on the grounds of the first endorsement. This is why the government changed the 25 years' prohibition on economic transactions of the *lal purja* to 10 years.

According to T.N. Adhikari, not a small number of ex-*sukumbasi* in his area, neglecting such endorsements of the *lal purja* paper, had already sold their *lal purja* as soon as they got it. By selling it, they can get more than several thousands and less than one lakh (a hundred thousand) rupees, which amounts to three years' income for the average *sukumbasi* family.

This means that the acquisition of *lal purja* gives the *sukumbasi* the lawful ownership of the land as well as a good money by selling their *lal purja*.

The Sukumbasi Ayog *and the Land Revenue Office*

Mr P (a fifty-one-year-old Brahman) is a high-ranking NC (Nepali Congress) officer in Pokhara and was chair of the Sukumbasi Ayog of Kaski district twice in the last five years. According to him, there are essentially two governmental institutions dealing with land ownership, the Land Revenue Office and the Sukumbasi Ayog. The former is the primary and long-lasting office which functions to register the transfer of landownership by economic transaction or inheritance. The latter is a secondary and ad hoc land office which examines *lal purja* applications and issues *lal purja*. He provided 300 *lal purja* and was ready to provide another 700 *lal purja* within his official term, but he could not fulfil the latter target because his appointment was suddenly terminated after the last national election.

Mr P informed us of an incident he witnessed which illustrates the cunning but lawful way in which local dwellers and Land Revenue officers cooperate to make money. When Hotel Fulbari was under construction, a group of seven families insisted on their joint ownership of 80 *ropani* (4.07 ha) of grassland contiguous to the hotel. According to Mr P, Land Revenue officers must have been bribed by those families who then sold the land to Hotel Fulbari for several lakh rupees as soon as the hotel opened. Jagannath Adhikari warns in a recent paper against a heavy loss of public properties in Pokhara: "A study conducted in 2002 regarding the loss of public properties (mainly chautaras, public land, and water ponds) showed that in a period of 23 years from 1978 to 2001, 66 per cent of chautaras, 92 per cent of water ponds, 66 per cent of public land plots and 72 per cent of public land area have been lost" (Adhikari, this volume).

DALIT AND GURUNG MAJORITIES IN THE SETTLEMENTS

Table 4.4 shows the contrast between the entire Pokhara population for 2001 by caste and the 1999 caste-wise distribution of the ex-*sukumbasi* and *sukumbasi* population in Pokhara. The largest group among the 1999 ex-*sukumbasi* and *sukumbasi* population is the Dalits (Untouchables) (34.1 per cent); Gurungs are second-biggest group (28.4 per cent). Bahuns, Chetris, and Newars are respectively 6.0 per cent, 9.3 per cent, and 6.7 per cent. Even though each of the three is a 'dominant caste' in the Pokhara population as a whole, it is correspondingly a minority among the ex-*sukumbasi* and *sukumbasi* population. The figures clearly show a heavy concentration of Dalits in the forty-one settlements. However, the proportion of caste/ethnic groups differs greatly from one settlement to another.

Table 4.4: Caste Breakdown of Populations of Pokhara and *Sukumbasi*

Castes	2001 Pokhara Population	1999 *Sukumbasi* Population	Difference
Bahun	22.8 (%)	6.0 (%)	(-) 16.8 (%)
Chetri	16.9	9.3	(-) 7.6
Gurung	21.3	28.5	(+) 7.2
Newar	10.1	6.6	(-) 3.5
Dalits	9.8	34.1	(+) 24.3
Others	19.1	15.5	(-) 3.6
Total	100.0	100.0	0.0

Source: Author's own fieldwork.

Seventeen of the settlements (see Table 4.5) show a clear tendency of caste-oriented concentrations, either Dalit or Gurung. The other twenty-four settlements show various combinations of castes and in fact each would seem to have its own idiosyncratic characteristics. For instance, Simal Bote (#2) is entirely composed of Dalit (Gaine) families. Mahendra Pul (#8), Tundako Patan (#6), and Prithvi Chok (#13) are dominated by Newars. Nonetheless, there are two weak tendencies. First, Dalits are the majority in such settlements as Shanti Ban (#14), Front of Hospital (#16), Simal Tunda (#28), Thanti Patan (#31), Amintara (#32), and Belbot (#40). Second, the following three settlements show somehow a balanced mixture of many castes: Sim Pani (#3), Ram Ghat (#15), and Dobilla (#35). Needless to say, those two tendencies can be commonly found in the settlements that stand on the economically worthless and naturally dangerous river bed.

Dalits in the Sukumbasi *Settlements*

In general Dalits in the *sukumbasi* settlements are among the poorest of the *sukumbasi*. However, there are some Dalit families that are far richer than the average *sukumbasi*.

According to our records, there are four Kasai (Newar Butcher caste) families in the Prithvi Chok Sukumbasi Settlement (#13) as well as twelve Miya families in Miya Patan Sukumbasi Settlement (#20). All these Kasai families run meat shops along the main street of Prithvi Chok and enjoy a near monopoly in the business of selling meat. All of them have their own good houses in Bagar. In the same way, all of these Miya families also hold their own houses of concrete blocks in Miya Patan. Some of them make a very handsome income by butchering water buffaloes, and the rests of them deal in glass bracelets (*chura*). However, these Kasais and Miyas are rare exceptions, and, though considered low caste, they are not included in official government lists as Dalits.

Most Dalits in Pokhara have been economically deprived as well as socially discriminated against for a long time. This is the reason why they

Table 4.5: Caste Majorities in 17 Settlements
(family number)

Settlement (#)	1st Major Caste	2nd Major Caste	3rd Major Caste	Total
Type I (Dalit Majority)				
Airport (#18)	Dlt 119 (64.0%)	Grg 32 (17.2%)	Mag 26 (14.0%)	186
Shiva Tol (#19)	Dlt 95 (49.0%)	Grg 84 (43.3%)	Ch 46 (23.7%)	194
Miya Patan (#20)	Dlt 21 (61.8%)	Grg 10 (29.4%)	Ch 2 (5.9%)	34
Gai Ghat (#24)	Dlt 17 (73.9%)	Grg 3 (13.0%)	Bra,Ch 2 (8.7%)	23
Pragati Tol (#21)	Dlt 51 (44.0%)	Grg 36 (31.0%)	Mag 12 (10.3%)	116
Shanti Tol (#34)	Dlt 37 (43.0%)	Grg 20 (23.2%)	Mag, Tam 8 (9.3%)	86
Mate (#39)	Dlt 15 (83.3%)	Grg 1 (5.5%)	Ch, New 1 (5.5%)	18
Type II (Gurung Majority)				
Amar Singh C.(#22)	Grg 24 (50.0%)	Dlt 7 (14.6%)	Mag 5 (10.4%)	48
Jana Priya T. (#23)	Grg 58 (75.3%)	Dlt 11 (14.3%)	Bra 4 (5.2%)	77
Kaji Pokhari (#26)	Grg 23 (56.1%)	Dlt 9 (22.0%)	Ch 4 (9.8%)	41
Rato Pairo (#29)	Grg 28 (40.6%)	Dlt 18 (26.1%)	Bra, New 5 (12.2%)	69
Masina (#36)	Grg 41 (80.1%)	Dlt 3 (5.9%)	Bra 3 (5.9%)	51
Khalte (#37)	Grg 27 (44.3%)	Ch 13 (21.3%)	Bra 13 (21.3%)	61
Type III (Ethnic Balance)				
Sarangkot (#4)	Grg 32 (23.9%)	Mag 32 (23.9%)	Dlt 32 (23.9%)	134
Old Bus Stop (#17)	Grg 67 (45.0%)	Bra 51 (38.1%)	Ch 37 (24.8%)	149
Hanuman Tol (#30)	Grg 37 (31/6%)	Dlt 37 (31.6%)	Mag 17(14.5%)	117
Kranti Tol (#33)	Grg 46 (41.1%)	Dlt 37 (33.0%)	Mag 10 (8.9%)	112

Source: Author's own fieldwork.
Abbreviations: Dlt (Dalit/Untouchable); Grg (Gurung); Mag (Magar); Tam (Tamang) Bra (Brahman); Ch (Chetri).

are to be found concentrated in the *sukumbasi* settlements. Encouraged by the more open atmosphere after 1990, Dalits in and around Pokhara have been rushing into the *sukumbasi* settlements seeking freedom from the traditional discrimination of their mountain villages.

During our 1998-9 research a considerable number of Dalit *sukumbasi*s informed us of their belief in Christianity. Despite the longstanding constitutional prohibition on proselytization, after the arrival of democratization several new churches have been opened in various places near the centre of the city. There are two main reasons why Dalit *sukumbasi*s are attracted to Christianity. First, their approach to the church improves their chances of receiving material assistance such as food, medicines, clothes, and even cheap loans in case of need. Second, since 1998 or 1999, Nepali Bibles have become widely available among Nepali Christians in Pokhara. Many *sukumbasi* Dalits are illiterate, but they can understand the contents of a book when it is read aloud and repeatedly by others. An old *sukumbasi* Dalit who had recently converted to Christianity said, "There is no equality among men under Hindu Gods but there is a human equality under the Christian God."

Gurung-Dalit Alliances in the Settlements

As described by Jagannath Adhikari (this volume), Gurungs in Pokhara have played a major role in boosting socio-economic developments in Pokhara, because they bring back substantial amounts of money from their traditional occupations as *lahure* (serving in foreign armies or working abroad). According to the 2001 census data in Pokhara (shown in Table 4.4), Gurungs comprise the second-largest percentage of the population of Pokhara (21.3 per cent) and are almost as numerous as the largest, the Bahuns (22.8 per cent). It is therefore not surprising to see Gurungs occupying the second largest position (28.5 per cent) among the *sukumbasis/hukumbasis*.

There are different stereotypes for each caste group in Pokhara (Yamamoto 1991: 12-14). When being spoken of respectfully, Pokhara Gurungs are referred to as *mukhiya* (village headman); when referred to with contempt, they are called *bheda* (sheep). Both nicknames reflect common perceptions or stereotypes. The former suggests that Gurungs are active and dominant, while the latter means they are also very collective-minded as well. Once Gurungs have a good leader from among themselves, they behave collectively like an army. By contrast Dalits are quiet, passive, and inactive. In a sense, the Gurung personality is the opposite of the Dalits'. In settlements where Bahuns and Chetris are just small minorities, it is easy for Gurungs and Dalits to form functionally interdependent and mutually advantageous alliances: Gurungs take the leadership roles and Dalits follow. Particularly when there are some Gurung *bhupu-lahure*s (ex-Gurkha solders) in the settlement, they have been pushed to become leaders by Dalits in cases of external confrontation. Examples can be seen in Table 4.2: all four leaders (#23, #26, #31, #36) are Gurung *bhupu-lahure*s who served mainly in India. These *bhupu-lahure*s have several features in common: (1) they were not high-ranking military officers; (2) their military pensions are very low and are not sufficient to buy land in Pokhara; and (3) they have some experience of military education (including knowing how to read and write, how to use weapons, and how to repair some machines or cars).

THE TRANSFORMATION FROM 'COMMUNITAS' TO 'COMMUNITY'

As shown in Table 4.6, the twenty ex-*sukumbasi* settlements can be classified into three different levels of development. In the first place, nine of the ex-*sukumbasi* settlements are fully developed and can be considered as nearly equal to a 'community'. We consider these nine ex-*sukumbasi* settlements as 'first-class' settlements because they are furnished with all

Table 4.6: Developmental Levels of 41 Ex-*Sukumbasi* and *Sukumbasi* Settlements

20 Ex-*Sukumbasi* Settlements	21 *Sukumbasi* Settlements
1st class: #3, #5, #8, #9, #10, #20, #33, #36, #37	1st class: none
2nd class: #6, #7, #15, #23, #25, #28, #31, #35, #40, #41	2nd class: #1, #4, #11, #12, #13, #14, #16, #17, #18, #19, #21, #22, #24, #29
3rd class: #34	3rd class: #2, #26, #27, #30. #32, #38, #39

Source: Author's own fieldwork.

the six items of both infrastructure and 'suprastructure'. Second, ten ex-*sukumbasi* settlements can be categorized as 'second class' on the grounds that each lacks a few cultural facilities (mainly suprastructure). Third, only #34 has been classified as a least developed ex-*sukumbasi* settlement because it lacks all six items. This can be considered as 'third class'. As for the twenty-one *sukumbasi* settlements, there is not any 'first-class' settlement. We consider that fourteen *sukumbasi* settlements are 'second-class' on the same grounds that they are short of a few items. In the same way, seven *sukumbasi* settlements lack five or six items and are considered 'third-class' settlements.

Two conclusions can be drawn from Table 4.6: (1) various developmental stages are evident not only in the twenty ex-*sukumbasi* settlements but also in the twenty-one *sukumbasi* settlements; and (2) there are no fundamental differences in the developmental level in the same class between ex-*sukumbasi* settlements and *sukumbasi* ones. Consequently the provision of *lal purja* is a necessary but not a sufficient condition for settlements to develop into a community. The relationship between a leader and his followers is one of the keys that decides the degree of development.

In a previous paper (Yamamoto 2001a: 169-75), I proposed a hypothetical model of "three developmental stages of *sukumbasi* settlements": (1) cradle stage, (2) the stage of constructing 'infrastructure', namely, toilets, piped water, and electricity, (3) the stage of constructing 'suprastructure', namely, shops, temples, and schools. In the following subsection I will describe the development processes of *sukumbasi* settlements, paying special attention to the role of leaders. I shall argue further that, in proceeding through the process of the three stages, any *sukumbasi* settlement is required to transform itself from 'communitas' to 'community'.

The Cradle Stage

This is the first stage when *sukumbasis* start to occupy empty land. At the time of our research such newly built settlements as Yandi (#42), Behind Hospital II (#43), Ram Ghat II (#44), Gai Kharka (#45), and Bacche Buduwa (#46) were examples of the cradle stage. It is plausible to consider that the settlements listed in the third class in Table 4.6 belong to this stage. In the very beginning the occupants of the settlement are individualistic rather than cooperative as they are not yet committed to settling down in the settlement for a long time. But almost immediately a *sukumbasi* settlement in the first stage acquires the following characteristics. First, assuming their own illegality, they have to live with a sense of fear that somebody may show up and request them to move on as the land belongs to them. Second, most *sukumbasi* settlements in this stage have actual experience of one or two conflicts against external opponents. On these grounds, the first occupants tend to welcome latercomers in order to reinforce their physical collective power to resist future threats. Third, the occupants come to learn the necessity of cooperation with one another in order to face external opponents collectively or to work together for the betterment of their settlement. One of the occupants gradually becomes an 'opinion leader' among the rest. This is the birth of 'proto-charisma' in the *sukumbasi* settlement. By this term I intend to convey that the leader does not have as strong leadership qualities as might be expected with 'charisma'; rather, it is a spontaneous and informal leadership generated by the existence of followers in the *sukumbasi* settlement. A proto-charismatic leader is essentially reliant on his kind and charming personality, and cannot depend on previous social status, profession, or birth. Particularly in cases of conflict over land, the emergence of such proto-charismatic leaders occurs quickly. Lastly, *sukumbasi* settlements in the cradle stage can be characterized as exhibiting 'communitas' in Victor Turner's (1969) sense. Each *sukumbasi* lives with fear and instability. This is why, in order to compensate for such a fear, each occupant tends to participate in a communal 'festive mood' (e.g. telling stories together of their successful confrontations with police) partly in order to strengthen internal cohesion against external threats. In memory of their victory over the police, the *sukumbasi* committee of #30 named their settlement as Hanuman Tol after Hanuman's famous victory in the Ramayana.

The 'Infrastructure' Building Stage

There are at least three items – good toilets, piped water, and electricity – needed to establish a basic 'infrastructure'. Those settlements ranked in the 'second class' in Table 4.6 are considered to be in the second stage. The major characteristics of *sukumbasi* settlements in the second stage are, (1) they begin to construct infrastructure to improve the settlement, and (2) they start their *lal purja* application. In this stage a newly born proto-charismatic leader is examined by his followers for his 'aptitude' for practical leadership of the *sukumbasi* settlement. After surviving together a series of physical confrontations against external opponents, community consciousness develops. In these circumstances, the environment tends to lead them to form their own '*sukumbasi* committee'. The proto-charismatic leader is usually elected as its first chairman.

Once a proto-charismatic leader has become the official chairman of the *sukumbasi* committee, he is expected to perform even more actively as a leader than before. He has to reconcile all the different opinions among his neighbours and persuade reluctant neighbours to make contributions towards the costs of constructing water pipes and a water tank and at the same time try to contact the Ward/City Office or external NGOs to assist their project financially. Since most *sukumbasi* are illiterate, a committee chairman is also expected to help illiterate neighbours prepare their *lal purja* applications. Sometimes, if the *Sukumbasi* Ayog or Municipal Office shows an indifferent attitude towards their requests, a committee chairman will take all the settlement dwellers to the office to apply pressure collectively.

The 'Suprastructure' Constructing Stage

Until they acquire a *lal purja* most members of the *sukumbasi* committee follow the chairman obediently because they all share the common goal of seeking their *lal purja*. Once they obtain the *lal purja*, however, the incentive to follow any communal order directed by the chairman decreases rapidly. We have already seen such an example in T.N. Adhikari's description of the *sukumbasi* committee of Male Patan (#7).

Shops, Hindu temples, and schools are regarded as the 'suprastructure' necessary for a community. After their basic infrastructural needs are fulfilled, ex-*sukumbasi* settlements (even some *sukumbasi* ones) tend to fulfil their 'suprastructural' needs. Those settlements ranked in the 'first class' in Table 4.6 are considered to be in the third stage. On the one hand, the better-off people in the settlement begin to compare their own settlement with its neighbouring middle-class communities. They want their settlement to have such cultural objects. On the other hand, the poorer people in the same settlement tend to be indifferent to the construction of such cultural monuments. We should not overlook a latent wealth difference between the committee chairman and his followers in the same settlement. His close supporters tend to be 'just a little wealthier' than the other followers. Plans to construct suprastructural monuments in the settlement may be a source of hot discussion in the settlement committee. This is one reason why the ex-*sukumbasi* committee is likely to be divided and may break up just after *lal purja*s are acquired.

Some points need to be clarified. When the poorer followers become more egoistic and less cooperative, they tend to focus on the wealth differences between the committee chairman and themselves. It is a rather expensive project to construct a Hindu temple, a school, or a communal house. The poor inhabitants are very reluctant to contribute donations for such plans. Hence the chairman of the committee tries to get some financial aid from external sources. Usually those projects are performed under a joint budget with half coming from communal donations by committee members and the other half from the Ward or Municipal Office.

The introduction of public funds means that the poorer group will attempt to keep a close watch on the appropriate use of the money by the committee chairman. If the chairman uses the money only for the communal project, they try to forget their suspicions and retain their respect for and trust in the chairman. But some chairmen seem to consider it quite proper to retain some money for their own private purposes as ex officio profits; thus it is very easy for poorer followers to have doubts about the misuse of public money collected in their name. When many of the committee members decide not to follow the chairman, the committee itself will be divided without any new leader until a new factional leader takes over the position of the former chairman. I have heard stories of this kind, indicating the 'public death' of the chairman, in several ex-*sukumbasi* settlements. It is noteworthy that of the nine ex-*sukumbasi* settlements placed in the first class in Table 4.6, there are only two that have managed to maintain active committee activities after their acquisition of *lal purja*s. In the other seven ex-*sukumbasi* settlements, committee activities have more or less ceased.

A Comparison of Three Natural Refugee Settlements

In this subsection, I will compare three adjoining settlements of Masina, Khalte, and Mate, paying attention to the importance of leadership.

Of all the nine ex-*sukumbasi* settlements in the first class, only Masina (#36) and Khalte (#37) have enjoyed continuous communal activities. Miya Patan (#20) nowadays does not have any committee, but the Islamic leaders of the Miya group seem to provide an alternative way to fulfil the necessary functions of the committee. Bagar (#5), Naya Bazar (#10), Sim Pani (#3), Mahendra Pul (#8), Sita Paila (#9), and Kranti Tol (#33) have retained their ex-*sukumbasi* committees, but their activities are limited to ceremonial occasions.

The fact that Masina enjoys vigorous communal activities depends mainly upon the stable and good leadership of its committee chairman. We should not overlook the special advantages with which this settlement has been blessed since its birth. Both Masina and Khalte were created in 1977 as government-permitted settlements especially for refugees from landslides in three villages. This means that the people of Masina have not had to waste their time and energy over land conflicts, but have been able to concentrate their time, energy, and money on their own internal development programmes.

Another factor, which can be seen in Table 4.5, is that the caste breakdown of Masina is Gurung (80.1 per cent), Dalit (5.9 per cent), and Brahman (5.9 per cent), while Khalte has Gurung (44.3 per cent), Brahman (21.3 per cent), and Chetri (21.3 per cent). Both Masina and Khalte are Gurung-majority settlements, but in Masina they have an overwhelming absolute majority and they all come from the same three villages in the same area. Thus Masina dwellers naturally tend to be able to achieve a high degree of cohesion. Compared with these two, all the other thirty-nine settlements are composed of more or less heterogeneous mixtures of various economic refugees who came from various villages in different areas. The advantage of a homogeneous Masina and the disadvantage of other heterogeneous settlements can be easily understood if we think of the concept of 'habitus' in P. Bourdieu's sense (Bourdieu 1977).

Most importantly, Masina has been blessed with two good leaders; the late B.R. Subedi (a Bahun, who was sixty-five in 1998) and P.S. Gurung (a sixty-year-old Gurung). Mr Subedi, an ex-village headman of Paire VDC, had all the four requirements for proto-charisma and furthermore, he had long administrative experience as an ex-village headman. He was a short and lean man, full of dignity. There was something charismatic about him. P.S. Gurung is a *bhupu-lahure* of the British Army and is also endowed with all the four characteristics for proto-charisma. There have been no fights between these two leaders. Not only P.S. Gurung but also all other Gurungs in this settlement respected B.R. Subedi as an ex-mukhiya, and P.S. Gurung himself has the respect of all the Gurungs as a cheerful, active, and smart *bhupu-lahure*.

The functionally complementary combination of these two proto-charismatic leaders was excellent. When the committee needs some funds for local projects, Subedi was good at persuading Pokhara Municipal Office and Ward Office to help and made use of the network accumulated while he was a village headman, while Gurung is also good at asking his rich friends, *bhupu-lahure* of the British Army, to donate some money. This joint leadership between Subedi and Gurung succeeded in making Masina the most developed community in its neighbourhood. Unfortunately B.R. Subedi died in 2002, but P.S. Gurung succeeded him as chairman and has continued to be active in developing the settlement.

Both B.R. Subedi (of Masina) and P.B. Gurung (of Khalte) were elected as representatives of Ward 18 in May 1998. This resulted from the political cooperation of the Masina and Khalte voters. The two newly elected ward members managed to ensure the construction of a concrete-paved road from the main street up to their area. Khalte is next to Masina, and not only geographically but also socially, it has always followed Masina's lead. This has been Khalte's unique path to success since its origin.

Mate (#39) lies in the vicinity of Masina and Khalte. All these three settlements were built for the refugees from the 1976 landslides. But Masina and Khalte dwellers tend to speak ill of the Mate people, saying, "They are not natural refugees but riders on the rescue of the natural disaster." Mate has a caste-wise population of Dalits (83.3 per cent), Gurung, Chetri, and Newar (5.5 per cent). This is the one settlement where the Dalits are in an absolutely dominant position. Mate was started in 1978, just a year later than Masina and Khalte, but it has not been provided with *lal purja* even though it has never suffered from land conflicts. There is no proto-charismatic leader, nor even a *sukumbasi* committee in this settlement. As a result, Mate is one of the least developed settlements of all the forty-one in Pokhara. This can be partially ascribed to the Dalits' lack of a tradition of leadership and the failure of any clear leaders to emerge in the time after the settlement was formed.

HUKUMBASI VERSUS *SUKUMBASI* IN URBAN SETTLEMENTS

The Nepali word *hukumbasi* seems to derive from the term *hukum* (order). The *hukumbasi* is one who pretends to be a *sukumbasi* in order to obtain a *lal purja*. I have observed that in Bacche Buduwa a rich man employed a few young men in order to guard his tent by turns. They were following his 'order'. Nowadays, however, a new type of *hukumbasi* certainly exists. A new *hukumbasi* usually intends to accumulate future wealth mainly for himself/herself, i.e. he or she is not working for someone else and does not employ anyone else. Particularly in urban *sukumbasi* settlements, a considerable number of such new *hukumbasi* coexist.

Based on our research experiences, I would suggest three situational but practical criteria for distinguishing a *hukumbasi* from a *sukumbasi*. First, the former is educated to SLC (school leaving certificate) level or above, while the latter, if educated at all, has achieved no more than class ten. Second, the former usually occupies a stable job as a 'salaried man' in a private shop (*kamdar*) or even as a 'public officer' (*sarkari, chaukidar*), while the latter is a labourer (*jyami, mistri, dakarmi*). Third, as a result, the living standard of the former is better than the latter's in many ways.

A Comparison of Two Leaders in Airport Settlement

In Airport *sukumbasi* settlement (#18) there are two leaders: Smiling Painter (a thirty-seven-year-old Tamang) and Tall Noble Chetri (a thirty-five-year-old Chetri) who lives next to Painter. In the first election for chairman of the Sukumbasi Committee of this settlement held in July 2000, Painter defeated Chetri. The settlement was started in December 1997. Chetri was one of the brave initial pioneers who cultivated this area as a new *sukumbasi* settlement. Painter came to this settlement around one week later after it was opened by Chetri and his group.

It seems to me that Painter has a more attractive personality than Chetri. Painter is a talkative man with a good sense of humour whereas Chetri is not. There is something warm about Painter who always wears the same dirty old leather jacket. Chetri is a very handsome man wearing a clean shirt and a Nepali cap, but he appears cold rather than warm. There is something fastidious about Chetri. From the viewpoint of neighbouring *sukumbasi*s, Painter is much easier to talk to than Chetri. Although both men are equally helpful to others, more neighbours started gathering around Painter than Chetri. Mr Painter always looks his interlocutor in the face with a half smile and talks in a soft voice. Chetri takes pride in his lineage, which Painter does not.

Mr Chetri is the eldest son of twelve children (five sons and seven daughters). His father owns one *bigha* (13 *ropani*) land but he has not yet had 'separation' from his father. He passed the SLC in 1981 and left for India to work. He worked for a coal company in Darjeeling for twelve years. In 1987, in Darjeeling, he had a love marriage. In his company in India there was another Chetri from Dhankuta who was a relative of the famous Surya Bahadur Thapa. Thanks to his introduction, he had a chance to meet with Surya Bahadur Thapa directly in 1993, and at this meeting Thapa found him work in a governmental dairy company in Kathmandu. This company transferred him to its branch in Pokhara. For the initial four years after his arrival in Pokhara, he and his family lived in a rented room (paying Rs.700 per month) near the Industrial Area.

One day in November 1997, his son (then ten years old) urged him to take him to the airport to see airplanes. There Chetri noticed the vast open grassland. While he was looking at the grassland, a Sarki male from Shiva Tol (#19) approached him. Chetri asked the Sarki if this was public or private. The Sarki man replied that it was public land. Then Chetri and Sarki started talking about the possibility of living on this land, and Chetri decided to call several ex-Gurkha soldiers he knew. The following evening, sitting on the ground in the grassland, Chetri and Sarki had another meeting together with two Gurung ex-Gurkha soldiers. All four wondered why no *sukumbasi* were living in the area despite the fact that a flood of *sukumbasi* were living everywhere in Pokhara. None of them could come up with any plausible answers. Then they decided they should try to stay in the area and wait and see what would happen. The Sarki man continued that it was impossible for a few men to live there alone. But if a group of people were to live there together it might be possible to hold on to the land. He suggested they invite more people to live there together with them.

The following night again a group of twelve people gathered on this grassland, and all of them talked about the plan of living together. From this night on they stayed on the grassland for more than a week, but nobody showed up to protest at their occupancy of the land. When Chetri was thinking about arranging the division of the whole land among each of the occupants, Painter appeared in the area for the first time and asked them to let him live in this place. There was a plenty of land and nobody objected. On the following day Painter came again with a group of Christians to the settlement. (Painter used to live in Kathmandu under the guardianship of an American Catholic father.) They brought a few boxes of used clothes and some food. Painter played the role of representative of the Christians and distributed all the presents as equally as possible to each *sukumbasi* family in the settlement. Every *sukumbasi* family seemed pleased with the gifts and with Painter's generosity. Chetri alone refused to accept even a single item saying that he was a Hindu, not a Christian. As one of the pioneers of this *sukumbasi* settlement, Chetri was not happy to see Painter's growing popularity and the two became antagonistic. In the first election for chairman of Sukumbasi Committee held in December 1997, Painter defeated Chetri by a considerable margin. This was the start of a cold war between Chetri and Painter. It can also be interpreted as a class war between the *hukumbasi* and the *sukumbasi*.

Painter informed me of his conviction that Chetri was not a *sukumbasi* but a *hukumbasi*. My observation led me to the strong impression that their mutual antagonism came not only from a difference of personality but also from an emotional conflict between two different social classes, the *sukumbasi* and the *hukumbasi*. Comparing the living standards between the Painter family and the Chetri family gives a good idea of the class difference between them. First, Painter has no formal education although he is able to read and write Nepali very well. His present occupation is a painter as well as a road salesman of his own drawings mainly for foreign sightseers. His income is very unstable (between Rs.500 and 1,000 per month). Mr and Mrs Painter have to buy most of their food in the market. There is no scope for them to save money for the future.

Chetri enjoys a far better occupation than Painter. He works for a government dairy company as a manager and has a monthly salary of Rs.2,500. His wife also works as a teacher in a private school for which she is paid around Rs.2,000. Both Mr and Mrs Chetri receive special allowances once a year equivalent to two months' salary. This means that the two jointly earn some Rs.4,500 per month on a regular basis. Before moving to the present settlement in June 1998, they used to live in rented accommodation. But they decided to move to the *sukumbasi* settlement in order to be able to pay for their children's education. Their children are aged ten and eight and attend a private English 'boarding' school. Such schools are two or three times as expensive as an ordinary government school. In order to pay the tuition for their two children, they manage to squeeze about Rs.1,600 per month out of their monthly income of Rs.4,500.

Mr Painter is in a much more disadvantaged position in relation to land, the main traditional form of wealth in Nepal. His father, who was landless, was a kind of indentured labourer to a big landlord in eastern Nepal. When he was around three, both parents died one after the other. He was raised by the landlord as a shepherd until he was eighteen. At that time he had a secret love affair with one of the three daughters of the landlord. When the landlord found out, he kicked Painter off the farm. This landlord is still an influential man in his VDC. This is why Painter has been unable to get any of the necessary official documents to prove that he is landless.

By contrast, Chetri's father, who also lives in east Nepal, owns a sizeable amount of land there. This means that, according to Nepalese tradition and law, he has an automatic right to inherit his share of his father's land. But he insists that he is a *sukumbasi* because at present he owns no land anywhere in Nepal. Even if he gets his share of his father's land as inheritance, his father has five sons. His share will be just two *ropani* which is not sufficient for his family to live on.

Class difference is also visible in some subtle differences between the personal belongings of the Painter family and the Chetri family. Whether it is in the quality of their shanties, the interior objects, the cooking utensils, their clothes, or daily food, the Painters' objects are less refined than the Chetris'. Needless to say, those differences in quality are the result of the

Table 4.7: Monthly Expenditure of the Chetri Family
(1999 monthly family income = 4,500 NRs.)

Items	Price in NRs./Unit	Amounts per Month	Payment in NRs.	(%)
(1) Rice	100/*pathi*	10 *pathi*	1,000	(21.7)
(2) Dal (beans)	15/kg	15 kgs	225	(4.9)
(3) Vegetables			500	(10.9)
(4) Chickens and/or eggs			200	(4.3)
(5) Spices			200	(4.3)
(6) Sugar	25/kg	5 kgs	125	(2.7)
(7) Milk	10/litre	15 litres	150	(3.3)
(8) Tea	50/packet	1 packet	50	(1.1)
Sub-total of food stuff			2,450	(53.2)
(9) Kerosene for cooking	10/l	15 litres	150	(3.3)
(10) Electricity, candle, oil			100	(2.2)
(11) Soap (body)	?		?	
(12) Soap (laundry)	?		?	
(13) Others	[including (11) & (12)]		300	(6.5)
Sub-total			550	(12.0)
(14) 2 children's school fees			1,600	(34.8)
Grand Total			4,600	

Source: Author's own fieldwork.

Note: 1 *pathi* = 4.56 litres.

difference in economic power between the two households. In this context, I am sure that Painter's hatred of Chetri is partly generated by his feelings of economic inferiority.

It is possible to make a rough comparison of the monthly expenditures between the two households, as shown in Tables 4.7 and 4.8. First, the so-called Engel's coefficient (the percentage of all monthly costs for foods as a proportion of monthly expenditure) shows a radical difference between the two families: 53.2 (Chetri) *vs.* 73.8 (Painter). Second, considering that cooked rice (*bhat*) with bean soup (*dal*) is the most significant staple food of Nepalis, what is spent by the Chetris on rice as a proportion of all food is 40.8 per cent, whereas for the Painters it is 56.4 per cent. In other words, the Painters' daily meals are more heavily dependent on *bhat*. Additionally, considering the quality of *dal*, what the Chetris spend on beans is around three times what the Painters spend. This means that the *dal* of the Chetris is much less watery than that of the Painters. Third, comparing school fees, the Chetri family has to sacrifice 34.8 per cent of their monthly budget, but the Painter family does not spend anything on school fees. From such a comparative viewpoint, the Chetri family is enjoying a better quality of everyday food than the Painter family. At the same time the former is

Table 4.8: Monthly Expenditure of the Painter Family
(1999 monthly family income = 2,000 Rs.)

Items	Price in NRs./Unit	Amounts per Month	Payment in Rs.	(%)
(1) Rice	25/kg	35 kgs	875	(41.6)
(2) Dal (beans)	40/kg	2 kgs	80	(3.8)
(3) Vegetables*			100	(4.8)
(4) Buffalo meat	100/kg	1 kg	100	(4.8)
(5) Spices	80/kg	1 kg	80	(3.8)
(6) Sugar	28/kg	3 kgs	84	(4.0)
(7) Milk	10/half litre	10 litres	200	(9.5)
(8) Tea	32/packet	1 packet	32	(1.5)
Sub-total of food stuff			1,551	(73.8)
(9) Kerosene for cooking	10/litre	10 litres	100	(4.8)
(10) Electricity, oil			100	(4.8)
(11) Soap (body)	8/piece	8 pieces	64	(3.0)
(12) Soap (laundry)	22/piece	4 pieces	88	(4.2)
(13) Medicine			0	(0.0)
(14) Others			200	(9.5)
Sub-total (others)			552	(26.2)
(15) Children's school fees			0	(0.0)
Grand Total			2,103	

Source: Author's own fieldwork.
Note: The Painter couple grow some vegetables in a narrow front garden on their plot.

investing a considerable amount of money in their children's education, whereas the latter could not afford to do so even if they wanted to.

WHY DO *SUKUMBASI* HAVE TO LIVE IN A SHANTY?

The Landless Class and Other Classes

In this section I outline the features of a typical *sukumbasi* family in Pokhara in comparison to those of middle-class families. A majority of *sukumbasi* families consist of a married couple and two children. The average monthly income is Rs.2,000 to 2,500 while the monthly expenditure on food is Rs.1,500 to 2,000. The Engel's coefficient of the average *sukumbasi* family comes close to 80 per cent. At the time of our 1998 research, a teacher (a thirty-two-year-old Giri male) at a public high school received a monthly salary of approximately Rs.2,000. By the summer of 2001 a teacher's salary was almost three times higher (Rs.5,000). In addition to this monthly salary, he is also given 'allowances' (*bhatta*) equivalent to three months' salary every year. Thus, averaged throughout the year, his salary can be estimated to be approximately Rs.6,000 per month. The average monthly income of the *sukumbasi* was around Rs.2,000 per family in 1998, which had not increased at all between the summer 1998 and the summer 2001. On these grounds, the average monthly income of this public school teacher in 2001 can be considered as almost triple of that of the *sukumbasi*. Teachers also have the possibility of private earnings from 'tuition'. Furthermore, this Giri male has his own house and family land. His wife grows some rice and various kinds of vegetables for domestic consumption on his family land. Hence he does not have to spend much money on food. Taking these points into consideration, it can be said that the living standard of the average *sukumbasi* is much worse than that of the average lower-middle class man like this teacher.

Almost twenty years ago I employed my first Nepali research assistants in Pokhara, Mr A and Mr B. Both have since become wealthy middle-aged men. In the summer of 1998 I asked them about their monthly income. Mr A (a thirty-two-year-old Bahun male with a BA from Tribhuvan University) owns a large shop for construction materials at Chiple Dhunga in Pokhara. He is able to save almost Rs.30,000 per month in his bank account. In 1996 he constructed a palatial mansion a few minutes' walk from his shop. On the other hand, Mr B (a thirty-eight-year-old Chetri male with an MA from Tribhuvan University) works for a foreign bank in Kathmandu as an accountant. His monthly salary is Rs.15,000, plus a bonus equivalent to six months' salary. Thus his monthly income is nearly Rs.23,000. He lives together with his wife and three teenage daughters in his own gorgeous house close to Tribhuvan International Airport. He has his own car and employs a chauffeur and sends his daughters to an expensive private English 'boarding' school. It is interesting to see him teasing his daughters by saying, "They are better in English than in Nepali."

It was said that the monthly salary of a minister of HMG was around Rs.5,000 in 1998, but it was subsequently raised to Rs.12,000. I would like to make a rough comparison of the monthly incomes of the four economic classes as follows: (1) the *sukumbasi* in the landless class; (2) a public school teacher in the (lower) middle class; (3) my ex-research assistants in the (upper) middle class; and (4) high-ranking government officers. Their monthly incomes go respectively 2,000 : 5,000 : 23,000 : 12,000 in Nepalese rupees. This cross-class comparison leads to the following conclusions. First, the official salary of high-ranking HMG officers (who are considered to be more than upper-middle class by the public) is much lower than that of the well-off upper-middle class in the private sector. This is why those high-ranking public servants are obliged to depend upon their income of ex-officio 'profits' to compensate for the inadequacies of their official salary. This is the fundamental cause of the pervasive *khaubad* (or 'eat'ism, as the Nepalis call it, i.e. corruption) in Nepal. Second, purely in terms of numbers, it looks as if there is not so much difference between the monthly income of the *sukumbasi* and that of the lower middle-class man. As far as living conditions are concerned, however, there is a huge gap. Without a stable well-paid job, without land to live on, without a house to live in, many *sukumbasi* have to survive from hand to mouth. There may be a cause-effect relationship in the gap between the well-off rich class and the poverty of the landless class when one looks at the entire Nepalese macro politico-economical system.

During my 1999 research I asked a Nepali house contractor to give an estimate for building a 'lower-middle-class' house near the Airport area in Pokhara. According to him a small flat-roofed house (concrete-blocks and tin-roofed), with a floor space of one *anna* would cost Rs.800,000 and 4 *anna* (= one fourth of a *ropani*) land for a residence plot costs Rs.400,000. In addition to the main house, an Indian-style toilet separated from the house but within the plot is also necessary. It would cost around Rs.20,000 to build a small Indian-toilet cottage with a tin roof separated from the house within the plot. Thus the total estimated cost was Rs.1,220,000. This is equivalent to approximately 610 months' or 51 years' income of the average *sukumbasi*.

Building a Shanty in the Settlement

Mr Fighting Blacksmith (aged thirty-nine) has been living in Rato Pairo (#29) since 1980. This settlement, which has 40.6 per cent Gurung and 26.1 per cent Dalit out of a total of sixty-nine families, can be ranked as the second class without *lal purja*. Mr Blacksmith is a Marxist and a member of the UML Party, which may be one reason why he was elected vice-chairman of the Rato Pairo Sukumbasi Committee. He is not so talkative but is able to offer his own opinion clearly and articulately.

Mr Blacksmith works as *jyami* and earns Rs.1,800 per month and his wife also earns Rs.2,200 as a *jyami*. (According to him, he has to take some days off to work for the UML.) They may be a 'better-off' family among the *sukumbasi*. They have three sons (aged sixteen, fifteen, and twelve), and all three go to school. His parents live in Chapakot VDC on the west side of Phewa Lake, and his father owns two or three *ropanis* of land over there. He has not yet had an inheritance separation from his father. He has never considered himself a *hukumbasi*. (This question almost made him angry.)

The land occupied by *sukumbasis* is officially designated *abyabasthit basobas* (non-regularized residence) and Pokhara Municipality has a regulation that nobody is allowed to build a concrete-block house on the land without a *lal purja*. But this regulation is ignored in practice by many *sukumbasis*. Mr Blacksmith is one of them. Five years ago he built a small flat-roofed house with a floor space of one *anna* on his 4 *anna* plot in Rato Pairo. I asked the same house contractor to come to Mr Blacksmith's house and give an estimate of all the necessary costs to construct the same-size and same-quality house at the market rate of 1999. His answer is listed in Table 4.9. It would cost around Rs.20,000 (leaving aside the cost of the land) to reconstruct exactly Mr Blacksmith's house. It is interesting to see the cost for Mr Blacksmith's house and that for a lower-middle-class toilet cabin are more or less the same.

I would like to reiterate the following points: (1) in 1999 it cost around Rs.800,000 to construct a lower-middle-class house (a tin-roofed concrete-block flat one *anna* in size) plus Rs.400,000 for a 4-*anna* plot. (2) the cost of a lower-middle-class Indian-style toilet cabin is around Rs.20,000, (3) a

Table 4.9: Costs for Constructing a House in Pokhara (1999)
(One-storey house of block-make roofed with tin plates)

Materials & Labour	Price in NRs./Unit	Amounts	Market Price (NRs.)
1. Blocks (4 inches)	10/piece	384 pieces	3,840
2. Cement (not for floor)	300/bag	6 bags	1,800
3. Sand	10/bag	50 bags	500
4. Bamboo	100/piece	10 pieces	1,000
5. Hay	25/bundle	40 bundles	1,000
6. Skilled labour	200/day	16 day·persons	3,200
7. Unskilled labour	100/day	8 day·persons	800
8. Door (frame & cover)	2,000/unit		2,000
9. Window	500/unit		500
10. Tin plate (7ft x 9ft)	300/piece	20 pieces	6,000
Total			20,640

Source: Author's own fieldwork.

sukumbasi house like Mr Blacksmith's (a tin-roofed concrete-block flat with a one *anna* plot) also costs around Rs.20,000; and (4) in later section we will see that a Magar in Airport Sukumbasi Settlement built a small shanty at the cost of Rs.5,000 in 1998.

Let us compare those costs in terms of the average *sukumbasi*'s monthly family income (Rs.2,000). A lower-middle-class house : a lower-middle-class Indian-toilet cabin : a better-off *sukumbasi*'s house : an average *sukumbasi*'s shanty are respectively equal to 400 : 10 : 10 : 2.5 months. This will provide my answer to the fundamental question, 'Why does a *sukumbasi* family have to live in a shanty?'

Needless to say, many *sukumbasi* newcomers cannot afford to pay even Rs.5,000 to build their own shanty. The minimum requirements for a newcomer are as follows: (1) soil or clay to act as the floor base of the building; (2) several logs to act as pillars; (3) two or three polyvinyl sheets (two for the side walls and one for the ground) or bamboo/straw mats as an alternative (the former is preferable because it is more waterproof); (4) if possible a few used tinplate sheets for a roof; (5) some wooden boards to make a door; and (6) a few iron wires or ropes for binding the logs. Often neighbours of the newcomer are willing to help collecting materials. They know the locations of such available materials from discarded old houses or buildings under construction, because they go around the town for their labouring jobs. The newcomers will go with their neighbours to visit the marked locations usually after dark, to collect what they need. In this way, most of the materials, except (1) and (3), are reutilized by the *sukumbasi*. If discarded materials cannot be found, the newcomer has to buy them.

The soils are the hardest materials to get in the urban area where a hill cannot be found. But to avoid water invasion into the shanty floor during the rainy season, every shanty should be constructed on a mound at least 10-15 cm high. For this purpose, the newcomer will have to spend a few hundred rupees to hire several labourers who commute between the settlement and the nearby Seti River. Pairs of labourers fill a bucket with sticky riverside soil and carry it using a shoulder pole from which the bucket is suspended.

After collecting all the materials, the newcomer starts his/her construction in the following order:

i. make a 10-15 cm high mound on the ground;
ii. make four holes on the ground to sustain the props;
iii. cross a pair of props with wires (the same operation is repeated for another pair of props);
iv. bury the four props in the holes on the ground, and lay the longest log between two crossing points of the props and fix the log to the crossing poles;

v. cover those poles with the polyvinyl sheets or straw mats and fix them to the props with wire so that they are not blown away in the wind; and
vi. make the front door and fasten it to the front props.

It usually takes two days to complete all six operations. In total it costs Rs.500-1,000 to make a shanty in the urban settlements. It is interesting to see how the number of volunteer helpers from among the neighbours grows as the operation progresses. Sometimes the newcomer celebrates completion of the construction by distributing sweets to those who have helped. It is also interesting to observe that the *sukumbasi* in the urban settlement always locks their shanties with a strong lock and an iron chain at the door when they go out for work. The contrast between the shabby shanty and the gleaming lock on the door looks very odd to the eye of the outsider. But it is clearly the best way for the *sukumbasi* to protect the personal belongings which they have accumulated by means of their sweat and tears.

Poor Sukumbasi *Families in Airport Settlements*

Mr Thin Woodshoes (a forty-one-year-old Magar male) lives in a small shanty, which is a minute's walk from Mr Painter. Mr Woodshoes lives in his shanty together with his wife (aged twenty-seven) and his three daughters (aged ten, eight, and three). Because he is an ex-leprosy patient and it has affected his feet, he cannot walk far. He works as a labourer, but because of his physical handicap he earns less than Rs.1,000 per month. His wife works very hard as a wool maker and earns around Rs.1,600 on a fairly regular basis. Thus, the monthly income of this family is less than Rs.2,600. The monthly expenditure of the household amounts to around Rs.2,400. If Mr Woodshoes is well, they can save about Rs.200. But if he needs medical attention, he earns less than usual and, what is worse, additional expenses are incurred. They will be forced to suffer a shortfall of Rs.500 to 600.

Looking around the inside of their shanty, I was astonished at its emptiness. All they had were three floor mats, some cooking utensils (a kerosene burner, a cooking pan, a kettle, two plates, three glasses, an empty Coca-Cola bottle, a box of matches, two candles, several seasoning pots), a pair of old wooden shoes for the husband, two rubber slippers, three or four used clothes hanging on a rope, and three books and notebooks for children. There was not a large locker which is usually found in such shanties (most *sukumbasi* use it as an all-purpose container). Nonetheless the Engel's coefficient of the Woodshoes is 42.5. It came as a surprise to see that this family suppresses its food expenses to less than 50 per cent of the total expenditure, when Mr and Mrs Painter's Engel's coefficient was, as seen above, over 70. This is because the Woodshoes have to squeeze Rs.500 (21.8 per cent) for school fees for two of their daughters. Despite their very low income, they have to reduce the quality and quantity of their daily food intake in order to use one-fifth of their monthly income for their children's education.

There are many single-person households in the Airport settlements. It is these single males who survive the 'hand to mouth' living. They are mainly non-skilled labourers (*jyami, kulli*) and their Engel's coefficient amounts to nearly 90 or more. There are two reasons for this: (1) their tendency to eat outside at shabby chophouses; and (2) their liking for alcohol. Around Old Bus Stop (#17) and Shiva Tol (#19) there are many such restaurants in which both cheap meals and *raksi* (distilled liquor) are available. In 1999 they charged around Rs.25-30 per meal and about the same for a glass of *raksi*. In this sense alcohol is very expensive. An average labourer earns Rs.100 per day. He usually eats only once. If he also drinks one or two glasses of *raksi*, he has only Rs.10 to 20 remaining. If he buys several cigarettes (one rupee each), there is not much left in his pocket. According to them, *raksi* is good to remove muscle fatigue after a day of hard labour. They also say that when it rains they get wet to the skin and it is easy to catch cold because the body gets so cold. *Raksi* makes the cold body warmer from the inside and protects them against the cold. From the viewpoint of these labourers, *raksi* is a necessary expense even though they live hand to mouth. In short, a *sukumbasi* couple, with school-age children, tend to suppress their Engel's coefficient below 60 or 65 for the sake of their children, whereas for a single male *sukumbasi*, the coefficient tends to exceed 90.

NGO ACTIVITIES IN *SUKUMBASI* SETTLEMENTS

Between 10 and 21 August 2004, I carried out fieldwork to investigate NGO activities in ex-*sukumbasi* and *sukumbasi* settlements in Pokhara and the results of my findings are summarized in Table 4.10. GONESA (Good Neighbour Service Association) has been operating its aid programmes in fourteen of the forty-one ex-*sukumbasi* and *sukumbasi* settlements since March 2003, CWIN (Child Workers In Nepal Concern Centre) in six settlements since July 2000, and RUPP (Rural-Urban Partnership Programme) in eight settlements since May 1999.

GONESA is a non-governmental organization established in Pokhara in 1998 and registered with the social welfare council in 1999. According to Bharat Raj Sharma, the present chair of GONESA in Pokhara, this organization is sponsored by an Italian millionaire. None of their written materials mention who he is, but nonetheless this organization has been most active in ex-*sukumbasi* and *sukumbasi* settlements in Pokhara. GONESA's programmes have several unique characteristics:

1. It builds a small school building with a tin roof and painted yellow and

Table 4.10: NGO Activities in Ex-*Sukumbasi* and *Sukumbasi* Settlements (Aug. 2004)

Area Names		GONESA	CWIN	RUPP
1	Pani Tanki			
2	Simal Bote			
3	Sim Pani			Since Mar. 2003
4	Sarangkot	Since March 2003	Since May 2003	
5	Bagar			
6	Tundako Patan			
7	Male Patan			
8	Mahendra Pul			Since July 2001
9	Sita Paila			
10	Naya Bazar			
11	Behind Hospital			
12	Mate Pani			
13	Prithvi Chok			
14	Shanti Ban			
15	Ram Ghat	Since March 2003		
16	Front of Hospital			
17	Old Bus Stop			
18	Airport	Since March 2003	Since May 2003	
19	Shiva Tol			
20	Miya Patan	Since March 2003		
21	Pragati Tol	Since March 2003	Since July 2000	
22	Amar Singh Chok	Since March 2003		
23	Janapriya Tol			Since May1999
24	Gai Ghat			
25	Kulako Dil A			
26	Kaji Pokhari			
27	Bijayapur			
28	Simal Tunda	Since March 2003		
29	Rato Pairo	Since March 2003		
30	Hanuman Tol	Since March 2003		Since July 2003
31	Thanti Patan	Since March 2003		
32	Amintara			
33	Kranti Tol	Since March 2003		
34	Shanti Tol			Since July 2000
35	Dobilla	Since March 2003	Since March 2004	
36	Masina*		Since March 2004	Since July 2001
37	Khalte	Since March 2003		Since July 2001
38	Samintara	Since March 2003	Since March 2004	
39	Mate			
40	Belbot			Since Mar. 2001
41	Phirke			

Source: Author's own fieldwork.

Note:*Masina is the only recipient of aid from three different NGOs (CWIN, RUPP and WOCAS) out of all the 41 settlements in Pokhara.

red, within or in the vicinity of the settlement compound from its own budget.
2. It employs two teachers (one teacher on a monthly salary of Rs.1,200, the other an assistant teacher on Rs.1,000) from capable candidates living within the same local community.
3. The two teachers are in charge of a class of 20-5 pupils (over 5 years old) from Sunday through Friday in the school building and teach them how to read and write in Nepali, as well as English and basic arithmetic.
4. After school, the teachers offer lunch to each of the pupils every day.
5. Sometimes, when necessary, the teachers offer first-hand medical care to the children.

CWIN, sponsored by international NGOs, was established in 1987. It is an advocacy organization to defend the rights of children in Nepal and to fight against child labour exploitation; it also serves as a watchdog organization against violations of child rights in the country. It runs various programmes for the rescue, socialization, and rehabilitation of children at risk, such as street children, child workers, orphaned, abandoned, and destitute children, victims of abuse and exploitation, children of jailed parents, children from slums and shanty towns. In Pokhara CWIN has been running classes for school dropouts between six and eighteen years of age in six ex-*sukumbasi* and *sukumbasi* settlements. It is interesting to observe that CWIN cooperates with GONESA in at least four slum areas by using the same classrooms in the afternoon that GONESA uses in the morning. CWIN also employs a teacher (at Rs.1,500 per month) for each of its classes.

RUPP was established in September 1997 as a joint effort of HMG (National Planning Commission, Ministry of Housing and Physical Planning and Ministry of Local Development) and the UN (United Nations Developmental Programme and Centers for Human Settlements). It aims to strengthen urban governance in order to boost local economies and livelihoods by enabling people to take advantage of the social and economic development opportunities that can be obtained thanks to improvements in rural-urban linkages. Since RUPP is mainly sponsored by the UN, its Pokhara office is situated in a building within the compound of Pokhara Municipal Hall. RUPP has been running capital-loan programmes in eight settlements in Pokhara, and its local 'Mothers' Club' (*Ama Samuha*) has been in charge of performing its actual loan operation, charging between 15 and 20 per cent interest.

WOCAS (Women and Community Awareness Society) is a government-registered organization which aims to advocate and help exploited women in Nepal. Unfortunately out of all the forty-one settlements in Pokhara, Masina (#36) is the sole recipient of aid from WOCAS. This is managed by the Mothers' Club in Masina. In Kathmandu, LUMANTI

(Support Group for Shelter) has been very active in providing *sukumbasi* families in the Kathmandu Valley with construction of their shanties and financial aid but it has not yet extended its operation to Pokhara. However, the leader of Hanuman Tol (#30) told us that he was now in contact with the office of LUMANTI and would be requesting help from it in the near future.

Taking Hanuman Tol (#30) and Masina (#36) as the prime recipients of development aid, since they both are in receipt of help from more than two different NGOs, we can see the significant role of leaders who can function as liaison officers between the settlement and external organizations. In order to clarify this point, I have made an additional table, Table 4.11, by combining Table 4.6 on developmental levels with Table 4.10 on NGO activities.

The results in Table 4.11 are very clear: (1) as the developmental level of the forty-one settlements goes down, the recipient ratio also goes down. As shown in the table, the recipient ratio of the first-class settlements is 66.7 per cent, that of the second-class settlements is 45.8 per cent, and that of the third-class settlements is 25.0 per cent. (2) twenty-one ex-*sukumbasi* (with *lal purja*) settlements enjoy a recipient ratio (61.9 per cent) almost twice as high as those settlements without *lal purjas* (35.0 per cent). As explained earlier, the acquisition of *lal purjas* depends heavily on the settlement leaders' qualities and efforts. By the same token, the data also demonstrate the significant role of local leaders in promoting the long-term development of their settlements. We also have to pay attention to the fact that, as a result of the differences in these local leaders' efforts, NGO assistance is helping to widen the gap between different ex-*sukumbasi* and

Table 4.11: NGO Activities and Settlement Development

Developmental Level	21 Ex-*Sukumbasi* (with *lal purja*)	20 *Sukumbasi* (without *lal purja*)	Recipient Ratio Between Classes
1st Class	(#3), #5, (#8), #9, #10, (#20), (#33), (#36), (#37)	None	6 out of 9 (66.7%)
2nd Class	#6, #7, (#15), (#23) #25, (#28), (#31), (#31), (#35), (#40), #41	#1, (#4), #11, #12, #13, #14, #16, #17, (#18), #19, (#21), (#22), #24, (#29)	11 out of 24 (45.8%)
3rd Class	#34	#2, #26, #27, (#30), #32, (#38), #39	2 out of 8 (25.0%)
Recipient Ratio with/without *lal purja*	13 out of 21 (61.9%)	7 out of 20 (35.0%)	

Notes: # : Non-recipients of NGO aid.
(#) : Recipient of single NGO aid.
(#) [boxed] : Recipients of double NGO aid.

sukumbasi settlements in Pokhara, rather than evening up the developmental levels of all settlements.

CONCLUSION

This chapter attempts to provide a comprehensive view of ex-*sukumbasi* and *sukumbasi* settlements in Pokhara. I would like to emphasize two conclusions: (1) all developmental processes in *sukumbasi* settlements can be seen in the context of a transformation from communitas to community; and (2) in this developmental process, the emergence and development of 'proto-charisma' on the part of the leaders plays a vital role in deciding the course the transformation will take.

The Transformation from Communitas to Community

Victor Turner is an advocate of the interpersonal concept of 'communitas' as opposed to Robert Merton's concept of 'social structure'. When social structure is defined as a set of social roles and social statuses which are recognized consciously and performed in an orderly manner in a social system, a 'communitas' can be defined as a group of interpersonal relationships which lack social structure or are characterized by deviation from social structure (Turner 1969: 209-18). Turner puts particular emphasis on three cultural aspects of communitas: liminality, marginality, and structural inferiority. Our Pokhara *sukumbasi*s are endowed with each of the three cultural aspects of Turner's communitas.

First, most *sukumbasis* are economic refugees. They are essentially 'wanderers' who have moved from one place to another, or 'drifters' without any roots. Second, *sukumbasi*s are consciously aware of themselves as the illegal occupants of land and are trying to cope with external opponents collectively. Most of them do not belong to any social institutions except for the Sukumbasi Committee. Third, as to structural inferiority, Turner himself cites 'outcaste' as an example of structural inferiority. The Gurungs are also considered structurally inferior in the Bahun-Chetri dominated political system of contemporary Nepal. The eminent geographer, Harka Gurung, has noted that Bahuns and Chetris make up 79.9 per cent of Nepali Congress MPs and 84.2 per cent of the UML's MPs (Gurung 1992). Even under the latest constitution, which defines the kingdom as Hindu, the Gurungs feel they are not free from domination by traditional Hindu ideology (Cox 1989; O'Neill 1994; Krämer 2001: 185-90).

As Turner relevantly points out, a revolutionary group is a typical example of communitas. Both the *sukumbasi*s and the Maoists can be seen to exemplify high levels of communitas. Hence it is no surprise that there should be a political 'nexus' between some *sukumbasi*s and the Maoists. It seems that in 2000 and 2001 the Maoists retained some considerable influence in the *sukumbasi* settlements in Pokhara.

'Autogenetic Leaders' in Transformation

I have proposed the concept of 'proto-charisma' as a key to grasping the emergence of leadership in the *sukumbasi* settlements. I cited some examples of proto-charisma, such as T.N. Adhikari's father, Mr Painter, B.R. Subedi, and so on. They have the following personal characteristics in common. First, they are good at reading and writing Nepali. Second, they are kind enough to teach and help *sukumbasi* neighbours to prepare those official papers necessary for their application for their *lal purja*. Third, they are articulate and good at attracting people. Fourth, they have enough spiritual strength to protest against external opponents, even against law enforcement officials. These personal characteristics are nothing to do with their past or present social statuses or formal educational careers (only Subedi is an exception here). Regardless of their own intention to be a leader, they 'naturally' happen to attract neighbouring people and take the role of opinion leaders among them. A proto-charismatic leader often emerges in the cradle stage of a *sukumbasi* settlement.

I have interviewed thirty *sukumbasi* leaders in different settlements at different times. Most of them possess the above-mentioned four characteristics. None of them have any position worth boasting about in terms of the social hierarchy. None of them has had a good educational career. Although many of them are ex-Gurkha soldiers who have served mainly in India, none of them has experienced an outstanding career except for an old ex-village headman in Masina (#36). Many of them are skilled labourers, pensioners, and small farmers, but none of their occupations are better than a small shop owner, a contractor, or a peon.

Max Weber introduced the concept of 'charisma' into the field of sociology, and he has proposed the concept of 'charismatic dominance' as one of the three types of dominance. Our proto-charisma is a 'primitive' stage of Weber's charisma. As Weber's 'charismatic dominance' is certainly different both from 'legitimate dominance' and from 'traditional dominance', the same is true of the proposed concept of proto-charisma. Edward A. Shils criticized Weber's lack of distinction between 'dominance' and 'leadership'. Shils considers that 'dominance' is conducted on the grounds of some 'enforcement' for the benefit (or interest) of a ruler while 'leadership' is performed on the grounds of followers' spontaneous obedience for the benefit of followers or for a mutual benefit between a leader and followers. This distinction seems very important in our research findings. Most of our proto-charismatic leaders have lost their leadership role after their followers succeeded in getting their *lal purjas*. Discrepancies emerge between a leader and followers (or committee members). On the one hand, the leader attempts to make his leadership stronger, but on the other, his followers do not like his dominance over them. In other words, our proto-charisma is nothing but 'primitive charisma': the leader loses his followers once he starts to behave as if he had 'real charisma'. It is very important to clarify that, once proto-charismatic leaders fail to demonstrate 'self-sacrifice' for the sake of their followers, the followers stop respecting him and do not follow his orders any longer. In this sense, the proto-charismatic leader is not furnished with 'magnetic charms' which make it possible for him to 'dominate' his followers absolutely without any conditions. *Sukumbasi* followers do not like being dominated and resist when they start to perceive that the leader may be using them for his own benefit.

It can be concluded that a proto-charisma fails to become a real charisma when a *sukumbasi* group transforms itself from communitas to 'community', that is, a legalized neighbourhood. B.R. Subedi of Masina (#36) looks exceptionally close to having possessed real charisma. However, I doubt that Subedi was furnished with the 'magnetic charms' that would have enabled him to 'dominate' his followers in a truly charismatic way. I suppose that his success as a leader depended heavily on the contribution of his partner P.S. Gurung, and on the propensity of the Gurungs to follow cohesively.

REFERENCES

Adhikari, J. 2007. 'Urbanization and Change in Pokhara, Nepal', in this volume.

Bourdieu, P. 1977. *Outline of a Theory of Practice.* Cambridge: Cambridge University Press.

Cox, T. 1989. 'Langtang Tibetans and Hindu Norms as Political Language: A Critical Perspective on Sanskritization Theory'. *Contributions to Nepalese Studies* 16 (1): 11-20.

Gurung, H. 1992. 'Representing an Ethnic Mosaic'. *Himal* (May): 12-23.

Karan, P. and H. Ishii. 1994. *Nepal: Development and Change in a Landlocked Himalayan Kingdom* (Monumenta Serindica No. 25). Institute for the Study of Languages and Cultures of Asia and Africa, Tokyo University of Foreign Studies.

Krämer, K.-H. 2001. 'How Representative is the Nepali State?', in D.N. Gellner (ed.), *Resistance and the State: Nepalese Experiences*, pp. 179-98. New Delhi: Social Science Press.

Merton, R.K. 1957 (1949). *Social Theory and Social Structure.* New York: Free Press.

O'Neill, T. 1994. 'Peoples and Polity: Ethnography, Ethnicity and Identity in Nepal'. *Contributions to Nepalese Studies* 21 (1): 130-45.

Turner, V.W. 1969. *The Ritual Process: Structure and Anti-Structure*. New York: Aldine Publishing Company.

Weber, M. 1978 (1968). *Economy and Society an Outline of Interpretive Sociology*, ed. G. Roth and C. Wittich, Vol. 1. Berkeley: University of California Press.

Yamamoto, Y. 1991. 'Pokhara no Caste Joke: Kaikyujoretsu no Fukakuteisei no Shiten kara (Caste Jokes in Pokhara: From a Viewpoint of Cognitive Uncertainty of Caste Ranking)'. *Kwassui Ronbunshu (Kwassui Bulletin)* 34: 9-21 (Kwassui Women's College & Junior College) (in Japanese).

——. 2001a. 'Nepal no Minshuka Undo to Toshi Slum no Keisei (Nepal's Democratization Movement and the Formation of Urban Slums)', in M. Fujimaki (ed.), Seikatsu Sekai toshite no Slum (Slums as a Life Arena), pp. 147-76. Tokyo: Kokonshoin (in Japanese).

——. 'Nepal no Minshuka to Toshi *Sukumbasi* Shuraku no "Communitas" teki Tokucho (Nepal's Democratization and Its Effect on the "Communitas" Nature of *Sukumbasi* Dwellers in Pokhara)', *Ritsumeikan Jinbunkagaku Kenkyusho Kiyo (Memoires of Institute of Humanities, Human and Social Sciences, Ritsumeikan University)* 76: 199-246 (in Japanese).

——. 2002. '*Sukumbasi* no Hinkon Seikatsu ni Miru "Ideology" to "Ninchishadan" (Ideology and Cognitive Shutdown in *Sukumbasis*' Deprived Conditions)', *Nanpo Bunka (Tenri Bulletin of South Asian Studies)* 28: 87-138 (in Japanese).

PART 2

MARRIAGE, KINSHIP, AND TRANSFORMATION OF INTIMACY

5

Abduction, Elopement, and Incest in Khas Society

HAYAMI YASUNO

INTRODUCTION

Conjugal unions in the Khas Brahman society of western Nepal divide into two categories: *biha gareko* (married) unions and *swasne lyaeko* (bringing a wife) unions.[1] This distinction corresponds to that made between those wives who have been married and brought to their husband's home with formal wedding rites and those who have been brought by consent but without any ritual. The former, referred to as *bivahita* ('married' women), retain their original caste status when married whereas the latter *lyaita* ('brought' women) are degraded within or from their caste (Höfer 1979: 73-4).

The term *biha* (marriage) is used almost as a synonym for *kanyadan* (the gift of a virgin), the most prestigious and most frequent form of marriage among the Brahmans. In *kanyadan* the father gives his daughter

---

[1]The people of Jumla, Dailekh, Accham, and Bajura are designated as Khas which consists of the Brahmans, the Thakuris, the Chetris, and the Untouchables. The Khas also include the Hamals who are the offspring of Brahman fathers and Thakuri mothers, the Khatris who are the offspring of Brahman fathers and Chetri mothers, and the Ghatris who are ex-slaves. Since the Chetris are referred to as Khasiya, Sharma suggests that they are the descendants of the ancient Khas (1971: 6, 1972: 56). What gave the area its cultural integration was the existence of the Western Malla kingdom which flourished during the twelfth to fourteenth centuries.

The fieldwork on which this paper is based was conducted at intervals over the past twenty years. Research in Ludku village of Sija Valley, Jumla district, western Nepal, was carried out between March 1983 and November 1984, July-September 1986, and July-October 1992. The research predates the rise of Maoism. Ludku village is inhabited by Upadhyaya Brahmans including their degraded descendants, namely, Jaisi Brahmans, Hamals and Khatris, and Ghatris. 'Ghatri' in this area corresponds to 'Gharti' in other areas in Nepal.

with a dowry to his future son-in-law and bears the high costs of the wedding for which a Brahman priest is indispensable. *Kanyadan* is a meritorious action on condition that no payment is received. If one asks for money or labour in exchange for the gift of a daughter, this is referred to as *chori bechera khane* (to subsist by selling a daughter) and, as in other parts of South Asia (Fruzzetti 1982), it is regarded as a sin. People know that brideprice marriage and 'buying with money' marriage, which are prevalent in the Karnali basin among the Chetris and the Thakuris respectively, contradict the *kanyadan* principle. However, their marriages are recognized as *biha* since they are carried out with rituals, however simplified those may be. *Biha* denotes a conjugal union wherein the wife does not lose her caste status. Apart from *kanyadan*, *biha* among Brahmans takes place as a result of the abduction of unmarried girls, who are forced to marry, and become a *bivahita*, with simplified rituals.

Marriage is, in principle, monogamous, but in practice, both polygyny, in which a man has plural wives, and the remarriage of women are found. In the case of women, the first marriage is normally carried out in the form of *kanyadan* before the girl reaches puberty but the second marriage is always a *lyaita* union. A woman can be a *bivahita* only once, namely, at her first marriage, but a man can repeatedly marry *bivahita* wives. Dumont posits that "all Indian castes distinguish, from the point of view of status or prestige, between two kinds of marriage: on the one hand, primary or main marriage: on the other, secondary or subsidiary marriages" (Dumont 1983: 109). The Ludku Brahmans thus recognize a type of perfect marriage, i.e. *biha* as the primary one, and a less reputable marriage which usually follows the perfect one, i.e. *lyaita union*, as the secondary one. From a male viewpoint, *bivahita* wives are 'principal' wives while *lyaita* wives are 'subsidiary' wives (see Good 1991: 183).

Elopements are publicly recognized as conjugal unions after the proper procedures have been followed (*jari*), though such unions are not celebrated with rituals and the wives concerned are 'degraded' in the sense that eloped and/or remarried Brahman women can no longer maintain their Upadhyaya status but become Jaisi Brahmans. It is said that *jari* is practised only by Chetris, but in fact, though it is most often seen among them, it is found among all castes (cf. Krause 2002: 382). In contrast to elopement, liaisons between married women and the agnates of their husbands are regarded as 'incest' and are socially punished.

From the woman's point of view, marriage and elopement imply going to the husband's place to live (*poila janu*) as the residential rule is virilocal. For women, monogamy is emphasized and remarried women are discriminated against as those having had 'two husbands' (*do poeli*), and are regarded as inauspicious. Impurity is the result of sexual intercourse on the side of the woman and the woman's status is determined by the number of male genitals (*linga*) she has had experience of. Remarried women are thus referred to as those who have a second genital (*dosro linga*).

Cooked rice (*bhat*) is not accepted from an eloped woman by her caste members since she has violated caste purity by having extramarital intercourse. As for the caste status of the husband in a *lyaita* union which involves elopement, he is not degraded unless he accepts cooked rice from the wife in question. In such a case the husband himself or his mother may cook to avoid pollution.

The principle of marriage is caste endogamy and lineage (and often village) exogamy[2] but hypergamy is permitted. Elopement leading to a conjugal union (*jari*) also obeys these rules.[3] *Bivahita* unions are usually endogamous but can sometimes be hypergamous. For instance, the union of a Brahman man and a Thakuri *kanyadan bivahita* can be found in Ludku. Women from the Chetri or the Ghatri caste who are married to Brahmans, however, cannot be regarded as *bivahita*s even though the marriages are the first ones for the women. Most hypergamous unions, including the remarriage of Brahman widows, are *lyaita*. Occurrences in Ludku of *kanyadan*, *jari*, and *lyaita* (excluding *jari* marriage) unions are shown in Table 5.1. It will be seen that among the Upadhyaya Brahmans most unions are *kanyadan* while one third of the Jaisi Brahman unions are *jari*.

Extramarital relations are categorized as abduction, elopement, and incest, and the distinction made between socially approved and prohibited unions is, as was noted, very precise and clear within Brahman society. Abduction and elopement are offences but can develop into conjugal unions. Incestuous unions, on the other hand, are to be dissolved. These three kinds of unions are viewed, in daily life, as negotiable in the order of things (cf. Comaroff & Roberts 1981: 133). They inevitably involve

Table 5.1: Different Types of Marriages in Ludku

Caste	Household	*kanyadan*	*jari*	*lyaita*	Total
Upadhyaya Brahman	58	70	5	7	82
Jaisi Brahman	19	14	7	2	23
Khatri	16	21	2	5	28
Hamal	3	6	0	1	7
Chetri	1	0	1	1	2
Ghatri	11	9	2	2	13

[2] Based on village exogamy, several villages are related to each other as wife-givers and wife-receivers (*chori lin din garne*) and are referred to as *kutumba* (affines).

[3] Hypogamous unions are socially frowned upon but a slight difference in caste status between a man and a woman tends to be dismissed. For instance, a few years ago, a married Upadhyaya Brahman woman from Ludku eloped with a Jaisi Brahman man. Also, a Ghatri man from Ludku took a Chetri woman to be his wife.

villagers' interests and usually incur disputes between the parties concerned.

The first resort in these disputes is to refer to the village fellows (*gaunle*) who are sometimes organized into *pancha* (ad hoc councils – the term *pancha* can be used to refer both to the council itself and to its individual members) or *kachahari* (caste courts). Both *pancha* and *kachahari* have the judicial authority to inquire into the case and punish offences with the exception of crimes. Since solidarity among villagers is strong, ways of settlement differ depending upon whether the dispute is inter-village or intra-village. The second resort is a higher authority or formal agency such as the police and law courts (*adalat*), or a *Masta* deity[4] through which a disputant puts a curse on his/her opponent. The villagers are indeed bi-legal and sufficiently skilled in using different legal codes to win a case. Indeed, some literate villagers manipulate the law courts while more traditional people believe that the deity will punish the rival.

In this chapter I shall examine cases concerning extramarital relations and the dispute process.[5] This data was collected in 1992; no doubt such processes began to operate differently after Maoists moved into this area.

TIPNE: ABDUCTION

Tipne is the violent abduction of an unmarried girl and the attempt to marry the girl in the form of *biha.* If such an attempt is successful, a Brahman priest is called upon to perform a simplified ritual to marry her to the man in question. The ritual is necessary because the girl in question will be otherwise degraded in terms of her caste status. In other words, she will not be a *lyaita* but a *bivahita.* It is important at this stage to note that *tipne* does not involve sexual intercourse, but it is considered to be a synonym of *jabarjasti* (rape) in the sense that there is no consent on the part of the girl. It is thus the violent attempt of a man to obtain for himself a *bivahita* wife.

Tipne occurs quite commonly since not all Brahman boys receive *kanyadan*, but it is not so successful in its objectives. In fact in Ludku there are only two instances of *tipne* marriages. The reason for this is that such violence needs supporters and attracts unfavourable attention. Moreover, the girl may be saved by others or run away before the ritual. Furthermore, the family and village members of the girl will not allow the man in question to marry her in such a way without opposition. This is because, if

---

[4]The local deities, Mastas, of the Karnali basin are believed to intervene in the human realm and to manifest themselves in mediums or *dhamis* (Gaborieau 1976; Campbell 1978). See Yasuno (1999: 83-92) for the role of a Hindu deity in dispute settlement.

[5]Pseudonyms are used in the following case studies.

the simplified ritual is carried out, it will no longer be possible for her to recover her *kanya* status. After all she is not polluted by an attempted *tipne* but her reputation is hurt (*be-ijjat*). If such an attempt is unsuccessful, payment of compensation (*jarimana*) is inevitable.

Case A is an illustration of *tipne* in which the abduction of an Upadhyaya Brahman girl from Ludku resulted in failure and incurred litigation. The abductor was an Upadhyaya Brahman who intended to marry the girl to his son. The case is reconstructed based on information given by several villagers who had participated in the dispute.

A. Tipne *and Legal Punishment*

> The girl in question was the only daughter of the former *mukhiya*, Pashupati Upadhyaya, who had died two years before. She was a ninth class student, not yet betrothed, and lived with her stepmother and young half-brother. Pashupati's younger brother, Deviprasad, had taken over the status of *mukhiya* and was taking care of her.
>
> One day in the month of Magh, 1992, the girl had visited her father's sister and was walking home accompanied by her cousin. As they approached Baktawara, a man named Kedar Upadhyaya stopped them and invited the boy to have a cup of yoghurt. The man was no stranger to the boy since the boy's mother's elder sister and the man's wife were ritual friends. When the boy left his cousin for a while, Kedar Upadhyaya's supporters appeared and captured her. She cried out but the boy, who was also seized by Kedar, could not help her. They took her to the house of her late father's parallel cousin who had married in Baktawara, and locked her up there, leaving a dog in front of the house. Kedar Upadhyaya went to look for a Brahman priest in order to marry the girl to his son.
>
> The boy escaped and ran back home. His mother, taking pity on the girl, took several villagers to Baktawara to stop anyone going in the house and ran to Ludku to report the occurrence. Deviprasad, the girl's father's younger brother was away from home but his wife, accompanied by several supporters from Ludku, went to Baktawara. She drove the dog away from the house with a stick and saved the girl. The family in whose house she had been kept did not resist because they did not want to have any dispute with the girl's family.
>
> The Ludku villagers' opinions were divided on the case. Some of them thought that the girl should be married to Kedar's son, but others said that the girl's opinion was more important than theirs and she obviously did not want to marry Kedar's son. They questioned Kedar as to whether he would marry his son to the girl or not but he did not answer. He pretended to be fasting and said merely that he would not talk for the three days of the fast. This attitude incensed the Ludku

villagers who advised Deviprasad's wife to report Kedar's violence to the police.

Kedar brought a horse and a castrated goat to Ludku at night and begged some of the village notables not to raise a lawsuit but to accept the livestock as compensation for his actions as well as a gift for marriage. One of the notables, who was the same age as Deviprasad, rejected the proposal, saying "Who can receive *jarimana* (compensation) to marry?" In addition, some Baktawara villagers went to Ludku and asked that no legal action be taken against Kedar and that the girl be married to Kedar's son. This request was also rejected.

Two months later Deviprasad's wife reported the event to the police in Sija who arrested Kedar, detaining him for several days. (His son, frightened, ran away to Nepalgunj.) But Kedar was released soon after because, it was said, the villagers of Baktawara had paid Rs.1,200 to the police. Deviprasad, who had heard the news of *tipne* in Nepalgunj, came home and complained to the police superintendent in Khalanga about the release of Kedar in exchange for a bribe, and he pressured the police in Sija to detain Kedar once more for a week.[6]

Deviprasad thought it might be dishonourable (*be-ijjat*) if he did not do anything. In the name of the girl, he raised a lawsuit against Kedar Upadhyaya's son. The complaint went as follows:

> On my way home from my father's sister's place, the man in question abducted me and attempted to force me to marry him. I request that he compensates me for the violence I incurred and, at the same time, for my jewellery (*gahana*) worth 39,000 rupees which he robbed me of at the time of abduction.

Kedar Upadhyaya defended, on his son's behalf:

> I am married to the girl in question. Since her natal family in Ludku has kept her and the jewellery which I gave her at the wedding, I request her natal family to return her and the jewellery to me.

The judge of the local court at Khalanga sentenced Kedar Upadhyaya's son to five days' imprisonment and a five hundred rupee fine for an attempted *tipne*. As for the robbery of the jewellery, however, he was found to be not guilty.

In case A, the *kutumba*'s attempt to abduct the girl from Ludku was not at first condemned by the Ludku villagers. The abductor was in fact given two options: either to marry or to pay compensation. The abducted party was not really listened to and the negotiations went on without direct talks

---

[6]See Caplan (1971) for cash and kind as two media in which bribes are paid.

between the parties involved. Notable, aged, or closely related villagers negotiated as representatives of the party abducted, acting not as *pancha*s but as informal mediators. The villagers of Baktawara were also acting as a cooperative body for the abductor in persuading the Ludku villagers to receive compensation and in paying a bribe to the police. This dispute was not settled at the village level but went to the police and law courts through the girl's father's brother. According to the local custom, to receive compensation was regarded as a contradiction of the *kanyadan* principle.

It is uncertain whether the Sija police in this case were influenced by bribes to release the accused, or by pressure applied through the *mukhiya*'s acquaintance with a person of higher authority. However, it does seem generally difficult for the police to function independently. Indeed, when I talked to the chief of the police station in Sija, which was established only in 1990, he said that the police received so many false accusations aimed at the harassment of rival disputants, that they could not take action properly.

Villagers understand that reporting an offence to the police and raising a lawsuit on the offence are two different and separate things. In the above case, the robbery of jewellery was added to the abduction cited in the original accusation. Adding another offence to the list is a usual tactic employed by the injured party. The purpose is to extract as much compensation as possible from the abductor. The punishment in this case was not so heavy but the decision made by the court was welcomed by Deviprasad and the Ludku villagers. Too heavy a punishment, in their opinion, would have incurred an appeal against the decision and a long fight in court – something they did not want to happen.

To return to the case in question, to avoid further attempts at abduction, the villagers made haste to marry the girl. Three proposals were received through the network of Ludku *kutumba*s. One of the suitors came quickly to see her and agreed to marry her. Soon after, the bridegroom returned with his village companions and carried out the wedding ritual in Ludku.

In such disputes, the terms *ijjat* (honour) and *be-ijjat* (dishonour) are often heard. The honour of the village and the honour of the girl must be upheld and therefore action must be taken against the abductor. In this case the girl's father's brother was a *mukhiya* and being literate as well as wealthy, was able to take legal action on her behalf.

THE DEFINITION OF *JARI*

In contrast to the abduction of an unmarried girl, taking away a married woman incurs the rage and possibly violent revenge of her husband. Such an aggrieved husband is entitled to demand compensation from the seducer and *pancha*s are invited by each of the parties concerned to decide on the amount. The *pancha*s' task in such a case is not to arbitrate but to conduct negotiations as the representatives of the husband and the seducer. These negotiations are seldom amicable, and are carried on without the presence of both the parties involved. Reconciliation between the parties does not occur until the compensation is paid.

Before describing the ethnographic facts of elopement and dispute settlement, I will briefly review the legal interpretations of the term *jari,* which is often defined as 'adultery'. According to Turner's dictionary (1931), *jar* means 'adulterer' and *jar katnu* is explained as

> to kill an adulterer. When the husband has killed the adulterer with his *khukuri* [sword] and cut off the woman's nose and hair, he proclaims openly in the village *'jar kate'* [I have killed the adulterer] and displays the blood-stained *khukuri.* This proclamation saves him from accusation of murder.

This interpretation of *jari* – in which an aggrieved husband is licensed to take blood revenge upon the adulterer and the unfaithful wife – seems to have similarities with Hodgson's quotation of an eminent court judge's statement on adultery:

> When a *Parbattia* [Parbatiya] has satisfied himself of the adultery, and the identity of the male adulterer, he may kill him before giving any information to the court or to the Sirkar: he must afterwards prove the adultery, and if he fails in the proofs, he will be hanged. (Hodgson 1880: 235-6)[7]

Punishment for adultery was different according to caste. The same judge stated:

> If a female of the sacred order go astray, and her paramour be not a *Brahman,* he is capitally punished: if he be a *Brahman,* he is degraded from his rank, and banished. If a female of the soldier tribes be seduced, the husband, with his own hand, kills the seducer, and cuts off the nose of the female, and expels her from his house. Then the *Brahman* or soldier-husband must perform the purificatory rites enjoined, after which he is restored to his caste. (Hodgson 1880: 241)[8]

Hodgson saw this practice of the Parbatiyas as an exception to Hindu laws. He noted:

> The Penal Law of Nepal, a Hindu state, is necessarily founded on

[7]The Parbatiyas at that time were considered to include the Brahmans, the Khas, the Magars, and the Gurungs. The Newars, Murmis, Kachar, Bhotias, Kirants, and other inhabitants of Nepal did not have the privilege of taking blood revenge in cases of adultery (Hodgson 1880: 242).

[8]Such punishment was practised also by the legal authorities of the state. Hodgson's memoranda show that he observed such executions during Dasain (Adam 1949-50).

> the *Shastras*; ... The only exception to the truth of the above general remarks are ... that, by the law of Nepal, the *Parbattia* husband retains the natural privilege of avenging, with his own hand, the violation of his marriage bed; ... (Hodgson 1880: 236)

The pictures of *jari* given by the judge-informant and by Hodgson were based upon the legislation prior to the Nepalese Muluki Ain of 1854, the Legal Code which was made by the order of Prime Minister Jang Bahadur. But did the punishment change after the institution of the Muluki Ain? According to Adhikari (1976: 109), "the punishment for adultery was the same both before and after Jang Bahadur's time. The aggrieved husband was allowed to cut down the adulterer". However, the Muluki Ain states, rather, that an adulterer should pay compensation to the aggrieved husband and a fine to the authorities while the aggrieved husband is allowed to kill the adulterer only in specific cases instead of claiming compensation. Fezas (1993: 14) points out that "[Jang Bahadur] did not suppress the customary killing of the wife's seducer by the injured husband, but tried to have it controlled by the state."

Höfer (1979: 79) regards the payment in question as a 'divorce payment' because "the adulteress belongs to her seducer (*jar*), that is, she is repudiated ...". In his view *jari* is a means to divorce and remarry. In the Muluki Ain the amount given as divorce payment depends only on the woman's caste, whereas the size of the fine results from the status disparity between her and her seducer (ibid.).

In 1963 a new legal code was instituted which proclaimed all citizens to be equal before the law. The new code "removed all caste discriminations from the *jari* laws and provided equal compensation for all castes" (Bennett 1979: 48). In 1975,

> the sixth amendment ... radically changed the nature of the provisions on adultery. The amended Code did away with the previous penalty of 'compensation' (up to Rs.1000/-) that the adulterer paid to the injured husband. In its place a fine of up to Rs.2000/- was instituted which is to be paid by the adulterous couple to the court rather than to the wronged husband. (ibid.: 50)

Thus, over time, the legal punishment for *jari* has changed from blood revenge to paying a fine to the authorities. However, in western Nepal, legal regulations are ignored and *jari* conflicts are usually resolved between the parties involved according to *riti-thiti* (group-specific traditions) without any official intervention. There, *jari* disputes are not referred to the law courts unless the parties have failed to resolve them according to their tradition.

The determining factor of *jari* in western Nepal is the elopement of the married woman. The question as to whether the woman has had sexual relations with the seducer is irrelevant. A woman's extramarital intercourse does not necessarily develop into *jari* whereas an elopement can take place without there having been any previous sexual relations. Such relations can start when the woman is staying at her natal home and provided that the relations with those other than husband's agnates are kept secret, they are referred to as 'secret love' (*bhitra prem garnu*) and are not regarded as punishable.

In the absence of divorce,[9] elopement is the only means by which a woman can justifiably leave her husband or in-laws for another man. She may have been deserted by her husband, failed to adapt to in-laws, or her husband may be mentally handicapped or too old. For the seducer, on the other hand, elopement is a means of marrying or remarrying since a man is permitted to have more than one wife. He may have failed to marry by *kanyadan*, lost his first wife, or be dissatisfied with his current wife. He may have no offspring and be eager to have a son, the offspring of a *jari* union being legitimated as the heirs of the father, though the lower-ranked sons cannot perform the funeral rites for their Brahman father.

Thus, *jari* marriage is generally negatively viewed since the wife is no more than a *lyaita* from whom cooked rice is not accepted. But this is only the formal view since in reality *jari* marriage serves a useful function in relieving the partners of the burden of a *kanyadan* marriage. In this sense *jari* is complementary to *kanyadan* marriage. More importantly, the husband does not lose his caste status by *jari* marriage unless he accepts cooked rice from his *jari* wife, and he still has a chance to marry a virgin (*kanya*) since men are allowed to marry repeatedly.

There are three main paths to elopement. Firstly, the young people from *kutumba* villages, whether married or not married, gather at the cattle shed at night to play, sing, and chat. Married women do not participate in such gatherings when living in their husbands' household (*ghar*), but they are often free to do so when staying in their natal household (*maiti*). They do this in the knowledge that they can find a future *jari* partner and develop a relationship at such a gathering. Secondly, some categories of people function as links between *kutumba* villages. The *bhauju* (elder sisters-in-law) or *mama* (mother's brothers) of the man or the lineage sisters of the woman may play the role of go-between in the search for *jari* partners. Such help is referred to as *phakaunu* (persuasion, seduction). Thirdly, a young man may 'steal' a married woman at night with the help of his friends.

---

[9]The villagers know of the concept of divorce but it does not exist in their custom. On this point, the Khas Rajputs of Sirkanda are different. According to Berreman (1972: 160-1), in their society, "a couple who do not get along well ... may go through a process called *chut*, divorce, which breaks the marriage bond." In this case the compensation is paid by the wife's family either to the husband or to his father.

If a married woman's elopement is revealed and the seducer (*jar*) is identified, her husband's or his family's first action is to insult, threaten, or beat the seducer helped by his village fellows. In such cases extreme violence is not rare. The aggrieved husband then has the option to take his wife back to his home (*bujhaunu*), but this solution is regarded as dishonourable or shameful since his wife has already been polluted by extramarital intercourse. Consequently, the Brahmans do not opt for this solution. Once the elopement is acknowledged as *jari* between the two parties, the aggrieved husband (*sai*) is expected to repudiate the woman and claim compensation. The date of payment is then set but the repudiation is not formally recognized until the receipt (*bharpai*) of the compensation has been written.[10]

Thus, *jari* in western Nepal signifies an elopement that leads to divorce and remarriage. The anger of *sai* against the *jar* is not allayed until the compensation has been collected. As mentioned above, the payment is a part of *riti-thiti* and the amount of compensation is also determined according to *riti-thiti* through negotiation between the two parties' representatives, i.e. *panchas*. If the two parties cannot agree on the amount, or if the adulterer pays nothing, the aggrieved husband will go to court or to a medium of the deity Masta. Strangely, the size of the fine is accepted among the villagers to be Rs.1,001, which may come from the amended amount of fine stipulated in 1975. If negotiations regarding the amount reach a stage of deadlock, the former husband asks for Rs.1,001. In other words he demands the amount written in the Muluki Ain and, by doing so, indicates that he will take legal action. In sum, *jari* is more a form of marriage or remarriage than short-term adultery. Furthermore, *jari katne* is not mere blood revenge taken on a seducer but the repudiation of an unfaithful wife through the collection of compensation from the seducer. In the following example, I describe the process of *jari katne* in which negotiation over the price is essential.

JARI KATNE: COLLECTING COMPENSATION

B. Jari Katne*: Collecting Compensation.*

On 6 Bhadra (22 August) 1992, five men from Bistawara came to Ludku to claim *jari* compensation. The following morning both parties reached an agreement on the amount, and the payment was made in rugs and cash. This *jari katne* negotiation was different from the usual

[10]Commenting on compensation in 'adulterous marriage' (*jari*) among the Limbus, Jones & Jones (1976: 106) note: "compensation is ordinarily paid only if the aggrieved husband can gather support from close relatives and influential people". In eastern Nepalese Hindu society, however, compensation is usually collected since only then is the previous marital relation regarded as dissolved.

practice in the following ways: (1) The negotiation was peaceful and incurred no violence; (2) the *pancha*s did not take any bribes; and (3) the *sai* did not appear at the final stage of writing the receipt. In most cases, *jar* and *sai* do not participate in the actual negotiation but rather exchange *tika* (ritual forehead mark) after the compensation has been paid.

The elopement which led to the *jari katne* had taken place one year before. Dipak Upadhyaya (thirty-one) took a married but childless woman of Bistawara to his home as his wife on 10 Bhadra 1991. Dipak had lost his wife during labour that same month and began looking for a wife soon after the period of mourning, visiting his *kutumba* villages. He found the said woman in her natal village with the help of his mother's brother. The woman's husband was mentally handicapped (*lato*) and she felt disgraced by this. Thus it was that a man looking for a wife and a woman wanting to divorce came to meet each other. After a short conversation in the cattle shed, both consented to elope. In fact, his friends accompanied her to Ludku, fearing that the Bistas might take revenge.

The people of Bistawara first came to Ludku on 28 Bhadra 1991 to claim compensation. As they had threatened the woman's natal family soon after the elopement, her brother later came to warn Dipak to pay the compensation, though the natal family usually keeps silent on the daughter's elopement.[11] Then the Bistas came in the month of Kartik and Dipak told them that he would pay the compensation only after having a baby with his new woman because he had lost his former wife and child in labour after paying compensation for her. Dipak had a daughter in Srawan and the Bistas found it out and sent a messenger on 11 Srawan (26 July) to ask the chairman of the Village Development Committee of Ludku, a member of the Congress party, to be an intermediary and to fix the date of payment.

Thus the five men came to Ludku to claim the compensation. The main spokesman was Kalodas, a fifty-year-old Congress party member. Another was the former husband's father's elder brother's son (aged thirty). The other three older men were the husband's *sakh* (agnates). In the meantime the chairman of the VDC had sent a man to look for Dipak's lineage brothers.

The meeting was held in the open air, near the burning ghat. Negotiations began slowly at around three o'clock. The reason for the delay

---

[11]Among Tamangs and Limbus, the natal family of the woman in question can claim the compensation. This is because marriage is contracted with the brideprice which the husband pays to the father-in-law. For instance, of elopement among Tamangs, Holmberg (1989: 60) notes "the seductive and forceful undertones of elopement and capture are overlaid in the finalizing themes of reciprocity through post facto exchanges".

was that they were mainly awaiting the arrival of Dipak's lineage brothers. The chairman did not know how much Dipak had prepared in payment. Neither side had stated the price. With the chairman's help, I was permitted to tape-record the whole exchange. The transcription of the tape was later checked by the chairman.

After the arrival of the lineage brothers, it became clear that all Dipak had prepared was a horse and Rs.1,000. The demands of the Bista group were gradually revealed. It became clear that they would not accept the horse because neither the father-in-law nor the former husband could look after it since the former was a widower with a small baby, and the latter was mentally deficient. Thus the Bista group demanded that Dipak pay compensation in cash (*nagad*) and cloth (*janes*).

The group from Ludku consisted of Tunga (the chairman of VDC), Manasa and Gaurisankar (Dipak's father's elder brother's sons), and Padma (a *sakh* who shares an ancestor with Dipak five generations back). In addition, there were some onlookers from another village whose names were Laksimi and Bhim. The Ludku party often suspended the negotiations and held private meetings to work on the strategy they would follow in the negotiation. The first separate meeting went as follows:

Tunga: We understand the Bistas' demand. They don't want to take the horse but will take cloth instead. They say they have no intention of going to *devata* (a deity) or to *raja* (law court). Manasa, you are a man of the 'family', tell us how much you can give them.

Manasa: What more can I tell you? What can I do if Dipak says he has nothing else to give? I am ashamed to attend this meeting. I haven't talked about this with my lineage brother, Dipak.

Gauri: We should ask Dipak whether he can pay the compensation in cash or not.

Laksimi: Nowadays demands can be anything up to Rs.25,000. So we'll have to offer at least Rs.10,000.

Tunga: We can't send them back empty-handed. You, brothers, must find out tonight where the money is and how much.

Padma: Dipak says he went to his friend in the village of Pabwais to ask for some money but got nothing.

Gauri: Dipak says he can't afford to pay more than Rs.1,000 and a horse.

Padma: But the Bistas don't want the horse. We've got to give them some *lyu* (rough rugs) and *ganecha* (pile rugs), and Rs.2,000-4,000 in cash.

Gauri: What will Dipak say?

Tunga: We don't need to ask him. We are the ones that will act as witnesses for him if he's taken to court, so he should go along with our decision. He is free to do whatever he wants, if he doesn't regard us as his *pancha*s. We've discovered that he has nothing but a horse to offer. You, brothers, must help him. You must provide him with the money.

Laksimi: It's been a year since he took the woman from Bistawara. We can't send the Bistas back empty-handed.

Tunga: He should alleviate the disgrace (*laji ko marnu*).

Manasa: I said that I couldn't help him when he came to see me.

Tunga: You can't say that you can't help him.

Padma: Brothers, you must at least bring Rs.6,000.

Tunga: The *jari* price these days is no less than Rs.5,000 in cash and Rs.4,000-5,000 in cloth.

Laksimi: Dipak may not agree to our decision.

Tunga, Padma, Manasa, Gauri, and the others returned to the meeting circle and sat down. The negotiation with the Bistas recommenced.

Tunga: Dipak has only got a horse and one thousand rupees to offer.

Kalodas: From what you're saying it seems like you've never been involved in *jari* before and that this is your first negotiation. But in fact, you should know the amount by now. After all, how many times have you taken or paid *jari* compensation? One of you has committed an offence. You have destroyed the family (*ghar uthaidine*). You must pay the compensation and we must take it. You don't have to give us too much but we, in turn, can't accept too little.

Padma: We're not hiding anything. We'll give you whatever he can afford but please don't demand too high a price.

Kalodas: You say that Dipak can't give us much. We say that the former husband can't accept too little. What can we do? We won't take much. Please don't give us less. We'll agree to a middle price since Dipak's offer does not meet with our demands and it is you who can decide the price. Please tell us how much cash and how much cloth you'll give us.

Padma: All right. I'll tell you the price. The *jari* compensation will consist of cloth worth Rs.6,000 and Rs.3,000 cash.

Kalodas: How can you offer us only Rs.3,000 cash and Rs.6,000 worth of cloth when the cost of *Dumini ko jari* [an impure caste woman's elopement's compensation] has reached Rs.15,000-20,000. Give us Rs.1,001 instead (according to the Codes). I am leaving for Bistawara now. In our village we have two *jari* cases in process. I will take you, the chairman, to show you how these negotiations go on.

The Ludku villagers once again gathered away from the meeting and their discussion went as follows:

Tunga: It's hard for us to go above Rs.3,000 cash and Rs.6,000 cloth.

Padma: Yes, because on top of that we've got to pay *jare patho* and *piune patho* (a goat for a feast). We will add another Rs.1,000 to make it up to Rs.10,500 and that's as far as we'll go.

Laksimi: As I see it, if the total value of the cash and cloth adds up to between Rs.10,000 and 12,000, it will be all right.

Padma: The moneylender didn't give Dipak any cash but he gave him a piece of pile rug (*ganecha*) worth Rs.4,000. And Dipak owns a piece of rough rug (*lyu*) worth Rs.2,000.

Tunga: Well, shall we go back to the negotiations? They've already said that they won't accept Rs.3,000 cash and the rugs which are worth Rs.6,000. The *ganecha* is worth Rs.4,000 and *lyu* is worth Rs.2,000. So, if we give the Bistas Rs.4,000 in cash in addition to them, the total will reach Rs.10,000.

Bhim: But the method of calculating *jari* compensation is different from normal financial transactions. If you've paid Rs.3,000 for goods, the goods will be calculated as being worth Rs.6,000. If you have paid Rs.6,000, the goods will be calculated as being worth Rs.12,000. The values doubles up according to *jari* calculation.

The group of Ludku villagers returned to the meeting circle.

Tunga: A man of honour (*ijjat*) doesn't abduct a married woman who is then called *arukako bigreko sindur* (a woman polluted by another) as a result of her actions. Money has its proper place but honour does too. I haven't been involved in *jari katne* negotiations for these four-five years so that I cannot tell you the price in the *jari* way. The *ganecha* will be worth Rs.6,000 and the *lyu* will be worth Rs.4,000.

Bista: We don't want *ganecha*. We want Rs.30,000 in cash.

Kalodas: If we'd claimed Rs.40,000 or 50,000 at the outset, we would barter with you. It would be shameful. As we've said, the former husband wants neither *ganecha* nor a horse but cash. First of all, we should agree on the cash and then we'll talk about *janes* (textile). I don't want *ganecha*. Please give me *lyu* and *kapada* (cloth) in its stead.

Laksimi: Why did the woman elope if her 'husband' was strong? If our 'man' had been strong, he would have married a single girl by himself.

Tunga: Your party, the husband, didn't pay any money for the woman. He just put *sindur* (vermillion) on her hair as a sign of marriage.

Bista: We need *jari* compensation.

Bista: Please tell us what you can and can't. Today the price of a castrated goat (*khasi*) is Rs.3,000 to 3,500. Our woman is worth more than a goat. You will be shamed if you say the *jari* woman's price is only Rs.3,000. If we bought a she-calf, we'd have to pay Rs.30,000 to 32,000. Let that be the *jari* price.

Tunga: It's easy for a housewife to give you something if there is plenty of food in her house. But if the larder's empty, how can she give you anything?

Kalodas: You've got to make Dipak 'hot'. The seed oil only runs when the hammer has become hot after hitting.

Laksimi: Have you heard Dipak's ideas on the matter? If you are not sure of his intentions, you will be disgraced.

Kalodas: Will you give us the price according to Ain (the Code) or the price according to Village tradition? We'll lose face if we fail to collect the *jari* compensation owed to us.

Tunga: And we will be shamed if we fail to pay the *jari* compensation. People will ask how the man could take the woman if he could not pay the *jari* compensation.

Kalodas: Let's judge things according to their true values. If you say you can't pay the price, we'll stop the meeting here and now. And we'll go to the highest authority. Let's put it to the deity and see the consequences of this wrongdoing.

Laksimi: The amount of *jari* depends on the ability of the payer.

Bhim: We beg you to accept the compensation which Dipak can pay now.

Kalodas: If Dipak says he won't pay the *jari*, we'll take out a lawsuit against him. And in that case you, the *pancha*s, will have to be the witnesses and say that Dipak has taken the woman from a man of Bistawara.

Tunga: Whatever we say, it's Dipak who has to pay the *jari* compensation.

When it began to get dark, all the negotiators went back to Ludku.

That night the five men from Bistawara were housed by Dipak's lineage brother. During the night Tunga and Padma persuaded Dipak and his lineage brothers to pay at least Rs.6,000 in cash and at seven o'clock the following morning the negotiations restarted. Dipak was asked to wait nearby for the outcome of the negotiations.

Kalodas: We'll neither take too much *jari* nor too little. Please give us the compensation according to custom. You should bear in mind that the father-in-law is widowed, that his small baby may die and that the *sai* (former husband) is in effect 'widowed' when you say you are not going to pay the compensation. Please let Dipak know what the ways of *santan* (descendants), *kul* (lineage), and *dharma* (religious duty) demand. Ludku has been the ruling village of the area since the days of ancestor Sankar Upadhyaya and its inhabitants have always obeyed the rules (*thiti*). If you don't pay the compensation and so break the rules, all the inhabitants will follow your example. The former husband and the former father-in-law have no power to raise a lawsuit. Furthermore you are our *ishta mitra* (acquaintances and friends) and we don't really want to accuse you of anything. If you do *jari katne*, please show yourselves to be honourable. May the deity punish such a man who does not pay the compensation after taking a woman from another, pleading that he has no money. Give us whatever he can afford and send us away if we ask for any more.

At 8:30, Rs.6,000 in cash and the *lyu* and *ganecha* were brought but the Bistas were not satisfied with them, so one of Dipak's lineage brothers gave an additional Rs.1,000. Then a receipt (*bharpai*) was written out by Padma on behalf of the former husband (*sai*), Manaraji Tiwari. The receipt specified the name, age, address, and the father's name of the *sai*, the woman, and of the seducer (*jar*). The *sai* stated:

> My wife (*bivahita swasne*) left me, *dosro linga pari* (having found the second genital), and eloped with Dipak Upadhyaya. I asked the latter for my jewellery (*gahana*) and clothes. The latter paid me back the total Rs.20,000 including my *gahana* and clothes, and I was satisfied with the payment. As I am mentally handicapped, my *hakdar* (right holder, i.e. close agnate), Gurubhakta Tiwari, with whom I share an ancestor dating back two generations, took Rs.20,000 on my behalf. Gurubhakta sealed this document with his thumb in the presence of witnesses. This document was penned as *bharpai*

> (receipt) of *jari katne* in the presence of the witnesses in the house of Dipak Upadhyaya. This *bharpai* was written to confirm that Gurubhakta would take responsibility if Manaraji Tiwari afterwards demanded *jari ghar gahana* (compensation and jewellery) from Dipak. 07 Bhadra v.s. 2049 (1992) [written by Padma].

> Two men from Bistawara and two men from Ludku including two spokesmen signed the document as witnesses. Both sets exchanged *tika*. The document was given to Dipak, who appeared for the first time at the meeting. After the *bharpai* was written, the Bistas demanded Rs.300 as village tax in addition to an offering to the deity (*devata dana*) and a goat for the feast (*jare patho, piune patho*). The latter two offerings are common in *jari katne* but the village tax is not. However, Rs.300 was paid but only Rs.50 was paid as *devata dana* and Rs.50 as *jare patho* and *piune patho*. The Bistas were again hesitant to accept so little and eventually two Rs.20 notes were added to make the amount acceptable. Thus in all Rs.7,440 cash, and *lyu* and *ganecha* were given and an agreement on the amount of Rs.20,000 was made. Dipak had in fact paid only Rs.700 for the *lyu* and Rs.2,500 for the *ganecha*!

It is useful to summarize the main features of the negotiation. The *pancha*s are, in principle, the representatives of the parties but they do not always voice the interests of the latter. An agreement is primarily made according to custom. The main spokesman is an experienced negotiator who is skilled in referring to these customs. The parties concerned have to obey the decision of the *pancha*s. In some cases, the *pancha*s of both sides collaborate with each other in order to extract a large amount of compensation from the seducer and take a certain portion of it as a bribe from the former husband. Other, smaller amounts of money called *jare patho* and *piune patho* are also given to the *pancha*s representing the former husband as a fee for their negotiations.

The payment of compensation consists of textiles, cloth, cash, and livestock, and the actual amount of payment does not reflect the amount stated on the document, the latter being a false figure. The reason for the false figure on the document is, according to the villagers, so that they can then use it as proof when claiming compensation if the woman in question re-elopes. Since, in the case of a second elopement, the amount of compensation is reduced to half that of the first one, it is better to write down a higher figure on the document of a first *jari*. It is said that a woman who has eloped more than three times is not worth claiming compensation over.

In addition to compensation, the *gahana* which the eloped woman is wearing must be returned to the former husband. This is because it was given to the bride at the wedding ceremony by the bridegroom or his family, though there is a great deal of ambiguity as to whether the jewellery belongs to the bride or her conjugal family.[12]

A woman who has eloped cannot retrieve her dowry from her husband. But what is the relation between *jari* compensation and dowry?[13] When I asked this question during the *jari* negotiations, the negotiators seemed to be amazed at my question and said that dowry and *jari* could not be seen as related. *Kanyadan* is, after all, a pure gift and a merit-making action and therefore should not be returned. The parents and natal family of the woman in question, who have given her as *kanyadan* to their son-in-law, should not be involved in her elopement. They must keep silent even after the elopement is revealed and are not allowed to meet her until the compensation has been paid.

In the negotiations, the aggrieved husband's party often threatens the seducer's party saying that the husband is ready to appeal to the law courts or to bring down a curse[14] and divine afflictions (*devata lagnu*) if the seducer does not agree to his demands. The seducer's disregard for a customary solution arouses serious hostility and prompts the aggrieved husband to make good such threats. If the negotiation for an anticipated amount of compensation ends in failure or if the payment is not made, the aggrieved husband will indeed resort to a deity (*devata*) or law court (*raja*). However, even if a lawsuit is instigated, its purpose is not to impose a legal punishment upon the seducer for adultery but to pressure him to pay the full compensation.

AN ATTEMPTED INCEST AND OATH-TAKING

In Brahman society adultery with a woman married in the village, i.e. sexual intercourse with one's mother-in-law, elder sister-in-law (*bhaujyu*), younger sister-in-law, or daughter-in-law (*buhari*) is regarded as inces-

---

[12]Accusation of the loss of the jewellery is not limited to the elopement. This is, as Bennett (1983: 170) points out, "a standard accusation made about the daughter-in-law" by her conjugal family. The eloping daughter-in-law is also readily blamed by her conjugal family for the theft of the jewellery.

[13]Dowry consists of three kinds of gifts: (1) clothing and jewellery which the bride retains as her personal property; (2) cooking utensils and eating vessels which become the property of the groom's joint family; and (3) gifts of clothing to female kin of the groom.

[14]The accuser will go to a deity to place a curse on the seducer. Such a curse is generally referred to as *pukar*, but if an individual promises to make an offering to or service for the deity in exchange for the god inflicting punishment upon his wrongdoer, the curse is referred to as *doeri*. It is believed that the god's afflictions do not cease until the wrongdoer and the victim are reconciled through the former's compensation for the latter's loss or damage. The wrongdoer also makes an offering to the deity in an attempt to lift the afflictions. The reconciliation in front of the deity is called *devata suddhaune* ('purifying' the deity). *Suddhaune* is an idiom used by local people to designate the ritual procedure. It is uncertain whether the deity itself is polluted or not.

tuous (*had nata*) and may involve excommunication of the parties concerned. Among other castes, however, such relations are not seen as incest. For instance, levirate marriage, i.e. remarriage with a brother-in-law, is common and even expected of widows in the Chetri caste and lower, impure castes.

Kinship is generally called *nata*, while members of a patrilineal group (*kul* or *thar*) are believed to share the substance of bone (*had*). Sexual intercourse between the members of a patrilineage (which includes, in the local understanding, in-married females) is referred to as *had nata* which literally means 'the kin who share a bone'. Of the term *had nata*, Krause reports a similar usage in Rara village of western Nepal:

> Nata denotes a relationship in which people share bodily substances [such as bone, flesh and blood] ... These substances are passed on directly from a father to his children and this theory of conception provides the basis for *bansa*, *kul* and *pariwar* [family] as exogamous units within which marriage and sexual relations amount to incest (*had nata lagne*). (Krause 2002: 436)

Women's membership is indicated not by a lineage (*thar*) name but by teknonymy. For instance, a woman is identified in terms of her relations: 'daughter of X' and 'wife of Y'. In other words, a woman belongs to her father's lineage before marriage and to her husband's lineage after marriage. At marriage, responsibility for (*kartabya*) and authority over (*adhikar*) the woman is transferred from her father to her husband. On the wedding day her father performs a funeral ritual symbolizing his daughter's death. Her husband's kin will henceforth have the duty to perform her funeral even if she dies while visiting her natal home. In the case of elopement, as was shown earlier, the woman's parents have to keep silent while her husband has the authority or the right to demand the compensation for adultery from her seducer.

Guidelines for a woman's behaviour towards her senior affinal males are very strict in Brahman society, her behaviour being one of respect-avoidance. A *buhari* has to hide her face with a black woollen veil, and is not permitted to gaze at her affinal senior males, which is regarded as shameless. Bennett describes similar prescribed behaviour patterns in Chetri society in the Kathmandu Valley: "A daughter-in-law usually pulls the end of her sari up to cover her head in front of her father-in-law, and she is expected to always do this in the presence of her husband's elder brother. This latter relationship seems to be the most restricted. A woman and her husband's elder brother may never touch each other" (Bennett 1983: 172). Such avoidance of bodily contact between *buhari* and *jethi* (elder brother of husband) is referred to as *na chune* or, 'not to be touched', in Jumla, just as impure castes are for pure castes.[15] If a man touches his younger brother's or son's wife, he must sit under an inverted bamboo basket like a prisoner for a day, take a bath to purify himself of the 'moral dirt', and give her a small amount of money as *dakshina.* In effect, respect-avoidance serves, as Bennett points out, "to eliminate suspicion of sexual relations between the daughter-in-law and her father-in-law or elder brother-in-law by replacing ambiguity with strictly prescribed mutual behaviour patterns" (ibid.: 172).

The one exception in the daughter-in-law's relations with affinal men is her relationship with her husband's younger brother (*devar*). With him, she may have a more relaxed, joking relationship, which is literally referred to as *thatta garne* (having a joke) and which can develop into sexual relationship. In this relationship, Bennett notes, a woman may have "some emotional outlet in her husband's family" (ibid.: 213).

Both sexual intercourse with one's brother-in-law and father-in-law and with one's own brother and father, are known as *had nata* incest. Incest with one's husband's elder brother is called *jethi nata* while that with one's own brother is *bhai nata.* There is no difference in the terms used to describe the offence or in the punishment used for 'intra-group' sexual offences and 'group-wife' sexual offences in Sija Brahman society.[16]

It seems contradictory that having sexual intercourse with one's elder sister-in-law with whom there is a 'joking relationship' and having sexual relations with one's younger sister-in-law with whom there is 'respect-avoidance' are both regarded as incest. However, in the absence of comparative data, I cannot judge whether this adjudged similarity is unique to Sija Brahman society or not.

The Muluki Ain of 1854 refers to three kinds of incestuous relations: incest with a sister or daughter, incest with one's mother-in-law or stepmother, and incest with the wife of an elder brother. As to the punishment for the third offence, the Ain prescribes that Brahmans be degraded from their caste standing and expelled from the country (Adhikari 1976: 108).

Incest is regarded as a sin (*pap*) or an act forbidden by *dharma* and the terms *dos* (fault, sin, guilt) and *aparadhi* (sinful, criminal, guilty) are used by the villagers to explain it. The villagers' reaction to this matter is not one of horror but of shame. Since incest may lead to the offender's excommunication or at least some form of punishment, the breach is variously redressed and often socially and politically manipulated. It can be

---

[15]When a bride first enters the groom's house, she is forced to touch her elder brothers-in-law. On the day of Holi she is expected to sprinkle them with water. Both rituals are referred to as *jethi chuwaune* (touching the elder brother-in-law).

[16]These distinctions are suggested by Goody (1956: 293) as one of the features of sexual offence in unilineal descent societies.

concealed and/or revealed for different reasons as I show in the following case.

C. A Case of Attempted Incest

> This episode began with Devi's allegation that she had nearly been seduced by a young man called Govinda. According to Devi, at midnight on 30 September, Govinda battered at the door of her house where she was sleeping with her young son, and said that he had something to give her. He tried to entice her away from her home but she refused to open the door. Then he ran away. Her allegation implied that Govinda had come to her with the intention to seduce her, but failed.
>
> Devi is a Jaisi Brahman, twenty-two years old, whose husband had been away in Nepalgunj for three months. Govinda, twenty-seven years old, was born in Ludku but had migrated to Rajapur with his wife several years before, where he had a son and a daughter. He had recently come back to see his mother in Ludku to ask for money to pay for land in Rajapur. The matter had kept him in Ludku for a few months. Although Govinda is older then Devi, their kinship relation is that of *devar-bhaujyu* (younger brother and elder sister-in-law). Govinda and Devi's husband share an ancestor who goes back five generations.
>
> On the night of 1 October, Devi visited Harigopal, a Dhadar Masta priest, and asked him to accompany her to Govinda's house. She also went to call for the former Pradhan but instead of the former Pradhan his son, Koptan, came. At the house of Govinda, Harigopal was told about what had happened. He said to Govinda, "Don't spread this episode around. She is your *bhaujyu*. Place five rupees here and tell her that you didn't intend to insult her." Govinda did so and in the presence of Harigopal and Koptan bowed at the feet of Devi.
>
> However, on 2 October, Devi's husband's elder brother, Noblal, who was a *mukhiya* (village leader) as well as a *dhami* (medium) of Tharpa Masta, was told of the episode and became angry. He visited the priest, the chairman of the VDC (a newly elected village leader), and Govinda to ask what to do about it. They agreed that Govinda should undergo an ordeal in front of Masta, either Dhadar or Tharpa. The reason for Noblal's dissatisfaction with the original settlement was unclear but his hidden intent seemed to be to extract some money from Govinda as an atonement for the attempted seduction.

On the evening of the same day I paid a visit to Harigopal. I did not know the exact details of the above incidents but I had heard rumours about them. After the ritual greetings, we started to talk of recent issues including the matter at hand when the chairman of the VDC dropped by, then Govinda's mother arrived, and soon after Govinda himself. Our conversation developed into an open discussion of the matter. Noblal then arrived. Govinda began by protesteing his innocence as follows:

> On the afternoon of 30 September I went to Noblal's house where Devi, her mother-in-law, and some other women were pounding rice into *chiura* (flattened rice). Devi asked me where I'd come from and I told her that I'd come from the village and asked her what she was doing. She said she was making *chiura*. I asked her to give me some and she laughed and agreed. She asked me why I hadn't been to her field hut to take *khir* (rice pudding) before. I said how I could visit her when she was alone at the hut and added that I would visit there only if Noblal *dajyu* was there. I asked her to give me some *khir*, if she was going to give me some. She said 'where can I get *khir*?' I said it was alright if she did not want to give me *khir*. I sat down and had a smoke. She gave me some *chiura* which I ate. She said she was going to cook some potatoes and invited me to have some. I accepted.
>
> I went back home and had some *roti* (bread) and then I went back to her house where she and her family were having a meal. Noblal's mother invited me to have some *bhat* but I refused because I was full. Then she offered me some *bhat* with yogurt, which I ate. Then uncle Panna came in and we chatted until late at night. Whilst I was there, Noblal's mother asked me for some *hashish*. So I prepared some and we, 'mother' and 'son', smoked it. Both of us went into a trance and I told her that I was going to go home. She gave me a torch because it was dark by then but because of *hashish*, I fell down in a rice field on my way home and the torch went out. I took the route that went past school, because I suddenly remembered that I'd been invited to join a drama rehearsal there. I passed by Karna's house (Devi's husband), and I tripped over a ladder leaning against his roof, making a noise as I did so. Devi shouted out, asking who it was. I was ashamed to hear her voice and ran away. I slept at Prem's house, a male friend of mine. So as you can see, Devi made up the story that I'd gone there to seduce her (*pasi lagnu*).

At that stage, the points at issue became clear to me. Devi gave the impression of having tried to tempt him with her affectionate attention, although the comments of Govinda's mother were indeed exaggerated: "Devi invited my son to her house and fed him *chiura*, *bhat* and *hashish* to accuse him of seduction." As the priest pointed out, why had she kept silent for a day if it was really an attempted seduction? She said that Govinda had come to seduce her two nights before but she only made the allegation later. She told the story to a Ghatri woman while cutting grass. The Ghatri woman told it to her own husband who told Devi's mother-in-law. If it *had* been a seduction, she should have first let it be known to her mother-in-law or her elder brother-in-law. The priest's wife said: "Devi should have seized him at that time or at least cried out for help and handed him over to the *mukhiya* or the police, as customs demand."

It is true to say that both Devi and Govinda showed some affection for each other. After all, *dewar* and *bhaujyu* are allowed to have a joke with each other. But Devi's behaviour appeared to have gone beyond the bounds of such a joking relationship. Noblal also admitted that his *buhari*, Devi, could have been somewhat overindulgent while her husband was away. But who should be to blame and be punished, and to what extent? If Govinda had battered at the door instead of stumbling over a ladder and running away, he would be to blame (*dosh*) and should be punished with a severe beating (*pitne*, *kutne*). If Devi had consented, both of them would be to blame. Furthermore, they should be ostracized from the village for having committed *had nata* incest. At the very least, they were to be criticized for showing a foolish lack of prudence about their *devar-bhaujyu* relationship.

The question arose as to the level at which the dispute should be settled. An intra-group solution was emphasized throughout the discussion because the matter was "that of house, of village, and of shame" as the chairman of the VDC pointed out. The matter was not to be disclosed to the public (*bahira na nikalne*), as Harigopal affirmed. "It is we who discuss and settle it, whether fault (*doshi*) is found or not. This is a matter to be solved at home by as small a number of *pancha*s as possible, without being brought to the attention of the the police." If Devi rejected the settlement made by the *pancha*s and went to a court of law, the *pancha*s would be disgraced (*gu khane*). Furthermore, the *pancha*s warned Noblal not to involve the people of another village in this dispute, saying that all of the *pancha*s would take the side of Govinda if he did so. In the end the *pancha*s declared that they themselves would impose a penalty (*sajay dine*) on Govinda by their own hand. Govinda agreed to this saying that he would be glad to be penalized (*sajay khanu*) by them, his brothers.

> After the meeting was over, I asked them for permission to be present at the ritual of the ordeal (*chuwasade*) which was to be held on the evening of the following day, and left to sleep. But early the next morning I was told that *chuwasade* had been carried out that very night. According to one of the *pancha*s, soon after our departure Devi, who was incensed by the ad hoc meeting, went to Harigopal's house and hit Govinda with a stick crying out that he was a liar. Then Noblal slapped her in defiance of the 'untouchable' status of their relationship. The

people around them tried to stop the brawl and there followed another meeting at Harigopal's house, where a *mukhiya*, a former school teacher, and the chairman of the VDC were invited as *pancha*s.

One of the *pancha*s who had been present at the meeting detailed the discussion to me. According to him, questioning revealed that each of the parties concerned had made three mistakes (*galti*). In Devi's case, she had (a) kept silent for a day after the incident took place; (b) asked Govinda for a cigarette, and (c) invited him to have *khir*. The mistakes that Govinda made were (a) to have given her a cigarette; (b) to have battered at the door of her house at midnight, and (c) to have tried to lure her away from the house saying, "Come out, *bhaujyu*."

On the matter of the gravity of their moral offence and the consequent punishment, the *pancha*s were divided. One party insisted on bringing both Devi and Govinda to a court of law and ostracizing them from the village, as both of them were transgressors (*doshi*) of the prescribed *devar-bhaujyu* relationship. The other party's view was that they had not actually committed incest (*kam ma bigareko chaina*), having simply been overfamiliar with each other (*mukh ma bigareko*). So they should touch a sacred object to prove their innocence (*nirdosi*) of *had nata* incest.

On top of their efforts to achieve a satisfactory settlement, the *pancha*s abused Govinda and Devi throughout the meeting with comments like, "Both of you are like dogs", "Dogs can do that", "Cattle can do that", and "You have disgraced us" (*mukh ma moso lagyo*). You have shamed our village". Concerning the relation of *devar-bhaujyu*, they said: "*Devar* and *bhaujyu* can have a joke with each other, but they should neither smoke together nor entice each other."

Eventually, both the moderates and the hardliners came to the decision that the parties should undergo *chuwasade*. Generally, a person performing *chuwasade* must ready himself/herself by fasting and bathing because he/she must be in a state of purity if he/she is to touch a sacred object. Unusually, however, the participants in the meeting did not wait until the next day but decided to carry out the ritual there and then. Harigopal, the priest of Dhadar Masta, brought a package of sacred bells, holy vessels, and canopies which he kept at his house. One of the *pancha*s first touched Govinda's head with the sacred package and Govinda made an oath (*kasam*), saying: "I am not guilty. Banish my descendants, deprive me of food, and kill me in half a day if I am guilty." Then he touched Devi's feet and apologized to her for going to her room at midnight to invite her outside. The *pancha*s fined him Rs. 500, but he was too poor to make the payment. Devi, in turn, made an oath while touching the sacred objects and said: "Banish me if I have told a lie (*jhuto*) and if Govinda did neither come to my place nor tell me to come out to take something. He looked down on me as a lonely wife and tried to lure me away from my house. Banish him in half a day. Let him have no release from rebirth (*ubo mukh*)."

After *chuwasade* had been carried out, a written agreement concerning Govinda's deed was made and signed by the *pancha*s. The paper specified the name, the age, the father's name and the address of Govinda, but told a different story from the facts. It stated that "at 11 o'clock of the night of 15 Asoj (1 October), Govinda went to Karka Neupane's house when his wife was out, and broke into the house to steal a silver anklet (*kalli*) and a golden ornament (*tilari*). When Devi came back home, Govinda ran away. She could not catch him and cried out for help. She reported to the *pancha*s that the above two sets of ornaments had been stolen by him. Afterwards the *pancha*s seized Govinda and searched him. He confessed to the theft and returned the ornaments to Noblal Neupane. This agreement has been written according to Govinda's statement. This paper can be referred to in response to any accusation made at court and is sealed with Govinda's right and left thumbs."

In this 'agreement' a theft was substituted for the alleged incestuous behaviour and the date that the incident took place was changed so that the one-day gap disappeared. Devi's response was also modified to the 'ideal' response expected of a modest wife. The aim of the paper was, according to the *pancha*s, to show that Govinda had indeed gone to Devi's house but without the intention of having an incestuous affair with her (*nata gota ma testo kam garne*). The agreement also confirmed that this was the final word on the matter and that Noblal, Devi, and Karka would be unable to take any further action.

Incest is so subtle and ambiguous that it is often difficult to distinguish between a wrongdoer and a victim. A dispute does not always follow an offence of incest. If the woman concerned is married, her disgraced spouse is a potential accuser in the case but an accusation is seldom made. This is because the matter is regarded as one of shame and disgrace, and could threaten the stability of a family or a patrilineage. Consequently, the parties concerned try to conceal it from the public and solve it in a quiet manner. Occasionally, however, a rumour spreads about incestuous intercourse, but even so, this does not mean that the matter has reached the public since nobody dares to allege that it is incest without good reason or a reliable witness. If a person external to the party or parties concerned makes an accusation against him/them, it is likely that his motivation comes from a previous feud or hostility. Concealed offences can escape social sanctions but a woman polluted by incestuous intercourse is not allowed to stay in her husband's household. Therefore, the usual solution for a woman is elopement.

Sex is a source of pollution and extramarital intercourse is thought to produce great impurity on the side of the woman. Impurity is transferred through commensality and therefore cooked rice (*bhat*) cannot be accepted from a 'polluted' woman. A man is polluted and liable to degradation only if he accepts *bhat* from such a polluted wife. It is obvious, then, that for men, pollution is not brought about by intercourse, though in the case of incest, *bhat* should not be accepted from either the woman or the man concerned. Social punishment for incest takes the form of withdrawal from commensality. Since the Nepalese constitution of 1959 proclaimed all citizens to be equal before the law, degradation as a penal sanction has been abolished (see Höfer 1979: 203). Nevertheless, degradation as a social punishment is still alive in western Nepalese Hindu society.

CONCLUSION

Extramarital relations are generally regarded as non-dharmic. Incest is an offence against culturally defined relationships and punished with beating, fines, ostracism, or exclusion from *bhat* commensality, with punishment differing according to status. Such liaisons are immediately dissolved by the community. Abduction and elopement, however, can develop into conjugal unions, though rituals are necessary if an abducted girl is to become a *bivahita* wife. If abduction fails, payment of compensation (*jarimana*) is traditionally imposed upon the abductor. A woman who elopes becomes a *lyaita* wife after being repudiated by her former husband in exchange for her new husband's payment of compensation (*jari katne*). The change in women's status as a result of extramarital relations can be summarized as in Table 5.2.

Failed abductions, elopements, and exposed incest necessitate social sanctions since they infringe marital norms and consequently cause social disputes. Hence the roles of *gaunle* (village fellows), *pancha* (ad hoc councils), and *kachahari* (caste courts) are foremost in confirming the processes of union or dissolution, settling disputes, and imposing punishments upon the offender(s).

Table 5.2: Change in Women's Status due to Extramarital Relations

Extramarital relation	Woman's status	Social sanction
Abduction (*tipne*)	*kanya* → *bivahita*	Fine (*jarimana*)
Elopement (*jari*)	*bivahita* → *lyaita*	Compensation (*jari*)
Incest (*had nata*)	degraded	*bi-bhat*,* *jarimana*

Note: *exclusion from cooked rice commensality

The extramarital process is also manipulated or managed by the parties concerned, the villagers involved, and the *pancha*s. In inter-village disputes over abductions and elopements (as conjugal unions are village-exogamous), offences are often exaggerated and a heavy punishment or large compensation is required. Adding false accusations such as robbery or theft to the main accusation of extramarital relations is not uncommon in lawsuits.

In intra-village disputes over incest, on the other hand, offences tend to be concealed and consequently no penal action is taken. Though it may arbitrarily be disclosed within the community, great efforts are made to prevent the brute facts emerging to the outside world. The substitution of the theft of jewellery for the original charge of attempted incest in the case C documents exemplifies this. Furthermore, the eventual solution is the polluted woman's elopement through which the responsibility for the woman concerned is shifted to another man in a different village.

These machinations comprise two factors: recognition of the penal consequences of the offence, and the shame and disgrace which such an offence brings upon a family and the community at large. To recover their honour, the suspected guilty party produces exaggerated and, often, false accusations in order to impose a heavy penalty on the rival. To maintain honour, on the other hand, efforts are made to conceal the offence, by substituting another unambiguous and less shameful offence in its stead.

The role of the *pancha* differs in inter-village and intra-village disputes. It has two faces. As Dumont (1970: 180) put it,

> caste justice is Janus faced: one face is turned towards the exterior, and this is penal justice; the other is turned towards the interior, and this is justice by arbitration, by conciliation, tending both to re-establish harmony within the group and maintain the authority of the panchayat. Indeed, it is noticeable that this authority, though strong when it is a matter of preserving the group's status, is weak in the other case.

The *pancha* in western Nepal, however, is not the same as a caste (*jat*) *panchayat* in India. Ludku's *pancha* is based upon lineage membership and therefore includes various castes such as Upadhyaya Brahmans, Jaisi Brahmans, Hamals, and Khatris. They are first of all *gaunle* (village fellows) and at the same time *dajyu bhai* (brothers). When disputes take place, neighbours gather and notables – elderly and respected villagers skilled in mediation – are invited. The *pancha* is not an institutionalized assembly but an ad hoc council (cf. Berreman 1972: 280). It is hard to make a distinction between informal mediators and *pancha*s. As case C shows, a gathering of villagers can be transformed into a *pancha* meeting. Some notables and even-tempered villagers are repeatedly invited as *panchas* to settle disputes, but they are not necessarily members of the council. Notables enjoy a high reputation, but usually take no part in village politics.

The *pancha* also has real authority to impose penalties on offenders. A fine paid by an offender goes into the hands of the *pancha*. *Raja* (law court) and *devata* (Masta deities) are recognized as higher authorities and these are resorted to with the *pancha*'s agreement, or as a private solution. Going to *raja* or *devata* is commonly resorted to by disputants, as is shown in the negotiation of *jari katne*.

The Masta deity is invoked in *chuwasade* rituals as a means of proving innocence, in which disputants touch a sacred object and swear that they are innocent of the charge. The deity is also invoked in cursing a rival (*pukar*). These invocations are based on the belief that the deity punishes the wrongdoer and administers justice in a way similar to the law courts.

REFERENCES

Adam, L. 1949-50. 'Criminal Law and Procedure in Nepal a Century Ago: Notes Left by Brian H. Hodgson'. *The Far Eastern Quarterly* 9: 146-68.

Adhikari, K.K. 1976. 'Criminal Cases and Their Punishments before and during the Period of Jang Bahadur'. *Contributions to Nepalese Studies* 3 (1): 105-16.

Bennett, L. 1979. 'Tradition and Change in the Legal Status of Nepalese Women'. *The Status of Women in Nepal*, Vol. 1: *Background Report*, Part 2. Kathmendu: CEDA, Tribhuvan University.

——. 1983. *Dangerous Wives and Sacred Sisters: Social and Symbolic Roles of High-Caste Women in Nepal*. New York: Columbia University Press.

Berreman, G.D. 1972. *Hindus of the Himalayas*. 2nd edn., revised and enlarged. Berkeley: University of California Press.

Campbell, J.G. 1978. 'Consultation with Himalayan Gods: A Study of Oracular Religion and Alternative Values in Hindu Jumla'. Ph.D. dissertation, Columbia University.

Caplan, L. 1971. 'Cash and Kind: Two Media of "Bribery" in Nepal'. *Man* 6: 266-88.

Comaroff, J.L. and S. Roberts. 1981. *Rules and Process: The Cultural Logic of Disputes in an African Context*. Chicago: The University of Chicago Press.

Dumont, L. 1970. *Homo Hierarchicus: The Caste System and Its Implications*. English edition. Chicago: The University of Chicago Press.

——. 1983. *Affinity as a Value: Marriage Alliance in South India, with Comparative Essays on Australia*. Chicago: The University of Chicago Press.

Fezas, J. 1993. 'Custom and Written Law in Nepal: the Regulations Concerning Private Revenge for Adultery according to the Code of 1853', in G. Toffin (ed.), *Nepal, Past and Present*, pp. 3-20. Paris: CNAS.

Fruzzetti, L.M. 1982. *The Gift of a Virgin: Women, Marriage and Ritual in a Bengali Society*. New Brunswick, N.J.: Rutgers University Press.

Gaborieau, M. 1976. 'Preliminary Report on the god Masta', in J.T. Hitchcock and R. Jones (eds.), *Spirit Possession in the Nepal Himalayas*, pp. 217-43. Warminster: Aris & Philips.

Good, A. 1991. *The Female Bridegroom*. Oxford: Clarendon Press.

Goody, J.R. 1956. 'A Comparative Approach to Incest and Adultery'. *British Journal of Sociology* 7: 286-305.

Hodgson, B.H. 1880. *Miscellaneous Essays Relating to Indian Subjects*, Vol. II. London: Trubner & Co.

Höfer, A. 1979. *The Caste Hierarchy and the State in Nepal: A Study of the Muluki Ain of 1954*. Innsbruck: Universitätsverlag Wagner.

Holmberg, D.H. 1989. *Order in Paradox: Myth, Ritual, and Exchange among Nepal's Tamang*. Ithaca and London: Cornell University Press.

Jones, R.L. and S.K. Jones. 1976. *The Himalayan Woman: A Study of Limbu Women in Marriage and Divorce*. Palo Alto, California: Mayfield.

Krause, B. 2002. *The Shahas of West Nepal: Political Autonomy and Economic Dependence in Former Nepalese Economy*. New Delhi: Adarsh Enterprises.

Sharma, P.R. 1971. 'The Matwali Chhetri of Western Nepal'. *Himalayan Review* IV. Kathmandu: Nepal Geographical Society. (Reissued in P.R. Sharma. 2004. *State and Society in Nepal*. Katmandu: Himal Books.)

——. 1972. *Preliminary Study of the Art and Architecture of the Karnali Basin, West Nepal*. Paris: CNRS.

Turner, R.L. 1980 (1931). *A Comparative and Etymological Dictionary of the Nepali Language*. New Delhi: Allied Publisher.

Yasuno, H. 1999. 'Popular Hinduism ni okeru Hyoi Cult no Ichizuke: Nishi Nepal no Masta Cult eno Bunseki-Shikaku wo Motomete (Spirit Possession and Popular Hinduism: A Study of the Masta Cult of Western Nepal)'. *JCAS Review* 2 (2): 71-96 (in Japanese).

6

'I Don't Mind Being Born a Woman': The Status and Agency of Women in Yolmo, Nepal

SEIKA SATO

INTRODUCTION: THE STATUS AND AGENCY OF SOUTH ASIAN WOMEN

"Why I had to be born as a woman, why I had to be born as a man, until today this question I've never thought of. With what I am, I am contented," said Dawa, a Yolmo woman in her mid thirties, replying to my question whether she believed in the saying that the reason why women suffer more than men as a rule is because of their own bad deeds in past lives.[1] This saying, which could be seen as deriving from Buddhist (and Hindu) teachings of rebirth, has wide circulation among contemporary Yolmo people. Dawa herself was also well aware of it, and right after the quotation above, had this to say: "[though] I also have heard people saying this many times, you see."[2] If this saying belongs to the stock of Yolmo common sense, her response also sounds rather commonplace as a Yolmo woman. Among those women whom I have had the chance to ask, almost no one expressed serious resentment against being born a woman in this life, nor did they question if the saying contained any truth at all.[3]

---

[1]For their thoughtful comments I am grateful to Keiko Yamanaka and other participants of the seminar where an earlier version of this paper was presented. I am especially in debt to David N. Gellner, whose generous input made this paper much better in many ways. The remaining errors and shortcomings are mine.

[2]The quote is from the interviews discussed in more detail below.

[3]This applies also to the case of an old Yolmo woman, whose life story is dealt with extensively in Desjarlais (2003). Her words in response to the question, what her life would have been like if

Even from this little fragment of conversation, it is possible to detect inconsistent layers of experience that being born a woman among the Yolmo entails. On the ideological level, women are said to be of 'lower' birth and inferior to men, and Yolmo women are themselves familiar with this discourse. Their self-esteem, nevertheless, does not seem to be affected by that knowledge at all. Somehow they appear to be quite contented with being born a woman; on a casual acquaintance, Yolmo women would hardly strike one as oppressed beings. They are generally cheerful, outgoing, assertive, friendly, as well as hard-working and liable to laugh often and extremely well. One might easily conclude that this high-spiritedness of Yolmo women is a reflection of their high status in society, which must be at least not substantially 'lower' than, and perhaps roughly equal to, that of men. But on closer scrutiny, this view does not hold good. As we shall see, they *are* of lower status, restricted, and disadvantaged in a number of respects, quite neatly in line with that teaching of rebirth, even if the form and degree of subordination must be admitted to be rather benign in the South Asian context, e.g. when compared with the situation found in the high-caste Hindu communities who are the neighbours of the Yolmo.[4]

This chapter is part of a broader attempt to explore women's lives – what they do, why they do it, and what it means for them to be born a woman – in a specific contemporary cultural/social context, which I here gloss as 'Yolmo'.[5] I do this by asking how these seemingly inconsistent layers of

---

she had been born a boy, are presented thus: "[t]his time, I was born a woman. I can't be a man. Maybe in the next life, maybe I can be born a man." I do not presume that we can detect in this any resentment against being born a woman *in this life*. What we may sense here is nothing more than a vague wish to be realized *in her next life*. After I finished writing this article, I encountered a Yolmo woman who stated that she *had* wished to be born a man. But this one statement I believe does not require any substantial changes in the argument I am pursuing here.

[4] Or, to borrow Ortner's words (1996c: 186) used for the Sherpas, the Yolmo may be described "as pretty good ... on a scale of gender inequality across world cultures".

[5] 'Yolmo' was originally the indigenous name of a locale on the southern slopes of the Himalayas, stretching across the border of Sindhupalchowk and Nuwakot districts, which after the advent of Janajati politics in the 1990s, has been increasingly asserted and accordingly begun to be recognized (for themselves as well as for outsiders) as a name of an independent ethnic group or a Janajati. Their population figure was presented as 579 in the last 2001 census, which definitely by far underrepresented the 'actual' figure (the present chairperson of Nepal Hyolmo Samaj Sewa Sangh, a Yolmo ethnic organization, claims that the figure should be above 50,000 at least). The extremely low return in the census could be due to the rather 'immature' state of ethnic consciousness among the Yolmo, or to some kind of deficiency in the counting procedure, or both. Their recent efforts to assert their 'Yolmo' identity in the context of Janajati politics can also be seen to be a newer version of their effort to separate themselves from the somewhat pejorative umbrella category for people of Tibetan origin, 'Bhote/Bhotiya', especially from 'Tamang' (see Sato 2004; also see Ramble 1997 for the discussion of 'Bhotiya' and its *non*-development of a shared identity). In its older version, they called (and many of them still call) themselves 'Lama' in the local context, and 'Sherpa' in the broader context of Nepalese or international society. An important point to note here is that, although it is true that they have their own language called 'Yolmo' (a dialect of Tibetan, hereafter Y.), they are of firm

experience articulate one another in Yolmo women's lives. Put in another way, how is it possible that these women do not *mind* being considered of 'lower' rebirth at all? When a Yolmo woman asserts that she doesn't mind being a woman, how can she do so, when she lives in a social environment where women are assigned lower status simply because they are women and many of them have to suffer in ways that men are not likely to? What does she mean by that remark exactly, in the first place? What does 'being born a woman' in Yolmo mean for herself and what kind of things does a Yolmo woman actually 'mind', then? These are the questions that I shall pursue here. It is beyond the scope of this chapter to provide satisfactory answers to them, of course. Rather, I would like to invite readers to share and think these questions through in the situation where Yolmo women are positioned or position themselves, which I suppose must be in many respects far from, but can still have a number of things in common with, that of 'our' own.[6]

Let me make a few notes to situate what I intend to do presently before proceeding. Studies of South Asian women have already accumulated in substantial numbers and continue to do so. Incipient feminist anthropology starting in the 1970s tended to focus on 'structure', in Lévi-Straussian, Marxist, or any other terms, and mainly concerned itself with articulating 'women's status' within the structure. The overall picture of South Asian women produced from this approach was quite grim. They were essentially portrayed as passive and submissive 'victims' of patriarchal systems, backed up by ideology and embedded in 'tradition', of which the favoured arena for study was that of 'rituals'.

The subordinate status of women was amply attested to in these works, but more recently the partiality of this picture began to be acknowledged. The 'subordination of women' is far from the whole story – women cannot be reduced, in any case, to 'victims', deprived totally of any capacity to act on their own, or to some 'commodity'-like thing, just 'given' and 'taken' by men. They are themselves actors; they have their own wills, feelings, and power, however modest or truncated, which definitely make a difference to the people surrounding them. Countering the dismal and static perception of female subjugation, women's 'agency' was brought to the fore and became

---

Tibetan Buddhist allegiance and share a number of cultural characteristics and relatively thick social ties as well as some feelings of belonging that bind these people (however loosely) together, it is also true that people from Yolmo do not constitute an isolated, homogeneous, primordial community. That is, any description generalized in the name of 'Yolmo' is bound to be an approximation. Concerning gender relations, I presume that many parts of what I present here as something 'Yolmo' cannot be necessarily generalized as such in the strictest sense on the one hand, and can have a lot in common with other Tibetan- or Tibeto-Burman-speaking communities such as Tamang, Sherpa, Nyeshangte, etc., and some even with caste Hindus, on the other. Below I shall try to mention these similarities and differences as far as possible.

[6]The fieldwork on which this paper is based was carried out between 1994 and 1997 and on several occasions thereafter.

the central subject matter of a number of works.[7] As a result of the effort to redress the overly grim picture of South Asian women, two seemingly incompatible polar images have been produced.

Valuable as such an approach is, focusing on the 'agency' of women has not always successfully avoided slipping into some kind of romantic voluntarism (cf. Des Chene 1997). Concentrating rather narrowly on explicating individual women's wills and actions, what they do and say from their own perspective, these works sometimes tend to lose sight of the fact that agency is embedded in structure, which constrains as well as is indispensable for the construction of agency in the first place. The agency of women, women's wills, needs, and capacities to act are liable to be stressed to such an extent that structure is extruded from the picture entirely; yet it is only in the light of structure that one can adequately position agency. Some of these works are not entirely free from the impression that they imagine agency as something that stands simply *outside of* or even *against* structure. It is as if, in crude terms, *the more* active the agency becomes, *the freer* it becomes from the structure, and as if a powerful enough agency could effectively *negate* the structure of women's subjugation, thus obliterating the actuality of women's subjugation itself.[8]

A case in point is Watkins (1996), where the "spirited" attitude of women is presented in order to testify to their equal standing to men among the Nyeshangte of west Nepal. It is plausibly stated in her account that among the Nyeshangte, who are similar in many ways to the Yolmo, women do enjoy (or have enjoyed)[9] *almost* equivalent status to men. But it is also apparent from what she actually writes that women *are* excluded, categorically or factually, from some prestigious areas of practice, such as Buddhist priesthood in the village and large-scale international trade. Nyeshangte women may well be spirited, as she depicts them, but this fact does not mean or presuppose that they are free from the structure that puts them in a rather disadvantaged status. 'Agent' is not to be mistaken as an atomic individual who is possessed with limitless 'freedom', as Western individualism would stipulate. Agency cannot be (re)produced without structure, though it cannot be entirely reduced to or derived from structure either. What should be examined, in order to understand women's lives in a specific cultural/social context, is *neither* structure *nor* agency, but *both* structure *and* agency at the same time, and the dynamic and complex relationships between these two.

---

[7] See Raheja & Gold (1994), Campbell (2000), Hayami et al. (2003), and Kitamura (2004), to name only a few.

[8] This kind of conception is what Ortner (1996b) was trying to get rid of, when she proposed the concept of "serious games" to grasp the mutual determinations of 'agents' and 'structures' adequately. See also Abu-Lughod (1990).

[9] She discusses the recent decline of women's status among them. But I doubt if what she saw as recent (and in connotation "foreign") developments can adequately be called "recent" at all.

What Watkins failed to recognize was this mutually constitutive relationship between agency and structure.[10]

Thus it is possible to restate the aim of this chapter as follows. I aim to bring to light how the agency of Yolmo women, which is revealed in and underpinned by their generally outgoing demeanour as well as their contentedness with being born as women themselves, is (re)constructed through the local structure of gender inequality in which they find themselves. In other words, my project is to connect (or to find how to connect) those two polar propositions, 'women as victims' and 'women as agents', their structural subordination and their capacity to act, to obtain a better understanding of women's lives in a specific local context. The local structure itself is a product of repeated and concerted practice by people belonging there and it is gradually being transformed through their very practice, but this process of structural transformation can be only obliquely addressed here. My central concern is the construction of Yolmo women's agency, the way it is related to, and produced and reproduced through the structure established in the present.

In the following section I will start with the structure in the context of everyday practice in a Yolmo village. In the second section, I will move on to the examination of women's agency (within the constraining structure) in the context of a life event, namely 'marriage'. I do this by presenting an unusually attractive narrative of a Yolmo woman about how she settled into – or rather, how she rigorously resisted settling into – her present marital bond. Not unexpectedly, marriage is a decision *for life*, though (or precisely because) it happens only several times at the most for any Yolmo individual (only once for the majority). The occasion constitutes one of the foremost opportunities for a Yolmo woman to exercise her agency, either overtly or covertly, in order to get what she wishes for (or to avoid what she does not) by all means. Thus it offers us an exceptionally rich arena to look into how far her agency can go.

A SKETCH OF GENDERED EVERYDAY PRACTICE IN YOLMO

Here, instead of trying to present a comprehensive overview of the structure, gendered as well as gendering (cf. Bourdieu: 1977, 2001), in Yolmo society, I have no choice but to limit my scope to focus rather narrowly on a sketch of their everyday practice of gender. That is, here I shall deal mainly not with

---

[10]Concerning this point see also Maggi (2001: 40-3). As she points out, the efforts to avoid this "either/or trap" were in fact already present in feminist anthropology at the outset (see Lamphere 1995: 96).

what they *say* but rather what they *do*. The reason for doing this is that the latter, as I understand it, is more essential for the structure of gender to be forged, confirmed, and maintained in Yolmo village life. By contrast, discourses on gender are rather scanty, not elaborated in content, and encountered only sporadically. Moreover, most discourse on gender is produced only in response to some kind of violation occurring in the sphere of gendered performance. The first thing the analyst needs to do in order to delineate gender among the Yolmo is to observe how they *do* gender, how their everyday performance articulates with gender distinctions. Space constraints preclude a comprehensive account of how they 'do' gender. I shall here confine myself to practice within individual Yolmo households.

The Gendered Organization of Labour in the Household

Most of the social activities of villagers, except for large-scale Buddhist rituals held occasionally at village temples, revolve around respective villagers' houses (Y. *khangba*),[11] which as a rule all members share and call as one's own (but also note that a household is frequently visited by non-members, from inside as well as outside the village, and is hardly a closed or isolated unit). A household (Y. *dongba*) in Yolmo village is a tight-knit unit, which in general consists of a couple (or agnatically related couples in some cases) and their unmarried children. All the members of a household are expected to share in virtually every sphere of life. Though it is now very common that at least some member(s) of the household are away for an extended period of time (discussed later in this section), a *dongba* is still typically imagined as a clearly demarcated and closely related stable group of people who live under one roof, eat together, take care of each other, cooperate in productive as well as reproductive labour, receive guests jointly, function as a sponsor in village temple rituals, and participate in festivities (wedding and village temple rituals included) as a corporate unit. The household can be considered "an atom",[12] the single most important unit which cannot be divided further and which operates as a relevant unit in almost all the social contexts where more than one household is involved in Yolmo village life.

Tightly knit as it is, if one looks *inside* any given Yolmo household, one will find that it is structured by an uneven distribution of labour as well as by a differentiation of status among its members. Labour distribution and status differentiation are structured mainly along the lines of gender and seniority. The degree to which gender structures these two domains is variable: the way in which gender affects status is rather clear-cut, whereas labour

---

[11] Houses are used for small-scale Buddhist rituals as well as for 'shamanic' ones at times (about shamanic healing practice in Yolmo, see Desjarlais 1994).

[12] This term 'atom' was used to characterize Sherpa households in Solu by Ortner (1978).

distribution is more flexible; nonetheless, these two domains are interrelated and are influenced by each other.

Let us begin with the domain of labour. The organization of labour in Yolmo is neither rigidly prescribed for every household nor strictly fixed as a rule in a given household. The first thing that determines 'who carries out which work when' is the necessity to carry out the job itself, and only secondarily is the gender of the person who happens to be available for that job taken into account. That is, essentially nobody would be barred from performing any kind of work if it turns out to be necessary for the person to perform that work. Work 'outside' (farming, herding, collecting firewood and fodder, etc.), as well as work 'inside (and around)'[13] the house (cooking, serving food and drink, attending to guests, brewing alcohol, house cleaning, washing, threshing grain, looking after small children, etc.), can be done in theory – and is in fact observed as being done – irrespective of the person's gender.

But this fact does not mean that various jobs are distributed evenly or that there is no discernible division of labour at all between men and women in Yolmo. If there are no *negative* prescriptions as to which work is not to be done by which gender, there are certainly preferences and an actually observable tendency as to which kind of labour is likely to get done by which gender. As for work 'inside', it is performed, if any 'female hands' are available, invariably by women in the household. It is only when none are available, when there is no choice (as when women in the household go out or fall sick, or no competent female member exists at all), that men do try to get it done themselves (possibly with poor outcomes). Speaking of work 'outside', there seems to be no clear idea that favours one gender over the other to carry it out. Nonetheless, at a subtler level than the case of work 'inside', the imbalance does seem to be present. While men do perform that work even when there *is* any female labour force available in his household, his share of work 'outside' will be at best equal, and probably less than that of his female counterpart. That is, it is not only the work that we would sum up as household chores, but also work 'outside' that women perform at least as hard as men. No ideology that 'outside' work should be reserved for men is found here. No woman (except those who are too old or too young to labour) can afford (or aspires) to be a 'housewife' in a modern sense of the word.[14] Women are expected to work both 'inside' and 'outside', which, in

[13]The distinction between work 'outside' *vs.* work 'inside' is made by Yolmo themselves. What is designated as work 'inside' actually includes work carried out immediately 'around' the house, including in stone-paved front yard and small vegetable garden.

[14]The sexual division of labour described by Clarke (1980) seems to be more clearly demarcated than what I present here. The difference may be related either to the historical and economic situation of the village Clarke worked in or to the earlier time period when his research was conducted.

short, amounts to an almost double work burden for women.[15] There is no denying that labour arrangements in Yolmo households are quite flexible and actually vary substantially depending on household composition, individual members' preferences and skills, or the necessities of the occasion. But it needs also to be stressed here that there *is* a tendency for women to be overburdened both with 'inside' and with 'outside' work.

There is also a relatively recent trend emerging from broader socio-politico-economical developments, which seems to 'fit' as well as to exacerbate already existent local patterns of gender-biased labour arrangements. Recently, more and more men have begun to leave their village for Kathmandu, parts of India, and other foreign countries, in most cases in order to earn money, and in a relatively small number of cases to attend school/college or to be Buddhist monks. Women too can and do go outside to work or study, along with their men or some even on their own.[16] But it is impossible to miss the overall gender imbalance in migration. With the increase of mainly male outmigration, the responsibility for running the family estate is falling more and more heavily on the shoulders of women who stay behind. Moreover, with the rapid increase in various opportunities which have opened up inside villages since the 1990s,[17] which extract male manpower even more from household labour, this trend now affects even those households with working adult male members.

Gendered Space Arrangements Inside the House

If the division of labour between genders in Yolmo households is rather practical and in fact relatively balanced, the status order between men and women in a household (including temporary visitors as well) is more prescribed than practical and more fixed than flexible. Status differences between genders (and within each gender) in Yolmo are most clearly represented in the space arrangement inside each house. Where one is seated in the main room of a house does and should reflect what and who one is in that house: one should take one's place in accordance with one's gender, rank, and role (whether member or visitor) in a given household gathering.

Every Yolmo house is built on virtually the same design with respect to its main room with the hearth, where most of the social activities take place

---

[15]See Acharya and Bennett (1981), a seminal study of the sexual division of labour across different ethnic groups in Nepal, which likewise found that women's workloads were invariably heavier than men's. See also Cameron (1998) for the Hindus in far western Nepal.

[16]It is known that quite a number of young women from Yolmo went to work at Rana Palaces in Kathmandu in the past. As for female outmigration for study on her own, I have not heard of any case so far, except those who have chosen to be nuns.

[17]I refer here to 'work' such as engaging in party politics or being active in governmental as well as (local or international) non-governmental organizations.

and which is often the only room that a house contains.[18] The organization of the main living space is shown in Figure 6.1 (directions are given as if facing the hearth). First, the space of the room with hearth is roughly divided into male and female halves, within which men and women, respectively, are normally seated. The left side of the hearth is understood to be female space and the right side male. Second, each of these spaces is differentiated by the roles and the order of rank, particularly elaborately in the case of the male half. The seat by the hearth along the *chöti*[19] (1) is for the seniormost male member of the household. Other male members or male guests should be seated in descending order of status (correlated with seniority, kin relations, and general personal prestige), starting from the seat by the hearth and ending by the bed along the *chöti* (2)-(3). Still lower-ranking male members or lower-ranking outsiders (such as agricultural labourers hired from outside Yolmo), if present, can be seated facing this line, opposite the *chöti* (7). On the bed adjoining the altar, specially highly honoured (male) guests may be seated,[20] such as Buddhist priests or monks (4)-(6). As for the female half, the differentiation is much more ambiguous and less hierarchically elaborated. The seat on the opposite side of the hearth from that of the senior-most male member, the 'corner' [of the house] as they call it, is for the woman who is in charge of cooking and distributing food to all, as a rule the seniormost female member of the household (8). In some cases, however, because the one who sits at the corner has to carry out the bulk of the cooking herself (this corner is the whole 'kitchen' in a Yolmo house), if the senior-most female member does not feel able to carry out the task (either because of age or sickness), she can give up her seat (temporarily) to another female member of the household. Although sitting at this corner certainly entails some status and prerogatives (as well as responsibility) for its occupant, the rest of the female space is not clearly differentiated. Difference, if any, is attributed to practical concerns. For example, a seat right in front of the hearth is much sought after, especially in winter, because it is very warm there (10). Or someone who helps in cooking or serving would occupy the space next to the 'corner' seat (9), but occupying the seat next to the senior-most female does not necessarily mean that the person is next to her in rank, as would be the case according to the logic of male space.

Villagers generally 'know' where to seat themselves, at least to which side of the hearth one should place oneself, though sometimes there are

[18]There is no specially preferred orientation for building houses according to the cardinal directions in Yolmo. The main concern seems to be the availability of space for the front yard, which is made invariably so as to adjoin the front door and window-side of the house.

[19]*Chöti* is a wooden altar-cum-cupboard, which is made (and a number of them beautifully carved) by local carpenters.

[20]Seats on the bed can also be used if there are too many male honoured guests to be fitted into the row along the *chöti*.

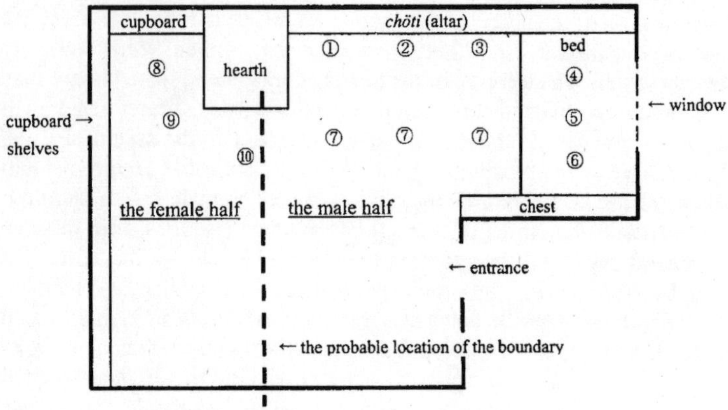

Key

- ① – seniormost man of house
- ②–③ – men in decreasing rank order
- ④–⑥ – Buddhist monks or especially honoured guest in decreasing rank order
- ⑦ – still lower rank men
- ⑧ – the 'corner', seniormost woman of house
- ⑨ – woman of lower rank
- ⑩ – woman of lower rank, female guests

Figure 6.1: Space Organization in a Main Room.

subtle negotiations or manipulations over where in each half to take one's seat or to make/let someone be seated when visiting someone else's house or when receiving guests at home. If someone should be uncertain or in case she or he takes the wrong seat (as children or visitors from outside Yolmo may do), he or she is generally shown where to sit.

We should take note that the boundary is an 'imagined' one, not physically demarcated in the house interior but just mapped onto the space through concerted and repeated seating practice by people. For one thing, 'transgression' of the boundary occurs, not infrequently, when some practical concerns make it necessary or more convenient to arrange things otherwise. As already stated, the 'corner' is the only place where one can cook, so if no female member is available for cooking, any man of the household is allowed to sit there. To take another example, an adult woman can sit and relax in the seat next to hearth on the male side, if no adult male who should be given priority is present (and none is expected to return soon).[21] For another thing, the boundary 'moves' in accordance with the needs of the situation. For instance, when there are too many male or female guests present in the house and it would be difficult for either men or women to be contained in respective gendered halves, they do not have to be compressed tightly within their own half, but can 'pour out' into the other half, resulting in the (temporary) shifting of the boundary. What these examples show is that male and female halves are not to be considered mutually exclusive 'blocks' that exist 'up there' in space. The boundary between gendered halves appears readily recognizable, but it is far from being fixed, and in fact it is quite fluid and fuzzy.

If the boundary is rather fluid, how is it possible that the boundary is maintained? What is it that makes us discern the male half from the female, or makes us see that every Yolmo house space *is* divided into two gendered halves?

It is not the rigidity or fixity of the boundary, but the repetitive nature of practice that inscribes and maintains the opposition between the two halves. The boundary may shift or transpose itself, but the practice of drawing and redrawing the boundary itself is continually exercised across different situations. Put another way, what is constant is the principle (and the practice activating that principle) of *no mixing* between men and women in seating arrangements. The boundary can be redrawn as the situation changes, but its presence should be reiterated and made plainly clear whenever both genders share the same space. What may initially look like an almost fixed dividing line running over the fireplace is actually just the most *probable* location of the sexual division of space, not the *normal* one.[22]

---

[21] Clarke (1980) reported an interesting example of 'transgression', that of childbearing women. They are said usually to go into labour at the seat of the senior-most male member of the household (1). If this is done just from practical necessity (the seat of the senior-most female member, which is basically the kitchen of a Yolmo house, is surely not a convenient place for this task) or for some other reason is an interesting question, which Clarke did not pursue. Children transgress the boundary all the time. Up to six or seven years old, children can sit wherever they please: in the men's row along the *chöti* or even on the bed without any censure, as long as nobody is present who should occupy these spaces.

[22] See also the description of house space organization presented in Clarke (1980: Chaps. 6 & 10). His argument is basically on the same lines as mine, but the difference lies in that he posited the boundary between gendered halves as something fixed in space. He did not seem to recognize fully the dynamics of boundary maintenance which I am discussing here. See also Ortner (1978: 74-5), which presents us with interesting material for comparison with the Yolmo case. The organization of house space among the Sherpas of Solu as described by Ortner looks similar to that of the Yolmo in many ways but lacks the boundary running straight through and dividing the space into two gendered halves (all men are seated along the walls while women are concentrated in the left side as well as the centre of the room). In this kind of arrangement in which men do not have to share the centre floor with women, in any case there appears to be neither room nor necessity for the boundary of gender to be actively maintained through

One case that illustrates this point clearly is the way in which a couple, a husband and wife, seat themselves. As a rule one does not see couples sitting next to each other, side by side, in 'public', either at home or when visiting others.[23] I have already mentioned that the seniormost couple (which in many cases is the only couple) of the household should sit on either side of the hearth. This means that they sit at a distance of some one and a half metres from each other, sandwiching the hearth (with the wife facing the hearth and the husband sitting with his back to the *chöti*), with no possibility of touching or showing any sign of physical intimacy. This cannot be interpreted as an arrangement forced on to them by the physical construction of Yolmo house interior, because, as a matter of fact, this way of taking seat is obligatory, or at least perfectly normal, for a couple under *any* circumstances. When a couple visits someone else's house, they without fail sit quite apart from each other. If a visiting male guest is seated along the rear line, this automatically takes him far away from his wife's position, which would likely be somewhere near the side of hearth. But this pattern is also observed even when the house is so packed with people that the men and women have to sit side by side along the male/female space boundary. In this circumstance too, husband and wife would not try to sit together: they take their respective seats far into their respective gendered halves. One's husband is one's 'man' (Y. *kyowa*) and one's wife is one's 'woman' (Y. *bhimi*), as the Yolmo call them. So, it would not be stretching the point too far to take this customary seating practice as attesting to the principle that 'man' and 'woman' must not be mixed and must be seated separately at all times.[24]

To summarize, space inside Yolmo house is structured by the transposable yet sustained opposition between male and female spaces,[25] with each again structured by the order of role and rank in different degrees of rigidity or elaboration. What is important for the present discussion is not differentiation *inside* each half but the *inter*-relationship in terms of which these halves are opposed as well as connected to each other. I stated earlier in

people's seating practice itself (while there is always room for each individual to negotiate their place *inside* each gender's space through seating practice, which Ortner duly described). See also Gaborieau (1991), for a discussion of spatial organization in the Parbatiya house in central Nepal.

[23] An exception is at one's own wedding ceremony, when newly wed couples are seated side by side. On other casual occasions (e.g. riding a bus, resting at a tea shop, etc.), they may sit together.

[24] This may also be interpreted as related to their aversion to bringing 'sexual' matters into public display.

[25] But note that this opposition or divide in space is a symbolic one and hardly constitutes any barrier to communication. Men and women seated on both sides of the boundary converse with each other with no difficulty, and eat and drink together. In short, they share one and the same social space.

this section that the spatial arrangement is a representation of the status difference between men and women. But how could this be the case? This should mean that the male half can be regarded as 'higher' than the female half and that this disparity reflects as well as produces status difference between genders. Actually, it is not so straightforward a task to make this case as it might seem at first. To an already 'cultured' eye, the unequal status ascribed to each half is more than apparent. The gendered division of space can be nothing but what effectively makes people realize and conform to the lowered/heightened status of their own gender, not just an opposition or distinction between men and women. But, how is it so?

Some signs of imbalance between the gendered halves can be detected in the organization of space itself. First, the male half, all in all, can be said to be for resting as well as restful. Speaking of what people do while sitting in the room, very often there is a clear contrast between both sides of the hearth. While the left side, especially the 'corner', is essentially a place to work, mainly cooking, the right side of the hearth is essentially reserved for resting. While sitting there, men do nothing but drink, eat, and socialize, unless they are engaged in some kind of religious work, such as making *torma* or reading sacred texts, which in Yolmo households is carried out only by men (on this point, see further below). The rear row of seats along the *chöti* is quite comfortable to sit in, too, with a relatively thick carpet and cushions lining the *chöti* to lean on, which are a kind of 'luxury' not available for those seated on the other side of the line.[26] But these privileges, to be allowed to just sit instead of working and to sit with relative comfort, are actually not necessarily the ones extended to *all* men occupying the male space. Those sitting in the row facing the *chöti* have no backrest either,[27] though they do not have to work like someone sitting in the female 'corner'. On the other hand, women not sitting in the corner can sometimes sit idly, doing nothing but chatting – though it is probable that they will occasionally give a hand to the woman working in the corner.

These signs, then, can be no more than correlatives of the unequal relationship. They do not in themselves *establish* the hierarchical opposition between the male and female halves as a whole. What constitutes the male half as 'higher' than the female half does not seem to be found in the seating arrangement itself, or, for that matter, in any other single domain of practice. Essentially speaking, one cannot in fact see any *ultimate* foundation for the

[26]In the early days of my fieldwork in Yolmo, I was almost without fail seated in the row along the *chöti*, but later, people began to treat me as a woman in this respect. I was seated somewhere facing the hearth where there was no backrest, which happened to strain my back badly sometimes.

[27]Because the household size in Yolmo is quite small, it is not likely that any male members will have to sit facing the *chöti* when non-members are not present. In other words, men usually get to sit in the row along the *chöti*.

disparity – but by no means does that mean that the inequality is not real. We should not look for a single, but for multitudes of practices and their interrelatedness, which taken together constitute female space as 'lower' than the male space. I shall briefly delineate some of them below.

One domain that can be taken to contribute to this inequality is the way in which food and drink are served among the Yolmo. As already stated, serving as well as cooking is done by women whenever possible. What is more directly relevant to the creation of gender status disparity is not who serves, but who are served and in what way, namely, the fact that as a rule *all* the women, irrespective of whether they are household members or guests, are served in a less respectful way than *all* the men, irrespective of whether they are household members or guests.

Whenever tea or alcohol, snacks or meals are served, women always receive their share later than men (but before children and low-ranking wage labourers from outside Yolmo). Everybody knows that the most respected is served first.[28] The order of serving is normally attuned to the order of rank among those present. Thus the customary practice of serving women later than men affirms, time and again, that 'woman' as a category is to be somewhat less respected than 'man' as a category. And it is also always true that women are served in a somewhat less formal manner. They get their tea in cups without saucers and their meal in one dish (i.e. in the same way as children and labourers from outside), unlike male counterparts who always get their tea in cups with saucers and their meal with the soup in an independent bowl. And while men are normally served food or drink on the long wooden table (Y. *solju*), women almost always have to do without one (that is, their cups and plates are put directly on the floor). A man would feel bitterly offended if he were treated without such paraphernalia, but it is taken as a matter of course that women are served in this way.[29] In Yolmo, men are taken as *naturally* deserving such signs of respects. Whatever rank he occupies in the given male gathering, any man is treated as higher in rank than any woman. Through this mundane food-serving practice, the status disparity between genders is constructed and reaffirmed.

Another domain that has crucial importance in the hierarchical construction of gender is that of religious/Buddhist practice. As noted earlier, Yolmo people are Buddhists and virtually every one of them practises the

---

[28]He who is served first does not begin to eat or drink immediately but waits until everyone is served. When all have received a share, he utters some mantras and offers tokens of the food/drink from his share to the gods. It is only after this offering that everyone starts to eat/drink together.

[29]I am aware of only one Yolmo woman who complained about this 'discrimination' against women. She told me that she herself would serve tea with saucers to everyone, male or female. But she did not seem to have tried to object to the order of serving or the gendered division of space, as far as I know.

religion in one way or the other, but the way people do this is quite varied, not only in accordance with their inclination, knowledge, and level of spiritual development, but also in accordance with their gender. In the version of Nyingma Tibetan Buddhism practised in Yolmo village society, women are categorically barred from pursuit of any 'higher' religious practice.[30] Buddhist priesthood, as well as managing the work of the village temple (Y. *goba*), is open only to male members of the village to this day.[31]

What we should note for the present discussion is the fact that pursuing (or giving managerial support, such as officiating as *goba*) religious practice is very prestigious and honorable in Yolmo village society. Acquiring religious knowledge (or serving as *goba* for the village temple) has been a principal way to gain social prestige among them, along with making lots of money.[32] Women do participate, sometimes quite eagerly, in religious practice, as they prostrate before *Lamas* (Buddhist masters) or sacred images, circumambulate *chortens*, or give donations to gain merit, but they are traditionally excluded from reading Tibetan sacred texts (though they could be blessed by having one touched to the head), from participating in text-reading rituals carried out in the village temple (though on a few occasions they are allowed to sit at the rear of the hall and observe the ritual), or from playing any other important roles in village temple ceremonials,[33] and hence, from obtaining any formal posts of authority, which were limited until recently to those pertaining to village temple organizations (Sato 2004: Chap. 2).[34] As a matter of fact, this exclusion is the other side of the coin that women tend to be more burdened with household (= secular) work than men. They turn out to be not just burdened more, but burdened more with less-valued work.

The exclusion of women from 'higher' religious practice is partly supported by, and itself reinforces, the ideology of karma mentioned at the outset of this chapter: that being born a human is a highly desirable and hard

[30]Women can be nuns, however. Nuns have, in theory, left the household/secular world, and so can be considered an exception to gender restrictions. But again, nuns are not regarded as equals of monks. See also Ortner (1989, 1996a) and Watkins (1996: 240).

[31]Again, there are various ways to pursue higher Buddhist practice open to men. One of the important factors is the person's patrilineal descent. For the special role played in Yolmo Buddhism by men from Lama clans, see Clarke (1980) and Sato (2004: Chap. 4).

[32]These two things are not necessarily separate but rather interrelated by a 'causal' link in many Yolmo people's thinking, i.e. wealth allows one the time to devote to religion, and piety is likely to bring merit and wealth. See Clarke (1980), also Sato (2004: Chap. 4).

[33]But as already mentioned, since households (*dongba*) operate as a sponsor of village temple rituals as a unit, women can also be said to participate in temple rituals as a member of the donor household.

[34]Since the mid 1990s, there has been a mushrooming of organizations in and across Yolmo villages, both governmental and non-governmental, some of which are funded through international connections.

to obtain birth (when compared to being born as, say, an insect or a dog), the saying goes, that being born a man is to be considered a superior rebirth than being born a woman, and that because women are of inferior birth they are not fit to participate in 'higher' practice. And this reasoning can also be put the other way round: because women do not carry out 'higher' practice, their status should remain 'lower' than that of men.

Backed by the multitude of gender-biased practices just considered, seating arrangements in Yolmo houses do start to appear as stratified, rather than just opposed, between male and female halves. The observable gendered opposition in space becomes nothing but the visual manifestation of the unequal gender relationship itself, projected onto concrete space and lived out in flesh. The main room of each house becomes an arena in which gender inequality is to be performed, displayed, and reproduced. Gender status disparity is *performatively* constructed through the interrelated practices, seating arrangements included (Butler 1990). No one domain of practice is enough for this task, no sound foundation for the inequality ever exists. But taken all together, in the chain of practices across domains acted out in time, the status difference does emerge strongly and indisputably.

What intrigues an onlooker like me is that one can find no trace of any grievance or resentment on the part of the structurally disfavoured party, namely, the women. They conform themselves to the established behavioural practice, they even attempt to make others conform to it by scolding on the spot in the case of children or by talking behind people's backs in the case of adults. The practice of hierarchical gender relations does seem to constitute part and parcel of every woman, her *habitus*. What she does, how she does it, what and how she perceives herself to be doing, and even what she *is*, are immersed in and not to be easily dissociated from her gendered habitus, which has been developed through years of upbringing.

The everyday practice of gender definitely has a central role to play in establishing and reproducing the Yolmo version of gendered/gendering structure embedded in every gendered person. But there are other domains of practice, which have crucial bearings on the constitution of gender in Yolmo society – marriage, for instance, is one such domain. Now we turn to this domain of practice in order to explore the way in which the agency of a Yolmo woman is exercised against the backdrop of her structural subordination. While Yolmo women generally do not seem to bear any grievance against their 'lower' status as women, not a few of them are known to have asserted their agency by resisting, in some cases really vigorously, their being married off.[35]

---

[35]Women who have admittedly exercised their agency in the opposite direction, that is, to marry a man of their choice, were much fewer.

A STORY OF EXTRAORDINARY RESISTANCE: LISTENING TO A YOLMO WOMAN

In contrast to the everyday practices revolving around a Yolmo house/household, marriage is a precondition of the renewal or creation of new houses/households over time.[36] Even if getting married cannot be anybody's everyday practice, it is the one event that has a profound impact on, and constitutes the bedrock of, almost everybody's everyday practice.

Marriage in Yolmo is an unmistakably gendered institution. Customarily, patrilineal descent is given precedence and virilocal marriage has been a rule among the Yolmo. Their favoured type of marriage is the so-called bilateral cross-cousin marriage. The bride must move from her natal home into her husband's house upon marrying, though her patrilineal clan affiliation remains intact throughout her life. She takes only some movable assets with her which she receives from her parents (Y. *mhonor*), such as jewellery in general. This may be quite valuable but is useless for earning a living in the agricultural economy. So she is virtually left empty-handed in terms of productive means and must depend on her husband in her marital home, though her labour contribution is bound to be substantial and in many cases essential for household (re)production (as discussed earlier). And it is the newly wed wife, not the husband, who must be dislocated from the natal home and struggle, in a number of cases quite badly, to get along with 'strangers'.[37] In short, she is destined to start living as a 'lower' status member of her new household all over again, in that she is a newcomer, with no productive means, in many cases of a younger generation, and as a woman. No doubt this kind of marital practice works rather *against* the woman, possibly more seriously and substantially than in the case of everyday practice itself.[38]

In the marriage procedure too, imbalances are quite apparent. The bride or her party is formally deprived of the initiative to make the contract. When a marriage is arranged, in principle it is the (prospective) groom's party that makes the proposal, not the bride's.[39] The bride's party, if not the bride herself, holds the right to say 'no' to the proposal, but their agency is not

---

[36]Inheritance is another key moment and vitally important institution. In Yolmo the bulk of the parental assets are divided equally among sons and the share of daughter(s) is as a rule quite limited, as is generally the case in Nepal. See further below.

[37]She may actually be acquainted with her husband or his family beforehand though, because marriage is in many cases contracted inside one's village or between nearby villages and because in either case it is very likely that the marriage is contracted between already related kin.

[38]This kind of marital practice is not limited to the Yolmo, but is actually widely shared among diverse groups of people in Nepal, including Hindu high-caste communities (cf. Bennett 1983).

[39]Some have been known to negotiate through informal channels, however.

allowed to go beyond that. In the now rather out-of-date practice of 'marriage by capture', which nevertheless is said to have occurred until quite recently, the imbalance is even more apparent. In marriage by capture the prospective groom's party 'drags and takes away' (Y. *tödi kerke*) the bride by force, physically denying the woman's agency.[40] There is no denying that there are and always were cases of so-called 'love marriage' among the Yolmo, where some kind of mutuality between the man and the woman is the foundation for their relationship. But it is important to note that the procedure for arranging marriage (making the formal proposal from the groom's side, etc.) is regarded as 'normal' among the Yolmo and accordingly most of them undergo the procedure eventually, if in a somewhat abbreviated form, regardless of whether the marital contract was actually secured by capture or 'love'.

The symbolic denial of a bride's agency is again an integral part of the Yolmo wedding process. The bride is not allowed to walk by herself from her natal home to her husband's but must be carried on someone's back (even if it takes a couple of days to reach the prospective groom's village), and it is very appropriate, if not obligatory, for her to weep, or at least to look sad at her wedding,[41] none of which apply to the groom. These facts we should bear in mind when we try to understand their lives or their 'life stories'.

Here I present a Yolmo woman's narrative of her life story, those parts of it relating to her marriage:[42] how she resisted getting married, how she got married against her will after all, and how she got (or did not get) along in the course of her marital life. Her experience of marriage, or for that matter the course of life itself, is by no means 'typical' of Yolmo women, still less of South Asian women. One could even say that her story is a rather exceptional one. But what makes her story so attractive for us lies precisely in its rather exceptional quality. Her extraordinarily firm resistance against her marriage, vividly illustrated in her own straightforward words (and through her lively voice, which can in no way be conveyed here), is the very thing which made her account worth listening to in depth. What should interest us most is this: the contradiction (or something which appears to be, in our eyes) that manifests itself in her narrative sharply and plainly, between the intensity of her suffering as a woman and the serenity of her own content-

---

[40]Speaking of the Yolmo, there seems to be always a possibility that 'capture' is staged, for one reason or another, with the complicity of the prospective bride or of her parents (see Ahearn 2001 for a description of a somewhat different pattern of marriage by capture).

[41]This expectation is presumably general to South Asia. One is reminded here of a scene from a recent film, *Bend it Like Beckham,* where this was stated in just these terms.

[42]The narrative reproduced here is the excerpts from interviews conducted in Kathmandu in August-September, 2003. The conversation was basically carried out in Nepali, with Yolmo vocabulary (or sometimes sentences) interspersed throughout.

ment with being born a woman.[43] Personal grief or sorrows, of course, take peculiar forms in each one of Yolmo women (or men, or us), but the sharper the contradiction appears to be, the better it is for the sake of the present discussion. It is via this contradiction, via trying to grasp how the contradiction sustains itself that we shall have a better chance to look into Yolmo women's lives.

Dawa's Story of Her Marriage

Dawa was thirty-six years old (according to Western calculation, that is, about my age), a wife and a mother of two children (one seventeen and the other thirteen years old) at the time of the interview. She was born in Yolmo but was subsequently taken to north-east India and brought up there by her parents, who set out to make money and stayed there for many years. Many other Yolmos did the same, both then and now. When she was around sixteen years old, she and her family came back with some money and re-settled in Yolmo.[44] It was not long before a proposal came for her and, eventually, she was married off.

The Marriage Proposed

When the prospective groom became very fond of her and had his relatives come and 'ask for' (Y. *langje*, Np. *magnu*) her for himself,[45] she was still quite young, seventeen or eighteen years old, although she does not remember her exact age at the time. For her part, she had no desire to get married to anyone, still less to him. "I was neither fond of him, nor was I thinking that I would marry anyone at that time." What she was planning for herself, as she relates to me now, was that she would stay on at her parents' house at least for several years, preferably learning to weave carpets, possibly going to live in India or in Kathmandu. But it turned out that her parents had different ideas. The young man was from the same village and of her mother's clan, thus he was her classificatory cross cousin. These conditions seemed to suffice for them to make themselves ready to 'give' their daughter to him. But before they made any decision, at least they did attempt to secure Dawa's own consent:

> [My parents] asked me, "Are you going or not going?" And when they asked, I somehow ... to me it seemed that if I cried really bitterly, Father and Mother would feel pity (Y. *ningcho*) for me and

---

[43]The quotation at the outset of this article was from the interview with the same person.

[44]The amount of money they brought back with them did not seem to be very impressive by Yolmo standards even then, but was anyway enough to build a new house in the village and to supply the family's needs for years to come.

[45]It is customary for a prospective groom to send someone else to ask, even if he initiated the proposal himself, as he did in this case.

> would not give me away [to anyone]. So, the more they inquired, the more I cried. The more they inquired, the more I cried ... from my mouth the words 'not going' didn't manage to come out.[46] And Father and Mother ended up thinking, "Hmm, my daughter must think good of the proposal, that's why she stays just crying, without uttering a word. All right, Daughter then, I will drink the *shyalgar*!"[47] Thus he drank it all up.

The proposal was accepted – even though she was desperately hoping that it would not be.

Running Away from the Wedding

Thus the date of the wedding (Y. *bhama*) was set and the preparations for the wedding got underway. But even in these circumstances, she had not given up her opposition and she had not agreed to marry this man yet. She recalls,

> ... on the day, when my wedding was the day after tomorrow, there was so-and-so's ... wedding. On that day, I washed myself and my clothes, folded them up, picked up a 100 rupee note from under Father's pillow, took up a sack, packed them in it, and put it underneath my bed. And then I went to the wedding. At the party, everyone said to me jokingly, "Eat! Eat the wedding![48] Now, the day after tomorrow, we are going to eat your wedding, too!" "Eat my wedding?! You won't get to eat my wedding at all! How would you? I shall never be at the wedding!" said I, also jokingly. "Are you thinking of running away or what? Where in the world could you run away? The wedding is the day after tomorrow. There is no way to escape now!" they said. "You watch where I shall be on the wedding day," I replied. Then, the day before the wedding, very early in the morning, I got up ... I used to bring two big baskets of firewood, fetching them from the forest, two baskets of firewood every morning. ... The reason why I did this was, I was pretending, you see, pretending in order to make my way to escape [from my

---

[46]Desjarlais points out that young Yolmo women often found it "difficult to speak their minds directly to more powerful elders" though they do communicate well, "particularly with other women of the same general age" (2003: 142). Of course, it depends on what they were trying to talk about. But this observation I suppose certainly holds good when it comes to talking about the kind of topic which concerns us here (namely, marriage, love, or sexuality).

[47]*Shyalgar* is a bottle of *chyang* (Y. distilled alcohol, usually made from millet. Note that the word is widely used for *non*-distilled alcohol in Himalayan regions outside Yolmo) with three small pieces of butter placed at its mouth, which is offered as a token of goodwill or respect. It is customary to offer *shyalgar* when making a respectful request. To drink from the bottle indicates that the request is accepted.

[48]Attending a wedding or other festivities is expressed as to '*eat*' (*sae*) in Yolmo, presumably connoting the enjoyable sensory qualities of those occasions.

> wedding]. ... Ever since the proposal came, I had been doing this, thinking this would help me escape. ... I used to stay in the forest for one to two, even three hours to gather two baskets of firewood. It didn't take me that long to gather firewood actually. But I was pretending, because [if I did this] Mother and Father would think later when I had run away that I was gathering firewood. And on the day I ran off, too, my parents thought ... "Dawa has gone off to gather firewood, that's the way she is, sometimes it takes her quite a long time to finish gathering firewood," and so they just stayed home doing nothing for three, four hours after I had left home. And in three, four hours I had already passed through Melamchi Pul.[49] I did not rest for a minute. From my village I ran and ran, until I arrived at Melamchi Pul.

Passing through Melamchi Pul, from Narkhola she got on the bus to Banepa, and from Banepa to Ratna Park, Kathmandu, and from Ratna Park to Baudha, at the eastern end of Kathmandu city. There were a number of people from Yolmo living there, including her 'sister' (maternal parallel-cousin, in this case) Pema from the same village, with whom she had made good friends. Pema was living with her brother, weaving and selling carpets on her own. She arrived at Pema's and that day they stayed up talking till late at night. "We will weave carpets, weaving carpets we two will make a lot of money, and making a lot of money we two will set up a [carpet] factory – that's how we two talked with each other."[50] But what they dreamed of was not to come true. "Well, the next day, Father arrived and took me back." Here is what happened when he came, as she related to me:

> Then [when Father arrived], I did not open the door. "If you force me to open the door," I was sitting at the window of the third floor you know, "If you dare to force me to, I will throw myself from the window and die!" I said. Father said, "Don't talk like that. Up [in the village, your] Mother has fallen unconscious, they [the prospective groom's party] say they will take your little sister in your stead."[51] ... from outside the door Father talked, from inside the door I talked. I had locked the door. So he said, "It's up to you, whether you marry or not. When we arrive up [in the village], how much they have already spent for the [preparation of] wedding, how much

[49]Melamchi Pul is a small bazaar in the bed of Melamchi River, some 2000 metres below her village.

[50]At that time, the carpet industry was booming and it offered a number of young (especially unmarried) Yolmo women one of the few options of waged employment.

[51]This way of putting the matter, though it does not happen often, does attest to the essential nature of marriage in Yolmo, that is, as a contract between two households, not between two individuals.

> *chyang* they have already made, I will pay for it. It's up to you, when we go back, you don't have to marry, you stay for a month or so, and then you may come here again and weave carpets." In this way, he persuaded (Np. *phakaunu*) me and took me back. And once he had taken me back by persuasion, when we arrived home, Father started to drink *chyang*, and Mother hadn't fainted, as it turned out ... Mother said to me, "Why did you do this? If you had told us that you wouldn't go in the first place, Father would not have drunk *shyalgar* then. You just stayed silent, so thinking you must have liked the proposal, *shyalgar* was drunk. So now, Daughter, don't behave like this, now they have already sent all their invitations to the wedding, they have got everything ready. You have no choice but to marry." Then, somehow, I understood that I had to do this marriage in any case. I thought: "For the present, the honour of Father and Mother must be saved." I hadn't been thinking of what effects Father and Mother would suffer, how they would have to be ashamed in front of people. "All right, I'll go" – but to myself I said: "Right now I'll marry him, but I won't stay long. For a few days I'll stay, and then I'll run away."

So she accepted, at last, to be married off. But before she was sent away from her natal home, she stole Rs.100 from her father again and kept the money with her, so that she could escape in the near future. She recalls, "I was thinking: I shall need some [money] for the bus fare, if not for food. At that time, I could even forget hunger."

Settling into Married Life

But she was not able to grasp a chance to run away very soon, because someone was posted to watch her '24 hours'. It was not that her husband and in-laws were harsh to her – on the contrary. She herself admits that they were kind and caring, that they almost indulged her "as if I were not a daughter-in-law, but a true daughter [of my mother-in-law]".[52] Still, she could not and had no mind to get along. With neither any chance to escape nor any intention of staying at her husband's, she frequented her natal home, just a few minutes' walk away. But she could no more find her place there either. If she visited often, Mother scolded her for coming and even told her not to come any more. "It is not good, people say, if a married daughter should stay [for a long time] at her natal home, you see," she explained. At stake here again was a matter of her parents' honour, the honour of those who had given their daughter away.[53] But this honour hardly mattered to her or was not

[52]It is not expected that the relationship between daughter-in-law and mother-in-law will be easy among Yolmos. She could be said to have been rather lucky in this respect.

[53]One may be reminded of the notion of *kanyadan* among Nepali and Indian Hindus (cf.

enough to make her give up her own wish. "At that time, I didn't care about Mother and Father's honour ... my heart was so childish."

In the course of time, she became pregnant. She did not seem to be able to avoid sleeping with her husband, even if she asserts that she had been refusing to talk with him ever since their wedding. "I didn't want to sleep in the same bed with him, but I fell to sleep [in the same bed] ... and while I was asleep, it turned out to be conceived." She poignantly points out that "it's a shameful story" that the baby was to be born even "without having any talk with him".[54]

The conception hardly changed her mind or attitude. She was determined to run away as before, which she actually realized during her first pregnancy, though she was taken back home quite soon. Still she persisted in trying to get out of the marital bond again and again. Her second escape was attempted five months after the baby was born. Here is her account of the incident and its aftermath, as well as those succeeding trials to escape, none of which succeeded in the long term:

> I left my five-month-old child behind; I left a baby who was still breast-feeding. It was at that time, you know, when he [her husband] and my brother came after me and took me back from Danda Khola, persuaded me, saying sweet words to me. There ... Khendu's father[55] said, "I understand [what you want], let's go back at the moment. After we two arrive up [in our village] again, we all discuss the matter. We two could go and stay in Kathmandu and weave carpets there."[56] And once we arrived up [in our village], where in the world could we go to weave!? Things got back all the same again. And then after that, I just stayed and stayed like that. Then bad fate, you see, another baby I conceived. Even with this baby in my stomach, I ran away. Later the baby was born. Even after this [second] baby was born, I ran away, taking this child with me. Once, I said even to the extent that I would throw this child away. ...

After many failed efforts to escape from the present marital life, finally at

---

Bennett 1983), even if among the Yolmo the virginity of the bride receives far less emphasis. One should also note here that the wife-giving party is as a rule respected by the wife-taking party in Yolmo society, contrary to the Hindu practice.

[54]March (2002: 212) writes that 'talking' can be used as a euphemism for 'having sexual intercourse' among Western Tamangs. But here Dawa's words should be taken at their face value, even if somewhat exaggerated, or we could not comprehend what she is talking about.

[55]Teknonymous usage, referring to her husband via her first-born child's name.

[56]Here, his interpretation of the reason for his wife's attempt seems to be not that she wanted to get a divorce from him but that she wanted to live somewhere outside the village (he does not seem once to have imagined breaking the marital bond with her, in any case). I cannot say whether he was right or not, after all, but it is quite probable that she had come to accept being married to him by this time and that she was rather resisting living a village life.

some point she changed her mind. That was when (or around the time when)[57] her third child, Nono, was born.[58] To continue her story:

> And I stayed and stayed like that, and Nono was born. Ever since Nono was born, I have not [attempted to] run away. At that point, I was beginning to understand ... after all, it must have been written on my forehead[59] that I shall marry [this man]. When I began to understand, I thought, "Now I understand how things should have been. Now I wish my children to have a bright future. Even if I don't like him, for the sake of the children's future I must think." Since then, I have stayed. Since then, I have not run away.

Her story of her long resistance against becoming a wife and a mother (of her wedded husband and his children) was thus concluded.[60]

Analysis

Dawa's settling into marital life, as recounted to me, was full of turmoil – a marriage which crushed her will, unwanted childbearing, and her extraordinarily stubborn resistance, most dramatically realized in the form of repeated attempts to run away from her husband's home. Through her almost diehard resistance, her 'agency' emerges so conspicuously that you can in no case fail to grasp it. But what is also acutely felt by us as we listen to her narrative is the magnitude of disappointments, difficulties, and sorrows, which she had no choice but to endure all through the years, until she, as it were, managed to *swallow up* and make her hope out of them. We cannot forget that it was exactly against the scale of her sorrows that her agency showed itself so impressively as to be almost heroic.

From *our* point of view, at a casual glance, we sense that her fate is something *typically female*. What she had to suffer seems to be one of those old sufferings of 'woman'; you could even say that hers was almost an epitome of them – a woman trafficked across one unit to another, her own will being subjugated for the benefits of larger society, constrained by her reproductive capacity, and positioned overall as inferior to men (cf. Rubin 1975). We might naturally anticipate, then, that with all her sufferings she

---

[57] At another point in the interview, she alternatively said that the change had occurred *before* Nono was born.

[58] Her second child died prematurely when just two months old.

[59] The notion that one's fate is written on the forehead is found throughout northern South Asia. For cases from the Nepalese Himalaya, see Desjarlais (1994), Ahearn (2001), and March (2002).

[60] Now she says that she cares for her husband very much as well as for her children. "After I bore three children, love (Np. *maya*) for him took root." What is narrated here seems like an extremely delayed realization of the saying quoted in Ahearn (2001: 75): *naso pasyo maya basyo*: 'The vein/hose [i.e. penis] entered, and love followed'.

should *naturally* bear some resentment or criticism against the way 'woman' is destined to be in the society where she lives, if not resist against her being classified as 'woman' in the first place. Or, if this anticipation might be going too far, we may well suppose, at the very least, that she should have thought negatively of her being a woman, that she should have wished, at one point or another, she were not a woman, but a man.

But we already know that this was not in fact the case. Every Yolmo woman I have encountered so far, Dawa herself included, looks too energetic and self-assured to sit and pity her own fate, no matter what hardships, mistreatments, or misfortunes befall her. The contradiction presented at the outset of this chapter, confirmed through our examination of their gendered everyday practice that constructs the 'lower' status of women, now looms still larger and sharper before us, instead of resolving itself smoothly into our compassion for a Yolmo woman's fate (even though we cannot help feeling it).

Let us try to see things from her point of view, conveyed through what she actually related. The reasons why she resisted against her marriage to the present husband are said to be twofold: (1) she did not want to marry *then*, and (2) she did not want to marry *him*.

The first point, the reason why she did not want to marry at all at that time, can be pretty clearly understood from the excerpts already reproduced here – she was not ready to leave her natal home yet *and* she wanted to earn money on her own. These two might seem contradictory to each other, but in fact they are not in the Yolmo context. An unmarried daughter belongs in theory to her natal home, that is, she is regarded as a member of her parents' household wherever she may actually live. This 'theory' constitutes the other side of the coin: she is strongly expected to contribute to her parents' household economy, if she ever earns money on her own. However, some obligatory contributions aside, staying at her natal house means nonetheless for a daughter to have considerable freedom; she can live a relatively carefree life as long as her parents stay active. Thus to stay on at their parents' home is generally a desirable state of affairs for young women, though everyone understands that this neither can nor should last forever. So, her wish to stay on at her natal home at the quite young age she was at the time is hardly peculiar; it is in fact a common attitude found among Yolmo women. To aspire to 'make a lot of money' on one's own is, on the other hand, if not peculiar, not a really common alternative for Yolmo women yet (whereas it is almost imperative for Yolmo men, except for those who pursue a religious career). It depends greatly on the individual woman's personality or domestic circumstances whether she tries to take up this path or not.[61]

[61] This does not mean those women who stay at home make no contribution to the household economy, of course. As we have already seen, in the village context, women rather than men tend to bear the bulk of all types of work.

About the second point, that she did not want to marry her present husband, she had this to say at another point in the interview:

> You can see very good-looking men [everywhere]. I thought, "Shit! How can I marry a man like him? I would go with [= marry] a good-looking man!" (laughter) A friend of mine also said to me, "Why would you go? ... His face is no good, why would you go with him?" Someone else also said he looked like a monkey, and so on. And I thought, "That's really true, why shall I go with a man like this? If I go, I will go with a beautiful, handsome man, with good-looking face." [But] it has to have been written on your forehead [to come true], you see. Yet in my thinking, I thought I would [marry a handsome man]. ...

Here she states that she did not want to marry her husband because he "was not handsome" in her (and some others') eyes. She also said succinctly on another occasion that "I've got no chance to experience the thing called love (Np./H. *pyar, prem*)."[62] Her youthful heart longing for 'love', coupled with a sort of repugnance felt against her prospective groom, lay behind her resistance. Since apparently she had no lover or particular man she especially liked when the proposal came (at least), her strong longing for something as abstract as 'love' might appear rather strange when one takes into account the then environment in Yolmo, where 'love marriage' was not really so common, if not unheard of. What is quite certain is that her wish for 'love'/'love marriage' can be seen to be a kind of forerunner of the present trend in Yolmo society (and in other parts of Nepal) in which, in general, young people's own likes and dislikes are being accorded far greater weight than before (cf. Ahearn 2001).

If there were two reasons for her to resist marriage, the targets that she had to resist were also twofold. Concerning the first point, her parents, especially her father who gave her away, should be a target to be resisted, which she actually did by attempting to run away from her wedding. It is significant, though, that there is no sign in her narrative that she bore any resentment or bitter feelings against her parents, either at the time or afterwards. On the other hand, concerning the second point, her husband should naturally be a target, and actually he became one. Repeated attempts to escape from her marital home are seen to be directed mainly at him.

There seems to be no room for resentment, still less rejection of having being born a woman to develop out of this course of reasoning. And in its own terms, this way of reasoning is sound indeed. For one thing, what Dawa had to suffer, the immediate cause of which is marriage against one's will, is not and has not been necessarily destined for *all* women in Yolmo. Even in

---

[62]The original word translated here as 'love' is *pyar* or *maya-prem* (Np./H.).

her generation, or older, there were a number of Yolmo women who were married with their own wishes not being ignored but reasonably considered, sometimes even to the man of their own choice. The kind of marriage we would call 'love marriage' seems to have been more or less present, if not prevalent, in Yolmo villages, where one finds a host of festive occasions for young men and women from surrounding villages to get together and observe each other. The symbolic passivity of the bride does not mean she has no way at all to manipulate the situation in her favour. For another thing, a marriage against one's will can and did happen not only to women but also to men. In Yolmo, marriage has normally remained essentially a contract between the wife-giving household and the wife-taking household, the transfer of a woman from the former to the latter, to this day.[63] And in respective groups, not only a prospective bride but also a prospective groom can be forced into marriage. The ultimate decision is to be made on behalf of each household as a whole, and it is usually the case that the prospective groom too does not hold a position of authority within his household.

If we focus on the fact that Dawa's suffering is not shared by women *as a whole* and yet can be shared also by some men, we could jump to the conclusion that her suffering and her being a woman are not related. That is to say, because she, as many other Yolmo women, had a not-too-bad chance to be married off happily if she was asked for her hand by the *right* man at the *right* moment, what she had to suffer has basically nothing to do with her gender.

But, as a matter of fact, there are some differences in the position where men and women find themselves. As already stated, marriage in Yolmo is heavily gendered as an institution in itself; it imposes a number of disadvantages on women, which men as a rule do not have to bear, such as her dislocation upon marriage, empty-handedness in productive means, and the generally heavier workload or 'lower' status accruing to her gender (one may also add the possibly traumatic experience of unwanted sex and childbearing). If so, one could rightfully say that being a woman *is* related to, if not the *sole* cause of, her sufferings. Certainly Dawa's fate was aggravated; her suffering must have been constituted by her gender, at least partly. She had to suffer worse because she was a woman. Then, why does this simple 'fact' not occur to her? How could she remain just contented with being a woman while she herself was acutely aware of her own fate as being far from satisfactory?

One reason should be sought in the just-mentioned fact that Dawa's gender is only partly to be blamed for her bad luck. What she underwent, she had to, because of several combined conditions which include her gender as

[63]Note that this kind of notion about marriage neither necessarily precludes the concept of 'love marriage' nor 'capture marriage', as long as the union is affirmed by both parties involved.

one of them. Another reason could be that her fate was realized the way it was *through her own decisions* in the final analysis. This may sound odd but note that she was not dragged into her marriage in the *literal* sense of the word, that is, by physical coercion. True, she was married off to her husband unwillingly, and she had no choice but to be taken back to her husband's house only to attempt to get out of there all over again. But what she did, she did because she was *persuaded* into doing so, not just because she was *made* to. I certainly agree that the kind of choice she was afforded cannot be adequately called a choice at all, but still I see a very thin line to be discerned between pure coercion and over-constrained choice.

The most important reason should be sought in the way she perceives what 'being a woman' in Yolmo entails. What does it mean for her to be a woman, anyway? What is it for her to be born and live as a woman, if it has nothing to do with the kind of turmoil that she underwent in her life?

This apparently is too big a question to be answered satisfactorily here. But I would like to suggest that we need to return to what was examined in the preceding section: namely, the construction of gender through everyday practice. I argued that the structure of gender in Yolmo society should mainly be explored not as a discursive construct, but rather as something formed and re-formed through gendered/gendering everyday practice, such as the division of labour, seating arrangements, serving order, Buddhist practice, etc. Repeated time and again, everyday practice constitutes their habitus, and their habitus produces what they do, as well as, in the long run, what they *are*. Gendered practice constitutes gendered habitus which generates gendered beings. Even if they hardly talk about or have any interest in talking about the practice for themselves, nonetheless it is readily recognizable that performing the practice in the right way or manner (Np./Y. *dhanga*), which is in many contexts gendered, is crucially important for them. They do not explicate the practice, but without fail they point out if inappropriate performance happens to occur – on the spot or behind the scene. Such phrases as "this woman [Y. *bhimi*] with no appropriate manner [to do things]!", "he turned out not to know the manner!", or most succinctly "this [bad] manner!", are common expressions that let people know when something has not been done in the way it should have been. Yolmo people take great care about doing things with good *dhanga*, in the manner proper to one's gender.[64]

If what constitutes a gendered person in Yolmo is in the main to perform this gendered everyday practice in an appropriate way and vice versa, it should be no wonder that Dawa had come to bear neither anger nor resentment against being born a woman, still less any will to do something to 'change' the state of 'woman' in her society. After all, everyday practice

[64]About *dhanga*, see also Desjarlais 2003.

itself, no matter that it positions women 'lower' than men, cannot be the *cause* of her misfortune, her misfortune cannot be *derived* from that. Having endured sufferings and resisted vigorously against them, as she actually did, does not necessarily bring about realization of the subordinated status of 'woman' in Yolmo society.

She bears no grievance against the practice also because the practice has already got *into* her, it has become part and parcel of herself. In short, she *is* a woman and she cannot, and does not, want to cease being a woman, the person carrying out things *with dhanga*, in an appropriately gendered manner. Howsoever severely she has to suffer, howsoever vigorously she resists her fate – these facts have basically no bearing on her conception of herself as a woman. They can have nothing to do with her gendered self-conceptions. So long as she performs everyday practice in an appropriate way, she is a Yolmo woman and does not have to be anything else.

CONCLUSION

I have tried to delineate the status and agency of women in the context of contemporary Yolmo society, namely, women's position in the structure that accords them inferior status, on the one hand, and individual women's acts and wills produced as well as constrained by this structure, on the other hand. The question that drove this paper forward was: How can Yolmo women seem so contented with being born a woman in their society, when being a woman means being 'inferior' to, as well as disadvantaged in a number of respects than, being born a man? Or, how is the generally assertive and high-spirited manner of Yolmo women, their active agency, being (re)produced? In other words, how is it possible for their agency to take the form that it appears to do, in the context of their structural subordination? Searching for the answer to these questions, firstly I sketched the outline of their structural subordination in the context of everyday practice, and then brought this picture into compelling contrast with a Yolmo woman's experience, which contains the extraordinary magnitude of sufferings as well as struggles, which turn out amply to attest to her agency. The extent of her sufferings and struggle, if far from representative of Yolmo women, gave us a clue to look into that seemingly contradictory relationship between the 'low' status and the 'active' agency of Yolmo women, which has been the central concern of this chapter.

One factor that sustains what is regarded as a more or less clear contradiction in each Yolmo woman's life is the simple, commonsense truth that every woman's sufferings are different, in degree or in kind. While each one of the women (or men, for that matter) suffers in her own way, they are one and the same in that they are 'woman' – there is no direct causal or logical chain(s) between one's gender and one's fate, after all. The 'chain' cannot be isolated in a neatly identifiable form, but is interwoven with many other kinds of 'chains', which do not allow themselves to be unravelled easily. Women's sufferings can be explained *only partially* by their being a woman.

Another factor is related to the embedded/embodied nature of gender. Objective gender structure is constituted through people's concerted practice (and exists as long as people's practice continues) and it is in turn embodied in a gendered habitus which constitutes – is part and parcel of – the gendered individual. In other words, one's gender is not something easily detachable from oneself. It is thus not at all surprising that few people ever attempt to reflect upon, still less negate, their gender. To do that could involve questioning the very way of being oneself, *who they are* in the first place. Under the imminent imperative of performing things in the right way, every day, any time, it is in fact highly improbable that people would delve into this kind of far-reaching questioning. Only from a sort of external position does the imperative begin to lose its self-evidence and one is likely to start seeing the order of things in a different light.

If a Yolmo woman never objects to being born a woman, we may point out one more reason for that. It is not only because her sufferings cannot be ascribed solely to her being a woman or because she was brought up that way and does not question the state of things she found herself in. It is also because her very wishes, longings, or dreams, at least some of them, are *made out of her being a woman,* as it were. If she aspires to marry "a beautiful, handsome man", for example, she does so precisely from the position of a woman, normatively heterosexual, in one way or another. Being born a woman is actually not just a source of her sufferings; it turns out to be what constitutes her desires and thus the very foundation of her joys, at the same time.

REFERENCES

Abu-Lughod, L. 1990. 'The Romance of Resistance: Tracing Transformations of Power through Bedouin Women', in P.R. Sanday and R.G. Goodenough (eds.), *Beyond the Second Sex: New Directions in the Anthropology of Gender*, pp. 311-37. Philadelphia: University of Pennsylvania Press.

Acharya, M. and L. Bennett 1981. *The Rural Women of Nepal: An Aggregate Analysis and Summary of 8 Village Studies (The Status of Women in Nepal*, vol. 2, pt. 9). Kathmandu: Centre for Economic Development and Administration, Tribhuvan University.

Ahearn, L.M. 2001. *Invitations to Love: Literacy, Love Letters, and Social Change in Nepal.* Ann Arbor: The University of Michigan Press.

Bennett, L. 1983. *Dangerous Wives and Sacred Sisters: Social and Symbolic Roles of High-Caste Women in Nepal.* NY: Columbia University Press.

Bourdieu, P. 1977. *Outline of a Theory of Practice*, tr. R. Rice. Cambridge: Cambridge University Press.

——. 2001. *Masculine Domination,* tr., R. Rice. Cambridge: Polity Press.

Butler, J. 1990. *Gender Trouble: Feminism and the Subversion of Identity.* London & NY: Routledge.

Cameron, M.M. 1998. *On the Edge of the Auspicious: Gender and Caste in Nepal.* Urbana and Chicago: University of Illinois Press.

Campbell, B. 2000. 'Properties of Identity: Gender, Agency and Livelihood in Central Nepal', in V.A. Goddard (ed.), *Gender, Agency and Change: Anthropological Perspectives*, pp. 102-21. London & NY: Routledge.

Clarke, G.E. 1980. 'The Temple and Kinship among a Buddhist People of the Himalaya'. Ph.D. thesis, University of Oxford.

Des Chene, M. 1997. '"We Women Must Try to Live": The Saga of Bhauju'. *Studies in Nepali History and Society* 2 (1): 125-72.

Desjarlais, R.R. 1994 (1992). *Body and Emotion: The Aesthetics of Illness and Healing in the Nepal Himalayas.* Delhi: Motilal Banarsidass.

——. 2003. *Sensory Biographies: Lives and Deaths among Nepal's Yolmo Buddhists.* Berkeley: University of California Press.

Gaborieau, M. 1991 (1981). 'The Indo-Nepalese House in Central Nepal: Building Patterns, Social and Religious Symbolism', in G. Toffin (ed.), *Man and His House in the Himalaya: Ecology of Nepal.* New Delhi: Sterling Publishers.

Hayami, Y., A. Tanabe, and Y. Tokita-Tanabe (eds.). 2003. *Gender and Modernity: Perspectives from Asia and the Pacific.* Kyoto: Kyoto University Press; Melbourne: Trans Pacific Press.

Kitamura, Y. 2004. *Indo no Hatten to Jenda: Josei NGO ni yoru Kaihatsu no Paradaimu Tenkan (Development and Gender in India: Women's NGO Practising Paradigm Change).* Tokyo: Shinyosha (in Japanese).

Lamphere, L. 1995. 'Feminist Anthropology: The Legacy of Elsie Clews Parsons', in R. Behar and D.A. Gordon (eds.), *Women Writing Culture*, pp. 85-103. Berkeley: University of California Press.

Maggi, W. 2001. *Our Women Are Free: Gender and Ethnicity in the Hindukush.* Ann Arbor: The University of Michigan Press.

March, K.S. 2002. *'If Each Comes Halfway': Meeting Tamang Women in Nepal.* Ithaca: Cornell University Press.

Ortner, S.B. 1978. *Sherpas through Their Rituals.* Cambridge: Cambridge University Press.

——. 1989. *High Religion: A Cultural and Political History of Sherpa Buddhism.* Princeton: Princeton University Press.

——. 1996a (1983). 'The Problem of "Women" as an Analytic Category', in *Making Gender: The Politics and Erotics of Culture*, pp. 116-38. Boston: Beacon Press.

——. 1996b. 'Borderland Politics and Erotics: Gender and Sexuality in Himalayan Mountaineering', in *Making Gender: The Politics and Erotics of Culture*, pp. 181-212. Boston: Beacon Press.

——. 1996c. 'Making Gender: Toward a Feminist, Minority, Postcolonial, Subaltern, etc., Theory of Practice', in *Making Gender: The Politics and Erotics of Culture*, pp. 1-21. Boston: Beacon Press.

Raheja, G. and A.G. Gold 1994. *Listen to the Heron's Words: Reimagining Gender and Kinship in North India*. Berkeley: University of California Press.

Ramble, C. 1997. 'Tibetan Pride of Place: Or, Why Nepal's Bhotiyas Are not an Ethnic Group', in D.N. Gellner, J. Pfaff-Czarnecka, and J. Whelpton (eds.), *Nationalism and Ethnicity in a Hindu Kingdom: The Politics of Culture in Contemporary Nepal*, pp. 379-413. Amsterdam: Harwood Academic Publishers.

Rubin, G. 1975. 'The Traffic in Women: Notes on the "Political Economy" of Sex', in R.R. Reiter (ed.), *Toward an Anthropology of Women*, pp. 157-210. NY & London: Monthly Review Press.

Sato, S. 2004. 'Kyodosei no Kindaiteki Jokyo: Nepal no Yolmo ni okeru "Minzoku" to sono Dojidai' (The Modern State of Community: Yolmos of Nepal in the Age of Ethnic Activism). Ph.D. thesis. The University of Tokyo (in Japanese).

Watkins, J.C. 1996. *Spirited Women: Gender, Religion, & Cultural Identity in the Nepal Himalaya*. NY: Columbia University Press.

7

Parental Wisdom *vs.* Youthful Romance: Getting Married in Two Nepali Communities

SARAH LEVINE

INTRODUCTION

With rising levels of education, young Nepalis are often still single at an age when their parents had already married and had several children.[1] In coeducational schools and colleges, and later on in the workplace, adolescents and young adults have the chance to form – albeit surreptitiously – romantic attachments to be nurtured as much by correspondence as by face-to-face contact (Ahearn 2001). In Nepal, as in India, young people, influenced by the mass media, as well as western-style education with its emphasis on self-development, are demanding a greater role in decisions regarding their own future, especially with regard to marriage.[2] As marriages based on personal choice, albeit with parental approval, become more common, new ritual forms are being introduced to accommodate them. Focusing on the female experience, this chapter looks at how marital unions have taken place over the past three decades in two communities in the Kathmandu Valley of Nepal, one composed of inner-city Newars and the other of Nepali-speaking Parbatiyas (hill people) who live in a semi-rural location about six miles away. Material is drawn from a study of the impact of women's schooling on reproductive and child health, and on children's acquisition of literacy skills, which was conducted in Lalitpur District between January 1997 and June 1998 (LeVine et al. 2001; LeVine et al.

---

[1]Funding for the research reported in this article was provided by the William T. Grant Foundation. In order to assure anonymity, all names have been changed. I would like to thank Emily Dexter, Meredith Rowe, Deepa Pokharel, Mridula and Ramendra Sharma, Mallika Shakya, and David Gellner for their comments.

[2]See, for example, Rao & Rao (1976), Osella & Osella (2002), and Medora (2003).

2004). The circumstances under which the marriages took place were of special interest because the women in the study most often identified marriage rather than, for example, personal choice or academic failure, as the reason for terminating their education.[3]

BACKGROUND TO THE STUDY

The 2001 census figures indicated that the Parbatiyas, the dominant ethnic group in Nepal who speak Nepali, a Sanskritic language, made up 32.4 per cent of the population. Uniformly Hindus, Parbatiyas are divided into three high (Thakuri, Brahman/Bahun, Chetri) and a small number of low occupational ('untouchable') castes. Newars constituted 5.6 per cent of the population, the majority of whom lived in the Kathmandu Valley (Gurung 2003: 5). Newars speak Nepal Bhasha/Newari, a Tibeto-Burman language, which suggests that their distant ancestors migrated into the Valley from the north-east rather than the south. Since at least the fifth century CE, the Newars have practised both Hinduism and Buddhism (Slusser 1982: 213); and Newars have their own complex caste system, which includes Buddhists as well as Hindus (Gellner & Quigley 1995). As Höfer (1979: 204) pointed out a quarter of a century ago, "Although [since 1963] there is no longer an inequality before the law based on caste affiliation, the system of relations constituting the caste hierarchy remains unchanged and is tacitly sanctioned." Although caste is now much more contested than it was when Höfer was writing, many traditional caste-based relationships (e.g. between priest and patron, patron and barber, or patron and sweeper) continue today.

Western-style education is a relatively new phenomenon in Nepal. In 1951, when the Ranas, who had run the country as their private fiefdom since 1846, were ousted it was estimated that less than two per cent of the population was literate and only half of one per cent of school-aged children were enrolled in school (Khaniya & Kiernan 1994). After the 'coming of democracy' (*prajatantra*) as the revolution of 1951 was popularly called, schooling spread quite rapidly so that forty years later, in 1991, 62 per cent of all fifteen year-olds in the country had been enrolled in school at some point (Stash & Hannum 2001). Poverty, caste and gender were still substantial barriers to access, however; levels of school attendance varied widely from district to district, and school dropout rates, especially for girls, remained high (Graner 1998). According to the 1991 national survey data, only 8.8 per cent of women of reproductive age (15-49) could read and write (Thapa 1996); again, even in Lalitpur district, one of the three districts of the

---

[3]Of 108 schooled women in the sample, 41 (38 per cent) reported that their schooling had been terminated by marriage.

Kathmandu Valley where Western-style education had been introduced earlier and school attendance had been more widespread than in other areas, 68 per cent of women in that age group had never been to school at all (Ministry of Health 1993). Following the return of multi-party democracy after the People's Movement (*jan andolan*) or revolution in 1990, successive governments made great efforts to broaden the educational base to include children who had been excluded. By the mid 1990s, all but the poorest low-caste children in the Kathmandu Valley were receiving at least a few years of formal education; furthermore the number of girls enrolled in school was now only slightly lower than the number of boys (ratio 1 : 1.2 for primary and 1 : 1.4 for secondary school) (CBS 1993). Like Liechty (2003: 212-16), we found that many fathers and mothers expressed the belief that educating children of both sexes and equipping them to become financially independent was their most important parental responsibility. When pressed, however, most admitted that in their view the arrangement of an offspring's marriage was even more important. This was particularly so in the case of a daughter.

According to Indic cultural traditions, at marriage a Newar or Bahun-Chetri girl leaves her father's house (Nw.: *thache*; Np.: *maiti*) and goes to live among 'strangers' in her husband's home (Nw.: *che*; Np.: *ghar*) where she is subject to the authority of her in-laws, at the bottom of the household hierarchy, and takes on her husband's kinship and ritual obligations. As the Newari proverb has it: 'One's own become other, others become one's own' (*thah katah, katah thah*). Infringements of *dharma* (her social and religious duty as prescribed by the scriptures) rarely go further than dawdling, after a visit to the temple, to chat with other women instead of hurrying home as she should. With the birth of a son, the young wife achieves a measure of respect and thereafter her status gradually rises until, when her son marries, she herself becomes a mother-in-law.[4] Concerned as parents usually are about their daughter's welfare during many years of subordination in her married home, they are as selective as their circumstances permit when choosing her husband.

THE STUDY

Material on which this chapter is based was collected from mothers of children aged four to nine who were enrolled in Kindergarten and Class One. Given our focus on measuring school-based literacy skills, we over-sampled women who had been to school: because schooled women could only be found in significant numbers in the high and middle castes, we drew our

[4]See Bennett (1983: 165-213), Levy (1990: 114-16), Kondos (1989), Gray (1995: 104).

sample from those castes. The subjects were born between 1950 and 1975 and got married between about 1965 and 1990. Age at marriage ranged from twelve to twenty-nine, with a median of eighteen years. Material is drawn from:

1. Open-ended interviews with twenty women, whose caste and socio-economic backgrounds were similar to those of the women in the study, concerning their personal experience with regard to marriage, separation, divorce, and widowhood, and the experiences of junior kin;
2. A survey questionnaire covering these topics submitted to 167 women aged 22 to 47.

THE TWO COMMUNITIES: SOCIAL CONDITIONS IN THE LATE TWENTIETH CENTURY

The Newars of Patan (N = 86)

The Newars, a people who include many distinct status and occupational groups, live in densely clustered settlements which are structured by kinship and affiliation to religion-based organizations (*guthi*). Although the majority are Hindus, a substantial minority are Buddhists whose form of Mahayana Buddhism is derived from that which flourished in the first millennium CE in northern India. Since Newar Buddhism has always existed side by side with Hinduism, the two traditions share many beliefs.[5] While the geographical origins of the Newars are not precisely known – their ancestors appear to have migrated into the Kathmandu Valley from all points of the compass over a long period of time – their culture has much in common with that of their Bahun-Chetri neighbours. Their Tibeto-Burman language, although structurally unrelated to Nepali, is heavily Sanskritized in its vocabulary. As a result of continuous contact with South Asian Indic culture, possibly by the fifth century CE and certainly by the end of the first millennium, they had begun to develop what, by the fourteenth century, had become their own exceedingly complex caste system (Riccardi 1980). Meanwhile, Buddhist as well as Hindu high castes had adopted brahmanical life-cycle rites.

Forty-five per cent of the women in our study were high-caste Buddhists (Vajracharya and Shakya) and twenty per cent were high-caste Hindus

---

[5]Traditionally, Buddhist Newars follow Vajrayana or Tantric Buddhism, a form of Buddhism that in medieval times was widespread in the Gangetic Plain. In the wake of Muslim invasions in the late twelfth century, it disappeared from India and survived in South Asia only in Nepal (Gellner 1992). By the seventeenth century at the latest, the last monks had married and metamorphosed into householder priests in the manner of Hindu Brahman priests. Their descendants own and occupy the residential courtyards of hundreds of temples and ancient monastic complexes in the three main Kathmandu Valley towns.

(Shrestha). The Vajracharyas and Shakyas are, in terms of their traditional socio-religious identity, domestic and temple priests; most of the Shresthas are Hindus who, under the Newar kings, enjoyed noble rank. Although denied noble status by the Parbatiya conquerors, they were – and still are – considered to be high-caste. The fourth Newar group (35 per cent) were the Maharjan/Jyapu belonging to a number of intermarrying agriculturalist sub-castes. Jyapus in this study are city dwellers, some of whom still go out from the city to work their fields each day. Some scholars have identified them as the descendants of the aboriginal inhabitants of the Kathmandu Valley and thus to have been less influenced by Indic culture than the Newar high castes (Pradhan 1981: 8; Toffin 1984: 19-20, 157, 587, 589). The majority of Jyapus in our study called themselves Buddhists.

The Bahun-Chetris of Godavari (N = 81)

The ancestors of the farmers of Godavari migrated into the Kathmandu Valley as soldiers in the army of Prithvi Narayan Shah, king of Gorkha, who defeated the last Newar kings in 1768/9 and were rewarded for their military service with irrigated fields from which, according to local lore, the inhabitants, Tamang peasants, had been chased away to rain-fed land on the tops of the surrounding hills. Today's Godavari landowners, who live in two-storey brick houses in widely dispersed settlements, each lineage on its own land, are orthodox Hindus belonging to two high castes, Brahman/Bahun (priests, according to the four varna scheme, but most are farmers) and Chetri (warriors or rulers, according to the varna scheme, but likewise most are farmers).[6] Three Parbatiya low occupational castes (tailors, leatherworkers, and ironworkers) also live in the area together with a mix of tribal people and members of a former slave caste (Gharti)[7] who are employed as labourers in the local marble quarry and other enterprises, which include a shirt factory and a beer-bottling plant. Only Brahmans and Chetris, who make up 23 per cent and 77 per cent of our sample respectively, are under consideration here. For the last several decades their acreage has provided these farmers with an inadequate cash income; thus most able-bodied men work off the land. Some are employed locally but most

[6]Chetris included a few Puri and Giri (who claim to be descendents of Brahmans who, after renouncing their caste to become wandering holy men – *sannyasi* –, later married and returned to householder life). These two groups are considered equal to Chetris with whom they frequently intermarry (Bouillier 1979).

[7]Gharti living in Godavari are reported to be descendants of Magar tribesmen who, having been given to their creditors as 'bondsmen' in repayment of debts which their families had incurred, were never redeemed. Although slavery was abolished in Nepal in 1924, most Gharti continued to live on the land and to work for their former masters. They form a separate endogamous caste.

commute to Kathmandu and Patan where they work at every level from office boy to high government official.

MARRIAGE, DIVORCE, WIDOWHOOD, AND REMARRIAGE AMONG THE NEWARS AND BAHUN-CHETRIS

Despite cultural differences, and despite their own sense that they are different from each other, Newars and Bahun-Chetris do in fact share a great deal. Furthermore, since everyone watches the same Hindi and Nepali films in which marriages are frequently depicted, both ethnic groups are increasingly pressured into accepting a pan-Hindu form of wedding ceremony. At the same time, there remains great diversity among the Newars, even among middle- and high-caste Newars, so that in their attitudes towards and expectations of marriage some high-caste Hindu Newars are actually closer to Bahun-Chetris than they are to other Newars.

Various forms of (first) marriage have been identified among the Newars, ranging from the ritually elaborate and expensive to elopement, with a number of simple forms falling in between. Pradhan (1981: 58) noted four forms in Bulu; Ishii (1995) found three in Satungal, as did Sakya (2000: 145) in south Kathmandu. Our Patan informants listed four:

1. marriage arranged through a designated go-between (*lami*) and ritually sanctified by a priest;
2. marriage arranged though a *lami* but without priestly sanctification;
3. 'love marriage' (*lav marij*) formalized by all the conventional rituals;
4. elopement.

Fürer-Haimendorf (1966: 49) noted two forms among the Bahun-Chetris, the first being a very elaborate, full life-cycle ritual and the second a much simpler rite known as 'worship of the lamp and water-jar' (*diyo kalash pujne*), which might also be used to legitimize an elopement or a second marriage. Bennett (1983: 71) reported that *swayambar*, in which the bride places a garland around the groom's neck, could be substituted for *diyo kalash pujne*. For at least the past half-century the costly and ritually complex form has been the most popular in both ethnic groups and four fifths of the women in our study were married in this way. Many were still in their early and middle teens when their parents, in the belief that they were doing as well as they possibly could for their daughters, had withdrawn them from school to marry them off.

Polygyny is fairly common in both communities and the process by which a man marries his second wife is much simpler than the one by which he married his first. If, instead of keeping his first wife with him, he divorces her, he may do so – whether formally or informally – with relative impunity.

For her part, a discarded wife's only option is to return to her natal home where she and her offspring are likely to be resented by her brothers' wives and children. Divorce initiated by a Bahun-Chetri woman is rare and much stigmatized, as is remarriage (Bennett 1983: 12, 258 n.11); however, the existence of Jaisi Bahuns, the descendants of Brahman widows, indicates that widow remarriage happened often enough in the past. Although divorce initiated by both sexes has been reported to be common among village Newars,[8] Ishii (1995: 120) found that it was relatively rare in Satungal, the village where he worked in the 1970s and 1980s; in the city it is rarer still and is very much frowned upon, especially in the case of Newar high-caste women.[9] Gellner and Pradhan (1995) suggest that it is uncommon among urban Jyapu women as well, and we also found this to be true.[10]

The marriage of a Newar girl differs from that of a Bahun-Chetri in one important respect. In effect it is her second marriage. Well before puberty, at age eight and often younger, all high-caste and some middle-caste[11] Newar girls undergo an elaborate rite known as *ihi* by which a father makes a formal offering of his daughter (*kanyadan*, the gift of a virgin daughter, the central rite of the Hindu marriage ceremony) to the god Narayan (Vishnu) represented by a *bel* or oak-apple fruit (Allen 1982; Kunreuther 1994).[12] Following this rite, which is performed by a priest, the parents are expected to host a feast for their relatives and friends. Because *kanyadan* is not included in her second (adult) marriage ceremony, *ihi* is regarded as a Newar girl's only true marriage. The rationale most often given for *ihi* is that, because it links a girl in marriage with a god, her status as a married woman is not

[8]See Fürer-Haimendorf (1966), Nepali (1965: 250), Pradhan (1981: 68-75), Toffin (1984: 120-1).

[9]See Quigley (1984: 253, 260), Lewis (1984: 296), Levy (1990: 131), Gellner (1991), and Tuladhar (1995).

[10]Only one Jyapu woman in the study admitted to having had a previous marriage that ended in divorce.

[11]Pradhan (1981) reported that none of the Jyapu women in Bulu, the village in the southern part of the Kathmandu Valley where she worked, had had *ihi*; Kunreuther (1994), who worked in Kathmandu and in Terathum in east Nepal, reported that "most" Newar girls undergo *ihi*. However, our data indicates that urban Jyapus are still in the process of adopting *ihi*. Whereas all the high-caste Newar women in our study had undergone the rite, this was true of less than one third (28 per cent) of Jyapu women. Most said that in their families it was simply not the custom to perform *ihi*. Financial constraints, i.e. that their families couldn't afford to celebrate the rite with a feast, do not appear to have been the problem since, although some high-caste families may provide lavish feasts for their daughters, other families, including Jyapus, generally take their daughters along to someone else's celebration of *budha/budhi jankwa* (old-age rites) or the establishment of a new *chaitya* where the main expense falls on the sponsor of that rite, or, in Kathmandu, attend a mass *ihi* celebration, which does not require one to hold a feast (Gellner, personal communication).

[12]For Hindus it is often said that the *bel* fruit represents Shiva as a witness to the marriage, and for Buddhists, Suvarna Kumara, the son of Shiva (Gellner 1991).

reduced by the death of her earthly spouse. Technically she does not become a widow and so avoids the restrictions to which a widowed Bahun-Chetri woman is subjected (Toffin 1977: 38; Pradhan 1981: 68; Allen 1996); most importantly, she is free to remarry. Although Ishii (1995) reported that remarriage was common among young village widows, it is as stigmatized for a high-caste Newar woman as it is for a Bahun-Chetri. Widows who are still of child-bearing age may choose to go this route, despite the stigma, but the only option for older widows is to live out their lives in a marginal position in their deceased husband's household (Gellner 1991).

ARRANGED MARRIAGE

The conventional marriage, which is how the large majority of our subjects got married, is arranged by the parents or senior members of the two families, and is between young people who are unrelated and usually complete strangers. The wedding itself is sanctified by a Hindu or Buddhist priest and celebrated by feasting. Whether or not Newar parents believe that *ihi* is the only true marriage their daughter will ever enter, for them, as for Bahun-Chetris, finding her a 'good' mortal husband is their primary concern.

For Bahun-Chetris, a go-between (*lami*),[13] who may be a man but is more often a woman, is central to the search and to the negotiations between the two families (Fürer-Haimendorf 1966: 48). Although frequently a relative, the go-between may be unrelated or even someone hired for the purpose. Most importantly, he or she should have a large circle of acquaintances, which, it is hoped, includes a family that is currently in search of a bride for their son – or a husband for their daughter. He or she also plays a formal role during the wedding ceremony itself. High-caste Newar parents have always called on a *lami* to find a bride for a son but it was only in the 1990s that they started to so find husbands for their daughters too. Some would let it be known within their social circle that they had a daughter of marriageable age and then wait for word to get around; but others would merely dress her in expensive clothes and show her off on celebratory occasions, especially at weddings. If, despite her finery, she failed to attract a proposal, there was nothing her parents could do about it. Thus, whereas virtually all Bahun-Chetri women over age thirty, unless they are seriously physically or mentally handicapped, are married, albeit to a widower or to a man who is himself compromised in some way, many Newar families include a spinster sister or aunt who, even though as a young girl she had no observable defects, may never have received an acceptable marriage proposal or even any proposal at all.

---

[13] The Godavari Bahun-Chetris have adopted the Newari word for matchmaker.

THE SUITABLE BOY: GENERAL REQUIREMENTS

Parents have a wide range of concerns when considering a potential son-in-law. As Fürer-Haimendorf (1966: 48) observed of the Bahun-Chetris he studied in the Godavari area in the 1950s, parents want husbands for their daughters in whose families "everything is normal and respectable and nothing has to be explained away". First, the young man should be from the same caste and sub-caste but from a different lineage. Each sub-caste conducts household rites in a slightly different manner and, given that married women are responsible for carrying out most domestic rituals, it is considered most important that an incoming bride be familiar with the ritual practices of her married home. If performed incorrectly, rituals could be ineffective, if not damaging to the health and welfare of the family. Second, there should be no traceable kin relationship between the pair, i.e. the boy must be at least seven generations removed from the girl on her father's side and four generations removed on her mother's side. Third, the boy's family should not be 'compromised' by divorce or an irregular marital union.[14]

Both Newars and Bahun-Chetris agree not only that the ritual status of the two families should be identical but also that their economic circumstances should be as similar as possible or else problems may occur later on (Bennett 1983: 147; Levy 1990: 130).[15] Marrying one's daughter to a man from a better-off family sometimes occurs but is frowned upon.[16] The reason usually given is that over the course of a marriage the bride's relatives must fulfil many material commitments to the bride and her children (Bennett 1983: 148-51; Ishii 1995: 134). Should the husband's family be wealthier, the bride's relatives will be unable to meet those commitments adequately and as a result will experience shame and resentment. On the other hand, since parents are anxious that their daughter live in her husband's house in

[14]Included here are unsanctified marriages by men of the patriline with widows or divorcées as these result in lowered caste status for the children of those unions; inter-caste marriages entered into by the candidate's close relatives are also cause for concern as the caste status of the children of these irregular unions is lower than the father's.

[15]Although Bahun-Chetri families are of equal ritual status when marriage negotiations begin, by virtue of *kanyadan* (gift of a virgin daughter, see below), the central rite of their wedding ceremony, wife-givers assume a subordinate position in relation to wife-takers. This is not true of Newars since *kanyadan* is not part of their wedding ceremony.

[16]Newly prosperous urban Jyapus who want to improve their caste status have been reported taking brides from poor but high-caste Shrestha village families. The quid pro quo involved is as follows: the girl goes to live in a wealthier home and the boy, by virtue or his father financing his entry into a Shrestha funeral organization (*guthi*) may be accepted as a Shrestha, or if not, then at least *his* son will be (Rosser 1966). However Quigley (1995: 90) claims that "while there is indeed a great preoccupation among Sresthas with this kind of mobility, its actual incidence is very limited."

the manner to which she has been accustomed in her natal home, for a boy from a poor family to marry a girl from a rich family is also disapproved of.[17]

In childhood, a Newar or Bahun-Chetri girl has a strong attachment to her mother's natal home which is represented by her mother's brothers (Nw.: *paju*; Np.: *mama*). After marriage she may remain emotionally very close to her mother; however, at the birth of her first child her relationship with her own brothers deepens. As her child's *paju/mama*, her brothers are required to attend and participate in all their nephews' or nieces' life-cycle rituals.[18] Meanwhile, from earliest childhood, a sister, who is believed to embody auspiciousness, has offered her brothers ritual protection, a role which she continues to fulfil throughout her life.[19] On the fourth day of the autumn festival called Tihar by Parbatiyas and Swanti by Newars, a married sister returns to her natal home to bless her brothers in a rite known as *Bhai Puja* to Parbatiyas and as *Kija Puja* to Newars; in return, her brothers give her gifts that are as lavish as they can afford.[20] A sister's ritual attention is considered essential to her brother's welfare, most especially to his reproductive success. Similarly, the ritual attention of her brothers is considered essential to the welfare of her children. This reciprocity of roles requires frequent contact and results in a strengthened relationship between a married woman and her brothers whose visits and emotional support should help ensure her welfare in her married home.

Among both Newars and Bahun-Chetris, the residential arrangement of choice is the three-generational joint family consisting of the patriarch, his wife and unmarried children, and his married sons with their wives and children who live together in one house in which all the married women share a single cooking hearth. Among the Newars, a son who separates when both his parents are still alive will definitely be criticized, unless his father has married a second wife. Only on the death of the patriarch should sons go their separate ways, meaning that – ideally – each son builds his own house on land behind the original house.[21] In the Bahun-Chetri case, by contrast, it is expected that sons will separate after some years of marriage, and no criticism is levelled against them. In rural areas new house sites are generally available so that sons can easily separate when they wish to. But given the shortage of land in urban areas, instead of building separate residences

---

[17]This may occur among Bahun-Chetris when a girl is handicapped in some way and a husband from her own economic background cannot be found.

[18]If a woman has more than one brother, ritual obligations to her children are shared among them and they take it in turns to attend ritual events in their sister's married home.

[19]See Bennett (1983: 248-52), Levy (1990: 415), Gellner (1995b: 228), Gray (1995: 85-93).

[20]Shakya and Vajracharya men are exceptions to the rule in that at Kija Puja they have to go to the house of their married sister (Gellner 1995b: 228).

[21]In practice there are cases in which parents and married sons separate their household. Conversely, it is not unknown for brothers to continue living together after their father's death.

Newars often divide the tall, narrow family house into small (sometimes tiny) flats. Although sisters-in-law no longer share a kitchen, they continue to live in very close quarters and competition and resentment may flourish as before. In many cases, it is to survive feuds with sisters-in-laws rather than mistreatment from her husband or parents-in-law that a Newar wife needs support from her natal kin.

As noted earlier Newars, like Parbatiyas, are forbidden to marry people with whom they are able to trace a kinship connection. Newar high- and middle-caste parents often prefer to marry their daughters in the immediate vicinity, not only for emotional reasons but because this will allow for easy access, both for the fulfilment of ritual obligations and for support from the natal home. Given the density of Newar settlements, they are frequently successful in their search (Gellner 1995a: 28; Sakya 2000: 140).[22] Thus in the early years of her marriage, when she is most in need of support from natal kin, many young Newar wives manage to visit their natal homes almost daily. By contrast, Bahun-Chetris are traditionally a rural people, and although migrants to the city can sometimes find suitable spouses for their offspring close by, in the countryside this is unlikely. Thus a new bride may find herself living at a considerable distance from her natal home, which she rarely has the opportunity to visit. Young Bahun-Chetri women often expressed a longing for contact with their families and a deep sadness that distance restricted it. In contrast with the Newars, of whom 38 per cent of our sample reported visiting their natal homes at least once a week, only 4 per cent of the Bahun-Chetris did so and 48 per cent reported making two visits or less each year (usually at the festival of Tihar in November and on Mother's Day in May). Again, whereas 34 per cent of the Newars reported seeing their brothers at least once a week, only 2 per cent of the Bahun-Chetris saw their brothers so frequently.

Kanchi, a Chetri girl from Godavari, was one of the fortunate ones. The youngest of six children, she was much loved. Her mother, Prabha, wept at the prospect of losing her. Her father, Sri Ram, and her three adult brothers were grave and sad. But Kanchi was eighteen and needed to get married. The married homes of Sri Ram and Prabha's other daughters were far from Godavari and, apart from the two months they spent in their natal homes after giving birth, they rarely saw their parents. Kanchi, Sri Ram, Prabha, and their sons decided, wasn't to marry more than one hour away. They asked the headmaster of the local primary school to be their intermediary; he had taught a great many children over the years, including Kanchi, and knew

[22] The 'marriage close at hand' model applies mainly to Jyapus, Shakyas/Vajracharyas, Udays, and Manandhars. For a long time Shresthas have preferred to marry over long distances (Ishii 1995: 125-7). Out of necessity, occupational castes who, because their castes or sub-castes are small, must also marry far away. Women from these castes, which make up approximately one third of the Newar population, may visit their natal homes infrequently.

everyone within a 3-mile radius. They had no luck the first year but early on in the second the *lami* suggested a boy whose home could be reached on foot in 30 minutes. Sri Ram accepted his proposal, the two young people were married in the conventional manner, and four months later Kanchi became pregnant. During her pregnancy she would often arrive in her natal home soon after daybreak and stay there until her husband came to fetch her home in the evening. "He refuses to let her spend the night with us," Prabha remarked with obvious satisfaction, the implication being that he had fallen deeply in love with her. Sri Ram stopped complaining about how much Kanchi's wedding had cost. The whole family was delighted, even self-congratulatory, at how well things were working out.

More typical was the experience of a young Chetri woman named Jyoti, who was married to Arun before she reached menarche. Impressed by the prospect of ten *ropani*s of irrigated land on which Arun's father grew three crops a year – unheard of in their own hill-farming community – Jyoti's parents had accepted his proposal. "They thought they were sending me to a good place," Jyoti said ruefully. She conceded that her widower father-in-law was a kind man, but even so, without an adult woman in the homestead to share the burden of work, during the first few years of her marriage she had often felt overwhelmed. As her husband's home was two days' walk away from her natal home, her brother had rarely been able to visit and she had been miserably homesick.

THE CANDIDATE'S PERSONAL ATTRIBUTES

Caste, kinship, correct marital history, economic status, and geographical location are the most important factors that parents bear in mind when considering marriage proposals for their daughters. Once they have ascertained as best they can that the boy and his family meet these criteria, they proceed to an appraisal of the candidate's personal characteristics. First, he should be no more than five years older than the girl. A wider age gap is to be avoided since it implies 'problems': he has been too long out on his own, perhaps working in India or the Gulf or studying abroad, and may not settle to the responsibilities of married life; or else he may have 'bad habits' such as drinking, gambling or, worse yet, drugs. Only very poor parents will give their daughter to a widower since he is likely to be much older than she and the father of several children. From the outset, her workload will be extremely burdensome and there is a strong likelihood that one day her own sons will quarrel bitterly with their half-brothers over their patrimony.

Second, a husband should have more formal education than his wife, a consideration which rarely presented a problem a generation ago, when few girls went to school and those who did studied for only a few years.

Although by the late 1990s almost as many girls as boys were studying in secondary schools and university, this is a recent development. Women recalled being taken out of school – including primary school – in the 1980s, because their parents were afraid that if they kept on studying their marriage chances would be negatively affected. "Men are afraid of educated women," one Sakya woman observed. "And even if they aren't, usually their mothers are. Women of an older generation are very conservative. Even those who can read and write are in two minds about an educated daughter-in-law ... If she has a job and earns a salary, the mother-in-law likes that, but she doesn't like it when the daughter-in-law expresses her own opinions."

A third consideration is the number of brothers a candidate has. Given the rivalry likely to develop in a joint household, the fewer sisters-in-law a young wife has to deal with, the better. If the prospective bridegroom is an only son, his wife will have no one to help her with domestic work; if he has several brothers, competition over resources of all kinds could be intense. Ideally, then, he should have just one brother.

Good health is a major concern but character is less so. The belief that marriage is the cure for youthful irresponsibility is widely held. "When the leopard changes his spots, no one's surprised," a Brahman woman remarked. "That happens all the time. If the family is good, then chances are the boy will turn out good as well." Looks are more important to boys than to girls and, as elsewhere in the subcontinent, a fair complexion is especially prized (Rozario 2002). In particular, Brahman women, whose distant ancestors are believed to have hailed from the south, confided how, as young girls, they had worried about rejection on account of their dark complexions. During negotiations, each party sees photographs of the other, but although theoretically a girl may also veto her suitor on the basis of looks, in fact this very rarely happens. A college-educated Bahun-Chetri woman observed, "That's gender inequality for you! A boy could have rejected me because he didn't like my photo but however much I may have disliked *his* photo, I couldn't have rejected him. The girl's parents don't care about the boy's appearance, only about his family and his job. If the family is respectable and the boy is employed, they're happy. Why would they care if his skin is black and spotty or his nose is too big?" Parents are concerned with the boy's family more than with the boy himself for two reasons: first, in a joint household, their daughter will spend many more daytime hours with her female in-laws than with her husband; second, the marriage will establish an alliance between the two families and the burden of maintaining it will be carried by their own sons, in their role as maternal uncle. In short, the parents look for a 'good fit' for their sons as well as for their daughters.

These days, a boy and a girl whose parents are in the process of negotiating their marriage may be brought by relatives for a 'meeting' in a neutral space such as a temple courtyard or a restaurant. While family members chat the young couple may steal glances at each other but they rarely exchange a word. Even if the boy tries to talk to her, the girl is usually too shy to respond. Again, although sometimes this 'meeting' takes place before the two families have reached a firm agreement, more often than not it only occurs afterwards. "So what would have been the point of talking to him?" said one highly educated Newar woman. She recalled that at age twenty-six, this was the first 'serious' proposal she had received and the level of anxiety in her family was palpable. (Had she educated herself out of the marriage market?) "Whatever I thought about him after I'd seen him wouldn't have made any difference. My parents and his parents had agreed and that was that."

THE ENGAGEMENT

According to Newar tradition, in order to finalize the marriage negotiations[23] the boy's family sends a tray bearing ten betel nuts, clothes, cosmetics, and toiletries to the girl. By contrast, once negotiations are concluded, Bahun-Chetris conduct a formal engagement ceremony known as *tika lagaune*. Escorted by a party of male relatives and friends, the bridegroom comes to the bride's house and, in the presence of the bride's family priest, the young couple garland each other and put red paste dots (*tika*) on each other's foreheads. The groom's party is then provided with a meal.

An engagement, which involves many gifts from the groom's family to the bride's family, may last days, weeks, or months, depending on the time of year and the astrologer's calculations. Although traditional parents like Kanchi's would not dream of allowing her to spend time with her betrothed, it is now the practice among more westernized parents to let their daughter meet the boy they have chosen for her periodically so that the two can get to know each other. Negotiations over the marriage of Parami, a twenty-one year old Shakya girl, who had completed two years of college, and Ratna Man, who had finished his BA degree and had entered his family business, were completed in January; however the astrologer determined that the wedding shouldn't take place until May. The two sets of parents – Parami's father headed a non-governmental organization and Ratna Man's father had a thriving craft export business – agreed that in the intervening months the engaged couple could talk as often as they wanted on the telephone and go without a chaperone to certain, carefully selected restaurants. (Cinemas, frequented mostly by poor people, were definitely out of bounds.)

[23]Many financial issues must be negotiated. On the groom's side, they include gold jewellery for the bride and whether or not to hire a band to accompany the wedding procession. On the bride's side, they include presents for the groom and the goods – jewellery, saris, clothing, and household items (*saman*, or *stridan* meaning dowry) – which she will bring with her to her married home. These things constitute her inheritance; after marriage a Nepali woman has no further claim on her father's property.

THE WEDDING

Although the schedule of events that make up a traditional wedding is not set in stone, the sequence, which is broadly valid for both high-caste Newars and Bahun-Chetris, is usually as follows:[24]

1. The bride's family gives a feast for their relatives and friends.
2. Accompanied by a brass band (musicians belonging to the untouchable Damai – tailor – caste wearing 'military' uniforms),[25] the groom and his male friends arrive at the bride's house.
3. Rituals of *swayambar* (garlanding)[26] and *kanyadan* (the gift of a virgin daughter) in the case of Bahun-Chetris, and *swayambar* in the case of Newars, are conducted by a priest.
4. The bride, wearing the red silk sari and gold jewelry that her husband has given her, takes tearful leave of her natal home and family, climbs into a palanquin (in the village) or a car decorated with pink streamers (in the city), and, with a brass band playing, is escorted to her new husband's home. Her dowry (*stridan/saman*), consisting of as much gold jewellery and ornaments as her family can afford to give her, a bed and bedding, cooking vessels, a closet, a trunkful of new clothes, and these days a TV, takes up the rear of the wedding procession (*janti*) on porters' backs or in a truck.[27]
5. On their arrival at the groom's home, bride and groom undergo a series of rituals; these are followed by a feast at which the groom's family introduces the bride to *their* relatives and friends.
6. The marriage is consummated within four days of the bride's arrival.

It is by this sequence of events, which Bennett observed in locations near

---

[24]Bahun-Chetri weddings may only occur in the seven months of the year that are regarded as auspicious. Newars also generally observe these restrictions, but, because upper-caste brides have undergone *ihi* and thus are considered to be already married, their weddings may in theory take place in the five inauspicious months as well; however, they rarely do so. For an account of elaborate Newar weddings from the 1950s, see Bajracharya (1959).

[25]Hiring brass bands to play at weddings is a relatively recent innovation introduced by Bahun-Chetris and adopted by high-caste Newars. The older women in the study did not have them at their weddings. Those Jyapu women whose weddings followed a highly elaborate form were accompanied to their new husbands' homes by traditional Jyapu flute bands. As a feature of Jyapu revivalism, Jyapu organizations (the Jyapu Samaj in Patan and the Jyapu Mahaguthi in Kathmandu) insist that wedding music be played by local Jyapus – both as a way of preserving the tradition and as a way of keeping costs down – rather than by a Damai brass band.

[26]In the ritual of *swayambar*, the bride formally 'chooses' her bridegroom by garlanding him, although in reality her parents have already selected him. *Swayambar* is a relatively recent innovation for Newars. Fifty years ago the bridegroom did not go to fetch his bride but rather, waited at home for his male relatives to bring her in the *janti*. When she arrived a joining ritual (*hwakegu*) was performed for the bride and groom (Sakya 2000: 247).

[27]Exactly what the *stridan* consists of is the subject of much discussion and gossip.

Godavari in the 1970s and Gray in the 1980s, that 93 per cent of the Bahun-Chetri women and 72 per cent of the Newar women in this study got married and that the majority of their younger relatives are still getting married. Among the emerging urban middle class, however, which defines itself primarily by patterns of consumption (Liechty 2003: 64-72), weddings are steadily becoming more extravagant. The night before Parami Sakya got married, her parents hosted a party in a downtown hotel. Parami, wearing a beautiful Varanasi sari, sat chatting with her female cousins while 700 relatives, friends, and colleagues of her parents (but no one from the groom's 'side') drank soft drinks, beer, and whisky and helped themselves to a lavish buffet. Next day, the groom arrived at the bride's home with his father, male relatives, and neighbours. After the *swayambar* ritual had been performed under the direction of a Vajracharya priest, a sumptuous meal was served to the groom's party and members of Parami's family, about forty guests in all. Throughout these proceedings, instead of being conventionally solemn (bridegroom) and painfully shy (bride), this young couple, who, it was reported, had already, during the course of their 'dates' over the months since their official engagement, 'fallen in love', appeared relaxed and happy. When the time came for the bride to be escorted to her new husband's home, she left her house, climbed into a black SUV decorated with pink streamers and, instead of weeping, grinned from ear to ear. Following the completion of the traditional rituals in the groom's home and a buffet supper given by his parents that in lavishness equalled the one given the previous evening by the bride's parents, the young couple departed on a four-day honeymoon.

By 2000, a few devout Theravada Buddhist parents had begun calling on monks as well as their traditional Vajracharya priests to perform their offspring's marriages; and a few, in addition to a feast for hundreds of friends and relatives, were offering a midday meal (*bhojanadana*) to up to forty monks and forty nuns (LeVine and Gellner 2005: 321).

Almost half the Jyapu women in the study (42 per cent) reported that their marriages had been arranged. Few, however, had been married in the ritually elaborate manner uniformly favoured by the high castes. Recalling her own girlhood, one remarked,

> My father died when I was a young child so from age ten I worked on construction sites in the dry season and gave my wages to my mother, and in the rains I worked in our fields. People knew I was a hard worker, and when I was fifteen a proposal came for me. My auntie was the *lami*. What the *lami* always looked for was a girl who worked hard and I was one of those. I was taken to see my husband's father who told me what work I'd have to do in his place. My mother thought it was a good place and told me so. As for me, what did I think? I thought, if it isn't this man, then it'll just be another. So I agreed ... I came here and my father-in-law put *tika* on my hus-

band and me and after that we were married. No priest came to the house and we didn't go to the temple either.

Poor and fatherless though she had been, she felt that her mother, with a *lami*'s help, had looked out for her interests and done well for her.

Today, as in the past, the parental hope is that a boy who grows up in a good family (meaning one in which the head of the household is firm but fair-minded and thus the level of conflict is low) will turn out to be a good husband. Although parents are less concerned with the bridegroom's personal characteristics than with his family's culture and traditions, it is their assumption that two reasonably attractive young people from similar backgrounds will be compatible and that understanding and a companionate love will gradually grow between them. These days, having spent many years studying and working with the opposite sex as well as watching Hindi films and soap operas on cable TV and reading Barbara Cartland romances, in the case of college-educated girls, and *The Joy of Sex*, in the case of college-educated boys, young people want more than companionship from marriage. They want romance, which in Nepal may be as much the outcome of parental care and youthful expectation as personal choice. A Brahman woman who had observed her two sisters, one who had a love marriage and the other an arranged marriage, remarked, "Three days after the wedding, you couldn't have told the difference – my sister Riva and her husband, Rajiv, who hadn't spoken one word to each other before their wedding day, were as crazy about each other as my sister Kamala and *her* husband, who'd met in college and were formally engaged for two years. Riva and Rajiv expected to fall in love, and so they did."[28]

Mothers were asked if, aside from the prestations that tradition specified they should receive from their relatives on ritual occasions, they received any financial (cash and major consumer goods) from parents and brothers with whom, as their children's *paju/mama*, they had a lifelong special relationship. Bahun-Chetri women were more likely than Newars to report having received financial help both from parents (77.7 per cent compared to 60.4 per cent) and from brothers (63.9 per cent compared to 53.4 per cent). Table 7.1 suggests that, despite much less frequent face-to-face contact, Bahun-Chetri women had more licence to call on their kin and their kin were more willing to respond positively than was the case with Newars. This may indicate the willingness of Bahun-Chetri parents and brothers, who rarely saw their daughters and sisters, to substitute financial support for face-to-face moral support. The Maharjans, with 73.3 per cent, were the only Newar

---

[28]Ahearn reports (2001: 75) that her Magar informants, citing the proverb *naso pasyo, maya basyo* (the vein/hose [penis] entered, and love followed), told her that, regardless of how a new bride might feel about her husband at the outset, once they had had sexual relations she would begin to love him.

Table 7.1: Patan and Godavari Mothers: Financial Help Received from Parents and Brothers (*mama/paju*)

	Maharjan (30)	Shakya (23)	Vajracharya (16)	Shrestha (17)	**Newar Total (86)**	**Bahun-Chetri (81)**
Financial help from parents	22 (73.3%)	13 (56.5%)	8 (50%)	9 (52.9%)	**52 (60.4%)**	**63 (77.7%)**
Financial help from brothers (*mama/paju*)	16 (53.3%)	13 (56.5%)	10 (62.5%)	7 (41.1%)	**46 (53.4%)**	**55 (63.9%)**

caste who came close to the Bahun-Chetris' 77.7 per cent positive response for receipt of parental help. This is interesting given that most Maharjan women were living in the same neighbourhood as their parents and saw them frequently thereby obviating the need to substitute financial help for face-to-face emotional support; again, more than half of the Maharjans (58 per cent) reported having had love marriages by which one might expect them to have alienated their parents. But whereas women from the higher castes who had had love marriages often reported having alienated their parents at least initially, this was rarely the case with Maharjans, in whose community love marriage and elopement were both common and accepted (see following section). This finding points to the possibility that, compared with married women in the Newar higher castes, Maharjan women have a closer – if not more dependent – relationship with their parents.

Although the two ethnic groups as a whole were ten percentage points apart with regard to financial help from brothers, Vajracharyas, with a 62.5 per cent positive response, were within only one percentage point of the Bahun-Chetris. This may reflect the fact that whereas love marriage was a not uncommon occurrence among women belonging to the other three Newar castes, only one Vajracharya woman reported having chosen her husband herself. Thus women belonging to this socially conservative group may have been able to call more easily – and with greater chance of success – on their families than the other Newars in the study.

DOMESTICATING ROMANTIC LOVE

Although 24 (28 per cent) of the Newars reported that they had chosen their husbands themselves, love marriage was very rare among the Bahun-Chetris: only two women in Godavari reported that they had husbands of their own choosing, and one of them, a Brahman woman named Prema, admitted she had regrets. Her husband, also a Brahman whom she'd met in secondary school, had turned out a n'er-do-well. Her parents, she conceded, would probably have made a better choice than she. In the younger generation, however, anecdotal evidence indicates that love marriage is becoming more common. In any event, a large proportion of both Bahun-Chetris and Newars reported having younger relatives who had had love marriages. Most of these marriages were between girls and boys from similar caste backgrounds and so, whatever their initial reservations, their parents had been able to arrange the marriage and get them married in the conventional way. Following the death of their father, an Upadhyaya Brahman woman who had had a major role in the upbringing of her much younger sister and was about to see her marry her college sweetheart, admitted that she liked the boy, but she expressed sadness that the boy came from a Jaisi Brahman family, i.e. his paternal grandfather had married a (young) widow and therefore the children of that union had 'lost caste'. "I never thought I'd see my sister, who comes from a *jharra* family such as ours [i.e. whose lineage is impeccably pure], marrying a Jaisi and giving birth to Jaisi children."[29]

In Patan, a young man named Sanup told me about how, having fallen in love with his college classmate, Pramila, he had been confronted by parental class- as well as caste-prejudice. A compliant only son who in the past had often told friends that he would leave his marriage up to his parents "who knew about how to arrange such things whereas he didn't", Sanup suddenly informed his family that he and Pramila intended to get married. Both young people were Brahmans, but because Sanup's family was from the city whereas Pramila came from the Tarai, Sanup's parents, assuming that they were impecunious provincials, refused to countenance the marriage. "People like us don't marry people like them," they told Sanup. They justified their snobbery on additional grounds: they were Purbiya Brahmans whereas Pramila's family were Kumai Brahmans;[30] their ancestors were believed to have come in different historical periods from different parts of north India and traditionally the two groups, each of whom considered themselves ritually superior to the other, did not intermarry (Bista 1967: 4). Sanup's parents admitted that in recent decades they had heard of Kumais accepting Purbiya brides for their sons. Perhaps nowadays some Purbiyas were also accepting Kumai brides for their sons but that hadn't yet happened in *their* family, and it wasn't about to happen now!

At this point Sanup threatened to elope with Pramila and since the young people were both well educated and might be able to make it financially on their own, this was no empty threat. Meanwhile, Pramila's parents, to whom

---

[29]Upadhyaya Brahmans embody and maintain the highest ritual purity in terms of marriage and food restrictions (Bennett 1983: 11). Jaisi Brahmans are the offspring of the union between an Upadhyaya Brahman and a Brahman widow or divorcée.

[30]Kumais, who traditionally provide the Shah kings with their chief priests (*rajguru*), are said to have come from Kumaon in modern Uttaranchal and Purbiyas from further to the east.

news of the romance had been 'leaked' by one of Pramila's brothers, had their own strong objections: the last thing they wanted was for their only, much-loved daughter to spend a lifetime being despised by her in-laws. After weeks of tension, Sanup's parents learned, through discreet investigations, that even though, in their view, Pramila's family were provincials, their economic status was just about equal to theirs; and so, reluctantly, they resigned themselves to overlooking differences in ritual status. Sanup's mother instructed Sanup to bring Pramila on a Saturday afternoon to a certain temple to which she came accompanied by her younger and altogether more 'modern' sister. After sending Sanup away, the two women interviewed Pramila at some length and when, after wandering about the neighbourhood feeling at once both defiant and apprehensive, Sanup returned to the temple, his mother informed him that Pramila had 'passed'. The next step was for Sanup's father to approach Pramila's parents. Preparations for the marriage could go forward, he informed them, so long as it was presented to their respective social circles as an arranged marriage. Meanwhile, the young people would have to accept the following restrictions: (1) they were not to see each other again until the wedding, which, since Pramila's maternal grandfather had recently died, could not take place until the year of mourning was over; and (2) if they met on campus, they were forbidden to talk to each other on the grounds that if they were seen doing so, there would be gossip about Pramila, and Sanup's parents would not countenance their son marrying a girl whose reputation (*ijjat*) had been sullied. However they could correspond with and telephone each other. Provided the young people accepted these stringent conditions, Sanup's parents were willing to permit the college romance to metamorphose into marriage. Meanwhile, even though, given that Pramila's family were Kumais and they themselves were Purbiyas, everyone who knew either side was perfectly aware that this had to be a love marriage, they went along with the fiction which Sanup's parents perpetrated: after scouring the country for suitable spouses for their offspring, the two sets of parents had decided that Pramila and Sanup were better suited for each other than any other candidates.

A Brahman woman voiced the concerns of many parents when she exclaimed, "Nowadays, young people are so free in their behaviour! If I had a daughter in the college, I'd be worried sick. It's so easy for a girl to lose her good name, and once that goes, who will marry her?" Young single women complained bitterly that parental determination to keep everything 'normal and respectable' can get out of hand. "Sometimes, more out of concern for family reputation than for their daughter's welfare, parents respond too quickly to gossip," a Shakya girl said angrily. "If they hear from somebody that their daughter has a 'friend', their first thought is to get her married to him as soon as possible. You daren't be seen even *talking* to a boy in case someone goes and tells your parents. Parents aren't concerned with *your* feelings, only with what other people *think*. So the next thing you know, they're making you *marry* the boy! You may not even like him, let alone love him but they won't listen. And if your so-called 'friend' *isn't* from the 'right' sort of family, that won't save you. Just to protect their *own* reputation, your parents will marry you off to some stranger who *is*."

Like Pramila, most of the high-caste Newar women who reported that they had chosen their partners themselves had fallen in love with boys from the 'right-enough' sort of family, enabling their parents to 'get them married' in the conventional way. By contrast, Jyapu women – almost half of whom had had love marriages – reported that they had simply eloped with their boyfriends. On arrival at the boy's home, the boy's father had put *tika* on the young couple and sometimes, but not always, invited his immediate relatives to a celebratory meal.[31] "And then we were married," one woman recalled with a shrug, years later. Sometimes the boy's family had taken a while to accept the relationship, which meant that the couple had had to stay with sympathetic friends while the boy negotiated with his parents. (If the boy's parents were adamant in their refusal to accept the girl into their household and the young couple could not afford to rent their own place, once they wore out their welcome with their friends, they would separate and the girl would return to her parents.) We were told that although for their part the girl's parents often put on a show of being outraged, they were usually reconciled within the year. "A mother always wants to see her daughter," one young wife explained.

Devi Maya, a poor Jyapu woman, still single at age twenty-eight, declared fiercely that she would never elope. She also reported that she had received seven marriage proposals and rejected them all. "Those men knew I was a good worker and that's why they wanted me, but they weren't what *I* wanted. Some were village people. ... Some were townspeople. ... One was a widower. ... Another had sent his wife back to her parents ... Two or three were heavy drinkers. All men drink at feasts of course and most get drunk as well, but those fellows who asked for me got drunk every day. Men like that always beat their wives. ..." Unlike three of her brothers whose marriages, although arranged, had been celebrated in a very simple fashion and without sanctification by a priest, she wanted a *pakka* (properly elaborate) marriage to a good man who wouldn't get drunk and wouldn't beat her and wouldn't despise her because her family was poor. "My *lami* will be a neighbour, not a relative – my aunts are all too close, they know our family business too well." They knew that she had three as yet unmarried and three married brothers, all of whom lived with their wives and children in the narrow parental house, and that the six quarrelled incessantly with their widowed

---

[31] For descriptions of Jyapu weddings, see Pradhan (1981), Toffin (1984), and Ishii (1995).

mother and with each other. "They wouldn't strike a good bargain for me." Devi Maya wanted a very good bargain. She wanted her *lami* to make sure that the wedding was done in style, just as it would be for a girl from a well-to-do, harmonious family that everyone respected:

> Together with the betel nuts, the boy would bring me nail polish, a sari, pretty underclothes. Then we'd have the *swayambar* and a party in my house. And then there'd be a proper *janti*. The boy would take me to his house in a taxi with his friends and relatives walking alongside. ... Even though it's expensive, his family would agree to hire a band to head the procession. ... And the following day, my in-laws would have a party for us, and then we'd go to the temple and the priest would put *tika* on the two of us. We'd spend four days at his house, and after that, four days at mine. And then we'd be married for good, for the rest of our lives.

Although upper-caste Newar women from rich families do sometimes remain single from choice, Devi Maya was well aware that in her case spinsterhood, without any prospect of an inheritance, was not an option. But she knew that because her family was poor, her father was dead, and her brothers were quarrelling with her mother, she had little hope of having a *pakka* marriage to a good man. For that, she needed a united family, one that was willing to scrimp and save and sacrifice for her, one that would stand behind her afterwards so that if she had trouble in her husband's home they would help her. But the reality was that, rather than making sure she married properly, her brothers were urging her to elope. "That way, I'd cost them nothing," she said bitterly. "No *bhoj* (feast), no saris, no *saman*, nothing at all."[32]

When she heard the word 'elopement', Devi Maya's aunt, who had been listening to the conversation, shook her head in disgust:

> Eloping is very bad. Those girls – they simply arrive with their boyfriends and there they are, without any formality at all. Usually a girl like that, she's been having trouble at home. She's been quarrelling with her mother and so she runs off with a boy without knowing anything about him. She just needs somewhere to go. But when she gets to his house she'll probably find he already has a wife – who gets mad as anything. And the in-laws don't want the girl either – "just another mouth to feed" is what they're thinking. So there she is, without any protection at all. Because she ran away from home, her brothers won't accept responsibility for her. They're not going to stand up for her later on and so when the boy doesn't

[32]Devi Maya's brothers' approach was, and no doubt still is, a common and sensible strategy among families who wish to avoid expense.

like her anymore, what can she do? If she's settled things with her mother, maybe she can go back home, but if she hasn't, where will she go? All she can do is elope with another man, maybe one who's even poorer than the first.

INTER-CASTE MARRIAGE

While parents acquiesce to the inevitable when, as in the case of Sanup and Pramila, a son or daughter falls in love with someone of the same caste, the parents of young people who fall in love across caste or ethnic lines are likely to oppose the match much more vigorously. Such marriages constituted the most flagrant violation of caste rules which, until its repeal in 1963, the Nepal Law Code imposed on all citizens. Under the old law code, hypogamy – marriage between a high-caste woman and a man of lower caste – was punishable by large fines, imprisonment, slavery, and even death (Höfer 1979: 71). Hypergamy – marriage between a high-caste male and a female of lower caste – was not illegal and was common, especially in rural areas. However, it too was socially penalized: the husband and family, including the children, of the incoming woman, did not eat the rice she cooked. If the incoming woman was from a higher caste than her husband, he and his family did eat the rice she cooked but the children of the union took their father's caste. As noted above, the offspring of a Brahman man and a Brahman widow or divorcée fell into a special category known as Jaisi, while the child of a Brahman father and a Chetri or a tribal mother fell into a lower category known as Khatri, often abbreviated today as 'K.C.', short for Khatri Chetri. Fürer-Haimendorf (1966) noted that in the 1950s a substantial proportion of Godavari households were the offspring or descendants of mixed-caste marriages. Although it is possible, after several generations of strategic marriage alliances, for a patriline to purify itself so that the great-grandchildren of a Brahman man and a Chetri or a Tamang woman achieve pure Chetri status, in the 1990s, many Godavari families still called themselves Khatri. It appears that in the intervening decades few had purified their lineages. Despite their legal elimination, almost everyone remains acutely aware of caste distinctions.

Inter-caste marriage results in ambiguous caste status for the offspring of the union and this is especially so in the case of a hypogamous union. Anita Shakya was in her fourth year of college when she eloped with Mohan, her Jyapu classmate. They had been discreet sweethearts for several years and although Anita's mother had eventually learned about the relationship, her alcoholic father remained in the dark. One day, after her father, in a drunken rage, gave her a beating, Anita eloped with Mohan to his family's house. His parents, who up to this point appear to have been in the dark about the relationship, were none the less delighted that their son had brought them a girl from a high caste family. Sakya reports (2000: 172-86) that by this time, the mid 1990s, Theravada monks were occasionally being asked to perform a ritually simple wedding ceremony for mixed-caste couples in the monastery; but even though Anita's mother was a devout Theravadin and Anita may have known about this option, she and Mohan did not avail themselves of it. Mohan's father did not call a priest to perform a wedding ritual; nor did he perform a domestic ritual either. Nevertheless, four days after Mohan brought Anita to the house they were considered by both families to be 'married'.

When Anita's father learned that his daughter had had a 'surreptitious marriage' (Sakya 2000: 175) with a Jyapu boy he declared that she was never to darken his door again. Her mother berated herself mercilessly for not having forced Anita to break off her romance and wept at the thought of her slender daughter, who had never worked in the fields in her life, planting rice seedlings in the summer sun. Members of her extended family, convinced that she had severely compromised the marriage chances of her female cousins, were aghast. What Shakya parents would permit their son to marry a girl whose 'cousin-sister' would soon be giving birth to a Jyapu child?

ALTERNATIVE RITUAL SOLUTIONS

From the viewpoint of Newar parents, a romance between a Buddhist and a Hindu, even if they are of equivalent caste status, is nevertheless problematic. Their concern, however, may be more with the offspring of the union than with the young couple. As half-castes, at feasts, where guests must be seated according to caste, how will they know where to sit? In the case of the son of a Shakya or Vajracharya father and a Shrestha or Uday mother, what *baha* will admit him as a member? What death *guthi* will come to burn them when they die? Most important, who will they marry? In fact, marriages between high-caste Hindus and Buddhists are sufficiently common to have resulted in the adoption of special ritual processes. Provided the approval of both families is obtained and both sets of parents can be present, both Buddhist and Hindu priests may be invited to perform wedding rituals. Although Sakya reports (2000: 145) that these are more likely to take place on different days, when Mina Shrestha and Vinaya Shakya got married, their family priests combined forces to perform the wedding rites. At age twenty-nine, Mina had been 'looked at' by a number of young men, all of whom had turned her down. Given that she was beautiful, highly educated, and came from a very good family, this could only be *explained*, her sisters decided, by her determination to marry a man she had chosen herself, and hence her off-putting behaviour with prospective suitors. She denied she had a boyfriend, much less divulged his identity, until one day, after she had been rejected by the latest in a succession of suitors, she told her parents that she wished to marry Vinaya Shakya. Vinaya, who worked in her office, had been pressing her to marry him for several years; but she had taken her time to consider his proposal and meanwhile, as a filial daughter, had submitted herself to being 'looked at' by half a dozen men from her own caste. When at long last the young people made known their intentions, both sets of parents adjusted quite quickly to the news and set about planning the wedding. On day 0ne, Mina's family would give a party for 500 friends and relatives in a rented hall. On day two Mina, accompanied by her entire extended family, would go to their neighbourhood temple, Batuk Bhairab, in Lagankhel, where they would be met by Vinaya, his father and his male relatives. There the *swayambar* ritual would be conducted by the Shrestha family's Brahman and the Shakya family's Vajracharya, after which Vinaya would take Mina to his home in a ribbon-festooned car. (Although Vinaya's relatives would accompany them on foot in the traditional manner, Mina and Vinaya vetoed hiring a brass band since in their view brass bands were noisy and distasteful.) On day three, Vinaya's parents would host a party for 500 of *their* friends and relatives in their home. Aside from having the *swayambar* performed by the priests of both families in a temple rather than by her own family's priest in her house, Mina's wedding was going to be exactly like the weddings of her sisters, both of whom had had arranged marriages. Furthermore, like her sisters and their husbands, after their wedding, Mina and Vinaya were going to live in a joint household with Vinaya's parents, his brothers and his brothers' wives.

Mina and Vinaya's wedding was six weeks in the planning; but Saruna Shakya and Sudhir Shrestha couldn't spare one week let alone six. Negotiations for the marriage between Saruna and a suitable boy had almost been finalized when, one Sunday, she informed her parents that instead she was going to marry Sudhir, whom she had got to know at work. Furthermore, since Sudhir was about to be transferred to Delhi and Saruna intended to go with him, they had to get married immediately. Her parents, who until then had been completely unaware of Sudhir's existence, were convinced that, given their daughter's self-confidence and implacable determination, if they withheld their consent she would elope. So, stunned though they were, on the following Wednesday they put on a full-scale wedding party at which, in the presence of hundreds of guests, Saruna and Sudhir garlanded each other in an ad hoc *swayambar* ceremony.[33] Sudhir's parents and relatives, who lived outside of Kathmandu, were not present. Despite this, and despite the

[33]Parents are able to put on wedding parties at very short notice provided (1) they hire a caterer, who, typically, is capable of providing an elaborate but standard menu for as many as half a dozen parties on the same evening, and (2) they can call on an army of female relatives to shop for the bride's *saman* and prepare many of the requisite ritual accoutrements.

fact that no priest had officiated, Sudhir and Saruna were regarded as man and wife.

Mina and Saruna were fortunate in that, even though the husbands they chose were from different castes and different religions, 'at least', like themselves, their sweethearts were high-caste Newars and thus their parents were able to set aside their misgivings. From the parental point of view, however, a marriage between a Newar and a Parbatiya is much more difficult to accept. A schoolteacher named Sushila Shakya fell in love with a Bahun colleague, Sachit Pandey. Knowing that Sachit would be unacceptable to Sushila's devout Theravada Buddhist family, the couple had no choice but to elope. After stopping at a Hindu temple to receive *tika* and a blessing from the priest whom Sachit knew, they made their way to Sachit's home where Sushila was introduced to the Pandey parents. Although at first they were upset that their son had defied them, given that the couple were living separately and the issue of commensality could be avoided, the Pandeys ultimately accepted Sushila as their daughter-in-law. But Sushila's parents were obdurate. Six years after the elopement, although they permitted their daughter to visit and they even baby-sat for their grandson from time to time, they continued to bar their son-in-law from their home. And, to their sorrow, unlike his Buddhist cousins, Sushila's little boy, as the son of a Brahman father, was not attending *buddhadharma* classes in the Theravada vihara.

Under the 1971 legislation that established civil marriage, all these mixed-caste couples could have registered their marriages in the Central Office of Lalitpur district and thereafter they would have been legally married. It appears, however, that to date, unless the woman needs to provide official evidence of her marital status in order to obtain a passport, few mixed-caste couples elect to go this route (Sakya 2000: 175). Rather, they – or their parents – prefer to adopt some variation, however minimalist, of the traditional wedding ritual.

CONCLUSION

More than four fifths of the women in the study (83 per cent) reported having had ritually elaborate and expensive weddings to young men, who, although from similar caste backgrounds, were complete strangers. Again, most of those women who had fallen in love with young men from the same background had also got married in the conventional manner of their caste. In the decade or so since the youngest women in the study married, however, the incidence of love marriages between young people belonging to different castes and religious traditions had steadily risen, a consequence of greatly increased unsupervised contact between young men and young women who were staying longer in school and then entering the labour force, and of the advent, through the mass media, of Western notions of romance. A Brahman woman with two college-going sons spoke for many when she confessed that it would be easier for her to accept a foreigner as a daughter-in-law than a Nepali girl belonging to a different caste. She, like many other high-caste and many middle-caste parents, deplored inter-caste marriage but admitted that she didn't know how to prevent it.

Most of the children about whose futures these women worried were still quite young and their marriages were many years off. As mothers, they wanted to do the best they could for their offspring and to most this meant arranging good marriages for them, including, in the case of many Jyapus, providing them with the kind of elaborate wedding that they themselves had not had. Even though some dreaded the expense, they believed that unless a daughter was properly provided for, her in-laws would not respect her and she would suffer in her husband's home. One Jyapu woman voiced the frustration she was facing with her eldest daughter in this regard. When the girl received her first marriage proposal, even though her parents considered it a good one and wanted her to accept it, she summarily turned it down on the grounds that the boy had less education than she did and he was too old-fashioned in his thinking. "She's been getting all these ideas from TV," her mother noted bitterly. Parents who were eager to provide their daughters with 'all the advantages', were discovering, to their hurt and chagrin, that they had minds of their own.

Although the majority of women (including most of those who had themselves married for love) emphatically *favoured* arranged marriages, when asked whether they *expected* to arrange the marriages of children of both sexes, only just over half (54 per cent) of the Patan mothers said yes. Godavari mothers, living 6 miles distant from the lures of city streets and better able to supervise their offspring, were more confident: almost three quarters (73 per cent) said they expected to arrange their children's marriages. Again, whereas 76 per cent of Godavari mothers said they expected to arrange their daughters' marriages in particular, only 56 per cent of Patan mothers were so confident. Asked what qualities they hoped their son-in-law would have (whether or not they had any say in choosing him), Godavari mothers most often said that he should have a good education, whereas Patan mothers stressed that he be 'understanding'. In response to the question, "What kind of girl would you want your son to marry?" Godavari mothers again stressed education, whereas Patan mothers more often hoped for a daughter-in-law who was 'simple and unspoiled'. Thus, while a rural mother was likely to see education – leading to employment – as the essential component of a good life, an urban mother, taking a high level of education as a given, had a more nuanced view. On the one hand she hoped that her daughter would marry a man who was more considerate of his wife's wishes than perhaps her own husband had been of hers; and on the other she wanted to save her son from marriage to a 'modern' young woman who she imagined would have unbridled consumer desires and little respect for her in-laws. Most especially, she wanted to protect *herself* from the conflict that was likely to arise between herself and a 'modern' daughter-in-law with a 'mind of her own'. Unlike rural Bahun-Chetri families who, when conflict escalates to an intolerable level, can separate their joint households with relative ease and thereafter, as close neighbours, live harmoniously, unless they were wealthy enough to buy land and build in the suburbs, an urban Newar family's only option is often to continue sharing a narrowly confined space.

To conclude, in the late 1990s, although parents might still believe that getting their daughter married 'well' was their most important parental responsibility, many admitted that the choice of groom might no longer be theirs to make. The decision would have to be made jointly – if it hadn't already been made. Typically, however, educated young women were cautious and pragmatic. Even if they wanted to select their husbands themselves, they knew that sooner rather than later a married woman would need the support of natal kin. Well aware that marriage without parental approval would precipitate a long and painful period of estrangement before they – let alone their husbands – would be welcome in their natal homes, instead of eloping they were more likely to stand their ground and negotiate. For their part, confronted by a daughter's determination to marry a man from a different background, the more modern their attitudes, the more likely parents were to accept the situation as a fait accompli and, rather than cutting her off as their own parents would almost certainly have done, to celebrate the union and arrange to have it sanctified by one of the new rituals.

REFERENCES

Ahearn, L.M. 2001. *Invitations to Love: Literacy, Love Letters, and Social Change in Nepal*. Ann Arbor: University of Michigan Press.

Allen, M. 1982. 'Girls' Prepuberty Rites amongst the Newars of the Kathmandu Valley' in M. Allen and S.N. Mukherjee (eds.), *Women in India and Nepal*. New Delhi: Sterling.

Allen, M. 1996. *The Cult of Kumari: Virgin Worship in Nepal*. Kathmandu: Mandala Book Point.

Bajracharya, P.H. 1959. 'Newar Marriage Customs and Festivals'. *South-Western Journal of Anthropology* 15: 418-28.

Bennett, L. 1983. *Dangerous Wives and Sacred Sisters*. N.Y.: Columbia University Press.

Bista, D.B. 1967. *People of Nepal*. Kathmandu: Ministry of Information & Broadcasting.

Bouillier, V. 1979. *Naître renonçant: une caste de Sannyasi villageois au Népal central.* Nanterre: Laboratoire d'ethnologie.

CBS. 1993. *Population Census 1991: Social Characteristic Tables,* Vol. I, Pt. VII. Kathmandu: HMG National Planning Commission Secretariat.

Fürer-Haimendorf, C. von (ed.). 1966. *Caste and Kin in Nepal, India and Ceylon.* Bombay: Asia Publishing House.

——. 1966. 'Unity and Diversity in the Chetri Caste of Nepal', in Fürer-Haimendorf (ed.), pp. 1-63.

Gellner, D.N. 1986. 'Language, Caste, Religion, and Territory: Newar Identity Ancient and Modern'. *European Journal of Sociology* 27: 102-48.

——. 1991. 'Hinduism, Tribalism, and the Position of Women: The Problem of Newar Identity', *Man* (N.S.) 26 (1): 105-25. Reissued as Ch. 11 in D.N. Gellner 2001, *The Anthropology of Buddhism and Hinduism: Weberian Themes*. Delhi: Oxford University Press.

——. 1992. *Monk, Householder, and Tantric Priest: Newar Buddhism and Its Hierarchy of Ritual.* Cambridge: Cambridge University Press.

——. 1995a. 'Introduction', in Gellner and Quigley (eds.), pp. 1-37.

——. 1995b. 'Sakyas and Vajracaryas: From Holy Order to Quasi-Ethnic Group', in Gellner and Quigley (eds.), pp. 209-39.

Gellner, D.N. and R. Pradhan. 1995. 'Urban Peasants: The Maharjans (Jyapu) of Kathmandu and Lalitpur', in Gellner and Quigley (eds.), pp. 158-85.

Gellner, D.N. and D. Quigley (eds.). 1995. *Contested Hierarchies: A Collaborative Ethnography of Caste among the Newars of the Kathmandu Valley, Nepal.* Oxford: Clarendon Press.

Graner, E. 1998. 'A Geography of Education in Nepal'. *Contributions to Nepalese Studies* 25 (2): 191-213.

Gray, J.N. 1995. *The Householder's World.* Delhi: Oxford University Press.

Gurung, H.B. 2003. *Social Demography of Nepal: Census 2001*. Patan Dhoka: Himal Books.

Höfer, A. 1979. *Caste Hierarchy and the State in Nepal: A Study of the Muluki Ain of 1854*. Innsbruck: Universitätsverlag Wagner.

Ishii, H. 1995. 'Caste and Kinship in a Newar Village', in Gellner and Quigley (eds), pp. 109-57.

Khaniya, T.R. and M.A. Kiernan. 1994. 'Nepal Systems of Education', in T. Husen and T.N. Postlethwaite (eds.), *International Encyclopedia of Education*, p. 4062. Tarrytown, NY: Elsevier Science.

Kondos, V. 1989. 'Subjection and the Ethics of Anguish: The Nepalese Parent-Daughter Relationship'. *Contributions to Indian Sociology* 25 (1): 113-34.

Kunreuther, L. 1994. 'Newar Traditions in a Changing Culture: An Analysis of Two Pre-Pubescent Rituals for Girls', in M. Allen (ed.), *Anthropology of Nepal: Peoples, Problems and Processes*, pp. 339-47. Kathmandu: Mandala Book Point .

LeVine, S. and D.N. Gellner. 2005. *Rebuilding Buddhism: The Theravada Movement in Twentieth-Century Nepal.* Cambridge MA: Harvard University Press.

LeVine, R.A., S.E. LeVine, and B. Schnell. 2001. '"Improve the Women": Mass Schooling, Female Literacy, and Worldwide Social Change'. *Harvard Education Review* 71 (1): 1-50.

LeVine, R.A, S.E. LeVine, M.L. Rowe, and B. Schnell. 2004. 'Maternal Literacy and Health Behavior: A Nepalese Case Study'. *Social Science and Medicine* 58: 863-71.

Levy, R. 1990. *Mesocosm: Hinduism and the Organization of a Traditional Newar City in Nepal*. Berkeley: University of California Press.

Lewis, T.T. 1984. 'The Tuladhars of Kathmandu: A Study of Buddhist Tradition in a Newar Merchant Community'. Ph.D. thesis, Columbia University (Ann Arbor: University Microfilms International).

Liechty, M. 2003. *Suitably Modern: Making Middle-Class Culture in a New Consumer Society*. Princeton: Princeton University Press.

Manderson, L. and P. Liamputtong (eds.). 2002. *Coming of Age in South and Southeast Asia: Youth, Courtship and Sexuality*. Richmond, Surrey: Curzon.

Medora, N. 2003. 'Mate Selection in Contemporary India: Love Marriages versus Arranged Marriages', in R.R. Hamon and B.B. Ingoldsby (eds.), *Mate Selection across Cultures*, pp. 209-30. Thousand Oaks: Sage Publications.

Ministry of Health 1993. *Fertility, Family Planning and Health Status Report*. Kathmandu: Ministry of Health, Family Health Division.

Nepali, G.S. 1965. *The Newars*. Bombay: United Asia Publications.

Osella, C. and F. Osella. 2002. 'Contextualizing Sexuality: Young Men in Kerala, South India', in L. Manderson and P. Liamputtong (eds.), pp. 113-31.

Pradhan, B. 1981. *Newar Women of Bulu* (Status of Women in Nepal, Vol. II). Kathmandu: CEDA, Tribhuvan University.

Quigley, D. 1984. 'The Social Structure of a Newar Trading Community, East-Central Nepal'. Ph.D. thesis, London School of Economics.

——. 1995. 'Sresthas: Heterogeneity among Hindu Patron Lineages', in Gellner and Quigley (eds.), pp. 80-108.

Rao, V.V. and N. Rao. 1976. 'Arranged Marriages: An Assessment of the Attitudes of College Students in India'. *Journal of Comparative Family Studies* 7: 433-53.

Riccardi, T. 1980. 'Buddhism in Ancient and Medieval Nepal', in A.K. Narain (ed.), *Studies in the History of Buddhism*, pp. 265-82. Delhi: B.R. Publishing.

Rosser, C. 1966. 'Social Mobility in the Newar Caste System', in Fürer-Haimendorf (ed.), pp. 68-139.

Rozario, S. 2002. '"Poor and Dark": What is My Future? Identity Construction and Adolescent Women in Bangladesh', in L. Manderson and P.L. Rice (eds.), pp. 42-57.

Sakya, A. 2000. 'Newar Marriage and Kinship in Kathmandu, Nepal. Ph.D. thesis, Department of Human Sciences, Brunel University, UK.

Slusser, M.S. 1982. *Nepal Mandala*. Princeton: Princeton University Press.

Stash, S. and E. Hannum. 2001. 'Who Goes to School? Educational Stratification by

Gender, Caste, and Ethnicity in Nepal'. *Comparative Education Review* 45 (3): 354-78.

Thapa, S. 1996. 'Infant Mortality and Its Correlates and Determinants in Nepal: A District-Level Analysis'. *Journal of the Nepal Medical Association* 34 (118-19): 94-109.

Toffin, G. 1977. *Pyangaon: Une communauté Newar de la vallée de Kathmandou: La Vie matérielle*. Paris: Centre National de Recherche Scientifique.

Toffin, G. 1984. *Société et religion chez les Néwar du Népal*. Paris: Centre National de Recherche Scientifique.

Tuladhar, S. 1995. 'Some Changing Aspects of Uday Marriage in the Kathmandu Valley'. MA thesis in Sociology, Tribhuvan University, Kathmandu.

8

Laments for Unfortunate Marriages: Domestic Violence in the Nepali Context

MAKIKO HABAZAKI

INTRODUCTION

It is said that domestic violence exists all over the world.[1] However, no widely accepted definition, not to mention a theory of it, has yet been established. As for those who are involved, it may occur between men and women, between women, or between men. The scope of the notion 'violence' may vary according to authors from the physical to the non-physical, including bullying by language, economic harassment, and so on.

Few anthropological articles take domestic violence as their main theme, because in order to deal with it we have to face the bare facts of violence, which can be encountered in the most private (i.e. domestic)

[1] I am grateful to H. Ishii, K. Nawa, and D. Gellner for their helpful comments and suggestions. I also thank K. Miyatake, T. Kuwayama, and H. Oda for their suggestions on earlier versions of this paper. I would like to express my thanks to Saathi, which granted me permission to conduct research interviews at the shelter. I wish to thank all the members of Saathi, and in particular Pramada Shah, Pramila Shah, and Kamini Chand. I am also grateful to Shanta Thapalia, Chhatra Kumari Gurung, Shashi Adhikary Raut, who are all LACC lawyers. I would also like to thank Nirmal M. Tuladhar, Mrigendra Karki of CNAS, and lawyer Nagendra Rai, as well as Anita Manandhar and Sumitra Manandhar Gurung, my advisers and friends. Thanks to Tomek Bogdanowicz for proof-reading this text. Above all, I am grateful to all the people I studied and interviewed, especially the women living in the shelter.

Materials for this paper were collected in March and April 2004 from interviews with the victims at the shelter in cooperation with Saathi. Open-ended interviews were conducted with all the residents individually. A questionnaire was prepared as a face sheet which mainly asked questions about life history. The women's home environment at both their maternal family and their husband's family homes was the main focus. Whilst the shelter has space for seventeen people, a total of twenty women were interviewed, as some sufferers came and left the shelter during that period.

space of all. In the anthropological literature, even when violence is taken up as a theme, scholars tend to focus on offering solutions or on institutions that mediate conflict; rarely do they pay attention to the actual victims of violence.[2] Tanaka (1998: 2) states that scholars have considered the theme to be difficult because of historical reflection which is aware of the fact that descriptions of violence in other cultures can give rise to the negative stereotype that they are violent, cruel, and barbaric. He also points out that anthropologists tend to think that the violence in each culture they deal with is exceptional and he suggests that they stay away from it both for their own safety and because of its complexity.[3]

Whilst an image of other cultures as being cruel or barbaric may possibly be propagated by cross-cultural research on domestic violence, it is also a fact that there are people who suffer from violence and as a consequence have lost all hope. Violence is a part, as well as a product, of culture. It is a highly personal experience. Some may regard certain behaviours as violence whereas others do not. If cultures differ, definitions of 'violence' will differ even more. Acceptable behaviour in one culture may be considered as abuse in another culture; the extent of 'violence' will vary according to culture.

In Nepal, especially in the case the Parbatiyas, although it is reported that domestic violence is serious, researchers have not been able to describe violence in ways that penetrate its core, nor have they been able to grasp the victims' situations or people's cognition of 'violence'. One of the reasons for this failure is that it takes place in the domestic sphere which is hard for non-family members to access.

Amongst high-caste Hindus, females are always inferior to males, and women can only obtain a high and secure status in their husband's household by mothering a son, who goes on himself to reach adulthood. A wife has to serve her husband as lord. It is "their dharma to be obedient, respectful, and pleasing to their husband" (Bennett 1983: 175).

When I stayed with a family of a Tibeto-Burman-speaking ethnic group, I witnessed a newly married wife crying after having been beaten by her husband. Yet she was hesitant to tell this fact to others, and nobody was there to help her. She was a Jirel. Notwithstanding this, after her husband left her, she was unable to prepare daily meals and her daily life disintegrated. Her mother-in-law refused to feed her, accused her of idleness, and eventually she left her husband's house.

The purpose of this study is to consider what kinds of phenomena are

---

[2]Recently a number of scholars who focus on domestic violence as their research theme have appeared. Some sessions on the theme of domestic violence were held by the American Anthropological Association in 1987, and by the Association for Social Anthropology in 1986 and 1988. See Counts, Brown, and Campbell (1992).

[3]For ethnographies dealing with domestic violence, see Babior (1993) and McClusky (2000).

recognized as 'violence' in Nepal and to explore the kinds of social backgrounds behind violence. I focus on domestic violence[4] and study it by means of interviews with residents of a domestic violence shelter. I will deal with them not as a social problem within each particular ethnic social group, but as one in the whole of Nepali society.

THE STATUS QUO OF DOMESTIC VIOLENCE AND ACTIVITIES TOWARDS ITS ERADICATION IN NEPAL

Policies towards Women and Legal Provisions in Muluki Ain

Movements opposing violence against women emerged in various countries particularly after the UN Declaration of the Elimination of Violence against Women (1993) revealed that violence to women is not a personal but a sociocultural problem formed historically by the unequal relations between men and women. In response to such global trends, actions to eliminate violence against women have emerged in Nepal without regard to cultural or ethnic differences. The government of Nepal, together with envisioning the establishment of a Family Court and a Mobile Court, is contemplating introducing acts to control domestic violence. The ninth five-year plan, begun in 1997, stated the necessity of empowering the economically weak, promoting gender equality, increasing women's access to political, economic, and social sectors, and enacting legal provisions to increase women's political participation (LACC n.d. a).

In 2002 the Parliament of Nepal passed the eleventh amendment to the Muluki Ain (Civil Law), changing women's property rights. It gives daughters an equal right to ancestral property as sons by birth, provided that they are not married and are over the age of thirty-five. It also admits the rights of widows to their husband's property, the property rights of divorced women, and the rights of divorced women to be fed by their former husbands. Moreover, it stipulates that women separated from their husbands, after taking their share of property, can adopt a child (or children), even if their former husband is alive or has a child by another woman. Furthermore, the previous restrictions on abortion have been

---

[4]There are a variety of terms used regarding such violence towards women, such as 'family violence', 'domestic violence', and 'violence against women', by Saathi, the NGO through which I carried out my field research. Some women in the shelter called their story of suffering *dukha ko kura*. Other women related only that they were beaten. One woman said that *pidit mahila* (oppressed woman) was identical to *domestic violence*. Their usage of the term 'domestic violence' was not consistent or uniform. Some used it to represent a state of human beings, others used it as a phenomenon from which they suffered. Nonetheless I will use the term 'domestic violence' in this chapter, as residents as well as staff at the shelter often used this term when speaking to me.

removed, effectively legalizing it up to twelve weeks. It has made punishments for rape more severe. Moreover, it has greatly improved marriage restrictions. Previously, the marriageable ages for women and men were sixteen and eighteen respectively, with the parents' consent, and eighteen and twenty-one respectively, without parental consent. Now for both women and men they are eighteen with parental consent, and twenty-one without. The gender distinction on this point has been abolished.

To prevent child marriages, punishments have been made heavier. In cases where a man marries a girl under the age of ten, he is fined between Rs.1,000 to 10,000, and is imprisoned for six months to three years. Where the girl married is between ten and fourteen, he is fined Rs.5,000, and imprisoned for three months to a year, and for girls between fourteen and twenty, he is either fined Rs.10,000 or imprisoned for six months.

As for polygamy, the amendment makes it clear that a man can neither remarry nor live with other women as long as his wife is alive and he has not divorced her, except in the following cases: (1) the wife suffers from severe venereal disease with no scope for a complete recovery, (2) she suffers from serious mental illness, (3) the governmental medical committee has proved that she is sterile, (4) her arms or legs are so paralysed that she cannot use them, (5) she has become blind, or (6) she has received a portion of his property according to the related Acts. Prior to the amendment, a wife's infertility for ten years was one of the conditions, but now the official medical committee has to certify her infertility (Sangroula & Pathak 2002: 110). Along with these changes, punishments have been made heavier; the fine for ignoring these provisions has been raised from Rs.1,000-2,000 to Rs.25,000, and the term of imprisonment has been increased from two months to between one and three years.

Domestic Violence Elimination Projects by NGOs

Some NGOs conduct activities to help eliminate domestic violence. Saathi and LACC (Legal Aid and Consultancy Centre) focus mainly on violence against women occurring within the family, and their efforts are directed to giving support to such women. Saathi runs shelters for victims of domestic violence and helps them to become self-sufficient. LACC mainly performs legal aid services for the protection of female rights.[5] Nepalese NGOs also provide social aid services to the victims of domestic violence.

Saathi, a non-governmental, non-profit organization established in 1992, aims for "the empowerment of women and children through the promotion of gender equity and equality based development" (Saathi n.d.). It has undertaken to combat violence against women in Nepal and conducts

---

[5] Although several support groups for women, such as ABC Nepal, Maiti Nepal, and RUDWOC, exist, only Saathi specializes in domestic violence.

projects to support victims and their children. They conduct awareness campaigns to enlighten society as to what domestic violence actually is.

LACC, established in 1987, offers free legal assistance to women in order to eradicate violence. Seventeen female advocates belong to the NGO, and they provide legal consultation, reconciliation, and legal actions. They started up the 'Women's Rights Helpline Project' and legal aid services on a radio programme in 1999. In addition, they publish leaflets and magazines which have helped to inform society at large about domestic violence in Nepal. According to the Helpline project, they were consulted 3,461 times between June 2000 and July 2003, with an average consultation time of thirty-three minutes. Those advised came from all over Nepal. Most of their complaints were about violence by husbands, and the subsequent partition of property, divorce, polygamy, and family disputes (LACC n.d. c).

Of those advised, 16 per cent were Bahuns, 29 per cent were Chetris, and 28 per cent were Newars; that is, 73 per cent were high-caste Hindus and Newars. Therefore, use of this service was particularly lopsided amongst the three caste/ethnic groups of Bahun, Chetri, and Newar.[6] In comparison to women's literacy rates in Nepal,[7] 53 per cent of them were 'literate', clarifying that most of them were well educated. Fifty per cent were residents of Kathmandu, 24 per cent from Lalitpur, 6 per cent from Bhaktapur, and 20 per cent from other areas.

The Helpline brings the problem of violence to public attention through its radio programme, and explains current legal provisions using case studies. Potential advice-seekers get information about this Helpline via the radio, as well as through word of mouth from friends and acquaintances. Thus most measures to support victims of domestic violence in Nepal are taken by NGOs.

The Current Status of Domestic Violence

Violence against women in Nepal ranges from sexual abuse, rape, and assault, to polygamy, child marriage, enforced divorce, trafficking, etc. Many instances of violence are recorded in *LACC LENS*, an occasional magazine of LACC, including those of wives chased out of the house because the dowry was poorer than the husband's side expected, wives beaten and driven out by the children of a co-wife and mother-in-law, wives slandered by the husband's family and finally becoming estranged from the husband, and the husband marrying another woman while the wife is absent giving birth in her natal home. All of the above cases have been

---

[6]LACC classifies only by six caste/ethnic categories, namely, Bahun, Chetri, 'Lower castes', Newar, 'Tibeto-Burmese', and 'others'.

[7]According to the Statistical Year Book of Nepal (CBS 2003a: 33) it is 48 per cent.

presented before a Nepali national court. Before resorting to a national court, sufferers sometimes appeal to the police or ask local intermediary organizations, such as neighbourhood associations, to arbitrate, which, either way, is settled by Nepali civil law.

Most women request separation from their husbands on the grounds of violence, polygamy, incorrigible infidelity, abuse caused by dowry disagreements, adultery disputes, beatings, and so on. They use legal means to attempt to recover their dues, their share of property that is held by their husbands, because it is difficult to solve such disputes through negotiations that do not entail legal action. In these instances, the abused wife may not seek a divorce but may wish to live away from the abusive spouse after getting her share of the property in order to escape from his violence. Estranged wives can receive monthly living expenses based on the earnings of their husband, until the property is distributed. Although according to state law women have the right to inherit their parents' property, due to the customary expectations in Nepali society they normally cannot claim it and do not receive it.

Prior to the eleventh amendment of the Muluki Ain, few unmarried women below the age of thirty-five in Chetri families in the Kathmandu Valley inherited their parents' land (Gray 1990: 214). Where customary law differs from civil law, the customary law of villages takes precedence. Thus, empowering women through civil law will not cause any rapid change in their ability to hold property in village Nepal, and it certainly will not prevent domestic violence without other social and cultural changes.

SHELTER FOR VICTIMS OF DOMESTIC VIOLENCE

The Saathi-managed Kathmandu shelter, 'Ashreya Shivir', which opened in 1995, is practically the only shelter for victims of domestic violence in Nepal. During a victim's stay at the shelter, daily necessities are provided free. Most women at the shelter have escaped from their homes and have no money, clothes, or daily necessities. Each individual is provided with a bed, which is the only space that can be considered her own private space. Otherwise, they live communally taking turns to cook and clean. There are some difficulties, which are peculiar to caste societies: in the case of either raw or cooked rice, whom one gives to, and whom one receives from could potentially become contentious issues. Training courses, such as making crafts or sewing, can be taken at the shelter, according to an individual's wishes. The shelter cannot be freely entered or exited; to go outside, permission must be obtained from the 'Madam', the chief of the shelter. Two women, who arrived as victims, now live at the shelter as residential staff and help to manage communal life, by purchasing daily provisions and so on. Women residents can stay there for up to six months. The NGO may seek a job for them, and it makes efforts to bring about a solution or negotiate a compromise between the resident and her husband. There was an exceptional case of an old lady who stayed at the shelter for over three years, because a job could not be arranged for her. Sometimes residents have mental problems and fear being isolated or not having anyone to help them.

Age and Caste/Ethnic Membership of Residents

Residents range in age from teenagers to those in their sixties. As for caste/ethnic membership, twelve women described themselves as Bahun-Chetris and most of the remainder stated that they belonged to a middle ranked caste/ethnic group, such as Rai, Tamang, or Gurung, etc. However, according to the staff some of these caste/ethnic membership claims are dubious. Sometimes those who call themselves Bahun-Chetri belong to lower castes. As mentioned earlier, caste differences can create problems when food is exchanged, which is particularly troublesome since the shelter is based on the principles of communal living, cooperation, and sharing work. For this reason, perhaps, many claim to be Bahun or Chetri even if they actually belong to a lower caste.[8]

Routes and Reasons for Coming to the Shelter

When they arrive women are asked their reasons for coming to the shelter. Whilst each woman claims to be a victim of domestic violence, the kind of violence varies from case to case. Out of twenty cases, nine women suffered physical violence at the hands of their husband or husband's families, five women suffered mental despair because their husbands were missing, one woman had nowhere to live after having been driven out by her husband, another claimed to be a victim of social discrimination resulting from her husband's death, another had been raped by an employer, and another had been incest-raped by a relative. Women who come to the shelter recognize that their suffering is due to domestic violence, and some have residential problems. The NGO administrative staff's decision whether to allow them to stay at the shelter or not is based on the availability of vacant beds and not the reasons provided by the women. Some women come to the shelter on their own or on the advice of an acquaintance, others are sent by other NGOs, by the police, or by a hospital. Amongst the latter cases, most are sent by the LACC.

---

[8] As women of all caste/ethnic categories are admitted to the shelter and as they all cooperate with each other, the caste/ethnic category is not an issue there. Some people told me that sometimes they do not give their real family names. However, in order to provide background, I will give assumed caste/ethnic identities.

Economic Conditions of Residents

Apart from a few exceptional cases, most women worked as housewives and did not earn money outside the home before coming to the shelter. Although there are a few cases in which a wife had to work elsewhere as a maid in order that her husband would not need to work at all, out of twenty women, seventeen did not have their own earnings. With the partial exception of those women from farming families, almost all are dependent on their husband's income. The occupations of the husbands of those at the shelter were as follows: labourers (7), office workers (6), farmers (4); of the remainder, one is a merchant, one unemployed, and one's occupation was not known. Compared with the general ratio of occupation in Nepal,[9] the proportion of labourers was higher. For women in such circumstances, earning enough money to be able to live independently is a serious problem.

Family Environment

The women's family environments and backgrounds varied. Of the sixteen women who were married, eight described their family as nuclear, i.e. a husband and wife; or a husband, wife, and children: seven cases are more complex including polygamous families, i.e. a husband, wife and *sauta* (co-wife), a husband, wife and husband's family (such as father-in-law, mother-in-law, brother-in-law, sister-in-law, etc.), a wife and her son's family. One case was not known. Of the four unmarried women, two lived with their parents along with their sisters and brothers, one woman lived with her father's brother's family, and one lived with her employer's family.

Regarding their home town, seven came from inside the Kathmandu Valley, twelve came from outside Kathmandu, and one woman's home town was unknown. However, for thirteen women, their place of residence just before coming to the shelter was in Kathmandu, and for four women it was in Lalitpur. Therefore most of the women lived in or near the capital city. Of the sixteen married women, six lived with their parents in their *maita* (natal home), two women had a stepmother or a stepfather, three only had brothers or sisters, and two were orphans, with three women's backgrounds unknown. For seven women, their natal home was in the same district where they lived. Although their natal home was not far from their dwellings, they hardly ever called on their parents' assistance. There seems to be no distinct pattern regarding the women's educational level; some women did not go to school, whilst others studied as far as college. In short, women from a variety of home environments and backgrounds were brought together at the shelter.

---

[9] In Nepal as a whole, 60 per cent depend on agriculture for their livelihood. In the Kathmandu Valley, 11 per cent are employed as labourers (CBS 2003a: 38-42).

TYPES OF VIOLENCE SUFFERED BY VICTIMS

Physical Violence by Husbands

Twenty-year-old Saili,[10] a Chetri woman, is an orphan whose parents passed away during her childhood, and she was brought up by other villagers:

> When I was ten years old, a villager took me to Kathmandu, and I was married at the age of thirteen. The woman of the house where I had worked had recommended marrying a certain man. At that time I worked there as a maid. At first I refused to marry, but I was married by force. The man threatened to kill me if I didn't marry him. But I didn't want to live together with him. He stalked me, abducted me to his room, and confined me, and I was married by force. When my child was born, he started to assault me. He often beat me to take money away from me. Also, during my second pregnancy he punched me again and again, and threatened to kill me in spite of the child in my womb. I reported his violence to the police, and he was held in jail. But he continued to assault me, so I escaped from him with my daughters. He seemed mad. He beat me when he was sober as well as when he was drunk. He is addicted to drugs. His father also always drinks alcohol. I heard that since childhood he had been violent. After the marriage my husband's violence improved, but later it became more severe. Sometimes I had to sleep outside because I could not buy the alcohol which he had ordered me to go and buy at midnight. One night he struck me and drove me out. After fleeing from my husband I had an operation on my heart. I think that my heart cracked because of his torture. He has left the apartment now. I don't know where he is. I lived in a friend's apartment for a short time, but she didn't have enough income to feed us all. A friend of mine told me about this shelter, so I came here by myself. I hate my husband. My daughter worries about our life and asks me to stay away from him as she knows everything that my husband did to me.

Pabita, a twenty-six-year-old Chetri woman, is a victim of physical violence:

> I was raised by my *phupu* (father's sister) after my parents died in a plane crash. When I lived in Butwal, she recommended marrying a man from the same caste. He came from Sindhupalchok to work in Butwal. As soon as we had performed the wedding ceremony at a temple, we moved to his house in Sindhupalchok. Then I found

[10]Throughout this paper pseudonyms are used.

> that a *sauta* and their daughters were there. I was very surprised to see the *sauta* because I had heard that my husband's marriage to me was his first. If I had known that he had another wife I would not have married him. In his house there was a father and mother-in-law, his sisters, the *sauta*, and their daughters. I lived together with them all. It was not long before he began to beat and kick me when he was drunk. He was also violent to his other wife. When he saw me talking to someone, regardless of whether they were male or female, he got angry and struck me. I lived there for two years. Then, along with only myself, he went to Kathmandu to get a job. He got a job as a driver, but I have never seen him doing any work. He always bought alcohol with money borrowed from friends and drank in the daytime. I tried to get work outside but he would not allow me. Whilst living in Kathmandu, his violence continued. I sometimes had to go to the hospital for the wounds to heal. Twice I reported suffering violence from my husband to the police. Once, following intervention by the police, he promised not to ever hit me, but he began to beat me again. I hate him.

Pabita's and Saili's cases are similar in that, in addition to suffering physical violence, both their husbands did not work and they lived in poverty.

Mental Violence – A Husband's Disappearance

Minu, a forty-two-year-old Limbu woman, came to Kathmandu from Ilam so that her property might be returned to her from a husband who had disappeared. She claims that her husband had used the dowry from her parents to build their house. She consulted the legal service on this matter and sued for restitution. Minu was very shocked to learn that her husband had deceived her and escaped:

> My husband was working at the taxation office in Ilam. He swindled me to get my property. He cheated me into marrying, even though he already had a wife and children. We lived together for a year after marrying. When I was three months pregnant with a child he gave me some medicine for an abortion. He told me that he was not able to support a child. He only married me for my property. When proposing he had said that I wouldn't have to work hard and he wouldn't give me any trouble, so I had never worried about him disappearing. After getting married, one day he said that he was going to work and he disappeared. ...

In the case of Samjana, a twenty-year-old Sherpa woman, her husband disappeared while she was pregnant. She delivered the child in hospital, but could not return to her apartment because of non-payment of the rent. So some staff at the hospital sent her to the shelter. At the time of the interview she had given birth just three weeks earlier:

> My husband disappeared on the 2nd of Magh (January-February) this year. As his father was sick, he left for his parents' home in Sindhupalchok, and told me he would come back in three days. But he did not return, and after two weeks I called his office. He was working at the office of a computer company. I was surprised that he had stopped working at the job. I had not at all heard that he had quit his job. It turned out that he had escaped. Although he had bought a lot of the month's food we required, he had left me only 50 rupees. As we are from different ethnic groups and both our parents opposed our marriage, we have not met each other's families. But he said that when the child was born in Baishakh (April-May) he would take me to his parent's home. The ideas he expressed were different to what was in his heart.

In Samjana's case her husband disappeared despite the fact that they had not quarrelled and had enjoyed a happy life with a stable and regular income.

Nani Maya, a twenty-five-year-old Rai woman, was eight months pregnant at the time of the interview when her husband had disappeared half a month earlier:

> We are from the same ethnic group, and met while working at a restaurant in Kathmandu, fell in love, and married. Since we did not fulfil the wedding rituals we talked about going to his family home to perform the rites and take wedding pictures. We had never quarrelled and he had never beaten me. Last month he went to a ticket counter to buy bus tickets to Dhankuta where his parents live, and since then he has not returned to our apartment. He had promised a marriage ceremony, but he has run away from me. I know nobody from my husband's family. Although when I asked his elder brother, who lived in Kathmandu, of my husband's whereabouts he would not tell me. I cannot call his village as the village office was destroyed by the Maoists, and there is no other place in the village I can call to ask about his whereabouts. He escaped. He disliked having his picture taken and so I don't even have any pictures of him. How can I find him? How can I?

Neither Samjana nor Nani Maya knows where her husband's family home is, neither of them has a picture of their spouse, nor do they have any idea how they should go about trying to find him. They said they felt that they could not do anything. Only Minu is looking for her husband. Most women living in the shelter have not even met their husband's families.

Mental Violence – A Husband's Neglect

Because she was completely ignored by her husband, Puspa, a thirty-three-year-old Bahun woman, became mentally sick. She married the partner chosen for her by her parents at the age of seventeen:

> My parents carried out the full wedding rituals and held a luxurious party for me. I had a large dowry, with gold, a sofa set, curtains, a bed, and a car. Although at the time I had wanted to go to school rather than get married, I was unable to refuse the marriage as they had decided it. They said that if I married him I would not suffer any troubles and would have a contented life. He is three years younger than me and in those days went to school. Although he did not want to get married, either, he also married me so as not to oppose his parent's intentions. Since the marriage, our life has not gone well. Whilst in the nine years we lived together he never struck me, he often ignored me, never speaking to me at all. Sometimes I asked him to talk to me, but he continued to ignore me. Even when I could not do anything because of a high fever, he would not even bring me a cup of water. Although my father-in-law took me to hospital and bought me medicine, my husband did not come to the hospital. All the time, for nine years, I suffered by being ignored by him. I became deranged, so I returned to my parent's home, but my natal family did not understand my suffering, so I was not able to live there.

After four years, Puspa is still mentally unstable and often bursts into tears or violently swears at other residents. Even now she continues to take tranquilizers. She appears to be suffering mental violence from her husband.

Incestuous Rape (had-nata-karani)[11]

The following cases concern violence not from a husband, but from an uncle, a relative, or other villagers. Salita, a forty-year-old Bahun woman, lived with the brides of two of her sons, a grandchild, and two daughters after her husband passed away seventeen years ago. One day she was raped by her husband's younger brother. At first other villagers were not aware of the incident, but since she had become pregnant and her abdomen gradually grew larger, they knew she had conceived a child.

> Villagers knew of my pregnancy for six months. To bear a child with one's own relative is so terrible that all the villagers stopped drinking any water which I had touched. Later they expelled me

[11]In the interviews, they explained their incidents using the terms *had nata* or *nata parne* for the relative and *karani* (rape).

> from the village and threatened to kill me if I returned to the village. They looked down on me. Although my daughters and sons still allowed me to live in the house, they were also under threat of expulsion from the village if they continued to live together with me. So I cannot go back to the village. I want to return there. My children reported that I had been raped to police. The brother who raped me escaped from the village and has not yet been caught. He is not deranged, but has bad inclinations.

Since villagers know of the incident she cannot enter the village, so through the NGO she sought permission from the villagers to live in the village again. However, the villagers would not give her permission. She suffered rape, and in addition has been sanctioned for incest by the villagers.[12]

Tulasa, a nineteen-year-old Bahun woman from Kanchanpur district, was raped by her mother's brother's son when she was thirteen years old. Since news of the incident spread all over the village and her school, she could no longer live there and ran away to her father's brother's house in Kathmandu. She cried as she spoke:

> After I came to Kathmandu, my uncle found out about it and got angry with me and assaulted me. I received a letter threatening to kill me and my parents if I talked about the rape to anybody. He is a bank manager, and since coming to Kathmandu I have lived in his house. I could no longer live there after he beat me, so I ran away. I don't have any friends in Kathmandu. Everybody on campus called me 'a wicked person', and spoke ill of me. My parents hate me for having done such a thing. My life has been broken. In my society, it is said that such a thing is a female crime, and the man is not blamed for incest. Although everyone tells me it's my sin, I show them that it isn't my sin through living independently. He must be killed or put in prison, but he is not at all accused in my culture.

At one point she considered committing suicide, but she persuaded herself not to, hoping to make everyone realize that it was not she who had been sinful. Now she is training in handicrafts in order to get a job. She suffered violence from her paternal uncle (*kaka*) as well as from her maternal cousin.

---

[12]In Parbatiya society, a respect-avoidance relationship exists between a woman and elder males of her conjugal household, whereas an affectionate relationship conventionally exists between a woman and her younger brothers-in-law (Bennett 1983: 173-4; Cameron 1998: 181-2). In some societies in Nepal, levirate marriage is preferred (Majupuria 1991: 95). However, the interviewees commented that sexual intercourse with a younger brother-in-law is strictly prohibited.

Evidently a woman who has been incest-raped is not treated with sympathy as a victim, but as a target for violence. The violence of being raped in this case led to further physical violence by the victim's uncle.

CULTURAL FACTORS THAT LEAD TO DOMESTIC VIOLENCE

Marriage and Domestic Violence

There are various kinds of marriage in Nepal according to district or caste/ethnic group. Ishii (1980: 98) has classified marriage in a Newar village into three types. Majupuria (1991: 93-4) mentions eight kinds of marriage, such as arranged marriage, marriage by capture, marriage by elopement among hill tribes, etc. LeVine (this volume) classifies marriages among the Newars of Patan into four types: arranged marriage with a *lami* (go-between) and ritual sanctified by a priest, arranged marriage by a *lami* without priest's rituals, 'love marriage' with conventional rituals, and elopement. Bennett (1983: 71) mentions that *lyaite* marriage, where a man takes a woman into his household with simple rites such as only a *deo kalas puja,*[13] or *swayambar,*[14] was also popular; thus there are a variety of marriage procedures. Among Parbatiyas an orthodox marriage is arranged between the bride's and groom's parents. Yasuno (2000: 66, also this volume) distinguishes *swasni lyaeko* (having taken a wife) and *biha gareko* (getting married) as being concerned with whether rituals are performed or not.

In the case of residents of the shelter, eight of the sixteen married women said that theirs was a 'love marriage'. They considered a 'love marriage' to be getting married without the consent of parents or guardians. Each case is divided into whether or not wedding rituals were performed. Four women stated that their marriages were arranged. Every woman had her parents' or guardian's consent, but none of the women had full wedding rites or were given a dowry. The marriage ages were low: six women were over seventeen years old when they married, four married between the ages of sixteen and seventeen, and three married under the age of sixteen.[15] (Three women's marriage ages were unknown.) As for *biha darta* (matrimonial registration), only two women had registered their marriages. Although all of them knew about the *biha darta*, most of their husbands refused to let them register.

---

[13] *Deo kalas puja*: the worship of a sacred water vessel with lamps.

[14] The ritual of putting a garland on a husband's neck demonstrates the choice of the man as a husband.

[15] By law it is now prohibited to marry under the age of eighteen years.

Pabita, who had escaped from her husband, insisted that she was disgusted to learn that he had another wife. In the case of Sarasvati, a thirty-five-year-old Tamang woman, a *lami* deceived her into marriage, telling her, "You'll only do easy work. It's not hard." In reality, her husband was fierce and he had a *sauta*. Kanchi, a twenty-year-old Chetri woman, was also deceived by a *lami* who told her that the housework would be easy, when in fact her husband beat her repeatedly and threatened to take a *sauta*.

One reason they decided to marry was that the housework would be easy, but after marriage they understood that was a lie, so they felt they had been deceived. As for *sauta*, they were not told by their husbands about them. It turns out that for residents in the shelter, their husbands had many secrets and lies.

Five women from the 'love-married' couples experienced the disappearance of their husbands. The remainder experienced physical violence, a husband's death, and a separation according to the wife's wishes. In the arranged marriages, there were no cases of a husband's disappearance, except one case where the husband ran away in order to avoid being captured by the police. Three of the women suffered physical violence, whilst one woman suffered being completely ignored by her husband.

Kaili, a twenty-year-old Chetri woman, married for love four years ago. She got married while working in Kathmandu, but ten months ago her husband left her when she became pregnant.

> I married for love at the age of sixteen. I was working after graduating from the ninth grade. At that time he was a friend of mine. One day [after we got married], I seriously scalded myself from face to neck, and was in hospital for two months. After I returned to the apartment, he often spent the night in his office not returning from there, and he gradually stopped talking to me. Whenever he came back we quarrelled. One day he told me he was to be transferred to a branch office, and that he would come to take me later. He said "Stay here" but he never came to pick me up. Whilst waiting for him for a year, our child was born. He hadn't beaten me but we quarrelled many times. He complained about the cost of my medical treatment as it is very expensive. As he heard that it would cost us more money for a doctor to cure my burns, I think he decided to run away from me.

In the love marriage cases, most women did not do anything to trace their missing husbands, as neither did they have pictures of them nor had they met their respective husband's family. In the arranged marriage cases, their husbands did not disappear, but rather the wives were deceived by husbands and go-betweens, and the former also violently abused them. Thus it is possible to see that arranged marriage tends to be connected to physical violence and love marriage tends to be connected to the mental violence of the husband's disappearance.

Polygamy and Domestic Violence

When residents retold their experiences, a word which cropped up frequently was *sauta,* meaning co-wife. Although Bahun-Chetri marriages are monogamous, it is widely known that much polygamy also exists. Socially and religiously, polygamy between Parbatiyas has often been approved, and according to Bennett (1983: 83), one fifth of high-caste males in Narikot village have a *sauta*. Some men have not only two wives, but three or more. Although Newar communities are mostly monogamous, examples of polygamy can also occasionally be encountered (Ishii 1980: 102).[16] There are a comparatively large number of cases in Parbatiya communities, and Bennett (1983: 187) points out the relationship between polygamy and economic conditions, as well as men's pride in having two or more wives. An acceptable reason for having a second wife is that the first wife is either infertile or dead. In the domestic hierarchy, the wives are not equal. The *lyaite* wife is assigned a lower position compared with the wife for whom a formal wedding has been performed. Sometimes a lower-caste woman is pushed around and robbed of her share of a husband's property by the first wife (Yasuno 2000: 118-19).

Six women in the shelter had husbands with *sauta*s. Of these, in one case the husband had a *sauta* with a son before marriage, in another case he had a daughter before marriage, and in some cases the *sauta* and children had already run away. In four cases, after the marriage the husband brought in a *sauta*. Of these four cases, two women did not have a child, and the other two had only daughters. It could be said that the failure to bear a son tends to be connected to the problem of multiple wives as in most cases the women did not have a son. In such cases, a former wife often has little power in the family.

According to the available statistics, in 2001, 5.7 per cent of males in the whole country had lived with more than one spouse (CBS 2003b: 39). Some 280,000 men had more than one spouse, so it can be concluded the system of polygamy still continues. In order to lawfully have multiple wives, they must formally divorce or fulfil certain conditions under the Muluki Ain. However, a lawyer said that it is easy for men to have multiple wives if they pay the penalty, which for wealthier people is not substantial. Practically speaking, polygamy is accepted in society, so if a wife wishes to have her husband punished for having other wives, she has to appeal to a

[16]This occurs when the husband and wife have reached an advanced age and the first wife has not borne a son.

state court. However, in practice this is difficult, as to bring such charges is costly and a lawsuit would take a long time.[17]

Even though polygamy is an accepted custom in Nepalese society, for the women, for whom it creates a problem, it can be extremely threatening. Of all the relationships a woman has in her husband's home, the most openly and bitterly antagonistic is with the *sauta* (Bennett 1983: 187). They often have negative feelings towards each other, and sometimes a husband will become the younger wife's ally during a quarrel between the wives. Husbands typically ignore such disputes, which focus on food, clothes, property, money, and the husband's affections (Deuba & Rana 2001: 47). Once a wife has borne a boy, the dominance of her mother-in-law will usually lessen, but the relationship with *sauta*s will never decrease. They are rivals over bearing a son, as well as for influence over the household economy (Bennett 1983: 187-8).

A wife will sometimes quarrel with her husband about the *sauta*. The reasons are usually his bringing in another wife, sharing his property with the *sauta*, his affection for her, etc. To bring a *sauta* into the household can result in bad treatment of the child and the mental and physical abuse of the wife. Kanchi, a twenty-year-old Chetri woman, had an arranged marriage without formal rites or a dowry:

> The *lami*, a female relative, said that he would not beat me, and that I wouldn't have to work hard in married life. He began to punch and kick me after about two years had passed. He began to beat me after hearing gossip from *amaju* (elder sister-in-law). In the household there were a father and mother-in-law, my husband, *amaju*, and I. He always beat me with a *khukuri* knife and fire-wood. He also threatened to bring a *sauta*. Not only him but also his entire family conspired against me. One day he brought a *sauta* and kicked me out, so I reported it at a police box. Then he kicked out the *sauta*, and confined me in a room so that I could not run away and beat me again. I escaped to my father's sister's house. I heard that he had had another wife before marrying me, but she had not been there when I came to the house. I would not have married him if I had known about the existence of a *sauta*.

In Kanchi's case, before a *sauta* came she suffered physical violence by her husband as well as by her husband's family. As the husband used to threaten her with 'bringing in a *sauta*', it is clear that for women the existence of a *sauta* is threatening.

Sarasvati, a thirty-five-year old Tamang woman, came to the shelter

---

[17]There were 135 reported cases of the crime of polygamy in 2054 V.S. (April 1997 to April 1998), 96 in 2055 (1998-9), 96 in 2056 (1999-2000), 75 in 2057 (2000-1), 50 in 2058 (2001-2) (CBS 2003a: 295).

because she had been injured and driven out by her husband, her *nanda* (her husband's younger sister), and the *sauta*:

> I got married ten years ago and came to my husband's house. His family had visited us with a *lami*, but I had refused to marry him. They then came to ask me to marry him through a *lami* who was the husband's mother's brother's wife (*maiju*). Since my family was poor, we had trouble with a lack of food. The *lami* told me I would not need to work hard, so my parents arranged the marriage. But it was a lie. After the wedding ceremony at my family house, I arrived at my husband's house and heard that a *sauta* had been there at one time. Nobody had told me about it. My mother-in-law and *nanda* probably drove her out and dumped her belongings. If I had known about it, I would not have married him. They deceived me. He took a third wife four years ago. She had two children and lived in the main house with the family. Then I was driven out and lived in a detached house alone. Since then he started to beat me. My husband and *sauta* often came to beat me and pulled my hair, dragged me around and beat me. Once after they had whacked me with some firewood, I was severely bruised and couldn't lift myself up and had to stay in bed for a month. Then one day they chopped me with a *khukuri*. The bracelet I was wearing broke and my arm bled. He wouldn't give me any medicine to care of my wound or give me any money either.

In her case the physical violence started when the *sauta* came, and one wife abused the other. Therefore, the problem of polygamy not only causes trouble for women but is also connected to domestic violence. Moreover, the problem can influence the relationship between a maternal family and daughter. In Kanchi's case, her father also had multiple wives as well as her husband, so she was told not to return to her natal home. Her mother had died when she was four years old, so she had a *sano mami* (stepmother) in her *maita* (natal family). She also admitted suffering physical violence in her maternal home, "I can't go back to my *maita* because of my stepmother. My father and she beat me." Sometimes a daughter will suffer from domestic violence by a stepmother. In such ways polygamy can be one of the reasons that cause domestic violence.

The Natal Family and Domestic Violence

In cases where a married woman cannot depend on her husband and his family, she may have to count on her natal family. After marriage a woman still has rights in her parents' home and can return and live there at any time, and in Bahun-Chetri households can receive permanent support from them (Gray 1990: 217).

However, sufferers of domestic violence in the shelter cannot count on the help of their natal families. There are cases where no support was given by a maternal family because the marriage was for love in spite of the parents' opposition, or the parents were not informed of the marriage. There are other cases where there was no support given by the wife's parents or from her brothers.

Sanu, a twenty-four-year-old Chetri woman, married a Newar man:

> After getting married, I lived with my husband, *sasu* (mother-in-law), and *amaju* (elder sister-in-law). I got acquainted with my husband whilst working together at a textile factory. Two years after getting married he began to strike me. Whilst he struck me he always said something offensive. I don't know why. I escaped from his violence and came to the shelter. Although my parents are anxious about me, they don't help me with my life. They told me to solve my own problem by myself, because in spite of their opposition, I married someone from a different ethnic group.

Sanu's father is a high school teacher and she is a well-educated woman having passed the School Leaving Certificate (SLC).[18] Her natal family is very poor. When she ran away from her husband's house, there was no place where she could live. So she asked them for help, but they refused to help her. Even if there is a problem in the husband's family, in love marriage cases a woman cannot return to her parent's home.

One woman's case is an example of an attempt to get her parents to come to her aid, only to be refused. Amanda, a twenty-year-old Magar, married a friend from the same ethnic group against her parents' wishes; they objected because he was not of the same economic level.[19] Amanda and her husband came to Kathmandu to get a job. Three years later he died in an accident, and then when she had trouble with living costs and finding a place to live, she came to the shelter with her son:

> Whilst my parents are wealthy, my husband was an orphan and was very poor. Therefore, my parents had said that it was useless to marry such a poor person, and opposed the marriage. I called to ask them to pick me up and take me back to my natal home, because after my husband's death I did not have any place to live. But they haven't come to Kathmandu. I think that the reason they would not pick me up is that I married a poor orphan.

---

[18] After ten years of schooling students take a unified SLC examination to certify their graduation.

[19] It is important to choose a spouse so that each family is economically well balanced (LeVine, this volume; Bennett 1983: 147; Ishii 1980: 101).

She bears a grudge against her parents who did not come to take her to the natal home. She also said that she regretted marrying for love against her parents' wishes.

After her husband disappeared, Lakshmi, a twenty-six-year-old Bahun woman, came to the shelter on the advice of a hospital, as she had trouble paying the rent for an apartment. She said she felt regret at marrying for love. She also feared being scolded by her elder brother and mother, and therefore refused to return to her maternal home. Neither Lakshmi nor Amanda suffered physical violence from her husband. However, in Lakshmi's case, her husband's disappearance with all their money could be said to comprise mental violence, as he must have known how much trouble this would cause her. Amanda also considers herself a victim, since she is despised by society as a widow. Both women had lost contact with their parents when they married; neither set of parents would offer help, in spite of their daughter's sufferings, because she had chosen a love marriage instead of parental guidance.

Some women suffer secondary damage from a step-parent even after having returned to their natal home, and others do not have the option to return as they have no parents but only brothers. The cases of Kanchi and Kaili described previously provide such examples. Sarasvati, whose case was mentioned earlier, said "There is nobody at my parents' home." For her "nobody" means no parents. She could not run away back to her family home even after suffering violence from her husband's family, even though her natal home is nearby. She said that her "... parents have passed away ..., if they were still alive I could return. But how could I live together with my brother's family without my parents? I couldn't. ..."

Women who leave their husbands and return to their natal homes are considered deviant, because such action is seen as a de facto divorce, and it is contrary to the norm. Further, such women cannot obtain the same position of respect or domestic power that a woman who has borne a child in her natal home receives. A divorced woman who returns to her parental family is a rival for the other wives living there (Gray 1990: 217).

Puspa, who suffered mental violence through her husband's neglect, was troubled by the lack of understanding by her parents and brothers, and eventually could not live with them. She had had good relations with them until she decided to return to her parent's home. As is the rule in Bahun-Chetri communities, she would sometimes visit her old home when her husband's parents allowed her to. However, after many years, when she was no longer able to bear her husband's neglect and returned home, her natal family would not incorporate her as a member of the family.

In Nepal, a natal family is expected to provide valuable support to a married daughter. If she cannot have their help, she is likely to despair for her life. These examples show how the cultural rules regarding relationships with a parents' home serve to make domestic violence a more serious problem in Nepal.

Mediation and Domestic Violence

In many South Asian communities there is a tradition of a Panchayat (a local or caste council) to settle problems and reconcile differences. At present in Nepal, there is of course a national judicial system as well as the traditional judicial system in each community, and people can use both. However, sometimes the national court judgements are different from those of the traditional courts. It has been pointed out that whilst the national court judgements are superior to others, they do not always have priority (Yasuno 2000: 106).

Regarding crimes of incest, there is a traditional regulation in the Muluki Ain of 1854 (Höfer 1979: 87-8), that it is a crime related to village society. Rules and fines, according to caste status, are also given, for cases of divorce due to adultery (ibid.: 79-80). However, there is no mention in the Muluki Ain about disputes and violence between family members, and these kinds of matters are not problems which are referred to traditional village courts.

When a dispute occurs in a family, typically a senior family member mediates. Women's disputes, in particular, frequently cause divisions in a family, and as long as the relations between brothers are good, a senior family member will mediate (Bennett 1983: 179). However, in the case of a violent husband or *sauta*, they do not come to mediate or attempt to reconcile differences.

In Kanchi's case, it was known in the village that her husband was violent and nobody regarded him as a sensible man. Despite this, she reported that, even though they heard her cry whilst suffering violence, none of the villagers or even her family helped her. Sarasvati's husband had a bad reputation throughout the village and often quarrelled and fought with other villagers. Although everybody knew he beat her, they never helped her. As domestic violence occurs in the household domain, which is veiled to outsiders, it is often difficult to find the violence. It is also not a problem that is taken up by customary law. Further, as it unfolds in private, even neighbours cannot intervene easily.

In Parbatiya society, an uninvited visitor is sometimes suspected of being a thief or even a witch, so rather than be regarded as meddlers they will often choose not to intervene (Bennett 1983: 2). Consequently, domestic violence is a problem that village societies cannot easily mediate. However, the case of Hajuri provides an interesting example of how an NGO group made the village society intervene in a family problem.

Hajuri, a Chetri woman in her sixties, had the opportunity to talk to her husband and his son (the child of a *sauta*) about her treatment at their hands through NGO mediation. Although the NGO requested that they should take her back, they repeatedly refused to accept her. However, at a meeting held in the village office attended by the chief of the village and a secretary, her husband and the son signed a certificate drawn up by the chief promising to take care of her. It stated that they would provide her with meals and a living space, and would not beat her. With the chief of the village mediating, these promises were made to Hajuri. It was effective because villagers joined the negotiations to settle a domestic dispute. Usually disputes between a husband and wife are not referred to the village office. However, in this case the NGO asked the village officer to be present.

Domestic violence in Nepal has rarely been considered a 'problem', so it is hardly surprising that intermediary organizations are lacking at the village level. Therefore, a suffering woman who is unable to solve her problem in village society must go to the police, NGOs, and a legal service which is part of the framework of the nation.

Divorce, Widows, and Domestic Violence

Nepalese society's opinion of women who have separated from their husbands is so severe that sometimes it may cause further distress to the victims. Although according to custom most women do not remarry, there are a few remarried women. According to the Muluki Ain of 1854, which may be taken as a legal formulation of high-caste norms, the acceptance of cooked rice from 'cord-wearer' castes and 'non-enslavable' castes is obligatory if the woman was married with full rites, but it is not obligatory if the wife was married before, or if she is a divorcée or widow. If, before the present marriage, the woman has been married three times or has had sexual intercourse with three men in her life, taking cooked rice from her is forbidden. Such a woman is regarded as *wesya*, a whore (Höfer 1979: 73). By contrast, in Newar communities, by tradition, it is comparatively less difficult than in Parbatiya communities for the wife to initiate the divorce. However, for women to remarry is difficult. There are few divorced women who have remarried. After divorce, most return to live in their parents' village (Ishii 1980: 97-102).

A remarried woman is discriminated against as a person with two husbands and she is considered inauspicious (Yasuno 2000: 67). Widows are also discriminated against, and in Parbatiya communities a widow's remarriage is not allowed. She is regarded as being engaged in an inauspicious matter and is looked upon with pity (Dhungana 2002).

In the case of the residents of the shelter, most women did not wish to divorce. The reasons they gave were that they feared discrimination resulting from divorce, or they hadn't ever considered 'divorce' for themselves as they hadn't registered their marriages. Amanda, a widow who dreaded discrimination, said that if she was to work at a Nepali house everyone would look down on her, and she hoped to get a job in a foreigner's house as they would not despise her. Saili, who had suffered severe violence, also did not wish to divorce. In Nepali society, becoming a widow or a divorcée means losing one's social position. Since this often results in becoming the object of social discrimination, it creates a situation in which many women feel that they have to continue to live with their husband and his family, even if they face violence from him or his family. Needless to say, economic restrictions also often exist. It is vital that husbands feed their family as most women cannot earn sufficient income to support themselves and their children. The way widows and divorcées are viewed by society, combined with economic dependence, leads to factors which suffocate the possibilities of 'empowerment' for victims of domestic violence.

CONCLUSION

There are various types of domestic violence among different caste/ethnic groups in Nepal. These types can be related to a number of social factors. It would doubtless be possible to find differences by caste/ethnic groups in how violence takes place if we probed into the matter in minute detail. But more important is the fact that domestic violence exists to some extent in any society without regard to caste/ethnic groups. It is not an exceptional phenomenon.

Women in the shelter where the interviews were conducted use the term 'domestic violence' (using the English words) for all the violence they have suffered, just like those around them including the NGO staff. The NGOs dealt with in this chapter accept as victims all the women suffering from the violence of someone of their family and kin. In practice they do not distinguish between violence within a family in a narrow sense and other kinds of violence. The term 'domestic violence' plays an instrumental role in their attitude not to refuse anyone who comes to the shelter, and to provide support for them to survive.

Article 1 of the UN 'Declaration on the Elimination of Violence against Women' (1993) states, "the term 'violence against women' means any act of gender-based violence that results in, or is likely to result in, physical, sexual or psychological harm or suffering to women, including threats of such acts, coercion or arbitrary deprivation of liberty, whether occurring in public or in private life." Though the social connotation of domestic violence is a little different from gender-based violence, the kinds of harm or suffering stated here are highly relevant to the former. It is therefore appropriate to consider the experiences of tortured woman with the above Declaration in mind.

The victims' grief, their sincere minds, and the substance of the violence they have experienced were clearly exemplified in the preceding narratives. Though material on and documentation of domestic violence in Nepal could certainly be better, I hope the discussion in this chapter has demonstrated that it is a problem shared by the whole of Nepalese society and is an area requiring further research. Even if certain kinds of violence may be accepted or overlooked in society, it is still a serious problem for the person suffering them.

There may be cases in which relations between a husband and wife or between a daughter and her parents are quarrelsome. But as far as they are under the roof of 'family', they are not usually disclosed and other people tend to refrain from intervening. Thus it is difficult to encounter actual cases of domestic violence, although it is said they are common in Nepal. But we can have a glimpse of their awkward situation as well as how they think about domestic violence through the victims' narratives.

Those who married for love did not easily reveal the fact of their suffering as they considered it to be dishonourable. Some women in the shelter regretted their love marriages. They thought that if they had not married for love, they would have been able to get their parents' help and good jobs. They told me that they had not understood what would happen in their future lives after a love marriage. One woman wept that her *maiju* (her mother's brother's wife), who had been like a mother to her, had never met her since she got married. Another lamented that she had never considered the possibility of losing her parents' support after marrying for love. Still another reported that she had never anticipated that her husband would disappear.

Love marriages and inter-caste/ethnic marriages are not new in Nepal. Inter-caste/ethnic marriages existed in the past, as can be attested by the existence of a provision for their punishment in the Muluki Ain. In arranged marriages, relatives on both sides are involved in the married life of a new couple. Also, the communities concerned come to know of the marriage well. In love marriages, a woman and a man themselves decide to marry, and they often start their conjugal life without the consent of their families. Moreover, the husband's side may remain ignorant of the marriage. One woman suspected that her husband had not informed his family. Another woman said that her husband had not only concealed his marriage from his family but had also hidden from her the existence of his first wife and their children. In contrast, on the wife's side, family members generally know of the marriage though often with objections. In short, there tends to be less social recognition and support for love marriages compared with arranged marriages.

Types of marriages seem to be relevant to modes of domestic violence. If a woman is deserted by her husband after being married for love, it is sometimes very difficult for her to find him because it often happens that she is ignorant of the exact address of his natal family, not to say its members. More profound mental violence is incurred in such a case than a similar incident in an arranged marriage. In this way, the difference between love and arranged marriages is related to the intensity of violence. 'Love marriages' and 'inter-caste/ethnic marriages' have been incorporated into Nepalese culture and society, though they used to be loaded with negative images. That the ties of love marriages are breakable is a part of the culture. Parents respond to their daughters' marriages consciously or unconsciously according to their cultural values.

The cases of domestic violence dealt with here give rise to the question what 'marriage' is. All the women in the shelter asserted that they were married. But in spite of their claims, it seems that few others knew of their marriages. Furthermore, husbands' perception of marriage may be different from that of the wives. Expressions such as 'I will never marry again' and 'I will never divorce my husband' are commonly heard from women. For them 'marriage' is a matter which takes place only once in their lifetime, while for men it is not necessarily so. What is considered by women as 'marriage' may be regarded only as cohabitation by their 'husbands', who for that reason consider that they can escape from it easily.

Although violence ranges from the physical to the mental, every case occurred in the sphere of family and kin, or in the private realm. People tend to think that the private realm is something totally cut off from the social sphere (thus abstaining from intervention). But we have to keep in mind that it is a realm heavily loaded with sociocultural values. Culturally confirmed, sanctioned, or sometimes overlooked actions and reactions can become offensive to their sufferers who are in many cases women.

Tanaka (1998: 14) distinguishes between 'ritualized violence' and 'physical violence'. According to him the former has certain cultural and social forms or expressions and the latter is committed in a sudden way. The former is approved of by the society and found in political contexts as well as in rites. 'Domestic violence' does not fit neatly into this classification. It is neither ritualized nor accidental. However, in a society in which most men believe they have the right to beat their wives (Cameron 1998: 170-1), domestic violence looks as if it constitutes one of the socio-culturally approved customs. On the other hand it is difficult to say that it has fixed forms or expressions, though as we have seen, it is related deeply with the society and culture concerned. Thus 'domestic violence' can be called 'sociocultural violence' since, given prevailing sociocultural norms, it has the potential to appear at any level of society.

It seems that often a husband's violence is considered as only 'bad luck' for the wife (Sangroula & Pathak 2002: 112). However, it is not a matter to be dismissed as simply as that, but must be considered as a serious problem for the society as a whole since the issue is deeply rooted in the culture of the society. It is necessary not only to deal with it with discretion as a private matter, but also to tackle it as a problem of the sociocultural structure of the whole society.

Domestic violence is serious for the women who suffer from it, sometimes threatening or destroying their lives, and causing social discrimination for the victims. It is most important to focus on the sufferers' torment because, even though it seems to be approved of by their culture, they experience deep sorrow and lament their circumstances.

REFERENCES

Babior, S.L. 1993. 'Women of a Tokyo Shelter: Domestic Violence and Sexual Exploitation in Japan'. Unpublished thesis, University of California, Los Angeles.

Bennett, L. 1983. *Dangerous Wives and Sacred Sisters: Social and Symbolic Roles of High-Caste Women in Nepal.* NY: Columbia University Press.

Bista, D.B. 1967. *People of Nepal.* Kathmandu: Ratna Pustak Bhandar.

Cameron, M.M. 1998. *On the Edge of the Auspicious: Gender and Caste in Nepal.* Urbana and Chicago: University of Illinois Press.

CBS. 2003a. *Statistical Year Book of Nepal 2003.* Kathmandu: HMG, NPC Secretariat.

——. 2003b. *Women in Nepal: Some Statistical Facts.* Kathmandu: HMG, NPC Secretariat.

Counts, D.A., J.D. Brown, and J.D. Campbell (eds.). 1992. *Sanctions and Sanctuary: Cultural Perspectives on the Beating of Wives.* Boulder: Westview Press.

Deuba, A. and P. Rana. 2001. *A Study of the Psycho-Social Impacts of Violence against Women and Girls with Special Focus on Rape, Incest and Polygamy.* Kathmandu: Saathi.

Dhungana, N. 2002. 'Inhuman Practices in Widowhood'. *Hamro Sansar: A World of Our Own* 1: 35-6.

Gray J.N. 1990 (1982). 'Chetri Women in Domestic Groups and Rituals', in M. Allen and S.N. Mukherjee (eds.), *Women in India and Nepal*, pp. 211-41. Delhi: Sterling Publishers.

Höfer, A. 1979. *Caste Hierarchy and the State in Nepal: A Study of the Muluki Ain of 1854.* Innsbruck: Universitätsverlag Wagner.

Ishii, H. 1980. *Newar Sonraku no Shakaikozo to Sono Henka: Caste Shakai no Henyo (Social Structure and Its Change in a Newar Village: Social Change in a Caste Society).* Tokyo: ILCAA, Tokyo University of Foreign Studies (in Japanese).

Kaino, T. 1998. 'Kazoku to Boryoku (Family and Violence)'. *Kenkyu Kiyo (Journal of the National Women's Education Centre of Japan)*, Vol. 2: 3-12.

LACC (Legal Aid and Consultancy Centre). n.d. a. *LACC Brochure*. Kathmandu: LACC.

——. n.d. b. *The Eleventh Amendment of National Code of Nepal (Muluki Ain) on Women's Right*. Kathmandu: LACC.

——. n.d. c. *'Lyak Mahila Hak Help Lainma Darta Bhaeka Kehi Satya Ghatana-haru (Some Events Reported to the LACC Women's Rights Help Line)'. LACC LENS* 10: 1-30.

Majupuria, I. 1991. *Nepalese Women*. Bangkok: Crafsmen Press.

McClusky, L.J. 2000. *Here, Our Culture is Hard: Stories of Domestic Violence from a Mayan Community in Belize*. Austin: University of Texas Press.

Saathi and The Asia Foundation. 1997. *A Situational Analysis of Violence against Women and Girls in Nepal*. Kathmandu: Saathi.

Saathi. n.d. *Saathi Brochure*. Kathmandu: Saathi.

Sangroula, Y. and G. Pathak. 2002. *Gender and Laws: Nepalese Perspective*. Kathmandu: Pairavi Prakashan.

Singh, M. 1996. 'Women's Socio-Political and Legal Status in Nepal', in *Red Light Traffic*, pp. 25-31. Kathmandu: ABC/Nepal.

Sri 5 ko Sarkar Kanun Nyaya tatha Samsadiya Vyavastha Mantralaya (HMG, Ministry of Law, Justice, & Parliamentary Affairs). 2059 v.s. (2002). *Muluki Ain (State Law Code)*. Kathmandu: Kanun Kitab Byavastha Samiti (Law Books Management Board) (in Nepali).

Tanaka, M. 1998. 'Boryoku no Bunkajinruigaku Jyoron (Introduction to the Anthropology of Violence)', in M. Tanaka (ed.), *Boryoku no Bunkajinruigaku (Anthropology of Violence)*, pp. 3-28. Kyoto: Kyoto University Academic Press (in Japanese).

Thapalia, S. 1995. *Customary Practices of Divorce in Nepal*. Kathmandu: Legal Aid and Consultancy Center.

Yasuno, H. 2000. *Nishi Nepal no Hyoui Cult: Popular Hinduism ni okeru Fuko to Funso (A Possession Cult in Western Nepal: Misfortune and Conflicts in Popular Hinduism)*. Tokyo: Keiso Shobo (in Japanese).

9

Drug Users of Dharan: Aspects of Marginalization

KHUSIYALI SUBBA

INTRODUCTION

I was sitting in a Drop-In Centre (DIC) in Dharan when a young woman came in to exchange needles. I was surprised to see her in the DIC, because I had presumed that only male drug users visited DICs. This DIC was established by an NGO called the Kirant Yakthung Chumlung/Punarjiwan Kendra (KYC/PJK or Kirant Limbu Association/Rehabilitation Centre), which, as the name implies, was founded by the Limbu organization, the Kirant Yakthung Chumlung. It provides needles to injecting drug users free of cost in order to prevent HIV transmission. Injecting drugs is popular among users because it leads to quicker intoxication at a reasonable price. But it makes one highly vulnerable to HIV transmission and other blood-related diseases. Due to lack of awareness as well as lack of money and the easy availability of needles in the market in Dharan, drug users share needles, which are often contaminated with different blood-related diseases. KYC/PJK has been working on drugs-related issues in Dharan for a long time. As well as distributing needles, it provides drugs education to users from different DICs. In December 2002, I was contracted by KYC/PJK for one month to assess the needle exchange programme.

One of the DIC staff members introduced me to Sunita Limbu, who was then twenty-two years old. After we had got to know each other, she told me her story:

> I started my schooling in Kalimpong at the age of 6 years. I was put in a hostel as my parents were working overseas. Hence, I have very little experience of a homely environment.

I went to Kathmandu after passing my school leaving certificate (SLC) and got enrolled in one of the expensive and reputed schools. I felt very lonely as I was new in the school and the environment of Kathmandu was also new for me. I had an uncle who was also studying there. He paid visits to my hostel, as he was my local guardian and I also had days out with him on holidays.

Unfortunately he was a drug user. He encouraged me to experience heroin, which I inhaled for the first time in my life. The first couple of times I was just experimenting for fun but slowly I became habituated. In the beginning my drug activities were secret but soon the school found out about it. I was rusticated. I came back to Dharan. My parents were in Brunei at the time. In Dharan, I met many other drug users, in whose company I felt comfortable to continue my habit.

I got married with a Newar guy who was also a user. I managed to live with his family for a few months, but our marriage broke up after eight months. His family did not accept me as their in-law as ours was an inter-caste marriage. They wanted to separate us. Eventually they sent their son to India for treatment and I returned to my natal home.

Although I was living with my family, they did not respond well as they were unhappy with my marriage. Moreover, I was a drug user which stigmatized them. While my father was alive, I had no problem getting money to support my drug use. After his death, I started selling household items to supplement my drug dose. In the end I left my natal home too and began staying with friends.

In various ways males exploit us and, in this scenario, the police come first. They keep us in custody if they see us in a group even though no offence has been committed. Once in custody, a policeman did approach me to spend nights away with him saying, "I will release you if you agree to spend nights out at my lodge."

In the same way petty drug dealers approach us to have a physical relationship in return for drugs. Even user friends blackmail us in return for drugs sometimes. In fact, males everywhere exploit females in every way.

... I manage my dose by carrying drugs from Jogbani for local dealers and sometimes I depend on my user friends.

I felt bad hearing her story. It is true that people do not have a positive attitude towards her because all drug users are considered antisocial. But it struck me that she was not solely responsible for her current condition. Maybe things were going badly in her immediate social environment.

Sociological theorists consider that every individual is bound by societal norms and values. When they deviate from such norms, they may be influenced in some way by the environment in which they live. But society generally considers them as antisocial beings.

Sunita introduced me to some other females who were using drugs but had not yet been exposed in public as users. Empirical research indicates that gender is one of the most significant intervening variables in drug use (Curran & Renzetti 1996). When females take drugs openly in a society like Nepal, where it is supposed that only males take drugs, it suggests a situation of rampant drug use, i.e. in this particular society drug use has grown out of control. My encounter with Sunita made me want to know whether drug use really is rampant in Dharan, and, if so, what could be the possible reasons for the problem.

In general it is assumed that people use drugs for entertainment, experiment, or to relieve discomfort and anxiety. Once they begin, gradually they become dependent. This may be true. But further questions occurred to me: What can be the reason for youths of Dharan to become dependent on drugs? Why do they feel discomfort with their lives? Moreover, why are the children of some specific cultural groups, such as the Rai, Limbu, Tamang, and so on, who have a tradition of service as Gurkha soldiers or other forms of overseas work, more likely to fall into drug addiction than the youth from other groups?

Rampant drug use may have destroyed the family as well as social life of several households, but it has not yet been accepted as a serious social problem either by the local community or by the government. To a large extent, users' families have to cope on their own. Other case studies, which provide the current scenario of drug users, are given below. Of course, there are several drug users who do not come from the Janajati groups, but since I come from a Janajati and Gurkha soldier background myself, I decided to focus on this aspect. There are two types of cases presented, those representing the users' point of view and those representing the parents'. Putting them together gives some idea of the social impact of the problem.

After completing my assigned work with KYC/PJK, I started my own study, which lasted for three months (January-March 2003). As I was born and brought up in Dharan, I was acquainted with several users but had never talked with them about personal matters. During this period I tried to get information about their drug habits, which was very tough as they didn't want to admit to being users. Females and beginners, those who are in the early phase of drug use, try to maintain their anonymity. Work experience with KYC/PJK helped me to become familiar with some of them. Once I had got to know them, they became a bond through which I could become familiar with others. In technical terms, I used the snowball method to collect information, because drug abuse is a very sensitive issue and it is hard to identify the people who use drugs for recreational and addiction reasons.

For the purposes of this study, I met people from different sectors, such as local inhabitants, intellectuals, politicians, NGO staff, teachers, and parents, in order to understand their views about the drugs problem in Dharan. Secondary sources of data were also utilized in order to gain a broader understanding of this issue. While collecting information, I accompanied users to their secret places where they usually inject in a group. Once I went with them to Jogbani (on the Indian border) to observe how they get drugs from the other side of the border. However, the users I knew did not take me to places where there would be other users who would not know me, nor did they take me to the place where their local dealer operated.

While I was doing my study, I told them clearly what I was doing and I provided assurances that their names would be kept confidential. Hence, pseudonyms are used for all informants in this chapter.

My discussion in this chapter could be taken as exemplifying an interactionist approach as it focuses on the ways in which people actually interpret and react to the values of the group of which they are members. I would explain the situation of vulnerability in Dharan as a consequence of historical marginalization.

GENERAL UNDERSTANDINGS OF DRUGS AND THEIR USE IN NEPAL

Societies in all parts of the world have used drugs which suppress pain and sorrow and also provide pleasurable sensations when consumed. The oldest are those obtained from the cannabis plant, the opium poppy, and the coca bush. Archaeological evidence indicates that cannabis cultivation dates back to 6,000 BCE; religious and mystical use of cannabis in Indian societies is reported from at least the seventh century CE (WHO 1990: 18).

The term 'drug' has caused much confusion as it has different meanings for different people in different communities. Drugs vary also in effect and toxicity, not to mention the manner in which they are used, from society to society. Thus definitions of drug use and misuse also change through historical periods or vary from one setting to another. What are acceptable practices in one culture may not be so in another. Thus, cultural values and group norms determine what forms of drug use are socially acceptable and what forms constitute a social problem. For instance, alcohol is a drug, as are caffeine and nicotine; these are commonly and widely used as aids to sociability and ordinary activity. Despite the scientific proof of its harmful qualities and habit-forming nature, society does not classify alcohol as a harmful drug (Parrillo et al. 1996). But some drugs and some users are socially defined as unacceptable, and it is these drugs and their users that constitute the so-called drug problem (Kornblum & Julian 1995).

From a scientific and sociological perspective, a drug is any substance that chemically alters the functioning of the brain or nervous system. The term psychoactive drug refers to a chemical substance that affects consciousness, mood, or perceptions (Parrillo et al. 1996). However, the Technical Report Series of World Health Organization (WHO 1980: 18) has defined drugs as "Any substance that, when taken into the living organism, may modify one or more of its functions." Similarly, drug misuse is defined as "use of a drug which is viewed as a problem by the society concerned. The society's view is on its assessment of the physical, mental or social harm caused by the use of a drug or on ethical or religious disapproval. Deviance from the norm is another criterion" (ibid.). According to the US National Institute on Drug Abuse, drug abuse is the use of a drug to an extent that causes harm to the user (Kornblum & Julian 1995).

Using the above definitions, we take drug misuse to be the use of unacceptable drugs and/or the excessive or inappropriate use of acceptable drugs in ways that can lead to physical, psychological, or social harm. It was not seen as a great social problem until the middle of the nineteenth century. By the end of the nineteenth century, drug abuse and addiction were being seen in many countries and were beginning to receive the attention of national governments as part of moves towards social responsibility (WHO 1990b).

In Nepal, the social tolerance for alcohol consumption is high. Nepalese society is composed of different caste and ethnic groups. Ethnic or indigenous groups of Nepal have cultural and religious value for alcohol use. Historically society has been segmented on the basis of its use. In the civil code of 1854, ethnic groups were placed in the Matwali or 'alcohol-user' category whereas high-caste groups were classified as Tagadhari (wearers of the sacred thread), who were traditionally supposed not to consume alcohol (Bista 1991). The use of alcohol ipso facto defined one as low status.

Although Tagadhari groups are supposed not to consume alcohol, the use of cannabis is related with their Hindu religion. Cannabis is assumed to be a favourite of Lord Shiva. Moreover, it is described in the Atharva Veda, one of the most ancient Hindu religious texts, that a number of Hindu saints took cannabis to overcome hunger and thirst, which helped their concentration during meditation (WHO 1980).

Hence alcohol and cannabis are historically and socially accepted drugs in Nepal, with different symbolic and social meanings. Their use is influenced by legend, tradition, and religious culture. But it has begun to be seen as a problem in the country as the cultural barriers of the consumption of drugs have almost disappeared. It is estimated that almost one half of the Nepalese population consumes alcohol. Those who are most attracted are among the younger generation. Some of the largest consumers are males from high-caste backgrounds (Dhital et al. 2001).

Whatever may be the importance of drugs, I treat them in here as a source of new social problems affecting each of us as well as society in different ways. According to Parillo et al. (1996), antisocial behaviour, broken relationships, family instability, crime and violence, poverty, unsafe streets and highways, worker absenteeism, and non-productivity, all frequently have drug-related causes. These problems have all been increasing in Nepal over recent decades.

To judge by the available literature, drug misuse in Nepal was not treated as a serious problem before the 1950s. It began to be seen as a problem in the country between the mid 1960s and early 1970s (Ivana. & Shrestha 2002). After the political changes of 1950-1 the government of Nepal adopted an open-door policy to establish relationships with the wider world. The new policy has had many consequences, such as increases in trade and commerce, an influx of foreigners, international migration, and so on. It has also brought with it significant changes in the socio-economic and political spheres. Along with this, Nepal faces new challenges, for example, greatly increased use of psychoactive drugs and their increasing availability in the market.

In the beginning drug users were found only in big cities like Kathmandu and Pokhara and the misused drugs were limited to alcohol and cannabis. Gradually new types of drugs were introduced into the market and they have partly replaced the old drugs. Simultaneously their use has spread to various places. For instance, in the 1970s cannabis was popular, in the 1980s heroin spread like an epidemic, and from the early 1990s psychotropic drugs such as codeine-based cough syrups (Phensidyl/Corex), opiates Buprenorphine (Tedijesic), and Nitrazepam/Diazepam became popular in Nepal (Ivana & Shrestha 2002). Today, cannabis, heroin, opiates, tranquilizers, and methaqualone are the most common drugs available in the country (Dhital et al. 2001).

Popular drugs in use in Nepal have been classified by UNDCP in the following categories (Dhital et al. 2001) (alcohol and tobacco are not included in their list):

Cannabis: *Ganja*, *Bhang*, *Chares*
Heroin: Smack, Brown Sugar
Opium & Opiates: Codein, Methadone, Morphine, Pethidine
Buprenorphine, etc.

Tranquilizers (sedative and hypnotic): Valium, Nitrazepam, Diazepam, Alprazolam, Ativan, Buscalm, etc.
Others: Glue, Boot Polish, Iodex, Kerosene, Petrol, etc.

According to a policy research study by UNAIDS, there were an estimated 40-50,000 drug users in Nepal excluding those using cannabis, alcohol, and tobacco. The majority of the drug-using population were young people of fifteen to thirty years (CWIN 2001). Injected drugs were the most popular. Many use multiple drugs such as mixtures of Diazepam, Norphin, and Avil. One estimate was that 96 per cent of users in Kathmandu were injecting drug users in 1996 (UNAIDS 2000).

DRUG USE IN DHARAN

As a local resident, I have witnessed and experienced considerable change in Dharan during my lifetime. I was aware there were several teenage drug users in my neighbourhood. However, until I began work in this area, I never realized the seriousness of the situation. I discovered that there were hundreds of youths destroying their lives, that several parents were going to be childless because the only child of the family was already HIV positive, thanks to their use of drugs. The FHI/Nepal report 2001 states there were an estimated 5,000 drug users in Dharan. This number seems to be quite high in comparison to other Nepalese cities, with the exceptions of Kathmandu and Pokhara. To understand the issue of drugs in Dharan, it is necessary to provide a brief historical overview.

General Overview of Dharan: Yesterday and Today

Dharan lies in the eastern part of Nepal and is situated in the foothills of the Siwalik and Mahabharat ranges immediately below Bijaypur hill. The hill previously was under the rule of the Limbu king, Sanglaing, during the latter half of the fourteenth century. His son, Punglaing, adopted Hinduism and named himself Amar Raya. Seven generations of his descendants, all with Hindu names, ruled there (Subba 1995). It was the last descendant, Vijaya Narayan (reigned 1584-1609), who named the place Bijaypur (Shrestha 1995). Dharan was a dense forest in the past. Some 110 years back, people of Bijaypur started to clear the forest. The term *dharan* means a place where two logs are placed together in order to create a convenient place to saw timber. There were many such *dharan* set up here, and hence the town was named Dharan (Jimee 2001).

In 1953 the British Gurkha Recruiting Camp was established in Dharan, and since that time the town began to expand (Karmacharya 1998). As the junction of two different ecological zones, hill and Tarai, it became a business centre. Hill people came down to sell goods, herbs, and fruits. Indian traders were the collectors of this hill produce. At that time there were about fifty or sixty households in Dharan. The majority of the inhabitants were Newars and they made their living from trade.

After the establishment of the British Gurkha Recruiting Camp and the malaria eradication programme in the Tarai, there was rapid migration to Dharan. The British recruiting camp provided many opportunities and facilities, which attracted people from the surrounding hills. Many of those who had served in the Indian or British armies did not go back to their original habitat after retirement. Instead they settled permanently in Dharan as it has a good geographical location, favourable climatic conditions, and increasing infrastructural facilities.

The population of Dharan was only 4,486 in 1952/4 (Jimee 2001). As migration took place from various places, the population increased and is now at 95,332 (CBS 2002). The Rais are now the biggest group followed by the Newars, the third largest group are the Limbus, considered closely related to the Rais as fellow Kirantis (see Table 9.1). With the growing population, several social changes took place. In the past few decades new social problems, such as drugs, burglary, prevalence of street children, violence, trafficking of women, etc., have arisen.

Drug Use

Of all these problems, drug use seems to be one of the most serious, and it is making the social environment more insecure physically as well as psychologically. Dilip Maskey (considered as an old drug user) remarked that, "There was a limited number of drug users in Dharan in my time. Those limited users mainly comprised the children of the local elite and of the Gurkha army men who were sent to study either in Darjeeling or in Kathmandu." Khalil Ahmad (1999) has written in his report, "Drug use became to be seen as great problem in Dharan only since 10-12 years before because the number of drug users increased drastically within this period."

A study published in 1997 revealed that there were 2,128 male and 255 female drug users in Dharan (KYC/PJK/Peace Corp Nepal 1997). According to a study four years later, there were an estimated 5,000 people abusing drugs in Dharan (FHI/Nepal 2001). According to KYC/PJK, 80 per cent of them were injecting drugs and 40 per cent were infected with HIV in 2002 (KYC/PJK 2002). The prevailing unsafe practice of injecting and sharing needles is the main cause of HIV transmission. According to yet another survey conducted by KYC/PJK in 2004, there are 3,888 drug users in Dharan (see Table 9.1). Kamal Tigela, the director of KYC/PJK, says, "The number of drug-using population is based on estimates as it is difficult to collect exact data. Drug use is a shameful activity, so no one wants to admit to being a drug user. This makes it very difficult to identify drug users. So, the number of drug users is based on the records of DICs. There may be more users than this."

Table 9.1 shows that of all drug users, Rais, Limbus, and Newars are numerically dominant in Dharan. Of them all, Rais outnumber the others. But in their respective community, the drug-using percentage is also high among the Limbus at 4.7 per cent. This is equivalent to the rate among the Rais and higher than the Newars. The table shows that Chetris and Brahmans are also influenced by drug use, but, as I had decided to restrict my study to those of a heavy army background, or those influenced by remittances, I did not include cases from these particular groups.

During my study, I noticed that drug users from ethnic groups were more open about their activities and could often be seen in the street in a

Table 9.1: Drug-Using Population of Dharan

S. No.	Ethnic Group	Population (CBS 2001)	Drug Users	% of the Total Drug Users	% of Drug Users in Their Respective Population
1	Rai	18,531	875	22.50	4.7
2	Newar	13,541	499	12.83	3.7
3	Limbu	10,725	501	12.88	4.7
4	Chetri	9,596	355	9.13	3.7
5	Dalit	7,805	320	8.23	4.1
6	Brahman	8,341	285	7.33	3.4
7	Tamang	6,773	269	6.91	4.0
8	Magar	3,329	134	3.44	4.0
9	Gurung	2,258	91	2.34	4.0
10	Bhujel	1,691	68	1.74	4.0
11	Marwadi	1,438	49	1.26	3.4
12	Sherpa	549	20	0.51	3.6
13	Sunuwar	455	17	0.43	3.7
14	Yakkha	188	7	0.18	3.7
15	Others	10,112	398	10.23	3.9
	Total	**95,332**	**3,888**	**100.00**	**4.1**
	(Injecting Drug Users)	(2,321)		(59.69)	
	(HIV+)	(994)		(25.56)	
	Drug Users in Total Population	**95,332**	**3,888**	4.07	

Source: KYC/PJK 2004.

group. It means that those from the so-called upper-caste groups (Brahmans and Chetris) are more likely to use drugs on their own. Umang Rai, in charge of the Drug Rehabilitation Centre established by KYC/PJK, said: "Parents of Brahman and Chetri drug users are more concerned for the treatment of their children than Rais and Limbus or any other ethnic group. ... After treatment, cases of relapse are rare among Brahmans and Chetris but higher among the ethnic groups." This may be due to the fact that many parents of Brahman and Chetri youth are relatively well educated, hold jobs locally, and remain at home all the time. Thus they notice the changing behaviour of their children, whereas most of the parents of the ethnic groups tended to be absent from home for long periods. Thus, their uneducated mothers may be unaware of their children's changing behaviour.

The ratio of the drug-using population in Dharan as a whole is 4.07 per cent. This is similar to the global ratio. Kamal Tigela said: "After 20 years there may be a generation crisis within these particular groups, if the growing trend of drug users remains the same. Most of the drug users use injections and there is a high risk of HIV transmission. Moreover, most of the drug users are the only child of their parents. If they get infected with HIV then it will result in a serious situation for that family."

FACTORS FOSTERING DRUG USE BY YOUTHS IN DHARAN

A drug user does not only destroy himself or herself but also the entire family and there will be no peace (Phanjoubam 1997). Drug users may have difficulty getting and maintaining employment to earn legitimate income for their regular dose. Hence they become involved in criminal activity which often involves violence and aggression. And this causes problems for their family.

Drug use also affects the economic and social life of the family as well as society. For instance, some users told me they normally spend Rs.40 per day in drugs. If they spend Rs.40 every day then it would be Rs.1,200 monthly. And it is not easy to manage such an amount daily for a drug user without being involved in crimes like stealing and selling goods. Likewise, if there were 3,888 users, the amount spent would be about Rs.200,000 daily. But economic factors are rarely calculated.

There are few resources in Dharan for income generation. The means of survival of the majority of households is based on remittances. Most families belonging to the above-mentioned cultural groups have more than one family member working overseas. Foreign employment has become a way of life. "You youngsters wouldn't have got these luxuries and opportunities to study if we had not served in the army" is a common phrase and the reality of Gurkha households.

Spending long periods of time living apart from the family has created a distance between parents and children. This distance may lead to various bad results. During my study, most of my informants cited family reasons for taking drugs. I found non-army, caste people condemning the children of Gurkhas for destroying their own children: "All these [our youth] have been spoiled by their contact with the children of Lahures [those working abroad] (*yo sabai lahure ko choraharu ko sangat le bigareko ho*)." Parents from the Janajati groups tend to accept that "our children get into it faster than others. It is due to our internal problem: we could not give them time [i.e. spend time with them]. This makes them free to do whatever they like and sometimes they get out of control." These contrasting views show up different ways of conceptualizing the same problem and may also reflect characteristic ways in which different castes and ethnic groups view each other. Some view unemployment and lack of awareness as playing a large part in creating the drug problem in Dharan. In *A Time Bomb under the City: Drug Abuse in Dharan*, published in 1999, Danish sociologist, Khalil Ahmad, argued that migration for economic reasons and cultural deviation had caused the drug problem in Dharan. He highlighted the higher income of Gurkha families and the remittance of oversees employers as the main factors.

All the above statements may have some truth in them, but I argue that it would be incomplete to generalize purely on the basis of high remittances. Some other factors are also at play. There are many rich people other than Gurkhas in Nepal, but they are less likely to come in for such severe criticism as indigenous groups like Rais, Limbus, and so on. My interest in this chapter is to discuss those factors that are rarely considered in this context. In order to give adequate considerations to this problem, I will present some of the narratives I collected in the field and then examine the issue according to various contexts.

Case Studies

CASE 1

I am Shyam Limbu. My father is a retired Indian Army soldier whose pension is not enough to cover the family expenses. So my mother makes alcohol to generate extra money to support my father. Thus I have been familiar with taste of alcohol from the very beginning as it was my mother's business. While I was young I sometimes secretly took some and drank it. Mother did not punish me even though I was caught sometimes. She just let me go with a scolding and told me not to do it again. My mother used to give me *tongba* (liquor made of millet) to drink during festivals such as Dasain and Tihar. In the same way, if I helped my mother in the fields, she gave me *tongba* to drink. Drinking alcohol and *tongba* is an integral part of our culture. In this way I have been familiar with *tongba* and alcohol from early age.

While I was studying in standard nine, some of my friends told me to take nitrocine tablets as it gives good experience. In order to try, I took a tablet. I felt cool and slept well. I felt excited and strong when I took it next time. I enjoyed the trip of the drug more than *tongba* or other types of alcohol. I started taking it regularly, as I thought it could be stopped whenever I needed to. But I did not realize how my dependency was increasing. I realized it only later, when I could not raise the money to buy an increasing amount of drugs. So I started selling my belongings, first my clothes and shoes, later other items from home. My family was unaware of my activity. They came to know it for the first time when I was imprisoned for taking drugs in a group. My family released me from custody that first time and advised not to take drugs again. But I did not stop and I have been in police custody several times for different drugs-related crimes. Every time I have been arrested my mother helps to get me released from custody. My brothers and sisters hate me and they don't want my mother to release me from police. But mother protects me and lends me some money regularly, because she wants me not to get involved in stealing things from the neighbourhood. My family wants to take me to a rehabilitation centre, but I do not want to go. I think I don't want to waste my mother's money for treatment because I know that it is not possible to give up the drug as long as there are other drug users existing in society.

CASE 2

My neighbours hate me because I'm a drug user. But this is not the only reason why they hate me: being a Dalit gives them an extra reason [he is a Damai, from the Dalit tailor caste]. Now I'm twenty-two years of age and have a son. I am the last child of my family. My elder brother and sister have been working in Hong Kong since 1998.

My family's economic status is high as my father had served in the British army and receives a pension. In the British Gurkha regiments, there was a provision to recruit some of specific caste groups to perform their caste-related work. From this provision my father was recruited and served for 22 years.

I went to an expensive private school to study where the majority of students were from rich families. I always felt inferior in front of other friends, as I was the only student of lower caste in the class. I have bitter experiences of exclusion in the neighbourhood when I was growing up: no one would let me enter their home. When I was studying in standard ten, my friend insisted that I should take tablets to have an experience of drugs. I resisted at the beginning. But soon I accepted, as I did not want to feel excluded from their group. And for a long time I could not separate from the group, as they were the dominant group of the entire class. Hence, slowly I started taking drugs just to keep company with my friends and became an addict to the extent that today I cannot live without injecting drugs. I did not pass SLC exam. My father insisted I should continue my study but I could not. Once I was taken to a rehabilitation centre, but after three days I managed to run away and return home. I did not want to stay under the rule of the centre as I had been habituated to freedom.

Two years ago my mother arranged my marriage with a girl of a poor family. But I'm not concerned about them. Because most of the time I spent managing money to indulge my drug habit. I have destroyed my status hence society would not accept me normally. So I want to die using drugs.

CASE 3

I am Binod Rai and 21 years old. I became a drug addict because of my own father. I blame my father because he was very strict in nature and it made me frustrated in life.

I am the first child of my parents. From an early age I was interested in music, especially playing guitar. But it was the activity my father hated most. He always wanted me to study as he did not get chance to study in his time. He always kept me inside the home. This made me often frustrated but I was helpless. After my SLC exam, I started going out with friends because my friends used to tease me for sitting at home like a girl. One day I stayed out overnight and this made my father very angry.

Next time, when I stayed out, my father slapped me in front of my friends and shouted at them too. This made me embarrassed. I left home quietly. He became more angry with me and announced that I was not allowed to go back home.

I stayed with friends and spent a month. During this period I did not visit home though I missed it very much. I became very upset with my family circumstances. I met some drug-using friends while living away from home. I tried the drugs as I heard it would reduce the tension. After a month when my father went back to his duty abroad, my mother took me back home. By this time my exam results had come out and I had passed. So I was sent to Kathmandu for further study. I was enrolled in one of the reputed schools in Kathmandu but again met some friends who were drug users. I did avoid drugs for several months but as time passed by, I started using them again, sometimes to keep company with friends and sometimes to relieve my own tensions. I failed my next set of exams and returned home. It made me more frustrated and I started using drugs openly. My father realized his mistake and took me to India for treatment. But it did not work as I soon relapsed and started using drugs again.

CASE 4

It's my bad fortune that took me here in this stage and that I have become an injecting drug user. Usually I inject four times a day. I started taking drug from cough syrup at the age of eighteen. I started it not for fantasy or any other reason for entertainment, rather it was my obligation.

My parents decided to marry me off to an army man when I was 17 years old. I was not happy with their decision because he was nearly twice my age. So I eloped with a guy of my choice who is the son of an ex British Gurkha. For a few months, my marriage went well and during this time I got pregnant. Gradually I noticed my husband's activities changing. He started being absent from home and made demands for big amounts of money to his mother. My mother-in-law always fulfilled his demand in the absence of my father-in-law as he was serving abroad. One day I came to know about my husband's drug-using habit and his involvement with another girl. I spoke with my husband about it, but it led to a cold war between us. On the other hand my mother-in-law started scolding me not to trouble his son. She used to say that I was the one who caused the fight with her son. It hurt me but I had to remain quiet.

One day a serious quarrel took place between us, during which my husband slapped and challenged me, if I dared to dress up like other girls and take drugs, then he would stop hanging around with them. It hurt me very much, hence I left home along with my newborn baby to my natal home. He may have spoken in anger, but this struck me very badly deep inside to my heart.

I was in a stressful situation since I returned to my natal home. Hence, to get rid of the stress I started taking syrup and slowly switched in to other drugs and became dependent on it. In the course of time, he came to take me back home, but I didn't go as I thought it was too late to do so. In this way I fell in to drug addiction. Now I am living at my natal home along with my son. People do not have a good attitude towards me, but I'm helpless as I'm habituated and can't live without it.

CASE 5

Police are the big dacoits. If they were strict, then the drug problem would not have been increased to this extent. For them, it's a good opportunity to be transferred to Dharan. They put drug users in custody and demand money from their parents for their release. It would be good if they were doing this sincerely. I would have given them a reward if they were able to charge the dealers ... if you don't believe me, then go and see the record file. How many dealers were arrested? They arrest only the addicts not the dealers. I guess they have consent with drug traffickers.

I'm a retired army man. I retired from my job in 1982 and went to Brunei for further service. I earned lots of money and spent it all on my family. My wife died due to cirrhosis as she was alcoholic. When I came back from Brunei she died and I was responsible for looking after the entire home. My two daughters and my elder son are married. But my younger son has become an addict. He started using it due to his friends' influence. My wife was also unable to control him as she herself was an alcoholic. My son bothers the entire family with his stealing and fighting in the neighbourhood. I decided to send him to Arab last year. When his blood was tested we knew he was infected with HIV. He is dying ... it kills me every time when I see his face but he does not understand my feeling.

The Sociocultural Context

Drug abuse is considered delinquent behaviour. Scholars adopting the broken home hypothesis often point out that children from single-parent homes are more likely to become involved in delinquent activities than children from two-parent homes. The common rationale offered for this hypothesis is that one parent is simply less effective in monitoring children's behaviour than two parents.

As already discussed, in Dharan foreign employment is a major source of earning a living for some groups like the Rais, Limbus, Gurungs, etc. They are either serving as Gurkha soldiers or working in Brunei, Hong Kong, Korea, the Arab countries, or elsewhere. As they work away from home for long periods, their wives hold the authority over the children and the economy in their absence. Although women hold an equal position to males in these societies, they are considered less strict in controlling their children's activities. And due to the lack of a strong person at home, who implements strict rules, children were found to take up wrong activities under the influence of their peer group.

Moreover, children's socialization phase often coincides with the period when their father is away. In the father's absence, they are pampered because mothers are less strict than fathers. Generally, the father's retirement coincides with the time when his children reach adulthood. This means that it is very hard for some of the younger generation to accept their father's authority.

Research indicated that parents' relationships and interactions with their children are correlated with the children's involvement in delinquency (Curran & Renzetti 1996). I also found that long parental absences creates a communication gap between parents and children. Generally, the father fails to acknowledge his children's problems. They spend large amounts for their education, but they never think about children's personal interests. They view themselves as providing everything that they did not get when they were young. And when they discover their child going off on the wrong track, they resort to traditional means of asserting authority, sometimes threatening or giving physical punishment. It makes children more frustrated. Bijaya Limbu, manager of a drug rehabilitation centre, remarked, "Drug addiction is a lifelong disease which is not curable but can be controlled. For that one needs to have professional assistance, not physical punishment."

Socialization is a long process through which the values and norms of society are learned. The children of a Janajati background grow up with alcohol as a normal part of their socialization. I discovered that drinking alcohol in small amounts, or even regular drunkenness, is not considered a big problem in these communities. This negligence creates great challenges later. When one woman was asked when she noticed her son taking drugs for the first time, she replied, "I never noticed him. I thought he was drunk. Later his older sister told me that he was taking other kinds of drug."

According to the interactionist approach, people's actions derive from their interpretations of what goes on around them; indeed many of these interpretations are learned through interaction with other people. The majority of the drug users interviewed mentioned family tension as one reason why they became dependent on drugs. Some users were found to be frustrated with their alcoholic parents. Some revealed that broken relations with their parents or fighting with each other had created family tensions. According to others, lack of opportunity and joblessness had pushed them to get involved in drugs.

One's social location in a particular society, i.e. one's social class, sex, and age, also influences one's expectations and opportunities as well as the probability that one will be involved in antisocial behaviour. "Sometimes I feel like turning the children of those people who hate us in society into addicts," said twenty-three-year-old Raju Tamang, thereby revealing his hatred of society. On the other side, many people refuse to regard the problem as their own and would like a drastic solution. They say things like, "I wish we could remove these addicts as we removed the street dogs ... very disgusting." We can see that there is growing hatred between the drug users and the rest of society. With few exceptions, society does not cooperate with drug users. This is one reason why drug treatment is less effective in Dharan. It is also one reason for relapse after the treatment, according to Umang Rai, who is in charge of a treatment centre.

The communication gap between the generations could be one reason for frustration. The new generation is living in a transitional period. As they are exposed to an alien culture at an early age, they cannot adjust to traditional ways of life at home. Outside the home they are exposed to many different influences, which are not acceptable to their parents. In this situation, they can neither ignore their parents nor avoid their friends. For some, those who are sent to live in a hostel from an early age, there is a lack of a family environment and parental affection. This leads them into wrong ways. Thus the gap between the generations, which is exacerbated by migration and the process of modernization, is another social-cultural cause of drug use.

Economic Context

Economic factors play an important role in determining addiction in any society. During my fieldwork, people frequently told me, "Joblessness in Dharan is the main reason for drug addiction." There is some truth in this. The situation of unemployment is very destructive for the youth as they have excess free time. It leads them to take drugs to have fun and pass the time. Nonetheless, I do not fully agree with this local common sense, as I did not meet any drug user who was both well educated and jobless. It is also important to bear in mind that in Dharan the average age of falling into drug addiction for the first time is fourteen to sixteen years (UNAIDS 2000). This is the time when young people who can afford it are preparing for their SLC, and generally for such youths it is not the time for earning, unless they have to. If they have to work, they are likely to drop out of full-time education. Some argue that access to money is another factor encouraging drug use in Dharan. This too is not fully acceptable as there are drug users who are from poor backgrounds.

One significant factor behind drug addiction may be unequal economic status. As already discussed, remittances are the main economic source for the majority of social groups in Dharan. Those who have foreign employment earn much higher salaries than those working in Nepal. This has made them economically sound. For instance, a lower-level army pensioner gets Rs.11,800 a month, whereas a high-class officer in Nepal gets around Rs.10,000. Besides their pension, the former work abroad. Even as industrial workers in the Persian Gulf they earn a minimum of Rs.20,000 a month, which is double the salary of any officer working in a Nepalese government office. It has raised the economic status of the former very high. But it has had a different impact on the two different groups.

First, as money earned abroad is rarely invested in order to generate income in future, it leads to a greatly increased purchasing capacity. This means that the children of those working abroad become habituated to an easy life. They can have whatever they want without any struggle. And so long as they get economic support from their parents who work abroad, the children prefer not to work. Low official salaries cannot motivate them to work in Nepal as they are not sufficient for their expenditure. In any case, getting official work is far beyond what they can achieve. Hence they want to go abroad and earn like their parents. I found that the idea of working abroad is an extremely influential factor which demotivates them from academic study.

Second, there is an impact on the children of poor backgrounds who are influenced to take drugs mainly in two ways. First, because of their lower economic status, they may not dare to say 'No' when rich friends insist that they taste drugs. Second, they feel their poverty even more because they cannot themselves offer others these expensive drugs. Hence, to cope with their frustration they start taking cheap substitutes and become addicted to them. There are still other factors, which will be discussed further below.

Economics may be seen as playing a significant role in drug use. The low cost, ease of access, and adequacy of supply may well explain the popularity of drug use with everyone, from the teenager to the elderly population (National Institute on Drug Abuse 1988). It could be one of the possible factors in increasing drug use. As the nature of drug use has changed over time and made a significant drop in price, the number of drug users has increased. For instance, heroin and opium were very expensive when they were in pure form and thus were far from easy for ordinary people to access. When they came in the form of injections, the price decreased significantly with the effect that the users of these drugs cut across social and economic lines.

The dealers have expanded their market to include the poor as well as females. In Dharan injection drugs are the drug of choice because of their low cost. Users generally share drugs that are available in ampoules if they don't have money to bear the cost alone. The recent trend is to use injection drugs in form of a mixture of Norphin, Avil, and Diazepam. Thus economic variables are another important part of the explanation for the increasing number of drug users.

State Policy and Practices

In general the drug problem in Dharan does not seem to be directly related with politics. Yet there may be an indirect connection because of the historical marginalization of specific groups. Prolonged marginalization has caused poverty, uneducation, rebellion movements, and many of the other problems that Nepal faces today. I would argue that Dharan's drugs problem is one of the consequences of this marginalization. Two examples of this marginalization can be given, one from national political history, one more local.

Nationally, some groups have had a continuous history of marginalization. Gurkha recruitment was evidence of historical marginalization. After the political unification in the eighteenth century, the Shah dynasty came into power to rule over Nepal. The Rana Prime Minister, Bir Shamsher, acquiesced in sending the Nepali manpower that was requested by British India. Gurungs, Magars, Rais, and Limbus were in prime demand. More than 27,000 soldiers were hired between 1886 and 1904. Roughly 200,000 were drawn to India during the First World War. Approximately the same number participated in the Second World War. Beginning in 1919, the

British started to compensate this loss by providing an annual present of Rs. one million to the Nepalese state. The amount was doubled following World War II. The Rana Prime Minister was awarded a gift of £1,750,000 for his help (Mishra 1987).

In fact Rana rulers sold these specific groups, not only because they were in demand, but also because they were available in increasingly larger numbers, in large measure due to the (by now) fast-paced weakening of the communal organization of resource use and the consequent immiserization of a substantial proportion of the households in the central and eastern hills (Mishra 1987). Another consideration for the central government was its fear of mutiny in recently conquered territory. Hence it wanted to maintain its hegemony by ensuring that a substantial proportion of the adult Janajati population was absent from the country. Further evidence comes from the civil code of 1854. In this code, Nepalese society was segmented on the basis of culture and religion. As mentioned earlier, high-caste Hindus were categorized as Tagadhari, occupying the upper positions in the hierarchy, and the hill indigenous people were classified as Matwali. Their position is lower than the Tagadharis. They are considered alcohol drinkers, in many instances martial in nature, and are never included in the mainstream, except in a military context.

Despite the fact that drug use is viewed as a matter of grave concern and a big social problem internationally, Nepal's government has not paid much attention to it. There is a plan to establish five residential treatment and replacement centres for drug users. And for the families of the users, who will be living in the hostel, awareness programmes will be also launched (NPC 2002: 468). However, although there is only one year left before the end of the Tenth Plan, no steps have yet been taken to implement the plan. This may be connected to the fact that many of Nepal's drug users belong to the hill ethnic groups.

The increasingly unstable political situation of Nepal has created several impacts on different societies. In my opinion the case of drugs in Dharan is also a result of this situation. I interpret it as a local level of marginalization. Dharan lies in the second place among the drug-taking communities of Nepal (FHI/Nepal 2001). But it has not received any attention from the government sector, whereas drug-related problems are a big social and health issue in Dharan. Some NGOs work in this field but their services are limited. A very limited number of users benefit from their services. It means that the growing issue of drugs is still out of control in Dharan. But to everyone's dismay, there is no effort by the government sector nor has any politician ever addressed the issue in public speeches.

In fact Dharan appears to have been marginalized from the central level planning and programmes from very early on. There are today no major government offices in Dharan, despite the fact that it is the most populated town in the entire district. It was the regional headquarters in the past, but government offices were shifted elsewhere. Moreover, the previously advanced trade and commerce did not remain the same as the transportation extended to remote areas and many businesses based in Dharan could not survive. In the absence of big government offices, businessmen did not feel secure about investing their money. The local inhabitants have been deprived of job opportunities. The economically active population migrate abroad or to other towns to earn their livelihood. Economic stagnation has created a feeling of isolation in Dharan.

There are basically three reasons for this political exclusion. Surya Nath Upadhaya, the first mayor of Dharan, said: "Dharan is intentionally isolated by politicians as it is a communist centre." Other politicians and intellectuals support his statement as this is the main reason why its contemporary issues are not getting attention from the government. It is known as a communist centre where the majority of people have supported the communist ideology from an early period. The communist party has won every election after the restoration of democracy in 1990, but apart from a short nine-month period, it has never controlled the central government. Thus, Dharan and its problems never get any attention from the central government. This can be taken as one reason for political exclusion.

Secondly, no political leader from Dharan has ever secured a powerful position in the central government. In Nepal, it is commonplace for politicians to provide as many facilities as they can to their voters or to the people of the area from which they were elected in order to secure their votes in the next election. They feel no hesitation in taking from the people of the other side in order to benefit their own people. Thus, in the Panchayat period, some leaders who were in power shifted many of the government offices from Dharan to their home place. And the rest were shifted after the restoration of democracy.

A third aspect of marginalization can be traced to the fact that sixty-two per cent of Dharan's inhabitants are hill/ethnic indigenous groups such as Rai, Limbu, Newar, etc. The Rais and the Limbus are the indigenous groups of the eastern hill region which came under the rule of the Hindu royal dynasties of Nepal during the sixteenth and seventeenth centuries (Regmi 1971). Most recently, they are ranked as one of the disadvantaged groups of Nepal (NEFIN 2004). These groups share a marginal position vis-à-vis the state, whose structures have been dominated since the establishment of the kingdom by a ruling class composed overwhelmingly of members of the high castes (Caplan 1995: 69). Thus, as state power is monopolized by the so-called high-caste groups, if a social problem is stereotypically identified with members of indigenous groups, it is likely that it will be neglected by the state.

This marginalization has had some direct and some indirect social impacts. As a direct impact, there is a lack of opportunities for jobs and businesses. This forces locals to migrate elsewhere to earn their livelihood; it requires them to be absent from home for a long time or to stay behind and remain idle and frustrated. As an indirect impact, such marginalization keeps the local society backward socially, culturally, politically, and economically. For instance, it prevents local people from receiving exposure to different people of different societies from whom they might learn much. It also affects their psychology. According to a study report, the majority of drug users in Dharan fall into the age range of fourteen to thirty and the majority are school dropouts (Ahmad 1999). When I asked a drug user why he dropped out of school, he said, *Dherai padhera ke garne? Jagir khana chaina. Dherai padhne le ke po gareko cha ra?* ("What will I do with more education? There is no way to get a job. Anyway, what have educated people ever accomplished?") It sounds, in his conception, as if education is for a job or for survival, and, since he can depend on being provided for by his parents, he can live without it. It indicates that psychologically they become poor, as they think they can do nothing here even with education. This is mainly because they do not see the importance of education at home and even in society they do not see any prospect of acquiring a job, nor do they see people of different status who vary from them. In fact, they lack any role model who might motivate them towards education or creative work. Today, going overseas and earning money is the only life goal of the children of this particular group.

Other Factors

After 1990 there were some considerable changes in Dharan. To achieve economic growth the private sector was encouraged to invest. The mass media and communication advanced with this provision. In 1997 satellite networking came to Dharan. It made people much more aware of global affairs. But children were influenced by it negatively, especially by entertainment programmes. Young men began to imitate movie heroes. Smoking and street fighting are very common in popular movies and exert a great influence on the life of the local youth. The notion of fashion was adopted, and was considered an integral part of modernization. Some started to use drugs in an attempt to be fashionable and modern; others started due to pressure of such 'modern' peers. At the same time, manpower agencies mushroomed and enabled many Nepalis to work in different foreign countries. Many people from Dharan migrated to different countries through those agencies. It has benefited them economically, but, as we have seen, many of their children went astray in their absence.

In 1994 the British government announced that it was going to hand over Hong Kong to China in 1997. It created a provision for Nepalis who had served in the British Gurkhas that their children born in Hong Kong could get Hong Kong citizenship (ID) if they applied before 1997. This caused a great migration to Hong Kong, not only of the children of Gurkha soldiers, but also many non-Gurkhas, who managed to obtain fake Hong Kong birth certificates. Many of those over sixteen years of age went to Hong Kong. It increased the amount of remittances flowing to Dharan. It helped to create an economically independent youth. Some of the young people working in Hong Kong got involved in drugs while there and, when they came back to Dharan, influenced others back home. In addition to the young people, parents too started going to Hong Kong instead of passing their retired life in Dharan. For some time the trend of having both the young people and the household head absent has been apparent. This, as we have seen, has led the younger people who are left behind at home to go out of control. In addition, people have become more individualistic; they are indifferent to the opinions of the wider society, because they do not have time to participate in it as they spend most of their time abroad.

With economic advancement, there is a trend among the wealthy to send their children either to India or to Kathmandu for study. Living in the hostel children are sometimes influenced by contact with 'the wrong sort' to take drugs or other kinds of misbehaviour. There is, in addition, the factor of geographical location, which means that drugs are easily available. Dharan is situated in the Tarai near the border with India. It takes merely an hour to go from Dharan to Jogbani on the border. Jogbani is the main route by which drugs enter east Nepal. In India, the drugs mentioned earlier are openly sold as they have legitimate medical uses. One can get them easily without a prescription. But in Nepal such drugs are banned unless one has a medical prescription. Hence many drug users get drugs from Jogbani themselves. The police administration in Nepal is not strict about drug trafficking. As one drug user said, "If there were no drugs in the market then how can one be addicted? But it is possible [to remove them] only if the police administration becomes strict on drug trafficking." The response of a high-level police authority to this is: "The low related narcotic drugs are simple and limited in coverage. Hence, we cannot be so strict."

Corruption remains another leading factor for promoting drug trafficking. Many parents take the view that, due to weak administration, their actions will have an impact only on the street-level deals and will do little to deter the major suppliers of arugs.

CONCLUSION

Drug misuse is not a street-corner problem, but an international one. It is a current problem around the world which is mounting every day. Every society will have a different combination of factors behind its growth. In this chapter I have argued that it cannot be seen simply as a social or a psychological problem. I have viewed it as one of the gradual results of historical as well current political problems.

In this paper I have discussed social, economic, political and geographical factors, and their own influence on the drugs problem. Today the number of drug users is increasing and some particular cultural groups are greatly influenced by it. These groups are among Nepal's marginalized groups. Drugs have become a problem as a result of their continuous marginal position. It would appear that the youth of Dharan did not see the Maoist rebellion as an outlet to express their frustration. The message of joining the Maoists has been primarily focused in the rural areas. These urban youth are unlikely to be able to find a place in such a movement. Mark Liechty (2003: Ch. 9) has described a drug addict from Thamel, Kathmandu, and this case describes a sense of hopelessness leading to addiction similar to what I have analysed for Dharan.

The situation of drug users in Dharan will not improve unless a new drug-controlling strategy is adopted. Historical factors must also be kept in mind while preparing such a strategy. The concerned communities must be involved while implementing plans and programmes. Government involvement is essential to tackle the problem. But at the same time, efforts are also needed from INGOs, NGOs, local society, academicians, political leaders, and so on. All this will only be possible if people realize that drug users are a reflection of their own society.

REFERENCES

Ahmad, K. 1999. *A Time Bomb under the City: Drug Abuse in Dharan*. Dharan: KYC/PJK.

Bista, D.B. 1991. *Fatalism and Development: Nepal's Struggle for Modernization*. Hyderabad: Orient Longman.

Caplan, L. 1995. *Warrior Gentlemen: "Gurkhas" in the Western Imagination*. Oxford: Berghahn Books.

CBS. 2002. *Population of Nepal: Village Development Committees/Municipalities (Eastern Development Region)*. Kathmandu: HMG, NPC Secretariat, CBS in Collaboration with UNFPA Nepal.

Curran, D.J. and C.M Renzetti. 1996. *Social Problems: Society in Crisis* (4th edn.). Needham Heights, Massachusetts: Allyn and Bacon.

Dhital, R., Y.B. Gurung, G. Subedi, and P. Hamal. 2001. *Alcohol and Drug Use in Nepal: With Reference to Children*. Kathmandu: Child Workers in Nepal Concerned Center (CWIN).

FHI (Family Health International)/Nepal. 2001. *HIV and Injecting Drug Use in Selected Sites of the Terai, Nepal*. Kathmandu: FHI.

Ivana, L. and A. Shrestha. 2002. *Empowering Women Substance Users*. Kathmandu: The Richmond Fellowship.

Jimee, G. 2001. *Urban Expansion in Nepal: A Case Study of Dharan*. Kirtipur: Central Department of Geography, Tribhuvan University.

Karmacharya, H.R. 1998 (2055 v.s.). *Dharan ka Pratham: Hijo ra Aja (Foundings and First Instances in Dharan: Yesterday and Today)*. Itahari: Siddhi Binayak Publications (in Nepali).

Kornblum, W. and J. Julian. 1995. *Social Problems*. Englewood Cliffs, NJ: Prentice Hall.

KYC/PJK. 2002. *Harm Reduction Program in Dharan Municipality*. Dharan: KYC/PJK.

——. 2004. *Situation Analysis of Drug Users in Dharan*. Dharan: KYC/PJK.

KYC/PJK/Peace Corps Nepal. 1997. *Dharan ma Lagu Padartha Durvyasan Sambandhi Samudayik Anusandhan (Cooperative Research on the Misuse of Intoxicating Substances in Dharan)*. Dharan: KYC/PJK (in Nepali).

Liechty, M. 2003. *Suitably Modern: Making Middle-Class Culture in a New Consumer Society*. Princeton: Princeton University Press.

Mishra, C. 1987. *Development and Underdevelopment: A Preliminary Sociological Perspective* (Occasional Papers in Sociology and Anthropology, Vol. 1). Kirtipur: Central Department of Sociology and Anthropology, Tribhuvan University.

National Institute on Drug Abuse. 1988. *Learning Factors in Substance Abuse* (NIDA Research Monograph Series, Vol. 84). Kathmandu: NIDA.

NEFIN. 2004. *Classification of Indigenous Nationalities of Nepal*. Kathmandu: Nepal Federation of Indigenous Nationalities.

NPC. 2002. *The Tenth Plan (2002-2007)*. Kathmandu: HMG, NPC.

Parillo, V., J. Stimson, and A. Stimson. 1996. *Contemporary Social Problems*. Needham Heights, Massachusetts: Allyn and Bacon.

Phanjoubam, T. 1997. *Drug Abuse and Illicit Trafficking in North Eastern India*. New Delhi: Vikas Publishing House.

Regmi, M.C. 1971. *A Study in Nepali Economic History*. Delhi: Manjusri Publishing House.

Shrestha, S.K. 1995. *Limbuwanko Aitihasik Adhyayan (A Historical Study of Limbuwan)*. Lalitpur: Kirant Publication Centre (in Nepali).

Subba, C. 1995. *The Culture and Religion of Limbus*. Kathmandu: K.B. Subba.

UNAIDS. 2000. *Drug Use and HIV Vulnerability: Policy Research Study in Asia*. Bangkok: UNAIDS Asia Pacific Inter Country Team.

WHO. 1980. *Drug Problems in the Sociocultural Context: A Basis for Policies and Programme Planning* (Public Health Papers 73). Geneva: WHO (World Health Organization); Albany, New York: WHO Publications Center.

——. 1990. *Preventing and Controlling Drug Abuse*. Geneva: WHO.

William, K. and J. Joseph. 1995. *Social Problems*. New Jersey: A Simon & Schuster Company.

10

Learning to be Silent: Change, Childhood, and Mental Health in the Maoist Insurgency in Nepal

JUDITH PETTIGREW

INTRODUCTION

On a hot sunny day in the spring of 1995, just weeks after his birth, I rocked Raju in a bamboo cradle on the veranda of his aunt's house and thought about his future.[1] I wondered how much of his life he would live in the Tamu (Gurung)[2] hill village he was born into and whether he might follow his uncle into the Gurkhas or his father to the United Arab Emirates as a migrant worker.[3] As I looked at his tiny sleeping face, I hoped that he would have more options to choose from than those of earlier generations.

---

[1] I am especially indebted to my informants and to 'Ramesh' who assisted me in conducting the research on which this paper is based. For comments on earlier versions, I am grateful to Sharon Hepburn, Mark Jordans, Brandon Kohrt, Don Messerschmidt, Sara Shneiderman, Deepak Thapa, and the editors of this volume. I would like to thank Mark Jordans for the use of a pictorial scale used at the Center for Victims of Torture, Nepal (CVICT), which I adapted to assess levels of fear. I am grateful to Mecha Gurung and Ocean Gurung for assistance with the translation of Nepali language materials and to Yarjung K. Tamu for advice on Tamu Kyui terms and cultural concepts. A British Academy Small Grant provided financial support.

[2] 'Tamu' is the singular of 'Tamu-mai', the term that the people who are better known as 'Gurungs' apply to themselves when they speak their own language, Tamu Kyui (a Tibeto-Burman language indigenous to the Tamu-mai). As this chapter is based on research carried out in a predominantly Tamu village and conducted primarily through Tamu Kyui, I use the term 'Tamu' throughout. Most conversations in this chapter took place in Tamu Kyui (and non-English words included in the text are Tamu Kyui unless otherwise indicated). I am responsible for translating them into English. Formal interviews conducted in April 2005 took place in Nepali and were translated into English by my research assistants and me.

[3] All personal and place names are pseudonyms. I have chosen to give the village a Tamu Kyui pseudonym rather than a Nepali one as, although official names are in Nepali, all Tamu villages have a Tamu Kyui name which is always used when speaking Tamu Kyui. Certain ethnographic details have been disguised in this piece in an attempt to protect the identity of my informants.

I imagined that he might, like his brother Dambar, receive part of his education in the city, but I expected him to spend at least his first twelve years in the village. Raju's socialization would follow a similar course to Dambar's, who was his age when I first arrived in 1990. Tamu Kyui would be his first language but once he went to school, he would quickly learn Nepali. At an early age, he would be taught to carry water in a small bamboo basket; would play on the village paths with neighbourhood children and look after the family's animals. I also wondered if tragedy and trauma would influence his life as it does for so many – such as the hazards of monsoon landslides, accidents in the forest, inadequately treated medical conditions or lack of opportunities to match educational achievements.

Raju is now ten years old. He is a shy, obedient little boy who speaks two languages, herds goats and plays mischievously with his friends. Unlike his brother he has grown up during the 'People's War'.[4] He is, as his mother explains, "Just a year older than the war". In addition to his usual duties, he sometimes sits by the courtyard gate at dusk and acts as a 'sentry' for his mother and *matheba* (elder mother),[5] to warn them of the arrival of Maoists.[6] At other times, he goes to a village shop to find out if the insurgents are in the village and if so where they intend to spend the night. He knows how to answer the Maoists' questions and what to say to conceal his family's possessions. Like Dambar, he plays with bamboo 'guns' but rarely pretends to be hunting in the jungle; instead he plays Maoists and soldiers, running around with other children mimicking the combatants he sees in the village on an almost daily basis. His play-group includes girls who carry and shoot 'guns' like the Maoist women who visit. Raju knows the names of a range of military equipment, especially that used by the insur-

[4]The Communist Party of Nepal (Maoist) declared a 'People's War' in February 1996 and now controls, to a greater or lesser extent, most of rural Nepal. For an overview see Thapa with Sijapati (2003).

[5]Raju's *matheba* – Dhan Kumari – is his grandfather's elder sister's daughter.

[6]Non-aligned villagers interact with various categories of Maoists. As well as the local activists, whom they live beside and may be friendly with, they encounter other party workers and members of the local militia, many of whom will be from other parts of the country. Senior Maoists in the area include the "commander", the political commissar who is responsible for decision-making and policy implementation. Other senior party members visit for specific programmes; some are liked and respected but others less so. Villagers evaluate them primarily on how they treat locals. Groups of the People's Liberation Army visit on a regular basis and stay a night or two when moving through the area. Although Maoists are not always in the village, and sometimes the security forces also visit, locals consider their area to be under Maoist control. When discussing the planned extension to a day-care centre, villagers remarked to me, "We have to get permission from the government. Our government is the Maoists." Permission might also be taken from the relevant office of the Nepal Government; however, this is considered less imperative because other than teachers, health workers, and occasional patrols by the security forces, representatives of the government no longer have a consistent presence in the area.

gents, and last year I watched him stop digging radishes, and using his hoe as a gun, pretend to spray the ground and walls of the kitchen garden with bullets. More recently, I overheard him make shooting noises while nonchalantly walking along a village path. When he was younger, I watched Raju's mother hit him to teach him the importance of silence, and he is now extra careful to be quiet in certain situations, observing carefully what is going on around him in a manner that is suggestive of a child older than his ten years.

The Anthropology of Children in War

Despite growing interest in the anthropology of war, relatively little ethnographic study has been undertaken during ongoing conflicts (for some exceptions see Nordstrom 1995, 1997, 1998; Olujic 1995; Sluka 1995). The ethnographic material on the wartime experiences of children is similarly limited (for exceptions see Olujic 1998; Povrzanovic 1997; Quesada 1998; and Suárez-Orozco 1987 on civilian children; Dickson-Gõmez 2002; and Peters and Richards 1998 on child soldiers; and Boyden and de Berry 2004 on armed conflict and displacement).[7] Children are both victims and combatants in war. Carelessly discarded bombs injure some; others are killed when their school becomes a battlefield, others play war games mimicking and elaborating what they have seen, and some choose to fight.[8] Writing about child and youth soldiers Korbin notes that they are

> ... not only conscripted but also may choose a more active than passive role in the hostilities swirling around them. Some children and youth fight because they believe in the cause, some are conscripted, and some join because they see this as a way to secure survival necessities such as food, water, and shelter in the absence of other avenues to obtain these resources. (Korbin 2003: 440)[9]

---

[7]This follows the general trend as research on the impact of war on children's lives has received minimal attention until recently (Barenbaum, Ruchkin, and Schwab-Stone 2004; Machel 2001). Conducting research on children involves additional ethical considerations, which may have played a role in deterring scholars from studying this topic. Most research, including that of anthropologists, is conducted post-conflict.

[8]Children who play in and around the village are particularly vulnerable to bombs and landmines. For example, in rural Somalia 75 per cent of the injuries incurred from mines were to children aged five to fifteen (ICRC 1994). There are frequent reports in the Nepali media of children killed or injured by bombs or landmines (*Himal* 2003, *The Kathmandu Post* 2003, *Kantipur* 2004, Nepalnews.com 2004). While there are no official records of numbers of landmine casualties, the Nepal Campaign to Ban Landmines (NCBL) reported that in 2004, 1,445 people were victims of explosions resulting in 1,056 injuries and 389 deaths. This included 90 children injured and 44 killed. In the first half of 2005, NCBL stated that 406 people were injured by explosions, of whom 52 were children. Those killed numbered 156 including 27 children (NCBL).

[9]There are multiple motivations for joining the Maoists. Some are clearly considered choices,

There is an expanding body of human rights and journalistic literature[10] on the impact of the Maoist 'People's War' on children as either civilians or combatants.[11] While this work points to the surface-level impacts of the insurgency on children, an ethnographic study recording the ongoing village level experience can document how the insurgency affects children's daily lives in more depth. This chapter on the impact of the 'People's War' on civilian children from non-aligned families in a Tamu hill village in west central Nepal attempts to address the gap in the literature on children in the conflict. Based on twelve short periods of fieldwork (of between two days and two weeks) carried out in 2002, 2003, 2004, and 2005 this piece focuses on three issues.[12] First, it examines the 'culture of terror' that has developed in a village that I refer to as 'Kwei Nasa'. Second, it explores adults' concerns about their children, addressing in particular the steps that caregivers take to protect their children.[13] While children growing up in the 'People's War' do so within an environment of community-wide conflict-related violence, their lives are framed by pre-existing structures of suffering (*dukha* in Nepali). This piece aims to examine the present situation in the context of existing distress and disadvantage, for

---

others serendipitous, and still others due to unavoidable contingencies. In addition to the reasons listed by Korbin, Nepali youths join to avenge the death of family members and friends; to address the structural inequalities of gender, caste, poverty, marginalization; because the Maoists provide opportunities, skills and subsistence; because they were under suspicion by the security forces and had few options but to join; in reaction to arrest and torture; because their friends joined; because they found the dancing and rhetoric at propaganda events appealing; they were attracted by the power acquired when carrying a gun; and so on. For further discussion of the motivations of young Tamu-mai for joining the Maoists, see Pettigrew (2003). For a similar discussion on youth motivation in Dolakha district in central eastern Nepal, see Shneiderman and Turin (2004).

[10]This literature addresses issues such as the number of child fatalities and injuries, the Maoist abduction and recruitment of children, the detention and torture of children, the need for the combatants to prioritize children's rights, sexual violence against children, the dangers of exposure to land mines, children from displaced families, the traumatization of children exposed to fighting, and the impact on education (see Amnesty International [2005]; CWIN [2004]; Human Rights Watch [2004]; Watchlist [2005]; Basnet [2004]). There is also a literature aimed at children (see HimRights 2005).

[11]The Maoists and the government both deny the recruitment and use of children. It is difficult to obtain estimates, but it is widely believed that approximately 30 per cent of the combatants are youths (SAIR 2004). When meeting the Maoists it is obvious that significant numbers are under eighteen, a fact that those asked do not deny. On the basis of personal experience I suggest that the numbers are higher. There are numerous stories of the security forces using children as informants, couriers, and messengers. The government insists that it is not possible to join the Royal Nepalese Army (RNA) until aged over eighteen, however, it is possible to enlist at age fifteen in order to follow military training (Watchlist 2005: 37).

[12]This research builds on earlier work which stretches back to 1990.

[13]My main informants are predominantly middle-aged, middle-income Tamu women. The perspectives contained within this piece are primarily, but not exclusively, those of members of this group.

example, poverty, inadequate healthcare, and poor educational opportunities.[14] Third, it considers children's interpretations and representations of Maoists and explores how the ongoing presence of the insurgents and their activities influence the day-to-day lives of village children. The chapter ends with preliminary comments on the impact of the insurgency on child development and mental health in general.[15]

Methodology

As the focus of this account is more on adults' concerns about their children, rather than children's experiences from their own perspectives, most of the data is based on participant observation and on informal and formal interviews (including eighty-five interviews on the impact of the conflict conducted in April 2005) with adult caregivers. The chapter includes some informal observational data on the children of my closest informants including those in the house I live in during fieldwork and in two neighbouring houses. Interviews were not conducted with children but two directed questions ("What do you think of the Maoists?" and "Do Maoists talk to you?") were asked to four children while participating in a shared activity. An additional question ("Have the Maoists asked you what you have in your house?") was asked of one child during a conversation with his mother where he was present (for a more detailed discussion on the general approaches used in conducting anthropological fieldwork in the Maoist insurgency see Pettigrew, Shneiderman, and Harper 2004).[16]

'Cultures of Terror'

The 'culture of terror' model is one of the main current anthropological approaches for the study of political violence (Taussig 1987, 1992; Green 1995; Suárez-Orozco 1987).[17] Michael Taussig – whose early ideas writers

---

[14]Violence has a long history in Nepal, which includes the violence of exclusion on the basis of caste, gender, class, or ethnicity; poverty and inadequate health care; poor educational opportunities or employment opportunities; and state-perpetrated violence such as the use of torture. What is new is community-wide conflict-related violence. The term 'structural violence' is frequently used to refer to these types of suffering; however, I have chosen to use the Nepali word *dukha* (suffering, trouble, hardship, pain) as it is the term used by locals to refer to these hardships and disadvantages.

[15]Although the security forces visit Kwei Nasa they do so rarely, so this chapter is primarily concerned with villager-Maoist interrelationships (for a discussion of villager-army relationships, see Pettigrew 2004).

[16]For discussions of conducting research on children in conflict, see Eyber and Ager (2004), Utas (2004), and Boyden (2004).

[17]I have reservations about the term 'culture of terror' because I consider it to be an imprecise term which requires further definition. Furthermore, it over privileges 'terror' at the expense of 'normality'. Despite my concerns, I retain it as I feel that it provides a useful framework within which to analyse what is going on in rural Nepal. For a critique, see Margold (1999).

such as Green, Sluka, and Suárez-Orozco have further developed – states that where political torture and murder become endemic, 'cultures of terror' flourish. Sluka suggests that "A culture of terror establishes 'collective fear' as a brutal means of social control ... When fear becomes a way of life ... a culture of terror has emerged" (2000: 22).[18]

'Cultures of terror', Suárez-Orozco states, have their "own vocabulary and grammar, cultural facts and artefacts". The vocabulary he discovered during research in Argentina, included words such as 'disappeared', 'torture centres', 'torture rooms', and 'electric prods' (1992: 240). A central aim of this chapter is to consider the 'culture of terror' as experienced in Kwei Nasa. In Kwei Nasa, as elsewhere in rural Nepal, daily life is lived in a 'shadow of fear'.[19] Prem Kumari, a fifty-year-old villager, sums up the situation:

> There is nowhere safe. Maoists come and ask for food and shelter at any time. They do not think about night or day or our daily tasks, they interrupt us at any time. No matter what they ask for, we have to give it, since otherwise, they can do anything to us. When they arrive, we are in danger in case the army visits and when they leave we are in danger if the army finds out that they have been in our houses. The army accuses us of being Maoist supporters and ... shout and threaten us. In nearby villages, they have even hit women. If the army comes while the Maoists are not here then we worry about the return of the Maoists since they can accuse us of spying. ... We also worry about bombs and landmines. These are dangerous things that children might unknowingly pick up and play with or that we might step on in the forest.

While the activities of everyday life, such as working in the fields, preparing food, going to school, walking to town, visiting relatives, playing, eating or sleeping, continue to occupy most people's daily lives in rural Nepal, at any moment a familiar routine can be pierced by unexpected terror and violence. Violence, as one of Linda Green's Guatemalan informants explained, is, "... like fire, it can flare up suddenly and burn you" (Green 1995: 109). A Kwei Nasa neighbour, Padam Sobha, referring to fear, explains:

---

[18]Sluka is referring here to state terror. However, his ideas can be applied equally well to an insurgency where civilians are exposed to the terror of both parties to the conflict.

[19]The Tamu Kyui term for fear is *nghiba* and the word for terrified is *nghinghinghan*. The latter, however, is not widely used (except by some elderly people) and instead most people use the word *lhe* [very] *nghiba* to describe extreme fear. When people stated they were *lhe nghiba* I translated this into English as 'very frightened', and when they stated that they were *lhe, lhe nghiba,* I translated this as 'terrified'. In formal interviews conducted in Nepali in April 2005, I used the Nepali term *dar* for fear and the words *dherai dar lageko* for 'very frightened' and *besari dar lageko* for 'terrified'.

> You can't say when you will be frightened. It all depends on the situation. Sometimes there is 100% fear and I feel sweaty, shaky, my heart beats fast and my stomach feels sick. At other times, there is no fear and then sometimes there is a little bit of fear. I am 100% frightened, especially at night and when walking to and from the town or another village. I don't often feel like this during the day but you can't say when you will be frightened.

Green suggests that "... with repetitiveness and familiarity people learn to accommodate themselves to terror and fear". Fear becomes routinized. Over the last few years, many people have told me that they have become used to their unusual circumstances. Curfews, army check posts, the militarization of life in Nepal, and living with the Maoists have all become habitual. Padam Sobha continues, "I was very frightened when the Maoists first came. I could not look at them without feeling terrified. Now I see them every day and most of the time I am not frightened. I am used to them." During recent interviews with eighty-five people on the impact of the conflict, many reported that while they remain frightened, familiarity with the situation has led to a decrease in fear. The majority of the time, people's greatest fears are not realized, such as death, abduction, or injury to themselves or their families, but the possibility is always there. The potential always exists for punishment for actions interpreted or re-interpreted as unacceptable. For example, villagers are sometimes permitted by the Maoists to make and openly sell alcohol, and at other times they are not. In general, experience shows that if the villagers do as the Maoists request, they are unlikely to be harmed.[20] The fear of being caught in the crossfire is ever present, but it is to an extent 'a fear in the back of the mind', since to date, although some people have had close escapes, it has not happened in this village.[21]

Comments about not being frightened are a reflection of what people feel, but at other times they are part of a process of denial.[22] Sometimes the risks are so great, the options for escape so small, and people so terrified, that to go on they tell themselves and others that they are not frightened. During late 2002, when large numbers of the Maoist People's Liberation Army (PLA) were regularly in the village, Dhan Kumari, who knows a little English and referred to the PLA using the English words 'Red Army', said to me, "When you were here in the monsoon we were frightened of

---

[20]Problems occur when the demands are excessive. In early 2005, Maoists killed an ex-Indian Army officer in a neighbouring village when he did not pay the large 'donation' requested.

[21]People in neighbouring villages have been injured in crossfire and others killed when the security forces erroneously thought them to be Maoists.

[22]There are multiple motivations for denial, including pride and the desire to appear to keep the 'heartmind' 'smooth' (see below).

them. Now we are not frightened. We had 400 of the Red Army stay and we are not frightened any longer." While familiarity had apparently decreased her fear, or so she said, she was in fact terrified. Struggling to manage the situation, she convinced, or attempted to convince herself and others, that she was not frightened. When she heard that a very large group of insurgents had arrived in the village, she was clearly terrified and became panicky, shouting angrily and rudely at others. Afterwards she admitted that she was extremely frightened.[23]

Socialization to terror enables people to survive in extreme situations. It is not possible to live in a constant state of alertness, so feelings of fear and chaos diffuse throughout the body but surface in dreams, bodily aches and pains, anxiety, denial, changed social relationships, illness, and behaviours such as increased alcohol consumption. Green notes that the routinization of terror "... allows people to live in a chronic state of fear with a façade of normalcy at the same time that terror permeates and shreds the social fabric" (1995: 108). A veneer of normality masks the fear that is never far away and normal abnormality best describes the situation.

KWEI NASA IN THE 'PEOPLE'S WAR'

Kwei Nasa is a large village of several hundred households located along the upper slopes and top of a ridge in the Himalayan foothills. It contains a health post, rice mill, post office, teashops that serve as general-purpose stores, and a kerosene distribution centre, but it has no electricity. Although most villagers are Tamu, Kwei Nasa is a mixed community which includes Dalits, and in nearby hamlets Brahmans, Chetris, and small numbers of Tamangs and Magars.[24] The primary occupation is farming and the staple crop is rice, but maize and millet are also grown. Many villagers have relatives in foreign armies or working overseas and remittances make a

---

[23]There are many reasons why people become terrified. In most cases, it is because they fear being caught in crossfire, or fear accusations and punishment from either side, or fear the abduction of family members. They are especially frightened of the security forces who do not usually have local connections like the Maoists, and are considered liable to "kill you easily". On this particular occasion, Dhan Kumari was frightened because she thought that my assistant and I might be accused by the Maoists of being spies. Other people did not evaluate this risk in the same way and felt that Dhan Kumari was exaggerating the danger. Dhan Kumari's fears must be considered in the wider context of her life as she feels very vulnerable (she is in her early sixties and her parents are dead; she is by choice unmarried, lives virtually alone, is often unwell, and has a medical history of anxiety). The topic of fear in general has received inadequate attention in anthropology. For an exception, see Green (1995).

[24]The Dalits are mainly Damai (Tailors) and Kami (Blacksmiths). Both groups are considered 'untouchable'.

significant contribution to the local economy.[25] Stretching below the village on either side of the ridge are the steeply terraced fields, some close to the village but others up to an hour's walk away. Agricultural work involves steep climbs and descents and long walks with heavy loads. Most consumer goods that people use come from the town.[26] Vegetables sellers visit each week and other merchants come less regularly to sell dry goods, glass bangles, and sundry items. In the winter months traders from the north sell herbs and turquoise and coral beads. For everything else people make shopping trips to the urban centre which is less than a day's walk away.

When I arrived in Kwei Nasa in the summer of 2002, it had been two years since I visited the village. At the time of a previous trip in 2000, Maoists were coming into the villages for 'donations' and guns and to give propaganda speeches and cultural programmes.[27] Interviews with middle-aged and older people revealed two recurring themes, their reluctance to believe that Tamu youth joined the Maoists and their surprise when they discovered women's participation. The Maoists had also become a catalyst that brought pre-existing unexpressed concerns to the surface. Talking about the guerrillas provided an indirect way of talking about conflict between neighbours and kin, and the fears associated with these conflicts (Pettigrew 2003). By 2001 a Maoist training camp was established in the area and stories proliferated about the comings and goings of the insurgents who operated openly in the area. The 'People's War' reached a new height in November 2001, when the Maoists withdrew from a several-month-long ceasefire and initiated a series of attacks across the country including ones targeted at Royal Nepalese Army (RNA) barracks. This confrontation marked a departure, since for the first time the Maoists directly challenged the army rather than just the police. In response, then Prime Minister, Sher Bahadur Deuba, imposed a State of Emergency, which effectively suspended most civil rights and for the first time deployed the army to fight the insurgents.

I returned to Kwei Nasa towards the end of a hot monsoon afternoon in July 2002. At first glance, things looked very much as before: women washing at the tap, children playing by the buffalo pond, a group of people clustered in the tea shop. As I approached, I was surprised to see so many unfamiliar faces; young men and women I had never seen in the village before. This is hardly surprising, I told myself, as I have been away for some time and as the first tea shop in the village, this place tends to attract

---

[25]Particularly in the Gurkha Brigade of the British Army and in the Indian Army. The largest proportion of those outside the country are migrant workers employed in India, the Gulf states, East Asia or South-East Asia.

[26]In an attempt to maintain anonymity I have chosen not to name this nearby urban centre.

[27]I place 'donations' in inverted commas as giving is compulsory.

visitors. I called out a greeting and the three casually dressed young men standing at the door replied. As I rounded the corner into the main street the usual collection of teenage boys were playing basketball, watched by a group of younger children standing on the sidelines, too little to be allowed to join in. "You've come," someone shouted out. "I have come," I replied in the informal way of Tamu greeting. I continued my journey through the village, stopping briefly to say hello at water taps and across the walls of courtyards. I noticed that Krishna Maya's tea shop was boarded up but otherwise things looked much as they did when I first visited twelve years before.

Several hours after arriving in the village, I sat on the opposite side of the hearth from a friend. Over a cup of tea I told her that I was thinking of visiting nearby villages to get details of army killings, which I knew from a meeting with a human rights organization had not been fully documented. Dhan Kumari looked horrified; she did a quick scan of the veranda and courtyard and told me in a hushed and hurried voice:

> You cannot go there, it is terribly dangerous, and you cannot talk about the killings. They are secret things. It is very dangerous to talk about what the army does. Do you not know that the Maoists are here nearly every day? They come and force villagers to feed them, there is no choice. Then the army comes and they blame people because they fed the Maoists. It is a very dangerous time now. ...

She stopped abruptly and tensed as we heard footsteps outside. "Stop talking," she said. "I don't know who it is." Dhan Kumari was notably relieved when she discovered that it was a neighbour. "Where are they? How many are there?" She asked him. "There are five," he replied. "Three men and two women – they have forced *Pade* [the president of one of the village women's committees] to open the committee house and that is where they are going to sleep tonight."[28] Dhan Kumari turned to me and commented:

> They don't all sleep at once; they take turns to sleep and turns to guard. At least one or two of them are always awake. Sometimes a Tamu woman comes, she speaks Tamu Kyui. She is from a far-off village and she is pregnant. We haven't seen her for a while and we wonder if she has been killed in a skirmish as she couldn't run fast enough.

On the second morning of my stay, I visited a tea shop to chat with the owner. It was midday and as most people were out in the fields we were alone except for her youngest daughter who was playing on the ground in

[28] *Pade* is a Tamu kinship term meaning 'second daughter'.

front of us making a 'tea shop' out of stones, sweet wrappings, and match sticks. In hushed tones, Durga told me about the visit of the Maoists to her shop the previous week:

> In the early evening a group arrived. They were heavily armed and they wore belts with bullets around their waists. One of the girls was very young – she couldn't have been more than thirteen. It upset me to look at her as she was about the same age as my eldest daughter. I am so glad that I sent Nani [eldest daughter] to live with my relatives in the town so there is no chance that the Maoists will forcibly recruit her. The leader of the group told me that they wanted food and to stay the night. I told them that I could feed them but I pleaded with them not to sleep in the house. I said, "If you stay here and the army arrives then all my family will be killed." One of them laughed and replied, "Then we'll die together." I begged them not to stay and they left after they had eaten.

She stopped talking briefly, and looking at her little girl, commented:

> It is hard to keep children safe nowadays. I have sent Nani to the town but can I protect Kaji [youngest daughter]? She is still little and does not understand and I am worried about her picking up bombs that the Maoists might leave behind. Recently they had bomb-making equipment in a house in our hamlet. One of them was reading by candlelight, she fell asleep, and the candle caught fire. She only woke up when her hair caught fire. They put the fire out but if she had not awakened, then there would have been a terrible explosion and everyone in the house and maybe even the area would have been killed or injured.

The next day we went to the lower secondary school to meet the teachers.[29] They give 2 per cent of their monthly salary to the Maoists and at the yearly festival of Dasain, they give 20 per cent.[30] "If we don't," an experienced middle-aged teacher stated, "they will hit us, kill us or break our

---

[29]The school is for classes one to eight. Classes nine and ten are held in the high school, which is an hour's walk away. Teachers and health workers are the only government employees still working in the villages and are vulnerable to threats and intimidation from both sides. Because of historical links between teachers and left-wing ideology, the security forces suspect them of being Maoist activists while the Maoists may consider them government spies. Caught between the demands of the Maoists to comply with their requests, and the demands of the security forces not to do so, they face extreme pressures.

[30]Teachers are required to give a proportion of their salary to the Maoists. How much they give varies but is often between 5 per cent and 15 per cent. Previously those in Kwei Nasa were giving a higher percentage. Teachers, however, are frequently reluctant to reveal how much they give and sometimes deny or downplay the amount demanded.

legs." In November 2003, the Maoists punished the science teacher at the high school for openly criticizing them. His face was blackened and a garland of shoes placed around his neck. One of the teachers commented: "We were forced to go there [to watch the punishment], but we couldn't watch, and so we turned away and didn't look." The teacher still works in school, but was frightened and colleagues wondered how much longer he would continue to teach in the area.[31] The school does not always close when there is a Maoist-called *bandh* (general strike) in the region but if they are asked by the insurgents to do so, the teachers comply.[32] The District Education Office told the teachers not to take risks and so the headmaster commented, "Even if one Maoist comes and asks us to close, then we close."[33] He continued:

> We teachers are brave as we have to deal with the Maoists. We are used to them as they come often to the school with their guns. We are also used to dealing with the security forces and their threats. In the past, the security forces threatened the teachers and forced us to cross out the slogans written by the Maoists. This put us at risk but now they do not do this. Recently some Maoists from the student wing came and told us to gather the students and they made a speech about the work of the student wing. One of them was a past student in this school. Nowadays if students are behaving badly and making a disturbance or not attending, it is difficult to control them because they might take revenge by joining the Maoists and returning to the school and giving us trouble. One boy passed class six but did not progress to class seven. Some time later, we saw him and asked him what he was doing. He replied, "Sir, I am with the Maoists now and have studied more than you have." They are not presently asking students directly to join them but they put them under indirect pressure to join.

Sometimes it is impossible to hold classes as the insurgents requisition the school building for cultural programmes. This puts the children and teachers at great risk should the security forces arrive.[34]

---

[31]This conversation took place towards the end of 2004. By spring 2005 he had left his post and the area.

[32]During a *bandh*, commercial and other services must shut down for a specified period. *Bandhs* are enforced by the threat of violence.

[33]Despite the comments of the Kwei Nasa headmaster stating that they are supported by the District Education Office, this is often not the case.

[34]Despite repeated calls by NGOs, INGOs, donors, and humanitarian organizations to respect schools as zones of peace, both sides requisition educational facilities. Maoist events are commonly held in schools (for a discussion of Maoist use of schools in Dolakha district, see Shneiderman and Turin 2004). Schools are usually the only large complexes (containing buildings and a flat courtyard/playground) in a village and are often strategically positioned on

The outside walls of the school and the nearby day-care centre are covered with Maoist slogans, and in the school grounds three out-of-district labourers were badly beaten by Maoist party workers who wrongly accused them of being thieves. As in other parts of rural Nepal, the children draw helicopters, guns and socket bombs and talk about the difference between the equipment of the security forces and those of the Maoists. They know who the local Maoist commander is and how he escaped capture by the security forces by dressing as a woman.

Children who attend the high school feel particularly vulnerable as they walk to and from school partly through a forest. An eighteen-year-old girl commented:

> Sometimes I am frightened to wear my school uniform as when the Maoists see it they know I am a student. They tried to get me to join their student wing but I did not join. I am so frightened that they will take me. Sometimes when we reach school there is no class and we have to go to meetings. We can't study and as I am doing my SLC (School Leaving Certificate) this year I am worried.

Another girl of the same age, who has a long history of activism, stated that prior to the escalation of the conflict she was the chairperson of the Maoist student wing. She participated in many programmes in the school and at one stage wrote a letter to the school administration requesting additional resources, which they provided. Her family members became angry, upset and frightened about her involvement, which made her fearful, and she resigned. Although no longer involved in the movement she is frightened of both parties to the conflict and feels vulnerable to the threats and intimidation of both.

One April morning, during the ceasefire of 2003, I accompanied a group of children to collect berries and edible ferns. As we searched along the banks of a dry stream bed I asked them what they thought of the Maoists. Raju and his friend Krishna were silent and Krishna looked uncomfortable. I repeated the question before Raju replied quietly, "We don't like them," and when asked why, he replied, in a whisper, "Because they have guns and they kill people", but then quickly added the comment widely cited by adults and children alike that "Maoists don't hurt villag-

---

top of ridges. Holding meetings or cultural (dance and drama) programmes at schools is potentially a good source of recruitment as well as providing a medium through which Maoist educational ideology can be promoted. Because of this, schools are prone to becoming battlefields. In a particularly disturbing incident in Doti district, four students were killed and five injured by the security forces during a clash with the insurgents, which occurred during a Maoist cultural programme (Amnesty International 2005; Basnet 2004; Watchlist 2005). For additional material on education in the conflict, the National Coalition for Children as Zones of Peace (CZOP) and the responses of NGOs and INGOs, etc., see cwin.org.np and savethechildren.org/countries/asia/nepal.asp.

ers."[35] Several other eight- to ten-year-olds questioned separately gave the same reply and some answered only in monosyllables. I asked a Dalit girl who initially stated: "I'm not frightened of them," but then said, "Yes, I am frightened because they have guns." A slightly older girl stated: "We shouldn't be frightened of them. If they know we are frightened they can give us more trouble." I asked the children if the Maoists talked to them and the Dalit children said, "No, they just talk to the big people," but the Tamu children said "Yes", and explained that they had been asked questions like, "Are there guns in your house?" The children always replied that there were none, which in most cases was true as family guns (for hunting) were hidden or had already been requisitioned by the insurgents.

Aside from the ubiquitous Maoist slogans, Kwei Nasa appears much as before the escalation of the conflict and in many ways it *is* much as before.[36] Each day villagers get up, work in the fields, eat, go to school, visit each other's homes, play on the paths, plan weddings and funerals, visit the health post, and walk to town. In public places, conversations are about everyday matters: people meet and discuss who has married, who has gone overseas for work, who has died, arrangements are made to work together and the cost of the expansion to the day-care centre is discussed. The women chatting and washing the mud off their legs at the village tap after a day of work in the fields pay no outward attention to the armed insurgents sitting listening to the radio just yards away. The small group of children playing at the bottom of the steps outside the shop ignore the young Maoist who requests supplies from the shopkeeper.[37] The villagers seem to be used to living with the insurgents.

Yet this apparent normality is also a façade. There is another side of Kwei Nasa where fear is communicated and people struggle to use what strategies they can to cope with their changed environment. Inside homes, adults talk together in hushed tones and children seated beside the fire listen in silence. Children of Raju's age are fully aware of the concept of *norbe ta* ('inner' or secret talk).[38] In the past, such discussion mainly

---

[35]This was both a denial and an acknowledgement of reality. By early 2003, Maoists had beaten visiting labourers in the village but had not physically harmed villagers.

[36]Although the slogans were originally painted by the Maoists, in a couple of places they have been crossed out by the security forces and derogatory terms referring to the soldiers replaced with derogatory terms referring to the insurgents.

[37]Maoists usually pay for items they buy at village shops, but sometimes they do not. For example, they sometimes demand 'donations' of rice from villagers and this includes shop-owners. It is not always clear why items are sometimes paid for and at other times not. Neither is it clear if demanding 'donations' of foodstuffs at particular times is party policy or individual whim, as some cadres occasionally act outside the official party line.

[38]*Norbe ta*, which translates literally as 'inner talk', is a Tamu Kyui term and is always conducted in that language. It refers to things that are to be kept in one's 'heartmind' (see below).

concerned private family matters. Nowadays this expanded concept includes friends, neighbours and other villagers – people who need to know about the movement of either side in order to keep safe. Seated around the fire, adults discuss which part of the village the Maoists are in and wonder about future visits to their hamlet. They question why certain parts of the village are frequently targeted and others not – which is likely to do with geographical proximity to potential escape routes. Throughout my visits this 'tracking' of the Maoists continued, with villagers quietly passing information to family, friends, and neighbours about the presence and movements or anticipated movements of the insurgents. Information is passed verbally using code words; for example, the Maoists are usually referred to using certain indirect terms.[39] What is important is that the term used is polite should the insurgents discover what it is. In public places information is passed via surreptitious glances, raises of the eyebrows, minute movements of the eyes, inclinations of the head or by referring to the movements of 'animals' on the paths or in the jungle.[40]

Children who play on the village paths tell their elders about the movement of strangers in and around the village.[41] This is an extension of the usual role of informing families and neighbours about the imminent arrival of guests. In the past, such information allowed a household to be prepared for a visitor; nowadays it is important to be forewarned of the arrival of the insurgents, to have time to take small measures to protect themselves and their families.[42] Children frequently volunteer unsolicited information about whom they have seen around the village. One day a neighbour laughingly told me that a group of village children seated at a resting place had stopped a young Tamu and told him that the Maoists had just walked past and were going in the same direction as he was, to which he replied that he and his friends were the Maoists.

The communal emphasis on sharing information and helping keep each other safe can be contrasted to the increase in levels of suspicion and mistrust. It is widely believed that the Maoists have an excellent local

---

[39]The strategies used are similar to those used by the NGO workers Adhikari (2003: 369-83) encountered in rural east Nepal. I have chosen not to list the approaches used in Kwei Nasa as they could be open to abuse by the Maoists or the security forces if they learned them.

[40]I have described elsewhere how villagers furtively advised me to take or avoid certain paths and parts of the village (Pettigrew 2004).

[41]From the stories that I have collected in other villages in the area and in different districts, it is clear that the army uses children to provide information about the movement of people in and out of villages, sometimes with tragic consequences. A villager visiting relatives in another part of the country was in a village when soldiers gave sweets to children who told them which house Maoists were sleeping in. The soldiers killed the Maoists and shortly afterwards the Maoists' colleagues wrote to the children's parents threatening to kill them. The family left for India the same day.

[42]For example, during times when there are restrictions on the making and/or selling of alcohol, this might involve hiding liquor or stopping the production process.

intelligence network. When I asked people how the Maoists acquired information, they replied, "Their spies are everywhere." Recently a frightened Dhan Kumari told me that two unknown children of Raju's age were in the village that day and admitted to local children that they were spying for the Maoists. When questioned further people acknowledged, albeit reluctantly, that some of the Maoists' information is provided by villagers. Dhan Kumari commented, "Other people tell them but this is secret."

The ethos of cooperation, communication, and helping keep each other safe coexists with the view of others as untrustworthy. This is not new, however, but is a pattern that pre-existed the 'People's War' (Pettigrew 2003). In the face of hardship, Tamu-mai stick together.[43] When confronted with difficult or painful situations they rely on each other for assistance and support. The other side of this enveloping and supportive ideology is that people make constant demands upon one another for various forms of assistance that cannot always be met. As McHugh (1989: 78) explains, it is rude to refuse and so people make excuses saying that they have prior commitments or that there is no more of a requested item. Outward harmony is maintained and resources protected, but at a deeper level, this behaviour – which everyone participates in – creates a widespread sense of mistrust. In the present situation the old polarities remain but the stakes are higher and mistrust deeper. Suspicion of potentially vengeful relatives, friends, or neighbours who might take advantage of the situation to denounce you to either side are added to by a heightened mistrust of strangers. This includes a range of potentially terrifying people, of any age and gender, including the insurgents and their spies as well as violent criminals who masquerade as Maoists.[44] While cultural constructions of Tamu youth have been strongly challenged in recent years (see Pettigrew 2003), the arrival (or perceived arrival) of child spies presents new challenges to understandings of childhood.[45] This is deeply unsettling to Dhan Kumari as it contradicts her desire to believe that Raju, now aged ten, is too young to be taken and reinforces her opinion that children of Raju's age are susceptible to indoctrination.

Trying to Keep Children Safe

Villagers questioned about how they keep their children safe provided very similar answers. A forty-six-year-old Dalit woman stated that she says to her children: "Don't tell anyone they [the Maoists] visit. They might kill

[43] As Macfarlane (2001), supported by McHugh (2001), notes, this ethos remains central even in urban centres.

[44] Several villagers have had very frightening encounters with thieves masquerading as Maoists.

[45] It is not within the scope of this chapter to address Tamu constructions of childhood and their interrelationship to the conflict. This must await further treatment.

you. Don't make a noise." A sixty-two-year-old Tamu woman stated, "I tell them not to go near them, do not follow them, and do not talk to them". A twenty-eight-year-old Tamu woman replied that she tells her children, "Not to speak about their visits". People tell their children not to talk to either side and if they have to, they must do so "politely". They must not reveal details of what goes on inside their homes such as preparing food for Maoists or what property they have. Caregivers try, often in vain, to keep their children at home and/or away from the places where they might encounter either side.[46] They also tell their children not to take sweets offered and many warn of the dangers of touching "unknown objects" that might explode. They acknowledge, however, that because it is very difficult to keep children safe they are extra vigilant. Small bits of information considered inconsequential in the past, such as the age and possible identity of strangers, are carefully noted in case they provide information about the movements or behaviour of either side.

Worries about security concern children as well as adults. In January 2004 Raju said to Dhan Kumari that he thought my research assistant, Ramesh, and I should not visit Kwei Nasa as the day after the news of our forthcoming trip was received a large group of the PLA arrived. His reaction was related to events of a year previously when hundreds of Maoists were in the village and he was told by Dhan Kumari to "guard" me should they come to the house. While he could not prevent their arrival, which occurred shortly after these instructions, clearly he felt partly responsible for my safety as over the course of the following hour, during which I remained hidden inside the house, he surreptitiously checked on me several times while supposedly playing with a toy car. The previous afternoon he overheard Dhan Kumari express her fears that the Maoists might think that we were spies and instructed us to remain inside the house, which she locked from the outside in the hope that this would deter them. When questioned, Raju refused to explain why he thought we should not visit. Dhan Kumari commented that he knew that both she and I were frightened the previous year and he was trying to protect us. Assal and

[46] Some strategies used by caregivers to protect children from the impact of the conflict raise child rights concerns. In a report on children in the conflict, Amnesty International stated "Children are often taken out of school for fear of recruitment and some are sent away to other districts, often unaccompanied. In addition, there have been reports of girls being married very young as parents fear that if their daughter is taken away by the CPN (Maoist) for some time she will no longer be marriageable" (2005). In 2002 I interviewed several rural women in an urban centre in the mid-west whose early marriages were arranged to ensure that they would not be recruited. Although caregivers in Kwei Nasa have similar fears for their female children, I have not encountered these practices. This may be because the threat of recruitment, while ever-present, is less extreme in this area. Furthermore, as large numbers of villagers live in the nearby urban centre those who send their children out of Kwei Nasa have family members with whom they can live.

Farrel (1992: 280) state that under conditions of war children are often frightened, not of losing their lives but of losing their families. This fear may express itself in selflessness which is partly due to the degree to which children's self-identity is bound to their immediate family. Secure surroundings create opportunities to learn a range of different roles, emotional idioms, and complex problem-solving skills. According to Barenbaum, Ruchkin and Schwab-Stone, conflict situations "... create an atmosphere where complex moral dilemmas are simplified and things split into good and bad which leads children to identify more closely with important others" (2004: 46). The growing ability to identify with others means that questions of responsibility and feelings of guilt are important to school-age children living in conflict zones (de Jong 2003). Some children may harbour plans for revenge or worry that they might have been able to prevent a traumatic event from occurring (Eth and Pynoos 1985). Children of this age may fear for the well-being of others, especially their siblings and parents (Pynoos and Nader 1988).

Teaching Children What to Say

Villagers are extra careful about what they say and to whom they say it. Silence is an important coping strategy and widely used by both sides. One evening, in the summer of 2002, when Raju was seven, his mother and I prepared vegetables for the evening meal and talked in vague terms about the recent arrival of two groups of Maoists in the village. Suddenly Raju asked in a rather loud voice, "Are you talking about the Maoists?" With barely a break in her conversation, his mother turned to him and said, "Do not talk about these things" and slapped him hard on his leg. Tearful, he retreated into the corner. When I later questioned Dil Maya about her actions, she explained that Raju had not yet learnt to be silent. "He must learn not to speak about certain things. It is hard for him but he must learn, as it could be a matter of life or death. Nowadays you cannot be sure with whom you are talking and so you must know when to be silent."[47] Three years later Raju is fully aware of the realities of village life in the 'People's War'. One evening Dhan Kumari, talking about the Maoists, said, "They ask children where their fathers are and if they have gold, guns and other things in their houses. Nowadays you have to teach the children what to say." I asked Raju, who was sitting beside her playing with a toy car, "Have the Maoists asked you what you have in your house?" "Yes, they have" he replied. "I always say we don't have any of those things." He then recited the answers he gives in which he denies the existence of guns and gold and downplays the number of possessions owned by his relatively well-off family. Recently he boasted that he "... knows what answer to give to any

[47]Not only had Raju spoken loudly but he had used the insurgents' names.

questions they ask," and he is proud that, unlike his elder brother, who only visits the village occasionally, he is viewed as *raba* ('street-wise', competent).

Raju is vigilant and his conversations in public places are particularly guarded. It is, however, harder to censor the conversations of younger children. One afternoon, walking through the village I met five-year-olds Nil Kumari and Man Maya on their way home from school. As we walked Man Maya started talking in a loud voice, "Mother, do you know that two Maoist girls came to our house when it was raining? They have gone now but they left their bags in our house. They said that they will be back in the evening with lots more people."[48] Not wanting to draw attention to what she said, I replied in a quiet voice that I knew what had happened and changed the subject. As she walked along holding my hand, I wondered if anyone else had overheard what the little girl had said. She had spoken very near a shop that is frequented by Maoists, and allegedly by army spies on occasion. Later I discussed this with Asha, her mother, who commented, "Man Maya is very frank and I can't stop her talking openly. It is dangerous but what can I do? She is still too small to understand." That evening Dil Maya backed up Asha's comments stating that "Five is too young to understand." She continued:

> By the age of seven or eight children can understand what to say and what not to say. Raju is nine and he understands very well, younger children are especially in danger as they can easily be tempted with sweets and then they will say things they shouldn't.

I asked another villager, Hom Bahadur, how he and his family kept their two small children under the age of five safe. He replied, "When they are about seven or eight they can understand and so it is easier to talk to them about what to do or not do and what to say or not as they understand the dangers. Before that age we frighten them of both sides as we hope they will stay away from them and not speak in their presence." Teaching children to be silent is not new, as children have always been taught about 'inner talk' – things that are secret and not to be discussed outside the immediate family or a close circle of confidantes. Children have also always been taught to be frightened of categories of beings such as witches, ghosts, and malevolent spirits. What is different now is the overwhelming emphasis on silence and fear as the primary defences against violence.

Faced with insecurity and competing ideologies, parental control is undermined and adults feel unable to protect their children. Some village children are educated in boarding schools in the town and while this is not

---

[48] Man Maya calls me "mother" as I am the same generation as her birth mother.

new, the numbers have increased since the escalation of the conflict.[49] Sometimes this is in response to general concerns about security while at other times it is in response to specific events. When the security forces visited the home of a middle-aged couple, their two teenage daughters were alone, questioned at length, and verbally harassed. On return, their parents sent their daughters immediately to town as they worried that they would become the brunt of dangerous unwanted attention.[50] However, not everyone has the means to protect their children in this way. Many people interviewed, particularly those from less well-off backgrounds, are unable to relocate and must continue to protect their children in the village as well as they can.

Fear of Recruitment

Although there are Maoist activists in the area, particularly in some of the surrounding hamlets where there are families with long histories of Maoist involvement, the overwhelming majority of people in the village do not support the movement. When I asked villagers, they were adamant: "We are not Maoists and we do not support them. They have made life very dangerous and difficult for us. No one in this village has joined them." It is, however, difficult to judge who has left the village for employment and who has left on the pretext of seeking employment and instead joined the Maoists or was recruited forcibly. Despite their assurances, villagers would not necessarily know who has joined, as Maoists are usually posted to locations outside their home area. In addition, villagers have good reason to conceal any connection their families may have with the guerrillas. If people from Kwei Nasa have joined, however, they have done so in secret and in very small numbers.

Maoists use various ploys to abduct children or to encourage them to join the movement. In a neighbouring village, they arrived during the festival of Tihar and invited teenagers to join them in festive singing and dancing.[51] A village woman explained, "We wouldn't allow them out of our houses as we thought it was a trick to get them to join the Maoists. We kept

---

[49]The majority of children and teenagers remain in the village. However, the ethnic profile of children in the school is changing. In September 2005 teachers pointed out that because so many families are sending their children out of the village, there are fewer Tamu children in the lower grades than prior to the escalation of the conflict.

[50]The security forces frequently harass young women. Amnesty International has documented an increasing number of cases of violence against women and girls including those of women shot dead allegedly following rape (2005). I encountered two such cases when visiting an adjoining district.

[51]Maoist cultural programmes include dancing which is appealing to many young people and therefore a good medium for recruitment. Villagers who have seen them considered the performances more impressive than the performances of local youth groups.

them in for three days, only the very small children went out." Chuckling, she added, "It was amusing seeing the Maoists and the tiny children dancing together but what could we do?"

All caregivers interviewed fear the recruitment of their children and strongly urge them not to join.[52] A thirty-one-year-old Tamu man tells his son, "Do not look at their activities, stay inside the house reading and play close by." A fifty-five-year-old Dalit woman replied, "I tell them to be quiet, as they can take you away." A thirty-five-year-old Tamu woman says to her children, "Do not go with them even if they try to persuade you." One of the ways adults deter their children from involvement is to watch them while the insurgents are in the village. When Maoists stayed in Dhan Kumari's house one of them lifted Raju up and threw him in the air. She commented:

> I was furious and immediately told him to stop. I don't like them getting too close to him and I don't want him to get too close to them. He understands well and knows not to go with them. He is frightened of them but as he is only a child, they might convince him. What if they took him? How would we live then?

Ideas about the vulnerability of children and their susceptibility to Maoist propaganda are expressed in ideas about the *sai* (heartmind) that governs emotions, volition and cognition and morality.[53] People talk of having a "full (happy) *sai*" (*sai toba*), a "small (unhappy, sad) *sai*" (*sai chyoba*), a "crying (unhappy, sad) *sai*" (*sai kroi*), a "full (satisfied) *sai*" (*sai mrei*). The *sai* is also the place of memory, thought, and competency. Capable persons are those who "within their *sai* are knowledgeable or capable" (*sai nor raba*). A child's *sai* (*kolmai sai*) is underdeveloped. Children do not know right from wrong as clearly as adults do. Capability may develop earlier than morality, however, and while Raju is *raba* when talking to Maoists about his family's possessions, he remains morally underdeveloped and vulnerable. Furthermore, his souls – which can easily fly out when he is shocked or distressed – are less integrated into his body than those of an

---

[52]For a recent report on child and community-led strategies to avoid children's recruitment in armed forces and groups in West Africa, see Save the Children (2005). The strategies cited overlap with some of those discussed here and include identifying and moving to safe places, avoiding separation from caregivers, changing children's attitudes to stop children wanting to join the fighters, providing schooling and skills training.

[53]McHugh likens the *sai* to the Western idea of personality when she writes: "The *sae* [*sai*] is believed to have fixed boundaries, which are given for each individual, in much the same way as are other personal attributes such as intelligence, beauty, height and so on. An individual's *sae* can be bigger or smaller, its size determined by one's life experiences. A description of the size of an individual's *sae* resembles our colloquial description of an individual's personality. Where the notion of the *sae* differs most from our ideas about personality is the connections that are drawn between internal states and external events ..." (1989: 78). The Nepali language equivalent of the *sai* is *man*.

adult are.[54] All round he is a more fragile being – vulnerable to fear, emotions, illness, being influenced by others and therefore susceptible to Maoist recruitment.

Distress is considered unsettling and the emphasis on communal solidarity means that there are powerful restraints against the expression of difficult emotions. The situation is similar to Robert Desjarlais's account of the social constraints on the communication of distress among the Yolma Wa of Helambu, where he states that villagers

> ... value the ability to "hold" one's heartmind – to "hide" one's thoughts within the body and not let on, when faced with grief, pain or anger, that one is hurting. ... Yolma Wa evince a "rhetoric" of silence, holding that they must hide their sorrows. ... Just as ... [they] disapprove of the social expression of personal turmoil, so they learn to shun it privately. A villager realizes ... that it is an entirely sensible strategy to avoid emotional distress and so keep the heartmind "clear". (1994 [1992]: 142)

The desire to control emotional expression means that people strive to hide their fear, which must be evaluated in the light of this cultural emphasis. That people admit to high levels of fear illustrates the extreme degree to which they are frightened. The 'silencing of fear' coexists with the 'silencing of dangerous talk' and so silence becomes one of the primary interactional patterns. Jagannath Adhikari, in his work in eastern Nepal, encountered this when he was greeted with silence while asking potentially sensitive questions and when making mundane comments (2003: 371).

Caregivers try to restrict their children's movements and encourage the development of competencies and morality through teaching and inducing fear, but with undeveloped *sai* there are limitations. Their task as caregivers is complicated by increasing numbers of people relocating to the towns, few visits being made by on-leave soldiers or town-dwelling relatives, and the cancellation or scaling back of many community activities. There are limited events to counteract the excitement and attraction of the Maoists. Caregivers are, however, largely successful, as few or any young people from the village have joined the Maoist movement, but determent requires ongoing vigilance.

---

[54]Bodies have multiple souls (*plah*). Men have nine and women seven. The fragility of people is expressed by the fragility of the *plah* and, as McHugh observes, "Beliefs about the *plah* convey a sense of the fragility of the person. *Plah* can easily fly out of the body and if all the *plah* are lost, the body's elements are no longer held together by the life force and the person will die. If some *plah* are lost, illness results" (1989: 79). Children are especially vulnerable to losing souls as they are easily frightened and their *plah* are less used to their bodily 'home', and prone to wandering. This concept is similar to the Nepali language concept of *sato jancha* (soul loss), which "is seen as occurring primarily in children ... [and] results from children being frightened by a frightening event they witness or by a spiritual event such as a *boksi* [witch] or *bhut* [ghost], etc." (Kohrt n.d.).

Caregivers actively discourage voluntary recruitment but forcible recruitment is harder to prevent.[55] Village parents meet young insurgents who have voluntarily enlisted but they also encounter those who have been forcibly recruited. Kwei Nasa adults are particularly distressed by the latter and thinking of these youths' caregivers, they think of themselves.[56] Purna Maya, who recently relocated to the town as she was frightened that her two teenage boys would be recruited, talked in mid 2004 about meeting Tamu female cadres:

> I can't advise them as I would usually advise young women. They are my daughters but they are on the wrong road and I cannot say anything.[57] I can only ask them where they come from but they do not reply fully. Instead, they just say "I am from a faraway village." I know from their accent which district they are from but nothing else. They speak to me in Tamu Kyui and I think about their parents, do they know or not? How they must worry for them. I feel this in my *sai*, my *sai* cries for them, those parents. Their children are the age of my children, how frightened they must be. We are moving to the town but my husband and I are only going because of our boys. They can be taken at any time and I am terrified for them. What would happen to them? They might be sent to a remote district far from here. They might suffer a lot, they might be killed, and they might have to kill people. I tell them to stay at home and not walk around the village too much. If they go out in the evening, I worry until they are back home. When large groups of Maoists come, I am terrified. They could be taken at any time and there would be nothing that we could do. On the outside we look normal, but on the inside we are shaking.

An older woman in another village talked about the aftermath of an ambush of the Maoists by the security forces and her thoughts about the parents of a dead insurgent:

> After the firing ended, other villagers and I came out of our houses. On the street in front of my house, I saw the body of a 13-year-old

[55]Stories about forcible recruitment are widely known. Last year a young Maoist who was forcibly recruited escaped in the area, and was hidden by an old man in his house for sixteen days. He finally made his way to town where he surrendered to the security forces who interviewed him for a day before returning him to his family in a far-off district.

[56]Some will have joined voluntarily, but once in the movement should they change their minds they will encounter difficulties leaving (as well as encountering problems returning home due to stigma). The distinction between 'volunteering' and 'being coerced into joining' may be very small as vulnerable youths may be pressurized into participating.

[57]In Tamu kinship terms all females of her daughter's generation are considered to be her daughters. The relationship is closer or more distant depending on the relationship between their clans.

boy who was part of the dance troupe; his guts spilled out on the road. I knew him well and fed him many times. I felt very upset when I saw him. When we feed a dog, it is grateful and wags its tail and he was like that. He was a Tamu from a far off village and a member of a clan closely connected to mine. He would not tell me where he was from, sometimes he said one village and at other times he said another. I felt very upset about his death as I thought about his parents and how young he was and wondered when they would find out that he was dead.

Fear and Fascination

During a visit to Kwei Nasa at the end of 2002, a group of insurgents appeared in Dhan Kumari's house. While entry was politely 'requested', it was obvious she was obliged to host the rebels, and although not required to feed them, she had to provide tea and accommodation. Dhan Kumari fears these situations partly because they bring Raju within the Maoist sphere of influence. While she stopped a cadre playing with him she could not prevent more subtle influences which play a role in attracting young people to the insurgents. Raju spent most of the day in the courtyard along with Man Maya, a little girl from next door. They watched the Maoists wash clothes, transcribe revolutionary songs into notebooks, kill and cook three goats, repair equipment, and dismantle, repair and clean guns. In the early afternoon, I noticed Raju and Man Maya watching intently as a teenage female cadre tried repeatedly to remove a cleaning cork that was stuck in the barrel of her weapon. Once it was freed, they stood beside her as she carefully took the gun apart and cleaned it piece by piece. She invited them to examine the weapon and with fascination both children peered down the barrel of the newly cleared rifle. By mid morning, Raju's earlier hesitancy had gone and he was clearly enjoying himself observing the activities of young people who in some cases were only six or seven years older than he.[58] It is not difficult to see why visits by Maoists provide fertile ground for recruitment as they create an air of excitement and activity, which is attractive to many young people. Since the discontinuation of development work in the village three years ago, the only people who have attempted to mobilize the youth are the Maoists.[59] To children (and indeed to many adults) large-scale visits by Maoists appear to evoke both fear *and* fascination. They interrupt the mundanity of daily life and with the courtyards full of people and numerous side-events taking place

[58]With one exception the members of the group billeted in the house were teenagers.

[59]All development work was carried out by an NGO. As this organization has royal connections, it is particularly unpopular with the insurgents and, in late 2002, its premises were ransacked and the staff forced to leave the village.

they are spectacles somewhat reminiscent of major community-wide events. Raju repeats the dominant narrative that he is frightened of the insurgents – and undoubtedly he is – but this is a partial picture. A more accurate representation of the emotions that Maoists arouse needs to acknowledge conflicting feelings such as fascination (albeit fleeting) *and* fear, which the Maoists draw upon in their attempt to attract recruits.

Restricted Movements and Clothing

The conflict has changed the movement of locals in the village and the surrounding countryside.[60] People fear being caught in the crossfire or mistaken for insurgents in the forest. By choice, villagers prefer to go into the jungle in groups, as it is a potentially dangerous place. While past fears related mainly to concerns about malevolent supernatural beings, present-day fears also relate to who else is in the forest.[61] The local landmarks, which act as mnemonic cues for people to remember the stories of people and events of the past, are added to in new and disturbing ways as the narratives of places where people died or other insurgent-related events occurred, and become imprinted into perceptions and memories of the landscape: for example, the place where a Maoist commander died; the path where a man from a neighbouring village was killed by the security forces; the bend on the road where the Maoists attacked an ex-serviceman; the place where the Maoists made a temporary medical post.[62]

When small numbers of Maoists are in the village, or neither side is present, children of Raju's age play freely. They venture less deeply into the forest, however, when they are at risk of meeting the opponents and are vulnerable to abduction or arrest or being trapped in the crossfire. Dhan Kumari has told Raju not to pick up strange packages or bags, but commented that this is difficult "as children are curious and like to look and pick things up". The death or injury of children by improvised exploded devices (IEDs) is common throughout the country. Last year Maoists laid mines to ambush the security forces on a road to the village. When the army did not arrive they removed them, during the process of which a cadre died when one of the ordinances exploded. The irresponsible use of explosive devices is a deep concern among the villagers. The day the two

---

[60] See Pettigrew (2004) and Adhikari (2003) for further discussion concerning the perceived risk related to wearing certain items of clothing.

[61] It is important, however, not to over privilege conflict-related fears at the expense of others. While they are there, people perceive and evaluate them differently. While walking through a forest after dark recently, en route to a neighbouring village, some of the group were more worried about wild animals than armed combatants, while for others it was the reverse.

[62] Space is an important concept in shaping local culture in an area like Kwei Nasa. I have written about this elsewhere (Pettigrew 1999).

female Maoists left their bags in Man Maya's house was, according to her father,

> the worst day of my life, I was terrified all day. I wanted to move the bags but I couldn't as I was sure they contained bombs. We left them where they had placed them but we were terrified that the army would arrive and find them and then we would die. I have never been happy to see the Maoists, but that day I was delighted when they returned to collect their bags.

Caregivers tell their children not to go to places like road heads, tea shops, or houses in certain hamlets where they might encounter Maoists. Practically, however, it is impossible for children to avoid most of these places. Dambar visits Kwei Nasa during his school holidays, and one day as he prepared to leave for the town I asked his mother if it was safe for him to travel. Dil Maya explained that the town-based teenagers returning to school travelled together in a large group, but even so, they were at risk in the forests. As the motorable road, which cuts several hours off the journey, had been re-opened after partial destruction during the monsoon, they were to travel some of the way by bus to avoid the most densely forested parts of the road. Despite the precautions, however, Dil Maya is never sure if it is safe for Dambar to visit and makes ongoing evaluations about whether or not he should come. During one of my stays last year, he did not visit as she thought it unsafe for him to do so. This spring, however, he accompanied a group of village youths into the uplands as the Maoists, including the commander, were out of the area. Dambar, now a town boy, is considered less safe than village-based Raju. One day I noticed him wearing combat trousers but when Ramesh and I told him not to wear them, he replied:[63]

> They are my father's. When he was on leave [from his job in the Gulf], he wore them and the Maoists stayed in our house. They thought that he was a Gurkha soldier and so he took them off as otherwise they would think that we were rich and ask for lots of money. The Maoists will know that I am too young to be a Gurkha so there's no problem.

Ramesh and I replied that he was not so much in danger from the Maoists as the security forces who might think that he was a Maoist. He replied that

---

[63]Combat dress is extremely popular in Tamu villages. This is partly because of the availability of cast-off British and Indian army clothing (and commercially available replicas) which is considered both high status and durable. In 2002, the government told the population not to wear combat dress as it put them at risk of being suspected of being Maoists. Because of this it is not as widely worn as previously. It remains popular, however, but in the case of a teenager it is particularly risky to wear. I know of one case where an on-leave soldier serving in the Indian Army, dressed in combat dress, was killed by the security forces who believed him to be a Maoist.

he did not have another pair of trousers. When we told Dhan Kumari she also told him to change his clothes and commented, "He doesn't live here and he doesn't understand the dangers so well." Shortly afterwards he found a change of clothing.

A 'Little Man'

James Quesada (1998) notes that Nicaraguan children living in adverse conditions are commonly regarded as adults and cites the case of a ten-year-old boy who was seen and treated as an adult male. Although Raju has a father and a brother, his *de facto* family consists of his mothers. Dhan Kumari and Dil Maya refer to him as the "man of the house" and symbolically bestow this role on him when they tell him to be a "sentry", "guard" me, or do a reconnaissance to the shop. This role was further internalized by him when he took responsibility for advising Dhan Kumari to cancel our visit.

Raju monitors and advises Dhan Kumari during her, at times, volatile interactions with Maoists.[64] Some months ago, two Maoists arrived one evening and asked her to cook for them. She said that she could give them rice and lentils but she could not prepare food as she "was too tired and too old" and so they should get it cooked elsewhere. After she said this one of them pointed his finger at her and spoke rudely and threateningly under his breath. She heard what he said and replied, "Why are you pointing your finger at me? If you are brave enough, shoot me, kill me now!" The other young man pulled his colleague away and said, "Mother, he is new, he doesn't know how to behave." They took the food and hastily left. Afterwards Raju told a still furious Dhan Kumari not to talk to them like that as "it was dangerous."

There is a partial reversal of caring roles in the house. Dhan Kumari has chronic back pain and over the last twelve months developed heart pain and breathing problems. Doctors in town diagnosed her complaints as anxiety but despite medication, it is worsening. Dil Maya and Raju give Dhan Kumari her tablets and provide necessary support when she is unwell, which is now almost a daily occurrence. Raju spends most of the time in Dhan Kumari's house and so it usually falls to him to assist her. Recently I watched him open packets of medication and bring her drinks. He provides more than practical support, however, as some months ago I overheard Dhan Kumari say to him, "You and I are living here in this dangerous time. Those with guns come and can do anything to us and no one would save us. Thieves also come and can kill us. Maybe one day we will be killed in our house. It is all up to our luck." In a shy but determined voice Raju whispered, "We will not be killed."

---

[64] For further discussion of the liberties that older women can take with Maoists, see Pettigrew (2004) and Adhikari (2003).

CONCLUSION: CHILDREN AND THE 'PEOPLE'S WAR'

A 'culture of terror' exists in Kwei Nasa, and fear, danger, insecurity, increased levels of suspicion, and the need to protect oneself and one's dependents are now predominant features of village life. Fear is unevenly experienced; at times it is overwhelming and at others it is minimal or absent. During the day, most villagers are apprehensive, but at night, the majority have moderate to very high levels of fear. In interviews with 85 people, only two stated that they were not frightened.[65] Out of 47 people asked to rate their fear level, 37 had a small amount of fear (1-2) during the day. At night, 25 were very frightened to terrified (4-5) and 17 were moderately frightened (2-3).[66] Formal assessments likely produce under-estimations, however, as the desire to 'smooth' the *sai* results in the down-playing of emotional distress. Individuals experience fear differently and some people are more fearful than others. These variations are linked to pre-existing personality, the impact of particular experiences and life situations, coping skills, and available resources including degree of support. Villagers are extra vigilant and make ongoing evaluations of danger and levels of security. To manage the situation people have developed a range of skills, most of which are adaptations and elaborations of pre-existing behaviours. People provide each other with information and support and communicate using coded messages, but at the same time, there is an increase in levels of suspicion and mistrust. Some people are unable to cope with the ongoing pressures and if they have sufficient resources they relocate to town. Others have no choice but to remain.

Providing food for Maoists has the greatest impact on household activities.[67] Requests for food interrupt daily activities and have economic costs, but most importantly, they place the household at risk.[68] The dangers

---

[65]In the first case a sixty-seven-year-old Dalit woman said that there was so much *dukha* in her life that she felt untouched by what was happening (her husband and other family members interviewed separately were, however, very fearful). The second woman, a forty-six-year-old Tamu, stated consistently that she was not frightened. I do not know this person well and so cannot corroborate this response with observational data.

[66]Levels of fear were evaluated on a scale of 0 to 5 using a *doko* (carrying basket) pictorial scale adapted from a scale used at the Center of Victims of Torture, Nepal in Kathmandu.

[67]Sixty out of eighty people interviewed stated that the greatest impact of the war on their household activities was the requirement to feed Maoists. The remaining answers included: disruption of schooling or fieldwork, threats by the security forces, having to provide firewood for either side, having to repair and make clothes for the insurgents (Damai [Tailor] women). Five people replied that there was no impact on their household activities. Four of these people were elderly women who do not have responsibility for running households. The fifth was a fifty-six-year-old householder Tamu woman for whom I do not have additional information.

[68]I asked several people to make rough estimates of how much rice they had provided for Maoists in the last two years. Each person stated that they had given approximately 20 kgs.

include the presence of weapons, and many villagers expressed surprise and horror that Maoists bring guns into kitchens. Villagers fear that weapons will go off in confined spaces and that family members will be injured and/or that the security forces will arrive and the interior of the house will be engulfed in fighting.[69] From a village perspective, guns should be outdoor objects relating mainly to hunting and army service. It is disrespectful and 'bad manners' to bring them into the most intimate social space where people relax and sit together as relative equals. When Maoists arrive in a household, all those who live in it come under scrutiny. Youths may be encouraged to join the insurgents and both Dhan Kumari and Raju fear this eventuality. Another villager described how frightened she was when "they held my child and teased me saying that they would take him". Younger children like Man Maya, below the age of seven or eight, may unwittingly reveal secrets while the Maoists are present.

Children in Kwei Nasa are growing up in the 'People's War'. They attend school, run errands for their parents, sing, dance, and play, but they do so in a radically altered context. To what extent does the description of the adult experience of the 'culture of terror' described above apply to children? Children like Raju are given responsibilities beyond their years and take other responsibilities upon themselves. They make careful judgements about when to speak, how much to say, and how to reply to interrogations about their family's material circumstances and daily activities. They are extra attentive, used to evaluating the level of danger and taking steps to diminish the potential impact of violence on their family members.[70] Growing up in a family devoid of adult males, Raju has become a 'little man' at age ten, a role that is both placed upon him and which he internalizes. Like adults, children experience fear unevenly and sometimes they are clearly more frightened than at other times. Their fears, however, are of a somewhat different nature than those of adults. As potential recruits to the Maoist movement, children and youths are targeted and so particularly experience the fear of compulsory recruitment and its consequences. While being interviewed several young women described this fear not only

---

They also provided additional unestimated foodstuffs including millet, maize, vegetables, lentils, tea, milk, sugar, and occasionally meat. For the less well-resourced, these demands are a particular burden. While the poorest people in the village are not asked to provide food or very infrequently, in all cases they reported that they had been required to make other contributions such as provide accommodation or firewood. For a general discussion of the economic costs of the insurgency, see Thapa with Sijapati (2003).

[69]This happened in a neighbouring village and resulted in the death of two villagers. The Maoists, who are trained to escape, did so.

[70]This view of children is similar to that put forward by Boyden in an article challenging assumptions about children's resilience during war. She argues that children should be seen as "... agents of their own development who, even during times of great adversity, consciously act upon and influence the environments in which they live" (2003).

in terms of being taken by force but also of the aftermath of becoming part of an army and being forced to fight and kill. Despite the normal abnormality of the village, much of Raju's life is mundane: he plays, undertakes chores, and goes to school.

The social and individual context of a child's life, along with factors such as age, personality, and previous life events, play a role in increasing or decreasing a child's risk of developing long-term conflict-related problems. Protective factors include such things as a supportive family environment, stable social relationships, and a social support system, economic well-being, the availability of school, recreational activities, and the presence of coping strategies. Continued attendance at school, for example, in conflict zones normalizes children's lives and the social role of student strengthens community cohesion (Dawes 2000; Kos and Derviskadic-Jovanovic 1998). Educational settings provide routines, clear expectations, rules, tasks, responsibilities, social interaction, and friendship. Achievement in school boosts self-esteem and coping skills (Kos and Derviskadic-Jovanovic 1998), and helps prevent isolation and withdrawal (Laor and Wolmer 2002).[71] While Raju and his peers attend school, frequent Maoist-called strikes disrupt learning and school-based activities and bring children into the insurgents' sphere of influence. Maoist programmes to further their educational ideals and to encourage potential recruits to the movement are commonplace. When Maoists punished a teacher, the assembled children witnessed the other teacher's inability to do anything but avert his eyes.[72] Frightened teachers are likely to have poor concentration and diminished energy for teaching, and as children take their cues from their adult caregivers, when they witness situations in which the vulnerability of their carers is exposed, they tend to become fearful and insecure themselves (Machel 2001).[73] Raju both acknowledges and denies his fear, and shows signs of behaviour which suggests that he is sometimes anxious and fearful. For those under the age of ten, the 'People's War' is all they have known. They are aware that they are growing up in an insecure

---

[71] A significant proportion of Nepali children, however, receive little or no education and so cannot take advantage of these supports. Most children in Kwei Nasa attend the lower secondary school. While continued attendance at school plays a protective role, the standard of education is often poor, classrooms are frequently overcrowded, and the surroundings often abysmal. I recently provided a small grant to the Kwei Nasa school as approximately a third of the students in grade one are from impoverished backgrounds and are without basic supplies such as school books, exercise books, pens, and uniforms.

[72] Raju was not at school that day. Other children who were required to watch were upset, confused, and frightened.

[73] A teacher quoted in the documentary film 'Schools in the Crossfire' (Basnet 2004) stated this very succinctly when he said, "We ourselves are living in fear. We are terrified. How can we impart knowledge in such a state? Students are also being killed, so they are also terrorized. How is it possible to learn anything in such a state of mind?"

and dangerous time, but they have nothing to compare it against, it is the totality of their lived experience. The situation has led to the development of competencies that are not only prized but, as discussed below, may have a protective role.

A 'culture of terror' institutes fear as a means of social control. Villagers feed Maoists and provide donations because they are frightened of the repercussions if they do not. When the Maoists are out of the village during ceasefires or, for example, earlier this year when the local cadre left for some weeks, their influence remains, and decisions such as building a clinic at the day-care centre, are made in the light of how the insurgents will evaluate them when they return. The security forces are feared deeply, but as they rarely visit their influence is minimal. Nonetheless, the possibility that they could appear at any moment remains, and being caught in the crossfire is a primary feature of the 'culture of terror'. Fear of the combatants parallels a fear of thieves who masquerade as Maoists and there is a widespread feeling of insecurity and potential or real lawlessness.

Suárez-Orozco notes that 'cultures of terror' have their "own vocabulary and grammar, cultural facts and artefacts" (1992: 240). In a previous publication, I suggested that the following words and phrases, which I translated into English from Tamu Kyui, should be included in the Nepali case: "frightened", "terrified", "forced to provide food", "forced to give money", "patrols", "helicopters", and "random firing" (Pettigrew 2004).[74] Recent research highlights the following additions: "fear of being killed", "threatened", "danger", "bombs", "abduction by the Maoists", "trembling", "heart beats fast", "difficulty breathing", "dizziness", "talk politely to both sides", "do what they say", "do not talk to either side or tell them anything", "do not go near them", "do not go with them", "stay at home". Most of the latter terms are told to children by their caregivers.

It is important, however, not to over privilege the 'culture of terror' concept. In multiple ways, on a daily basis, people interact with and make decisions against this background, whether it be something as small as noting that a number of Maoist party workers are in the village through to negotiating with the commander about the extension of the day-care centre, or hearing from a neighbour about the arrest of another neighbour by the security forces. However, this does not account for the sum of all experiences in the village. Not every decision is made with the conflict in mind, and there are events such as deaths, healing rituals or marriages, which are organized much as they were in a pre-conflict era. This overriding 'culture of terror' coexists with other 'cultures' such as the 'culture(s) of rituals' and

---

[74] I have deliberately chosen to present these terms in English as they remain current and some of them could be open to abuse by the Maoists or the security forces if they discovered them. For the same reasons I have omitted some terms as they refer to strategies that help keep people safe.

the 'culture(s) of work'. These 'cultures' may be affected by the 'culture of terror'; for example, a recent discussion by the Maoists regarding the potential prohibition of share cropping impinges on the 'culture of work', as do the Maoists' occasional pronouncements that death rituals should be conducted with less expenditure. There are, however, spheres of life which are unaffected, unevenly affected, or only occasionally affected. The 'culture of terror' model applies, but to present it as the umbrella within which *all* of daily life is lived is to overemphasize it.

Psychosocial Impacts

Children are a highly vulnerable group, and living in a conflict-affected area can have a lasting impact on cognitive, moral and psychological development as well as interpersonal relationships and coping abilities (Pynoos and Nader 1988; Sack et al. 1993). Children may display more war-affected symptoms than adults (Chimienti, Nasr and Khalifeh 1989).[75] Somasundaram and Jamunanantha (2003) writing about Sri Lanka suggest that common symptoms of conflict trauma in children include (in descending order): sleep disturbances, irritability, war vocabulary, decline in school performance, war games, hyper alertness, aggressiveness, clinging, anti-social behaviour, sadness, separation anxiety, and withdrawal. Children in Kwei Nasa have some of these symptoms as they play war games, know and use war vocabulary and are hyper-alert. It is possible that there are other indicators of the impact of conflict: for example, Dil Maya and Dhan Kumari worry about Raju's poor school performance, but without additional research, this information is inconclusive.[76] Behaviour such as playing war games, however, can often be a normal response (Mark Jordans, personal communication). These games may simply be a form of mimicry, they may provide an outlet for feelings such as distress or anger, may allow a child to create a place in his/her mind for a particular event, or they may merely reflect the type of games that children like to play. They become a possible cause for concern when, for example, they involve

[75]Some scholars suggest that considering the suffering caused by political violence in terms of trauma is an inappropriate medicalization of human distress (Bracken, Giller, and Summerfield 1995; Summerfield 1998). There is a detailed literature on the interplay between culture and trauma which focuses on issues such as how cultural factors influence the expression of trauma and the treatment of suffering, the appropriateness of western psychological models in non-western contexts, the limitations of an approach which focuses on psychopathology and neglects environmental and relational aspects of well-being and development, and the limitations of a universalistic development and child protection model. Aside from some brief comments below it is not within the scope of this chapter to address these issues in any detail (for further discussion see Boyden 2003; Boyden and de Berry 2004; Bracken and Petty 1998; Kleinman and Good 1985; Summerfield 1998; Tol et al. 2005).

[76]Poor school performance is noted in other parts of the country and in some districts School Leaving Certificate results have deteriorated (Basnet 2004).

hurting other children, when a child is unable to express or deal with her/his own anger or the anger of others, or when anger or revenge become part of a child's emotional development.[77] Evaluations of what is dysfunctional, however, should only be made taking accepted cultural norms and practices into account.

Not all children exposed to conflict develop psychological symptoms and conclusions about the impacts vary (Barenbaum, Ruchkin, and Schwab-Stone 2004).[78] Some contend that the effects are enduring (Stein et al. 1999), while others state that the majority of children exposed to war show no evidence of clinical disorder (Cairns and Dawes 1996) or they have symptoms that are fleeting or short-lived (Weine et al. 1995). Muldoon writing about Northern Ireland notes that just as children's experiences of conflict are highly variable so also is the impact on their adjustment. Furthermore, "... children's conflict experiences may be more likely to result in acting out or externalizing behaviours than in anxiety or depression, despite the latter reactions being more commonly expected" (Muldoon 2004: 465). Muldoon concludes that mental health represents only one aspect of the potential impacts of conflict on children as other social divisions and inequalities such as poverty and deprivation generally accompany political violence.

The overwhelming emphasis taken by many medical, psychiatric, and psychological researchers is on intrapsychic functioning. This perspective is premised on ideas about childhood which are based on universalistic child development and well-being models that pay inadequate attention to diverse cultural constructions and experiences of childhood. Not only are the social, cultural, and relational aspects of children's lives ignored but the impacts are generally viewed negatively. While children are perceived by many writers to be more vulnerable than adults because they are believed to have fewer survival strategies, anthropologists have pointed out that this is not necessarily so and the reverse may apply as there are usually fewer social prescriptions concerning children's tasks and roles. As Boyden (2003) notes, a smaller amount of attention is paid to children and they can more easily undertake tasks that adults cannot perform. Raju arouses less

---

[77] In a study of seventy Nepali boys aged six to nine, Kohrt et al. (2005) found that boys orphaned by the conflict and living in an institution had more severe aggression problems (recorded by the Behavioral Assessment Scale for Children-BASC) than boys of the same age at boarding schools. These children also displayed other symptoms which suggested that they may have been traumatized. For example, they had lower daily salivary cortisol levels than other boys, which may suggest childhood Post Traumatic Stress Disorder (PTSD).

[78] Estimates of the incidence of symptoms range from 22 per cent in Israeli children after scud missile attacks (Laor et al. 1997) to 48 per cent of Cambodian children exposed to shelling (Kinzie et al. 1986) to 70 per cent of Kuwaiti children following five months of military occupation (Nader et al. 1993) through to 93.8 per cent of displaced children during the Bosnian war (Goldstein et al. 1997).

suspicion than an adult when he sits on the courtyard wall playing with his catapult while surreptitiously doing 'sentry duty' for Dhan Kumari.

While it is important to consider the potential impact of living in a conflict zone, it is essential to position the present suffering in a wider context. Life in hill villages has always been difficult and frequently dangerous. During a visit to Kwei Nasa in 2003, I found that people were deeply affected by the death of six villagers from monsoon-related floods and landslides. In the fifteen years that I have conducted research, there have been many tragedies including accidents in the forest, falls from cliffs and steep paths, drowning, the death of women and infants during childbirth, the deaths and injuries of villagers working overseas. The effects of war or violence are not new either.[79] Several families I know have lost male kin serving in the Indian or British armies. High numbers of men from villages like Kwei Nasa lost their lives while serving in the First and Second World Wars. While these may be geographically and temporally distant, the losses of war and the affects of political violence are within living memory.[80] The suffering created by disadvantage and inequality is also ever-present and includes, depending on one's situation, caste, gender, class, and ethnic exclusion, poverty, poor infrastructure and governance, inadequate health care, and poor educational and/or employment opportunities. The impact of the latter means that Raju is growing up without a consistent father figure, as his father visits only every couple of years and his uncle no longer comes since he is a retired town-dwelling ex-Gurkha and a target for Maoist extortion. Although Raju sometimes stays with his uncle, his day-to-day social world, aside from school, is almost exclusively female. He looks forward to the visits of my research assistant as they provide an opportunity for him to identify with a man. On the day Ramesh leaves Raju disappears, as it is too painful for him to say goodbye. The lack of a consistent father figure has, I suggest, a greater impact on Raju's development than the insurgency.

Living in the 'People's War' does, however, mark a disjuncture, as community-wide political violence is differently evaluated to other sorrows. Dil Maya notes that Raju is a year older than the insurgency and his life tainted by growing up "in the war". This she contrasts to Dambar's upbringing, whose early years took place "in a time of peace". Raju with his underdeveloped *sai* is especially vulnerable to recruitment, landmines, crossfire, or apprehension as a Maoist. His *plah* (souls) are less integrated

---

[79]Domestic violence is also a feature of village life although I have no systematic data on it. Violent crime, although rare, is now perceived to be a real threat particularly from thieves masquerading as Maoists.

[80]Older men often retell the stories of the hardship and suffering experienced by the Gurkhas in World War II to the young. Up until his death in the late 1990s Dhan Kumari's father, a retired high-ranking officer, recounted these stories on a daily basis.

than those of adults are, and he is more susceptible to fear and emotional distress. Raju's *sai* in other respects has developed early, as he is *raba* (competent) beyond his years. As competency is highly valued, this is a source of pride for Raju as well as for Dil Maya and Dhan Kumari. This positive evaluation is supported by the literature which suggests that if the risks do not pose a threat to the child or his/her family a limited degree of exposure can lead to "self protective, adaptive cognitive styles" that facilitate more effective functioning (Jensen and Shaw 1993). Adaptive responses, however, do not mean that psychological distress is absent (Miller 1996).

Routinization and acclimatization may play a role in individual responses to conflict stress (Zimmern 1941; Ziv and Israeli 1973) resulting in a degree of resilience to long-term exposure to violence (Cairns 1996). If this is the only context a child has experienced then what occurs is viewed as normal, everyday reality (Jensen and Shaw 1993). The armed insurgents he saw on the street as a toddler while walking holding his grandmother's hand or in the courtyard when he was playing were, for Raju, 'normal' village characters. Similarly, instructions to "check for Maoists at the shop" in the same sentence as being told to "buy torch batteries" are routine. He knows that the appearance of Maoists is not 'normal' and contains dangers, but to him they are part of usual daily reality. As noted above, a supportive family environment, stable social relationships, and the presence of coping strategies helps diminish the impact of conflict. Although Raju lacks sufficient male role models, he is loved and cared for by Dil Maya and Dhan Kumari and a wider circle of kin and friends. They are unable to protect him from the difficulties of village life but they assist him by providing him with the skills he needs to survive.

When questioned about the impact of the insurgency on their children, caregivers in Kwei Nasa emphasize the dangers they face such as abduction, injury from explosive devices or crossfire, and they worry about disrupted education.[81] They observe that children spend time making 'guns' and playing war games, although like Povrzanovic's (1997) Croatian informants they do not attempt to interfere with or stop these activities. Children are susceptible to emotional distress and caregivers acknowledge that they are sometimes fearful of what is happening around them. Their less than fully developed *sai*, which makes them vulnerable, also offers a measure of protection, as being less aware than adults they are not as prone to anxiety and worry. When questioned about the emotional impact of the insurgency on Raju, Dhan Kumari is somewhat troubled. She admits that Raju experiences fear, but points out that he "is with us all the time".

---

[81] A detailed understanding requires children's self-evaluation of the impact of the conflict on their lives. I am in the process of developing a project which will focus on these questions.

Fundamental to the Tamu world view is the idea of interrelatedness and interdependence. People need each other for the practical demands of life, but they also need each other to survive as social and emotional beings, particularly at times of personal distress. Dhan Kumari states that family support helps keep Raju safe from injury and abduction and counteracts any emotional stress he might have. She also points to the competencies and protective skills that Raju has acquired and compares him favourably with his elder brother, who is less conflict-*raba*. Caregivers find it difficult to talk about the psychological impact of the conflict on their children partly because they are not used to doing so. That frightened adults may somatize their distress is acknowledged, as Dil Maya cites this as the underlying cause for Dhan Kumari's ailments, recently corroborated by medical opinion. Children with immature *sai*, however, are considered less susceptible to the internalization of distress. War games are seen by most to have their origins in mimicry but are not evaluated as possible psychological outcomes of the conflict. The disregarding of these impacts is partly because caregivers are not used to looking for them.[82] However, it is also because close examination of this and other conflict-related behaviours demands acknowledgement of the full extent of the challenges faced and calls into question parents' abilities to protect their children in this deeply altered time of danger, insecurity, and fear.[83]

---

[82] Those individuals deeply distressed by the conflict are acknowledged as such. In another village I met a youth shot by the security forces during an ambush, because he was the only young person in a group of villagers and, therefore, a suspected Maoist. Both he and other villagers evaluated him as conflict-affected, pointing out his changed behaviour and mood swings.

[83] This paper was written in 2005 and so the situation described, and the terminology used (e.g. Royal Nepalese Army, not Nepal Army), are those of the period before the Jan Andolan II (People's Movement II) of April 2006.

REFERENCES

Adhikari, J. 2003. 'Living on a Tightrope: Adaptive Strategies of Grassroots Development Workers in a Maoist-Conflict Area'. *Studies in Nepali History and Society (SINHAS)* 8: 369-83.

Amnesty International. 2005. 'Nepal: Children Caught in the Conflict' (http://web.amnesty.org/pages/npl-260705-action-eng).

Assal, A. and E. Farrel. 1992. 'Attempts to Make Meaning of Terror: Family, Play and School in Time of Civil War'. *Anthropology and Education Quarterly* 23 (4): 275-90.

Barenbaum, J., V. Ruchkin, and M. Schwab-Stone. 2004. 'The Psychosocial Aspects of Children Exposed to War: Practice and Policy Initiatives'. *Journal of Child Psychology and Psychiatry* 45: 41-62.

Basnet, D. 2004. *Schools in the Crossfire* (documentary film). Kathmandu: Images Nepal and Centre for Investigative Journalism/Himal Association.

Boyden, J. 2003. 'Children under Fire: Challenging Assumptions about Children's Resilience'. *Children, Youth and Environments* 13 (1) (www.colorado.edu/journals/cye).

——. 2004. 'Anthropology Under Fire: Ethics, Researchers and Children in War', in J. Boyden and J. de Berry (eds.), *Children and Youth on the Front Line: Ethnography, Armed Conflict and Displacement*, pp. 237-58. Oxford: Berghahn Books.

Boyden, J. and J. de Berry (eds.). 2004. *Children and Youth on the Front Line: Ethnography, Armed Conflict and Displacement.* Oxford: Berghahn Books.

Bracken, P.J., J.E. Giller, and D. Summerfield. 1995. 'Psychological Responses to War and Atrocity: the Limitations of Current Concepts'. *Social Science and Medicine* 40 (8): 1073-82.

Bracken, P.J. and C. Petty. 1998. 'Introduction', in P. Bracken and C. Petty (eds.), *Rethinking the Trauma of War*, pp. 1-8. London: Free Association Books.

Cairns, E. 1996. *Children and Political Violence.* Oxford: Blackwell.

Cairns, E. and A. Dawes 1996. 'Children: Ethnic and Political Violence – A Commentary'. *Child Development* 67: 129-39.

Chimienti, G., J.A. Nasr, and I. Khalifeh. 1989. 'Children's Reactions to War Related Stress: Affective Symptoms and Behaviour Problems'. *Social Psychiatry and Psychiatric Epidemiology* 24: 282-7.

CWIN (Child Workers in Nepal Concerned Centre). 2004. '*Children and Armed Conflict*' (www.cwin-nepal.org).

Dawes, A. 2000. 'Cultural Diversity and Childhood Adversity: Implications for Community Level Interventions with Children in Difficult Circumstances'. Paper presented to the conference 'Children in Adversity: Ways to Reinforce the Coping Ability and Resilience of Children in Situations of Hardship', September, Oxford University.

Desjarlais, R.R. 1994 (1992). *Body and Emotion: The Aesthetics of Illness and Healing in the Nepal Himalayas.* Delhi: Motilal Banarsidass.

Dickson-Gõmez, J. 2002. 'Growing Up in Guerrilla Camps: The Long Term Impact of Being a Child in El Salvador's Civil War'. *Ethos* 30 (4): 327-56.

Eth, S. and R. Pynoos. 1985. 'Developmental Perspective on Psychic Trauma in Childhood', in C. Figley (ed.), *Trauma and Its Wake*, pp. 36-52. New York: Plenum Press.

Eyber, C. and A. Ager. 2004. 'Researching Young People's Experiences of War: Participatory Methods and the Trauma Discourse in Angola', in J. Boyden and J. de Berry (eds.), *Children and Youth on the Front Line: Ethnography, Armed Conflict and Displacement*, pp. 189-208. Oxford: Berghahn Books.

Goldstein, R.D., N.S. Wampler, and P.H. Wise. 1997. 'War Experiences and Distress Symptoms of Bosnian Children'. *Pediatrics* 100: 873-8.

Green, L. 1995. 'Living in a State of Fear', in C. Nordstrom and A. Robben (eds.), *Fieldwork under Fire: Contemporary Studies of Violence and Survival*, pp. 105-27. Berkeley: University of California Press.

Himal. 2003. 'Bombs and Landmines in the Corn and Paddy Fields'. *Himal* (December) 16: 1-15.

Human Rights Watch. 2004. 'Between a Rock and a Hard Place: Civilians Struggle to Survive in Nepal's Civil War' (http://www.org.reports/2004/nepal2004/).

HimRights. 2005. *Farewell to Firearms: A Pictorial Report.* Kathmandu: HimRights.

ICRC (International Committee of the Red Cross). 1994. *Children in War.* Geneva: ICRC.

Jensen, P.S. and J. Shaw. 1993. 'Children as Victims of War: Current Knowledge and Future Research Needs'. *Journal of American Academy of Child and Adolescent Psychiatry* 32: 697-708.

de Jong, J. 2003. *Trauma, War, and Violence: Public Mental Health in Socio-Cultural Context.* New York: Kluwer Academic.

Kantipur 2004 'No Treatment for Wounded Children'. 23 January (www.kantipuronline.com).

The Kathmandu Post. 2004. 'Looked Like a Beautiful Doll, Exploded'. 15 February (www.nepalnews.com).

Kinzie, J.D., W.H. Sack, R. Angell, S. Manson, and B. Rath. 1986. 'The Psychiatric Effects of Massive Trauma on Cambodian Children: I. The Children', *Journal of American Academy of Child and Adolescent Psychiatry* 25: 370-6.

Kleinman, A. and B. Good. 1985. *Culture and Depression.* Berkeley: University of California Press.

Kohrt, B. n.d. '*Manma asar parcha* – it strikes the mind: Conceptions of trauma in Nepal', (manuscript in preparation).

Kohrt, B.A., D.J. Hruschka, R.D. Kunz, H.E. Kohrt, V.G. Carrion, and C.M. Worthman. 2005. 'Low Cortisol Levels and Disruptive Behaviors in Mongolian and Nepali Boys'. *Foundation for Psychocultural Research.* Los Angeles: University of California.

Korbin, J.E. 2003. 'Children, Childhoods, and Violence'. *Annual Review of Anthropology* 32: 431-46.

Kos, A.M. and S. Derviskadic-Jovanovic. 1998. 'What Can We Do to Support Children Who Have Been through War?' *Forced Migration Review* 3: 4-7

Laor, N. and L. Wolmer. 2002. 'Children Exposed to Disaster: The Role of the Mental Health, Professional', in M. Lewis (ed.). *Child and Adolescent Psychiatry: A Comprehensive Textbook*, pp. 925-37. Philadelphia, PA: Lippincott Williams and Wilkins.

Laor, N., L. Wolmer, L.C. Mayers, A. Gershon, R. Weizman, and D.J. Cohen. 1997. 'Israeli Preschool Children under Scuds: A 30-Month Follow-Up'. *Journal of American Academy of Child and Adolescent Psychiatry* 36: 349-56.

Macfarlane, A. 2001. 'Sliding Down Hill: Some Reflections on Thirty Years of Change in a Himalayan Village'. *European Bulletin of Himalayan Research* 20-1: 105-10.

Machel, G. 2001. *The Impact of War on Children*. London: Hurst and Co.

Margold, J. A. 1999. 'From "Cultures of Fear and Terror" to the Normalization of Violence: An Ethnographic Case'. *Critique of Anthropology* 19 (1): 63-88.

McHugh, E. 1989. 'Concepts of the Person among the Gurungs of Nepal'. *American Ethnologist* 16: 75-86.

——. 2001. 'Sliding, Shifting, and Re-Drawing Boundaries'. *European Bulletin of Himalayan Research* 20-1: 113-17.

NCBL (Nepal Campaign to Ban Landmines). 2005. (www.nepal.icbl.org).

Miller, K.E. 1996. 'The Effects of State Terrorism and Exile on Indigenous Guatemalan Refugee Children: A Mental Health Assessment and an Analysis of Children's Narratives'. *Child Development* 67: 89-106.

Muldoon, O.T. 2004. 'Children of the Troubles: The Impact of Political Violence in Northern Ireland'. *Journal of Social Issues* 60 (3): 453-68.

Nader, K.O., R.S. Pynoos, L.A. Fairbanks, M. al-Ajeel, and A. al-Asfour. 1993. 'A Preliminary Study of PTSD and Grief among the Children of Kuwait following the Gulf Crisis'. *British Journal of Clinical Psychology* 32: 407-16.

Nepalnews.com 2004. 'One Minor Killed in Blast'. 14 June.

Nordstrom, C. 1995. 'War on the Front Lines', in C. Nordstrom and A. Robben (eds.), *Fieldwork under Fire: Contemporary Studies of Violence and Survival*, pp. 129-53. Berkeley: University of California Press.

——. 1997. *A Different Kind of War Story*. Philadelphia: University of Pennsylvania Press.

——. 1998. 'Terror Warfare and the Medicine of Peace'. *Medical Anthropology Quarterly* 12 (1): 103-21.

Olujic, M. 1995. 'The Croatian War Experience', in C. Nordstrom and A. Robben (eds.), *Fieldwork under Fire: Contemporary Studies of Violence and Survival*, pp. 186-204. Berkeley: University of California Press.

——. 1998. 'Children in Extremely Difficult Circumstances: War and Its Aftermath in Croatia', in N. Scheper-Hughes and C. Sargent (eds.), *Small Wars: The Cultural Politics of Childhood*, pp. 318-30. Berkeley: University of California Press.

Pettigrew, J. 1999. 'Parallel Landscapes: Ritual and Political Values of a Shamanic Soul Journey', in B. Bickel and M. Gaenszle (eds.), *Himalayan Space: Cultural Horizons and Practices*, pp. 247-70. Zürich: Völkerkundemuseum Press.

——. 2003. 'Guns, Kinship and Fear: Maoists among the Tamu-Mai (Gurungs)', in D. Gellner (ed.), *Resistance and the State: Nepalese Experiences*, pp. 305-25. Delhi: Social Science Press.

——. 2004. 'Living between the Maoists and the Army in Rural Nepal', in M. Hutt (ed.), *Himalayan 'People's War: Nepal's Maoist Rebellion*, pp. 261-83. London: Hurst & Co.

Pettigrew, J., S. Shneiderman, and I. Harper. 2004. 'Relationships, Complicity and Representation: Conducting Research in Nepal during the Maoist Insurgency'. *Anthropology Today*, February, 20 (1): 20-25.

Peters, K. and P. Richards. 1998. 'Fighting with Open Eyes: Youth Combatants Talking about War in Sierra Leone', in P.J. Bracken and C. Petty (eds.), *Rethinking the Trauma of War*, pp. 76-111. London: Free Association Books.

Povrzanovic, M. 1997. 'Children, War and Nation: Croatia 1991-4'. *Childhood* 4 (1): 81-102.

Pynoos, R. and K. Nader. 1988. 'Psychological First Aid and Treatment Approach to Children Exposed to Community Violence: Research Implications'. *Journal of Traumatic Stress* 1 (4): 445-73.

Quesada, J. 1998. 'Suffering Child: An Embodiment of War and Its Aftermath in Post-Sandinista Nicaragua.' *Medical Anthropology Quarterly* 12 (1): 51-73.

Robben, A. 1989. 'Habits of the Home, Spatial Hegemony and the Structuration of the House and Society in Brazil'. *American Anthropologist* 91 (3): 570-88.

——. 2000. 'The Assault on Basic Trust: Disappearance, Protest and Reburial in Argentina', in A. Robben and M. Suárez-Orozco (eds.). *Cultures under Siege: Collective Violence and Trauma*, pp. 70-101. Cambridge: Cambridge University Press.

Sack, W.H., G. Clarke, C. Him, D. Dickson, B. Goff, K. Lanham, and D. Kinzie. 1993. 'A Six-Year Follow-Up Study of Cambodian Refugee Adolescents Traumatized as Children'. *Journal of the American Academy of Child and Adolescent Psychiatry* 32: 431-7.

SAIR (South Asia Intelligence Review). 2004. 'Nepal: Arming the Children', March (www.satp.org/satporgtp/sair/).

Save the Children. 2005. *Fighting Back: Child and Community-led Strategies to Avoid Children's Recruitment into Armed Forces and Groups in West Africa*. London: Save the Children.

Shneiderman S. and M. Turin. 2004. 'The Path to Jan Sarkar in Dolakha District: Towards an Ethnography of the Maoist Movement', in M. Hutt (ed.), *Himalayan 'People's War': Nepal's Maoist Rebellion*, pp. 79-111. London: Hurst & Co.

Sluka, J. 2000. *Death Squad: The Anthropology of State Terror.* Philadelphia: University of Pennsylvania.

——. 1995. 'Reflections on Managing Danger in Fieldwork: Dangerous Anthropology in Belfast', in C. Nordstrom and A. Robben (eds.), *Fieldwork under Fire: Contemporary Studies of Violence and Survival*, pp. 276-94. Berkeley: University of California Press.

Somasundaram, D. and C. Jamunanantha 2003. 'Psychosocial Consequences of War: Northern Sri Lankan Experience', in J. de Jong (ed.), *Trauma, War, and Violence: Public Mental Health in Socio-Cultural Context*, pp. 205-58. New York: Kluwer Academic.

Stein, B., D. Comer, W. Gardiner, and K. Kelleher. 1999. 'Prospective Study of Displaced Children's Symptoms in Wartime Bosnia'. *Social Psychiatry and Psychiatric Epidemiology* 34: 464-9.

Suárez-Orozco, M. 1987. 'The Treatment of Children in the "Dirty War": Ideology, State Terrorism and the Abuse of Children in Argentina', in N. Scheper-Hughes (ed.), *Child Survival: Anthropological Perspectives on the Treatment and Maltreatment of Children.* Amsterdam: Reidel.

——. 1992. 'A Grammar of Terror: Psychocultural Responses to State Terrorism in Dirty War and Post-Dirty War Argentina', in J. Martin and C. Nordstrom (eds.), *The Paths to Domination, Resistance, and Terror*, pp. 219-59. Berkeley: University of California Press.

Summerfield, D. 1998. 'The Social Experience of War and Some Issues for the Humanitarian Field', in P.J. Bracken and C. Petty (eds.), *Rethinking the Trauma of War*, pp. 9-37. London: Free Association Books.

Taussig, M. 1987. *Colonialism, Shamanism and the Wild Man: A Study of Terror and Healing.* Chicago: University of Chicago Press.

——. 1992. *The Nervous System.* London: Routledge.

Thapa, D. with B. Sijapati 2003. *Nepal's Maoist Insurgency, 1996 to 2003.* Kathmandu: The Printhouse.

Tol, W.A., M.J.D. Jordans, S. Regmi, and S. Sharma. 2005. 'Cultural Challenges to Psychosocial Counselling in Nepal'. *Transcultural Psychiatry* 42 (2): 317-33.

Utas, M. 2004. 'Fluid Research Fields: Studying Excombatant Youth in the Aftermath of the Liberian Civil War', in J. Boyden and J. de Berry (eds.), *Children and Youth on the Front Line: Ethnography, Armed Conflict and Displacement*, pp. 209-36. Oxford: Berghahn Books.

Watchlist on Children and Armed Conflict. 2005. 'Caught in the Middle: Mounting Violations against Children in Nepal's Armed Conflict'. January (www.watchlist.org/reports/nepal.report.20050120.pdf).

Weine, S., D.F. Becker, T.H. McGlasthan, D. Vojoda, S. Hartman, and J.P. Robbins. 1995. 'Adolescent Survivors of "Ethnic Cleansing": Observations on the First Year in America'. *Journal of the American Academy of Child and Adolescent Psychiatry* 34: 1153-9.

Zimmern, E.M. 1941. 'War Strain in Children'. *British Medical Journal* 4177: 124.

Ziv, A., A.W. Kruglanski, and S. Schulman. 1974. 'Children's Psychological Reactions to Wartime Stress'. *Journal of Personality and Social Psychology* 30: 24-30.

Ziv, A. and R. Israeli. 1973. 'Effects of Bombardment on the Manifest Anxiety Level of Children Living in Kibbutzim'. *Journal of Consulting and Clinical Psychology* 40: 287-91.

PART 3

TRANSNATIONAL LINKS INSIDE AND OUTSIDE NEPAL

11

The Development of Local Entrepreneurship: A Case Study of a Tourist Area, Thamel in Kathmandu

IZUMI MORIMOTO

INTRODUCTION

The main purpose of this chapter is to examine the process of the creation of Thamel, Kathmandu,[1] and to show how the activities of local entrepreneurs[2] as agents for the regional formation of a tourist area coincided with the development of international tourism. From a broader perspective, this process can be seen as the process of involvement in the global market and the process of the economic, cultural, and political marginalization of the Third World in global core-periphery relationships. The regional formation of tourist areas, especially in the Third World, has often been looked at in terms of economic dependency on capitalism. However, tourism in local areas has developed as the outcome of a complex interplay of factors that

---

[1]The main data presented in this paper appeared in the seventh chapter of my doctoral dissertation (Morimoto 2001: 96-141) and was first presented in public at the conference in Japanese Association for South Asian Studies at Tokyo University in 2000. I am grateful to David Gellner, Hiroshi Ishii, Keshav Lall Maharjan, Katsuo Nawa, Seika Sato, and others, for their helpful and constructive comments and criticisms on various earlier versions of this paper. I would like to express my deepest gratitude to all the people of Thamel who helped me during my fieldwork in Nepal, without whose kind help I could not have carried out this work at all. However, I am responsible for any errors or shortcomings.

[2]The word 'entrepreneur' can be translated either as *byabasayi* or as *byapari/bepari* in Nepali. The meanings of these two words are not the same in the local context. People in Thamel tend to distinguish *bya(be)pari*, who sell or trade, from *byabasayi*, who try to develop some industries. For example, people who keep hotels are called *byabasayi*, whereas people selling miscellaneous goods such as precious stones in shops and small souvenirs on the street are called *byapari* and would never be called *byabasayi*. In this chapter, the word 'entrepreneur' means *byabasayi*, various types of which can be observed, as described below.

have taken place between capitalization by the global market and local adaptation to it. The local process of tourism development is not necessarily explained simply by positing the core-periphery relationships of 'world system' theories.

It should be emphasized that as a tourist area Thamel is different from many other famous tourist areas, such as luxury resorts in the Third World, in that most local businesses in Thamel have grown up not because of investment from developed countries, but through investment mainly by local Nepalis, occasionally by Indians, and (only recently) by Chinese. Taking into consideration the importance for Third World countries to have relationships with developed countries, even lopsided colonial relationships, in order to attract international investment and tourists (Britton 1991), it might be thought that the lack of a colonial past could be a handicap to Nepal for tourism development. In order to examine how Thamel has been developed, it is important to focus on local entrepreneurs who have to make business opportunities mainly by themselves.

To consider these circumstances, I will focus on the business strategies of local entrepreneurs who participate in tourism, especially the hotel industry. I will explore how they have created Thamel as a major tourist area in Kathmandu, the most important gateway for global tourism in Nepal. In other words, I will explore how these entrepreneurs have participated actively in the global market.

This chapter is based on fieldwork conducted mainly in Kathmandu from October 1995 to January 1997. The follow-up research in Thamel was undertaken for about one or two months each year from 1998 to 2004. The data used in this chapter was collected from many associations, such as Hotel Association Nepal and Thamel Tourism Development Committee, and from observation and interviews with local people, such as hotel entrepreneurs, who have played essential roles in developing Thamel as a tourist area.

TOURISM STUDIES AND ENTREPRENEURSHIP

Before the prevalence of mass tourism among people in developed countries, Christaller (1963) argued that tourism could be a means of achieving economic development in peripheral regions since the flow of rich tourists from the 'metropolitan' centre should inject foreign exchange and generate jobs. On the other hand, Britton looked at tourism's role in Third World development from the dependency paradigm perspective and at the same time pointed out that paradoxically the tourist industry would seem to suffer from a country not being a structurally dependent colony because of difficulties in attracting foreign tourism capital which brings with it foreign air carriers, international-standard accommodation, and wholesale tour packages (Britton 1982: 347-54). Many other geographers have also indicated that tourism development in less-developed countries or areas perpetuates not only economic but also political and cultural inequalities in core-periphery relationships of the world system.

The core-periphery model, whether approached from a modernization or a dependency perspective, provides a valuable and fundamentally geographical framework for contextualizing and comprehending spatial disparities in power and levels of development (e.g. Frank 1969). Tourism studies in the Third World have used this model extensively, usually from a dependency perspective and on an international rather than a domestic scale (Weaver 1998: 292). Most studies of the economic impacts of tourism rely on single case studies, so it is difficult to account for the varying effect of local contingencies on the geographical differences in entrepreneurial activity. Little has been done on themes such as the process of firm formation or the development of entrepreneurial skills in tourism (Ioannides 1995: 57). However, this does not mean that the influence of tourism development in local areas of the Third World has no significance. Most tourism studies do not investigate the actual circumstances among local people associated with small businesses about tourism development. The reason why such small businesses and activities by local people have not received much attention is that it is very difficult to recognize and theorize such actual circumstances because of their very instability and small size. In reality, there are plenty of small entrepreneurial activities, so-called economic activities in the informal sector, in Third World countries such as Nepal. These small, local activities play a significant role in forming a tourist area in the Third World, especially in the case of a locality that has emerged without any orderly town development, such as Kathmandu in recent years.

The term 'entrepreneur' is used here to refer to a person who undertakes capitalistic activities, often involving various risks. Much attention has been paid to the characteristics of entrepreneurs, organizational behaviour, and the role of markets, but the cultural contexts in which these phenomena occur have not been systematically addressed (Hitchcock 2000: 205-6). However, as Dahles (1999: 13) points out, small entrepreneurs are not driven solely by the profit motive, since the desire for prestige and constraints, such as obligations consequent on the membership of a particular social group, may also influence behaviour. 'Non-economic' values are important for entrepreneurs to make decisions on what and how to do entrepreneurial activities (Ateljevic and Doorne 2003: 126). In such cases, entrepreneurship may be regarded as a profit-seeking initiative directed towards resolving ill-defined problems in complex and structurally uncertain contexts by developing business strategies within their societies. In

Nepal, as Zivetz (1992: 43-5) indicated, entrepreneurship is the product of culture, and as such is also vulnerable to change. The tensions involved in political restructuring and cultural redefinition require that the individual entrepreneur and his/her community also engage in significant internal redefinitions. As entrepreneurship is founded on culture, it is crucial for understanding entrepreneurship in Nepal today to investigate its cultural and historical background. The emergence of industrial entrepreneurship depends in large measure on how much sociocultural room there is for the innovator to emerge. Equally important are the nature and degree of economic incentives in the prevailing market and policy situation which determine whether the innovator will choose industry over other investment options (Zivetz 1992: 1).

A tourist area is created as a consequence of entrepreneurial activities to meet various demands of tourists. Researching a tourist area we are able to analyse how entrepreneurship has been created and developed in tourism. Since tourism is one of the most attractive industries in recent years in many places, especially in the Third World, this promises to be especially fruitful. By focusing on local entrepreneurship in a tourist area, this chapter aims in addition to contribute to Nepalese studies, particularly as regards the country's modernization and industrialization.

TOURISM DEVELOPMENT IN NEPAL: A HISTORICAL PERSPECTIVE

Nepal remained isolated from the rest of the world until the mid-twentieth century and relatively few international tourists were allowed to enter the country except pilgrims and traders from India and Tibet. Nepal has attracted international tourists since the government officially opened the country to the world in the 1950s. International tourism developed into one of the most important industries for the Nepalese economy in the 1980s. HMG Nepal expects it not only to earn much-needed foreign exchanges but also, or rather, to create job opportunities.[3] Recently political instability, especially that caused by the Maoist insurgency, has had a serious impact on tourism in Nepal. Despite this problem, HMG Nepal has recognized tourism as one of the most important basic industries, and has designed its policies, plans, and programmes in order to improve the existing situation.

As Britton has pointed out, the dependency of tourism industries on foreign imports is common in the Third World tourism (Britton 1982: 338-40), and Nepal is no exception. But it would be a mistake to homogenize the Third World countries. This is made clear if we compare the

[3] See *The Eighth National Plan* (1992-7) (NPC 1992: 436-61).

percentage of tourism income between Nepal and the Caribbean islands which are very popular with Western people as seaside resorts. Nepal earns 2.9 per cent of its GDP from tourism (estimated data in 2001),[4] whereas in some Caribbean islands tourism accounts for around 80 per cent of their GDP.[5] There are several reasons for this difference between Nepal and the Caribbean islands, but the main reason is that Nepal does not have historical lopsided colonial relationships which lead to huge foreign investment and mass tourists.

The characteristics of tourism in Nepal have changed since the country opened its doors formally to the world in 1951. At first, the main visitors were Western elite Alpinists and academic scholars who went to the Himalayas. The growth of interest in mountaineering was followed by the development of Nepal's tourist sector during the 1960s and 1970s. In the same period, as Figure 11.1 shows, young tourists from Western countries, especially from the United States of America, started to come and stay in Kathmandu. They were known as hippies. There was a difference in the style of tourism between Western Alpinists and hippies. The difference between these two groups expressed itself spatially. Hippies gathered in Jhoche, known as 'Freak Street', in the centre of Kathmandu city area. Their lodgings were mostly parts of private houses let out by local Newars. On the other hand, many mountaineers and scholars took their lodgings in old Rana palaces along main roads because they had huge gardens suitable for preparing climbing equipment for expeditions.

In the 1980s the number of international tourists increased significantly all over the world. Nepal also had more tourists from Western countries as well as other developed countries like Japan. It can be said that mass tourism in Nepal started in the 1980s. The Nepalese government began to recognize the importance of tourism for economic development in Nepal, as was shown in the Seventh Plan (1985-90) (NPC 1986: 623-40). During this time, tourism in Nepal became more and more diversified according to tourism resources in Nepal and mass tourists' demand as, for example, adventure travel such as trekking in the Himalayas and going on safaris in the Tarai (Zurick 1992: 611-15), joining in eco-tourism and study tours in the mountains and local villages, and visiting resorts in the mountains, riversides, and subtropical jungles, and so on. As more and more mass tourists came to Nepal, Thamel grew and developed as a tourist area.

In 1998, the Nepal government held the Visit Nepal Year 1998 to develop tourist industries and make local people more aware of the importance of tourism. Consequently in 1999, Nepal had 491,504 tourists, the

[4]See *The Tenth National Plan* (2003-8) (NPC 2003).

[5]See World Tourism Organization 1998.

largest number it had ever had. However, since then the number of international tourists has decreased drastically. In 2002 it fell to nearly half that of 1999 (Nepal Tourism Board 2003). Such a serious decline in the number of tourists is due not only to political instability, which has become acute in Nepal, but also to the overall decline in the total number of international tourists everywhere since the terrorist attack on the World Trade Centre buildings in New York in 2001.

Figure 11.1 shows the number of international tourists who visited Nepal from 1962 to 2002. The black bars show the number of Indian tourists who visited Nepal by air. There is no data on Indian tourists who visited Nepal by land, such as automobile tourists, pilgrims, traders, migrant workers, and so on, because they are admitted across the international border with Nepal freely. HMG Nepal promoted a campaign to attract more Indian tourists so that the number of Indian tourists continued to grow until 1998. Since 1999, however, their numbers dropped because of political instability in Nepal, as seen in the political movement of the Maoists, the hijacking of the Indian Airlines flight IC814 in December 1999, and the royal massacre of June 2001. After the hijacking all Indian

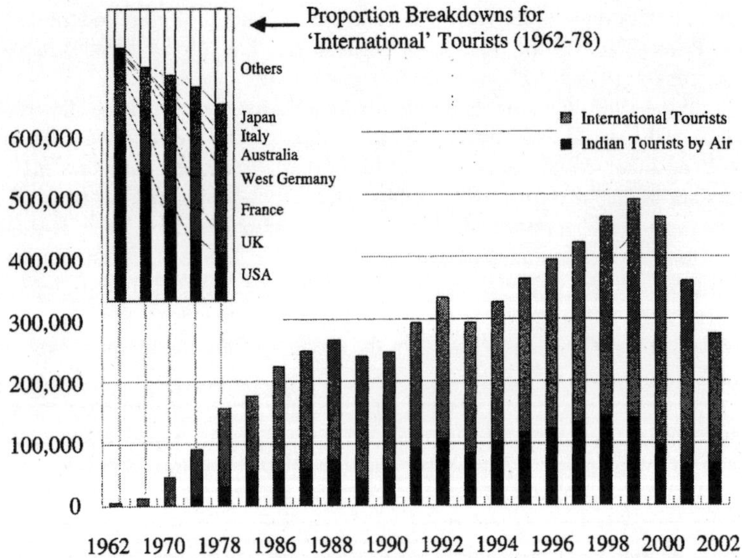

Sources: Ministry of Culture, Tourism & Civil Aviation 1985, 2002.

Figure 11.1: Number of Tourist Arrivals in Nepal.

Airlines flights to and from Kathmandu ceased for five months. The grey bars show the number of international tourists excluding Indians. This number increased until 2000, but since 2001 it has also decreased for similar reasons. However, there can be also seen some differences between Indian tourists and other international tourists. For example, Indian tourists appear to be more affected by political instability in Nepal than other international tourists.

Figure 11.2 shows another difference between Indians and others, namely, the seasonal factor. The main reason lies in the different purposes for visiting Nepal. Because many international tourists, except Indians, like to enjoy the view of mountains or to trek in the mountains, they prefer the dry season to the rainy season. On the other hand, many Indian tourists, who can visit Nepal without visas, like to visit Nepal to avoid the heat of summer at home even though it may be the rainy season in Nepal. Indian tourists also like to go shopping and sightseeing in Pokhara and Kathmandu. HMG Nepal began a campaign in the Seventh Plan (1985-90) (NPC 1986: 623-40) to attract Indian tourists precisely in order to flatten out the seasonal imbalance in tourist arrivals.

The difference between international and Indian tourists in spatial preference was easy to observe during my investigation between 1995 and 1997 in Kathmandu. Indian tourists prefer to stay in standard hotels, which are generally operated by Indians in New Road, at the centre of Kathmandu's shopping district, or in luxury hotels, while many international tourists prefer cheap hotels and lodges in Thamel, which is known as the budget tourist area in Kathmandu. Other international tourists choose to stay at luxury hotels. Thamel, the study area of this chapter, is different from another old tourist area, Jhoche, also called 'Freak Street', as men-

Sources: Ministry of Culture, Tourism & Civil Aviation 1999, 2002.

Figure 11.2: Tourist Arrivals by Month in 1999 and 2002.

tioned earlier. As Liechty (1996: 107) has pointed out, the new tourists seek to distance themselves from the hippies of 'Freak Street' and look for hotels that are an alternative to the dark and dirty 'flophouses' of Jhoche. Nowadays hippies can hardly be seen either there or elsewhere.

This chapter examines how such a budget tourist area, as Thamel has been created. It is necessary to recognize that the term 'tourist area' here does not mean the places where tourists can enjoy their purposive activities written in disembarkation cards, such as trekking or sightseeing, but rather where tourist industries such as hotels, restaurants, travel agencies, and souvenir shops have accumulated.

THE STUDY AREA: THAMEL IN KATHMANDU

This section gives some background information of Thamel in the context of the urbanization in Kathmandu.

Figure 11.3 shows the city areas of Kathmandu in the nineteenth century. The light grey part shows the city area. It was the centre of Kathmandu city in the nineteenth century, which was densely populated by Newars. As Karan and Ishii (1996) have pointed out, there was a degree of social segregation in the traditional residence patterns of Kathmandu city. High-ranking officials and priests tended to live in close proximity to the palace; traders, artisans, and craftsmen occupied the outer ring; and low-caste scavengers and sweepers lived in the dwellings beyond this area. Surrounding the inner core, an outer city that developed during the Rana period has been laid out (Karan & Ishii 1996: 191-6). The old palaces of the Ranas, whose family ruled Nepal as the hereditary Rana prime ministers for a century from 1845, are shown as dark grey areas in Figure 11.3. They built numerous palaces with extensive grounds outside the inner city of those days. Servants and employees working under the Ranas started to live nearby, schools and stables for the Ranas were set up around the palaces, and main roads were built to link the palaces with other palaces and the city centre.

The roads contributed to the development of business areas as well as residential areas. From the 1950s, the population of Kathmandu city began to increase and occupy vacant lots. The larger palaces are now used as public buildings such as government offices, schools, colleges, hospitals, and embassies, and some of them are also used as hotels, shopping malls, and restaurants aimed at the rich including foreigners. It could be said that the urbanization of Kathmandu today flows from the town development under the Rana regime even though that development was not planned well.

Also seen in Figure 11.3 is Thamel, located just outside the inner city

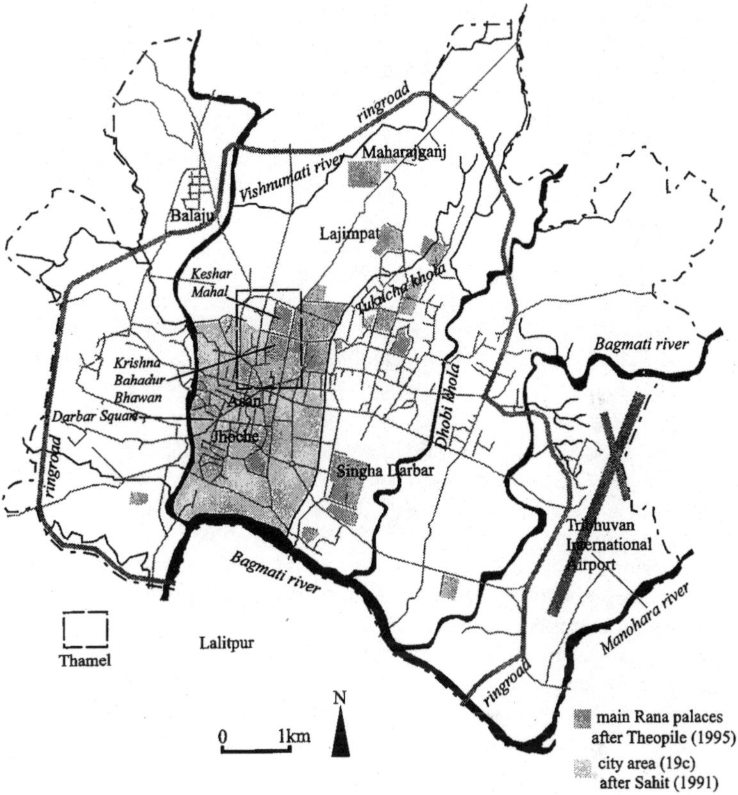

Figure 11.3: Study Area Thamel in Kathmandu.

in the nineteenth century. There are two magnificent old Rana palaces, Keshar Mahal and Krishna Bahadur Bhawan, which are now used as government offices. The latter opened as the first international hotel in Nepal in the mid-twentieth century, before being converted into government offices. There are also many Rana palaces with fine botanical gardens in Thamel, though they are not shown in the figure.[6] Compared with the palaces shown in the figure, the other palaces in Thamel are small, and therefore were exempt from confiscation by the Nepalese government after

---

[6]Details of the Rana palaces in Thamel are given in the section 'The Development of a Tourist Area and Entrepreneurship in Thamel'; see also Figure 11.6.

the collapse of the Rana regime in 1951. The Ranas still live in some of these palaces. Others are used by people who purchased them from the Ranas for their residential houses or other purposes, such as hotels and restaurants for international tourists. The fact that there were many Rana palaces in Thamel shows that at least when tourists started to come to Nepal in the 1950s, Thamel was not as densely populated as it is now. This does not mean, however, that Thamel was just vacant land. Urban infrastructure, such as electricity, telephone lines, and so on, was already in place, due to the presence of the palaces. With urbanization and migration from the mountain areas, the Kathmandu city area expanded even outside the Ring Road which was completed in 1986.

Since 1992 many policies to encourage private investment, foreign investment, technology transfer, and so on, have been designed. These policies have increased the participation of the private sector in business activities including tourism industries. Hotels, restaurants, shops, and offices related to tourism have increased rapidly even in hidden-away places where most tourists would have a hard time finding them.

During the hippy boom in Jhoche, Thamel gradually became a tourist area. At that time the area called Thamel was just a single street about twenty or thirty metres long. In the 1980s the boom in mass tourism began in Nepal and it brought many tourists to Thamel, one decade after the oldest accommodations had been opened there. As global mass tourism increased, this local shift created various new opportunities for local people to participate in business activities related to tourism. Thamel became a densely populated area crowded not only with international tourists, mainly backpackers, but also local entrepreneurs and their employees, and became one of the busiest areas in Kathmandu.

THE HOTEL INDUSTRY IN NEPAL

The Development of the Hotel Industry in Nepal

The Royal Hotel, the first hotel of international standards in Nepal, opened in the middle of the 1950s (Peissel 1966: 39-51). The building, Krishna Bahadur Bhawan, which is now a government office, faced Kantipath next to Darbar Marg. Only around 1967 did low-budget lodges open in Jhoche (Liechty 2001: 80-1), in the inner core of Kathmandu city, to attract hippies, while some other luxury hotels with fine gardens opened in the outer core of Kathmandu city.

Since the 1950s, the number of accommodations has grown, especially after democracy was achieved in 1990. The types of accommodation have become more and more diverse to meet the demands of the different types of tourists, such as mountaineers, hippies, and mass tourists. The different types of hotels are distributed in different social and geographical spaces – the luxury starred hotels and resorts, budget hotels, and budget lodges (Liechty's 'flophouses') in Kathmandu, and the luxury resorts in the mountains and subtropical jungles of the Tarai, or the teahouses along trekking routes. As for Thamel, it has earned a reputation among tourists as an area for cheap accommodation and good restaurants; on the other hand, it is known as a business area for local entrepreneurs, and also one of the most disreputable places for local people (Liechty 1996: 114-27). As I will discuss in the next section, Thamel has attracted local entrepreneurs, and at the same time, Thamel is the place which 'good' people keep away from because it is notorious for its 'low life'.

Figure 11.4a shows the number of hotels in Nepal. It is important to consider that not all hotels are included in this figure. Only the formally registered hotels are shown. Budget accommodations, especially in rural areas, tend to be run without registration. The reason why the number of hotels has increased significantly from 1985 to 1995 is not only that many hotels were newly opened but also that many, which had not done so before, took out formal registration.

Comparing the number of hotels from 1985 to 2002, we can see the success of decentralization of the hotel and related industries which has

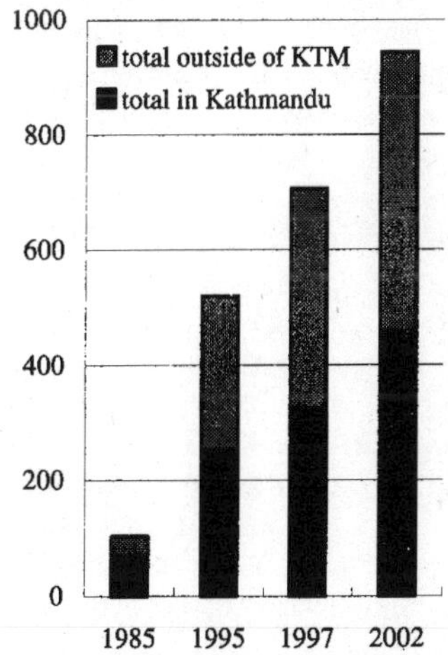

Sources: Ministry of Culture, Tourism, & Civil Aviation 1985, 1995, 1997, 2002.

Figure 11.4a: Number of Hotels in Nepal.

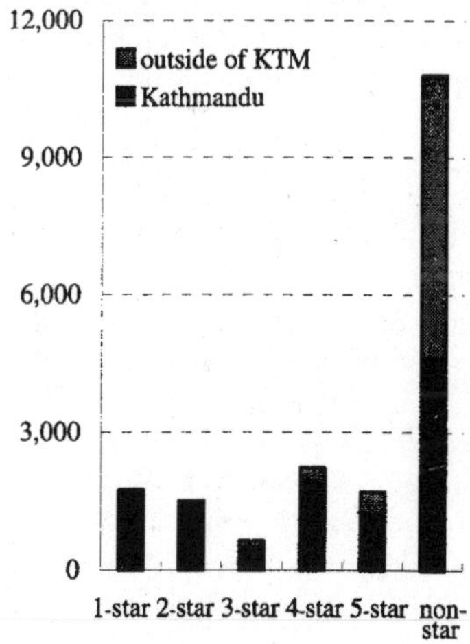

Source: Ministry of Culture, Tourism, & Civil Aviation 1997.

Figure 11.4b: Number of Beds in Nepal in 1997.

been promoted by the government since the 1970s.[7] Around half of all hotels in Nepal are outside Kathmandu, in places such as Pokhara, Chitwan, and others.[8]

With regard to the number of beds in Nepal, however, as Figure 11.4b indicates, a distinctly uneven pattern of regional development can be seen, in that most of the beds in starred hotels are concentrated in Kathmandu. Generally tourist accommodations outside Kathmandu are affordable to budget tourists. Although recently resort-type accommodations have started to be built outside Kathmandu, the number is still very small. These figures suggest that there is still very uneven regional development of the hotel industry in Nepal, both as regards quality and as regards the number of hotels.

The Distribution of Hotels in Kathmandu

Figure 11.5 shows the distribution of hotels in Kathmandu. This data is based on the Nepal Business Yellow Pages 2000. One black dot indicates one hotel. Although all hotels may not be included in the yellow pages, and the phone numbers of very small and unstable hotels are unrecorded, this data should be much more reliable than official government data, because almost all hotels in the Kathmandu city area have telephones installed even though they are operated without registration.

Hotels in Kathmandu are concentrated in particular locales. Each tourist area has its own characteristics. These characteristics are classified into some groups by scale and quality: large and luxury hotels for international tourists including Indians; standard hotels run by Indians for Indian tourists in shopping areas; small and cheap hotels for mass tourists; and very small and cheap ones for hippies.

Comparing the scale of different types, the average number of rooms in each hotel is 115 in Darbar Marg, 35 in Thamel, 30 in Jhoche, and 74 in Lazimpat. Darbar Marg is the central area in Kathmandu, where not only 4- or 5-star hotels, but also international financial companies and airline offices are located. Some of the starred hotels in Darbar Marg offer their standard rooms for US$120 per night, and suites for US$300 (in 2000).[9] Kantipath, nearer to Thamel, is the same as Darbar Marg. In Lazimpat, known as the exclusive residential area, there are many starred hotels, embassies, and old Rana palaces. On the other hand, hotels in Thamel are characterized by their low cost. A minimum room charge I found in

[7]Since *The Fourth National Plan* (1970-5) (NPC 1970) has been issued.

[8]See *Nepal Tourism Statistics 2002* (Ministry of Culture, Tourism & Civil Aviation 2002).

[9]Rooming charges in starred hotels dropped significantly after 2002 because of political instability, SARS, and so on. Some 4- or 5-star hotels offered their standard rooms for only US$40 per night through certain travel agencies when I stayed there in 2004.

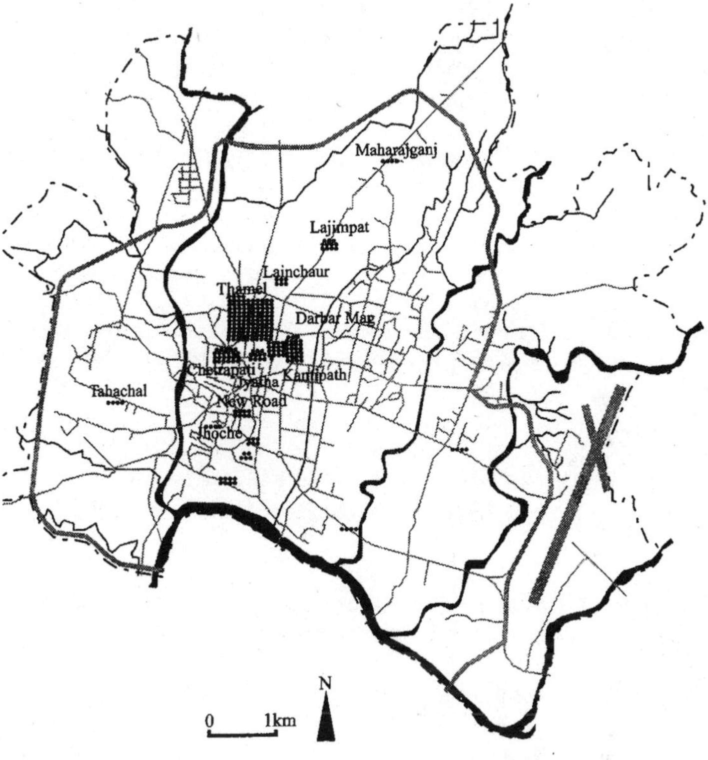

Sources: Nepal Business Yellow Pages 2000; Hotel Association Nepal 1998.

Figure 11.5: Distribution of Hotels in Kathmandu.

Thamel (in 2000) was only Rs.60 (about one US dollar). Hotels in Jhoche are also characterized by their low cost, both in the 1960s and 1970s and today. Even today the place has the image of hippy culture, as suggested by the signboard with the words 'Freak Street' in Darbar Square.

As noted earlier, the distribution of hotels in Kathmandu shows the spatial concentration. Darbar Marg, Kantipath, and Lazimpat are characterized by high quality and large scale. On the other hand, Thamel and Jhoche are budget tourist areas. Looking at it in the historical context, hotels have been located in Darbar Marg and Kantipath since the 1950s. In Jhoche cheap budget lodges began operation in the 1960s and 1970s. After the expansion of Thamel, many Jhoche 'flophouses' were closed and some were rebuilt as budget lodges or local residences.

In general, whether high quality or not, many accommodations are concentrated around Darbar Marg. The main reason is that, perhaps because of the proximity of the royal palace, it has the best concentration of infrastructure. Near Darbar Marg there was also vacant land in Thamel. These geographical advantages gave Thamel effective opportunities to develop tourism (Shrestha 1995). On the other hand, there was no room to develop in Jhoche which was already densely populated by Newars. The Bishnumati river which runs past the west of Jhoche prevented expansion in that direction (see Figure 11.3). In Thamel, by contrast, there were large vacant lots and old Rana palaces with fine gardens when mass tourism started in Nepal. Tourists staying in Thamel can avail themselves of all the facilities, such as international airline offices, banks, quality restaurants, and bars in Darbar Marg just a few minutes' walk away. Such geographical proximity to Darbar Marg gave Thamel a further key advantage in its development as a tourist area.

THE DEVELOPMENT OF A TOURIST AREA AND ENTREPRENEURSHIP IN THAMEL

This section examines how hotel entrepreneurs have been agents for the development of Thamel as a tourist area, or in other words, how local entrepreneurs have entered and adapted themselves to the global market.

The Regional Formation of a Tourist Area

Local people say that Thamel with its large vacant land, bamboo groves, and woods was haunted by supernaturals before tourists came. This story is sometimes told simultaneously with that of a brave man, Bhagwan Bal, who defeated demons and brought peace to Thamel (e.g. Lama 1998, 1999). Before the tourist boom, the area called Thamel was a small settlement north of the Kathmandu city area, around a Newar Buddhist monastery, Bhagwan Bahal, known as Than Bahi in Newari and honorifically called Vikramasila Mahavihara.[10] But now Thamel has expanded and the name refers to an area of approximately one square kilometre (see Figure 11.6).

Local place names such as Narshing Camp, Jyatha, Bhagwan Bahal, and so on, are included in the tourist area, Thamel. As the tourist area expanded, some nearby localities were absorbed into it. Thus it is not surprising that several places, which would not have been considered part

---

[10]See Locke (1985: 404-13). The word Thamel is a short form of the Newari term *thane bahil*. Thus Than Bahil means 'the large Buddhist temple in the upper Kathmandu city area' (Shrestha 1987: 50). This etymology suggests that Thamel, though outside the city, was attached to the northern half of it.

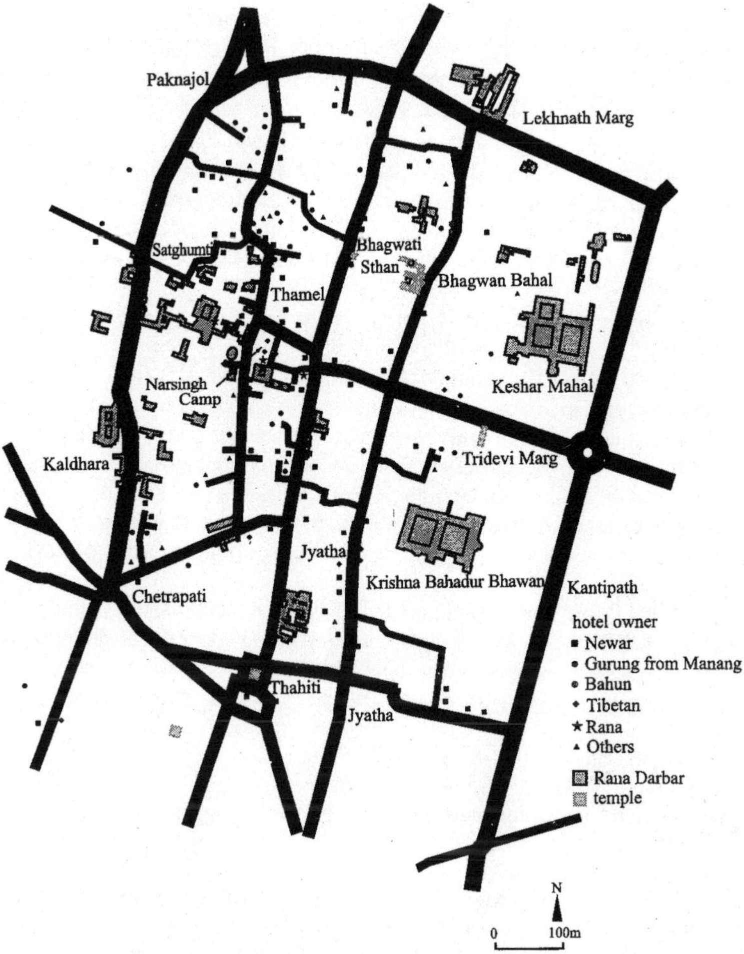

Source: Observation and interviews (1996-7).

Figure 11.6: Distribution of Hotels in Thamel.

of Thamel previously, have acquired more than one name as evident from the signboards of hotels and restaurants, such as Jyatha-Thamel and Chetrapati-Thamel. In Kantipath the first international hotel opened in the mid-twentieth century. There were some old hotels in Jyatha near Kantipath which opened before Thamel was developed as a tourist area. Today these old hotels give their addresses as Jyatha-Thamel. Thamel has been so successful that even Jyatha-Kantipath hotels feel the need to add '-Thamel' to their addresses instead of '-Kantipath'. And moreover, some of them give their address as 'Thamel-Kantipath', which suggests that their local identity is still Kantipath, distinguished from the new tourist area, Thamel.[11]

The prevalence of Newari words such as Thamel, Jyatha, Thanhiti, and Bhagwan Bahal, shows that Newars used to live there. On the other hand, the English names, for example, Narshing Camp and JP School, and many Rana palaces, prove that several Rana families also used to live in Thamel. As discussed earlier, the southern part of Thamel was densely populated by Newars who had been settled there for a very long time; however, its northern part was vacant and some Rana palaces were built there in the nineteenth and early twentieth centuries. In this sense Thamel may be said to have marked a border between the inner core and the outside of the city in those days.

In the 1960s local people started to buy the Rana palaces, which had beautiful chalk walls, though grown a little dirty, high ceilings, large rooms, and fine gardens with beautiful trees and fine fountains. Local people had imagined such old palaces as the residences of rich, modern, and upper-class people represented by the Ranas. Several local rich people living in neighbourhoods such as Asan bought Rana palaces as their new residence and moved to Thamel. Since the 1980s the price of real estate has risen exponentially in Kathmandu. Not only Newars living in Kathmandu, but also many people from outside Kathmandu bought land. There was still a considerable amount of vacant land in Thamel as mentioned above. Tibetans and Gurungs from Manang[12] started to buy land without specific plans for future use. As Spengen (1987: 242) remarks, when they bought land in Thamel, the price was not as high as it was to go in the 1990s. And then Gurungs from Manang tried to establish a more respectable presence in

[11]There is another example of old hotels in Thamel-Kantipath. This old and starred hotel, a part of which is in Thamel, faces Lekhnath Marg from which it obtains its address. It is surrounded by a high wall demarcating it from the budget tourist area of Thamel. This hotel marks a clear boundary between the budget and the quality tourist hotels, so I excluded it from my data collection in Thamel.

[12]They are popularly known as Manangis or Nishangtes but call themselves 'Gurungs from Manang' in Thamel. So I use the term 'Gurungs from Manang' as the name of their social group in this chapter.

Kathmandu by purchasing legitimate businesses – hotels, grocery shops, jewellery shops, and so on – in Thamel (Watkins 1996: 89).

Figure 11.6 shows the distribution of hotels in Thamel based on my intensive research from 1996 to 1997. There were 143 hotels in this area. Each mark indicates hotel owners' social category (*jat*), for example, a caste, an ethnic or a religious group.[13] There are many *jat*s such as Newars, Gurungs, Bahuns, Tibetans, and Ranas, to which hotel owners in Thamel belong. Figure 11.7 shows how these hotels have developed over the years. All the hotels that I could find during my survey from 1996 to 1997 are recorded in this figure. Rana palaces shown in Figure 11.6 are those I could find during my research. Some palaces have already collapsed and vanished or been merged into other buildings, and so may have been overlooked. There must have been more Rana palaces than indicated in Figure 11.6. Another fact to be pointed out is that quite a few hotels had closed by that time. When a hotel closes, however, new managers often come to rent the buildings from the owners and open a new hotel. In Figure 11.7, a black circle indicates a hotel operated by the owner and a white circle indicates a rental hotel. In a rental hotel, the managers have taken a lease for some years on the buildings and are running them as hotels.[14]

According to Figure 11.7, the first accommodation in Thamel, among those which still exist today, opened in 1968. The owner of this guest house, whose parents had previously bought a Rana palace, at first rented some of the unused rooms out when non-hippie tourists appeared in the neighbourhood. This was not unusual in the 1960s and 1970s. It is said that there were seven hotels in Thamel in the 1970s. Of these, four were run by owners of Rana palaces who used some spare rooms for tourists.[15] Since the old Rana palaces had more than enough rooms for their family use and they also had beautiful large gardens suited for hotels or restaurants, there was no need for a large investment nor any knowledge of hotel management to enter the hotel industry. The only thing they had to do was to keep the rooms clean and quiet, and to keep the hippies at a distance. At this time almost all the hotels and restaurants were near the oldest hotel, the Kathmandu Guest House, in Thamel. Some of the restaurants established in those days have expanded their businesses to run hotel or resort businesses today.

The oldest hotel in Thamel in Figure 11.7 started with only 13 rooms, had expanded to 120 rooms by 1997, and today is one of the largest hotels

---

[13] Nowadays the word *jati* is often used to mean an ethnic group in contrast with *jat* which denotes a 'caste'. But the people of Thamel usually use the word *jat* for both caste and ethnic group. So here I use *jat* as a category of social groups in Nepal in general.

[14] 'Hotel owner' here refers to a person who owns a building and property for accommodation whether he or she operates it as such or not.

[15] This information was based on my interviews in 1996-7.

year		
1968	●	120.0
1969		
1970		
1971		
1972		
1973		
1974	●	54.0
1975	○	26.0
1976	●●	34.5
1977		
1978		
1979		
1980		
1981	●○○○○○	38.6
1982	●●	23.5
1983	●○	42.0
1984	●●○	28.0
1985	●	18.0
1986	●●○○	29.3
1987	●●○	28.7
1988	●○	20.0
1989	●●●●○○○○	21.1
1990	●●●●●●●○○○	32.4
1991	●●●○○○○	21.9
1992	●●●●●●●●○○○○○○○○○○	20.4
1993	●●●●●○○○○○○○○○○	20.4
1994	●●●●●●●●●●●●●○○○○○○○○○○○○	21.6
1995	●●●●●●●●○○○○	25.8
1996	●●●●●●●●○○○○○○○○○○○○	20.8

Source: Interviews in 1996-7.

Notes: ● owner's hotel

○ rental hotel

* an average no. of rooms/hotel

Figure 11.7: Number of Hotels Opened in Thamel.

in Nepal. The owner's family established three other accommodations including a resort-type hotel, and the owner became a member of a decision-making organization for tourism development at the national level in 1997. As tourism developed in Nepal, this family acquired new knowledge and business opportunities, developed their entrepreneurship, and on the whole prospered. The reason why this family succeeded in the tourism business was not only that some members of the family went abroad to study tourism management, but also that they developed their entrepreneurship by accumulating experience at each stage of capitalism in modern Nepal. Another hotel owner operated for a while in Thamel, moved out, and opened a new standard hotel in another part of Kathmandu. Of course, there were also many entrepreneurs who were not so successful and had to close their hotels.

Thirty-one hotels established in the 1980s continued in operation until 1996-7, including fifteen rental hotels. Eight of the thirty-one owners came from outside Kathmandu. By contrast, during the beginning period (from the 1960s to the 1970s), four out of five hotel owners were Newars and all had lived in Kathmandu for a long time. In the next stage, mass tourism began and the social background of the entrepreneurs in the hotel industries diversified: not just Newars, but Gurungs from Manang, Bahuns, Ranas, Chetris, and others began to participate. To cope with the changes in tourism in Nepal, entrepreneurs had to invest in buildings and facilities for a new type of tourist in Thamel who demanded modern styles, not the dimly lit budget lodges where they hit their heads against low ceilings as in Jhoche. During this period, some entrepreneurs, including the Ranas, still transformed their residences into accommodations. However many entrepreneurs, such as Gurungs from Manang and Tibetans, had by then accumulated sufficient capital through other businesses, such as foreign trade in Asia and the carpet industry (Spengen 1987), to be able to invest their profits in real estate in Thamel. Some of them built new, specially designed hotel buildings. They were also able to develop the ideas they got through running their businesses and from experiences in foreign countries to establish and manage hotels in Nepal.

After the democratization of 1990, in just six years, from 1990 to 1996, 107 new hotels were established. Of the 107 hotel owners 42 were from outside Kathmandu. And in this period many local entrepreneurs started to make larger investments to improve the quality of their hotels in order to attract more tourists. As a result some hotels became famous for 'tourist standard', and not for backpackers-style cheap accommodation. As the number of tourists went up, many entrepreneurs who were looking for opportunities built and started hotels one after another.

According to my later survey in 2000, there were 179 hotels in Thamel, and of these, 19 were reopened and 42 were newly opened. Nine hotels closed in the previous three years. Based on my latest survey in 2004, there were 165 hotels, thirty of which were reopened and twenty were newly opened. Thirty-four hotels closed between 2000 and 2004. My observations after 1997 also indicate that the number of standard-type hotels had increased in Thamel, and several signboards written in Mandarin Chinese had appeared, anticipating the arrival of Chinese tourists in Nepal. I could also observe many reopened hotels in Thamel. For example, there were nineteen such hotels in 2000 and thirty in 2004. There are several reasons why hotels change their signboards so often: some hotel managers had to give up their hotels as a result of mismanagement in their other entrepreneurial activities, some moved their hotels into better buildings and facilities, while others tried to raise their rental fee when their clients renewed their contracts. Also, there were many rental hotels which made it easier for entrepreneurs to start or give up their rental hotel business. Thus the hotel industry in Thamel is characterized by its instability.

In the 1960s and 1970s it was possible to enter the hotel industry without any knowledge of hotel management. By the 1980s, however, tourists began to demand quality. Rooms had to be prepared for tourist use, and newly or rebuilt buildings with hotel facilities were required. As examined above, in the late 1980s, more international tourists came to Nepal as the Nepalese government encouraged the development of tourism as a basic industry. By then some entrepreneurs had accumulated wealth both from hotels and through other entrepreneurial activities and were able to invest in accordance with the demands of new tourists in Thamel. On the other hand, the old type of entrepreneurs continued to open their unused rooms for other tourists with only a little investment and knowledge of hotel management.

The Nepalese democratization brought economic liberalization to Nepalese society, and many people began to look for entrepreneurial opportunities. Tourism was one of the most rapidly growing industries. As the number of tourists increased, more business opportunities were created. But entrepreneurs also had to struggle for survival in competition with other entrepreneurs. Some invested to improve their facilities, such as private bathrooms equipped with 24-hour running hot and clean water, bright rooms with fluorescent tubes and telephones, and so on. Meanwhile, others kept their old-style accommodations with common bathrooms, cold and red water, and gloomy dormitories with 40-watt bulbs. An entrepreneur who owned an old-style hotel opened in 1982 told me why he had not invested in private bathrooms: the chronic shortages of water and electricity, even in the city area, meant that modern facilities would be meaningless.[16]

---

[16]As mentioned above, in the early days of tourism Thamel's infrastructure was relatively more developed. However, the shortage of facilities has become serious in Thamel today, because of overcrowding in the city generally.

If entrepreneurs in Thamel wanted to keep standard quality, they had to supply electricity and water constantly by using their own generators and wellwater, or by purchasing water from water wagons at their own expense. Many entrepreneurs who could not afford these facilities had no choice but to keep their facilities basic, as in the past, or worse than before because of overcrowding and environmental pollution. Many budget tourists still looked for these accommodations of the old type.

It is interesting to contrast Thamel with the tourist area of the city of Pokhara in mid-western Nepal. 'Damside' in Pokhara was developed by entrepreneurs mainly from two groups, the Thakalis from Tukuche, western Nepal, and the Gurungs, almost all of whom were ex-Gurkha soldiers (see Morimoto 1998). There were forty-five hotels in 1996. Of these eleven were owned by Thakalis and twenty-two by Gurungs. There are some differences in the development of Thamel and Damside. Thamel has attracted many entrepreneurs from all over the country and severe competition between them has brought definite improvement in the overall level of hotel accommodation. By contrast, the members of just two groups played the leading role in the formation of Damside and many of them ran their hotels using family labour and in their own family style. Even when the number of tourists declined, they kept their old signboards up even as the writing on them gradually wore away. They continue to live there even without any tourists, because many of them, though not all, had just offered the unused rooms in their own houses as accommodation. Thamel, on the other hand, provides unique opportunities for local hotel entrepreneurs to develop their skills and strategies through severe competition in the tourism market. At the same time, Thamel faces similar problems as Damside. The smaller entrepreneurs, such as restaurants, internet services, souvenir shops, and so on, have to survive on local custom as tourism declines year by year.

The Development of Entrepreneurship in Thamel

The formation of tourist areas has been encouraged by two agents: international tourists as well as local people especially engaged in tourism industries. As Liechty pointed out, tourist areas such as 'Freak Street' and Thamel are not simply 'tourist ghettos', if by these words we mean spaces only of, by, and for tourists, but rather translocalities, spaces in which a variety of Nepalis and a variety of foreigners interact playing roles (wittingly or otherwise) and where multiple imaginations of 'others' meet (Liechty 1996: 101). Thamel can have various meanings depending on situations. As examined above, tourism development in Thamel offers plenty of opportunities for the creative local entrepreneurs, large or small. Now I would like to examine how local entrepreneurs adjust their entrepreneurial activities to tourism development.

There were 143 hotel owners in Thamel in 1996-97, as shown in Tables 11.1 and 11.2. Thirty-eight owners came from outside the Kathmandu Valley. This included twenty-six owners who were Gurungs, of whom twenty-two were Gurungs from Manang, north-western Nepal. Kathmandu had a population of 675,341 in 1991 and the number of Gurungs was 18,488 or 2.7 per cent. On the other hand, out of 105 owners who came from Kathmandu 68 were Newars. The large number of Newar owners is not surprising, given that there were 258,280 Newars in Kathmandu in 1991, i.e. 38 per cent of the city's total population, and given that Kathmandu was originally a Newar city. There were also twelve Tibetan hotel owners who gave their home town as Kathmandu, though some of them were born in Tibet. Tibetans are also a minority group in Kathmandu just like the Gurungs. Compared to their proportion in the total population of Kathmandu, their numbers as hotel owners could be said to be very high. Why, then, have so many Gurungs from Manang and Tibetans built hotels in Thamel?

It is important to consider the sociocultural backgrounds of the local entrepreneurs. According to my interviews, almost all of the Newars come from the Kathmandu Valley and they had their own land near Thamel. As previously stated, Gurungs from Manang have prospered by trading with Asian cities such as Hong Kong, Singapore, Bangkok, and so on. They invested the funds accumulated by their international trade in real estate in Thamel before Thamel became famous as a tourist area in the 1980s. So they were able to buy land at a relatively cheap price. Tibetans also have bought land using funds accumulated from the carpet industry, which emerged as one of the Nepal's key export industries from the 1960s.

Table 11.1 shows that Newars born in Kathmandu were the largest group of hotel owners in Thamel, and Gurungs who came from Manang the

Table 11.1: Hometown of Hotel Owners by *Jat*s

Jat	in Kathmandu	other places
Bahun	12	2
Chetri	2	1
Gurung	1	25
Newar	68	2
Rana	5	0
Sherpa	1	2
Tamang	1	2
Tibetan*	12	0
Others	3	4
Total	105	38

Source: Fieldwork during 1996-7.
Note: *Some of them were born in Tibet.

Table 11.2: Number of Hotel Rooms by Owners in Thamel

Jat	No. of hotels	No. of rooms	Average
Bahun	14	234	16.7
Chetri	3	50	16.7
Gurung	26	737	28.3
Newar	70	1,669	23.8
Rana	5	63	12.6
Sherpa	3	116	38.7
Tamang	3	48	16.0
Tibetan	12	395	32.9
Others	7	247	35.3
Total	143	3,559	24.9

Source: Fieldwork during 1996-7.

second largest. Those whose home town is Kathmandu have a clear advantage in the hotel industry as hotel owners. Table 11.2 shows the number of hotel rooms according to the owners' *jat*. It can be seen that Sherpas built relatively larger hotels, which opened in the 1980s and 1990s, while Rana hotels had an average of only 12.6 rooms, because they were offering parts of their private houses as accommodation. There are obvious differences between social groups in their ways of carrying out entrepreneurial activities. It could be said that the reasons why Sherpas,[17] Tibetans, and Gurungs from Manang could build larger hotels than others were their experience as entrepreneurs and the capital accumulated from their involvement in the modern industries of Nepal. Furthermore, some of them made large amounts of money by smuggling gold, as well as, in some cases, trafficking in contraband.

Table 11.3 illustrates the circumstances of hotel management in Thamel. In Thamel as a whole, half of the hotels are operated by their own owners, and the other half by hotel managers who rent the buildings from owners on a contract basis. Bahuns and Chetris do not have so many of their own hotels and they tend to rent hotels from others to enter into the hotel industry. By contrast, Newars own seventy hotels, so that many entrepreneurs rent hotels from Newars. Leaving Newars out of the consideration, owners tend to let their hotels to managers from their own ethnic group. As for Gurungs from Manang, according to my research, entrepreneurs discuss what and how they would invest, and make decisions about a new business with their families and relatives. They then utilize their social networks to begin new enterprises. For example, sometimes they build hotels using their group-rotating credit system. By contrast, hotel manage

[17]Different from Tibetans and Gurungs from Manang, Sherpas have played an important role in mountaineering in the Himalayas since the 1920s, before Nepal opened her doors to foreigners. They can be said to be pioneers in tourism development in Nepal.

Table 11.3: Hotel Management in Thamel

Jat of hotel manager	No. of hotels									
	Hotel owners operating their own hotel	(%)	Hotel owners who let out their hotels as rental hotels							Total
			Newar	Gurung	Bahun	Chetri	Tibetan	Rana	Others	
Newar	34	(57.6)	17	1	2	0	3	1	1	59
Gurung	12	(60.0)	2	6	0	0	0	0	0	20
Bahun	5	(25.0)	7	2	4	0	1	0	1	20
Chetri	2	(20.0)	4	0	3	0	0	0	1	10
Tibetan	7	(87.5)	1	0	0	0	0	0	0	8
Rana	3	(100)	0	0	0	0	0	0	0	3
Others	7	(34.8)	5	5	0	1	1	1	3	23
Total	70	(54.4)	36	14	9	1	5	2	6	143

Source: Fieldwork during 1996-7.

ment by Ranas tends to be different from others. As suggested by Tables 11.2, 11.3, and 11.4, their hotels are relatively small and low in quality, in other words, budget lodges in the old style of Thamel. They have lived in Thamel for several generations, but do not seem to have social networks like the Gurungs, at least not such as can be mobilized for business. Because they happened to be in Thamel they opened their vacant rooms for tourists after observing others' success in the hotel business. In Nepalese society the Ranas are associated with political and economic power. The Ranas in Thamel today do not show any signs of developing entrepreneurship in the field of tourism. On the other hand, local people say that the successful Ranas who have lived in Thamel have already sold their properties at high prices to others and used the funds to buy land in newly developed areas elsewhere in the city.

The largest hotel in Thamel had 120 rooms and was operated by a Newar. The second largest had 100 rooms and was also run by a Newar; the third one had 95 and was run by a Marwari. We can say these three are exceptionally big as the fourth largest hotel had 62 rooms and many others much less. Table 11.2 shows the average number of rooms of the hotels in Thamel including the top three to be 24.9 (less than 35, or the average figure mentioned above based on the Nepal Business Yellow Pages). The difference in the quality of hotels in Thamel is illustrated in Table 11.4. Going by the average number of hotel rooms, Gurungs from Manang tend to operate larger hotels than others. Generally the average number of staff is roughly in accordance with the number of rooms. For example, Gurungs have the largest number of rooms and staff. On a rough calculation, Gurungs from Manang have one member of staff per room. By contrast, the Ranas have one member of staff per three rooms. Thus there are differences in the style of hotel management and in the quality of services provided to tourists.

When members of staff are broken down by gender, there is a clear division of services. Usually the hotels owned by Newars, Bahuns, Chetris, and Ranas restrict female staff to cleaning and doing the laundry. For example, the oldest hotel in Thamel employed ten female staff in 1997. Almost all of them were cleaning staff who wore a black and red sari uniform, like farming women from Bhaktapur. By contrast, in hotels run by Gurungs from Manang or by Tibetans, there were female receptionists at the front desk; and they also had female staff as waitresses in the restaurants. Although there is a division of work between men and women, there are not so many job opportunities for women in Thamel. A Newar entrepreneur who employs female hall staff in his restaurants told me that getting a job in Thamel was much more difficult for females than for males. According to his explanation, local people outside of Thamel recognized Thamel as a 'low-life' place, so if young girls work in Thamel, they might

Table 11.4: Hotel Rooms and Staff in Thamel

Jat of hotel manager	No. of hotels	No. of hotel rooms				No. of staff					
		Total	Average	The largest	The least	Male	Average	Female	Average	Total	Average
Newar	59	1,553	26.3	120	3	610	10.3	149	2.5	759	12.9
Bahun	20	359	18.0	28	10	158	7.9	45	2.3	203	10.2
Gurung	14	483	34.5	48	18	391	27.9	111	7.9	502	35.9
Chetri	10	191	19.1	32	10	73	7.3	17	1.7	90	9.0
Tibetan	8	238	29.8	25	2	100	12.5	32	4.0	132	16.5
Rana	3	34	11.3	15	9	8	2.7	3	1.0	11	3.7
Others	29	701	24.2	95	10	347	12.0	99	3.4	446	15.4
Total/average	143	3,559	24.2	51.9	7.7	1,687	11.8	456	3.2	2,143	15.0

Source: Fieldwork during 1996-7.
Note: *Gurung* call themselves Gurung from Manang.

be seen as prostitutes. Therefore, he told me, employers in Thamel tend not to hire females. Besides, I was also able to observe that it was not only the parents of 'good' young girls who prevented them from entering Thamel; 'Good' girls themselves tended to avoid even walking into Thamel. These images prevent many females from taking up tourist work in Thamel. At the same time, Thamel attracts many young Nepalis who want to interact with Westerners or experience what is called 'modern culture', i.e. dance restaurants and massage parlours.

Zivetz (1992: 190) pointed out that in Nepal economic innovation was considered deviant and, as a result, has been confined to minority or socially marginalized communities in Nepalese society. In this case study, two minority groups, Gurungs from Manang and Tibetans, were distinguishable from other social groups in that they came to invest heavily in the hotel and related industries to improve the quality of their hotels earlier than other groups, in accordance with global tourism development. On the other hand, some of the local people tended to consider their enterprises as part of their usual life and tried to cut costs to increase their saving or because of budgetary limitations. Some of them succeeded in developing their enterprises by competing with others for further development. On the whole, however, as Zivetz argued, it was easier for minority or socially marginalized communities in Kathmandu to enter into new industries and develop their entrepreneurship, or economic activities, in accordance with the change of global tourism. Some of the Gurungs from Manang and the Tibetans have continued their other businesses in which they were engaged before entering tourism, and look for more profitable economic opportunities. Some of the entrepreneurs in Thamel have started businesses in profitable new areas such as pashmina factories, trading companies, and manpower businesses. Thus, for them, hotel management is just one of their business outlets and one aspect of their entrepreneurship.

Thamel as a Translocality

For many Nepali people, the word 'tourist' signifies not simply a traveller, but a sort of person understood as a racial/caste/ethnic, and possibly, class category of person/species (Hepburn 2002: 613). We need to consider what 'tourists' means in the Nepalese social context. It can be said that the meaning of the 'tourist area', such as Thamel, might be different for international tourists and for the Nepali people. Even among the local Nepali people, it may mean different things. As mentioned above, Thamel has various reputations for both, such as a cheap accommodation area for tourists, as a business area for local entrepreneurs, or one of the most disreputable places for local people. To understand Thamel we need to examine the relationships between international tourists and local people, and also to examine the tensions between local entrepreneurs and local people in the context of Nepalese society. There are also tensions among entrepreneurs who have various sociocultural orientations according to their own social groups.

One of the business strategies can be found in the signboards on the streets. We can find some familiar names on the streets of Thamel, such as Imperial Hotel, Holiday Inn, and so on, though they have no business ties with the world-famous chains of hotels whose names they bear. It could be said that such names, familiar to international tourists, but not to Nepalis, were used as local entrepreneurs' strategies to attract foreigners. For example, Hotel California was named after the Eagles' song from the 1970s. The manager of this hotel had operated another hotel before, which he had called White Lotus, with its Buddhist associations. To take another example, the name of Hotel Horizon presumably derives from the famous novel about Shangri-La, *Lost Horizon*, written by James Hilton in the 1930s. In addition there are some shops named Shangri-La too. So what can be found in Thamel is not only Nepalese culture but also foreign cultures, or what could be called global culture.

Some entrepreneurs have employed Indian architects to design modern and luxury hotels, while others have designed their hotels to represent Tibetan, Buddhist, or Hindu images, and so on. According to my interviews with local entrepreneurs, these strategies of building designs and furnishings were not only to attract foreigners but also to represent their own identities.[18] In the 1980s and 1990s particularly, many hotel owners and managers set out both to represent their identities and to project certain images which foreigners expected to find in Nepal.

As for tourist images of Nepal, international tourists tend to recognize such landscapes as a homogenized Nepali culture, or Oriental culture, even though those landscapes reflect local entrepreneurs' own cultural identities as well as their business strategies. As Bishop (1989) shows, the image of Tibet as Shangri-La has been constructed through texts by Westerners from the eighteenth to the twentieth century. Moreover, it can be said that the Buddhist image of Kathmandu has been constituted through Western travellers, who encounter Tibetan exiles and frequently confuse Nepal and Tibet (Moran 2004). In Kathmandu there are many Tibetan monasteries which hold regular teachings for Western tourists. In these circumstances, when local Tibetan or Gurung from Manang entrepreneurs display their own cultures in the decor of their hotels, on the whole this meets with the expectations of Western tourists.

As for the local Nepalese sociocultural situation, it is important to mention the emergence of the Thamel Tourism Development Committee, a non-official body that was set up in 1989 by local entrepreneurs. This

---

[18]Tiwari (1994) also pointed out ethnic identities in the context of ethnic conflict in Thamel.

committee tries to maintain public order and hygiene, and organizes some events to stimulate tourism in Thamel. They have sometimes organized big events for tourists and local people engaged in tourism, such as food festivals, Christmas, and New Year events, and so on, in cooperation with local entrepreneurs. These events can be recognized as part of the landscape of translocality that embodies entrepreneurial strategies and cultural re-definitions of various social groups in Thamel.

CONCLUSION

In this paper I have examined how local entrepreneurs have created Thamel as a major tourist area in Ḳathmandu and, simultaneously, how they have participated in a process of involvement in the global market economy.

While Thamel has been created by global tourism, it can also be said that local entrepreneurs have significantly contributed to create a tourist area 'under the tourist gaze' (Urry 1990). Local entrepreneurs adopt the global capitalist cultures while at the same time displaying their own cultural and religious identities, both to other people in Nepal and to international tourists. I would like to suggest that these points are the important aspects of the process by which local entrepreneurs have experienced tourism as a part of globalization. On the one hand local entrepreneurs use their own networks oriented towards their caste or ethnicity, but on the other hand they are not averse to making strategic alliances with other groups when they think it appropriate.

Some tourism studies emphasize that ethnicity also acts as a powerful cohesive force that may help a group to maintain control over vital resources by excluding outsiders (Hitchcock 2000: 222). This chapter partly agrees with this viewpoint, as local people in Thamel made use of their sociocultural backgrounds to reduce business risks and to get more profit from their tourist- and hotel-related activities. On the other hand, however, many business relationships between people of different social groups can also be observed when they rent or lease hotels. The same was true when local entrepreneurs organized the Thamel Tourism Development Committee in order to develop Thamel for their mutual benefit. In doing so they were influenced by other businesses in Nepal, by international tourists oriented to the global market, and by the privatization that was being encouraged by national development planning in Nepal.

Zivetz (1992: 228) pointed out that industrialization has indeed chipped away at the historical monolith of Chetri-Brahman-Newar control over Nepal's economic resources and political life. This case study from Thamel may be said to illustrate in a small way the same process.

Tourism started only in the middle of the twentieth century in Nepal, and therefore there was no preordained position for it within traditional Nepalese social structure. There was room for various groups to enter the tourism business and to try new entrepreneurial activities. On the other hand, many Western tourists sought the image of Shangri-La in Nepal, or Tibetan wisdom, which is very far from the self-image of most Nepali people (Gellner 2003: 5). It may well be, then, that this transposition of the image of Tibet on to Nepal makes it easier for the Tibetans and Gurungs from Manang to enter the tourism business and cash in on their Buddhist identities, just as the success of the Sherpas as climbing companions and assistants depended in large part on their Buddhist background (Ortner 1999). In order to survive in severe competition, especially in the 1990s, local entrepreneurs have used their sociocultural backgrounds as a resource to develop their entrepreneurship. As a result of such entrepreneurial strategies, Thamel has become the place where the various cultural images of Nepal imagined by foreigners and represented by Nepalis themselves are displayed.

REFERENCES

Ateljevic, I. and S. Doorne. 2003. 'Unpacking the Local: A Cultural Analysis of Tourism Entrepreneurship in Murter, Croatia'. *Tourism Geographies* 5 (2): 123-50.

Bishop, P. 1989. *The Myth of Shangri-La Tibet, Travel Writing and the Western Creation of Sacred Landscape*. London: The Athlone Press.

Britton, S. 1982. 'The Political Economy of Tourism in the Third World'. *Annals of Tourism Research* 9: 331-58.

——. 1991. 'Tourism, Capital, and Place: Towards a Critical Geography of Tourism'. *Environment and Planning, D: Society and Space* 9: 451-78.

Christaller, W. 1963. 'Some Considerations of Tourism Location in Europe: The Peripheral Regions – Underdeveloped Countries – Recreation Areas'. *Regional Science Association Papers* 12: 95-105.

Dahles, H. 1999. 'Tourism and Small Entrepreneurs in Developing Countries: A Theoretical Perspective', in H. Dahles and K. Bras (eds.), *Tourism and Small Entrepreneurs: Development, National Policy and Entrepreneurial Culture: Indonesian Cases*, pp. 1-19. NY: Cognizant Communication Corporation.

Frank, G.A. 1969. *Latin America: Underdevelopment or Revolution.* NY: Monthly Review Press.

Gellner, D.N. 2003. 'Introduction: Transformations of the Nepalese State', in D.N. Gellner (ed.), *Resistance and the State: Nepalese Experiences*, pp. 1-30. Delhi: Social Science Press.

Hepburn, S. 2002. 'Touristic Forms of Life in Nepal'. *Annals of Tourism Research* 29 (3): 611-30.

Hitchcock, M. 2000. 'Ethnicity and Tourism Entrepreneurship in Java and Bali'. *Current Issues in Tourism* 3 (3): 204-25.

Hotel Association Nepal. 1998. *Tariff 1997-8*. Kathmandu: Hotel Association Nepal.

Ioannides, D. 1995. 'Strengthening the Ties Between Tourism and Economic Geography: A Theoretical Agenda'. *Professional Geographer* 47 (1): 49-60.

Karan, P.P. and H. Ishii (eds.). 1996. *Nepal: A Himalayan Kingdom in Transition*. Tokyo: United Nations University Press.

Lama, G. 1998. 'From Freak Street to Thamel a long Journey: Nepal Tourism'. *The Kathmandu Post (Sunday Post)*, 15 March.

——. 1999. 'How Hippies Discovered Nepal'. *Map of Greater Thamel September-December 1999*. Kathmandu: Thamel Tourism Development Committee.

Liechty, M. 1996. 'Kathmandu as Translocality: Multiple Places in a Nepali Space', in P. Yaeger (ed.), *The Geography of Identity*, pp. 99-130. Michigan: The University of Michigan Press.

——. 2001. 'Consumer Transgressions: Notes on the History of Restaurants and Prostitution in Kathmandu'. *Studies in Nepali History and Society* 6 (1): 57-101.

Locke, J.K. 1985. *Buddhist Monasteries of Nepal*. Kathmandu: Sahayogi.

Ministry of Tourism and Civil Aviation. 1985. *Nepal Tourism Statistics 1985*. Kathmandu: HMG

——. 1995. *Nepal Tourism Statistics 1995*. Kathmandu: HMG.

——. 1997. *Nepal Tourism Statistics 1997*. Kathmandu: HMG.

Ministry of Culture, Tourism and Civil Aviation. 1999. *Nepal Tourism Statistics 1999*. Kathmandu: HMG.

——. 2002. *Nepal Tourism Statistics 2002*, Kathmandu: HMG.

Moran, P. 2004. *Buddhism Observed: Western Travelers, Tibetan Exiles and the Culture of Dharma in Kathmandu*. London and NY: Routledge Curzon Taylor & Francis Group.

Morimoto, I. 1998. 'Nepal, Pokhara ni okeru Tourist Area no Keisei to Minzoku "Kigyoka" no Katsudo (Activities of Ethnic Entrepreneurs in the Formation of a Regional Tourist Area in Pokhara, Nepal)'. *Geographical Review of Japan* 71 (4): 272-93 (in Japanese).

——. 2001. 'Kokusai Tourism wo meguru Nepal Chiikizo (International Tourism and Geographical Images of Nepal)'. Doctoral thesis submitted to Ochanomizu University (in Japanese).

NPC. 1970. *Chautho Yojana (The Fourth National Plan)*. Kathmandu: HMG.

——. 1986. *Satau Yojana (The Seventh National Plan)*. Kathmandu: HMG.

——. 1992. *The Eighth National Plan*. Kathmandu: HMG (unofficial translation).

——. 1998. *The Ninth National Plan*. Kathmandu: HMG (unofficial translation).

——. 2003. *The Tenth National Plan*. Kathmandu: HMG (unofficial translation).

Nepal Business Yellow Pages. 2000.

Nepal Tourism Board. 2003. http://www.welcomenepal.com/ (official home page)

Ortner, S. 1999. *Life and Death on Mt. Everest: Sherpas and Himalayan Mountaineering*. Princeton: Princeton University Press.

Peissel, M. 1966. *Tiger for Breakfast: The Story of Boris of Kathmandu*. London: Hodder and Stoughton.

Sahit, B. 1991. 'Nepalko Pratham Janaganana 1910-1913 Janasankhyako Itihas tatha Bastika Bikas Sambandhi', in J.C. Regmi (ed.), *The First Census of Nepal 1853-1856*, pp. 1-106. Kathmandu: Office of Nepal Antiquary.

Shrestha, K.P. 1987. *Sthannam Kosh (A Dictionary of Place Names)*. Kathmandu: Nepal Rajkiya Pragya Pratisthan (Royal Nepal Academy).

Shrestha, P.M. 1995. *Regulating Growth: Kathmandu Valley Tourism* (Annex 9). Kathmandu: IUCN.

Spengen, W. van 1987. 'The Nyishangba of Manang: Geographical Perspectives on the Rise of a Nepalese Trading Community'. *Kailash* 13 (3/4): 131-277.

Theophile, E. 1995. 'Neoclassical Nepal: The Rana Palaces', in A. Proksch (ed.), *Images of a Century: The Changing Townscapes of the Kathmandu Valley*, pp. 108-25. Kathmandu: GTZ/UDLE.

Tiwari, A. 1994. 'Thamel Ethnic Card Between Tourism and Consumerism'. *Spotlight* 26 August: 16-21.

Urry, J. 1990. *The Tourist Gaze: Leisure and Travel in Contemporary Societies*. London: Sage.

Watkins, J.C. 1996. *Spirited Women: Gender, Religion, and Cultural Identity in the Nepal Himalaya*. New York: Columbia University Press.

Weaver, D.B. 1998. 'Peripheries of the Periphery Tourism in Tobago and Bermuda'. *Annals of Tourism Research* 25 (2): 292-313.

World Tourism Organization. 1998. *Tourism Economic Report*. Madrid: World Tourism Organization.

Zivetz, L. 1992. *Private Enterprise and the State in Modern Nepal*. Madras: Oxford University Press.

Zurick, D.N. 1992. 'Adventure Travel and Sustainable Tourism in the Peripheral Economy of Nepal'. *Annals of the Association of American Geographers* 82 (4): 608-28.

12

Re-examining Transnationalism from Below and Transnationalism from Above: British Gurkhas' Life Strategies and the Brigade of Gurkhas' Employment Policies

TAEKO UESUGI

INTRODUCTION

In any discussion about the variety of Nepalese culture and society, Gurkha soldiers occupy a unique position. They are not differentiated from other Nepalis either along ethnic/caste lines or by locality. It is their shared experience and memory of service in foreign armies or foreign police forces that differentiates Gurkhas from other Nepalis.

The Gurkhas' role in the development of Nepalese society and culture in the modern times is difficult to compare to that of other Nepalis. Gurkha employment has deprived Nepal of its young manpower, especially during two world wars. However, the Gurkha community has become a cradle nurturing pan-Nepalese identity, and at the same time played a role in bringing Western lifestyles and values to Nepalese society. Former studies on Gurkhas, therefore, have focused on the history of their employment, their representation in the colonial context and in Nepal, their identity, post-retirement life, and so on.[1]

On the other hand, for migration studies the employment of Gurkha soldiers provides a distinctive case study which is well worth close scrutiny

[1]See, for example, Caplan 1995; Des Chene 1991; Hutt 1993 (1989); Omissi 1998; and Uesugi 2000.

and cross-cultural comparison. In this chapter I examine a receiving state's commitment to the transnational ties of labour immigrants and the latter's commitment to state policies. I do this by analysing the post-war employment policies for Gurkha soldiers in the service for the British Army and how these have changed in the period covering the latter half of the 1990s up to 2003.[2]

Since the 1990s, migration studies in anthropology have developed within the framework of 'transnationalism', a term for the process or phenomenon whereby multiple ties or interactions are constructed and maintained across national boundaries by people or institutions. Discussions of transnationalism have tended to focus on "meso-level" (Faist 1997: 188) factors of international migration, migrants' transnational ties and network. Neither the macro nor the micro approach to migration studies has received enough attention.

In much of the literature transnationalism has been referred to as being caused by the grassroots activity of individual migrants or non-governmental institutions such as multinational corporations, NGOs, and so on (Basch et al. 1994; Ebuchi 2000: 303-4; Otani 2002: 134; Pries 2001: 3). On the other hand, states are also important actors in the process of transnationalism. As Basch et al. (1994) report, the Haitian government itself instigated transnational networks between overseas emigrants and the home country. Guarnizo and Smith (1998) suggest that one should distinguish transnationalism deriving from 'above' from transnationalism coming from 'below'. Following them, Portes and others have formulated the two types of transnationalism as "transnational activities initiated and conducted by powerful institutional actors, such as multinational corporations and states"

[2]Permission from the Brigade of Gurkhas made it possible for me to collect data in 1997/8, 2001, and 2003 and to write this paper. I would like to thank everybody concerned. Among them, special thanks go to Prof. L. Caplan of the School of Oriental and African studies, Asst. Prof. B.A. Hussainmiya and Dr H.Sato of the University of Brunei Darussalam, Dr D. Gellner of the University of Oxford, Mr Y. Imai and Ms Y. Nakamura of Japan Broadcasting Corporation, Mr P.K. Prasai of the Royal Nepalese Embassy in the United Kingdom, Gen. (retd.) Sir S. Cowan, Lt. Col. (retd.) A. Langlands of the Brigade of Gurkhas, Col. B.J. Hawgood of Gurkha Policy Headquarters, Mr G.J. Edgerley-Harris of the Gurkha Museum, Lt. Col. N. Rowe, Lt. Col. B. Rawat, Maj. G.M. O'Keefe, Maj. M.R. Little, Maj. P.C. Bullock, Maj. (QGO) B. Gurung, Maj. (QGO) K. Thapa, Maj. (QGO) N. Gurung and Sgt. B. Gurung of the 1RGR, Maj. (QGO) P. Thapa of the Headquarters The Brigade of Gurkhas, Lt. Col. D.J. Rowe, Lt. Col. I.N.A. Thomas, Lt. Col. I.A. Rigden, Maj. (QGO) L. Bantawa, Maj. (QGO) H. Rai, Capt. T.W. Pike, Capt. (QGO) T. Tamang, Sgt. G. Rai of 2RGR, Padre P. Wright of 2 Infantry Brigade, Gen. A. Mehta and Brig. C.B. Khanduri of the Indian Army, Pandit P.P. Gaire, Pandit A. Dahal, and Pandit S. C. Niraula, Mr P.G.C. Brown of Gurkha Children's English School, Mrs L. Dix and Mr R. Thapa of Hornbill School, Mr V. Khadka of BFBS, Mrs B.K. Gurung of Gurkha Kindergarten School, and Mr Y.B. Gurung of Gurkha Army Ex-servicemen's Organisation. It should be stressed that the views in this paper are the author's own and do not represent those of the British Army or the Ministry of Defence.

and "those that are the result of grassroots initiatives by immigrants and their home country counterparts" (Portes et al. 1999: 221). Further, they stressed the necessity of discussing the interaction between the two types of transnationalism (ibid.).

However, the role of migrant-receiving states in transnationalism has not been discussed much. Needless to say, past migration studies have paid enough attention to the receiving states' border controls, laws of citizenship, and other regulations as key factors determining the inflow of migrants. The formation and maintenance of migrants' transnational ties by receiving states, however, has been largely overlooked.

As Tilly pithily expressed it, "Networks migrate" (Tilly 1990: 84). Therefore, if a receiving state is to succeed in controlling the inflow of migrant workers, it is obliged not only to devise conventional immigration controls, but also to be involved in the formation and maintenance of migrants' transnational ties, networks, and social fields, i.e. migrants' transnationalism. The above-stated two types of transnationalism (Guarnizo & Smith 1998; Portes et al. 1999: 221) need to be examined with more focus on the role of a receiving state.

That is why I deal with the formation and implementation of employment policies in a specific context of contracted migration where the role of a receiving state is clearly discernible. In this chapter I describe and analyse the formation and implementation of post-war employment policies of the Brigade of Gurkhas and their change around the time of the Hong Kong handover. The policies clearly exemplify the receiving state's commitment to the migrants' transnationalism and show how a receiving state's transnational policies can articulate with migrants' life strategies. The term 'Gurkha' denotes Nepali men who are employed in foreign armies, police forces, or security companies.

This chapter is organized as follows. The first section describes the outline of the Gurkha employment and the policies of the Brigade of Gurkhas following the conclusion of the Tripartite Agreement (TPA) in 1947.[3] The second section deals with the Gurkha transnational networks and culture nurtured by overseas employment. The third section reports on the change in employment policies at the time of the handover of Hong Kong with a special focus on the Anglicization of Gurkha children's education in the camps. The fourth section explores the background to the change in the education policy, taking into account the changing politico-economic circumstances in Nepal. In the final section, I propose that the interaction between a receiving state and labour immigrants be incorporated in the discussion of the two types of transnationalism.

---

[3]For acronyms see 'Abbreviations' at the end of the volume.

TRANSNATIONAL EMPLOYMENT POLICIES

The History of Gurkha Employment

It was in 1815, in the midst of the Anglo-Nepalese War (1814-16), that Gurkha soldiers officially started to serve under the British Crown.[4] The first employer was the East India Company, later replaced by the Indian Army after the Mutiny, and then by the British Army and the Indian Army after the Independence of the Dominion of India.

The independence of India in 1947 brought about the full-fledged contract migration between the employers, the British Army and Indian Army, and the supplier of Gurkhas, Nepal. Since then Gurkha soldiers have been regular soldiers in the British Army. The Tripartite Agreement concluded in 1947 provides the basis for employment policies until today. It regulates the terms and conditions of Gurkha employment such as pegging the level of Gurkha pay to the pay code of the Indian Army, the ceiling of recruitment, facilities for providing Gurkha soldiers with Hindu pastoral care, and so on. In 1947 the Singapore Police also started to employ Gurkhas.

The Mission of Gurkha Soldiers in the British Army

Since 1815, the Gurkhas have guarded the security of British colonies and Commonwealth nations, and other overseas interests of the UK. They have fought on almost all the battlefields where the colonial Indian Army and British Army have been engaged, including the First and Second World Wars.[5] The post-War British Army assigned the Gurkhas the mission of defending Malaya and later Sabah and Sarawak until 1971, and thereafter the border control of the British colony of Hong Kong until 1997. In 1986, one Gurkha battalion took part in the campaign to recover the Falkland Islands. After the handover of Hong Kong, the headquarters of the Brigade of Gurkhas moved to the UK. At present (October 2003) Gurkha units are also deployed in Iraq, Afghanistan, Sierra Leone, the Falklands, and other countries.

Since 1962 one Gurkha battalion (about 800 men) has been stationed in Brunei. The British Gurkhas have served also in Canada as the training company of the Queen's Own Rifles of Canada since 1995.

Composition of the Brigade of Gurkhas

In 2003 about 3,500 Gurkha were employed by the British Army. The Brigade of Gurkhas consists of Royal Gurkha Rifles, corps units (Queen's

---

[4]On 24 April 1815, the Sirmoor Battalion was formed. The battalion, together with other regiments, was to be organized into the Second King Edward VII's Own Goorkhas and later into the First Battalion The Royal Gurkha Rifles (House of Commons 1989: x).

[5]The Gurkhas have never been deployed in Northern Ireland.

Own Gurkha Logistics Regiment, Queen's Gurkha Engineers, and Queen's Gurkha Signals), and other smaller units. The Royal Gurkha Rifles recruits boys of particular ethnic groups and castes (Gurung, Magar, Rai, Limbu, Tamang, Thakali, Ṣunwar, Thakuri, and Chetri) who have completed class eight in the Nepalese national education system. On the other hand, the corps units can recruit Nepali boys who have passed the School Leaving Certificate.[6] An applicant who wishes to be a Gurkha soldier must possess a Nepalese citizenship certificate issued by a district in Nepal. Nepali nationals living in a foreign country (e.g. India) can also apply. Since rural Nepalis regard service in the British Army as one of the most desirable overseas jobs, about a hundred applicants compete for each place. In 2003 the British Army planned to recruit 275 men.[7]

The System of Ranks

Gurkhas are promoted to the rank of officer through a career track different from that of British officers. Gurkha officers are of three kinds: Queen's Gurkha Officer (QGO), Gurkha Commissioned Officer (GCO), and Sandhurst-commissioned officer. QGOs are paid based on the pay code of the Indian Army and their status was inferior to that of British officers until 1995.[8] GCOs are equal with the British officers regarding status but they are paid based on the pay code of the Indian Army. Only Sandhurst-commissioned officers enjoy equal payment and status with their British counterparts.[9]

Every Gurkha starts his career from the rank of Rifleman, so Gurkhas are promoted to an officer's rank in their mid thirties at the earliest. The most senior rank achieved by a Gurkha officer is that of lieutenant colonel.

QGOs provide the majority of the officers in the Brigade of Gurkhas. In 1997, QGOs constituted about 92 per cent of all Gurkha officers in the Royal Gurkha Rifles.[10] Most of them are platoon commanders, troop commanders in the corps units, or the second-in-command of rifle companies (House of Commons 1989: xxxvi-xxxvii). They act as middlemen mediating between British officers and Gurkha servicemen.

---

[6] Clerks and technician recruits may come from *jats* other than those from which infantrymen are recruited (House of Commons 1989: xxvii). Those who seek recruitment as clerks and technicians normally apply in writing in response to advertisements (House of Commons 1989: xxxviii).

[7] *Kathmandu Post*. 2003. 'Maoists restrict boys from applying for British Army', 10 October.

[8] As described below the status of the three kinds of officer was equalized in 1995.

[9] However, they have to carry out their normal recruit training and thereafter serve a period with a unit before being selected for Sandhurst (House of Commons 1989: xxxvi). Therefore Gurkha Sandhurst-commissioned officers are older than their British counterparts.

[10] Source: The Brigade of Gurkhas 1997. In the same year, Sandhurst-commissioned officers provided about 4 per cent and GCOs 5 per cent of the total Gurkha Officers in the Royal Gurkha Rifles.

Double Allegiance

Since Gurkha soldiers are regular soldiers of the British Army, they swear allegiance to the Queen and her officials at the Attestation Parade (House of Commons 1989: xxviii-xxix). At the same time, they are allowed to be loyal to the King of Nepal. In 1947, FM Montgomery said to J. Nehru, "While the soldier (i.e. Gurkha) would obviously be under the discipline of the British Army, his primary allegiance would be to Nepal and nothing could or should be done which might come in the way of that allegiance" (Nehru 1947). In 1997 I found pictures of the then Nepal's King and Queen, Their Late Majesties King Birendra Bir Bikram Shah Dev and Queen Aishwarya, on the wall of the Sergeants' and Warrant Officers' Mess in Church Crookham, UK, where the Headquarters of the Brigade was located at that time.[11]

The Construction and Maintenance of Transnational Ties and Social Field from Above

While in the service in the British Army, Gurkha soldiers maintain economic and emotional ties with their families living in Nepal.[12] For sergeants and below, only one three-year-accompanied tour in fifteen years of service is permitted. An 'accompanied tour' means that their wives and children come to the camp to live with them. When their families are not living together with them in the camp, Gurkhas write letters, make phone calls, and send gifts and money to their families in Nepal. Therefore, it can be said that the employment policies of the Brigade of Gurkhas allow Gurkhas to build and maintain transnational ties with their families.

Reuniting Gurkha Identity with Nepal through Cultural Policies

The Brigade has had a cultural policy of symbolically reuniting Gurkhas with their country of origin, Nepal.

Firstly, the Brigade's religious policy focuses only on Hinduism, which is Nepal's national religion, although there are not a few Buddhists and followers of other religions. For example, of the 275 Gurkhas who enlisted in 2002, 144 declared that they were Hindus, 73 Buddhists, 54 Kiranti dharma followers, and 4 Christians.[13] The Brigade employs three Hindu religious teachers in a civilian capacity. The larger camps have their own Hindu temples. The religious teachers hold Hindu ceremonies every day, and each Sunday one Gurkha company takes its turn to attend the ceremony. Gurkha soldiers attend ten compulsory hours of classes on moral under-

---

[11]Even in 2002, one year after the massacre of Their Late Majesties, I found the same pictures on the wall of the Gurkha Children's English School in Tuker Lines, Brunei.

[12]Some Gurkha soldiers' families live in Sikkim, India.

[13]The data was given in a personal communication by Gen (retd.) Sir S. Cowan.

standing, given by a Hindu religious teacher, each year. The Brigade has formal holidays at the times of Hindu festivals such as Dasain and Tihar. The dates are determined by reference to the calendar sent by the Almanac Committee in Kathmandu so that synchronicity with Nepalese time can be maintained. Gurkhas are allowed to take leave of absence for Hindu family ceremonies. Beef is excluded from their meals. The Brigade explains that their religious policies aim to observe the article of Muluki Ain which prohibits inducements to religious conversion (Brigade of Gurkhas n.d.). The religious teachers also provide newly recruited British officers with lectures on Hindu culture and tradition. Gurkhas are represented as Hindus also to British officers.

Secondly, the use of the Nepali language is admitted in various spheres of regimental life. Although the language of command is English, the Nepali language (previously known as Gorkhali) has been used as the lingua franca of Gurkha soldiers of diverse ethnic backgrounds. *Parbate*, the magazine that was started in 1950 in Singapore as one of the measures to observe TPA, includes pages in Nepali (The Brigade of Gurkhas 2003a). The British Forces Broadcasting System (BFBS) broadcasts radio programmes in Nepali for fifteen hours a day. The Nepali programmes include Nepali songs, quizzes, question and answer sessions with Nepali MPs, and so on.

In the schools for Gurkha children in army camps after the Second World War, at least until 1998, the curriculum was based on Nepal's national curriculum and subjects were taught by Nepali teachers in Nepali.[14] The background to the introduction of the Nepalese style of education was the fear that without it Gurkha children would not adapt to Nepalese society on their return.[15] Even British officers are obliged to master spoken Nepali when they join the Brigade of Gurkhas. After completing a Nepali conversation course, they must go trekking in the Himalayas as a part of their training accompanied only by Nepali porters.

With the Nepali language and Hinduism at their core, the Brigade's cultural policies perpetuate symbolic ties between the Gurkhas and their mother country, and facilitate their reincorporation within their mother country.

---

[14]Unlike British Gurkhas, Gorkha children of the Indian Army have been educated in Hindi in camp schools (personal information from Prof. Ram B. Chhetri, Tribhuvan University).

[15]According to a document dating from the latter half of the 1950s, the British Army concluded at that time that the admission of Gurkha children to the British Army Children's School (BACS) was untenable for the following reasons: (a) BACS were heavily loaded with a commitment which cannot stand an increase without lowering their efficiency; (b) Gurkha children, like British children, need educating for life in their own country, which is not the UK; and (c) Gurkha children who receive Western education without its academic qualifications are only being trained as discontented unemployable expatriates (Public Record Office, WO16493). These seem to have been the reasons given for establishing a Nepalese style of education in the Gurkha camps.

Transnational Employment Policies and the Interest of the State

The personal transnational ties discussed above also provide Nepal's national economy with an important source of foreign exchange. Nepali servicemen working for foreign police forces or armies send money home to their families. Gurkhas end their term of service in Nepal and are supposed to stay there after retirement. Thereafter, foreign currency flows into the country in the shape of pensions. The British Ministry of Defence estimated the value to Nepal of British Gurkhas at about 30 million pounds sterling annually (House of Commons 1989: xxvi).[16] The *Kathmandu Post* reports that British Gurkhas bring home 56 million pounds sterling annually in the form of remittances and pensions (18 October 2003). Therefore, the Nepalese government has tried to continue this contracted labour migration, sometimes suppressing criticism on its employment policies.[17]

The transnational employment policies of the Gurkhas are not inconsistent either with Britain's national interests, at least in the financial sense. Through such policies the British Army can obtain quality workforce at low cost, controlling the inflow of the labour immigrants (i.e. Gurkhas) into the British Army according to its military demands at the same time.[18] For example, in its verdict of 21 February 2003, the London High Court ruled that Gurkha pensioners do not need equal pensions with their British counterparts for the reason that after retirement they are supposed to live in Nepal where the cost of living is much lower.[19] Their nationality justifies the Gurkhas' low pension.

The Involvement of the Nepalese Government in Gurkha Cultural Policies

Some official documents provide evidence that the Nepalese government has long been involved with the formation of cultural policies for the Gurkhas. In 1930 HMG Nepal proposed dispatching religious representatives to the Gurkha settlements in India, fearing that anti-Rana activists or Buddhist activists might undermine the Gurkhas' loyalty to the Nepalese government.[20] Furthermore, on the request of Nepalese government, the

---

[16]The year of this estimate is not made clear.

[17]For example, at a private meeting with British MPs, the delegates of the Nepalese Government to Downing Street criticized Mrs Blair who, as Cherie Booth QC, led the legal team for Gurkha veterans to secure equal pension with their British counterparts (*The Sunday Times*, 19 May 2002).

[18]The Defence Committee pointed out that a cost per man per year for the Gurkha battalion is 13,380 pounds sterling while that of the British battalion is 17,140 pounds sterling (House of Commons 1989: lxx).

[19]*Kathmandu Post* (Online edition), 23 February 2003.

[20]The proposal for the scheme emanated from a man called Bal Krishna Kasaju who submitted a memorandum to the then Nepalese Prime Minister. The then Chief Secretary

TPA of 1947 includes articles related with the Gurkhas' religious faith (Symon 1947):

1. The Gurkha troops should not be used against Hindus or any other unarmed mob.
2. The British government will assist in the observance of the religious susceptibilities of Gurkhas in the wearing of the *khukuri* in any stations to which Gurkhas may be posted.
3. All Gurkha officers and soldiers who serve in the British Forces Overseas will not be punished religiously.[21]
4. Priests are attached to units of the British Gurkha Regiment in a civilian capacity.

Policy Making from 'Below'

Despite what has been described so far, Gurkhas were never a silent target of these transnational employment policies. Although they are excluded from the table of discussion and negotiations between the two concerned states, the leaders of the Gurkha soldiers have also been involved in the process of forming employment policies of particular kinds. By the term 'Gurkha leader' I mean Gurkha officers, the Gurkha Majors (GMs) above all, and the religious teachers.

Gurkha Major

The Gurkha Major (GM) is selected from among the best of the senior Queen's Gurkha Officers. In 1997 there were eight GMs in the Brigade: one GM for each of two battalions of Royal Gurkha Rifles, one for each squadron of corps units (Queen's Own Gurkha Transport Regiment, Queen's Gurkha Engineers, and Queen's Gurkha Signals), one for Headquarters of the Brigade of Gurkhas, and two for British Gurkhas Nepal.[22]

---

to the Government of Bengal suggested the background for his manoeuvres as follows. Kasaju disliked the separatist tendency of the Hillman's Association in Darjeeling, which he saw as connected with the "All-India Budhist [*sic*] movement", led by a Nepali Buddhist, "Dr Dharmacharya", and the spread of Buddhist influence on Hinduism (Deputy Secretary, GOI, Foreign and Political Department 1930). See Maharjan (2007) on the activities of Dharmacharya and other Nepali Buddhists.

[21] This article is thought to have been added mainly at the request of the British Army. Hindus of Nepal were not allowed to go overseas. If they did so, they were considered to have lost their caste, and had to purify themselves and pay a fine to the ruler on their return (Banskota 1994: 149). Actually such a religious punishment was imposed on a retired Subedar-Major, Santbir Gurung, who returned from UK to Nepal (for the details of this incident, see Banskota 1994: 149; Farwell 1984: 44; Gould 1999: 173-5). Therefore, the article was necessary for the Gurkhas to be reincorporated into Nepalese society and for the British Army to secure the employment of Gurkhas.

[22] The Queen's Own Gurkha Transport Regiment was reorganized into the Queen's Own Gurkha Logistics Regiment in 2001.

For a British commanding officer a GM acts as a right-hand man and a "principal adviser on all specifically Gurkha affairs, including cultural, religious and family matters" (House of Commons 1989: xxxvii). He participates in decision making on Gurkhas' welfare as a member of the Gurkha Welfare Meeting in camps and a member of an annual meeting of commanding officers and GMs.[23] He can participate in everyday negotiations, such as giving permission for an accompanied tour, renaming the Dasain festival, raising the educational standards of children's schools, and so on.[24] In short, the GM is a middleman who mediates between the UK's state policies and the Gurkhas' lives, and between British officers and Gurkhas.

The Hindu Religious Teacher (Pandit)

As stated earlier, the Brigade employs three *pandits*, or Hindu religious teachers. They are civilians unlike their counterpart army chaplains, and are all Nepali men of Brahman caste. The required retirement age of a *pandit* is fifty, which means that religious teachers are employed longer than ordinary Gurkhas and retain influence on cultural matters for a longer period. All the religious teachers' fathers were also *pandits* of the British Gurkhas. The religious teacher of the Second Battalion of the Royal Gurkha Rifles is the fifth generation of his family to work as *pandit* for the Gurkhas. That is to say, their families have been involved with Gurkha religious life and have cumulated abundant knowledge on Gurkha community for generations.

The Defence Committee also states that the role of the *pandits* "is still of great importance in maintaining the Gurkha soldier's cultural identity" (House of Commons 1989: xxxii). They also familiarize newly recruited British officers with Hindu culture and tradition. It can be said that they act as a bridge between the Gurkhas and British officers. Further, the swearing of allegiance to the British Crown is presided over by a *pandit* at the Attestation Parade (House of Commons 1989: xxxii). *Pandits* not only maintain the Gurkhas' cultural identity as Hindus but also their loyalty to the British Army.

---

[23]In 2002 other members of the Gurkha Welfare Meeting in Tuker Lines, Brunei, included the second in command of 1RGR as the chairperson, the GM, the headteacher or deputy headteacher of the Gurkha Children's English School, a medical doctor or a midwife from the clinic in the camp, a representative of BFBS, and the supervisor of the Gurkha Kindergarten School.

[24]The annual meeting of Gurkha Majors in 1995 decided that the name of the festival should be changed from the Indian 'Dashera' to the Nepali name 'Dasain'. The background was the nationalistic feeling of Gurkha servicemen.

The Representation of Gurkha's Collective Identity by Gurkha Leaders in Dasain

In order to build an 'umbrella' Gurkha identity from various ranks and ethnic backgrounds, Gurkha leaders concentrate their men's multiple identities sometimes into a Nepali national identity and at other times into a Gurkha identity, which may be considered a pseudo-ethnic identity. The Dasain festival exemplifies such cultural politics by the Gurkha leaders, as will be described below.

The Dasain festival, a Gurkha version of festivals celebrated in the autumn in many regions of South Asia, is the most important official festival of the Brigade of Gurkhas. I attended the Dasain ceremony of the First Battalion of the Royal Gurkha Rifles (1RGR) in 1997 and that of the Second Battalion of the Royal Gurkha Rifles (2RGR) in 2003. The Gurkhas' Dasain is considered to re-enact two stories, the slaying of the demon Mahishasura by the goddess Durga and the battle between the exiled Prince, Ramchandra, and the King of Lanka. Special ceremonies are held for ten days, and Gurkhas get four days' holiday. Most of the expenditure for the festival is funded from the monthly donations of Gurkha servicemen to the President Regimental Institute. A GM is assigned to lead a Dasain Committee which is responsible for the successful organization of Dasain in each location.[25]

During Dasain GMs and *pandits* try to reinforce the national identity of Gurkhas. The GM of 1RGR explained that the purpose of Dasain was to maintain Nepalese culture. Also, the GM of 2RGR, showing me the draft of a Dasain speech he had delivered to his men, said, "I have to tell the soldiers what Nepalese culture is. Otherwise the younger generation will soon forget it."

A religious teacher also claimed in his speech delivered to the Gurkhas in Dasain:

> Even in a foreign country, we Nepalis defend the honour of Nepal and take pride in ourselves. We, who have grown up in Nepal full of beauty, will not forget our culture no matter what corner of this globe we live in. All wise persons cherish their own art and culture as invaluable riches.
>
> Nepali people have been known as Gorkha from old times all over the world. They have made temples and statues of gods both in war time and peace time if they had none of them. They have set a great value on their own traditions, cultures, customs, and norms. These have been our treasures. Among these 'treasures', there is a

[25] According to a personal communication from Gen. A. Mehta of the Indian Army, in the case of Gorkha regiments in the Indian Army, Dashera (the north Indian name for the Dasain festival) is held under the leadership of Indian and Gorkha officers.

> festival which demonstrates unity in our diverse family life. That is Dasain. We Nepali are diverse, but we are one in such matters as festivals, traditions, and life styles. Dasain does show this unity best of all.

During Dasain icons and items representing the nation and the national culture are used. For example, in 1997, it was requested that Gurkha servicemen of 1RGR wear *daura suruwal* and *topi* at some Dasain ceremonies; the cultural show commenced with the national anthem of the Kingdom of Nepal; and Nepalese and British national flags were printed on Dasain cards of 1RGR.

To put it briefly, during Dasain, Gurkhas are represented as nationals of the world's only Hindu kingdom. The Dasain festival is a cultural performance demonstrating the Gurkhas' umbrella identity and its desirable culture, the Hindu culture.

Such a representation of Gurkhas' collective identity is 'consumed' also by British officers as an ethnic attraction. During Dasain, British officers are invited to parties. They are treated to Nepalese cuisine together with Gurkha soldiers and their families. The climax of the Dasain festival is its cultural show held on the eighth day. The British officers and their wives are entertained with Nepalese ethnic dances and songs. The last programme in the cultural show is the Hall Dance on the stage. British officers, their wives, and Gurkha servicemen dance together till past midnight.

By representing their national culture in this most impressive way, at Dasain or on other occasions, the Gurkhas seem to succeed to some extent in demonstrating their coherence and their equality with their British counterparts, at least in the cultural sense.

As discussed in this section, Gurkha leaders themselves are involved with the formulation and endorsement of transnational employment policies. Especially through cultural policies based on Nepal's national culture, they have demonstrated who they are, reinforced the coherence of the Gurkhas, maintained their transnational position based in two nations, and reproduced the links between the Gurkhas and the British.

TRANSNATIONAL NETWORK AND CULTURE

Expansion of Gurkhas' Transnational Network

While the Brigade's transnational employment policies have promoted 'two-nation transnationalism', global employment opportunities and the deployment of Gurkhas around the world have continuously extended their transnational networks and unintentionally led to the emergence of a 'multi-nation transnationalism'.

Since 1900, when Gurkha servicemen of the British Indian Army were deployed across the 'black water' to China for the suppression of the Yi He Tuan rebels at the time of the Siege of the Legation in Peking, Gurkhas have continued to widen their theatre of operations around the globe. In addition, as stated above, their employer is not limited only to the British Army. Active soldiers are employed by the Indian Army, the Singapore Police, and they are also deployed in Brunei and Canada. Even after retirement they work for the Royal Brunei Armed Forces, private military companies, and other overseas employers. The fear of being outcasted, either by one's peers or by a strict Hindu regime, and the practice of *pani patiya* ritual (through which soldiers and traders going abroad were re-admitted to their caste on return to Nepal), which were serious concerns for Gurkha soldiers at the beginning of the twentieth century, are no longer a problem.

Such globally dispersed stationing of Gurkha soldiers has proliferated the transnational network of family and friends, which can be evidenced by the exchange of letters, electronic mail, gifts, Dasain cards, visits, and so on. For example, one Gurkha wife has five sisters and three brothers; of the five sisters, four are wives of British Gurkhas and the fifth is the wife of an Indian Gorkha. Of her three brothers one is an Indian Gorkha. During vacations Gurkha kin exchange visits across national boundaries. As a result, a transnational life strategy is deeply embedded in the Gurkha community. For example, they hold transnational families; and functions of a family, like child rearing, tend to be carried out by members of an extended family or relatives dispersed across national boundaries. In one case, a daughter of a Gurkha officer was being taken care of by his wife's sister whose husband is a retired Gurkha officer.

Sometimes radio programmes of the BFBS function as a kind of transnational noticeboard for Gurkhas. For example, a Gurkha wife sent a love letter for her husband stationed in Sierra Leone to a BFBS station in Brunei from Nepal. Her letter was broadcast in Brunei and the contents of the programme were sent to Sierra Leone through the Internet to be broadcast there again. In this way, her message was handed to her husband, and further, it was heard by her friends and many anonymous listeners. The programmes of the BFBS nurture a transnational community, encouraging its members to share a common language, common experiences, and common memories.

Transnational Military Culture

Therefore, the Gurkhas' so-called Nepalese culture is not just a replica or miniature of national culture lived in Nepal's soil. It is a culture constructed in a specific context of transnational military labour migration. Let me take Hindu ceremonies as another example of the reality of transnational military culture.

Hinduism as Duty Religion

The particularities of Hinduism, the national religion of Nepal, are revealed by the way it is practised in Gurkha camps. First, its military aspect is underlined. In his speech to the Combined Guest Party attended by the British High Commissioner, Brunei, a Gurkha Major said:

> Dasain, being a celebration of victory, has a special significance for the Gurkhas. At the same time, being a martial race, we have special devotion to pray to Durga Devi for provision of strength, courage, good will, and victory over the evil powers of the world. To the Gurkhas, the goddess Durga Devi plays a vital role in our lives. We pray to her for victory and protection against our enemies.

One Gurkha Other Rank, who had just come back from Iraq after a three-month mission in 2003, expressed his original interpretation of Dasain, which was, one may suppose, very different from the interpretation found in civilian Dasains in Nepal: "Why do we celebrate Dasain? Because the aim of Dasain is a fight for freedom." Considering that "fight for freedom" is one of the slogans of the leaders of the US-led allied forces in the Iraq war, he seemed to find that his mission in Iraq had something in common with that of Prince Ramchandra. He also found a common thread between the Dasain festival and a children's TV programme:

> The theme of Dasain resembles the story of the kids' TV drama, 'Five Rangers' (in English). As you know, in the drama, five rangers, called 'Red Ranger' and 'Blue Ranger' for example, are incorporated into the most powerful warrior. In the same way, also in Dasain, nine Durgas are incorporated into the most powerful being.

In sum, he used his experiences in the course of duty to construct an interpretation of Dasain with a focus on its military aspects.

Second, Hinduism is constructed also as duty religion of soldiers who serve in a foreign army. A religious teacher said:

> Our religion is Hindu and all our rituals and rites are conducted according to [the] Hindu way. In various occasions we perform our day-to-day practice and festivals in our own way with some special Nepalese cultural touch. My teaching and preaching to Gurkha soldiers are based on Hindu philosophy which always emphasize the Karma, I mean duty and service. Gurkhas are serving for another country. They are ready to die for other nations. Why are they ready to die for other nations? They are risking their life. Why? If they die they get money, but it is of no use to them. But Gurkhas are ready to die. What philosophy is working behind

> [them] to perform their duty? Our religion is teaching them that your duty is your religion. Duty always comes first. Soldiers must obey, be loyal, be brave, have courage, have discipline, and be ready to die. We are teaching our soldiers these things as religion. It is very important. Because they are religious people. They believe in gods. So that is why they follow our preaching. So religion is very important in regimental life. The regiment belongs to the British Army. But the people who work in it are Nepali citizens. How can we coordinate these communities? The co-ordinating force or mediator between the two communities is the Gurkha Hindu faith and tradition. That is why Hindu faith is very significant in regimental life. It works internally. You can't see openly but it works very internally and is inspiring.

The third aspect to Hinduism being as a duty religion is that it is sometimes distinguished from personal religion. Some Gurkhas regard Buddhism as their personal religion and Hinduism as a duty religion which surpasses personal religious faith in the workplace.[26] Although some Buddhist Gurkhas refrain from attending Hindu ceremonies, the distinction between a religion of duty and a personal religion sometimes mitigates the conflict which the Brigade's monolithic religious policies generate. One Buddhist Gurkha said:

> I am a Buddhist. Both my father and mother are more dedicated to Buddhism than me. Buddhism prohibits killing creatures. However, we kill goats and buffaloes here. I join the Dasain ceremony only because it is my duty. I am a Buddhist.

Since Hinduism is the duty religion of the Brigade, British officers, most of whom are Christians, also attend Dasain and play a vital role. The Commanding Officer of 2RGR rewards a decapitator for his distinguished service in animal sacrifice on the ninth day of Dasain by putting a white turban around his head in close cooperation with the GM. Other British officers also present money and whisky to the decapitator. After the *Mar* ceremony, British officers receive blessings from the religious teacher first, before the Gurkha officers.[27]

Hinduism, the national religion of Nepal, is reinvented as a religion of duty in the context of transnational military labour migration. Therefore, it

---

[26]While the Brigade officially implements only Hindu religious policies, religious pluralism is admitted in camp. Pettigrew and Tamu (2002) report that a Tamu (Gurung) soldier once worked as a shaman in a camp with the approval of the GM and British officers. The distinction between duty and personal religion should be examined in the light of this practical religious pluralism.

[27]The *Mar* ceremony is held on the ninth day of Dasain. In the camp in Brunei, goats, ducks, and a buffalo are sacrificed.

might be more appropriate to call the Nepalese national culture observed in Gurkha camps 'transnational-national culture'.

CHANGES IN CHILDREN'S EDUCATION AROUND THE TIME OF THE HONG KONG HANDOVER

The years since the 1990s have witnessed drastic changes in the circumstances of Gurkha employment, and Gurkhas overtly began to demand a policy change in accordance with their multi-nation-anchored transnational life strategy.

Improvement of Terms and Conditions Accompanying the Hong Kong Handover

Along with the end of the Cold War in the latter half of the 1980s and the handover of Hong Kong in 1997, the Brigade implemented a huge downsizing of the Brigade of Gurkhas. In 1994, prior to the handover, the number of Gurkhas were reduced from 8,000 to 3,400. Around that time the Brigade improved terms and conditions to mitigate the damage and shock which the downsizing might otherwise have caused. These policy changes include:

(1) Equalization of three officers' status, i.e. Sandhurst-commissioned officer, GCO, and QGO;
(2) Improvement of post-retirement job training;
(3) Equalizing the take-home pay of Gurkhas to that of British servicemen by adding overseas allowances to Gurkhas' salaries;
(4) Permission for accompanied tours of duty in the UK, Falklands Islands, and other postings;
(5) Anglicization of Gurkha children's education in camp;
(6) Grant of citizenship to Gurkha children who were born in Hong Kong before the handover (Subba 2004: 15).[28]

---

[28]The grant of Hong Kong citizenship opened for the concerned Gurkhas a path to emigrate abroad after retirement. The demands of the Gurkha Army Ex-Servicemen's Organization (GAESO), one of the Gurkha veterans' organizations, showed, that emigration abroad was one of the serious concerns for retired Gurkhas (GAESO 2001). Later, there were further developments. In 2003 it was reported that the (British) Defence Ministry, Home Office, and the Foreign and Commonwealth Office had started a review of immigration laws to grant Gurkhas the right to settle in the UK as 'special cases' (*Nepalnews.com* Arc828). Consequently, in 2004, former Gurkhas started to work as drivers for a bus company in West Wales (*The Times*, 16 June 2004). Furthermore, it was reported in 2004 that the UK government would act on the issue of providing British citizenship for retired Gurkhas soon (*Nepalnews.com*, 12 September 2004). It was on 29 September 2004 that Gurkhas finally were allowed to apply to settle in the UK and gain British citizenship (BBC News, 30 September

These policy changes, ranging from improvement of terms and conditions, change of policies on families, and assistance in post retirement life, have been evaluated to have made a deep impact on Gurkha life. How did these policy changes come into being and what was the background to the policy changes? In order to answer these queries I would like to focus especially on the Anglicization of Gurkha children's education in the camps, because it seems to reflect well the Gurkhas' life strategy and to affect their transnational national culture.

The Process of Anglicization of Children's Education

In 1998, accompanying the huge downsizing of the Brigade of Gurkhas, the schools established by the British Army exclusively for Gurkha children were abolished except for one elementary school in Brunei. At the request of Gurkha parents, the best teachers from the five abolished schools were selected and employed at the remaining school in Brunei. Further, the Service Children's Education, a defence agency, changed the name of the remaining school from 'Gurkha Children's School' to 'Gurkha Children's English School (GCES)'. The language of instruction was switched from Nepali to English, the Headteacher from a Nepali to a British civilian, and its curriculum from Nepal's national curriculum to the British national curriculum combined "with the best Nepalese practices" (Barton 2000).

The change in the education policy was explained as necessary to prepare Gurkha children for their future education (Barton 2000). What was their 'future education'? In 2002, the second British principal said that most Gurkha children go back to Nepal after their fathers' accompanied tours end. Therefore 'future education' meant the education they would receive after they went back to Nepal.

However, at that time (2002), further development was already under way. Since accompanied tours in the UK, the Falklands, and other camps have been permitted from 1997, more and more Gurkha pupils have begun to attend state-maintained schools in the UK or camp schools for British service children. As a result, it has become an urgent need to minimize the gap between children's education in the camps. One Gurkha officer remembers that from around the year 2000 Gurkha officers started to discuss the solution. He asserted, "We definitely need a good English school." Finally, the amalgamation of the two schools, GCES, and Seria Service Children's School (Seria SCS), the school in Brunei mainly for the British servicemen, was proposed in an annual meeting of Commanding Officers and GMs. Since the amalgamation was considered as being financially feasible, from late 2001 Brunei Garrison Headquarters started to

---

2004). Now it seems that the incorporation of Gurkhas into the British labour market and society in general will become the focus of Gurkha issues in the near future.

amalgamate the two schools and adopt the standard UK curriculum for all Gurkha pupils. It was in September 2003 that the amalgamation was realized and a new school, Hornbill School, was established.

The staff of the new school were selected from the two former schools. Both the Headteacher and Deputy Headteacher of the new school had filled these posts in the former Seria SCS and are British civilians; the Assistant Deputy Headteacher in the new school is a Nepali civilian and the former Deputy Headteacher of GCES. Every class is delivered in English and based on the British National Curriculum. For example, British history is taught with some references to historical events related to Brunei, Nepal, and other parts of the world (Hornbill School 2003: 16). Nepali language classes are taught by Nepali teachers and by a Hindu religious teacher as an extra-curricular subject.

Some Gurkha children who are going back to Nepal after the termination of an accompanied tour are taught separately in a class exclusively for Gurkha children. Others are educated in mixed classes with British children.

The aim of Hornbill School is "to prepare pupils for life in a multicultural society by developing an ethos and curriculum which reflects and values cultural diversity, recognizes and counters racial prejudice of all kinds and fosters racial understanding and harmony amongst all [*sic*] society" (Hornbill School 2003: 26). When I visited the Hornbill School in September 2003, a special Dasain assembly was going on with attendance of all pupils including British servicemen's children, all the teachers, and some parents.

Thus, in these five years, in a series of stages, the Nepalese national education for Gurkha children was integrated into the British multicultural education. This policy change was supported by many Gurkha parents as raising the educational standard and symbolizing the accomplishment of equalization in education for Gurkha children and that for British service children.

It should be noted that the Anglicization of Gurkha children's education was materialized by the initiative of Gurkha officers, the leaders of labour immigrants, and middle- or low-level administrators of employment policies.

THE TREND OF EMIGRATION IN NEPAL

In this section I explore the background to the Anglicization of Gurkha children's education in the camp introduced between 1998 and 2003; the socio-political circumstances in Nepal; and the mass trend of overseas labour emigration which accelerated in the 1990s. Year by year, Nepal's national domestic economy is becoming more and more dependent upon remittances from overseas labourers. The current political turmoil and the high rate of unemployment are some of the factors pushing people from remote villages to urban areas and from Nepal to foreign countries. According to one estimate, in 1998 there were 90,000 Nepali labourers in Gulf countries, 15,000 in West European countries, and 13,000 in East and Southeast Asia.[29] The 2001 Census reported that about 760,000 Nepali migrants lived in foreign countries.[30] An article in 2004 reported that approximately 1.2 million Nepalis lived in more than forty countries in the world and this number was increasing exponentially.[31] Another article in the same year reported that according to an official statistic of the Department of Labour and Employment Promotion, the total outflow of labourers in the period of the first nine months of the fiscal year (starting from mid July 2003) stood at 72,003.[32] As a result, the annual remittances from overseas Nepali workers were said to be around NRs.100 billion.[33]

Under such circumstances, the wealthier families tend to send their children to private schools which provide instruction in English and claim to offer a higher standard of education than the government public schools. The private schools affiliated with the Private and Boarding Schools' Organization of Nepal (PABSON), one of the private schools' organizations, number 8,500. About 30 per cent of Nepali pupils attend private schools and about 150,000 people work for the private schools.[34] Parents send their children to private schools hoping they will enter universities and get jobs on more advantageous terms and conditions in foreign countries, especially the Commonwealth countries. Currently, more and more educational institutions are offering the Ordinary (O Level) and Advanced level (A Level) courses, qualifications for higher education authorized by the University of Cambridge.[35]

Gurkha soldiers are among those wealthier Nepalis. One soldier who sent his two boys to a private school in Kathmandu said, "If we live in Nepal, we can get along with Nepali language. However, since our country is a small one, we cannot get jobs there. We have to search for jobs overseas and English is necessary in foreign countries." Although the future ambitions of Gurkha children may vary from being a soldier to a medical doctor or an athlete, Gurkha servicemen claim that their children need a good education for their future career. One retired Gurkha officer said,

---

[29]*Kathmandu Post*, 21 November 2002.

[30]CBS, n.d.

[31]*Kathmandu Post*, 10 October 2004.

[32]Ibid., 21 April 2004.

[33]Ibid., 21 April 2004. The year of this estimate is not shown.

[34]Ibid., 15 January 2003.

[35]Ibid., 28 May 2002.

"There are no Gurkha parents who send their children to public schools in Nepal." In order to pay the expensive tuition fees of private schools, they work overseas and send money to their families in Nepal, both while in service and even after retirement. Furthermore, the downsizing of the Brigade accompanying the Hong Kong handover created plenty of Gurkha veterans who are fathers of school-aged children and so had to earn money for their education. Thousands of retired Gurkha servicemen are working legally or illegally even in Japan.[36] One ex-serviceman, who sends his son to a private school in Nepal and is working in Tokyo, told me:

> I would like my son to enter university in an English-speaking country such as Canada or Australia. He would like to study Business Administration. After graduation, he can work for a local company. If he marries a local girl, he will be able to be a permanent resident there.

Therefore it is understandable that active Gurkha soldiers also want the Gurkha school in a camp to follow the system of education in Nepal. Such an orientation was realized in the change of children's education in a camp through the involvement of Gurkha officers who are leaders of the Gurkhas and middle- or low-level policy actors of employment policies. They succeeded in satisfying the educational needs of Gurkha children and their parents' ambitions, by means of the Anglicizing of camp education.

CONCLUSION

In the Brigade of Gurkhas, the transnational employment policies have been implemented. Firstly, the employment policies of the Brigade build and maintain transnational ties between Gurkhas and their families living in Nepal and reinforce the Gurkhas' sense of belonging to Nepal. Secondly, they secure the allegiance of Gurkha soldiers to the British Army, while retaining their allegiance to their mother country, Nepal, at the same time. Thirdly, they reunite Gurkhas symbolically to Nepal through cultural policies, which promote the faith of Hinduism, and the use of various national icons and items and the Nepali language at camp schools, in radio programmes of the military broadcast, and in the magazine of the Brigade. In the Gurkha schools in camps, especially, Nepali teachers taught Gurkha children in Nepali based on Nepal's national curriculum until 1997. These policies have been promoting a transnationalism from above that is anchored in two nations.

Such transnational employment policies have constructed a divide

---

[36]See Minami (2003) for Nepalese workers in Japan.

based on nationality in the British Army and a transnational-national Nepali community of soldiers whose culture and terms and conditions of employment are clearly distinguished from those of their British counterparts.

The Nepalese government has also been involved in the construction of the transnational employment policies through state-level discussion and negotiations. As Guarnizo and Smith have pointed out (1998: 7), many nation-states that have experienced substantial emigration are entering a process of actively promoting transnational reincorporation of migrants into their state-centred projects. This applies also in the case of Nepal and the Gurkhas.

However, what deserves attention here is that both a migrant-sending state (Nepal in this case) and a migrant-receiving state (the UK in this case) have committed to the incorporation of migrants (Gurkhas in this case) to the sending state in order to maximize their national interest. Migrants' allegiance to and transnational ties with their sending state (i.e. Nepal in this case), which were prime concerns in the discussion on transnationalism, have been constructed and maintained through policy making and implementation by the receiving state (i.e. the UK). The policies that the receiving state adopts in order to regulate immigration include not only border control, the law of citizenship, or treatment of asylum seekers, but also instigation of immigrants' transnationalism.

Furthermore, the policies have been constructed not only from 'above', i.e. by the two governments. Gurkha leaders are also involved in the formulation and implementation of some kinds of employment policies as middle- or low-level administrators. Through their administration they concentrate their men's multiple identity sometimes into Nepali national identity and at other times into Gurkha identity to make a collective identity out of various ranks and ethnic/caste backgrounds. The employment policies of the Brigade of Gurkhas show that transnationalism is a dynamic process influenced by interaction among multilevel actors, i.e. concerned "trans-territorial nation-states" (Guarnizo & Smith 1998: 8) and labour migrants.

On the other hand, the global expansion of Gurkha employment and deployments has continuously widened the reach of their destinations, which has had the inevitable consequence of nurturing their 'multi-nation-anchored transnationalism' and 'transnational national culture'. It should be noted that Nepalese culture as constructed and demonstrated in the Gurkha regimental life is constructed in the specific contexts of military labour migration, and is not just a replica of the culture 'lived' in their home country.

Therefore, it follows that a change in the situation around migration can lead to modification of transnationalism from below as well as restructuring of employment policies from above. Actually such a change is now going on in regard to the issue of Gurkha children's education in army camps.

The background to the change in Gurkha children's education can be found in the politico-economic circumstances in Nepal. The current political turmoil, the high rate of unemployment, and the resultant mass trend of emigration from Nepal have created a preference for instruction in English in Nepal among wealthier Nepalis. Rather, I would say that it is an overall restructuring of people's strategies for obtaining the most favourable kinds of "cultural capital" (Bourdieu 1979) in the age of globalization. Gurkha parents are among such Nepali parents. They did not miss the opportunity to have their life strategy reflected in the policy change at the time of Hong Kong handover and accomplished the Anglicization of their children's education in the camp (cf. Subba, this volume, on increased migration to Hong Kong from 1994). This change in educational policy exemplifies also the flexibility of Gurkha transnational national culture.

A migrant-receiving state evolves transnational employment policies and commits itself to working with the life strategies of labour migrants. Conversely, migrants themselves exercise their autonomy by strategically committing themselves to 'transnationalism from above'. They have to work with existing employment policies and strategize to have their requirements reflected in the policies from above. This chapter demonstrates, I hope, that by focusing on the process of formation and implementation of transnational employment policies for labour migrants, it is possible to analyse the dynamic interactions and negotiations involved in migrants' sense of belonging, transnational ties, and life strategies.

REFERENCES

Anderson, B. 1991 (1983). *Imagined Communities: Reflections on the Origin and Spread of Nationalism*. London: Verso Edition.

Banskota, P. 1994. *The Gurkha Connection: A History of the Gurkha Recruitment in the British Army*. Jaipur: Nirala Publications.

Barton, D. 2000. *Dear Parents* (The cover letter of the school prospectus). Seria: Gurkha Children's English School.

Basch, L., N.G. Schiller, and C.S. Blanc. 1994. *Nations Unbound: Transnational Projects, Postcolonial Predicaments and Deterritorialized Nation-States*. NY: Gordon & Breach.

BBC News, 29 September 2004. 'Gurkhas Win UK Citizenship Rights' (http://newsvote.bbc.co.uk/mpapps/pagetools/print/news.bbc.co.uk/2/hi/uk_news).

Bourdieu, P. 1979. *La Distinction: Critique Sociale du Jugement*. Paris: Editions de Minuit.

Brettell, C.B. 2000. 'Theorizing Migration in Anthropology', in C.B. Brettell and J.F. Hollifield (eds.), *Migration Theory: Talking across Disciplines*, pp. 97-135. NY: Routledge.

——. 2003. *Anthropology and Migration: Essays on Transnationalism, Ethnicity, and Identity*. Walnut Creek: Alta Mira Press.

Brettell, C.B. and J.F. Hollifield. 2000. 'Migration Theory: Talking across Disciplines', in C.B. Brettell and J.F. Hollifield (eds.), *Migration Theory: Talking across Disciplines*, pp. 1-26. NY: Routledge.

The Brigade of Gurkhas. 1997. *The Khukri – The Journal of the Brigade of Gurkhas* 49.

——. 2003a. *Parbate* (magazine of the Brigade of Gurkhas). (http://www.army.mod.uk/brigade_of_gurkhas/hqbg/parbate/index.htm).

——. 2003b. *Religious Festivals*. (http://www.army.mod.uk/brigade_of_gurkhas/religious_festivals/index.htm).

——. n.d. 'Religion, Religious Festivals and Holidays', Brigade of Gurkhas Standing Instruction 3 (67).

Caplan, L. 1970. *Land and Social Change in East Nepal: A Study of Hindu-Tribal Relations*. London: Routledge & Kegan Paul.

——. 1995. *Warrior Gentleman: "Gurkhas" in the Western Imagination*. Providence: Berghahn Books.

CBS n.d. 'Table 12: Population Absent from Household and Destination Abroad by Country of Destination and Sex for Regions and Districts'. *Population 2001*. Kathmandu: NPC Secretariat (http://www.cbs.gov.np/pop/html/tab12.htm).

Cohen, S.P. 1971. *The Indian Army: Its Contribution to the Development of a Nation*. Berkeley: University of California Press.

Collett, N. 1994. 'The British Gurkha Connection', in M. Hutt (ed.), *Nepal in the Nineties: Versions of the Past, Visions of the Future*, pp. 98-105. Delhi: Oxford University Press.

Deputy Secretary, GOI, Foreign and Political Department. 1930. 'Religious Representative Scheme' (sent for Comment by the Deputy Secretary, GOI, Foreign and Political Department to Chief Secretaries of Bengal, United Provinces, Bihar, and Orissa, and Assam), NO. F, 190-X/30.6 August 1930. L/P & S/12/3005, Coll. 21, IOLR.

Des Chene, M.K. 1991. 'Relics of Empire: A Cultural History of the Gurkhas, 1815-1987'. Ph.D. thesis, Stanford University. Ann Arbor: University of Michigan International.

——. 1993. 'Soldiers, Sovereignty and Silences: Gorkhas as Diplomatic Currency'. *South Asia Bulletin* 13 (1-2): 67-80.

——. 1999. 'Military Ethnology in British India'. *South Asia Research* 19 (2): 121-35.

Ebuchi, K. 2000. *Bunka-jinruigaku: Dento to Gendai* (*Cultural Anthropology: Tradition and Modernity*). Tokyo: Hosodaigaku Kyoiku Shinkokai (in Japanese).

Faist, T. 1997. 'The Crucial Meso-level', in T. Hammer, G. Brochmann, K. Tamas, and T. Faist (eds.), *International Migration, Immobility and Development: Multidisciplinary Perspectives*, pp. 187-217. Oxford: Berg.

Faist, T. 2002. *The Volume and Dynamics of International Migration and Transnational Social Spaces*. Oxford: Oxford University Press.

Farwell, B. 1984. *The Gurkhas*. London: Allen Lane.

GAESO (Gurkha Army Ex-Servicemen's Organisation). 2001. 'Plight of Gurkhas: Racial Discrimination and Human Rights Violations by the United Kingdom' (delivered at the 57th Session of the UN Commission for Human Rights). Geneva: Palais des Nations.

Glick Schiller, N. and G. Fouron. 1999. 'Transnational Lives and National Identities: The Identity Politics of Haitian Immigrants', in M.P. Smith and L.E. Guarnizo (eds.), *Transnationalism from Below*, pp. 130-61. New Brunswick: Transaction Publishers.

Gould, T. 1999. *Imperial Warriors: Britain and the Gurkhas*. London: Granta Books.

Guarnizo, L.E. and M.P. Smith. 1998. 'The Locations of Transnationalism', in M.P. Smith and L.E. Guarnizo (eds.), *Transnationalism from Below*, pp. 3-34. New Brunswick: Transaction Publishers.

Gurung, H. 1997. 'State and Society in Nepal', in D.N. Gellner, J. Pfaff-Czarnecka, and J. Whelpton (eds.), *Nationalism and Ethnicity in a Hindu Kingdom: The Politics of Culture in Contemporary Nepal*, pp. 495-532. Amsterdam: Harwood Academic Publishers.

Hornbill School. 2003. *Hornbill School Prospectus*. Seria, Brunei Darussalam: Hornbill School.

House of Commons, Defence Committee. 1989. *First Report: The Future of the Brigade of Gurkhas*. London: Her Majesty's Stationery Office.

Hutt, M. 1993 (1989). 'A Hero or Traitor?: The Gurkha Soldier in Nepali Literature', in D. Arnold and P. Robb (eds.), *Institutions and Ideologies* (SOAS Asia Reader), pp. 91-103. Richmond, Surrey: Curzon Press. (1st pub. in *South Asia Research* 9 (1) in 1989 and rpt. in *The Khukri – The Journal of the Brigade of Gurkhas* in 1991.)

——. 1997. 'Being Nepali without Nepal: Reflections on a South Asian Diaspora', in D.N. Gellner, J. Pfaff-Czarnecka. and J. Whelpton (eds.), *Nationalism and Ethnicity in a Hindu Kingdom: The Politics of Culture in Contemporary Nepal*, pp. 101-44. Amsterdam: Harwood Academic Publishers.

Iyotani, T. 2002. *Globalization towa Nanika: Ekijoka Suru Sekai wo Yomitoku* (*What is Globalization? Analyzing the Liquidization of the World*). Tokyo: Heibonsha (in Japanese).

Kathmandu Post (Online edition).
(http://www.nepalnews.com.np/contents/englishdaily/ktmpost/)

5 September 2001. 'Ex-Gurkhas to Sue British Officials Today'

28 May 2002. 'Young People Drawn towards O-A Level Studies'

8 August 2002. 'Ex-Gurkhas' Wives to Knock British Court's Door'

11 October 2002. 'Need for Paradigm Shift in Higher Education' by Nitya Nanda Timsina.

21 November 2002. 'Inward Remittance, Mainstay of Economy'

28 November 2002. 'Primary Curriculum to Include English'

28 November 2002. 'Ex-Gurkha PoWs Win Compensation'

4 December 2002. 'Govt to Protect Nepalis Working Abroad'

15 January 2003. 'Follow Code of Conduct in Toto: PABSON'

22 January 2003. 'Foreign Employment Boom Continues'

23 February 2003. 'GAESO Says Its Concerns Are Addressed'

1 March 2003. 'The World of Lahures'

14 March 2003. 'Sign 22-point Code of Conduct for Peace Talks'

30 March 2003. 'Maoist Dialogue Team Comes out in Open: Pledges Sincere Endeavour for Success of Peace Process'

12 May 2003. 'Maoists for End to Gorkha Recruitment'

28 August 2003. 'Gurkha High School'

10 October 2003. 'Maoists Restrict Boys from Applying for British Army'

18 October 2003. 'Gurkha Recruitment'

21 April 2004. '400,000 Nepalis Working Abroad: Rate of Workers' Outflow, however, Declines'

10 October 2004. 'NRN Movement: Current Status and Challenges Ahead'

Kennedy, P. and V. Roudometof. 2002. 'Transnationalism in a Global Age', in P. Kennedy and V. Roudometof (eds.), *Communities across Borders: New Immigrants and Transnational Cultures*, pp. 1-26. London: Routledge.

King Birendra Bir Bikram Shah Dev. 1997. 'Message from His Majesty King Birendra Bir Bikram Shah Dev to the "Brigade of Gurkhas" on the Occasion of Bijaya Dashami 2054 B.S., *Parbate* 49 (6): 1.

Maharjan, K.L. 2007. 'The Spread of Vihar Buddhism among Rural Newars in the Kathmandu Valley', in H. Ishii, D.N. Gellner, and K. Nawa (eds.), *Social Dynamics in Northern South Asia*, Vol. 2: *Political and Social Transformations in North India and Nepal*, pp. 193-238. Delhi: Manohar.

Mahler, S.J. 'Theoretical and Empirical Contributions toward a Research Agenda for Transnationalism', in M.P. Smith and L.E. Guarnizo (eds.), *Transnationalism from Below*, pp. 64-100. New Brunswick: Transaction Publishers.

Marcus, G. 1995. 'Ethnography in/of the World System: The Emergence of Multi-sited Ethnography'. *Annual Review of Anthropology* 24: 95-117.

Mason, P. 1974. *A Matter of Honour: An Account of the Indian Army, Its Officers & Men*. London: Jonathan Cape.

Minami, M. 2003. 'Zairyu-Nepal-jin-Rodosha no Ethnic Community to Network (Ethnic Community and Network of Nepali Labourers in Japan)', in H. Shoji and T. Mishima (eds.), *Kokusai-imin no Jizon-senryaku to Transnational-*

network no Bunka-jinruigaku-teki Kenkyu (*Cultural Anthropological Studies on International Migrants' Strategy for Survival and Transnational Network*). [Heisei 12–14 nendo kagaku kenkyuhi hojokin (kiban-kenkyu B[2]) Kenkyu-seika-hokokusho (study report: JSPS grants-in-aid for scientific research 2000-2)], pp. 85-108. Suita: Kokuritsu Minzokugaku Hakubutsukan (National Museum of Ethnology) (in Japanese).

Nehru, J. 1947. *Note on an Interview with FM Montgomery on the Employment of Gurkha Troops in the British Army and Other Important Matters*. 24 June 1947. L/WS/1/1025, pp. 3 (242)-12 (238).

Nepalnews.com (newsflash) (http://www.nepalnews.com.np/archive/)

7 August 2002. Arc 444. 'British Gurkhas Can Sue British Government'

15 August 2002. Arc 449. 'GAESO Files Case at London Court Seek Compensation for POWs'

16 September 2003. Arc 828. 'Gurkhas' Settlement in UK'

6 November 2003. Arc 897. '10,000 Pounds Payment to Ex-Gurkhas'

4 September 2004. 'British PM Raises Gurkhas' Hope for Citizenship'

Nishizawa, K. 1985. *Nepal no Rekishi: Tai-Indo-Kankei wo Chushin ni* (*Nepal's History: With a Special Focus upon Relationships with India*). Tokyo: Keiso-shobo (in Japanese).

Omissi, D. 1998 (1991). '"Martial Races": Ethnicity and Security in Colonial India, 1858-1939', in P. Karsten (ed.), *Recruiting, Drafting, and Enlisting: Two Sides of the Raising of Military Forces* (The Military and Society: A Collections of Essays 1), pp. 101-27. NY: Garland Publishing.

Otani, H. 2002. 'Transnationalism', in T. Ayabe (ed.), *Bunka-jinruigaku Saishin Jutsugo 100* (*The Newest 100 Technical Terms of Cultural Anthropology*), pp. 134-5. Tokyo: Kobundo (in Japanese).

Pettigrew, J. and Y. Tamu. 2002. 'Healing Here, There and In-between: A Tamu Shaman's Experience of International Landscapes', in P.A. Baker and G. Carr (eds.), *Practitioners, Practices and Patients: New Approaches to Medical Archaeology and Anthropology*. Oxford: Oxbow Books.

Pfaff-Czarnecka, J. 1997. 'Vestiges and Visions: Cultural Change in the Process of Nation-Building in Nepal', in D.N. Gellner, J. Pfaff-Czarnecka and J. Whelpton (eds.), *Nationalism and Ethnicity in a Hindu Kingdom: The Politics of Culture in Contemporary Nepal*, pp. 419-70. Amsterdam: Harwood Academic Publishers.

Portes, A., L.E. Guarnizo, and P. Landolt. 1999. 'The Study of Transnationalism: Pitfalls and Premise of an Emergent Research Field'. *Ethnic and Racial Studies* 22 (2): 217-37.

Poudel, K. 2001. 'Changing Order'. *Spotlight* (Online Edition) 21 (17), 9-15 November (http://www.nepalnews.com.np/contents/englishweekly/spotlight).

Pries, L. 2001. 'The Approach of Transnational Social Spaces: Responding to New Configurations of the Social and the Spatial', in L. Pries (ed.), *New Transnational Social Spaces: International Migration and Transnational Companies in the Early Twenty-first Century*, pp. 3-33. London: Routledge.

Public Record Office, WO16493. *Education of Gurkha Children: Policy.*

The Queen's Own Rifles of Canada. 1999. 'The Queen's Own Rifles of Canada: Gurkha Company' (http://www.qor.com/gurkha.html).

Sangraula, Y. 1999. 'Who Are Dying in Kargil?'. *Awake Weekly Chronicle* (Online Edition), 21 June 1999 (http://www.nepalnews.com.np/contents/englishweekly/awake/1-86/f-pagers.htm).

Sassen, S. 1996. *Losing Control? Sovereignty in an Age of Globalization.* NY: Columbia University Press.

——. 2001. 'Spatialities and Temporalities of the Global: Elements for a Theorization', in A. Appadurai (ed.), *Globalization*, pp. 260-78. Durham: Duke University Press.

Seria Service Children's School. 2002. *Seria S.C.S. Prospectus.* Seria, Brunei Darussalam: Seria Service Children's School.

Shogakkan, Random House Eiwa Daijiten Henshuiinkai (ed.). 1975 (1973). [personal-ban] *Shogakkan Random House Eiwa Daijiten (The Random House English-Japanese Dictionary).* Tokyo: Shogakkan.

Smith, E.D. 1997. *Valour: A History of the Gurkhas.* Staplehurst: Spellmount.

Subba, K. 2007. 'Drug Users in Dharan: Aspects of Marginalization', in this volume.

Symon, A.C.B. 1947. No title. (A letter to Lt. General His Highness Maharaja Sir Padma Shumshere Jung Bahadur Rana, G.C.S.I., G.B.E., K.C.I.E., Prime Minister and Supreme Commander-in-Chief of Nepal, 7 November 1947. Memorandum of Agreement, 9 November 1947.) IORL/WS/1/1206.

Takekawa, S. 2002. 'Globalization to Fukushi-kokka (Globalization and Welfare State)', in T. Kajita and M. Ogura (eds.), *Globalization to Shakai-hendo (Globalization and Social Change)*, pp. 121-50. Tokyo: Todai-shuppankai (in Japanese).

The Times. 16 June 2004. 'Former Gurkhas Surrender the High Ground for a Life on the Buses in Wales'.

Tilly, C. 1990. 'Transplanted Networks', in V. Yans-McLaughlin (ed.), *Immigration Reconsidered: History, Sociology, and Politics*, pp. 79-95. NY: Oxford University Press.

Uesugi, T. 1998. Preliminary Report 'Anthropological Study on Religion and Socio-cultural Networks among the Gurkha in the United Kingdom'. Typewritten manuscript submitted to the British Army and the School of Oriental and African Studies, University of London.

——. 2000. 'Eikoku-rikugun Gurkha-hei no Dasain: Gaikokujin-heishi no Guntai-bunka to Shudanteki-identity no Jiko-hyosho (Dashain of Gurkhas in the British Army: Foreign Soldiers' Military Culture and Self-Representation of Collective Identity)'. *Asia-Africa Gengo Bunka Kenkyu (Journal of Asian and African Studies)* 60: 113-58 (in Japanese).

——. 2001. 'Rhetoric and Ideology of the British Gurkhas' Cohesion: An Analysis of "Gurkha Dimension" and *Dashain* Festival'. *Ritsumeikan Journal of International Relations and Area Studies* 18: 83-113.

——. 2002. 'Eikoku-rikugun Gurkha-ryodan no Shukyo-seisaku: Genchijin-heishi to Futatsu no Kokka (Religious Policies of the Brigade of Gurkhas, the British Army: Native Soldiers and Two States)', in K. Yamaji and M. Tanaka (eds.), *Shokuminchi-shugi to Jinruigaku* (*Colonialism and Anthropology*), pp. 445-68. Nishinomiya: Kwansei-gakuin-daigaku Shuppankai (in Japanese).

——. 2003a. *Reproducing Gurkhaness: Children's Schooling and Hindu Religious Ceremonies in Brunei*. Typewritten manuscript submitted to the British Army.

——. 2003b. 'Gurkha Children's Schooling in Brunei'. *Gen-bun-ken* (*Studies for Modern Culture*) 79: 20-43, Tokyo: Senshu-daigaku Gendai-bunka-kenkyukai, Senshu Univ.

——. 2004. 'Transnational na Koyo-seisaku to Rodoimin no Seikatsu-senryaku: Hong Kong Henkan ni Tomonau Eikoku-rikugun Gurkha-ryodan no Koyo-seisaku no Henko (Transnational Employment Policies and Migrants' Strategy for Survival: The Change in the Employment Policy of the Brigade of Gurkhas, the British Army, around the Time of Hong Kong Handover)'. *Zinbun Gakuho* (*The Journal of Humanities*) 90: 169-214 (in Japanese).

Vertovec, S. 1999. 'Conceiving and Researching Transnationalism'. *Ethnic and Racial Studies* 22 (2): 447-62.

Yamanaka, K. 2000. 'Nepalese Labour Migration to Japan: From Global Warriors to Global Workers'. *Ethnic and Racial Studies* 23: 62-93.

13

'Bowling Together': Social Networks and Social Capital of a Nepali Migrant Community in Japan

KEIKO YAMANAKA

INTRODUCTION

On Sunday, 23 February 2003, in Tomita City[1] of Aichi Prefecture in central Japan, I participated as the chief guest in the Winter Bowling Championship 2003, sponsored by Tamu Dhi Nagoya (a branch of the Gurung Association). Fourteen teams of Nepali men residing in this region (referred to below as Tokai) occupied seven of the bowling alley's forty lanes, competing for the championship while their friends and families cheered from the gallery. Typically, members of an ethnic group such as Gurungs and Magars, or residents of cities such as neighbouring Hamamatsu and Shizuoka, formed teams. As they energetically bowled, the Nepalis exchanged good-natured jokes with one another about their scores and frequently shouted hurrahs for a member who made a 'strike'. Next to this congregation of about a hundred Nepali bowlers and spectators, and paying no attention to them, were many groups of Japanese families and friends enjoying their Sunday afternoon outing. Among them were four teams made up of middle-aged Japanese men and young, short-skirted

[1]This city name is a pseudonym, as are all personal names in this study. I wish to thank Gerald Berreman, my husband, for having introduced me to Nepal, offering his support throughout this research, and his editorial assistance on this paper. I am deeply indebted to many Nepali friends in Japan and Nepal without whose cooperation this study would have been impossible, but who must remain anonymous. I would also like to acknowledge helpful comments by the editors of this volume and by Keshav Maharjan and other participants in the 'Workshop on Social Dynamics in Northern South Asia' held in the Research Institute for Languages and Cultures of Asia and Africa, Tokyo, 25-7 June 2004, where this paper was originally presented.

Filipino women, competing among themselves. The Nepalis constituted just another group of happy players among the crowd of mixed nationalities who packed the bustling entertainment centre on that Sunday. Their nationality group was physically indistinguishable from the Japanese, but in the crucial legal respect of their visa status, they were sharply distinct. Most of the Nepalis were undocumented migrants who had overstayed their visas in order to remain as employees in small factories and construction sites scattered throughout the Tokai region.

In his 1995 article titled, 'Bowling Alone: America's Declining Social Capital', political scientist Robert Putnam (1995) discusses the importance of group interaction in leisure club activities and town meetings for maintaining healthy community ethos and promoting democratic governance. According to Putnam, dense networks of organized reciprocity and civic solidarity resulting from community interaction constitute a basis for developing grassroots democracy and effective governance among a citizenry. Drawing an analogy with notions of human capital as enhancing individual productivity, he defines "social capital" as "features of social organization such as networks, norms, and social trust that facilitate coordination and cooperation for mutual benefit" (Putnam 1995: 67). Citing Alexis de Tocqueville's remark in his *Democracy in America* (1969), Putnam observes that American society was once characterized by prolific social services. However, the rapid social change and new technologies that have occurred – especially since the 1960s – have fundamentally transformed American society into one dominated by isolating individualism. As a result, fraternal and philanthropic activities have sharply decreased. Instead of 'bowling together' with friends and colleagues, Americans today find themselves often 'bowling alone'. This suggests to Putnam that contemporary America faces a serious political crisis because it is losing many shared traditional grassroots institutions that have made the country strong and effective in pursuit of democratic governance.

By applying the notion of social capital to the Tokai Nepali community, the lively bowling scene described above sheds light on how it is that this migrant community of some 500 members mobilizes its 'networks, norms, and social trust' for collective goals. Elsewhere I have documented a series of community activities in which I took part from 1998 to 2000 among subgroups of this Nepali community (Yamanaka 2003a). They included formal events, such as the Annual Program (February 1998) and Dasain Festival (October 1998) sponsored by the Nepalese Welfare Society of Japan (Nepal Sewa Samiti), a Summer Bowling Championship organized by Tamu Dhi Nagoya (July 1999) and a Charity Nepalese Music Show by the Mount Everest Club (June 2000). In addition, there were informal gatherings such as the opening ceremony of a Nepalese food store (September 1998) and the wedding reception for a Nepali couple (February

1999). The list could be expanded if it were to include numerous small-scale meetings and gatherings that take place on Sunday afternoons in different locations for a variety of purposes.[2] Many of these activities are socially oriented, addressing issues of self-governance, social welfare, and national and ethnic identity that are important to 'guest workers' living and working abroad. This is a surprising and impressive achievement for an undocumented, therefore 'illegal', migrant community that suffers social isolation and is constantly under threat of deportation by the authorities.[3]

These vibrant and prolific activities by Tokai Nepalis contrast sharply with the paucity or absence of such social services among the more than 10,000 members of the Brazilian 'legal' migrant community in Hamamatsu City, Shizuoka Prefecture, which I have studied since 1994 (Yamanaka 1996, 2000b, 2003b). This is not to suggest, however, that Brazilians in Hamamatsu have not attempted to organize their community.[4] A few years after their arrival, many Brazilians began to turn to religion, hobbies, arts, and sports to enrich their lives that had theretofore been focused on saving money in order to return to Brazil as soon as possible. Since the early 1990s, there have been several organizations responding to specific interests in the Brazilian population, including the Catholic Church, Brazilian businesses, and Portuguese-speaking schools for children. Throughout the city there are small groups of Brazilians whose members pursue hobbies, arts, crafts, sports, etc. Yet, none of these organizations and their activities have addressed issues of self-governance, social welfare, or cultural preservation for the entire Brazilian community. Not one has evolved into a city-wide collective that would unite its members for achievement of their social and political goals.[5]

The striking contrast in goals, types, and ranges of community activi-

---

[2]In addition to these weekend activities, migrant groups mounted a donation campaign for ailing and injured compatriots, and contributed to homeland charities. In addition, a number of subgroups published magazines in Nepalese languages whose articles were written and edited by Nepali migrants.

[3]Minami (2003a) has also listed community organizations in Nepali communities in Tokyo and Tokai and discusses in detail his observations about their activities.

[4]In the mid 1990s, an attempt was made to establish a Brazilian organization unified by collective cultural activities. In his ethnography, *Brokered Homeland: Japanese Brazilian Migrants in Japan*, Roth (2002) describes a popular but short-lived Brazilian cultural centre launched in downtown Hamamatsu by a young Brazilian man. It failed primarily because of weak leadership and resulting financial difficulty. Since then there have been several attempts to establish a pan-Brazilian association in Hamamatsu, but none has garnered enough support to succeed.

[5]Elsewhere, I have described a small group in Hamamatsu, ALA Brasil, made up of fifty Brazilian families where activities are intended to assist their children enrolled in a public Japanese school (Yamanaka 2003b). This, however, is an exception to my observation of the scarcity of such community activism among Brazilians in the city.

ties observed in the two migrant communities in Tokai – Nepalis and Brazilians – suggests different modes, methods, and strategies of migrants in their social adaptation to the host society. The small undocumented Nepali community has developed a number of organizations to serve shared community needs and concerns, whereas the large documented Brazilian community has produced many groups intended to satisfy their individual interests.[6] In this chapter, I will pursue explanations for the pervasive community activism among Nepalis in Japan by focusing on migration systems, especially social networks and social capital, that are established in their community. Their migration and community building in a foreign country cannot be understood, however, without reference to the historical context of foreign military service among the ethnic minority groups from which the majority of Nepali migrants have been drawn, and the changing political climate in Nepal. Because an adequate understanding of their migratory process requires a fuller explanation of the changing social, economic, and political contexts in Japan, the receiving society, I will also discuss that country's growing civil society actions, especially the activities of pro-migrants groups that are relevant to the community activism of the immigrant Nepalis.

RESEARCH AND DATA

The data upon which this analysis is based was collected in Japan and Nepal between November 1994 and May 2004. During this decade, I conducted surveys, interviews, and observational studies on Nepali migrant workers in Hamamatsu, a city of half a million in western Shizuoka Prefecture, 257 km. south-west of Tokyo. Contiguous and to the west of Hamamatsu and its satellite cities lie Toyohashi, a city of 350,000 and its neighbouring cities in the eastern part of adjacent Aichi Prefecture. These cities host the headquarters of several major automobile and motorcycle companies, such as Suzuki, Yamaha, Honda, and Toyota, together with thousands of subcontractors that supply the parts assembled by the companies to become vehicles. Migrant workers, both documented and undocumented, find the Tokai area attractive because of chronic labour shortages there among small-scale employers.

In addition to these studies in Japan, between 1994 and 2000 I visited Kathmandu, Nepal's capital, and Pokhara, the country's fourth-largest city

---

[6]Muslim migrants from Bangladesh, Pakistan, and Iran, most of whom are undocumented, have built a mosque as the centre of their community throughout northern Kanto region (east of Tokyo) where they have settled (see Sakurai 2003). However, a comparison with their modes of social adaptation in Japan is beyond the scope of this study.

five times, for interviews with returnees from Japan. The survey and interview data thus collected in both countries include information about the migration experiences of 159 men and 30 women.[7] That data is supplemented by informal interviews with more than fifty informants who provided contextual information. The data reveals that the majority of Nepali migrant workers in Japan are from the Tibeto-Burman-language-speaking ethnic groups of Nepal's middle hills, nowadays known as Janajatis, such as Gurungs and Magars in the west, and Rais and Limbus in the east – the groups from which most British and Indian Army Gurkha soldiers have been drawn. Because these Nepali migrants, both men and women, often come from families that include former or current soldiers in the British or Indian Armies, they tend to be relatively well educated and familiar with foreign employment. Many have achieved the School Leaving Certificate (SLC – equivalent to completion of high school) which has allowed them to advance to post-secondary education. Prior to arriving in Japan, these men and women had engaged in a variety of occupations, including business in retail, tourism, or trade, or had been professionals or public servants, teachers or social workers, farmers, migrant workers, students, or ex-Gurkha soldiers.

MIGRANTS' SOCIAL NETWORKS AND SOCIAL CAPITAL

International labour migration is a response to differentials in labour and wages across national borders (Borjas 1990). The rapidly developing and integrating economy of Asia since the 1960s has resulted in growing economic disparity between a few rich countries (i.e. Japan, Singapore, Hong Kong, Taiwan, Korea, Malaysia, and Thailand) and their many poorer neighbours in East, South-East, and South Asia. The gross structural inequalities embedded in the global economy largely account for the rising waves of labour migration and the rapid emergence of integrated labour markets across national borders (Yamanaka 1999). The uneven distribution of material conditions in the region therefore explains how a migration flow begins. However, it fails to address why it moves from one selected country to another, for example, from India to Britain and from the Philippines to the United States. Nor does it address the question of how migration, once begun, is sustained over time while demands for labour at the destination points fluctuate widely.

Migration systems theory has evolved in response to these questions unanswered by economic theories of international labour migration. Operating at the intermediate level between individuals and social struc-

---

[7]For research methods employed in this study and findings from analysis of the Nepalese data, see Yamanaka (2000a, 2003a).

tures, a migration systems approach pays major attention to interactive processes and social institutions of migrants that link both ends of migration (Kritz & Zlotnik 1992; Massey et al. 1987). While driven by push-pull factors specific to a particular historical-structural context, such as colonial ties and military bases, the migrants actively mobilize social ties based on kinship and region to their advantage. A result is rapid development of extensive informal social networks that connect migrants (and their kinsmen and friends at origin) to others of shared origin at destination, and with one another once they reach their destination (Boyd 1989). The networks also enable migrants to transport social capital that is embedded in their social relations at origin to sister communities at the destination.

Sociological analyses of "social capital", defined by Portes (1998: 6) as "the ability of actors (migrants) to secure benefits by virtue of membership in social networks or other social structures" have focused on "relationships between actors, or between an individual actor and a group" (Portes 1998: 18). "To possess social capital, a person must be related to others, and it is those others, not himself, who are the actual sources of his or her advantage" (Portes 1998: 7). The internalized values of shared community enable members to identify give-and-take situations and oblige them to engage in the exchange of goods and services. By simply being part of the same social networks, migrants can thus accrue from other migrants of shared origin benefits such as employment information and assistance in obtaining housing and a job at destination. In exchange, the latter can expect the former to repay his social debts in the future. According to Portes (1998: 7-8), another source of social capital can be found in Marx's analysis of class consciousness among the industrial proletariat. Workers share a common fate based on their class and the resulting "bounded solidarity" which is the source of social capital that leads people of shared conditions to collective actions. Similarly, migrant workers develop bounded solidarity when they identify their ethnicity and class (and legal status in the case of undocumented workers) to be the source of their exploitation. In their struggles to improve their working and living conditions, migrants organize their limited resources to resist their employers and the state, which sets immigration policy. The enthusiastic, often altruistic, efforts of community leaders in these situations become collective resources for their members. The latter are able to appropriate the leaders' initiatives and actions for their collective interests. In return, the leaders receive community-wide recognition, status, and honour for their dedication and commitment to collective goals.

Examples of immigrants' social networks and social capital abound in international migration literature. At the turn of the twentieth century Japanese immigrants in Hawaii, the West Coast USA, and Brazil commonly organized mutual-help organization based on associational ties in their home prefecture (*Kenjinkai*). Surrounded by racial hostility and an unfamiliar culture, they bonded together to preserve Japanese culture and language, to support each other at times of death and birth, and to share recreation together on holidays and religious celebrations (Fujita & O'Brien 1991: 101). Since the 1980s sociologists have paid considerable attention to economic resources and opportunities embedded in immigrants' community ties. Lacking access to mainstream institutions, immigrants often mobilize their social capital in the forms of rotating credit associations, merchants' unions and industrial cooperatives. Examples are provided by the Chinese in New York (Zhou 1992), Cubans in Miami (Portes 1987), and Koreans in Los Angeles (Light & Bonacich 1988). In other examples, immigrants' associations aim to combat institutionalized economic and racial inequality in their employment and occupations. One such example is community-based labour unions organized by low-wage immigrant workers in the garment industry in San Francisco and New York. Comprising Chinese, Korean, and Mexican women, these organizations succeeded in the mid 1990s in achieving economic justice from exploitative companies by campaigning, demonstrations, and bargaining (Louie 2001).

In short, the twin concepts of social networks and social capital help to explain immigrants' initiative and solidarity that "are bounded by the limits of their community" (Portes 1998: 8). Although negative characteristics, such as exclusion of others and restrictive membership rules, are inherent in these homogeneous and closed social networks, the social capital available to members enables them to benefit from their collective resources, actions, and opportunities. The social dynamics built into immigrants' institutions help to explain why migratory flows, having once begun, continue regardless of fluctuations in labour demands, tightening governmental regulations, and hostile public attitudes towards the emergent migrant community. This is because family and community ties sustain the flow of migrants into the receiving country, while the growing ethnic economy absorbs incoming migrants as tractable and inexpensive employees.

POLICY, MARKET, AND ADAPTATION

In 1990, in response to a growing demand for unskilled workers and an increasing number of undocumented workers, Japan implemented an immigration policy that granted second and third generations of foreigners of Japanese ancestry (*Nikkeijin*), long-term residence visas for a stay of up to three years with unlimited access to the labour market. The same law defined unskilled labour by foreigners without Japanese ancestry as illegal.

The new law was intended to attract *Nikkeijin* as culturally familiar substitutes for what was perceived to be an alarming influx of foreign Asians, most of whom were unauthorized migrant workers from countries deemed culturally incompatible with Japanese (e.g. Bangladesh, Pakistan, and Iran). Spouses and children of *Nikkeijin* immigrants would also be permitted to stay, usually for up to one year. Renewal of visas in this category could easily (and therefore frequently) be done, as a result of which the *Nikkeijin* and their families could remain even longer than initially permitted.

Pulled by an explosive demand for labour in the manufacturing industries and pushed by economic and political instability in Latin America, more than 200,000 *Nikkeijin* from Brazil and substantially fewer from Peru arrived in Japan within the next five years. This large and sudden influx of unskilled migration occurred and continued throughout the 1990s despite the fact that since the early 1990s the Japanese economy entered a serious recession that forced many employers to lay off their *Nikkeijin* employees. In 2001, 266,000 Brazilians were registered as long-term residents, of whom 45 per cent were females and 15 per cent were children under fourteen years of age (Yamanaka 2003b). Most adult *Nikkeijin*, males and females, work as temporary labourers in automobile or electronics firms. Most are actually employed by labour brokers who in turn dispatch them to firms owned by small- to medium-sized subcontractors to large automakers or electronics companies (see below).

In his analysis of the rapid growth and sustained flow of the Japanese-Brazilian population in Japan, Higuchi (2002, 2003) discusses complex mechanisms of labour recruiting and brokering that link labourers in Brazil and employers in Japan across their national boundaries. Such mechanisms of intermediaries were developed in response to changing characteristics of demands for foreign labour during the prolonged economic recession from the mid to late 1990s. The automobile-motorcycle industry which the Hamamatsu-Toyohashi area hosts is marked by a well-defined division of labour comprising a pyramidal hierarchy of dependency between automakers, such as Toyota and Honda, and their numerous contractors and subcontractors. This relationship, often referred to as a "dual industrial structure" or "segmented labour market", is one in which automakers supply materials for the manufacture of parts to contractors who then, through a hierarchy of subcontractors, supply finished parts to the makers who assemble them into vehicles ready to be shipped to markets (Clark 1979: 64-73; Kondo 1990: 51-7).[8] Automakers and their higher level subcontractors are able to attract Japanese workers with higher wages,

---

[8]This subcontracting system entails a huge number of subcontractors. Ito (1993), for example, cites one major car manufacturer which is supplied by 47,308 subcontractors comprising three layers of contractorships.

more recent technologies, and better fringe benefits than lower level subcontractors can afford. As a result, shortages of Japanese labour have been concentrated among the latter. As a rule, the lower in the subcontractors' hierarchy, the smaller the firm size, the more severe are the labour shortages. Foreign workers are hired to counteract the shortages.

Labour brokers (*haken* or *assen gyosha*) and their networks across the Pacific play a critical role in the distribution of foreign workers by matching them with the subcontractors' labour demands regardless of their community or region of origin. In this process, migrants are uprooted from the social networks and sources of social capital in their places of origin, and are therefore required to build their social ties afresh among those whom they encounter at destination (Higuchi 2002). This recruiter-led "market-mediated" migration system (Higuchi 2002), combined with a discriminatory immigration policy, determines the ways in which foreign labour is incorporated into the segmented labour market according to legal status, ethnicity (or nationality), and gender.[9] It also shapes the ways in which migrant workers are incorporated into the host society.

In the early to mid 1990s, because of their legal status *Nikkeijin* Brazilian workers were assigned to firms of large- to medium-sized subcontractors with more than 100 employees. Without proper visas and Japanese ancestry, other workers, mostly from East, South-East, and South Asia, were placed in firms of small- to medium-sized subcontractors. In the late 1990s, however, when the economic recession deepened, labour demands for Brazilian workers dropped dramatically. The large- to medium-sized subcontractors who had formerly hired Brazilians no longer did so, relying instead on their Japanese labourers.[10] Small- to medium-sized firms, on the other hand, became more dependent than before on Brazilian-dispatched workers to meet large fluctuations in demand. In response, labour brokers have developed a system of "just-in-time (on demand labour) delivery" of Brazilians similar to the "just-in-time parts delivery" which is one of the core components of lean production that characterize the Japanese automobile industry (Higuchi & Tanno 2003: 40). Illegal workers were, as a result, replaced by the legal Brazilians and were forced to move to, or remain in, mini- to small-sized firms where wages and working conditions were the worst of all.

---

[9]In addition to legal status and ethnicity, gender makes a major difference in wages, working conditions, and fringe benefits. In fact, gender makes a larger difference in all of these benefits than do nationality or legal status (see Yamanaka 2003c).

[10]According to Higuchi and Tanno (2003: 38), facing the prolonged recession, the larger firms reorganized assembly lines to make production processes more efficient and revised working hours to attract Japanese workers. As a result, Japanese workers many of whom were female and aged, entered the labour force once occupied by foreign workers.

In the market-mediated migration systems by which workers are recruited in Brazil and matched with employers in Japan, Brazilians have been uprooted from their kinship and friendship networks in Brazil, which are the source of their social capital. Upon arrival in Japan, they and their families have faced the task of building their social ties afresh with the Brazilians they encountered in their neighbourhoods, workplaces, and other institutions, such as church, children's schools, and shopping centres. In the early to mid 1990s, when massive numbers of Brazilians migrated to Japan, labour brokers housed them in apartments they rented for them. This was because housing discrimination was rampant as a result of which foreign workers could not rent an apartment by themselves. This meant that when they lost a job, they lost their housing. This subletting system increased the broker-employers' control of their employees, including their geographical and occupational mobility and their private lives. Although most Brazilians had relatives and friends who had also migrated to Japan and kept close contact with them, their social networks were geographically widely scattered because they had depended on job brokers for their employment. This helps to explain, at least in the initial stages of Brazilian community building, the absence of organizations to serve the needs and interests of the entire Brazilian population.

Lacking brokers' assistance, Nepalis depended for migration heavily on social networks and social capital based on kinship and community ties. Higuchi (2002) calls this type of migration system "reciprocal". Once in Japan, they relied for employment and social adaptations on relatives and friends who had already settled in the country. A result has been the emergence of an ethnically and socially homogeneous Nepali migrant community, comprising mostly Janajati groups from western and eastern Nepal. Because of the close ties and inclusive social values among members (see the following section), the Tokai Nepali community has been able to generate firm solidarity away from home, and in the face of hostile immigration policies, despite the fact that it hosts many subgroups, each with a distinctive history, language, and customs. This does not mean, however, that the migrant community is free of personal conflicts and group frictions. Lacking resources and services available to citizens, an undocumented migrant community can be more burdened than other groups with interpersonal problems and inter-group tensions. Nonetheless, this relatively unnoticed Nepali community in Tokai has succeeded in constructing a community life which resembles that in which they would have participated had they remained in Nepal (Yamanaka 2003a). Such activities include religious celebrations, cultural performances, community association meetings, wedding receptions, and various types of sports and recreation.

NEPALI MIGRANTS' SOCIAL NETWORKS AND SOCIAL CAPITAL

According to the Japanese Bureau of Immigration Control (1996), in May 1996 there were 284,500 undocumented visa overstayers in Japan from all over the world, almost all of whom were illegally employed. The majority were from Asia, the highest number being 51,580 Koreans, followed by 41,997 Filipinos, 41,280 Thai, and 39,140 Chinese. The estimated 3,000 Nepali overstayers are therefore but a drop in the ocean, posing little threat to Japan's immigration control. It is significant, however, that despite its small numbers the population of Nepali overstayers grew rapidly in the ten years following 1986. Prior to 1989, the accumulated excess of entries over exits remained at less than 1,000, but by 1995 it had grown to 2,665, and by the year 2000 to 3,888 (Minami 2003a: 86). In the late 1980s Bangladeshis and Pakistanis entered Japan without difficulty because their home countries had exchanged mutual visa exemption agreements with Japan.[11] Unlike their two South Asian predecessors, the Nepalis have never enjoyed the privilege of visa-exempted free entry into Japan.

Throughout the world, undocumented migrants have relied heavily upon their informal social networks for safe entry and socio-economic adaptation in the new country (e.g. Massey et al. 1987; Menjívar 2000). In Malaysia and Thailand, for example, despite rigid immigration control by governments, national borders have been porous. This is not only because migrants can cross them offshore by small boats or overland on foot, but also because they share with the locals similar languages and religions. Unlike these South-East Asian countries, Japan is an island country to which migrants must arrive by air or the open sea and the nation does not share its language with others. Moreover, Japan's immigration policies are restrictive. Because of these three facts – Japan's geographic, cultural, and legal barriers – unskilled migrants without Japanese ancestry, including Nepalis, must employ multiple strategies that depend on migration brokers, social networks (e.g. relatives and friends already in Japan), and social capital (e.g. information, advance knowledge, and assistance for housing and employment upon arrival).[12]

The following analysis of Nepali systems for migration to Japan will begin with a description of the massive economic disparity between Japan and Nepal that pushes migrants from Nepal and pulls them to Japan. This economic inequality must be understood in the context of non-economic

---

[11]The Japanese government cancelled its visa exemption agreements with Bangladesh and Pakistan in January 1989.

[12]Nepali migrants also used agents operating underground in Nepal in order to obtain official documents (see Yamanaka 2000a: 78-80).

forces that have long linked the two countries, especially following Nepal's opening to the international community in the 1950s.

Economic Disparity and Non-Economic Ties

Japan and Nepal stand at opposite ends of the world economic continuum. Japan's 1995 GDP was 833 times as large as Nepal's and its per capita GDP was 143 times that of Nepal (Yamanaka 1999: 474). In 1993, Japan exported machinery and steel products worth US $67.8 million to Nepal. Nepal in return exported to Japan US $4.1 million worth of clothing, carpets, and craft goods. Japan was the top supplier of foreign aid to Nepal in 1994 at US $1,815 million. In the forty-two-year period, 1951-93, it also invested US $20 million directly into the Nepalese economy (Japanese Ministry of Foreign Affairs 1996). Japanese devoted their efforts to a wide range of economic and social development programmes including agriculture, forestry, water, electricity, roads, and bridges, health, and medicine, etc. (Hidaka 1967).

Cultural relationships between the two nations have been equally one-sided.[13] Japanese people have visited Nepal in significant numbers since the 1960s for mountain climbing and trekking in the Himalayas, and jungle tourism in the Tarai. In 1995, for example, 26,510 Japanese visited Nepal, while 2,686 Nepalis visited Japan (Japanese Ministry of Foreign Affairs 1996). The Japanese visitors were attracted to Nepal not only by tourism and fascination with Himalayan mountains and peoples, but by a growing concern with social and ecological issues of health, education, gender, religion, community development, and environmental preservation. By the 1990s, interested Japanese citizens had formed more than eighty grassroots, non-governmental organizations in Japan dedicated to such issues in Nepal. In addition, since the 1950s Japanese scholars have been active in research on the cultures and environments of the Himalayas. Their studies have provided voluminous information and knowledge critical to understanding Nepal's diverse ethnic communities, their social and economic systems, and changing ecological environments (Hidaka 1967; Ishii 2001).

Migration History and Communal Values

Nepal is made up of many ethnic groups each with its distinctive history, language, and religion (Berreman 1963; Bista 1996). The 1991 Nepalese national census lists sixty ethnic and caste groups within Nepal's 18.5 million population (CBS 1996). Despite this extraordinary ethnic heterogene-

[13]It should be noted that many Japanese feel an affinity with Nepal and Tibet as a result of the similarities of their Buddhism with Japanese Buddhism – especially the Shingon sect. This affinity is vividly suggested by Hidaka (1967) with the astounding map of all Japanese routes in Nepal during those sixty-seven years in the appendix. (See also 'Route Map of the Japanese Scientific Expedition for Nepal, 1958', in Kawakita 1960, Appendix.)

ity, the country's economic resources and political power have been historically monopolized by upper-caste, Nepali-speaking Hindu elites (Brahmans and Chetris), accounting for 29 per cent of Nepal's population.[14] As ethnic minorities lacking political clout in national politics, many Tibeto-Burman-language-speaking, multi-ethnic, multi-lingual, Buddhist/ 'animistic' groups have relied for 190 years on recruitment into the 'Gurkha Brigades' of the British and Indian Armies for economic survival (Cross 1985; Des Chene 1991, 1993; Pahari 1991; Caplan 1995; Uesugi, this volume). The four groups – Magar, Gurung, Rai, and Limbu – from which most Gurkha soldiers have been drawn, comprised 14 per cent of the total Nepali population in 1991.

For the past 190 years, the tradition of military service in the British and Indian Armies has provided families and communities of such Gurkha soldiers with a steady source of cash to supplement their subsistence economy based on terrace farming and cattle herding in precipitous Himalayan pastures. Soldiers' remittances and retirees' pensions were for many years sufficient to enable sending families to enjoy higher living standards than non-sending families (Hitchcock 1966; Pignède 1996; Caplan 1967; Macfarlane 1976). Throughout the Asia-Pacific region where most of these troops were stationed, the Gurkha tradition resulted in the construction of extensive information networks, often called "the Gurkha Connection" (e.g. Banskota 1994). The centre of these networks has been Hong Kong, once home to more than 10,000 Gurkhas and their families. Massive Gurkha recruitment ended, however, in the early 1990s when Britain drastically reduced its Gurkha Brigades in anticipation of Hong Kong's return to China in 1997. In 1991 there were slightly more than 7,400 Gurkhas serving in the British Army in Hong Kong and Brunei (Collett 1994), but after July 1997 British Gurkhas were reduced to 2,000 in London and 1,000 in Brunei.

At the individual level, during their fifteen or more years of military service in the British or Indian army, the young soldiers were exposed to foreign military organizations, regulations, and technologies (Uesugi 2001). Although limited to military expeditions and experiences within them, Nepali soldiers were also able to witness diverse cultures and ideas outside of Nepal. Upon retirement, ex-soldiers returned to their home villages, where they often exercise leadership in community politics and contribute to economic development (Hitchcock 1963, 1966; Höfer 1978; Des Chene 1991). Foreign military service has also resulted in the formation of many Gurkha mutual benefit organizations and associations in the areas of health, education, political activism, and other common interests.

---

[14]There are also disadvantaged Hindu 'untouchable' Dalits comprising 8.7 per cent of Nepal's population (e.g. Chhetri 1999: 58).

In studying the adaptation of ex-soldiers to urban living in Pokhara, Pettigrew (2000: 21) finds Doherty's (1975: 131-3) four organizing principles of Gurung society to be useful:

> *Generation*: primary identification with a generation, and with an age group within it. The direction given by this principle is lateral, towards group orientation.
>
> *Egalitarian-competitive*; there is stratification but it is modified through group participation; and through special arrangements, as for marriage, if it becomes unbalanced. Power and status are scarce and in demand, but they are shared.
>
> *Inclusion*: one's identity is importantly defined by membership in a group, and by participation with equals within this group.
>
> *Reciprocal-successional*: emphasis on the development of give-and-take situations and on the orderly succession to power. Prestations and counter-prestations are continually offered. Relationships between generations, and generational succession to power, have this pattern.

According to Doherty (1975), these communal values allowed Gurung businessmen to support each other in expanding their business ventures during the 1970s. Thirty years after his research, Pettigrew (2000: 22) found that the same values remained important among the Gurungs but that they were becoming less group-oriented. In Pettigrew's view, this was because retired ex-soldiers and their families had adjusted to urban environments where impersonal and individualistic attitudes were increasingly dominant. Such value erosion notwithstanding, these collective values of Gurkha groups highlight the consistency over time of the communal values that emphasize inclusion, reciprocity, and participation in community affairs.

Gurkha and Thakali Connections

Throughout the 1990s the recruitment of 'global warriors' was decreasing. However, their 'culture of emigration' continues today in Gurkha communities, producing massive numbers of 'global workers' in response to rising labour demands in East and South-East Asia and the Middle East (Yamanaka 2000a). In the late 1980s, Japan enjoyed an unprecedented period of economic growth which resulted in massive demand for an unskilled labour force to be employed in jobs shunned by Japanese. Nepali visitors and migrants to Japan before 1988 saw a golden opportunity for employment there, and sent the news to fellow Nepalis in Hong Kong and Nepal. In the mid to late 1980s, some members of the British Gurkha Brigades in Hong Kong visited Japan on their annual three-month vacation during which they worked to earn money. Other Nepalis, often members of Janajati groups, arrived in Japan as students, businessmen, professionals, or tourists, and many of them worked during their short stay.

My informants in Japan and Nepal have repeatedly recalled that a pioneer migrant to Japan was a Thakali man who came in the early 1980s in order to learn karate. According to Minami (2003a: 89), in the 1950s a number of Japanese anthropologists conducted field research in high Himalayan communities, studying their cultures and ecology (e.g. Kihara [ed.] 1957; Kawakita 1960). As a result, some of them established close relationships with Thakali communities in Thak Khola, a high valley in north-western Nepal, near the border with Tibet (e.g. Iijima 1961). For many generations, Thakalis and Manangis, among others, were active in trans-Himalayan trade, bartering salt from the Tibetan highlands for grain and other goods from Nepal's middle hills (Bista 1996). Over the years they have developed a tradition of keen entrepreneurship and have thereby accumulated considerable wealth. The Japanese research teams left a legacy among Thakalis by establishing networks of social ties and cultural exchange, that Minami (2003a: 89) calls the "Thakali Connection". Although comprising a small number, the connection was sufficient, by the 1970s, in its effect to bring a trickle of elite Thakalis to Japan. Some of them studied there and became medical doctors and prosperous entrepreneurs in Nepal. By the 1980s, this Thakali connection had encouraged a number of young, ambitious Thakali men to migrate to Japan for employment.

Upon their return to Hong Kong, Nepal, and elsewhere, these Janajati migrant workers reported to their relatives and friends Japan's extraordinarily high wages (at least by Nepalese standards), severe labour shortages, and relatively relaxed immigration controls. Among those who heard the good news were Newars, a Tibeto-Burman-speaking group indigenous to the Kathmandu Valley, and the two upper Hindu castes, Brahmans and Chetris. The three groups have long comprised a power-broker elite, historically monopolizing the country's economic resources and political power. The majority of them, however, are subsistence farmers who have faced increasing economic difficulties. They have also found migration to be attractive and have lost no time in going to Japan.

Migrants' Strategies

In 1990 the Japanese Embassy in Kathmandu tightened its visa issuance policy in response to immigration reform taking effect that year. Thereafter some visa applicants, in order to evade increased scrutiny at that embassy, travelled to countries where fewer questions would be asked. At that time, Germany did not require Nepali visitors to have visas for short stays, so many Nepalis flew there to apply for visas to Japan. Other such 'intermediary' countries included the UK, USA, Middle Eastern countries, Australia, Hong Kong, Korea, and other Asian countries. Analysis of my data indicates that more than 40 per cent (n=54) of Janajati respondents, compared to 24 per cent (n=14) of the Brahman, Chetri, Newar group respondents, obtained visas in such intermediary countries. In addition, 34 per cent (n=44) of Janajati respondents, compared to 22 per cent (n=13) of the Brahman, Chetri, Newar group, reported previous service in the British/ Indian Army, or employment in the Middle East, Asia-Pacific, Europe, or the United States. This data highlights the power of the Gurkha Connection which had grown out of the tradition of emigration and foreign employment among Janajatis, a main source of which had been British Gurkha service.

After a substantial population of Nepali men had arrived in Japan in the late 1980s, a trickle of women began to follow. A few had accompanied their husbands to Japan, but most arrived later as wives (sometimes sisters, cousins, and aunts) of earlier male arrivals. Having established employment and housing, the men were able to use savings to send for the women, often through channels provided by well-established professional or clandestine recruiters in Nepal. The analysis of my data suggests that by the mid 1990s a new cycle of immigration had begun, whereby relatives, not only non-working wives but also school and college graduate brothers of Nepali immigrants, were able to enter Japan. Women migrants usually work in factories side by side with their male relatives or in service establishments such as restaurants and laundry shops. By working abroad and remitting their savings to their families in Nepal, migrant women have broken the custom of being left behind at home to take care of the children and the old while tending crops and animals (cf. Aryal 1991).[15] The increasing presence of women in the Nepali community in Japan indicates that not only do some migrants enjoy the company of their family members, but some others have been able to establish a family in Japan with a newborn child.[16]

Workers with No Rights

For sojourning foreign workers, the ultimate goal of migration is to save a large sum of money and return home as soon as possible. Japan is a 'heaven' for achieving this goal, according to one Nepali immigrant. Its underground labour markets are, however, far from heavenly in their

[15] Literature on female migration to the US indicates that those who become employed experience enhanced status vis-à-vis their husbands as a result of their financial contribution to their households (e.g. Kibria 1993; Hondagnue-Sotelo 1994). This finding is worth examining in future studies of Nepali migrant women.

[16] Japan implements the principle of *jus sanguinis* (law of blood) in granting citizenship. A child born to foreign parents in Japan is therefore not entitled to Japanese citizenship.

treatment of illegal workers. The Japanese workplace is often ridden with labour exploitation and occupational hazards. Small-scale employers, lacking capital and credit, frequently neglect safety codes, postpone paying salaries for months, and sometimes go out of business without paying their employees. Illegal workers have no recourse but to seek a new employer. Verbal abuse and rude behaviour by employers are other forms of mistreatment commonly encountered. Many illegal workers also find the work they are assigned to be excessively demanding or the wages to be unacceptably low.

In addition to difficult working conditions, Nepali illegal workers suffer severe social invisibility and personal isolation. As day labourers, their lives are spent working in factories or construction sites for ten hours a day, six days a week. The limited time and clandestine nature of their presence in Japan prevent them from making friends outside the Nepali community. This remains true for the majority of Nepalis even after they have learned to speak and understand the language. Fear of apprehension by authorities is pervasive, inhibiting their participation in Japanese public activities. As illegitimate aliens, they are denied access to inexpensive health and medical care. This poses a serious threat to the many who perform hazardous jobs in workplaces that are often devoid of adequate safety measures. A relatively few Japanese, non-profit organizations, labour union activists, social workers, and medical personnel and other volunteers play critical roles in helping to overcome legal problems and in providing professional services in cases of labour exploitation, bureaucratic problems, and social and medical emergencies.

Democracy and the Ethnic Minority Movement

Following a short-lived attempt at democracy (1951-60), Nepal's authoritarian regime (called the Partyless Panchayat Democracy) for thirty years suppressed the needs and voices of the country's extraordinarily heterogeneous population. In April 1990, a massive popular political movement replaced the Panchayat system with a multiparty system (Khadka 1993; Brown 1996; Hoftun, Raeper, & Whelpton 1999). In November of the same year, the nation established a constitutional monarchy with sovereignty vested in its citizens. The new constitution guaranteed democratic principles, most notably freedom of speech, assembly, and religion.

The sudden 1990 establishment (restoration) of multiparty democracy inspired Nepali citizens in all walks of life – diverse ethnicities, religions, regions, languages, classes, and ideologies – to assert their rights, participating in national and local politics for the first time in thirty years. Long oppressed ethnic minorities also established political parties and organizations in order to promote their collective interests and cultural identities

(Hangen 1999; Hoftun, Raeper, & Whelpton 1999: 320-30).[17] It was in the context of these volatile moments in Nepalese history and the rapid social change of the late 1980s and early 1990s, that many young, relatively well-educated Nepali men departed for Japan. Upon arrival, they found themselves surrounded by an unfamiliar culture and a hostile immigration policy that defined them as illegal workers and visa overstayers.

Self-Help Organizations

Although it is difficult to determine how such profound political transformations in Nepal influenced the political views of migrants in Japan, they were clearly aware of the arrival of democratic society in Nepal. An essay published by Dipak Man Tamang, a Nepali immigrant working in Tokyo, in *Vimarsha*, a popular weekly Kathmandu magazine, indicates his view of why Nepali citizens had to seek overseas employment.[18] In it he described the plight of an undocumented worker in Asia's wealthiest country, and went on to criticize Nepal's political leaders:

> My address has changed again. This is the fifth time that my address has been changed. My next address would probably be in my country. The reasons for frequent change in my addresses are many. I quit the first two jobs because of low salary scale. I had to work eleven hours a day and would get a wage of 800 yen (US $7.21) per hour, which was far from satisfactory.[19] Retrenchment in factories where I worked also made me switch jobs occasionally. Now the situation has deteriorated to such an extent that many Nepali friends are prepared to work for just 500 yen (US $4.50) per hour. The economic glitter of Japan now seems to be bursting like water bubbles. ...
>
> Had the rulers, feudal lords, and dictators who ruled our country in the past, been honest enough to have some sense of nationalism, we would not have had to lead a wretched life now. How sad, they all turned blind eyes to the social, educational and economic uplifting of the people. As a result, today our people are condemned to work 16 to 17 hours a day in faraway places. It is the primary responsibility of the government to create an atmosphere whereby all Nepalis, without any discrimination, may contribute to the task of nation building. Unfortunately, it was not the case in the past and the present does not seem very different either.

---

[17]The ethnic groups commonly identified as Mongols are also and interchangeably identified as Janajatis (which itself is glossed as equivalent to *adivasi* or indigenous).

[18]The essay was published on 27 July 1993. The author himself translated the essay for me, from Nepali to English.

[19]In 1993 the exchange rate was 111 yen per US dollar.

In Tokyo in the early 1990s, Tamang, though a lawyer by training, was employed as a factory worker, facing many problems arising from his foreign and illegal status. With his friends he organized the Nepalese Help Organization (Nepali Sahayog Sangh).[20] The aim of the organization was to establish mutual help among the estimated 700-900 Nepali migrant workers in Japan at that time. By telephone and word of mouth, they contacted every Nepali they could, announcing the formation of the organization. In response, some 200 Nepalis attended meetings held every Sunday afternoon in Yoyogi Park, Tokyo.[21] Members wrote the organization's constitution stipulating its structure, staffing, finance, and activities. They elected a President and ten Executive Committee members to administer the organization. Tamang served as President for the first three years. Given the frequent injuries and illnesses among Nepali workers, the organization often had to call for donations to provide medical treatment for those in need. Later, Tamang moved to Hamamatsu where he organized a similar mutual help association.

When Tamang returned to Nepal in 1993, his colleagues in Hamamatsu and its vicinity continued his legacy by creating the Nepalese Welfare Society of Japan (Nepal Sewa Samiti) in 1995. An important characteristic of this organization was its policy of including all Nepali migrants in the area, regardless of ethnic and caste background. A Sewa Samiti leader of Newar ancestry, in conversations with me in the late 1990s, repeated the organization's emphasis on the importance of an all-Nepali association: "We are all Nepali here (in Japan), not Newars, Gurungs, or Thakalis. In the past some groups created rules so that they could pass job information only to their ethnic members. Those who violated the rule were fined. This was very bad. Instead of exclusion, we should help each other because we all have no visas."[22]

Two years after Sewa Samiti's successful launching, those who were concerned about the preservation of Nepalese culture established the Himalayan Club. In the same year, those who were interested in sports created the Mount Everest Club. Members of these two associations were drawn from both Janajati and non-Janajati groups, many of whom were members of the Sewa Samiti. The three associations often cooperated with each other in organizing programmes. For example, in February 1998, members of the Himalayan Club performed plays, songs, and dances at the Sewa Samiti's Annual Programme, while in June 2000, leaders of the Sewa Samiti gave opening speeches for a music concert organized by the Everest

[20] Interview with Dipak Man Tamang, 12 January 1997, Kathmandu. I am indebted to Minami (2003a: 105) for the Nepali name of the organization.

[21] The park was later closed by the Tokyo metropolitan government because on weekends it attracted a large congregation of foreign workers of diverse nationalities.

[22] Interview, 23 January 1998 in Tomita City.

Club. Although the impact of the 1990 Democracy Movement on these organizations' call for a socially integrated Nepal is unclear, the principle was clearly appealing to the 200-400 Tokai Nepalis who attended their events.[23] To the dismay of many Nepali members, however, the pan-ethnic Sewa Samiti ended in 1999 when it discontinued many of its activities. According to Minami (2003a: 90), divisions along ethnic lines became intense during the 1999 election for the organization's President. One faction supported a high-caste Hindu candidate while the other supported the incumbent Magar candidate. The latter won the election. This process and its outcome generated lasting splits and disillusion within the organization.

Ethnic Associations

An important consequence of the 1990 Democracy Movement in Nepal has been a strong social and political movement spread among a diverse set of the Janajati populations (i.e. such Tibeto-Burman-language-speaking groups as Magars, Gurungs, Tamangs, Rais, Limbus, Sherpas, etc.). The 1990 Constitution establishing freedom of religion and expression suddenly released tremendous cultural energy among many ethnic minority groups.[24] As early as July 1990, the Nepal Federation of Nationalities (NEFEN) was founded in Kathmandu, comprising seven nationalities, and had grown to thirty-nine nationalities by September 2001 (Minami 2003b: 10). Janajati groups were a major force within this new ethnic movement. Even in the years prior to the Democracy Movement, some Janajati intellectuals were calling for cultural awakening among Mongol groups throughout Nepal.

Hangen (1999), who studied the Mongol National Organization (MNO), founded in 1989 in eastern Nepal as a small ethnic political party, found a number of important characteristics of this organization. It regards the long reign over Nepal by high-caste Hindus as the main source of Mongols' cultural marginality, low social prestige, and political under-representation. At the heart of the MNO's ideology is an assertion that Mongols are the original inhabitants of Nepal (and are therefore also known as Janajatis) and that they form the majority of its population. In contrast, they declare that the Hindus ('Aryans') arrived in Nepal only several hundred years ago as refugees from northern India when it was conquered by Muslims. Despite their numerical minority position, according to MNO, Hindus were able to dominate Nepal's politics and economy

[23]It should be added that some Nepalis chose not to attend these community events and activities for fear that such a congregation of undocumented migrants would attract the attention of Japanese authorities.

[24]The 1962 Constitution had also included freedom of religion. The 1990 Constitution, however, established a multiparty political system in which citizens could exercise their religious rights more openly than before.

as a result of which they imposed the Hindu religion and language on the Mongols. In order to establish equality with the Hindus, MNO leaders proposed expansion of Mongol political power in national politics. They hoped to achieve that goal by inspiring many Mongol groups to join in generating a pan-Mongol identity and culture. However, Hangen (1999) points to a serious contradiction inherent in the MNO's ideology and strategy, namely, that Mongol identity is not one of unity because each of the nearly forty Mongol groups claims its own history, language, and culture.

This new ethnic movement in Nepal quickly reached the Nepali community in Japan, which is composed mostly of Tibeto-Burman-language-speaking groups. Minami (2003a: 90) reports the establishment of fourteen Nepali ethnic associations in Japan since 1995, each of which promotes its own identity and culture, while retaining its affiliation with the pan-Nepali association, Sewa Samiti. Many of these are branches of the ethnic associations that already existed in Nepal (Minami 2003a: 90). For example, Tamu Dhi Nagoya is an association established in 1996, serving Gurungs in the Tokai area. It organizes religious and social activities specific to the Gurungs, while providing entertainment opportunities for all Nepalis in the area, one of which is the bowling competition in which I participated in February 2003. It coordinates its activities with those of the Tokyo branch, which was established in 1995. These two branches cooperate with the Gurung Association in Kathmandu in publishing the magazine *Tamu Dhi* for distribution in Japan.

An important development following the demise of the Sewa Samiti in 1999 has been the establishment of the Nepalese Indigenous People's Association (Nepal Adibasi Samaj) in Tokai. This association, comprising all Tibeto-Burman ethnic associations as well as individual members, has been active in nurturing Janajati identity and culture in Japan for the past five years. It has organized a number of religious and social celebrations (e.g. the Buddha's birthday and Indigenous People's Day) and political lectures by prominent speakers from Nepal (e.g. Gore Bahadur Khapangi in 2001 [Minami 2003b: 11] and Krishna Bhattachan in 2003).

JAPANESE NGOs AND SUPPORTERS

To this point, I have discussed the contexts of Nepalis' migration that have enabled them to sustain migration flows to Japan and to engage in community activism there. I now turn to a consideration of the social contexts in Japan that have given the migrants support for their social adaptation and protection of their rights. Since the 1990s, and especially after the 1995 Great Hanshin (Kobe) Earthquake, Japanese citizens have become increasingly interested in organizing themselves to defend their rights. With the influx of foreign workers from Asia and Latin America since the mid 1990s, therefore, issues of migration, human rights, and multiculturalism have become key concerns for many sectors of Japanese civil society. The growing importance of pro-migrant activism in Japan can only be understood in the Asia-wide contexts of Japan's immigration policies and the government's relative tolerance for its citizens' activism.

Lack of Rights for Migrants

In most Asian countries, states treat migration as a law and enforcement problem, while viewing migrants as mere 'manpower' or a 'commodity'. As a result, a European style of public policy, where governments have focused on institutionalized social services as the main sphere of immigrant incorporation, has failed to take hold in Asia. Instead, the first step towards social incorporation has been initiated by community-based organizations (CBOs) and non-governmental organizations (NGOs) (Yamanaka & Piper 2006).[25] These citizens' groups have responded to the social and economic problems faced by migrants, precisely because the state ignores their rights and welfare. In Japan, since the late 1980s, there have been many citizens' networks, women's groups, religious organizations, local labour unions, and professional associations that assist migrant workers (Roberts 2000; Shipper 2001; IMAGE 2004). It is in the social context of rising public concerns for migrants' rights and emerging multiculturalism in Japan, that Nepali migrants have been able to establish cooperation with a number of dedicated NGOs and individuals in Tokai.

Securing Japanese citizens' cooperation becomes even more crucial for undocumented migrants, because their resources to solve socio-economic problems and defend their rights are much more limited. As discussed in an earlier section, under the deepening economic recession, undocumented migrants have been increasingly concentrated in the smallest and weakest segments of the manufacturing industries. As a result, unemployment and violations of tneir labour rights are frequent. Outside of the workplace, business establishments often exclude, or discriminate against, foreign customers by demanding official documents or proof of a Japanese citizens' financial guarantee, as a condition for providing services to them (e.g. a cell phone subscription). In addition, governmental law enforcement has been tightened as the economic recession has become prolonged. Politicians and other authorities have targeted undocumented migrants as

[25] It should be noted here that the governments of Singapore and Malaysia are intolerant of civil activism for migrants' rights. By contrast, following the British colonial legacy, the Hong Kong government is relatively tolerant of such activism. The governments of Japan and Korea are more tolerant of pro-migrant activism than the governments of Singapore and Malaysia but less tolerant than the Hong Kong government (Yamanaka & Piper 2006).

suspected sources of crimes that threaten Japanese citizens. In the increasingly adverse economic and political environment, migrants' needs for civil society's assistance have greatly increased.

Citizens' Groups and Individuals

In Tokai, Nepalis have established close relationships with a number of NGOs over the years. As early as 1990, the Herusu no Kai (Hamamatsu Overseas Labourers Solidarity), comprising labour unionists, religious groups, and other concerned citizens, began consultation and mediation services for legal and illegal foreign workers caught up in labour disputes. Among them Nepalis were a national group that often brought labour disputes and other problems to the organization for consultation and help towards resolution. Throughout the 1990s their cases were frequently mentioned in Herusu no Kai's bimonthly newsletters. In Nagoya, the capital of Aichi Prefecture, the Sasajima Hiyatoi Rodo Kumiai (Sasajima Day Labourers Union) is one of the major NGOs to which many Nepalis have entrusted their labour dispute cases. According to its leader, Mamoru Yoshikawa, in recent years about 60 per cent of the labour dispute cases with which his organization dealt were brought by Nepalis.[26]

Another area of great concern to undocumented migrants is health and medicine. In the mid 1990s, in response to the lack of inexpensive health care for foreigners, a number of Hamamatsu's health professionals and civil activists launched the Medical Association for Foreigners-Hamamatsu (MAF). In collaboration with volunteers, local hospitals, professional associations, and community organizations, they provide uninsured foreign workers with free annual check-ups. Behind the launching of the MAF was the well-publicized case of Jeevan Shrestha, a Nepali man who fell ill in Hamamatsu in 1993 and whose life was saved by major heart surgery performed in a local hospital by Dr Hiroshi Taniguchi, who became deeply concerned with the issue of foreigners' health care. The moral and financial dilemma that the Shrestha case brought to Dr Taniguchi and his colleagues when they made the decision to operate on the illegal, and essentially indigent, immigrant patient, led him to seek an alternative way to meet the medical needs of foreigners. A result of his efforts, with the assistance of Herusu no Kai and a city Rotary Club, was the founding in October 1996 of a free annual medical check-up programme that has continued every October up to the present (Yamanaka 2005). In his private practice Dr Taniguchi opens his clinic to uninsured foreigners at nominal expense, every Saturday afternoon. This has contributed immensely to health care for foreign residents in the area, including Nepalis.

In addition to these citizens' organizations, Tokai Nepalis have estab-

[26]Interview on 9 February 2002, Nagoya.

lished contact with many Japanese citizens. They include a bowling trainer who helps Tamu Dhi Nagoya to host its semi-annual bowling competition, a Buddhist priest who conducts religious rituals at celebrations such as the Buddha's birthday, weddings, and other important public undertakings, and a researcher who has volunteered to help with translation and documentation for visiting guest speakers from Nepal (Minami 2003c: 12). There are many more Japanese supporters of Nepalis if the list is expanded to include personal friends, work colleagues, and generous employers. In recent years, as a result of their prolonged stay, a few single Nepali men have developed relationships with Japanese women which have culminated in marriage. Consequently they have been able to legitimize their visa status and thereby contribute to the community with their access to resources unavailable to the migrant community. These resources include not only the benefits restricted to citizens, but also their spouses' social networks, social capital, and financial credits. These organizational and personal ties with Japanese are essential for Nepali community activists when they organize events and activities often held in public places.

Migrants' Initiatives and Rewards

The undocumented Nepalis as illegal aliens were well aware of the legal and social constraints on their residence, employment, and overall freedom. Leaders of community organizations, therefore, made special efforts to cultivate rapport with Japanese NGOs and citizens sympathetic to their plight. They frequently called upon these Japanese for advice and help in times of crisis. They also invited them to organized Nepali community events as honoured guests, requesting public speeches, and thanking them with gifts and awards. Rajendra Sharma, an active member of the Sewa Samiti, explained in an interview why he and others were committed to organized activities:

> We lack freedom here because we don't have proper visas. We have many problems. For example, those who have just arrived are so afraid of being arrested that they stay in apartments of their friends for weeks. Because Japan has been in recession for years by now, unemployment is rapidly increasing among us. Job hunting is difficult. Unpaid wages frequently occur. But we have nowhere to report abuse cases. Nepalis are afraid of the Japanese authorities and therefore do not want to have anything to do with them. So they often put group pressure on someone who has been injured at work so that he will not bring the case to the Labour Bureau for the compensation to which he is entitled.[27] It is sad. We

[27]Japan's Labour Standards Law makes no reference to workers' legal status in its protection of their rights.

> need to educate ourselves. We also need to be in touch with Japanese because we are unable to help ourselves. (Interview, 11 October 1998, Hamamatsu)

In most instances, the collective initiatives of Nepali organizations described by Sharma have been provided by a small but dedicated number of community leaders. While Sharma and others appear to believe in the value and necessity of these community agendas and the importance of acting on them, their dedication has taken a toll on their personal lives and savings. On top of their demanding long hours of work, these community leaders regularly spend several evening hours communicating with other members for planning and coordination. On Sundays – their only off day – they travel to attend meetings that are usually held in other cities. One might wonder what motivates them to volunteer for such heavy and costly community service for which they receive very little, if any, monetary reward. The following quote from an interview with Dinesh Gurung, a leader of the Gurung Association, Nagoya Branch, and a construction worker, provides a clue:

> After work, I am tired but have to do this and that – writing, copying, calling ... lots of things. They take time. Sundays – almost every Sunday – I have to go to committee meetings. The Gurung Association does not pay for transportation, but I have to go to Toyohashi, Nagoya, Hamamatsu, and sometimes Yokohama and Tokyo ... lots of money. But I am collecting experience and knowledge in Japan. I meet many important Nepalis and Japanese such as the Nepalese Ambassador to Japan, Japanese NGO workers, and others. I also learn the Japanese language. I am helping the Association and get more things than money. These people get to know me and they will help me when I need their help. I am not wasting my time here. (Interview, 25 July 1999, Tomita)

CONCLUSION

This study of social networks and social capital of Nepali migrants in Japan highlights the importance of cultural, historical, and political forces that shape their migratory process and social adaptation at their destination. Although regional economic disparity was the major cause of their migration, such 'colonial' ties as the "Gurkha Connection" and "Thakali Connection" laid the foundations of Janajati migration networks in East Asia in the middle to late 1980s (Minami 2003c: 12). These social networks bridged Nepal to Japan, transporting social capital crucial for migration, employment, and adaptation. Upon arrival undocumented Nepalis were faced with hostile immigration policies and increasing unemployment. In response, they united in order to collaborate for their economic and social survival. A call by the Tamu Dhi Nagoya organization for Tokai Nepalis to 'bowl together' twice a year was therefore an effective means for the migrant community to maintain social participation among its ethnically diverse members. While entertaining themselves in the bowling lanes, Nepali migrants were acting together in a manner which promoted cooperation to their mutual benefit and contributed to their self-governance. In so doing, they were constructing and reconstructing their social networks and accumulating their social capital in order to meet the new challenges and constraints created by the rapidly changing economic and political environments in both Japan and Nepal.

The research highlights two key issues relevant to the analysis of the migratory process and consequent social adaptation. The first issue is the exclusionary immigration policy of Japan that has engendered two contrasting migration systems: the market-mediated migration system of the Brazilians, and the social-network-driven migration system of the Nepalis. Brazilians of Japanese descent, who are fully documented immigrants, depended largely on labour recruiters who matched them to employers' demands regardless of the migrants' social relations at origin. A consequence was the relative absence of organizations that would address the collective concerns of the entire population in the city where they have settled with their families. In contrast, the undocumented Nepalis have relied heavily on social relations that are grounded in their communal principles and ways of life in Nepal.[28] These divergent paths taken by the two migrant communities also reflect the lack of Japanese policy on the social incorporation of immigrant residents. Being documented but without citizenship rights, more than 250,000 Brazilians and their families encounter mounting problems in the areas of health care, public housing, children's education, and racial discrimination. Despite a lack of concerted community actions among Brazilians, Japanese civil society has responded spontaneously and vigorously in an effort to eliminate such legal inequality based on nationality. Civil society action has resulted in incremental changes in policy and the attitudes of local governments towards the Brazilian population (Yamanaka 2003c, Yamanaka & Piper 2006). In

[28]Nepali workers have migrated to Korea as legal industrial trainees since the early 1990s. The Korean Small Business Association has recruited them in Nepal regardless of their ethnic or regional origin. This suggests that, like Brazilians, they have few social networks and little community-based social capital available to unite them. Existing studies reveal active collective engagements by Nepali workers to enhance their rights in Korea (e.g. Lim 1999, 2003). The ways in which Nepali workers organize themselves despite the market-mediated migration systems that have brought them to the country, would be a valuable topic for future research.

contrast, without official permits to reside and work in Japan, and with little attention or concern for their rights from policy makers, Nepali migrants must cultivate and rely on the moral support of Japanese citizens who happen to be concerned about their plight. Nepalis' impressive ability to organize effectively has thus had no impact on state policy and therefore does not contribute to change in the structural inequality from which they suffer.

The second key issue relevant to the migratory process being addressed here is that in the fifteen-year history of the Tokai Nepali community in Japan, there have been visible and significant changes in the community's patterns and strategies of collective adaptation. In the face of a hostile and unfamiliar environment, Nepali migrants of diverse ethnic backgrounds were able, during the first ten years, to unite in Japan based both on ethnic and national identity, but this changed in the late 1990s as a result of the rapid development of ethnic politics in Nepal. The establishment of ethnic associations among Janajati groups in Tokai, combined with the demise of the pan-Nepali mutual help association there, the Sewa Samiti, gave rise in 1999 to a Janajati ethnic organization, the Adibasi Samaj, exclusive to Janajati members. This signalled an emerging ethnic division between the majority Janajatis and the minority Brahman-Chetris. In addition to this communal falling out, many Nepali migrants have 'assimilated' into Japanese society as a result of their prolonged stay, acquiring the Japanese language and ways of life. The basis for Nepali 'bounded solidarity' is crumbling. According to a recent returnee from Nepal, "they [Tokai Nepalis] have become 'individuals' and don't care for the community any longer".[29] These changes in collective and personal patterns of adaptation clearly suggest the increasing fragmentation and erosion of group solidarity within the Tokai Nepali community. They also indicate the emergence of new strategies being employed by Nepali migrants for their social survival in Japan. Future research will be needed if we are to understand the nature of these evolving strategies and modes of collective and personal adaptation in response to the deepening economic recession in Japan, combined with the rapidly deteriorating political order in Nepal that is a result of the current civil war (Thapa 2002; cf. Ogura 2007).

---

[29] Interview, 4 July 2004, in Tomita City with a recent returnee from Nepal. In the early 1990s, he had worked in the Tokai area. After returning to Nepal and running a business in Kathmandu for ten years, he remigrated to Japan in December 2003 and continues to work in the Tokai area.

REFERENCES

Aryal, M. 1991. 'To Marry a Lahuray'. *Himal* (July/August) 4 (3): 18-19.

Banskota, P. 1994. *The Gurkha Connection: A History of the Gurkha Recruitment in the British Indian Army*. Jaipur: Nirala Publications.

Berreman, G.D. 1963. 'Peoples and Cultures of the Himalayas'. *Asian Survey* 3 (6): 289-304.

Bista, D.B. 1996 (1967). *People of Nepal*. Kathmandu: Ratna Pustak Bhandar.

Borjas, G.J. 1990. *Friends or Strangers: The Impact of Immigration on the U.S. Economy*. New York: Basic Books.

Boyd, M. 1989. 'Family and Personal Networks in International Migration: Recent Developments and New Agendas'. *International Migration Review* 23 (3): 638-80.

Brown, T.L. 1996. *The Challenge to Democracy in Nepal: A Political History*. London: Routledge.

Caplan, L. 1967. *Land and Social Change in East Nepal*. Berkeley: University of California Press.

——. 1995. *Warrior Gentlemen: "Gurkhas" in the Western Imagination*. Oxford: Berghan Books.

CBS (Central Bureau of Statistics). 1996. *Statistical Pocket Book*. Kathmandu: HMG, National Planning Commission Secretariat.

Chhetri, G. 1999. 'A Sociological Analysis of Dalit Occupational Caste Group in the Hills of Nepal', in R.B. Chhetri and O.P. Gurung (eds.), *Anthropology and Sociology of Nepal: Cultures, Societies, Ecology and Development*, pp. 56-68. Kathmandu: Sociological and Anthropological Society of Nepal (SASON).

Clark, R. 1979. *The Japanese Company*. New Haven: Yale University Press.

Collett, N. 1994. 'The British Gurkha Connection in the 1990s', in M. Hutt (ed.), *Nepal in the Nineties: Versions of the Past, Visions of the Future*, pp. 98-105. Delhi: Oxford University Press.

Cross, J.P. 1985. 'Introduction', in S. Tucci, *Gurkhas*, pp. 8-34. London: Hamish Hamilton Ltd.

Des Chene, M. 1991. 'Relics of Empire: A Cultural History of the Gurkhas, 1815-1987'. Ph.D. thesis, Stanford University. Ann Arbor: University of Michigan International.

——. 1993. 'Soldiers, Sovereignty and Silences: Gorkhas as Diplomatic Currency'. *South Asia Bulletin* 13 (1-2): 67-80.

Doherty, V.S. 1975. 'Kinship and Economic Choice: Modern Adaptations in West Central Nepal'. Ph.D. thesis, University of Wisconsin - Madison. Ann Arbor: University of Michigan International.

Fujita, S.S. and D.J. O'Brien. 1991. *Japanese American Ethnicity: The Persistence of Community*. Seattle: University of Washington Press.

Hangen, S. 1999. 'Making Mongols: Identity Construction and Ethnic Politics in

Ilam District, Nepal', in R.B. Chhetri and O.P. Gurung (eds.), *Anthropology and Sociology in Nepal: Cultures, Societies, Ecology and Development*, pp. 69-80. Kathmandu: SASON.

Hidaka, S. (ed.). 1967. *Nepal Himalaya Tanken Kiroku: Nepal to Nihon, 1899-1966* [Nepal and Japan: A Survey of Japanese Activities 1899-1966]. Tokyo: Kodansha (in Japanese).

Higuchi, N. 2002. 'Kokusai Imin no Soshiki-teki Kiban: Iju System-ron no Igi to Kadai (Organizational Foundation of International Migrants: Significance and Problems of Migration System Approach)' *Sociology* 47 (2): 55-71 (in Japanese).

——. 2003. 'Migration Process of *Nikkei* Brazilians', in M. Yamada (organizador), *Emigración Latinoamericana: Comparación Inter-regional entre América del Norte, Europa y Japón*, pp. 379-406. The Japan Centre for Area Studies (JCAS) Symposium Series 19. Osaka: National Museum of Ethnology.

Higuchi, N. and K. Tanno. 2003. 'What's Driving Brazil-Japan Migration? The Making and Remaking of the Brazilian Niche in Japan'. *International Journal of Japanese Sociology* 12: 33-47.

Hitchcock, J.T. 1963. 'Some Effects of Recent Change in Rural Nepal'. *Human Organization* 12: 75-82.

——. 1966. *A Mountain Village in Nepal*. New York: Holt, Rinehart & Winston.

Höfer, A. 1978. 'A New Rural Elite in Central Nepal', in J. Fisher (ed.), *Himalayan Anthropology*, pp. 179-86. The Hague: Mouton.

Hoftun, M., W. Raeper, and J. Whelpton. 1999. *People, Politics and Ideology: Democracy and Social Change in Nepal*. Kathmandu: Mandala Book Point.

Hondangue-Sotelo, P. 1994. *Gendered Transitions: Mexican Experiences of Immigration*. Berkeley: University of California Press.

IMAGE (International Migration and Gender Study Group). 2004. *Gendai Nihon Shakai ni okeru Kokusai Imin to Gender Kankei no Saihen ni kansuru Kenkyu (Research on Reconfiguration of International Migrants and Gender in Contemporary Japan: Toward Empowerment of Migrant Women and Formation of their New Subjectivity)*. Tokyo: Institute for Gender Studies, Ochanomizu University (in Japanese).

Iijima, S. 1961. *Nepal no Nogyo to Tochi Seido (Agriculture and Land-System in Nepal)*. Asian Economic Study Series No. 18. Tokyo: Institute of Asian Economic Affairs (in Japanese).

Ishii, H. 2001. 'Japanese Studies on the Himalayas and Nepal'. *European Bulletin of Himalayan Research* 20 (1): 165-208.

Ito, M. 1993. 'Nihonteki Torihiki Kanko: Keizokuteki Torihiki no Kino to Hyoka (Japanese Business Customs: Functions and Assessment of Continuous Business Relations)', in T. Itami, T. Kagono, and M. Ito (eds.), *Nihon no Kigyo System (Japanese Corporation Systems)*, pp. 74-94. Tokyo: Yuhikaku (in Japanese).

Japanese Bureau of Immigration Control. 1996. *Honpo ni okeru Fuho Zanryusha no Kazu ni tsuite (Numbers of Illegal Alien Residents in Japan)*. Tokyo: Japanese Bureau of Immigration Control.

Japanese Ministry of Foreign Affairs. 1996. *Kingdom of Nepal*. Tokyo: Japanese Ministry of Foreign Affairs.

Kawakita, J. (ed.) 1960. *Tibettojin: Choso no Tami (Tibetans: Peoples of Platform Burial)*. Tokyo: Kadokawa Shoten (in Japanese).

Khadka, N. 1993. 'Democracy and Development in Nepal: Prospects and Challenges'. *Pacific Affairs* 66 (1): 44-71.

Kibria, N. 1993. *Family Tightrope: The Changing Lives of Vietnamese Americans*. Princeton: Princeton University Press.

Kihara, H. (ed.). 1957. *People of Nepal Himalaya*. Kyoto: Kyoto University FFRS.

Kondo, D.K. 1990. *Crafting Selves: Power, Gender, and Discourses of Identity in a Japanese Workplace*. Chicago: The University of Chicago Press.

Kritz, M.M. and H. Zlotnik. 1992. 'Global Interactions: Migration Systems, Processes, and Policies', in M.M. Kritz, L.L. Lim and H. Zlotnik (eds.), *International Migration Systems: A Global Approach*, pp. 1-16. Oxford: Clarendon Press.

Light, I. and E. Bonacich. 1988. *Immigrant Entrepreneurs: Koreans in Los Angeles 1965-82*. Berkeley: University of California Press.

Lim, T. 1999. 'The Fight for Equal Rights: The Power of Foreign Workers in South Korea'. *Alternatives* 24: 329-59.

——. 2003. 'Racing *from* the Bottom? The Nexus between Civil Society and Transnational Migrants in South Korea'. *Asian Survey* 43 (3): 423-42.

Louie, M.C.Y. 2001. *Sweatshop Warriors: Immigrant Women Workers on the Global Factory*. Cambridge: South End Press.

Macfarlane, A. 1976. *Resources and Population: A Study of the Gurungs of Nepal*. Cambridge: Cambridge University Press.

Massey, D. et al. 1987. *Return to Aztlan: The Social Process of International Migration from Western Mexico*. Berkeley: University of California Press.

Menjívar, C. 2000. *Fragmented Ties: Salvadoran Immigrant Networks in America*. Berkeley: University of California Press.

Minami, M. 2003a. 'Zairyu Nepal-jin Rodosha no Ethnic Community to Network (The Ethnic Communities and Networks among Resident Nepali Workers in Japan)', in H. Shouji and T. Mishima (eds.), *Kokusai Imin no Jizon Senryaku to Transnational Network no Bunka Jinruigaku-teki Kenkyu (Anthropological Research on Survival Strategies and Transnational Networks of International Migrants)*, pp. 85-108. Osaka: National Museum of Ethnology (in Japanese).

——. 2003b. 'Minzoku naishi Senjumin Undo to Maoist Mondai: Magar no Jirei kara (Ethnic or Indigenous Peoples' Movement and Maoist Problems: The Case of the Magar)'. *Kaiho (Newsletter)*, 179: 10-11. Tokyo: Nihon Nepal Kyokai (The Japan Nepal Society) (in Japanese).

——. 2003c. 'Risou no Shakai Kukan wo Motomete: Kokka wo Choetsu Suru Nepal-jin Rodo Imin (Seeking Ideal Social Spaces: Nepali Migrant Workers who Transcend the Nation-State)'. *Minpaku Tsushin (Minpaku Correspondence)*, 103: 11-12. Osaka: National Museum of Ethnology (in Japanese).

Ogura, K. 2007. 'Maoists, People and the State as Seen from Rolpa and Rukum', in H. Ishii, D. Gellner, and K. Nawa (eds.), *Social Dynamics in Northern South Asia*, Vol. 2: *Political and Social Transformations in North India and Nepal*, pp. 435-75. Delhi: Manohar.

Pahari, A. 1991. 'Ties That Bind: Gurkhas in History'. *Himal* (July/August) 4 (3): 6-12.

Pettigrew, J. 2000. '"Gurkhas" in the Town: Migration, Language, and Healing'. *European Bulletin of Himalayan Research* 19 (Autumn): 7-39.

Pignède, B. 1996 (1966). *The Gurungs: A Himalayan Population of Nepal*. Kathmandu: Ratna Pustak Bhandar.

Portes, A. 1987. 'The Social Origins of the Cuban Enclave Economy of Miami'. *Sociological Perspectives* 30: 340-72.

——. 1998. 'Social Capital'. *Annual Review of Sociology* 24: 1-24.

Putnam, R. 1995. 'Bowling Alone: America's Declining Social Capital'. *Journal of Democracy* 6 (1): 65-78.

Roberts, G.S. 2000. 'NGO Support for Migrant Labor in Japan', in M. Douglass and G.S. Roberts (eds.), *Japan and Global Migration: Foreign Workers and the Advent of a Multicultural Society*, pp. 275-300. London: Routledge.

Roth, J.H. 2002. *Brokered Homeland: Japanese Brazilian Migrants in Japan*. Ithaca: Cornell University Press.

Sakurai, K. 2003. *Nihon no Moslem Shakai (The Moslem Society in Japan)*. Chikuma Shinsho 420. Tokyo: Chikuma Shobo.

Shipper, A. 2001. 'Pragmatism in Activism: Organizing Support for Illegal Foreign Workers in Japan' (Civil Society in the Asia-Pacific Monograph Series). Cambridge: Program on US-Japan Relations, Harvard University.

Thapa, D. 2002. 'The Maobadi of Nepal', in K.M. Dixit and S. Ramachandaran (eds.), *State of Nepal*, pp. 119-60. Kathmandu: Himal Books.

Tocqueville, A. de. 1969 (1835). *Democracy in America*. ed. J.P. Mayer, tr. G. Lawrence. Garden City, New York: Anchor Books.

Uesugi, T. 2001. 'Rhetoric and Ideology of the British Gurkhas' Cohesion: An Analysis of "Gurkha Dimension" and *Dashain* Festival'. *Ritsumeikan Journal of International Relations and Area Studies* 18 (March): 83-113.

——. 2007 'Re-examining Transnationalism from Below and Transnationalism from Above: British Gurkhas' Life Strategies and the Brigade of Gurkhas' Employment Policies', in this volume.

Yamanaka, K. 1996. 'Return Migration of Japanese-Brazilians to Japan: The *Nikkeijin* as Ethnic Minority and Political Construct'. *Diaspora* 5 (1): 65-97.

——. 1999. 'Illegal Immigration in Asia: Regional Patterns and a Case Study of Nepalese Workers in Japan', in D.W. Haines and K.E. Rosemblum (eds.), *Illegal Immigration in America: A Reference Handbook*, pp. 471-99. Westport, Connecticut: Greenwood Press.

——. 2000a. 'Nepalese Labor Migration to Japan: From Global Warriors to Global Workers'. *Ethnic and Racial Studies* 23 (1): 62-93.

——. 2000b. '"I Will Go Home, but When?" Labor Migration and Circular Diaspora Formation by Japanese Brazilians in Japan', in M. Douglass and G.S. Roberts (eds.), *Japan and Global Migration: Foreign Workers and the Advent of a Multicultural Society*, pp. 123-52. London: Routledge.

——. 2003a. 'Transnational Activities for Local Survival: A Community of Nepalese Visa-Overstayers in Japan'. *Kroeber Anthropological Society Papers* 89/90: 146-67.

——. 2003b. 'Feminized Migration, Community Activism and Grassroots Transnationalization in Japan'. *Asian and Pacific Migration Journal* 12 (1-2): 155-87.

——. 2003c. 'Feminization of Japanese Brazilian Labour Migration to Japan', in J. Lesser (ed.), *Searching for Home Abroad: Japanese-Brazilian and Transnationalism*, pp. 231-59. Durham, NC: Duke University Press.

——. 2005. 'Migration, Differential Access to Health Services and Civil Society's Responses in Japan', in S. Jatrana, M. Toyota and B.S.A. Yeoh (eds.), *Migration and Health in Asia*. London: Routledge.

Yamanaka, K. and N. Piper. 2006. *Feminized Migration in East and Southeast Asia: Policies, Actions and Empowerment. Occasional Paper 11*. Geneva: United Nations Research Institute for Social Development.

Zhou, M. 1992. *New York's Chinatown: The Socioeconomic Potential of an Urban Enclave*. Philadelphia: Temple University Press.

14

From *Tika* to *Kata*? Ethnic Movements among the Magars in an Age of Globalization

MAKITO MINAMI

INTRODUCTION

This paper focuses on the activities of Nepali migrants living either outside Nepal or in the refugee camps in Nepal, and on how they construct their ethnic identity.[1] I shall examine how networks of ethnic organizations are formed across national borders and how various movements in Nepal and abroad develop through mutual inspiration and contact. Three Magar cases are discussed: the Nepali immigrants in Darjeeling and Sikkim in India; the Nepali migrants to Bhutan who returned to Nepal from Bhutan and live in refugee camps; and Nepali immigrants in Hong Kong.

The legal status of these three Magar groups varies; they are Indian citizens, refugees, and Hong Kong denizens respectively.[2] Also, the

[1]I wish to express my gratitude to 'The Resona Foundation for Asia and Oceania' (No. 1517) and the JSPS Grant-in-Aid for Scientific Research (No. 1257126) for supporting this research. I am very grateful to the Magar communities, in particular such individuals as Gore B. Khapangi, M.S. Thapa, Bam Kumari Budha, and Sanjog Lapha in Nepal, C.K. Pulami and Ambar B. Saru in the refugee camps, Shanti Rana and Banu Thapa in India, Hum B. Thapa in Hong Kong, and Bhim Thapa and Gobinda Gharti in Japan. I am also grateful for data collection to Manichan Chantyal, S.B. Subba, and Ram B. Shrestha, and for translation to Hitomi Hongo. For comments on an earlier draft I am grateful to participants in the workshop on 'Social Dynamics in Northern South Asia' organized by Hiroshi Ishii and David Gellner at ILCAA, Tokyo University of Foreign Studies.

[2]Hammar (1989: 84) defined denizens as "foreign citizens who have a secure permanent residence status, and who are connected to the state by an extensive array of rights and duties". The denizens are usually granted civil rights and social rights, but not always granted full political rights.

process, timing, and scale of the three cases of migration are different. What is common to all three groups is a strong centripetal force based on their shared ethnicity. While their movements are connected and constantly influenced by the ethnic movements in their home country, the migrants themselves also play a key role in selecting which aspects of the home movements will be taken up and propagated in their new situation.

The largest amount of research on overseas Nepalis has been done in India, a neighbour with strong historical ties to Nepal where Nepalis can travel freely without documentation (Timsina 1992; Magar 1994; Hutt 1997; Samanta 2000; Upreti 2002; Sinha & Subba 2003, among others). In Bhutan, the Nepali immigrants have been studied in connection to the refugee issues (Dhakal & Strawn 1994; Hutt 1994, 2003). On Nepali migrants to other parts of the world, there is a study in Fiji (Griffin 1987), and a study of Nepali Christian migrants across the world (Perry 1997). After the 1980s, Nepali migration to countries beyond South Asia began in earnest, but there are few studies on overseas Nepalis, except a general introduction by Dhungel (1997) on Nepalis in the USA, some pioneering research by Yamanaka (2000, 2003) on migrant workers in Japan, and a study by Seddon et al. (2001) on foreign labour migration and the remittance economy in Nepal. Especially lacking is research on migrant workers in the Gulf countries despite the large number of the Nepali workers in these countries. While the present chapter does not fill in these gaps, I will try to give a broader perspective on the ethnic movements of the Magars in the age of globalization by presenting and comparing the most up-to-date states of the ethnic movements in the three geographically different places in the world.

ORIGINS OF THE ETHNIC MOVEMENTS

As a result of the democratic movement in 1990, absolute monarchy was abolished in Nepal and a new constitution was introduced. The new constitution specifies that Nepal is a multiethnic, multilingual, democratic, independent, indivisible, sovereign, Hindu and Constitutional Monarchical Kingdom (4-1), guarantees the freedom to form unions and associations (12-2c), and declares that each community shall have the right to preserve and promote its language, script, and culture (18-1). With these rights ethnic groups, known as Janajatis, who had been placed in the middle rank in the traditional caste hierarchy, and the Dalits (untouchable castes), who had been placed in the lowest positions, were empowered to establish their own 'ethnic' or 'caste' associations. In 1990 seven ethnic associations established an overarching federal association, which they called the Nepal Janajati Mahasangha (Nepal Federation of Nationalities: NEFEN), to campaign for their rights as citizens of Nepal (Fisher 1993; Gellner 1997: 20-3). The ethnic movements of NEFEN, with the support of various NGOs and other groups, found their place in the framework of the global indigenous population movements: its representatives attended the UN convention for indigenous people and the UN convention for the elimination of all forms of racial discrimination. In this process, the NEFEN, which had grown to forty-eight ethnic groups by June 2004, changed its name to Nepal Adivasi Janajati Mahasangha (Nepal Federation of Indigenous Nationalities: NEFIN). Over the period of fourteen years since NEFIN's foundation, several campaigns have borne fruit, such as recognition of the existence of unique ethnic groups by the government. The first population census that reported the population by caste/ethnic groups (classified into twenty-six ethnic groups) was carried out in 1991. The number of ethnic groups recognized by the census increased to forty-four in 2001. Population by mother tongue had been recorded even before the democratic movement, but increasingly detailed classification of the languages was made with each new census. In 1981, the populations by mother tongue were classified into eighteen languages with fourteen Janajati languages. The number increased to thirty-three with twenty-four Janajati languages in 1991 and to ninety-two with seventy-five Janajati languages in 2001. These numbers remain tentative as even a minority language with fewer than ten speakers is included in the statistics.

In 1997, the Rashtriya Janajati Bikas Samiti (National Committee for the Development of Nationalities) was established within the Ministry of Local Development. It provided an official definition of 'Janajati' and named sixty-one ethnic groups for the government to recognize. The purpose and structure of the committee and the list of ethnic groups were announced in the Government paper (*Nepal Rajpatra* 23 Asar 2054 [1997]), which was reprinted in Pradeep Thapa Magar (2000: 82-8). The number was later modified to fifty-nine (Gellner & Karki 2007). In short, the ethnic groups in Nepal began to assert their differences from each other and to make claims based on their ethnic identity, so that the government could no longer ignore them.

BUILDING ETHNIC MOVEMENTS

The Chantyals

The Chantyals are an interesting case in point. Previously they had called themselves the Chantyal Magar and regarded themselves, and were recognized, as a subgroup of the Magars. In 1989, however, they established the Nepal Chantyal Sangha (Nepal Chantyal Association: NCA) as a unique ethnic group separate from the Nepal Magar Association. They joined NEFEN in 1993. I visited the office of the NCA central committee in March 2001, just before the census. The association had prepared a large number of their own questionnaire sheets, and the committee was discussing how to carry out their own census using members of the committee, who planned to visit the villages in the areas of their origin to give guidance to the villagers on how to fill in the census forms.

The aim of the association was to push the population of Chantyals over the 10,000 mark. In order to achieve this goal, as de Sales (2003: 64) has pointed out, they had to teach the villagers that they were "no longer the Magar, but the Chantyal". In their original census form, the association is instructed to write Chantyal in the column 'name and *thar* (clan)', and then the form lists twelve clan names as 'our *thars*'.[3] These efforts were rewarded, as Chantyals were listed separately in the population census 2001, and were no longer included in the ambiguous category of 'others'. The total Chantyal population was recorded as 9,814 (the 74th largest group in the country) and the number speaking the Chantyal language as a mother tongue was recorded as 5,912 (the 38th largest language) (CBS 2002).

Table 14.1 is based on a photograph (I took with permission in 2001) of a list of supporters displayed on the wall of the office of the NCA central committee, which was rearranged by the country of residence of the supporters and by the amount of donation. As shown in the table, Japan stands out both in the number of supporters and in the size of their donations.[4] In fact, the Chantyals are well known among the Nepali undocumented workers in Japan for their success in inviting the members of their ethnic group to Japan, raising funds by rotating credits (*dhikur*). Thus ethnic movements in Nepal today are supported from abroad by their own diaspora communities.

---

[3]The clans were listed as follows: Khadka, Gharti, Garbja, Gyapchan, Jhiraja, Dandamare, Tathapja, Purane, Potlade, Budathoki, Bhalnaja, and Side, and so on. The original has the word *adi* at the end, which suggests that in fact there may be more than twelve Chyantyal clans.

[4]In Japan, there were about 3,880 undocumented immigrant Nepali workers in 2000. Among them, Thakali, Tamu (Gurung), and Magar in 1995, Marphali Thakali in 1996, Sherpa in 1997, Tamang in 1998, Chantyal in 1999, and Limbu, probably in 1999, organized their own ethnic associations for mutual aid, information exchange, and friendship. I estimate that the Magar population in Japan numbers about 400 to 500. Sixty-five members of Nepal Magar Sewa Samiti, Tokai (Nepal Magar Service committee, Tokai region) contributed about 2,460,000 Japanese Yen in 2001, to purchase land to construct a Nepal Magar Association central committee office. Eleven members of the same association also donated about 210,000 Yen to reprint *Ancient Magar and Akkha Script* by M.S. Thapa Magar in 2002. There are, furthermore, scholarships financed by the Magar diaspora communities for Magar students and journalists.

Table 14.1: Number of Supporters of the Nepal Chantyal Association by Present Residence and Donation

Present residence	Number of supporters by donation (Rs.)				
	over 20,000	20,000-10,000	10,000-3,000	3,000-1,000	Total
Japan	23	36	19	2	80
UAE			1	45	46
Bahrain				22	22
Germany		1	16		17
Brunei		2	4		6
Hong Kong			5		5
South Korea			2		2
USA		1			1
Qatar		1			1
Switzerland			1		1
Sub total	23	41	48	69	181
Nepal		1	1	26	28
Total	23	42	49	95	209

Notes: Rs.75 is equal to about 1 US $.
The highest donation is Rs.42,882, and the lowest one is Rs.1,000.

The Magars

The Nepal Magar Sangha (Nepal Magar Association: NMA) also provided detailed guidance on filling out the census form. At the Seventh National Convention of the NMA held in March 2001 in Dharan, a board member of the Association gave a speech – in Nepali – to several thousand Magars gathered from all over Nepal:

> Let's write the Magar language as our mother tongue in the census form. It does not matter if you can't speak a word of the Magar language. Rather than writing Nepali as your second language, write the names of the languages of our neighbouring Janajati, such as Rai, Limbu, and Gurung. For our religion, let's write Buddhism and not Hinduism. You shouldn't hesitate. The NMA announced the Magar Buddhist declaration at the conference in Jhapa district in 1998.

In their journal *Langhali* (Villager), issue 7, published in time for the National Convention, the association asked all Magars to write 'Magar' for their caste/ethnic group (*jati*), 'Magar language' for their mother tongue or the language in use, and *Bauddha dharma* (Buddhism) for their religion. In addition, the NMA requested people to check whether the census-taker filled in the form in accordance with their answers, and to spread this request to other Magars in their neighbourhood.

Many other ethnic associations carried out similar exercises in an attempt to provide standardized responses and guidance for replies to census questions about ethnicity, mother tongue, and religion. Interestingly, the National Committee for the Development of Nationalities, a government organization whose staff members consist of the leaders of the ethnic movements, gave similar or even more explicit guidance. The Committee's guidance states:

1. Write your *jati*, language, and religion only after consulting your ethnic association;
2. If the census takers are found to write on the form in pencil, stop him/her immediately, because the religion and language might be modified later;
3. If you see or hear about the census takers filling out the form without visiting every household, report this to your ethnic association, and stop him/her immediately;
4. If the census takers are not a Janajati, or if he/she does not understand the mother tongue, or if the one being questioned does not understand Nepali, the ethnic association should send a translator as a volunteer.

(*Langhali*, no.7, 2001: back cover)

In this way, the census became an integral part of the identity politics of ethnic groups. The initiatives they undertook may well have had an effect on the statistics, especially those concerning religion and mother tongue.

The results of these campaigns are reflected in the dramatic increase of Magar language speakers from 32 per cent (in 1991) to 48 per cent (in 2001), as shown on Table 14.2. At the same time, in the population as a whole, Hindus decreased from 87 to 81 per cent, while the Buddhists increased from 8 to 11 per cent. Mother tongue and religion are ascribed a highly political meaning in Nepal and the figures for both are of extreme interest to ethnic movements. However, the degree of Nepalization of the Magars is revealed by the facts both that such an explicit speech had to be made and that all twelve of the Magar speakers at the event spoke in Nepali.

DECLARATION OF BUDDHIST FAITH BY THE NMA

In 1998, the Nepal Magar Association declared that the Magars are Buddhist. The theoretical grounds for this declaration are to be found in a book published in 1993 entitled *Prachin Magar ra Akkha Lipi* (Ancient Magar and Akkha Script) by M.S. Thapa Magar, who is a lawyer and also the President of the Rashtriya Janamukti Party (National People's Liberation Party). In this book, he modified the details of Brahmi script and 'reconstructed' Akkha Lipi, a script for the Magar language, and he argued that

Table 14.2: Population Change of Magars and Magar Language Speakers

Year	Magar popn. [1]	Ratio to all popn. (%)	Magar language speaker's popn. [2]	Ratio to all popn. (%)	Magar language maintain ratio (%) [2]÷[1]×100	Nepal all popn.
1952/4	–	–	273,780	3.3	–	8,256,625
1961	–	–	254,675	2.7	–	9,412,996
1971	–	–	288,383	2.5	–	11,555,983
1981	–	–	212,681	1.4	–	15,022,839
1991	1,339,308	7.2	430,264	2.3	32.1	18,491,097
2001	1,622,421	7.1	770,116	3.4	47.5	22,736,934

Gautam Buddha is the ancestor of the Magars, and that the Magars were originally Buddhists.[5] With the publication of this book, the history of the Magars, which the author claimed to trace back to the Buddha himself, and the fact that Magar culture has a unique script, were widely announced.

The declaration was more than just about the issue of religion or conversion to Buddhism. There is a strong motivation behind the movement that the Magars should cease to be Hindus and should promote social reform. The NMA recommends that important life-cycle rituals should be performed by Magars themselves, rather than asking Hindu Bahun priests to do them. The aim is (1) to be independent religiously and also not to support Bahuns financially and (2) to assert intellectual freedom from Bahunism (*Bahunbad*). According to Magar activists, Bahunism implies worshipping Bahuns as sacred beings, and trying to imitate Bahuns in one's own conduct. Gore Bahadur Khapangi Magar, former President of the NMA and also the former General Secretary of Rashtriya Janamukti Party, often uses the phrase "Smile like a Magar and not like a Bahun" in his speeches, which is meant to warn people against following Bahuns blindly.[6]

Another recommendation for becoming more Magar is to learn and speak the Magar language.[7] The Magar language has a limited geographical distribution in the districts of Palpa, Tanahu, Nawalparasi, and Udayapur, and the number of people who speak the language is rather small, even among the Magars themselves. The statistic of 32 per cent users of the mother tongue in the total Magar population in the 1991 census is probably close to the actual ratio (see Table 14.2). Khapangi often says, "Learn a word of the Magar language before you die, so that you die as a Magar." His words reflect the endangered state of the language.

The national broadcasting station, Radio Nepal, began broadcasting news in the Magar language in 1994, and the first novel written in the Magar language titled *Rewas* (Custom) by Sanjog Lapha Magar was published in the following year. The first Magar language film *Simarekha* (Borderline), with Nepali subtitles was in the theatres in 1998, which

---

[5]The Akkha script is almost the same as the Brahmi script, in which the Asokan pillars were written in the third century BC, in India.

[6]Ahearn (2001) discusses Magar ethnic identity and gender by analysing a speech by Khapangi from 1993. We are informed that by that date, he had started to urge his audiences "not to follow Hinduism, 'the Brahmans' dharma', but instead to revert back to Buddhism". See also S. Lapha Magar and R. Rana Magar (2003).

[7]In the Magar language, there are various dialects. Eastern Magar is spoken mainly in Udayapur and Sindhuli districts, whereas western Magar is spoken mainly in Palpa, Tanahu, and Nawalparasi districts. The Magar language is also often taken to include two other languages, which seem to be quite different in their genealogy, namely, Kham spoken in Rolpa district and Kaike spoken in a few villages of Dolpa district. The NMA accepts all Magars including the speakers of Kham and Kaike.

attracted the public attention partly because of the appeal to Magarism (see de Sales 1998). The FM radio station, HBC94fm, featuring the aforementioned Sanjog Lapha as the DJ, airs an hour-long programme (*Kanung Lumpphes*: Our Platform) in the Magar language on Thursdays from 7 p.m. A textbook of the Magar language has not been revised since the edition by K.J. Baral Magar (1980),[8] but a Magar dictionary is being compiled by Sanjog Lapha et al.

STEP-BY-STEP WITHDRAWAL FROM THE DASAIN FESTIVAL

In relation to the Buddhist declaration, a very symbolic step was recommended, namely a boycott of the Dasain festival. Dasain is the major national festival in Nepal, and although it is a Hindu ceremony, it has also been celebrated in the Magar villages as a local tradition. The boycott of Dasain seems to be a movement that the Kirants (Rai and Limbu) started by 1991, which then spread to many other ethnic associations. The NMA had also insisted on the boycott even before the declaration of Buddhist faith.[9] The central committee of the NMA sent a request to boycott Dasain to district branches in 1996, which provoked debates in many regions in Nepal. For example, the Vice-President of the NMA Tanahu district committee raised an objection to this request, saying that it is not acceptable to abolish traditional customs and cultural activities. Rather, he said, we should try to reduce the excessive spending by cutting the number of plates in feasts (*Kantipur*, 22 September 1996).

In the Magar village in the Nawalparasi district, where I have been conducting research since 1986, some people agree with the boycott of the Dasain festival using the same arguments as the one given by the NMA. Their claim is that the festival is not a Magar festival. On the contrary, it is a memorial of the conquest of the Magars and the murder of a Magar king by a Hindu king. So can a Magar possibly celebrate such a holiday? In this village, where the journal of the NMA has never reached, this is a minority opinion and the festival is still enjoyed without restriction. The religious aspect of the festival, however, had already been toned down shortly before

[8]The publisher of this book is Suresh Ale Magar, who was the first General Secretary of NEFEN, currently under arrest and in custody as a supporter of the Maoist insurgency (June 2004).

[9]In the book of P. Thapa Magar (2000: 90-1), we can see nine kinds of appeal handbills prepared by various ethnic associations. Above all, it is interesting that he reprinted the handbill made by a Kirant association called Sabaikirant Yakthung Chumlung in Assam in 1992. It has been hitherto said that the boycott Dasain propaganda came from Kirant groups in East Nepal, however, it may also have spread from India.

I arrived in 1986. Until then, six neighbouring Magar villages used to take turns to perform a *nachan,* dances and songs of a Hindu epic, in front of the *kot* (literally 'fort', here meaning royal shrine) of Bhawani (the goddess Durga).[10] The *nachan* is no longer performed in my study village and neighbouring villages have also abandoned it.

The *jajmani* relationship, in which a village or an individual household makes a contract with a Bahun priest living outside the village to perform its household ceremonies, was still observed in 1986. It has completely disappeared in the last ten years even though there was no explicit pressure from the NMA. Even without a contract, the Bahun continued to come to the village on the day of Nag Panchami, to give out printed amulets and to tie a sacred string on the wrist of everyone.[11] Later, however, a very juvenile Bahun replaced him, and the custom no longer exists today. Thus, breaking away from 'Bahunism' has already progressed further than the NMA expected. For the villagers, who have no knowledge of Buddhism, the declaration of the Buddhist faith by the NMA was too foreign. They had no idea about what they were expected to do with Buddhism. At least in my study village, everybody speaks the Magar language on a daily basis, and they do not ask any rituals of the Bahuns. Funerals are administered by *kutumba* (the brother of the wife or mother, i.e. the wife-giver).[12] The policies of the NMA have already been put into practice even by those who have not become Buddhists.

The Buddhist movement among the Magars is so far limited to the level of discourse, and little practical guidance on what constitutes Buddhist belief or practice is presented to the people. This is because Buddhism is only a means in this movement. The real goal is to plant anti-Bahunism in the mind of the Magars. If that is the case, it may not be appropriate to view this movement as an anti-Hindu religious movement or as opposed to the caste system. For example, the NMA recommends a life independent of Bahuns, but it does not suggest doing away with ceremonial music played by the Damai, a Dalit caste whose traditional occupations are tailor and musician at weddings. Neither are the Magars' discriminatory attitudes toward the untouchable castes criticized. In this sense, even though the

---

[10]According to Hitchcock (1980: 92-4), songs of a similar *nachari* "consist of excerpts from the Ramayana and from the life of Lord Krishna". To specify the name of the Hindu epic and to compare these performances with similar dances and songs among other Magars (for example, de Sales 1986), further analysis of the handwritten text, photographed by myself, will be necessary.

[11]On the fifth of the brightening lunar fortnight in Saun (July/August), snake gods (*naga*), who control rainfall, are worshipped.

[12]Most villagers still have the naming ritual for a newborn baby carried out by a Bahun. Recently, however, a few Magars in my study village quit this custom, and asked a Magar with some knowledge of Sanskritic astrology to do the naming, thus saving themselves the trouble of a two-hour walk to the Bahun village.

Buddhist movement by the Magars is a historical event comparable to the neo-Buddhist movement of Ambedkar in India, its stance on the abolition of the caste system remains ambiguous.[13]

NEPALI REFUGEES FROM BHUTAN IN THE REFUGEE CAMPS

Nepali migrants to Bhutan (called *Lhotshampa* by the Bhutanese government) were expelled from southern Bhutan during the period of 1990 to 1994. According to the UNHCR, 100,400 refugees live in seven camps in eastern Nepal (figures for January 2002). If we go by an estimate by C.K. Pulami Magar, President of the Bhutan Magar Sangha (Bhutan Magar Association: BMA), 17,000 to 19,000 of these refugees are Magars.

Historically, the western half of present Sikkim and Darjeeling belonged to Nepal from 1774 to 1816. Because of the lack of a clear notion of national borders even after 1816, and because the border between Nepal and India is still open today, many Nepalis migrated to West Bengal, Sikkim, north-east India, and Myanmar mainly from eastern Nepal. Nepali migrants to Bhutan settled in southern Bhutan, which was virtually unpopulated at the time.

The process by which they became refugees can be summarized as follows. Around 1985 the government of Bhutan changed the citizenship right laws (National Law 1958) and began an assimilation policy to the dominant Drukpa culture. The Nepali and other ethnic groups in Bhutan began a protest movement, which the government met with arrests, imprisonment, and torture. Government pressure against the democratic movement became still harsher when the illegal Bhutan People's Party was established in June 1990. The refugee problem also began in this period.

The complete picture of ethnic movements in the refugee camps is not clear. In the case of the Magars, it was around 1996 that the BMA was established by Magar refugees in the camps. According to Pulami, there were no associations based on Magar ethnicity in Bhutan. He became familiar with the policy of the NMA central committee only after he started living in the refugee camp. The most shocking moment for him was when the NMA declared that the Magars were originally Buddhists in 1998, because, as Hindus, they were expelled from Bhutan for revolting against Buddhist culture. Pulami regretted their ignorance and said, "If we had

[13] Ambedkar, who was an Untouchable Mahar from Maharashtra and became the first Minister of Law in the independent Indian government, converted to Buddhism as a protest against the caste system in 1956. About 200,000 Mahar caste people followed him and converted to Buddhism collectively (Sanghrakshita 1986).

known that we were actually Buddhists before 1990, the present situation would not have happened. We could have lived as the most ideal Bhutanese nationals as Buddhists. We made the mistake of following the Hindu high-caste groups, who lead the democracy movement."

The Magars in the refugee camps have constructed a Magar Buddhist temple in order to propagate Buddhism among the Magar refugees. A Magar refugee was installed as a full-time, celibate monk.[14] The BMA proceeded to spread the Akkha script, and had given classes to 1,500 Magar students by 1996 (Magar 1996). Pulami published 2,000 copies of a new textbook *Akkharika Magar Guide Book* in 2003, since the original text *Ancient Magar and Akkha Script* by M.S. Thapa Magar has long been out of print and is still difficult to obtain even after it was reprinted in 2002.

The refugee camps are perhaps one of the very few places in Nepal where the Akkha script is taught for practical use. The spread of the script and Buddhism in the refugee camps is definitely more rapid there than among Nepali Magars. One of the reasons may be that the Bhutanese refugees who were born in the Buddhist kingdom know what a Buddhist temple is like and possess some basic knowledge of Buddhism. Also, there are Buddhist temples and monasteries of the Limbus and the Sharchops (other Bhutanese ethnic groups) in the refugee camps, where the refugees can learn about the religion. The source of motivation among the Nepali refugees is their hope of returning to Bhutan as early as possible, by becoming good Buddhist Bhutanese.

Life in the refugee camps always leads to the common goal of repatriation to Bhutan. Therefore, study of the Dzongkha language, which is the official language of Bhutan, is compulsory in all schools in the refugee camps. The singing of the national anthem of Bhutan by students before class was observed there, just as in schools in Bhutan. It is interesting that rotating credit associations called *dhikur*, which were introduced to the camps by Nepali neighbours, are organized on the basis of villages in Bhutan, rather than with neighbours in the camps or with connections based on ethnicity. This means that they expect to return to the same village in Bhutan in the near future, taking back their common kitchen wares, which were purchased with *dhikur* money. By contrast, BMA activities are a cultural movement which promotes the Buddhist identity of the Magar as Bhutanese citizens, rather than for economic mutual help. The aims of the NMA happened to coincide with those of the Magars in the refugee camps, whose ultimate goal is their repatriation to Bhutan.

---

[14]On the altar are displayed, from left to right, a framed picture of Durga, a picture of Krishna, an image of the Buddha, lamps, water vessels, a poster of Buddha behind the image, a picture of Shiva, and a picture of a Taiwanese sage. The image of the Buddha and the picture of the sage were given by visitors from Taiwan.

NEPALI IMMIGRANTS IN DARJEELING, WEST BENGAL, AND SIKKIM

As mentioned earlier, Nepal had a historically close relationship with north-east India. Nepali people seem to have moved into the unsettled forests in Darjeeling district, West Bengal, and Sikkim. As a result, the proportion of Nepalis in the population was already high early in the nineteenth century. The population of Darjeeling in 1991 was 1.3 million, of whom 0.6 million (49 per cent) have Nepali as their mother tongue. According to Banu Thapa Mangar, General Secretary of Akhil Bharatiya Mangar Sangha (All India Mangar Association: AIMA), the Mangar population in Darjeeling was at least 45,000 by the 1950s.[15] In the neighbouring state of Sikkim, in 1991, there were 260,000 (64 per cent) Nepali speakers in a population of 410,000. The population of Mangars in Sikkim is supposed to be 10,000 to 20,000 today, according to Gobinda Thapa Mangar, board member of the Akhil Sikkim Mangar Sangha (All Sikkim Mangar Association).

Ethnic movements among Nepali migrants to Darjeeling began in the years between 1920 and 1940, when the Kirantis, Newars, Damais, Viswakarmas (Kamis), and Tamangs, all formed their own ethnic/caste associations. According to Kano (2001: 247), the Sherpa Buddha Association was established in Darjeeling in 1924, while a Limbu Association called Yakthung Hang Chumlung was founded in Kalimpong in 1925 (Subba 2002: 9). The Mangars also formed the Mangar Samaj Darjeeling (Mangar Society Darjeeling) a little later in 1939. When we see that the Langhali Pariwar, the predecessor of the present NMA in Kathmandu started in 1971, and the oldest foundation of the Tharu Kalyankarini Sabha in Nepal dates back only to 1949, it seems that ethnic movements in Nepal originated in Darjeeling.[16]

Although further details of the development of these ethnic movements in their early stage are not known, a revival of ethnic movements began in the 1990s. In relation to the Mangars, the All Sikkim Mangar Association (1933), the Siliguri Jalpaiguri Mangar Samaj (Siliguri Jalpaiguri Mangar Society) (1997), and the Dooars Mangar Lapha Sangha Kendriya Samiti (Dooars Mangar Friend Association Central Committee) (2001) were

[15]In India people usually use 'Mangar', not 'Magar'. It was commonly used in the early part of twentieth century among the colonial administrators writing Gazetters (for example, see O'Malley 1999).

[16]Chalmers (2002: 35) writes that Nepali literature published in Banaras "played a pivotal role in the creation of a modern Nepali public culture and in the development of a fully articulated sense of Nepali identity."

established and they acted independently of each other. However, in 2002, board members of the Mangar associations in Darjeeling, Kalimpong, Kurseong, Sikkim, Dooars, and Siliguri gathered to plan the foundation of the All India Mangar Association (AIMA). In this process, all Mangar citizens in India, estimated to be 100,000 to 200,000, were unified into a nationwide association. In order to achieve this project, Banu has often visited the NMA Central Committee in Kathmandu to consult with leaders of ethnic movements, and also to learn about the Magar culture since 2000. The office of the AIMA is located in Kalimpong, while the Second National Convention of the AIMA was held in Jaigaun in February 2004. According to Shanti Rana Mangar, an executive member of the AIMA, about 5,000 Mangars in India attended this convention, including people from places such as Dehra Dun, Delhi, Meghalaya, and Assam.

The AIMA has a definite goal: to persuade the Central Government of India to recognize the Mangars as a Scheduled Tribe (ST). In Sikkim, the Mangars had already been classified as an Other Backward Class (OBC) in 1995, along with the Gurungs, Rais, Limbus, Tamangs, Sunuwars, and Bhujels.[17] The Mangar language was also recognized in 1995 as one of the official state languages of Sikkim, along with the Newari, Rai, Gurung, Sherpa, and Tamang languages. All these were added to the established state languages, Nepali, Bhutia, Lepcha, and Limbu (which had this status from 1977). However, because of the limited opportunities available to OBCs in the spheres of quotas for government job, entrance for higher education, and for investment loans, Mangar activists seek to attain the status of ST, since then they would receive preferential treatment.[18]

Upon requests from the ethnic associations, the Sikkim government nominated Limbu, Tamang, Gurung, Mangar, Rai, Sunuwar, and Bhujel groups as candidates for classification as STs, and submitted the list to the Central Government of India in September 2001. Of these candidates only the Limbus and the Tamangs were recognized as STs in 2002. The AIMA currently organizes a variety of cultural programmes, which represent their tribal status and backwardness, aimed at government recognition at the next nomination. The message by the Mangar Samaj in Kalimpong, and frequently mentioned by board members of the AIMA, expresses their self-image:

> Please think that: the people, who play *deusi* song in a cave, are us.

---

[17] Scheduled Tribes (ST) in Sikkim are Lepcha and Bhutia including Chumbipa, Dopthapa, Dukpa, Kagatey, Sherpa, Tibetan, Tromopa and Yolmo, according to a stipulation of 1978. The Scheduled Castes (SC) of Sikkim are Kami, Damai, Lohar, Sarki, and Majhi.

[18] Turin (2004: 194) has already mentioned that, "in Darjeeling ethnic activism rather appears to be related to attaining the status of OBC or ST which then provide the community with a quota of position in the administration of Government of India."

> The people who play *madal* drum and perform a *maruni* dance twisting his/her waist, are us.[19]
>
> The people who carry the *khukuri* with them, and fight for their country, are also us.
>
> However, the people who remain backward, in spite of being honest, sincere, hardworking, and brave, why they should be us?

The activities of the AIMA aim to reveal the origin and historical background, homeland, customs, religion, traditions, festivals, originality of the dances and songs of the Mangar, and to reproduce the traditional Mangar lifestyle by constructing model villages. They chose a valley located between Kalimpong and Darjeeling for a model village, where almost all of the 300-400 villagers still speak the Mangar language in daily life. Then they consulted with the NMA Central Committee in Kathmandu about the traditional style of the houses. Most of the board members of the Mangars were born and grew up in cities so they know neither the traditional dances and songs of the Mangar, nor authentic costumes needed for them. As a result, the NMA Central Committee became an adviser, and explored the essentials of the Magar culture for the Indian Mangars. They plan to train young Mangar people in the authentic dances and songs of the Magar by inviting the professional dance team, the 'Sorathi Culture Club', from Kathmandu.

The main aim of the ethnic movements of the Mangar in India today is to obtain recognition as an ST. Since newly recognized ST members, the Limbus and Tamangs, are Buddhists, the Mangars take a cautious attitude about declaring their religion as Buddhism. Till now, they have been unable to come to an official agreement on their religion; the association's magazine *Sehecha Lam* (Beautiful Path) 1(1) 2004 announces, without referring to Buddhism, that "Each Mangar family should maintain *Mangarat* (Mangarland) religion of Mangar *jati.*" Interestingly, they insist neither on Buddhism nor on boycotting Dasain, and have pictures of a pig sacrifice during the Dasain festival in their magazine.

Board members of the AIMA are not always concerned with the teaching and propagation of the Akkha script. In Sikkim, however, Mangar language classes using the Akkha script are scheduled to be introduced in primary education by the government. Darpan Publications in Darjeeling had an original font of the Akkha script made, and 200,000 textbooks in the

---

[19] *Deusi* is a song sung by men, who go from door to door begging money and singing in the evening of the fourth day of Tihar, the day for worshipping bulls (Goru Tihar). Maruni is a dance performed by men dressed up as women, which had originally been performed by the Rais. However, it is said that the Maruni dance had become popular in garrison bases of the British Gurkha regiments and was brought back to Nepal by ex-servicemen. The name of the dance is a parody of the word *taruni* (young woman).

Mangar language were being printed (in October 2003). They were also looking for teachers able to speak, read, and write the Mangar language using Akkha script.

As is well known, Nepali immigrants in India founded the Gorkha National Liberation Front in 1986, and thereafter started the movement demanding autonomy for Darjeeling and recognition of Nepali as a language to be included in the Eighth Schedule to the Constitution of India. As the result of these actions, an autonomous council called the 'Darjeeling Gorkha Hill Council' was approved in 1988, and limited autonomy, concerning industry, tourism, transportation, and water resource management in the district, was granted. Moreover, Nepali was recognized as the eighteenth Eighth Schedule language of India in 1992, along with Konkani and Manipuri.[20]

At the same time, as we have seen, Nepali migrants in West Bengal and Sikkim organized their own ethnic/caste associations, and each of them began to revive their culture and traditions. The caste groups are not exceptions. For example, the Bahun, Chetri, Sanyasi, Jogi, and Newar (not a caste group but an ethnic group, as they have their own internal caste hierarchy), all obtained the status of Other Backward Classes in Sikkim in September 2003. When I asked Banu, "Do you feel any hesitation about becoming a ST, which is sticking an image of backwardness to your people?" he said, "This is India here. A high government official is no doubt a high government official, even though he comes from an untouchable caste. People will obey his commands. Here, the position of the person is significant, more than being ST, SC, or OBC." For that reason, the AIMA argues that the younger generation of Mangars can obtain greater access to higher education by means of ST recognition.

MAGAR MIGRANTS IN HONG KONG

When Hong Kong was returned to Chinese sovereignty on 1 July 1997, the garrison base of the British Gurkha regiments in Shek Kong withdrew. However, a considerable number of ex-servicemen stayed on, finding employment as guards and in other such services. Denizenship was issued by the Hong Kong government for Nepali children who were born in Hong Kong before 1983, while their fathers had been stationed there. With

[20]To be accurate, the languages mentioned in the Eighth Schedule to the Constitution of India are not the official languages of the Union. They are recognized as the principal languages of India, which were originally fourteen languages in 1950. The Eighth Schedule now includes twenty-two languages including Sindhi, added in 1967, the three above-mentioned languages in 1992, and the Bodo, Santhali, Maithili, and Dogri languages in 2003.

increasing political instability at home, these 'Hong Kong IDs (Identity Card holders)' began to return to Hong Kong. They invited their spouse and family members in Nepal to Hong Kong. For this reason, the population of the Nepali migrants in Hong Kong now amounts to about 50,000, while the total population of Hong Kong is 6.8 million. Among the Nepalis, the Magars are estimated to be up to 20,000, according to Hum B. Thapa Magar, Chairman of Magar Sangha Hong Kong (Magar Association Hong Kong: MAHK).[21]

Although Gurkha regiments were stationed in Hong Kong from just after the Second World War until 1997, the establishment of Nepali associations there is a very recent phenomenon. According to Hum, the first was the British Gorkha Ex-servicemen's Association, founded in 1994 to work for improvement in the position of ex-soldiers. In the census year of 1996, the number of societies among the Nepali immigrants began to increase; then the Hong Kong Adivasi Sangha (Hong Kong Indigenous People's Association) and the MAHK were founded in 1997. In the list of 'ethnic minority self-help groups' made by Oxfam Hong Kong and uploaded on their website, there are eight Nepali organizations including two ethnic group associations (Tamu [=Gurung] and Magar respectively).[22]

The MAHK had already held large-scale cultural programmes, such as the *Lakhan Thapa Smriti Sanjha* (Lakhan Thapa memorial evening) in February 2001, the *Arun Smriti Sanjha* in 2002, and the *Master Mitrasen Smriti Sanjha* in 2004. The programmes were named in memory of Magar heroes who had been honoured by the NMA Central Committee. In the case of the programme in 2001, the MAHK gave a donation of Rs.50,000 to the fund to erect a bronze statue of Lakhan Thapa in Nepal.[23] Using the programmes as an opportunity, the MAHK invited not only Magar musi-

---

[21]The website (http://www.oxfam.org.hk/hkpoverty/) of Oxfam Hong Kong reports the number of Nepalese immigrants as 12,500 (2001). On the other hand, *Nepal Post Overseas* 2 (7): 4-5 (2000), which is a Hong Kong-based monthly magazine, claims that "Even though the number of Nepalese immigrants in Hong Kong was announced to be 17,700, it should actually be two or three times more. Perhaps it may amount to over 50,000."

[22]They are the Far East Overseas Nepalese association, Hong Kong Nepalese Federation, The Nepalese Association, Tamu Association of Hong Kong, Hong Kong Gurkhas Forum, Hong Kong Nepalese Women's Association, The Association of the Gurkhas' Sons and Daughters Hong Kong, and Magar Association Hong Kong.

[23]See Lecomte-Tilouine (2003) about Lakhan Thapa. Arun Thapa Magar was a popular singer, who died in 1999 at the age of forty-six. Master Mitrasen Thapa Magar was born in Dharamsala in 1895 and is known as a great poet, singer, stage writer, Buddhist preacher, and the first translator of Tolstoy into Nepali. At the Seventh National Convention of NMA, pictures of King Birendra and Queen Aishwarya (both died in June 2001), a biography of Lakhan Thapa (Magar 1997), a drawing of Magar poet Jit Bahadur Sinjali (see Lecomte-Tilouine 2003), and a biography of Master Mitrasen (H.B. Bura Magar 1998) were placed at the foot of the stage. At the inauguration ceremony, those pictures were decked not with a *kata* but with a garland. The pictures were not offered red *tika* powder.

cians but also ethnic movement leaders, like Khapangi, M.S. Thapa, and Balkrishna Mabuhang who was the former General Secretary of the NEFEN, to Hong Kong to deliver speeches, as was already the Magar association's practice in Japan. I was given an opportunity to attend the programme in 2004, which consisted of the performances of traditional Magar dances and songs, modern Nepali pop music, and a play by the dance team organized in Hong Kong. Four musicians were invited specially for the occasion from Nepal. The concert hall holding eight hundred chairs was almost full.

In May 2001, representatives of the MAHK, including Hum, were invited as chief guests to Tokyo to attend a cultural programme named Golden Nite 2001, which was organized by the Nepal Magar Sewa Samiti, Tokyo. Dance teams from Hong Kong also occasionally gave performances at cultural shows in Macau and in UK at the invitation of the Magar associations of the respective country. The networks and activities of the MAHK extended to different parts of the Magar diaspora all over the world.[24] The fact that the MAHK representatives have a secure legal position as Hong Kong denizens makes it possible for them to contribute financially to social services, and also to visit Nepal and maintain intimate relations with the representatives of the NMA Central Committee. It should also be noted that the MAHK network has always been based on and efficiently supported by the individual networks of ex-servicemen; Hum himself is one of them. The case of the Magar community in Hong Kong clearly shows the importance of 'The Gurkha connection' as Yamanaka (2000: 76-7) has called the network.

Even though the Nepali immigrants in Hong Kong are legally and financially more secure compared with those in other countries, they are still a minority group and subject to protection by the Hong Kong government, NGOs, volunteers, and so on. This dependence on other institutions is particularly because of their disadvantage in Cantonese literacy. They therefore have actively tried to show traditional Nepali or Magar dances and songs as their unique culture before local audiences on various occasions. It is their way of reiterating the fact that they are also Hong Kong's denizens, and of promoting the presence of Nepalis in Hong Kong. They are seldom concerned about whether they are Buddhist or not. On the other hand, they try to abstain from activities which might lead others to think

[24]According to an interview with Sila Ale Magar, who was one of the singers invited from Nepal for the cultural show in 2004, she had been performing in Malaysia, Qatar, Bahrain, Belgium, and Luxembourg, besides twice visiting Hong Kong (*Kaanung Eem* [Our Home] 7 (3): 53). For migrants, live music shows by performers from the home country are so exciting that popular Nepali musicians have begun to travel all over the world today, just like consolation tour groups in war times. In August 2004, she was also invited to perform in Japan by the Tamu association, Tamu Dhiin (Tamu Home), Japan.

that they are Hindus: for this reason MAHK has never planned any events related to Dasain.[25]

CONCLUSION

I have reviewed some Magar ethnic movements in three geographically and politically different areas. To summarize, I would like to characterize the ethnic movements as 'from *tika* to *kata*?' as in the title of this chapter. What I mean by this phrase is that the Magars are not expected to receive *tika*, an auspicious sign in Hinduism on their foreheads. They should rather receive *kata*, which is a white or light yellow silk cloth, around their neck as is usually given to an image of the Buddha for prosperity, respect, and safety in Tibetan Buddhism. Consequently, the boycott of Dasain and the Magar Buddhist declaration are emphasized as the very core of their movements. I also use '... to *kata*?' as with what might be taken to be a cynical meaning: receiving and giving *kata* has been till now the one and only practice of Buddhism for the Magars, as if it were proof of their being Buddhist. The promotion of the Buddhist movements by the NMA is limited to the level of discourse, in which ritual practices and manners of Buddhism are rarely mentioned. The motivation for their conversion has not come from belief in the Buddha, but from the denial of Bahunism and the hope for social reform.

I have argued that the significance of Buddhism for different groups of the Magar migrants varies due to the difference of host countries and migrants' social positions. The group for whom Buddhism means the most in practice are the Bhutanese Magars in the refugee camps in Nepal. They called themselves Buddhists following the NMA's declaration. By doing so, they hope to realize their repatriation to Bhutan as soon as possible. On the other hand, the Mangar immigrants in India, whose goal is to obtain Scheduled Tribe status recognition, may well take a neutral stance both for the boycott of Dasain and for conversion to Buddhism: they have to discuss more strategically what should be the essentials of the Mangar culture in order to meet required conditions of ST, such as 'tribal-ness,' backwardness, and peculiarity. In the case of the Magar immigrants in Hong Kong, it is difficult for them to find significance in calling themselves Buddhists. In spite of these different attitudes toward Buddhism, the *kata*-giving ceremony is commonly practised at events organized by Magar ethnic activists.[26] The *kata* has become a symbol of the Magar ethnic movements as well as of the resistance to the established social system.

---

[25] It is the same with the Magar Sewa Samiti, Tokyo/Tokai, in Japan.

[26] *Kata* is a white or light yellow silk cloth. *Kata*-giving ceremonies at public events of the Magars have been observed in India, Nepal, Hong Kong, and Japan, except in refugee camps.

Self-consciousness (*chetana*) of the Magar ethnic identity spreads from Kathmandu to overseas Magars, through various media.[27] The motivations for these ethnic movements, based on their ethnic awakening, have aspects unique to each place, such as repatriation to Bhutan, ST recognition in India, and their presence as a minority in Hong Kong. Diaspora associations are commonly recognized by the NMA Central Committee as branches and their members support the NMA in return, thus deepening the relationship between home and abroad. In fact, Magar literature, music, cinema, and journalism are stimulated by information and financial support from abroad. Leaders of ethnic movements in Nepal also visit foreign countries like Hong Kong and Japan in order to give speeches and to acquire knowledge of the situation of indigenous people around the world.[28]

Lastly, I would like to report a recent incident, which demonstrates the symbolic power of *tika*. In October 2002, the King of Nepal appointed Khapangi as the Minister of Women, Children, and Social Welfare in the Lokendra Chand interim Cabinet. Khapangi had filled the post for eight months until Chand resigned and new Prime Minister Surya B. Thapa was appointed. Following the custom, he visited the royal palace with other cabinet members during the Dasain festival just after his appointment, and was given *tika* by the King in person.[29] This meant that he celebrated Dasain with the blessing of the King, who is an incarnation of the Hindu god Vishnu.

Since Khapangi has always insisted that Nepal should "establish a decentralized federalist government with the 'politics of proportional representation' (Eng.)" (Ahearn 2001: 8) and should be declared a secularist state, and he has supported the Magar Buddhist declaration, many newspapers criticized him for betraying his own words and past activities. As a response to the criticism, Khapangi explained, "When the other person holds out his right hand for handshake, will you refuse it, just because you don't have such custom of handshake in your culture? *Tika* is an expression

[27] To deal with ethnic movements in relation to globalization is beyond the scope of this paper.

[28] For example, in Japan, Khapangi (in 2001) and M.S. Thapa (in 2002) were invited by the Nepal Magar Sewa Samiti, Tokai/Tokyo. Krishna Bahadur Bhattachan, a sociologist and an active leader of ethnic movements, was invited in 2003 by the Thakali Sewa Samiti (Service Committee), Tokyo/Nagoya. Nepal Adivasi Samaj (Indigenous People Society), Tokai and Tamu Dhiin Japan jointly invited Om Gurung, a radical anthropologist and present General Secretary of NEFIN in 2002.

[29] King Gyanendra had appointed the nine members of the new cabinet including Khapangi on 11 October, and he gave *tika* on 15 October, the day of Vijay Dasami. I suppose that Khapangi did not consider the meaning of *tika* carefully, being in a festive mood just after his abrupt appointment. I also think that the critical political situation made it harder to refuse. The other Magar Minister, Narayan Singh Pun, was appointed after Dasain, so he was able to avoid this test of allegiance.

of greeting and politeness just as a handshake." He also said, "I was appointed a Minister as a representative of Rashtriya Janamukti Party. The platform of the party does not oppose anyone's religion" (*Indigenous Voice National Weekly* 29 Sept. 2003). His remarks were not, however, enough to convince many Janajatis, because there was a precedent that a Muslim minister refused to receive *tika* from the king during his tenure as a minister.

As I mentioned earlier, since ordinary Magars did not willingly accept conversion and most of the Magar villages still continue to celebrate Dasain by exchanging *tika*, Khapangi's case didn't create much of a problem. After the resignation of the cabinet, however, he was branded as a pro-monarchist and seems to have lost his influence rapidly among Magar ethnic activists. Because of this, and no doubt for other reasons as well, the Rashtriya Janamukti Party split into two factions, the majority led by M.S. Thapa, and the rest, by Khapangi. Then the latter split away from the party and formed an independent Rashtriya Janamukti Prajatantrik Party (Democratic People's Emancipation Party) on 1 January 2004. Moreover, Khapangi had to decline the nomination for the candidacy of President of the NMA Central Committee at the Eighth National Convention in March 2004. As a result, he ended his four terms (twelve years) of service in the NMA as the President. The *tika* from the King consequently worked as a test to measure his allegiance. Indirectly, Khapangi's acceptance of *tika* from the King led to the disintegration of both the Nepal Magar Association and the Rashtriya Janamukti Party.

REFERENCES

Ahearn, L.M. 2001. '"We Were Kings Here Once": Gendered Constructions of Magar Ethnicity in a Speech by Gore Bahadur Khapangi'. *Himalayan Research Bulletin* 21 (1): 7-10.

Caplan, L. 1995. *Warrior Gentlemen: "Gurkhas" in the Western Imagination.* Oxford: Berghahn Books.

CBS. 2002. *Population of Nepal: Population Census 2001 - National Report.* Kathmandu: HMG, NPC Secretariat, CBS in collaboration with UNFPA Nepal.

Chalmers, R. 2002. 'Pandits and Pulp Fiction: Popular Publishing and the Birth of Nepali Print-Capitalism in Banaras'. *Studies in Nepali History and Society* 7 (1): 35-97.

de Sales, A. 1986. 'The Nachane of the Kham-Magar: Ethnographic Notes on a Group of Religious Dancers', in K. Seeland (ed.), *Recent Research on Nepal: Proceedings of a Conference Held at the Universität Konstanz*, 27-30 March 1984, pp. 97-111. München, Köln, and London: Weltforum Verlag.

——. 1998. 'Simarekha, a Historical Borderline?' *European Bulletin of Himalayan Research* 15-16: 78-85.

——. 2003 (2000). 'The Kham Magar Country, Nepal: Between Ethnic Claims and Maoism', in D. Thapa (ed.), *Understanding the Maoist Movement of Nepal*, pp. 59-88. Kathmandu: Martin Chautari.

Dhakal, D.N.S. and C. Strawn. 1994. *Bhutan: A Movement in Exile*. Jaipur: Nirala Publications.

Dhungel, R.K. 1997. 'Nepalese', in D. Levinson and M. Ember (eds.), *American Immigrant Cultures: Builders of a Nation*, pp. 645-51. New York: Simon & Schuster Macmillan.

Fisher, W.F. 1993. 'Nationalism and the Janajati'. *Himal* 6 (3) (March/April): 11-14.

Gellner, D.N. 1997. 'Nationalism and Ethnicity in the World's Only Hindu Kingdom', in D.N. Gellner, J. Pfaff-Czarnecka, and J. Whelpton (eds.), *Nationalism and Ethnicity in a Hindu Kingdom: The Politics of Culture in Contemporary Nepal*, pp. 3-37. Amsterdam: Harwood Academic Publishers.

Gellner, D.N. and M.B. Karki. 2007. 'The Sociology of Activism in Nepal: A Preliminary Report', in H. Ishii, D.N. Gellner, and K. Nawa (eds.), *Social Dynamics in Northern South Asia*, Vol. 2: *Political and Social Transformations in North India and Nepal*, pp. 361-97. Delhi: Manohar.

Griffin, C.C.M. 1987. 'Nepalese in Fiji'. *Domodomo* 3: 16-27.

Hammar, T. 1989. 'State, Nation and Dual Citizenship' in W.R. Brubaker (ed.), *Immigration and the Politics in Europe and North America*, pp. 81-95. Lamham: University Press of America.

Hitchcock, J.T. 1980 (1966). *A Mountain Village in Nepal*. (Fieldwork ed.). New York: Holt, Rinehart & Winston.

Hoftun, M., W. Raeper, and J. Whelpton. 1999. *People, Politics and Ideology: Democracy and Social Changes in Nepal*. Kathmandu: Mandala Book Point.

Hutt, M. (ed.). 1994. *Bhutan: Perspective on Conflict and Dissent*. Gartmore: Kiscadale Publications.

Hutt, M. 1997. 'Being Nepali without Nepal: Reflection on a South Asian Diaspora', in D.N. Gellner, J. Pfaff-Czarnecka, and J. Whelpton (eds.), *Nationalism and Ethnicity in a Hindu Kingdom: The Politics of Culture in Contemporary Nepal*, pp.101-44. Amsterdam: Harwood Academic Publishers.

——. 2003. *Unbecoming Citizens: Culture, Nationhood, and the Flight of Refugees from Bhutan*. Delhi: Oxford University Press.

Kano, K. 2001. *Sherpa: Himalaya Kochi Minzoku no Nijusseiki (Sherpa: Histories of Himalayan People in the 20th Century)*. Tokyo: Meikeido (in Japanese).

Lecomte-Tilouine, M. 2003. 'The History of the Messianic and Rebel King Lakhan Thapa: Utopia and Ideology among the Magars', in D.N. Gellner (ed.), *Resistance and the State: Nepalese Experiences*, pp. 244-77. Delhi: Social Science Press.

Magar, C.K. Pulami. 2003 (2060 v.s.). *Akkharika Magar Guide Book*. Damak: Akkalika Gyahot Sipal & Renja Bauddha Sipal.

Magar, H.B. Bura. 1994. *Is Gorkhaland a Reality or Simply Mirage?* Kathmandu: Pushpawati Bura Magar.

——. 1997. *Rastraka Gaurwa Tatha Nepalko Pratham Sahid Lakhan Thapa Magar: Duitiya (Lakhan Thapa Magar (2): The Pride of the Nation and the First Martyr of Nepal)*. Kathmandu: Pushpawati Bura Magar (in Nepali).

——. 1998. *Bahumukhi Pratibhaka Dhani: Mastar Mitrasen Thapa Magar (Master Mitrasen Thapa Magar: A Person of Multiple Talents)*. Kathmandu: Pushpawati Bura Magar (in Nepali).

Magar, K.J. Baral. 1980 (2037 v.s.). *Magar Kura Kuta Jatmo Ngakke? (How to Speak Magar Language?)*. Kathmandu: Suresh Ale (in Magar).

Magar, K. Sinjali. 2004. 'Swa. J.B. Thapa: Ek Paricay (Late J.B. Thapa: An Introduction)', *Seheca Lam (Good Path)* 1 (1): 27-8. Kalimpong (in Nepali).

Magar, M.S. Thapa. 2059 v.s. (2002) (2049 v.s. [1993]). *Prachin Magar ra Akkha Lipi (Ancient Magar and Akkha Script)*. Kathmandu: Briji Prakashan (in Nepali).

Magar, P. Thapa. 2000. *Lathuwa Nabanne Kaida (Ways not to be Foolish)*. Kathmandu: Lapha Pariwar (in Nepali).

Magar, R.B. Thapa. 1996. 'Bhutani Sarnarthiharuko Katha ra Sibirbhitrako Vyatha (Story of Bhutanese Refugees and Trouble in the Refugee Camp)', *Kanung Lam (Our Path)* 2 (2): 3-6 (in Nepali).

Magar, S. Lapha. 1995. *Rewas (Custom)*. Kathmandu: Lapha Pariwar (in Magar).

Magar, S. Lapha and R. Rana Magar (eds.). 2003. *Nepalko Rastriya Chintan: Gore Bahadur Khapangi Magarka Rajinaitik Antarwartaharu (Consideration on the State of Nepal: Political Interviews to Gore Bahadur Khapangi Magar)*. Kathmandu: Durga Prasad Gurung (in Nepali).

O'Malley, L.S.S. 1999 (1907). *Bengal District Gazetters: Darjeeling*. Delhi: Logos Press.

Pfaff-Czarnecka, J. 1999. 'Debating the State of the Nation: Ethnicization of Politics in Nepal – A Position Paper', in J. Pfaff-Czarnecka, et al. (eds.), *Ethnic Futures: The State and Identity Politics in Asia*, pp. 41-98. Delhi: Sage Publications.

Perry, C.L. 1997. *Nepali around the World: Emphasizing Nepali Christians of the Himalayas*. Kathmandu: Ekta Books.

Samanta, A.K. 2000. *Gorkhaland Movement: A Study in Ethnic Separatism*. Delhi: A.P.H. Publishing Corporation.

Sanghrakshita 1986. *Ambedkar and Buddhism*. Glasgow: Windhorse Publications.

Seddon, D., J. Adhikari, and G. Gurung. 2001. *The New Lahures: Foreign Employment and Remittance Economy of Nepal*. Kathmandu: Nepal Institute of Development Studies.

Sinha, A.C. and T.B. Subba (eds.). 2003. *The Nepalis in Northeast India: A Community in Search of Indian Identity. Delhi*: Indus Publishing Company.

Subba, J.R. 2002. *History and Development of Limboo Language*. Gangtok: Sukhim Yakthung Mundhum Saplopa.

Timsina, S.R. 1992. *Nepali Community in India*. Delhi: Manak Publications.

Turin, M. 2004. 'Mark Turin', in P. Onta (ed.), *Nepal Studies in the UK: Conversations with Practitioners*, pp. 187-210. Kathmandu: Chautari Books Series 15.

Upreti, B.C. 2002. *The Marginal Migrants: A Study of Nepali Emigrants in India*. Delhi: Kalinga Publications.

Yamanaka, K. 2000. 'Nepalese Labour Migration to Japan: From Global Warriors to Global Workers', *Ethnic and Racial Studies* 23 (1): 62-93.

——. 2003. 'Transnational Activities for Local Survival: A Community of Nepalese Visa-Overstayers in Japan', *Kroeber Anthropological Society Papers* 89/90: 146-67.

PART 4

NEPAL AS VIEWED FROM THE INDIAN HIMALAYAS

15

Issues, Activism, and Responses to Research in the Indian and Nepalese Himalayas: A Comparison

GERALD D. BERREMAN

INTRODUCTION

During the past ten years I have shifted the focus of my forty-seven years of anthropological research in the Indian Himalayas to include the adjacent Nepal Himalayas. More specifically, I have expanded my attention from India's central Himalayan states of Uttaranchal[1] and Himachal Pradesh, to include Nepal's western and central districts as well. In both countries I have been mainly interested in the peoples, cultures, and circumstances of the mid-montane regions of the Himalayas – the 'middle hills' as they are called in Nepal. I have attended relatively little to the submontane Tarai[2] and the high mountain peoples, and will therefore largely omit them from this discussion.

My primary research during this past decade has been devoted to comparing and contrasting social, political, and environmental issues and responses to them in the two nations' Himalayan districts. I have attempted to understand how people's definitions of, and responses to, issues that concern them differ – if they do – in the two countries and how those differences may be accounted for, while remaining mindful of the context:

[1] Until recently, Uttaranchal comprised the Himalayan districts of Uttar Pradesh (those between Himachal Pradesh and Nepal). During the years of agitation for statehood it was usually referred to as Uttarakhand.

[2] An exception is my 1967-8 urban study of ethnic and caste interaction in the old Paltan Bazar of Dehra Dun, a city of then 165,000 (now several times as populous), located in the Tarai at the foot of the Garhwal Himalayas and now the capital of Uttaranchal (Berreman 1972a).

their historical, environmental, social, economic, and political similarities and differences, as well as their interactions (see Ramachandaran 2002). It is this research that I will summarize here.

THE CENTRAL MID-MONTANE HIMALAYAS AS A CULTURE AREA

Hindus of the central Himalayas occupy a region and, for my purposes more importantly, they share a culture and society often known as *Pahari* (of the mountains). This was asserted long ago by Grierson in his *Linguistic Survey of India* (1916), when he categorized all of the Indo-Aryan languages of the Himalayas as "Pahari", and subdivided them into three related groups:

> In the extreme East there is Khas-Kura or Eastern Pahari, commonly called Naipali, ... Next, in Kumaon and Garhwal, we have the Central Pahari language, Kumauni and Garhwali. Finally in the West we have the Western Pahari languages spoken in Jaunsar-Bawar, the Simla Hill States, Kulu, Mandi, and Suket, Chamba, and Western Kashmir. (Grierson 1916: 1)

Speakers of these languages can be said to constitute a Pahari 'culture area' in that they share distinct patterns of learned, shared, and transmitted characteristics – within a region bounded roughly by the Tarai and Indo-Gangetic Plain to the south and by the high Himalayas and Tibet to the north, while to the east and west, the region fades more gradually into, respectively, the Buddhist Tibeto-Burman-speaking areas including Bhutan and Burma to the east, and the Islamic areas of Kashmir, northern Pakistan and Afghanistan to the west and north-west.

I am aware that the term 'culture area', formulated by anthropologist Clark Wissler (1950: 219-59) to describe the diverse native peoples of North and South America, has come to be considered an anachronism. It clearly is an over-simplification and rigidification if it is used in 'cookie-cutter' fashion to delineate discrete cultural territories. However, used in the manner of clines, to indicate variation along a continuum, it seems to me to be valid and useful. Dropping the term has simply resulted in resurrection of the concept in other guises. I have elsewhere enumerated many of the characteristics of the Indian Pahari culture area.[3] Some of the most distinctive ones are Pandava worship,[4] buffalo sacrifice,[5] *bedarat* (the

[3]Berreman (1960b, 1963: 344-51, 1970: 75-82, 1983a). See also, P.C. Joshi (2000).

[4]Ibid. (1963: 381-5).

[5]Ibid. (1972b: 378-9, photo #30, follows p. 196).

Himalayan rope-sliding ceremony),[6] terrace cultivation of *chaulai* (amaranth), among many other crops,[7] *bia* (traditional 'bride-price' marriage),[8] and absence of Vaishya and Shudra varnas (the latter assimilated to the 'untouchable' Dom [Shilpkar] category).[9]

In their comprehensive volume, *The Himalayas: A Syllabus* (1995: 115-78), Lewis and Riccardi define and describe the characteristics of "Four Ethno-Geographic Regions" of the Himalayas, two of which are of direct relevance here:

1. "Mid-Montane Pahari Region" (pp. 132-46): "middle hills from 2,500-7,500 ft. [above sea level] beginning east of Kashmir through the Panjab hills, Garhwal, Kumaon, Jumla, and central Nepal; considerable overlap from west of Kathmandu Valley to the eastern Nepalese hills".
2. "Mid-Montane Tibeto-Burman Region" (pp. 146-58): "hills from 2,500-7,500 ft. [above sea level] from west Nepal across to West Bengal, Sikkim, and Bhutan to Arunachal Pradesh".[10]

Anthropologist and native-born Pahari, P.C. Joshi, asserts that "The three dominant cultural areas constituting Uttarakhand [are] Kumaon, Garhwal and Jaunsar ...".

> The agitation for Uttarakhand as a political identity has aggressively emerged on the forefront ... on the political canvas and received mass support. ... The movement was a political struggle to achieve autonomy in the form of statehood to Uttarakhand [ultimately Uttaranchal]. It was at the same time a nativistic movement where people were trying to find a niche in the pluralistic cultural field of India. The agitation for a separate state at its core was also an attempt to redefine the essence of hillness – Pahari against plains culture. One of the prominent slogans stated, "*Koda, jhangora khayenge, Uttarakhand banayenge*" ["We will eat buckwheat and millet in order to make Uttarakhand"].[11] (P.C. Joshi 2000: 2)

---

[6]Ibid. (1961, 1963: 386).

[7]Ibid. (1963: 46-7, 1978a: 327-8).

[8]Ibid. (1963: 128-9), L.D. Joshi (1929: 40).

[9]Shilpkar means literally 'manual worker'. It is often used interchangeably with Dom to refer to the *achut* (literally, 'untouchable') castes and as an epithet directed at them (Berreman 1963: 200-4). It encompasses the "occupational castes" as defined in literature on Nepal (Chhetri 1999).

[10]The two of their "Four Regions" that are not directly relevant here are described as "The Submontane Region" [Tarai], and "Tibetan Highlands Region".

[11]The 'essence of hillness' is, literally, the essence of being Pahari.

The border between the Indian Himalayas and Nepal, like many, if not most, national borders in the world, is an artifact of colonialism, in this case the British-Nepal war of 1814-16, which pushed the border that Nepal had extended west to roughly the Tons River, back eastward to the Kali, its present location. It is a political, rather than an ethnic or cultural boundary. Linguistic and cultural features vary, cline-like, as an irregular continuum throughout the length of the Indo-Nepalese Himalayan arc.

The Himalayan people I know best are India's Pahari: the Himalayan Hindu, Indo-European speaking, Brahman and Kshatriya (Baman and Thakur) subsistence farmers, and low-caste artisan/service castes (Dom or Shilpkar), who populate small villages on the mountainsides and in the occasional valleys, between altitudes of approximately 700 and 2,700 meters above sea level, i.e. Lewis and Riccardi's "mid-montane Paharis" (Berreman 1963, 1972b). Their precise equivalents in Nepal, are the high-caste Hindu Bahun, Chetri, and the low "occupational" castes (Chhetri 1999).

Because I believe that most readers of this volume will be more familiar with Nepal than with Himalayan India, and because I am more familiar with the latter, I will begin with an overview of my research and the ethnography of that region.

THE SOCIOCULTURAL CONTEXT

My most intensive ethnographic experience in the Himalayas has been in 'Sirkanda'[12] village and its immediate area of about a 4-mile radius known as Bhatbair. I began research there for fifteen months in 1957-8, living much of the time in the village, and I have continued with frequent shorter visits of varying duration over the following years, most recently in fall 2000. It is a Garhwali village (the term refers to the Pahari region, dialect, and culture of which it is an example), situated at an altitude of about 1,800 metres above sea level, near the crest of a ridge overlooking the steep, partially terraced ravine of the Bandal River 800 metres below. There the river comprises the north-eastern boundary of Dehra Dun district with Tehri Garhwal district. At the time of my initial research Sirkanda had a population of about 385, roughly half of whom at any given time resided in field houses and cattle sheds (*chans*) located up to 12 miles from the central settlement. It was without electricity, running water, and roads, a long day's trek from the mountain town of Mussoorie to the north-west, or from Dehra Dun to the south-west. A number of people, mostly women, had never been to either. Bhatbair comprised some ten villages, at least

[12] 'Sirkanda' is a pseudonym. All other place names are actual.

fifteen smaller settlements, and about 2,000 residents (Berreman 1963: 9-37, 1962).[13]

In Nepal's middle hills, Tibeto-Burman-speaking Buddhist or 'Mongol' peoples (also known and self-described as 'Janajati' or 'Adivasi') are by far the most populous and diverse ethnic category (see Hangen 1999; Gurung 1997: 527; Gaenszle 1997: 368). They share the rural space and livelihood, but not the culture or social organization, of the Hindus, and are a major force in the political dynamics of the nation, both in the countryside and in the remittance economy. However, they are scarcely present in the mid-montane regions of India with which I am most familiar. There they are Bhotiyas, encountered only at higher altitudes (see Pant 1935; Hoon 1996), or they are labourers from Nepal. As a result I know less about them and have therefore unavoidably slighted them in this paper.

If asked their identity when outside of their region, a person of Sirkanda will gauge their reply by the context of the encounter and their estimate of the questioner's identity or knowledge: if judged to be totally unfamiliar with the area such as a Pardesi (a foreigner or south Indian), the reply will likely be 'Pahari' (of the mountains); if adjudged to be a knowledgeable Desi (Indian of the plains) or a Nepali or non-Garhwali Pahari, the reply would be 'Garhwali'; if identified as an unfamiliar fellow Garhwali, it would be 'Sirkanda *wala/i*' (Sirkanda person) or perhaps some term of intermediate scope such as 'Bhatbair *wala/i*'. Terms designating major Pahari subcultural areas are widely recognized and used (e.g. Garhwali, Kumaoni, Kinnauri, Jaunsari), as are ethnic terms (e.g. Gaddi, Gujjar). A historic ethnic term for high-caste Paharis is Khas (or Khasiya). Both of these designations – Pahari and Khas (Khasiya) – are rejected by some, mostly by expatriates, as being derogatory and even false, on the grounds that they are 'tribal' designations implying backwardness and Hindu unorthodoxy. For others they are identities carried with pride (Berreman 1963: 14-20, 138-9; Bista 1996: 70-8; Joshi 1990).

[13]During 1957-8, one family of Muslims was living in Bhatbair, some distance from Sirkanda. I saw them only once, at a regional fair, and would have been unable to distinguish them from the Hindu Paharis if they had not been pointed out to me. Prior to the traumatic 1947 partition of India and Pakistan, there had been a number of Muslim families in Bhatbair. Sirkanda people said they had nothing against them – "they're just Pahari farmers like us". During the partition, a group of Sikhs on horseback and carrying guns rode through Sirkanda asking about Muslims. "We told them 'there aren't any around here,' and then we got in touch with the Muslims and warned them to flee – for our safety as well as theirs. We had seen bodies in the river." I have visited several times a Muslim Gujjar settlement in a sal forest in the Siwalik Hills south of Dehra Dun, whose members, together with the cattle (and sometimes goats and sheep) that provide the staples of their subsistence, and most of their possessions, move annually in the spring, a month's trek to higher elevations where pasturage is available for their livestock. Some of them pass through Sirkanda en route and arrange to pasture their herds and flocks on fallow Sirkanda fields for a few days or more in exchange for the resultant manureing of the fields.

It will be clear from the brief description of the Pahari system of castes (*jatis*) and caste categories (varnas) that is to follow, that this system is similar to, but distinct from, the Sanskritic system found throughout most of north Indian Hindu society. I will refrain from describing that 'Sanskritic' system because it has been described so widely and well that I am confident that most readers of this volume will be as familiar with it as am I (see Srinivas 1962; Kolenda 1978). It will be equally clear to those who know Nepal, that the Pahari system is virtually the same as the Hindu Nepali system. My description of what I purport the system to be will inevitably convey a Garhwali bias, for it is in the context of that culture that I learned it.

Pahari society shares with pan-South Asian Hinduism the *jati*/varna (i.e. caste/caste-category) system, but its expression differs from that found elsewhere in northern India in that: (1) it has only two, rather than the conventional three, 'twice-born' varnas; and (2) it has no once-born varna.[14] The twice-born Pahari varnas are, Baman (Brahman, the priestly varna) and, ranked closely below it, the subsistence farming Kshatriya (royal/warrior) varna, known and addressed, with profound but unacknowledged irony as Thakur (landlord), or Rajput (royal), but in some areas referred to as *jajman* (this last, presumably because they are the Bamans' ritual clientele).[15] The population of Thakurs far outnumbers all others in these hills (as it does among Nepali Hindus as well). The categorical Pahari term that embraces both of the twice-born varnas is Bit or Bith.

The twice-born varna that is 'missing' in Pahari society (as compared to the Sanskritic four varna system), is the Vaishya (mercantile) varna, ranked immediately below the Kshatriya. Also 'missing' is the once-born Shudra varna that in Sanskritic Hinduism comprises mostly artisan or 'occupational' castes – often called *choti* (little), or *kamzor* (weak) *jatis*. These are collectively ranked fourth and last in the Hindu varna system, far below the Vaishya, but far above the despised and gravely polluted varnaless, *achut* (literally 'untouchable') castes often called *nich*, (literally 'low' but perhaps better translated as 'despicable').

It may seem paradoxical that while the Pahari system lacks the Vaishya and Shudra varnas, it does not lack the castes that would comprise them or, more accurately (since castes are everywhere regionally circumscribed marriage networks), the system does not lack the *sorts* of castes that would

---

[14]As most readers will also know, the ritually purest varnas are called 'twice born' because their male members are ritually 'reborn' (at approximately the age of puberty) to full adult status with the caste responsibilities and the entitlements that accompany them. Lesser castes do not have this privilege (nor do women!).

[15]This refers to the extensively researched Jajmani system of exchange of goods (or services) for services among castes in (nowadays mostly rural) India. The early and authoritative classic on the subject is Wiser's *The Hindu Jajmani System* (1936).

comprise them. In the absence of Vaishya castes, their roles in Pahari society are generally filled by merchant/moneylenders of non-Pahari Vaishya castes – often Marwari 'Baniyas' (Rajasthani merchant/money-lenders) – or by entrepreneurial Paharis, most often Thakur/Rajputs.

Castes that would rank as Shudras in the Sanskritic four varna system are found in the Pahari system to have been relegated to the debased *achut*, (lit. 'untouchable') category, excluded altogether from the varna system. Pahari castes of this category are generally referred to by the derogatory term Dom, but also by the descriptive and equally derogatory term Shilpkar ('manual worker' or artisan).[16] Castes that in the Sanskritic varna system would be respectable, 'clean' Shudras, but that in the Pahari two-varna system are consigned to the gravely polluted 'untouchable', non-varna Dom/Shilpkar status, include blacksmiths, goldsmiths, stonemasons, carpenters, tailors, weavers, and others.[17] Those that would be in the Dom category even if there were a Shudra varna, include shoemakers/leather-workers, barbers, basket makers, and various kinds of drummers/musicians and entertainers/performers. Among Dom/Shilpkar castes in general there is a conspicuously wider range of ranks than is found among Baman or Thakur/Rajput castes (Berreman 1963: 200-17: cf. Chhetri 1999).[18]

These despised castes, denied membership in the caste system (and therefore symbolically excluded from Hinduism), have generated a system of their own comprising subsets of castes, ranked into categories that resemble mini-varnas. The fact that they exist among the very castes that are virtually excluded from legitimacy in the broader society, suggests that these castes have responded to their dire situation by constructing their own

[16]This use of the term Shilpkar suggests that manual labour, rather than – or in addition to – ritual pollution, is a criterion for their status.

[17]An example may clarify the dynamics of the juxtaposition of caste and ethnicity: my Sirkanda friend, Safri, a Pahari blacksmith (Lohar) and therefore a Dom, many years ago managed to marry his eldest daughter, Kamaldi, to Prem Das, a Lohar from Nagal, a village at the border of the Garhwali and Desi culture areas. Prem Das was by ethnicity a Desi and therefore by caste a Shudra. I once went unaccompanied to visit the young couple and, seeking directions to their house in his village, I resorted to inquiring for directions from a shopkeeper. I was surprised when, having steeled myself for the expected abrupt, disdainful response to such a request regarding a Lohar, I was instead matter-of-factly escorted to a location from which the shopkeeper could point out the blacksmith's home and shop. I had not been thinking of the disparity in caste status of the husband and the wife, in their contrasting ethnic settings. When I remarked on this to Prem Das, he recounted his own dismay when he first visited his parents-in-law in Sirkanda only to there become the unsuspecting victim of untouchability.

[18]A remarkable nineteenth-century British civil servant, whose knowledge of Pahari culture remains unsurpassed, wrote 120 years ago that "according to popular estimation, [Pahari Doms] are divided into four grades, all equally impure and outside ordinary caste life, but furnishing certain distinctions from occupation and the like ... so that no link in the chain of social distinction between the highest and the lowest will be wanting" (Atkinson 1882: 444; cf. Berreman 1963: 214-17).

independent social structure, patterned on that of the dominant society, without its sanction – or even its awareness (cf. Berreman 1963: 181-3, 190-1, 232-3, 1972a: 572-3). This is consistent with processes manifest among the same castes in the realms of religion, ritual practice, and community caste-council (Panchayat) governance. There too, those who are excluded have created their own roles and institutions: priests, exorcists, rituals, deliberative and judicial councils, mutual assistance arrangements, festivals, and entertainments. It seems likely that this pattern of response to societal denigration and exclusion is a widespread phenomenon by no means limited to South Asia. That is, in the context of denigration, deprivation and exploitation, the disadvantaged – in this case 'untouchables' – have risen to the occasion to protect their interests, by creating a parallel universe of social, religious, political, and perhaps even economic components, a universe of the oppressed, that virtually reproduces that of their oppressors.

THE COMPARATIVE RESEARCH: INDIAN AND NEPALESE HIMALAYANS

I turn now to my research comparing Himalayan peoples of India and Nepal in their perceptions and actions regarding some significant social/political issues. I will do so by posing some questions that I have attempted to answer, and some issues I have attempted to understand, followed in each case by my conclusions – or perhaps more accurately, simply my thoughts – with respect to each of them. It cannot be expected, nor do I believe that my conclusions and generalizations will apply uniformly throughout such complex societies as these with respect to such complex issues as I will address. Rather, I hope that by raising these questions and proposing responses to them, I may challenge others to their own research and perhaps superior responses.[19]

The questions follow; the length and scope of the 'answering' responses vary widely.

Question 1: Why has Nepal Incurred a Maoist Insurgency, while Himalayan India has Not?

I ask this question first, and reply to it at the greatest length and with the most citations, because misgovernance, injustice, and inequality, and the responses they have elicited among their victims, are paramount and urgent issues in the Himalayan regions of both Nepal and India – as they have been worldwide.

[19] Apologies to Arnold J. Toynbee (1947) and his theory of the role of "challenge and response" in shaping human history!

Let it be acknowledged at the outset that the differential scale of the two nations – their relative geographic demographic, political, and economic size and complexity, together with the countries' contrasting histories (colonial India and Nepal's tortured political history) – largely account for their citizens' differential expressions of resistance.[20] These differences are, however, so complex and long range as to be beyond detailed analysis in this chapter. In any case, they have been extensively documented by others.

A number of more specific and immediate contributing factors can be posited in response to this timely and tragic question. Prominent among them are the fact and nature of Nepal's current and recent monarchies, combined with the country's political instability over the last century and a half, including the failure of its experiments with democracy since the 1950s. These events have been gravely exacerbated by economic crises in the context of pervasive and extreme rural poverty resulting from population pressure on inadequate, fragmented, maldistributed land, and the alarmingly bleak prospects for the country's increasing number of educated urban youth, together with the dangerous juxtaposition of stark ethnic and class divisions within the society.

Nepal's situation can be contrasted with India's experience of colonialism and its overthrow, followed by democratic governance, shaken but not shattered by the turbulence of ethnic and regional conflicts and religious extremism. Although India is plagued with many of the same problems that face Nepal – notably in its vast rural sector – it has developed an infrastructure and an industrial capacity, coupled with a middle class to manage it, that has nurtured an economy and government which, although vulnerable, have managed to survive. I will here present some thoughts on the subject.

In officially Hindu Nepal, despite their numerical minority, Bahuns, Chetris (and, in Kathmandu and its environs, Newars) are overwhelmingly dominant educationally, economically, administratively, and politically,[21] leaving the majority Janajati/Mongols to remain as subsistence farmers and tourist guides at home, or foot soldiers, security guards and labourers in India and abroad (Yamanaka 2000).

In officially secular India, Paharis tend to occupy a social, economic, and political position relative to Indians of the Indo-Gangetic Plain (Desis),

---

[20] On the issue of sociocultural complexity, see Berreman (1978b).

[21] The Tibeto-Burman-speaking Newar comprise a wide variety of "caste blocs" and occupational specialists, roughly comparable to Hindu caste categories (varnas), which in turn can be divided according to their venue – as urbanites and as rural agriculturalists (Jyapu or Maharjan). Among the former are priests, merchants, and bureaucrats, as well as lower status artisans and other specialists, and lowest of all, sweepers. As Newars, indigenous to the Kathmandu Valley, all have been recently declared to be Janajati despite the fact that the urban segment comprises largely a social, political and economic elite (see Gellner 1997b).

which in many ways corresponds to that of the position of Nepal's Janajatis relative to its Hindus. In other words, India's Desis dominate and denigrate Paharis in much the same way that Nepal's Hindus treat Janajati/Mongols, though less severely.

The lesser severity is a consequence of the fact that the Nepalese ethnic split is more profound and pervasive than the Indian one. India's Paharis are, after all, Hindus – albeit 'rustic' ones in the minds of their co-religionist Desis. Paharis regard Desis as arrogant and domineering, but they are fellow Hindus nonetheless. They speak closely related, 'Indo-Aryan' languages, and their caste-based social systems are basically similar. In short, they do not suffer the ethnic chasm that separates Hindus and Janajatis/Mongols in Nepal, with their unrelated languages, their differing religions, and their divergent social structures.

Nepal's Janajati/Mongols comprise a vast, essentially disenfranchised majority within a powerful, privileged, minority-dominated society and nation. India's Paharis are a small minority in a huge majority-dominated nation. Social class – wealth *versus* poverty, education *versus* illiteracy, political power *versus* vulnerability – compound the difference. Janajati/Mongols, on the whole, are severely economically disadvantaged, frustrated and resentful, but there has been enhanced access to education among some, and foreign residence by a few. As a result, there has been increased awareness of alternatives. They have recognized the possibility of, and visualized the means to achieve, social, economic, and political equality and justice. A number of authors have analysed these issues as they occur in Nepal, notable among them Bhattachan and Pyakuryal, from whom a brief excerpt is worth quoting:

> Bahun-Chhetris, whose total combined population, according to the census of 1991, is 29 per cent of the total population of Nepal, but control about 70 to 90 per cent of the total key political, bureaucratic, military, and police positions. The remaining 71 per cent of the total population have been deprived of these positions for the last two centuries. Therefore, majority of the ethnic and low caste groups are in direct conflict with hill Bahun-Chhetris.[22] (Bhattachan & Pyakuryal: 1996: 27)

[22]The "remaining 71 per cent" of the population is, of course, not made up entirely of Janajatis. Gellner reports (personal communication) that recent figures suggest the probable proportion of Janajatis in the total population to be 42 per cent, and that the "low caste groups" to which Bhattachan and Pyakuryal refer are Hindu Dalits, the despised, disadvantaged, exploited, 'untouchable' (*achut*) castes that perform ritually polluting but secularly essential services in both Nepal and India (Chhetri 1999; Upadhyay 1990; Human Rights Watch 1999). The "ethnic groups" to which they refer presumably include Muslims, Hindus of Indian ancestry resident in the Tarai, and scattered smaller, ethnically distinct groups (see Bista 1996).

A result has been the tragic, desperate, but expectable Maoist insurgency. I say 'expectable' with the advantage of hindsight, but others have come to the same conclusion with foresight. Among the earliest and most detailed accounts of the origins, development, and probable future of Maoism in Nepal are those by Nickson (1992), and Mikesell (1993). Both combined their accounts with a comparison of the similarities between the Maoism of Nepal, led by the Nepal Communist Party's Masal faction, and that of Peru's Sendero Luminoso. In conclusion, Nickson, who produced the more detailed of the two accounts, observed that:

> Sendero Luminoso and Masal have emerged in [two] countries with many structural similarities. Both political parties appeared at a time when each of these countries was emerging from a long period of authoritarian rule during which the standard of living of those living in the poorest rural areas had stagnated despite the official rhetoric of priority concern for these sectors. ...
>
> The future prospects of Maoism in Nepal will ... depend largely on the extent to which the ... government addresses the historic neglect and discrimination of the small rural communities which still make up the overwhelming bulk of the population of the country.
>
> If, as seems extremely likely, the [governing] Nepali Congress Party fails to deliver serious structural improvements in land tenure and in service delivery by the public administration, then, in the face of deteriorating living conditions in general, and growing unemployment of secondary school leavers in particular, the fragile centre-ground of Nepali politics may well begin to disintegrate, thereby widening the degree of tacit support for revolutionary solutions such as that proposed by Masal.
>
> ... It would seem that, contrary to global trends, the medium-term prospects for Maoism in Nepal are by no means exhausted. (Nickson 1992: 383-4)

Mikesell, in a brief essay in *Himal* magazine, 'The Paradoxical Support of Nepal's Left for Comrade Gonzalo', also anticipated parallel violent responses to similar circumstances in Peru and Nepal:

> There are ... ample forms of masked violence present in Nepali society, and perhaps the type of sectarian violence espoused [by the 'Shining Path'] is but a short step away. These masked forms of violence include expropriation of lands, rural debt, rent servitude, high child mortality, misappropriation of resources, inflation, corruption in favour of a few, labour migration, and trade of women for prostitution. Besides the communist movement, these factors are also giving rise to new forms of Janajati consciousness

> and nationalist movements in the hills. If respected as a cry for recognition, autonomous development and substantial change, they could evolve into a positive force; if ignored or suppressed, they could lead to sectarian violence. (Mikesell 1993: 32)

That article elicited a sharp letter of rebuttal by Skar, "No Shining Path in Nepal", in which he cited his extensive experience in Peru as the basis for asserting that "*I do not see Nepal as being on the brink of a violent future*", whereupon he proceeded to justify his ill-fated prediction (Skar 1994: 7, italics in the original).

Gellner (1997a: 26), citing Dahal (1995: 166-7), writes:

> Although "ethnic awareness has become an ubiquitous aspect of political life in Nepal after democracy", he [Dahal] argues that "ethnic problems show the characteristics of a non-peasant, urban phenomena [*sic*]. In other words, ethnic politics has no base at the grassroots level and pose no immediate danger to political stability and national integration."

Having contrasted Dahal's views with others that are less sanguine about the prospects for ethnic peace (an earlier version of Bhattachan & Pyakuryal 1996), he concluded with his own observation that

> ... [A]lthough Nepal certainly faces very great economic and ecological problems, the worst fears of some commentators about the politicization of culture may well prove to be unfounded. With the more pluralist model of national culture that has already emerged, it is to be hoped that, despite increasing demands for a place at the national table, few ethnic activists, and fewer still of their potential followers, will wish to depart from it altogether. (Gellner 1997a: 28)[23]

For further insights into these and related issues in their historical context, see Gellner (1997a), Lecomte-Tilouine (2004), and, from a Marxian perspective, Mikesell's *Class, State, and Struggle in Nepal: Writings 1989-95* (1999), especially his 'Social History of the *Jaana-Andolan*: A Critical Analysis' (87-116), 'The Class Basis of the Movement: Historical Origins and Present Significance' (191-212), and 'The Next Step: Cultivating the Roots of Rebellion' (213-30).[24]

---

[23] In closing a 1993 letter to the editor of *Himal* magazine, Gopal Gurung, President of the Mongol Jana Andolan National Organization in Kathmandu had this to say: "The Mongol National Organization wants real democracy, provincial government, secular country and human rights, not only in a constitution but in practice. There will be a blood bath in this Himalayan Kingdom if the minority but powerful Hindus neglect the majority of the indigenous Mongol people." (G. Gurung: 1993: 5).

[24] The term 'Marxian' (suggesting a less doctrinaire use of Marx than does the term 'Marxist') is *my* characterization of Mikesell's work, not his. I derive it from the usage of Eric Wolf, who

In addition to the items cited and quoted above, there are extremely significant accounts based on interviews and observation of one or both sides of Maoist *vs.* Police/Army encounters by journalists Onesto (1999-2000, 2005)[25] and Ogura (2004, 2007), by anthropologist de Sales (2000), by Gersony (2003), who is a consultant to Mercy Corps International, and by Bevacqua (2004), "chief economist for Merrill Lynch and Commerz Securities in Tokyo from 1993-2002, [who, in 2003] travelled extensively through central and south Asia in order to observe first-hand how US foreign policy in the post-9/11 environment was affecting the lives of ordinary people ... " (p. 6). Dipak, is "a writer in Nepal who received a special invitation from party comrades in Rukum to witness the Rukumkot Raid [on the night of 1 April 2001], firsthand". His account of that "widely acknowledged ... topmost military action to date", is available in Dipak (2001). In the same journal and issue is a brief summary based on "accounts from the Nepali and Western press", of a range of events in and around "the People's War", during July 2001, under the headline "Nepal: People's War Confronts the King's Army". Other Significant items include a critique of the Maoist agenda, from the left, by Shrestha (1997), an essay by Thapa (2002), and thirteen essays by a variety of authors, including the editor, in Hutt (2004). The last of these includes, as appendices, three valuable documents: "A. The Forty-point Demand of the United People's Front (February 1996); B. Full Text of Prime Minister Sher Bahadur Deuba's Message to the Nation (27 November 2001); C. Full Text of King Gyanendra's Address to the Nation (4 October 2002)".[26]

---

writes, for example: "I have drawn freely on concepts taken from the storehouse of Marxian ideas" (1982: 386), and "Since Karl Marx's name is such a bugaboo, it is important to focus on his ideas rather than on the polemics surrounding them. Vernon Venable's *Human Nature: The Marxian View* (1945) is, to me, still the best all-round introduction to the subject" (Wolf 1982: 394).

[25]Onesto (1999-2000): 'Dispatches: Report from the People's War in Nepal,' by journalist Li Onesto, is a series of reports published almost weekly, in twenty-two parts between 18 July 1999 and 13 February 2000, in the *Revolutionary Worker*. Now that series, together with her interview with Prachanda, General Secretary of the Communist Party of Nepal (Maoist), is available as a book (Onesto 2005). It comprises her unique eyewitness reports, interviews and numerous photographs from her "travel into the guerrilla zones of [the western middle hills] of Nepal" in the spring of 1999. "I travelled and lived with members of the People's Army and interviewed political and military leaders, guerrilla fighters, relatives of those killed in the war, and villagers in areas under Maoist control. I embarked on this three-month journey with the aim of capturing the passion, voices, and faces of the peasants who are waging what they call a 'People's War'. I was the first foreign journalist to be given such access by the Communist Party of Nepal (Maoist) the party leading this revolution," she reports (Onesto 2005: 2).

[26]The initial issue of *Himalaya* (formerly *Himalayan Research Bulletin*), published by the 'Association for Nepal and Himalayan Studies' is titled 'War on Terrorism, War as Terrorism, and Nepal's Maoist Insurgency' (Brower 2003) (published Sept. 2004). Received too late to be incorporated in the text of this chapter, it comprises six current scholarly research papers followed by 'Comments' and a 'Roundtable Discussion', both of which emanated from

To return to the question of why there has been no insurgency in the middle hills of India that comes close to matching that of Nepal, it must be acknowledged that this is in part a self-fulfilling contrast. That is, by limiting the territories to be compared in this essay to the Pahari mid-montane region of India and the middle hills of Nepal, I have excluded India's, long-term confrontation with separatists (and Pakistan) in Kashmir, the lingering contestation with China over the adjacent Aksai Chin region (Fisher, Rose & Huttenback 1963), and the long and bitter insurgency in the north-east hill states adjacent to Myanmar. As recently as 3 October 2004, for example, Associated Press reported:

> Gauhati [Assam – 2 October 2004]
> In a shattering series of attacks, suspected separatists hit nine targets – a railroad station and eight markets – with bombs and gunfire across two states in northeastern India [Assam and Nagaland] on Saturday, killing 44 people. ... More than three dozen insurgent groups have been active, and the region is home to one of Asia's longest-running separatist conflicts, dating to shortly before India gained independence from Britain in 1947. ...
>
> [It] has alsc been the scene of an insurgency that has killed 15,000 people since Naga rebels began fighting for a separate nation almost six decades ago. The rebels want special status for Nagaland state ... where most of the 2 million Nagas – most of them Christians – live in predominantly Hindu India. ...
>
> Insurgent groups in India's northeast are pushing demands ranging from independent homelands to autonomy within the nation. The rebels say they are seeking to protect their ethnic identities [and protect their natural resources].
>
> (*San Francisco Chronicle*, 3 October 2004: A8)

There have been other well-documented autonomy movements, both violent and non-violent, throughout the north-eastern hill states (Sarin: 1980), in the new north-central state of Jharkhand (Munda & Mullick 2003), in Kashmir (Asia Watch 1993; Ahmad 1996; Behera 1996), and elsewhere in India (Gough & Sharma 1973). Kumaon and Garhwal (adjacent to Nepal), which comprised the eight lightly populated Himalayan districts of Uttar Pradesh, India's most populous state, were the scene of agitation for statehood under the name Uttarakhand, since shortly after India's independence in 1947 (Aryal 1994b; Pande 1995; Dhoundiyal et al. 1993). The state was finally established, under the name Uttaranchal, in 2000, four turbulent years after its widely heralded announcement. Although that agitation included some violent incidents, in the Pahari

---

conference papers in 2002. It is a key resource on its topic. It will be followed by a second issue, titled 'Nepal's Maoist Insurgency, Part II'.

region there has not been organized, militant, and sustained violence at all comparable to what has been happening and continuously accelerating since 1996 in the middle hills of Nepal.

A major difference between the agitation and insurgency in India and Nepal is simply that in India, these actions have been aimed at achieving various degrees of political autonomy for ethno-territorial groups. By 'various degrees' I mean agitations ranging from demands for statehood *within* the nation (e.g. the successful agitations for Uttarakhand/Uttaranchal in the Himalayan middle hills, and for Jharkhand in central India), to movements for *secession from* the nation (e.g. the unsuccessful agitations for Nagaland in the north-east, and Khalistan within what is now Punjab). In Nepal, by way of contrast, the insurgency is aimed at nothing less than overturning the monarchy and assuming governance of the nation as a democratic socialist state.

This difference has major international consequences in that Nepal's revolution raises in the minds of 'great powers' the spectre of significant change in the regional – perhaps global – balance of power. As a result it has attracted financial and military assistance to the Royal Nepalese Army by India, Britain, and the United States, unprecedented in modern times (Onesto 2005). The US has taken the ominous step of declaring the Maobadi a terrorist organization, an action that has no doubt exacerbated security concerns in China.

This situation, heretofore rarely confronted in the foreign press, is addressed directly and incisively by Bevacqua (2004). His essay, 'Nepal and the "War on Terror"' is based on government documents and his own experiences and inferences. A few paragraphs will suggest its nature:

> Soon after launching their rebellion [in February 1996], the Maoists' 'influence spread rapidly, largely because the government failed to provide adequate services or to punish corrupt and abusive local [government] officials.' That was the assessment of the U.S. Congress when it stepped up military aid to the government of Nepal in 2002. Indeed at the present time, after eight years of combat, the Maoists fully control at least five of Nepal's 75 districts, and control most of the countryside in all the rest. Only the Kathmandu Valley and provincial capitals remain in the government's hands, along with the national park that includes Mt Everest [in 2003].
>
> Deep and unmitigated poverty is the underlying source of strength for the Maoists. Even in areas in which poverty has been alleviated somewhat, such as in the Kathmandu Valley, the memories of it remain vivid. ...
>
> ... [T]he government seems unable or unwilling to tackle the

> daunting level of poverty in the country despite massive foreign aid that makes up nearly 30% of the national budget. ...
>
> The key problem – and the one the Maoists exploit the most in gaining support in the countryside – is the unequal distribution of land ownership in the country. The bottom 40% of farming households operate only 9% of farm land, while the top 6% own more than 33%. ...
>
> ... In the face of growing poverty and a government unwilling to make reforms, the rebels feel justified in taking up arms.

Bevacqua goes on to report that on the international level circumstances and prospects are equally grim:

> [I]n the wake of 9/11 the Nepalese government began an international campaign to raise foreign assistance for their 'war on terror'. For 2002, U.S. aid to Nepal ... was initially set at $27.5 million [up from $5.3 million total for the previous six years]. But after then-Prime Minister Deuba met with President Bush in May 2002, the Bush administration asked Congress for an additional $20 million in military financing – $15 million for helicopters and $5 million for night-vision goggles and armour, and communications equipment. Only $14 million was actually spent that year, but the administration nonetheless requested $37 million in aid funds for 2003.
>
> The U.S. is not acting alone of course. Last year UK provided 6.5 million pounds (approximately $10 million) to finance hardware purchases. India has provided training, helicopters and transport vehicles.
>
> The growing support the Maoists receive from average Nepalis shows that many now believe there is no alternative route to real change in the country. The rebels are, unfortunately, often as unsavoury as the government. They use violence and the threat of violence not only to weaken the government and prove it is incapable of governing, but also to coerce support from villagers and intimidate potential opponents.
>
> All observers, even the U.S. government, agree that neither side [Maoists or RNA] will ever succeed militarily.
>
> ... In the end average Nepalis will be the losers.

The question remains: Why has there been no movement such as that described above for Nepal, in culturally and environmentally similar India?

In challenging Mikesell's assertion (1993: 31) that "the conditions exist in the hills of Nepal for a Shining Path-like movement, equally sectarian and equally violent," Skar (1994: 6) announced: "*I do not see Nepal as being on the brink of a violent future*" (italics in the original). He followed that report from his "clouded crystal ball",[27] with a tortured explanation and rationalization of it, whereupon he concluded: "This kind of process is not applicable to Nepal, where there is no clear-cut dual society and instead exists a multiplicity of ethnic groups. In Peru, basically class and ethnicity are overlapping categories while in Nepal they are not."

It is precisely the ethnically dual society (Bahun/Chetri *vs.* Janajati/Mongol), with its associated stark class division that largely accounts for Nepal's Maoist movement. By way of contrast, it is the relatively homogeneous nature of India's Pahari society, with its overwhelming social, economic, and demographic preponderance of the Bahun/Thakur population (at the expense of the small minority of low, 'occupational', 'Dom' castes) that has contributed heavily to preventing a similar movement there.

My disagreement with Skar is not about the dynamics of Maoist movements, nor the existence of a multiplicity of ethnic groups in Nepal. Rather, it is his fundamental claim, as stated in the final six words of his concluding sentence quoted above: "In Peru, basically class and ethnicity are overlapping categories, while in Nepal they are not" (Skar 1994: 4). I would substitute: "In Peru, basically class and ethnicity are overlapping categories, *'as they are in Nepal'*". That similarity, I believe, largely accounts for the similarities Mikesell describes between the Peruvian Sendero Luminoso (Shining Path) and the Nepali Maobadi (Maoists), and that accounts for the fact that Skar was so wrong in his prognostication.

My answer to the question posed (Why the Maoist insurgency in Nepal and not in India?) is, in short: Nepalese Maoism is primarily a result of the fact that Nepal has had the ethnic and class divides in the context of severe poverty and differential power, epitomized in its monarchy, that moved subsistence farmers of the middle hills to desperate measures. The Pahari region does not have that combination of conditions, at least not to anywhere near a comparable degree.

Question 2: Why has India's Pahari Region Spawned a Grassroots Anti-deforestation Movement (Chipko), while Nepal has Not?

Pahari Chipko

There has been a long history of anti-deforestation activism in the Pahari region, as has been well documented by Ramachandra Guha in his aptly titled book, *The Unquiet Woods: Ecological Change and Peasant Resistance in the Himalaya* (1990). It is not surprising, therefore, that in 1973 a grassroots anti-deforestation movement, Chipko Andolan, had its begin-

[27]"The Clouded Crystal Ball" is a phrase formerly used by *The New Yorker* magazine to identify amusing quotes of egregiously erroneous predictions gleaned from published sources.

nings in response to a brazen attempt by commercial timber merchants to cut down a local forest near Chamoli town in Garhwal district. Chandi Prasad Bhatt, an employee of a local transport agency, is credited with initiating the action, when he proposed that local villagers interpose themselves between the axemen and the trees, by literally 'hugging the trees' (Chipko means 'stick to'). They did so, the axemen desisted and departed, and a movement was born. At about the same time, a similar protest was mounted at Silyari in Tehri Garhwal district, inspired by the soon-to-be-famed Gandhian environmentalist, Sunderlal Bahuguna.

Despite its nationwide, and ultimately worldwide, publicity, as an active grassroots force, Chipko remained confined largely to those two districts. But its impact has been widespread. It has inspired environmental activism throughout the world – activism that has not been limited to its goal of saving the trees. It has also undertaken opposition to destructive limestone extraction, and to big dam construction (notably the Tehri Dam in Garhwal), and active advocacy of such social issues as female and child protection and anti-liquor agitation. The literature by and about its actions, activists, and advocates has been so prolific, and its thirty-year history is so complex, that it cannot be adequately summarized here. I have had a special interest in it in view of the fact that it originated in the districts with which I am most familiar. I have therefore contributed substantially to that literature, dating from a very brief monograph (*Himachal: Science, People and "Progress"* 1979), followed by pursuit of the subject in some detail for more than a decade thereafter. In several journal articles and book chapters I have provided accounts of the rarely described political context of the origin and evolution of the movement (see Berreman 1983b, 1985a, 1985b, 1987, 1989).[28]

The movement has been motivated by mountain farmers' determination to protect trees and other natural resources upon which they depend, from the commercial devastation that has long been rampant, and in recent years, increasing throughout the mid-montane region. Forests are essential for the resources they provide – fuel for warmth and cooking, fodder and forage for livestock, compost for fertilizer, building material, medicinal herbs, wildlife habitat, and – because all rural folk are nowadays dependent in part on the money economy – surplus forest products for sale. Forests are also essential for the environmental protection they offer in conserving water and minimizing erosion and landslides. Chipko has attracted the support of environmentalists, temperance activists, and feminists (for it has been widely described as, to a significant extent, a women's movement) in India and abroad.

---

[28]Berreman 1983b and 1987 are similar to one another; the first was published in Sweden, the second in India. (In the light of the differential access and distinct audiences, I try to publish my work on South Asia *in* South Asia as well as in the West, when possible.)

The movement is credited with having proposed and supported legislation to limit deforestation – legislation that was ultimately successful despite fierce opposition from commercial timber interests – in prohibiting in 1981, for a period of fifteen years, commercial logging in all forests above 1,000 metres above sea level (which includes virtually all of the forests of the Himalayan mid-montane region).[29]

Almost simultaneously, action to limit destructive limestone extraction was energetically pursued. The extraction (euphemistically termed 'quarrying') is accomplished by simply blasting the face of the mountain and trucking away the resulting limestone debris, a process that was destroying the face of the outer ranges of the Himalayas in several regions (including the steep hills immediately adjacent to Dehra Dun, now the capital city of Uttaranchal). A related destructive and dangerous feature is the process of reducing limestone to a form that can be used to make cement and other materials. The limestone is burned for many days in huge outdoor ovens, discharging enormous amounts of toxic smoke and particles, with the result that once pristine environs of Dehra Dun have become virtually smog-bound, its air a threat to all who breathe it, and its rivers diminished and dangerously polluted with organic and inorganic poisons (Kapoor 1983: 'The Doon Doom').

The disappointing – even tragic – side of this story is that the legislation – regarding both deforestation and limestone quarrying – has been largely unenforced and therefore ignored, while the fifteen-year moratorium on timber cutting has expired. Trucks loaded with timber and limestone can be seen emerging regularly from the mountains into the Tarai, and the dynamite blasts of limestone quarrying can be heard every day of the week. Barren hills, landslides, immense grey cliffs where mountainside forests recently stood and the acrid smoke-filled air over the adjacent Tarai are testimony to the devastating work of the timber and limestone industries.[30]

Why no Nepali Chipko?

In her 1994 article on the Chipko movement, investigative journalist, Manisha Aryal, concluded that the movement had "collapsed" and that it

---

[29]Many primary sources on Chipko are cited in Guha (1990) and Aryal (1994a), as well as in my own articles on Chipko cited above.

[30]"The Central Himalaya, also known as Uttarakhand ... once described as the valley of Gods is today a land of deserted confluences, denuded forests, receding glaciers, and fleeing and migrating population. This tranquil land of salubriously sequestered forests and salutiferrous vegetation is today threatened with ecological imbalances, upheaval, agitations [for statehood], and neglect due to commercialized planning, sudden mechanization and unregulated transformations" (Dhasmana 1990 (1982)). This is by a loyal and dedicated (expatriate) Pahari scholar, who is an uncompromising critic of, and advocate for, his people and region.

had "singularly failed to provide a catalytic charge in other parts of the Himalaya". She followed with these remarks:

> Perhaps it is in the adjacent hills of Nepal, east of Uttarakhand – where grassroots activism is most remarkable for its absence – that Chipko's legacy can be best applied. ...
>
> Rural Nepal, which contains the largest chunk of the populated and destitute midhills of the Himalayan region, has still to learn to look away from donor organizations, international agencies, government bureaucracy, and political parties, and into ways of developing from within. And Chipko certainly has some lessons.
>
> (Aryal 1994a: 9)

Nepal has produced no Chipko or Chipko-analogue to confront deforestation. The explanation seems to be quite simple: there has not been even an approximation of the amount of environmentally destructive commercial timber (and other natural resources) extraction in Nepal Himalaya that has plagued the Pahari region of India. An exception is to be found in some forested areas bordering the Tarai, and those surrounding three or four Himalayan urbanized areas, most notably Kathmandu and Pokhara.[31] There commercial timber extraction is to be found, but on a much smaller scale than in India, not only absolutely, but relative to the areas and populations affected. Deforestation in rural Nepal is primarily the result of necessary timber consumption-for-use by mountain villagers (and, sadly, promiscuous but economically important consumption by and for tourists) rather than by rapacious commercial timber entrepreneurs, as is the case in India. There is therefore little motive for a Nepalese Chipko movement.

Those who are concerned and active in forest conservation are primarily non-governmental organizations, United Nations agencies including the United Nations Development Program (UNDP), foreign governmental development agencies, and missionary organizations. To my mind, the most effective among all of the foreign projects has been the Nepal-Australia Forestry Project (Griffin 1988), a major source of whose success can be inferred from the title (and content) of Griffin's, Chap. 2.1: "Australians in an Advisory Role". The operative word is "Advisory". Other such programmes tend to employ Nepalis mainly as menials and drivers of the foreigners' off-road vehicles that are often and aptly referred to as 'development tanks'. The programmes, research, and publications of the International Centre for Integrated Mountain Development (ICIMOD) also continue to make important contributions.[32]

---

[31] Within the Tarai, broadleaf hardwood sal forests are also cut commercially with devastating results (as they are in the Indian Tarai as well), but this is beyond the scope of this paper.

[32] "Established in 1983, ICIMOD aims to promote sustainable development in the Hindu Kush -Himalayan Range of Afghanistan, Bangladesh, Bhutan, China, India Myanmar, Nepal, and

Before leaving this question, I think it important to provide context by describing the divergent descriptions and analyses of the Himalayan environment (and specifically of Nepal's forests) that emerged on the environmental scene as famously set forth by Erik Eckholm, in *Losing Ground: Environmental Stress and World Food Prospects* (1976), and the influential, radically revisionist (and to me convincing) interpretation published by Jack D. Ives and Bruno Messerli in *The Himalayan Dilemma: Reconciling Development and Conservation* (1989; see also Metz 1991). The former view attributes massive erosion in the Himalayas, and devastating flooding in the plains, to recent rampant deforestation in the Himalayas (Eckholm 1976: 40, 76-84). Ives and Messerli describe the geological history of such flooding, erosion, and landslides, which long antedate human agency in deforestation, and they document the more modest degree of contemporary deforestation than had been generally believed, together with its relatively minor impact in most of the country on erosion and downriver flooding. In short, the devastating Himalayan environmental crisis that Eckholm foresaw, and which became conventional environmental wisdom, was found by Ives and Messerli and others to be a substantial exaggeration:

> We believe that the environmental deterioration in Nepal has been overdramatized, that correlations have been represented as cause and effect that have often been confused, and that a perceived super-crisis has evolved in the popular press, the conservationist literature, and even in the mainstream scientific writing. ... Our primary aim has been to challenge what we perceive as a series of ingenious but unsupportable linkages connecting massive landscape changes by the subsistence farmers with increased flooding and siltation on the Ganges Plain.
>
> ... We have concluded that the causes of the crisis are not environmental but relate to the social, economic, institutional, and political situations in which the Himalayan region finds itself. While the ultimate effects may be similar – that is, an environmental catastrophe – clarity on this point should result in more rational and more effective responses. (Ives & Messerli 1989: 211)

In short, Himalayan deforestation in India is primarily attributable to commercial timber harvesting imposed from outside the region, sold, processed, and consumed there by commercial interests headquartered in the north Indian plains, with labour recruited mostly from the plains, even for work in the mountains.

Pakistan. ... Most activities are carried out by or through collaborating institutions and organizations in its member countries" (ICIMOD 1997).

In Nepal, to the extent that deforestation exists (which is a matter of debate), it is primarily a consequence of local patterns of use, and is therefore either not perceived as a problem, or not thought to be amenable to change. Where there *is* exploitation of forest resources under conditions similar to those described above for India, it may well generate similar responses. It may contribute significantly to the inequalities, injustices, and resentments that have motivated and fuelled the Maobadi insurgency.

In the end, the realization of Aryal's recommendation that rural Nepal's "destitute midhills ... has still to learn to look away from donor organizations, international agencies, government bureaucracy, and political parties and into ways of developing from within" (Aryal 1994a: 9) may prove to have emerged from the hills and ravines of Rukum and Rolpa's Maobadi rather than Garhwal's Chipko.

Question 3: Given the Absence of Grassroots Challenges to Deforestation in Nepal, as Compared to India's Chipko, Why have Big Dams Evoked Grassroots Opposition in Both Countries?

The experience of, and response to, construction of big dams in the Himalayas of both Nepal and India is epitomized by the grassroots opposition that has been mobilized against construction of the Tehri Dam in Tehri Garhwal, India, and Arun III in Nepal.[33]

In both countries these dams (and others) have been planned, financed, and construction undertaken without participation of those Himalayan people who will be affected, and in fact in the face of their opposition. Grassroots opposition stems from the fact that the dams will in both cases displace many people: entire villages will be inundated together with their fields, pastures, and sacred places, their residents moved to unspecified, unfamiliar locations and environments. Even many of the villages that have not been scheduled to be inundated and displaced will lose fields and pastures and will be separated by the catchment lakes from others as well as from their relatives and familiar environs – often by many miles. In both places there have been no plans for employment of local people in the dams' construction, and in many areas no plans to provide electricity the dams will generate to local people. Among those who are knowledgeable about such things, opposition also stems from the fact that the dams are on or near earthquake fault lines, poised ominously above innumerable villages and towns downriver. In addition, geologists and hydrologists have reported that they will fill with silt decades before their announced obsoles-

[33]For Tehri Dam, see Negi (1990). For Arun III, see Bhattarai (1993), Pandey & Bell (1993), and Pandey (1995). For a geographically broader view on the issue, see Aryal (1995), Agarwal, Chopra, & Sharma (1982), which includes 'Is Tehri Dam a Time Bomb?' (p. 66), and Agarwal & Narain (1985). A detailed case study of dams and their impact in South India (Karnataka), that is relevant to the entire subcontinent and beyond, is Sharma & Sharma (1981).

cence. Perhaps the silver lining to this is that a lake filled with silt is no longer a lake, which eliminates the threat of a bursting dam!

Facing similar problems, people living in the vicinity of both the Tehri Dam and the Arun III have responded with grassroots activism in opposition to the dams, and organization to mobilize resistance against their construction (in India, this has fallen within the programme of Chipko). That the resistance has been effective is demonstrated by the fact that funding and legislative support for both of these large dams has been jeopardized. In the case of Arun III, a series of smaller dams has been substituted at the insistence of the World Bank, which has made a turnabout in its policy regarding the funding of dams. The same fate seems likely for the Tehri Dam, although India's more powerful enabling economy and its players' vested interests, combined with the symbolic association that these massive structures have with national pride, may overcome that auspicious threat.

Question 4: What are the Circumstances and Responses of Dalit Nepali Hindus and Newars to their Social Status Compared to Dalit (Dom) Pahari Hindus of India?

Nepali Dalits

Low Hindu castes of Nepal, the "occupational" castes (Chhetri 1999), or simply the 'untouchables', have begun to adopt the appellation 'Dalit', as the similarly despised and disadvantaged castes in India are now known. They comprise the forgotten, or more accurately, the ignored and avoided, population of Nepal (Dahal et al. 2002). Despised and rejected by their high caste co-religionists, excluded from their temples and rituals, denied a place in the Hindu varna system and consigned by tradition to a de facto position beneath that system as lowest of the low, they are relegated to the most polluting and onerous occupations. Avoided as well by others, Buddhists and Hindus alike, virtually ignored by the society's governing and administrative agents – even by most social scientists – they are in every sense the pariahs of the society; shunned by all, while being indispensable for their skills and labour, by most. They do not participate in the agendas that such movements as the Chipko and anti-big dam organizations promote. They are not welcome or even allowed to do so nor, consequently, can they imagine any benefits to themselves for doing so – no benefits, that is, beyond avoiding the violent wrath of those who exploit them (cf. Berreman 1963: 84-6, 220-6, 233-56).

There are few – some, but few – indigenous social welfare services available to them; a few more foreign and international agencies and NGOs, and finally, several missionary organizations that are likely to expect or require as a quid pro quo, that they join in the alien gospel. A substantial number do just that, thereby becoming the proverbial 'rice Christians'.

Pahari Doms

Low-caste Indian Paharis, known collectively as Doms, or now as Dalits, are in much the same situation as their Nepali equivalents. The major difference is that in India, the Pahari Dalits have a community of millions of fellow citizens of their own social status throughout the nation. Although Pahari Dalits are beyond the reach of many of the social agencies whose interests and activities work on behalf of Dalits in the plains, there is the potential that these agencies will reach into the Himalayas to incorporate Pahari Doms in their clientele. Dalits have been the focus of concern of a number of foreign religious, non-governmental, and aid and development agencies as well as Indian ones.

Most important, symbolically as well as factually, is that India has its 'reservation system', analogous to 'affirmative action' in the US (Galanter 1984; Berreman, forthcoming). Although that system of 'compensatory discrimination', as it is often described, has scarcely reached the mountain-dwelling Pahari Dalits (and in fact has not been consistently pursued or rigorously enforced anywhere in the nation) it has set a precedent and therefore has the potential for its implementation. It is, after all, a constitutionally mandated programme to enhance the opportunities for Dalits and other 'backward classes' – including women – to obtain higher education, legislative representation, and other benefits of the democratic, egalitarian society that India claims to be.

In Nepal there have been recent, preliminary efforts toward initiating a reservation system, but there is, to my knowledge, no legislation there comparable to that in India – no legislation requiring such compensation and privileged access for disadvantaged minority communities and little or no commitment to the idea of an egalitarian society. If it is somewhere on the books, it is certainly not enforced.

Question 5: What have been the Responses by Social Scientists, the Media and Publics of India and Nepal, to Social Science Research Conducted in Their Himalayan Regions?

Indian Responses to Pahari Research

There has been at least a 120-year history of 'modern' reporting and research on the peoples and cultures of the Indian Himalayas, beginning with that by British and Indian civil servants in the form of Gazetteers, governmental reports, memoirs, and the like – even fiction. These have been supplemented by the contributions of interested Indian and British missionaries, mercenaries and travellers to various periodicals (e.g. *Panjab* [later *Indian*] *Notes and Queries* 1883-7). While many of these were ethnocentric to say the least, others like Atkinson's *Himalayan Gazetteers* (Atkinson 1882) were credible, even remarkably authoritative, ethnographic accounts.[34] Contemporary anthropological and sociological works are so numerous as to stock entire bookstalls at annual meetings of South Asia scholars in India and the United States, with new and recent publications.

It is impossible to generalize about how scholars, publishers, and reviewers have responded to the wide range of published offerings on Pahari societies, cultures, and social issues, but some trends can be observed and some examples marshalled to support those observations. While scholarly books are generally ignored by reviewers, a few are reviewed, usually perfunctorily. Some of these are lauded and some criticized or vilified. It seems that a disproportionate number of those in the last category are accounts of India's Pahari societies. It may not be an exaggeration to assert that there is a tendency for the vehemence of criticism to vary directly with the degree of accuracy and completeness of the ethnography. I will describe four examples. The first two concern ethnographic books, responses to which will be presented at some length. The following two concern ethnographic doctoral dissertations which were unpublished, have therefore reached a limited audience, and will be more briefly treated. A fifth brief genre comprises a kind of postscript. It refers not to a single work, nor does it pertain to the Pahari region. Rather, it is presented as a context for understanding the venom to which scholarly work is vulnerable in India. It demonstrates that the fate of the preceding Himalayan examples, though characteristic to the region, is not unique to it.

Case One: *Polyandry in the Himalayas* (1975) is an ethnographic book by Y.S. Parmar, Ph.D., Chief Minister of Himachal Pradesh, a native of that Himalayan state, and a social anthropologist who has specialized in the ethnography of its Pahari Hindu population. A distinctive feature of that society – one shared with Jaunsar-Bawar in western Uttaranchal and, in fact, throughout much of the western Pahari region of Himachal Pradesh – is the prevalence of – in fact, preference for – fraternally polyandrous marriage or, as it is more accurately termed, polygynandry (the marriage of a group of brothers to one or more women).[35] Parmar's book is an updated

---

[34]In the memoir category, I would recommend *A Summer Ramble in the Himalayas* (Edited by 'Mountaineer' [Mr Wilson of Mussoorie] 1860), and in the fiction category, *The Wild Sweet Witch* (Philip Woodruff [pseudonym for Philip Mason] 1947). Both are grounded on intimate knowledge of Garhwal and its people. Wilson's book comprises his edited version of notes provided him by an anonymous "well-valued companion during much of his ramble", while Wilson himself was described in the Introduction as being "quite fond of natural history and inquisitive as to the habits and customs of the people which he has portrayed with skill in this account" (iii) (see especially pp. 159-232). Mason was in the Indian Civil Service for twenty years (1927-47), several of which were spent as District Commissioner of Garhwal District. His novel, set in the Pahari heartland, is a gripping read and a vivid, accurate, depiction of its subject matter.

[35]See *Himalayan Polyandry: Structure, Functioning and Culture Change, A Field-Study of*

version of his dissertation submitted in 1944 to the University of Lucknow. Its Foreword is by the then Prime Minister Indira Gandhi, who describes the book as "a commendable effort ... [for] polyandry is the subject of much ill-informed comment. ... By putting it in its proper historical and economic context, the author gives us a deeper understanding of the manner in which societies evolve institutions to enable them to deal with the basic problems of living and surviving" (vii).

Professor S.C. Dube, Director of the Indian Institute of Advanced Study, wrote its thoughtful Introduction, which concluded, "*Polyandry in the Himalayas* is an important book and it will be read with admiration and respect" (xii). No such luck; not, at least, in the legislature and the popular press. *The Overseas Hindustan Times* (22 May 1975: 3) was one of many newspapers to report on what its headline described as "Feminine Wrath over CM's Book":

> [Parmar's] book ... describing the matrimonial options open before the hill women ... caused some feminine fulminations in the [Himachal Pradesh] Assembly. All four women legislators of his own party staged an indignant walkout, denouncing the insult done to their 'simple artless' sisters living in the Himalayan valleys, when Speaker Kultar Chand Rana disallowed an adjournment motion on the subject ... and three male colleagues came forward to join them in the ceremonial protest. Taking strong exception to certain observations ... which they alleged projected a wrong picture of the hill women, they said the book should be banned and copies already in circulation confiscated. ... While some of these practices must have been prevalent in the past, what ruffled the critics was that the observations in the book, 'based mostly on half-truths and legends' made it clear nowhere that the customs had long since ceased to exist. The result was that the Himalayan woman was portrayed to the outside world as a footloose promiscuous siren.

Jaunsar-Bawar, by Lucknow University anthropologist, the late D.N. Majumdar (1962). "In fact, the Jaunsari family system is not only polyandrous but a combination of fraternal polyandry and polygyny. All men of each generation who are brothers marry together with one or, as is usually the case, more than one wife. ... In principle and in practice, all the brothers form an inseparable group as 'fraternal husbands' in the name of the eldest brothers. The wives, on the other hand, join the union individually, one after another. ... This form of marriage may, therefore be known as 'polygynandry', and this union a polygynandrous family unit instead of being known by the popularly used term 'polyandrous'" (Majumdar 1962: 72). In 1982 I visited the large Pahari village of Lakhamandal, by the Jamuna River in tehsil Chakrata of Dehra Dun district, where Majumdar had studied polyandry. There I interviewed families ranging from a large Rajput family that comprised two husbands (brothers), four shared wives and eleven sibling offspring, to a small low-caste Bajgi (musician) family, consisting of an elderly couple, their two sons sharing one wife, and an infant son. Neither family was exceptional in the village. See Berreman (1962, 1975, 1980).

Naqvi (1975: 10) noted, within a longer report on the subject, that in addition to their objection to Parmar's discussion of polyandry, the legislators objected to his report that in Pahari marriage, 'bride price' (*reet*), rather than dowry (which has also been called 'groom price'), was traditional and usual.[36] "Several other books have been written in similar vein," Naqvi wrote, including the government's 1961 census, which reported on the prevalence of *reet* marriage in some regions. "Whatever may be the merits or demerits of the book, the controversy has certainly increased its sales. And his detractors allege, Parmar's reason for publishing this book was to make money. … "

One cannot but marvel at the notion that academic monographs make money.

Case Two: My own book, *Hindus of the Himalayas* (1963), is an ethnographic account of a Pahari (Garhwali) village and its region based on fifteen months' research from 1957 to 1958. The second edition (1972b) includes material gathered in numerous visits to the village during 1968-9, while I was primarily engaged in a study of urban society and social interaction in Dehra Dun city (1972a).

Sixteen years after the book's initial publication, it, and I personally, came in for vehement criticism similar to that experienced by Dr Parmar. Public attention was directed to the book when, on 11 May 1979, I was awarded an honorary doctorate by Garhwal University, in Srinagar, Garhwal, during its locally publicized 'first ever convocation'. It was a time of intense tension in the region to which I, and all concerned with the convocation, fell victim.

My fellow honoree was Hemavati Nandan Bahuguna, a forty-year party stalwart in Indira Gandhi's Congress (I), and a long-time member of Parliament from Garhwal. He had been Mrs Gandhi's right hand in several roles, including as Chief Minister of India's most populous state, Uttar Pradesh (1973-6), and Secretary-General of Congress (I) (1979-80), until May 1980. At that point he resigned both his membership in her party and his seat in Parliament, to found the opposition Democratic Socialist Party. Over Mrs Gandhi's vehement opposition he won back his old seat under his new party affiliation by defeating Mrs Gandhi's hand-picked candidate in a by-election occasioned by his resignation (Berreman 1983b, 1985b).

The convocation was held in the midst of all this and was therefore highly politicized. Neither the University nor I could avoid being tarred by the political brush. At the time, Mrs Gandhi was temporarily out of office as a result of having lost in a special election she had called in the expec-

---

[36]It must be noted that under Khasa customary law, "The payment of bride-price and formal entry as wife in the husband's house are enough [necessary and sufficient] for the purpose [of accomplishing a valid marriage]" (L.D. Joshi 1929: 40; see also, Berreman 1963: 128-9).

tation of solidifying her prime ministership. She lost to the lacklustre Lok Dal opposition party and its equally lacklustre candidate, Morarji Desai, who had appointed the University's governing Vice-Chancellor who was in turn officially responsible for designating the two honorary degrees. The University was then caught between competing factions: the Congress party and the Communist Party of India (CPI) had joined hands in opposition to the Lok Dal, with which the University and those responsible for the event were identified. The local Srinagar newspaper, vehemently anti-Lok Dal, anti-University, and allied with city elites, expatriate politicians, and local activists, went on the warpath. My book, *Hindus of the Himalayas*, largely overlooked or long forgotten and never the focus of media attention or more than passing review, was suddenly 'discovered' and I walked into a maelstrom. I will here provide a sampling of the resultant self-explanatory commentary.

> *The Times of India*, 26 May 1979: 'Storm in UP House Over Book on Hill People', by Our Correspondent, Lucknow, 25 May:
>
> The UP higher education minister, Dr Shivanand Nautiyal, today assured the vidhan parishad [state legislature] that the alleged CIA agent, Mr Gerald D. Berreman, who was recently honoured with a doctorate by Garhwal University, would not be allowed to tread the 'sacred' land of Uttarakhand in future, which he had desecrated in his book entitled 'Hindus of the Himalayas'. In an emotion-choked voice, Dr Nautiyal, who hails from a town in the Garhwal Himalayas, said he would initiate government action for banning circulation of the book. According to him, Mr Berreman had not only ridiculed the customs of hill people but also carried 'insinuating' tales about their sex life.
>
> Dr Nautiyal[37] said a high-level inquiry would be ordered into the matter and all those guilty of recommending award of an honorary degree to Mr Berreman [six Garhwali Anthropologists and Sociologists: Professor. Anoop Chandola, Dr R.S. Negi, Dr M.M. Dhasmana, A.P. Singh, B.M. Chanduri, S.C. Panch Bhai] would be punished. Amid continuing applause from all sections of the House, he added that the government would request Garhwal University to withdraw the honorary doctorate.

[37]Nautiyal, Minister for Higher Education of Uttar Pradesh, who at the Convocation had posed with me in small group photographs without comment, was subsequently called by the Governor to account for his words before the Legislature. A copy of his letter in reply, dated 2 July 1979, was forwarded to me by a friend of the Governor. In it, Nautiyal wrote: "I am really sorry that so much heat has been generated by this issue"; "this matter was raised on the floor of the Legislative Council and feeling the sentiment of the Members I promised to look into the whole matter"; "I myself have not seen the book".

> Mr Sinha [CPI] said that Mr Berreman had tried to poison the minds of people living in the plains against the people of the hill regions. ... Immediately after Mr Sinha finished his speech during zero hour, several members rose simultaneously and demanded that the 'dirty book be banned and its author not allowed to enter the state'.
>
> Demanding that ... the honorary degree be withdrawn, ... Mr. Brahm Dutt (Cong-I) disclosed that a senior member of the staff of Garhwal University, had initiated a move to appoint the alleged CIA agent as visiting professor to the university in lieu [*sic*] of his own appointment in a similar capacity to California University. [!]
>
> [But] Mr Hari Krishan Awasthi (Independent) ... said that the government should be careful before trying to intervene in the academic matters of a university which was an autonomous body.

None of the allegations were true, and none of the threats were carried out.[38] However, one can understand from the rhetoric here and in the case of Dr Parmar the attitudes, beliefs, embarrassments, and suspicions held about Pahari culture and those who report upon it. Expressions of such views are especially frequent among expatriate Paharis (but also by others) when confronted with ethnographic accounts of contemporary rural Pahari life.

When, in 1993, I was doing follow-up research in the area, I stopped by Dehra Dun and went to the Nataraj Publishers and Bookstore, to look at their books and talk with my acquaintance, Mr Arora, its proprietor. I noticed that he had no copies of my *Hindus of the Himalayas* on display.

---

[38] I am deeply indebted to Alok Sinha, IAS, former District Magistrate of Garhwal who, when I arrived in Mussoorie for my Chipko research in the fall of 1981, was on the faculty of the IAS Academy there. He contacted me to say that he had been the officer commissioned to look into the allegations surrounding my honorary degree. He had reviewed my Central Intelligence Division file, the newspaper accounts, and my publications, and had filed his report that the charges were entirely spurious. He and his wife, Rita Sinha, IAS (who had been Deputy Magistrate of Garhwal, and was in 1981-2, a Ph.D. candidate in Geography at Chandigarh University), became my fast friends based on our shared interests. It was they who introduced me to Lakhamandal on the right bank of the Jamuna river in the middle hills of Himachal Pradesh. I am indebted as well to two academics who came to my defence in print as well as personally: poet/Sanskritist/anthropologist, Dr Ved Prakash Vatuk (1979), and linguist, Professor Anoop Chandola (1980). Others who did so in person or in letters to academic and political figures included, Professor K.N. Sharma (a sociologist), and courageously during the event, Garhwal University faculty members, Dr Atul Saklani (a historian), Miss Gupta (a sociologist), Professor Paliwal (a botanist), Professor K.P. Nautiyal (an archaeologist), and Dr Bartwal (a political scientist). When, in 1981, the Minister of Home Affairs had summoned me from Dehra Dun to Delhi, to decide whether to allow me to pursue my Chipko research, he told me that eminent US Indianist anthropologist Harold Gould, who happened to be in India at the time, had voluntarily approached him and offered effective testimony on my behalf.

When I inquired about it he replied, and showed me, that he had copies, but kept them out of sight, under the counter. He feared the passions that had been aroused by the furore in the newspapers' political rhetoric nearly fifteen years before, that still resonated there.[39] He suggested that those passions might have infected 'Sirkanda' villagers as well.

Despite his concerns, I went to the village as usual, and was welcomed and hosted during that sojourn as always. As one Rajput man commented when I mentioned that I had been warned in Dehra Dun of possible hostility in the village as a delayed result of the furore, he dismissed the idea in words something like this:

> That was all politics; nobody here pays any attention. What do those people know? Two men came here riding horses a few years ago. We never trust city-folk who show up on horses. These men said they were newsmen. They asked a lot of questions about you; offered people two and a half rupees apiece for photos you had given them. Some people sold them one or two. They demanded to be fed but disparaged what we gave them, then demanded to see people they said you had named in your book. But most of them weren't names of people in this village. They even sent for the tailor in Domgaon (five miles away) because he had one of those names. He came in a hurry – maybe thought he would make some money. But when he got here he turned out to be the wrong man and he got nothing. He was pretty angry. [The names the writer had asked about were pseudonyms used in the book to protect people's identities.] Then they rode away on their horses. We never saw them again – never will. You were here for 2 or 3 years and have returned time and again. You're always welcome.[40]

Case Three: This is the first of two responses to graduate students' Himalayan ethnographic dissertations. 'Religion and Ritual in Rural India: A Case Study in Kumaon' (1982) was a Ph.D. by Tribhuwan Kapur submitted to the University of Delhi (Department of Sociology, Delhi School of Economics) and supervised by Professor André Béteille. It is a detailed account focusing primarily on religion, but with substantial ethnographic

---

[39]In 1993 the book was reprinted in New Delhi by Oxford University Press, where it was touted on the dust jacket as having "come to be widely regarded as [*sic*] classic". The same publisher reissued it in paperback in 1997 and 1999. Its notoriety no doubt contributed to its belated recognition and sales.

[40]The two men were in fact local writer/political agitator, Kunwaar Prasoon (who had been complicit in the degree imbroglio), and a photographer. They produced a scurrilous article retailing the claims others had made (see above), adding a few of their own, and illustrated with several photographs of mine (without acknowledgement) which they had purchased in the village (see Prasoon 1979). A strong rebuttal appeared five months later in the same publication, by one of those who had nominated me for the degree (Chandola 1980).

context, in a Kumaon village and its region, based on eighteen months of participatory research in two phases during 1979 and 1980-1.

I became involved when I was asked by Professor Béteille and his Department of Sociology to read the dissertation. They were sceptical about the author's data, and especially his accounts of what they regarded as grossly non-Brahmanical, non-Sanskritic rituals and behaviours of these Himalayan Hindus: their exorcisms, animal sacrifices, myths and legends, and aspects of their social structure. The professors wanted to know: is this young man telling the truth? Is what he reports believable? Could he have been the victim of deception, or of alcohol- or hashish-induced fantasies, or dietary-deficiency delusions, or worse, could he have been inventing his data? His years of postgraduate work apparently hung in the balance.

I read Tribhuvan Kapur's dissertation drafts, talked with him repeatedly, and came to know his family. His mother is a prominent sociologist, his father a recently retired brigadier. He had grown up in Kumaon (site of his dissertation research) where his father had been stationed. I found nothing in his dissertation or his discussions with me that was inconsistent with the range of beliefs and practices in Pahari culture as I knew it. He had become ill in the field, reportedly as a result of an inadequate diet, and so retired from it for a time, but nothing led me to believe he was misled or confused. I told his dissertation mentors there was nothing in his account that is not to be found widely in Pahari culture, and in fact, little that is not found in folk Hinduism of north India at large.

I attribute his advisers' scepticism to their lack of experience in the contexts into which Kapur had immersed himself, and above all, their ethnocentric beliefs about the nature and content of daily life in the rural mid-montane region. "Brahmans don't *do* such things," one of the professors proclaimed. I urged them to see for themselves if they had lingering doubts. They evidently had none, for Kapur was awarded the doctorate without further ado.

Case Four: 'Land, Labor and Status: The Social Implications of Ecologic Adaptation in a Region of the Western Himalayas of India' (1970). Nikki Nitzburg, Ph.D. dissertation, Department of Anthropology, Harvard University.

Nitzburg's dissertation includes ethnographic material on Hindus of high and low castes, as well as non-Hindu populations in Spiti, Himachal Pradesh, and while most of the area is north and west of the Pahari culture area, the dissertation includes its north-western periphery. Her research covered caste interaction, marriage patterns, and many other topics. While pursuing her research, and thereafter, Dr Nitzburg (then a graduate student) was harassed in every way, with insinuations and accusations by administrative personnel, officials, and others who purveyed rumours that she spent her research time carousing with liquor and sex among her informants. This was quite clearly a case of gender stereotyping, discrimination, and exploitation of a young, foreign woman pursuing research alone, in a relatively remote area. She was ultimately driven from her commitment to research and teaching in and about India, and from anthropology and academia altogether, by the lingering character assassination and the career destruction she had experienced in India.

Case Five: The four responses to scholarly monographs described so far are representative of widely held uninformed, ethnocentric attitudes and beliefs about peoples of the middle Himalayan hills. Such responses are expressed, not only by Indians of the North Indian plains, but by many Himalayan expatriates as well; not only by the lay public, but by some anthropologists and sociologists too. The following is a vivid example, drawn not from written work, but from a personal experience at a professional meeting:

When, in 1996, I gave a paper at the eighty-third Indian Science Congress in Patiala, my presentation was along the lines of the present part of my contribution to this volume. I had closed with some remarks about the objections levelled at *Hindus of the Himalaya* (Berreman 1963, 1972b; Chandola 1980; Prasoon 1979; Vatuk 1979). I mentioned specific charges that had been brought against me and the book, one being that I had written that among the Garhwalis I have known, a buffalo is occasionally ritually sacrificed. Other charges included the fact that they generally practise 'bride price' (*reet* or *bia*) marriage, and that polygyny is not unusual. When I had finished and the chairman called for questions, a gentleman leaped to his feet, dashed to the podium and in a rage announced that he was a Garhwali and that he was outraged by the book which was full of such 'lies'. "Garhwalis do not sacrifice buffaloes, only Nepalis do that," he shouted. "Either you are not telling the truth, or the people were lying to you, or you were not talking to Garhwalis but to Jaunsaris [Paharis who, like those about whom Dr Parmar wrote, inhabit the hills west of Garhwal and are routinely disparaged by Garhwalis]. Yes, Jaunsaris may do those things; they are known to follow such practices and even polyandry." He continued his tirade, then suddenly turned his wrath in another direction by announcing that: "The scriptures endorse buffalo sacrifice; you don't know that! *Our goddess Durga killed the demon Mahishasur with the vajra given her by Lord Shiva, when it was in the form of a buffalo. All Hindus know that*!" With that, he stormed out of the room.

I refrained from pointing out to the audience the apparent inconsistency between his claim that buffalos are not sacrificed by Garhwalis and his assertion that such sacrifice is scripturally endorsed; nor did I point out that my book contained a photograph of such a sacrifice, which I had taken in a Garhwali village. But I did assure the audience that the man was not a shill whom I had induced to stage the performance in order to illustrate my assertions regarding expatriate Paharis' attitudes toward their mountain-dwelling fellows. Later, when Dr Lakhbir Singh of Punjabi University apologized for the outburst, I learned that my accuser was a senior Delhi University anthropologist, J.S. Bhandari.

This incident recalls a happier one, on a related subject, that I think bears telling:

In 1981, during my 'Chipko research year' in the mountain town of Mussoorie, I encountered my former language teacher, the elderly Pundit, Mr Dimiri, who had grown up in a village a couple of days' walk from sacred Badrinath and in fact had officiated in the temple for a year in his youth. He joined me for tea in a local shop. After initial pleasantries, he turned serious, saying, "Berreman, a foreigner has written a scandalous book about Garhwalis, do you know about it?" I studied his face to see if he knew, but he clearly did not, so I replied, "Yes, it's no doubt *my* book!" "You have seen it?" he asked. "Mr Dimiri, I *wrote* the book," I replied, " It was the thesis I was researching in 1957-8 when we first met". These are my notes on the rest of that conversation:

B: Have you read the book?
D: No.
B: Have you seen it?
D: No.
B: Then why do you think it's scandalous?
D: Everyone says it is.
B: Had anyone you know read it?
D: No, probably no one had seen it, but many have heard of it. What did you write that was thought scandalous?
B: You should ask your friends, *I* don't think *anything* in it is scandalous. [silence]
B: ... Well, OK, one of the main things was that I said that Garhwalis sacrifice buffaloes.
D: Oh, now I see! You should not have said that.
B: But it's true. In a Garhwali village in Saklana, not far from 'Sirkanda' [he knew I had worked there], I saw a buffalo sacrificed and people said it was not unusual. I have a photo of it and the photo is in the book. [more silence]
B: Mr Dimri, when you were a boy did people sacrifice buffaloes?
D: [His eyes lit up, and he gazed out over the valley in a manner that I interpreted as nostalgic:] *Zaroor* [for sure], we sacrificed *so many* buffaloes when I was a boy!
B: So, that's what I was saying.
D: But that was 50-60 years ago, they don't do that any more.
B: ~~Well,~~ what if you walked to a village that is 25 miles from the road, would they sacrifice buffaloes there nowadays?

D: A village 25 miles from the road? Oh, *yes* – everything's just like when I was a boy, 25 miles from the road!

B: That's the kind of village I'm talking about.

D: Oh! ... Still, you should not have said it!

B: I guess you're right, but anthropologists are supposed to tell the truth, the whole truth.

D: These people here aren't anthropologists!

B: Right. Thanks for the talk Panditji. *Phir milenge*. [we'll meet again.]

While writers and writings dealing with Himalayan societies and cultures in India seem to be exceptionally vulnerable to vehement – even vitriolic – critique, such responses are by no means limited to Himalayan topics. By way of illustrating their broader reach I offer the following examples of responses to perceived Orientalism (Said 1978) in Western publications on India.

> 'Wrath Over a Hindu God: US Scholars' Writings Draw Threats From Faithful' (Vedantam The Washington Post 2004).
>
> A professor of religion at Emory University [Paul Courtwright] ... immersed himself in the story of Ganesha the beloved Hindu god with the head of an elephant. Detecting provocative Oedipal overtones ... he wrote a book setting out his theories in 1985. Nineteen years later, thanks to an Internet campaign, the world has rediscovered Courtwright's book. ... [H]e has received threats from Hindu militants who want him dead. "Gopal from Singapore said, 'The professor bastard should be hanged,' " said Courtwright, incredulous. "A guy from Germany said, 'Wish this person was next to me, I would have shot him in the head.' A man called Karodkar said, 'Kill the bastard. Whoever wrote this should not be spared.' Someone wanted to throw me into the Indian Ocean."
>
> Other academics writing about Hinduism have encountered similar hostility, from tossed eggs to assaults, to threats of extradition and prosecution in India.
>
> The attacks against American scholars come as a powerful movement called Hindutva has gained political power. ... Its proponents assert that Hindus have long been denigrated and that Western authors are imposing a Eurocentric world view on a culture they do not understand. ...
>
> In November [2003] Wendy Doniger, a University of Chicago professor of the history of religion, who has written 20 books about India and Hinduism, had an egg flung at her by an angry Hindu when she was lecturing in London ... [See Braverman 2004]

> In January [2004], a book about the Hindu king Shivaji by Macalester College religious studies professor James W. Laine provoked violent outbursts [Laine 2003]. One of Laine's collaborators in India was assaulted, and a mob destroyed rare manuscripts at an institute in India where Laine had done research. The Indian edition was recalled, and India's prime minister warned Laine not to "play with our national pride." Officials said they want to extradite the Minnesota author to stand trial for defamation, and the controversy has become a campaign issue in upcoming parliamentary elections. ...
>
> Many Indian scholars have rushed to the defense of the American authors. They say the controversy over the books is part of a larger pattern of political violence against scholars in India. (Vedantam 2004)

This is not to say that criticism, even that expressing passionate resentment and wounded pride, is not understandable or should be suppressed. After all, Courtwright is reported to have written that Ganesha's "trunk represented a limp phallus ... and [Lord] Shiva's power is represented by ... an erect phallus" [see Courtwright 1985: 121].

> ... New Jersey entrepreneur Rajiv Malhotra argued that Doniger and her students had eroticized and denigrated Hinduism, which was part of the reason "the mainstream misunderstands India so pathologically." ...
>
> Malhotra quoted passages from Courtwright's book that offended him, [for example]: "Although there seem to be no myths or folktales in which Ganesha explicitly performs oral sex, his insatiable appetite for sweets may be interpreted as an effort to satisfy a hunger that seems inappropriate in an otherwise ascetic disposition, a hunger having clear erotic overtones" [Courtwright 1985: 111]. (Vedantam 2004)

While these quotations are surely taken out of context, it is hardly surprising that devout Hindus would take strong exception to such statements by scholars whose unfamiliar academic religion is apparently Freudianism. It is not the fact of criticism and objection that I see as characteristic of Indian – as contrasted with Nepalese – responses to scholarly writing about their societies and cultures, but their unbridled virulence – and the fact that they are so readily triggered, in such a wide diversity of contexts, including those less obviously provocative than these. One must acknowledge, of course, that vehement rhetoric in response, even to dispassionate analyses of their faiths, is employed by fundamentalists and zealots of every major religion in many countries – like the United States, Afghanistan, and Israel

– even as their targets may justly be accused of purveying – even epitomizing – Orientalism.

Nepali Responses to Himalayan Ethnographic Research

While it is risky to generalize about entire societies and cultures, I do see a tendency towards a characteristic contrast between the responses to Himalayan ethnography in India and Nepal. The contrast is this: among Indian Hindus there is widespread embarrassment, scepticism, denial, rejection, even hostility, combined with a certain lurid fascination with religious beliefs and practices that are considered unorthodox at the least and immoral at most. The semi-mysterious Paharis are thought to be 'guilty' of such behaviour. Expatriate Paharis are often embarrassed and secretive of them. In Nepal, it seems, everyone is familiar with the fact of diversity in the religious practices of other Himalayan people, for they are the stuff of daily life. When confronted with unfamiliar customs, their responses tend to range from disinterested tolerance to interest, curiosity, and even enthusiasm to know more about them (enhanced, perhaps by the fascination they often hold for free-spending foreign tourists – especially where erotic temple carvings and bloody animal sacrifices are concerned).

In short, in Nepal I did not encounter the kind of suspicion by scholars and the hostility by journalists and local citizens when confronted with ethnographic accounts of Himalayan peoples – Hindu and Janajati – with which I have become familiar among plains Hindus and expatriate Paharis in India (as described above). In Nepal, anthropological books, monographs, and periodicals, comprising ethnographic descriptions (in English) of most of the country's ethnic groups, are stocked and prominently displayed in both scholarly and popular bookstores, without negative comment.[41] At the same time that in Dehra Dun my book was being concealed under the counter, if carried at all, in Kathmandu it was displayed, often in quantity, in practically every bookstore – Pilgrim Books offered a copy, erroneously identified as a first edition, for US $100! There is little evidence in Nepal for what I have elsewhere called the "plainsward mobility" exhibited by many Paharis, i.e. the adoption of plains standards of belief and practice in pursuit of status enhancement (Berreman 1963: 134-7).[42]

This is not to say that all such accounts are embraced without criticism

---

[41]Probably at least 95 per cent of the ethnographic works published in Nepal are in English.

[42]Like Srinivas's term, Sanskritization, for Hindu status emulation (1966: 6), 'plainsward mobility' is my term for this Himalayan manifestation of status emulation. Sociologists Robert Merton and Alice Rossi (1957), following Hyman (1942), called this widespread phenomenon "reference group behaviour", and pursued its dimensions in detail (see Berreman 1964, especially 232-7).

in Nepal, but it is to say that when criticism is mounted, it tends not to be laced with the rancour, the hostility, that is common in India.

To demonstrate that Nepalis are not Pollyannaish (though, indeed, anyone who knows them will need no such demonstration), I will give an example of frank, sharp, and empirically based, but clearly in part emotionally driven, criticism. Perhaps the most frequent academic criticism in Nepal is that which has been termed "academic colonialism" (Saberwal 1968; Berreman 1969). The term, as is probably obvious and is in any case well known, refers to the domination of social science (or any academic domain, usually in former colonies and in societies with 'developing' economies and infrastructures), by American and European academics. Such domination entails the overwhelming advantages of abundant research funding, and standardization of scholarly quality as being that of the Euro-American nexus: in education, medium of instruction and communication, access to publication, choice of topics for research, and eligibility for funding and employment – in fact, absolute overall domination of the academic discipline worldwide. Nepali anthropologist Dilli Ram Dahal, Ph.D. from University of Michigan, writes from his post in the Centre for Nepal and Asian Studies in Kathmandu:

> Of the many works published by foreign anthropologists on Nepal [this by a well-known anthropologist] is one of the most widely read.
>
> Even as the decolonized subcontinent closed up to anthropological research ... never-colonised Nepal ... opened up to welcome social scientists. ... Picking up where British residents and representatives ... had left off, Western ethnographers began conducting detailed studies of Nepal's many population groups.
>
> With few Nepalis engaged in the discipline, it can be said that the anthropological portrayal of the 'real Nepal' has been a project of Western social scientists. What they have had to say has by and large been accepted with little questioning ... Bound as they are to their own cultural blinders and career-driven as many academics tend to be. ... The honest social scientist must, first and foremost, protect and honour the persons which are the subjects of his/her necessarily intrusive study. All too often, research can jeopardize the very community which has helped advance the career of the scholar. ... My intention by focusing on one study, is to caution those who would accept unquestioningly all Western anthropological works which seek to pass judgment on one community or the other. (Dahal 1996: 50)

Dahal then undertakes to uncompromisingly criticize the study of a Mongol community in a hill district in eastern Nepal, by the anthropologist referred to above. Lacking space to render his argument and evidence, I will simply excise a number of key sentences in order to convey the thrust of his argument:

> The [group's members] are characterized as an innocent and naïve people, in stark contrast to the Brahmins who are portrayed as cheats or otherwise dishonest in their dealings.[43]
>
> I want to establish that his truth is at best partial and selective. …
>
> I had an opportunity to do research [there] and came upon certain details which were not reported by [the author] and developed certain interpretations with which I feel able to challenge [the author's] general thesis. …
>
> All this suggests, disturbingly, that the author of a study which has informed and helped form the worldview of numerous social scientists engaged in the Central Himalaya was selective in his use of the full range of information available. It is difficult not to conclude that the selection was based on his desire to prove a hypothesis he brought with him to the field site.
>
> In the case of Nepal, there is no doubt that [this author's] work has had an impact on subsequent studies, and unwittingly he has helped shape the argumentation of many young Western social scientists who came later. Here, then, is the classic case of a society, without social scientists of its own, defined on the basis of someone who is from without. (Dahal 1996: 51)

This Nepali scholar has demonstrated a sharp critical sense with a documented critique that avoids the kind of thoughtless suspicion, denial, and rancour that has characterized some of the examples above. This is consistent with my experience of teaching and research in Nepal and specifically in Tribhuvan University.

Accounting for the Differential Responses in India and Nepal to Ethnographic Accounts of Peoples of Their Respective Himalayan Middle Hills

An explanation for the contrast between Indian and Nepalese responses to accounts and analyses of Himalayan societies seems to me not far to seek.

In a brief but classic essay, the late anthropologist, Agehananda Bharati (1978), has described vividly how, to most Indian Hindus (and many others as well), the Himalayas are a remote and unfamiliar, yet hallowed, near-mythical land, featuring the sacred Ganga, Jamuna, and their sources, Gangotri and Jamnotri, the temples and sacred spaces of Badrinath and

[43] Dahal is himself a Brahman.

Kedarnath, Haridwar and Rishikesh. In fact, virtually every river and mountain peak represents the abode of gods, and the geography of their exploits. Hindus who visit the mountains, on pilgrimage or sightseeing tours, are nowadays transported by bus, scarcely noticing the mountain people seen, if at all, in fleeting glimpses through dusty windows, or encountered in hasty purchases from hectoring snack vendors at the infrequent stops. More generally, people's knowledge of the Himalayas is derived from TV or films. Bharati reported that one popular film included a background image of "a highly stylized peak [that] was meant to be, I presume, Mount Kailasa, the abode of the Hindu and Buddhist divinities; but actually resembled one of the more elaborate whipped-cream sundaes" (1978: 77). It is clear that he regarded this depiction of the holy mountain as a metaphor for Indians' perceptions of and beliefs about the Himalayan people and culture.

In short, most Indian people's understanding of the mountains and their Pahari population is vastly romanticized, mythologized, idealized. Their factual knowledge of the Himalayan people is virtually nil. When they do glimpse them, or see a documentary that includes them, they are likely to be shocked to discover that they are not learned pundits, pious pilgrims, and ascetic sadhus, but hard-working subsistence farmers living in ways that strike them as being the very antithesis of the way residents of their Holy Land should live.

Small wonder, then, that when confronted with an ethnographic account that accurately describes the daily lives, the livelihoods, the unfamiliar, even mysterious customs of the Paharis, people of the plains, including journalists, politicians, and ordinary folks, are often appalled, offended, and disbelieving, combined, perhaps, with a certain lurid fascination. And no wonder that Pahari elites, or Pahari expatriates who have left all of that behind when they migrated from the hills to the cities of the plains and the relatively genteel lifestyle there, are often embarrassed and defensive and in vehement denial. No wonder researchers' accounts are greeted with scepticism, hostility, and denial. Perhaps it is not surprising that even Mr Bhandari, expatriate that he was, in spite of being the anthropologist that he was, responded as he did to my presentation in Patiala – an outsider confronting him with the stark disparity between his idealized past and his rejected ethnic present.

In India, then, the Himalayas are not only a geographically remote hinterland, but its Pahari population is, to most people, culturally unfamiliar and socially peripheral – in a word, they are in every way marginal to the larger Indian society. In Nepal, by contrast, the Himalayas are the heartland, the physical and psychological homeland of most of the Nepali people, Janajati/Mongols and Hindus alike. Its unique hill and mountain environment is their familiar territory. Its people and their cultures comprise the familiar centre of Nepali culture and society. They are not merely spectators of the Himalayas, they are of the Himalayas, they are its people.

As I approach my conclusion, I want to pose a final question, one that, like the introductory portion of this essay, is not explicitly comparative. Rather it pertains specifically to my characterization and analysis of the situation of the Pahari residents of India's Himalayas, the area and people I know best.

Question 6: What is the Broader Relevance of Indian Attitudes towards Pahari Research, and What do Those Attitudes Reveal about (mis)Understandings of the People and Their Culture?

In addition to the anthropologists and their critics whose views I have described above, there are at least three categories of people whose points of view about Paharis are of interest here: (1) Hindus native to the Indo-Gangetic plains; (2) expatriate Paharis – those whose roots are in the hills but who have migrated to the plains; and (3) Paharis who live in the hills and follow a rural Pahari way of life.

Based on my familiarity with rural Paharis, I will take for granted that the dominant Bamans and Thakurs are generally confident that they live a viable, honourable, albeit difficult, way of life as hard-working farmers. As to the Doms, they deeply resent and deplore their caste situation (Berreman 1960a, 1971, 1972c), but regard it as no worse than that of Dalits throughout India, so far as they know of it. I will therefore limit myself here to the first two categories, Hindus of the plains and expatriate Paharis.

In 1982, three years after the traumatic honorary degree imbroglio at the University of Garhwal, at a professional meeting in New Delhi, I encountered the young Punjabi anthropologist who had comprised the University's Department of Anthropology at the time of the troubles, but had been strategically 'out of station' during those events. He drew me aside and handed me a short cyclostyled manuscript that he assured me would interest me, while asking that I tell no one where I had got it; it could jeopardize his job. It proved to be a paper delivered by Dr M.M. Dhasmana at a scholarly conference earlier that year. (It was published five years later as 'Changing Milieu and Development Strategies in Garhwal', Dhasmana 1987.) In it the author described what he termed the 'migrant syndrome'. As a Garhwali Pahari himself, he observed that:

> In the socio-cultural history of Uttarakhand, nothing could be more unfortunate than the 'migrant syndrome' characteristic of its population. From time immemorial it has been … characteristic of the people of Garhwal and Kumaon, specially of the elites. … The inhabitants of Uttarakhand always claimed to be immigrants. … [As soon as] a person attained some status in socio-economic field, he claimed to have migrated from different parts of the country. …

> The migrant claim was a race for social status and an attempt to sever links from the Trans-Himalayan culture. (Dhasmana 1987: 202)

Under the British, he explains, educated Garhwalis migrated to cities of the plains as government employees:

> Not everyone of them revealed their origin. Some ... dropped their agnatic clan titles and adopted the common caste titles prevalent in the plains.[44] Since the early fifties of this century, the Garhwalis have fared considerably well. ... They are [now] not shy of their origin and are proud to call themselves as the Garhwalis. People who had dropped their clan titles have reverted to their usage. But this attitude has not been of any help to ... their region. ... A new concept in the migrant syndrome has become the status symbol today. This is the concept of being a Garhwali but settled outside of Garhwal. ... Many of the new generation of Garhwali settlers have almost forgotten their language, rituals and social customs. (ibid.: 203)

I agree that, as Dhasmana implies, expatriate Garhwalis have often adopted the prejudices of the plainsmen toward their fellow Garhwali Paharis, as being unorthodox, uneducated, and Jangli (rustic), and have therefore either concealed their heritage or distanced themselves from its realities in favour of a pristine, mythologized image that would be quite unrecognizable to their mountain-dwelling cousins. This is clearly the source of the legislators' and journalists' objections to Parmar's *Polyandry in the Himalayas*, and to my *Hindus of the Himalayas*, as well as the scepticism directed at Kapur's dissertation on Kumaoni society and religion, and the hostility exhibited to Nitzburg's dissertation research (Berreman 1983a: 251-6).

The broader bases for these reactions to Himalayan ethnographies are implied by the title of Bharati's article quoted above: 'Actual and Ideal Himalayas: Hindu Views of the Mountains'. That is, such reactions are responses to the incongruity between firmly held stereotypic beliefs and expectations about Himalayans on the one hand, and the stark realities confronted in ethnographic accounts, on the other. As Bharati puts it, "to all Hindus except those who live there, the Himalayas tend to be ascriptive rather than actual mountains"; "the Himalaya is a state of mind" (1978: 78). "The Hindu attraction to the ascriptive Himalayas", – which Bharati calls "the *rishi* syndrome" (ibid.: 81) – is largely responsible for hostility and denial in response to disillusive Himalayan ethnographic research and its authors.

---

[44]'Agnatic clan titles' are defined by Dhasmana as "The trans-Himalayan practice of deriving clan names from the place of settlement of forefathers" (1987: 211).

Those who are afflicted with that syndrome are unaware of the realities of life in the mountains, and unbelieving when confronted with accounts of those realities (as Kapur found out, even in the case of his learned dissertation committee), and they are often outraged as well, as Dr Parmar and I found out. Ethnography, if it is good ethnography, tells the truth, and the truth sometimes hurts, especially if one is schooled or socialized in mythology.

When I asked Pahari villagers about the disparity between the realities of their lives and outsiders' stereotypes about them and their rugged, sacred homeland, they responded by saying, in effect:

> We have to work to bring up the crops, tend the livestock and see to our families in these rocky mountains. That is our life. We require meat now and then for strength to do our work, we can't waste it fasting. We can't spend our time praying, who would plough the fields? Where is the water for daily bathing? Who can afford the expensive rituals and greedy Brahmins. Let those who belittle us come and live with us, as you have done. We shall see how pious their lives will be! (from my field notes, 1958)

Professor P.C. Joshi, who was "born in Kumaon ... 'educated' by Jaunsaris and worked in Garhwal" (2000: 20), writes that:

> When Himalaya is imagined, it is Uttarakhand, the home of Lord Shiva and Parvati (Nanda), giver of India's lifeline the Ganges and Yamuna, that is imagined about which the Skandha Purana says "In a hundred ages of the Gods I could not tell thee of the glories of Himachal. As the dew is dried up by the morning sun, so are the sins of mankind by the sight of Himachal."
>
> But these are celestial metaphors; on the ground are living beings with blood, bone and marrow, the Pahari, who have inhabited these mountains for ages. *Uttarakhand is therefore both* devbhumi *(the abode of gods) and at the same time the home of Paharis the hill dwellers*. (P.C. Joshi 2000: 3, emphases added)

CONCLUSION

By way of a brief conclusion, I will indulge in a gross, but I think suggestive, oversimplification by comparing India's Paharis with Nepalis of the middle hills, as seen in the minds and actions of the dominant populations of their respective homelands. To do so, I will simply list some words (in this context, necessarily English) that I believe characterize widely shared perspectives – images – held by members of the socially, politically, and economically dominant populations of India and Nepal, vis-à-vis their rural Himalayan countrymen. The list amounts to a casual word-association exercise that reflects a fundamental contrast that comprises a subtext underlying this entire essay:

Paharis	*Nepalis*
Hinterland	Heartland
Periphery	Centre
Unfamiliarity	Familiarity
Remote	Proximate
Minority	Majority
Fantasy	Reality
Ideal	Actual
Prejudice	Pride
Mystery	Knowledge
Suspicion	Confidence
Them	Us

People's responses to Himalayan ethnographic descriptions, like their responses to one another, tend to manifest the kinds of contrasts described in this chapter and summarized by these contrastive word-pairs. Nepalis, although riven by the Hindu-Janajati/Mongol divide, and by caste, ethnicity, and class, are culturally, psychologically, and geographically located at the centre of their Himalayan society and culture. By contrast, Paharis are culturally, psychologically, and geographically on the periphery of the larger society of which they are a part. The respective self- and public definitions of the two societies' members – the nature and degree of their self-confidence and public respect – are, in turn, largely products of these contrasts.

Knowledge of one another, I think, is the basis for inter-group understanding, while understanding is a prerequisite for mutual respect. I do ethnographic research and writing with the hope, if not the conviction, that it will provide knowledge that can pave the way to understanding that, in turn, may make a contribution towards social equality and justice. That is what the anthropologist's 'cultural relativism' is all about; *not* the claim that whatever people in a society characteristically do is therefore acceptable cross-culturally (or even within that society), *nor* that it is necessarily tolerable, but absolutely that *it is explicable*. That is the rock bottom premise of anthropology as I see it, and the prerequisite for any application of the insights provided by our anthropological research and imagination. To understand that is to make a significant step towards being able to do something about achieving the kinds of societies whose customs and requirements would rest lightly and equally on all of their members.

REFERENCES

Agarwal, A., R. Chopra, and K. Sharma (eds.). 1982. 'Dams', in *The State of India's Environment 1982: A Citizens' Report*, pp. 57-69. New Delhi: Centre for Science and Environment.

Agarwal, A. and S. Narain (eds.). 1985. 'Dams', in *The State of India's Environment: 1984-85: The Second Citizens' Report*, pp. 99-120. New Delhi: Centre for Science and Environment.

Ahmad, E. 1996. 'A Kashmiri Solution for Kashmir'. *Himal South Asia* (November/December) 9 (8): 16-24.

Aryal, M. 1994a. 'Axing Chipko: Forest Policies and the Seeds of Discord'. *Himal* (January/February) 7 (1): 8-23.

——. 1994b. 'Angry Hills: An Uttarakhand State of Mind'. *Himal* (November/December) 7 (6): 10-21.

——. 1995. 'Dams: The Vocabulary of Protest'. *Himal* (July/August) 8 (4): 11-21.

Asia Watch & Physicians for Human Rights. 1993. *The Human Rights Crisis in Kashmir: A Pattern of Impunity*. NY: Human Rights Watch.

Atkinson, E.T. 1882. *The Himalayan Districts of the North-Western Provinces of India*. Allahabad: North-Western Provinces and Oudh Press.

Behera, N.C. 1996. 'J & K (& L & D & G ...): Making and Unmaking Identities'. *Himal* (November/December) 9 (8): 26-33.

Berreman, G.D. 1960a. 'Caste in India and the United States'. *American Journal of Sociology* 66: 120-7.

——. 1960b. 'Cultural Variability and Drift in the Himalayan Hills'. *American Anthropologist* 62: 774-94.

——. 1961. 'Himalayan Rope Sliding and Village Hinduism: An Analysis'. *Southwestern Journal of Anthropology* 17: 326-42.

——. 1962. 'Pahari Polyandry: A Comparison'. *American Anthropologist* 64: 60-75.

——. 1963. *Hindus of the Himalayas*. Berkeley: University of California Press.

——. 1964. 'Aleut Reference Group Alienation, Mobility and Acculturation'. *American Anthropologist* 66 (9): 231-50.

——. 1969. 'Academic Colonialism: Not so Innocent Abroad'. *The Nation* 209 (16): 505-8.

——. 1970. 'Pahari Culture: Diversity and Change in the Lower Himalayas', in K. Ishwaran (ed.), *Change and Continuity in India's Villages*, pp. 73-103. NY: Columbia University Press.

——. 1971. 'Self, Situation and Escape from Stigmatised Ethnic Identity', in *1971 Yearbook of the Ethnographic Museum, University of Oslo*, pp. 11-25. Oslo, Norway: Universitetsforlaget.

——. 1972a. 'Social Categories and Social Interaction in Urban India'. *American Anthropologist* 74 (3): 567-86.

——. 1972b. *Hindus of the Himalayas: Ethnography and Change.* Berkeley: University of California Press.

——. 1972c. 'Self, Situation and Escape from Stigmatised Ethnic Identity', in K.S. Mathur and S.C. Varma (eds.), *Man and Society*, pp. 95-108. (Silver Jubilee Number of *The Eastern Anthropologist, 1972.*)

——. 1975. 'Himalayan Polyandry and the Domestic Cycle'. *American Ethnologist* 2 (1): 127-38.

——. 1978a. 'Ecology, Demography and Domestic Strategies in the Western Himalayas'. *Journal of Anthropological Research* 34: 326-68.

——. 1978b. 'Scale and Social Relations'. *Current Anthropology* 19 (2): 225-45, and 19 (3): 624-5 'Reply'.

——. 1979. *Himachal: Science, People and "Progress"* IWGIA Document 36. Copenhagen, Denmark: International Work Group for Indigenous Affairs.

——. 1980. 'Polyandry: Exotic Custom *vs.* Analytic Concept'. *Journal of Comparative Family Studies* 9 (3): 377-83.

——. 1983a. 'The U.P. Himalaya: Culture, Cultures and Regionalism', in O.P. Singh (ed.), *The Himalaya: Nature, Man and Culture*, pp. 227-65. Delhi: Rajesh Publications.

——. 1983b. 'Identity Definition, Assertion and Politicization in the Central Himalayas" in A. Jacobson-Widding (ed.), *Identity: Personal and Socio-Cultural*, pp. 289-318. Uppsala Studies in Cultural Anthropology 5. Uppsala, Sweden: Acta Universitatis Upsaliensis. Stockholm, Sweden: Almqvist & Wiksell International.

——. 1985a. 'Internal Colonialism and Fourth World Movements in the Indian Himalayas', in J. Brosted, J. Dahl, ... and H. Kleivan (eds.), *Native Power: The Quest for Autonomy and Nationhood of Indigenous Peoples*, pp. 104-36. Bergen, Norway: Universitetsforlaget AS.

——. 1985b. 'Chipko: Nonviolent Direct Action to Save the Himalayas'. *South Asia Bulletin* 5 (2): 8-13.

——. 1987. 'Uttarakhand and Chipko: Regionalism and Environmentalism in the Central Himalayas', in M.K. Raha (ed.), *The Himalayan Heritage*, pp. 266-300. Delhi: Gian Publishing House.

——. 1989. 'Chipko: A Movement to Save the Himalayan Environment and People', in C.M. Borden (ed.), *Contemporary India: Essays on the Uses of Tradition*, pp. 239-66. Delhi: Oxford University Press.

——. forthcoming. 'Caste and Race: Reservations and Affirmations', in B. Natrajan and P. Greenough (eds.), *Beyond Durban: The Global Fate of Caste and Race.* Hyderabad: Orient Longman.

Bevacqua, R. 2004. 'Nepal and the "War on Terror"'. *JPRI Working Paper* 100 (http://www.jpri.org/publications/workingpapers/wp100.html).

Bharati, A. 1978. 'Actual and Ideal Himalayas: Hindu Views of the Mountains', in J.F. Fisher (ed.), *Himalayan Anthropology: The Indo-Tibetan Interface,* pp. 77-82. The Hague: Mouton.

Bhattachan, K.B. 1987. 'Sociology and Anthropology Curriculum and the Needs of Nepal'. *Occasional Papers in Sociology and Anthropology* 1: 11-28.

Bhattachan, K.B. and K.N. Pyakuryal. 1996. 'The Issue of National Integration in Nepal: An Ethnoregional Approach'. *Occasional Papers in Sociology and Anthropology* 5: 17-38.

Bhattarai, B. 1993. 'Arun III, Nepal's Reluctant Narmada'. *Himal* (March/April) 6 (2): 37.

Bista, D.B. 1987. 'Nepal School of Sociology/Anthropology'. *Occasional Papers in Sociology and Anthropology* 1: 6-10.

——. 1996. *People of Nepal* (sixth edition). Kathmandu: Ratna Pustak Bhandar.

Braverman, A.M. 2004. 'The Interpretation of Gods'. *University of Chicago Magazine*, December 2004: 32-6.

Brower, B. (ed.). 2003. 'War on Terrorism, War as Terrorism, and Nepal's Maoist Insurgency'. *Himalaya* 22 (1).

Chandola, A. 1980. '*Hindus of the Himalayas*: A Rebuttal [to Prasoon] from America'. *Ravivar* (*Sunday*): Febuary 1980: 10-16 (in Hindi).

Chhetri, G. 1999. 'Occupational Caste Groups in the Hills of Nepal', in R.B. Chhetri and O.P. Gurung (eds.), *Anthropology and Sociology of Nepal: Cultures, Societies, Ecology and Development*, pp. 56-68. Kathmandu: Sociological and Anthropological Society of Nepal.

Courtwright, P.B. 1985. *Ganesa: Lord of Obstacles, Lord of Beginnings*. Oxford: Oxford University Press.

Dahal, D.R. 1995. 'Ethnic Cauldron, Demography and Minority Politics: The Case of Nepal', in D. Kumar (ed.), *State Leadership and Politics in Nepal*, pp. 148-70. Kirtipur: CNAS, Tribhuvan University.

——. 1996. 'The Fallout of Deviant Anthropology'. *Himal South Asia* (May) 9 (2): 50-1.

Dahal, D.R., Y.B. Gurung, B. Acharya, K. Hemchuri, and D. Swarnaker. 2002. *National Dalit Strategy Report, Part I: Situational Analysis of Dalits in Nepal*. Kathmandu: National Planning Commission, HMG/Nepal (www.nepaldalitinfo.20m.com/archives/analyse2002.pdf).

de Sales, A. 2000. 'The Kham Magar Country, Nepal: Between Ethnic Claims and Maoism'. *European Bulletin of Himalayan Research* 19: 41-72.

Dhasmana, M.M. 1987. 'Changing Milieu and Development Strategies in Garhwal', in M.K. Raha (ed.), *The Himalayan Heritage*, pp. 200-14. Delhi: Gian Publishing House.

——. 1990 (1982). 'Transformations and Development in Central Himalayas', in K.M. Gupta (ed.), *Himalaya, Man and Nature*, pp. 26-9. Delhi: Lancers Books.

Dhoundiyal, N.C., V.R. Dhoundiyal, and S.K. Sharma (eds.). 1993. *The Separate Hill State* (Vol. II, English). Almora: Shree Almora Book Depot.

Dipak, 2001. 'Rukumkot Raid: A Live Broadcasting'. *Revolutionary Worker* (29 July) 23 (13): 8-9.

Dixit, K.M. 2002. 'Insurgents and Innocents: The Nepali Army's Battle with the

Maobaadi'. *Himal South Asia* (June) 15 (6): 28-38; reissued in D. Thapa (ed.), 2003 *Understanding the Maoist Movement of Nepal*, pp. 299-314. Kathmandu: Martin Chautari.

Dixit, K.M. and S. Ramachandaran (eds.). *State of Nepal.* Lalitpur, Nepal: Himal Books.

Eckholm, E.P. 1976. *Losing Ground: Environmental Stress and World Food Prospects.* NY: W.W. Norton.

Fisher, M.W., L.E. Rose, and R.A. Huttenback. 1963. *Himalayan Battleground: Sino-Indian Rivalry in Ladakh.* New York: Praeger.

Gaenszle, M. 1997. 'Changing Concepts of Ethnic Identity among the Mewahang Rai', in D.N. Gellner, J. Pfaff-Czarnecka, and J. Whelpton (eds.), *Nationalism and Ethnicity in a Hindu Kingdom: The Politics of Culture in Contemporary Nepal*, pp. 351-73. Amsterdam: Harwood Academic Publishers.

Galanter, M. 1984. *Competing Equalities: Law and the Backward Classes in India.* Berkeley: University of California Press.

Gellner, D.N. 1997a. 'Introduction: Ethnicity and Nationalism in the World's Only Hindu State', in D.N. Gellner, J. Pfaff-Czarnecka, and J. Whelpton (eds.), *Nationalism and Ethnicity in a Hindu Kingdom: The Politics of Culture in Contemporary Nepal*, pp. 3-31. Amsterdam: Harwood Academic Publishers.

——. 1997b. 'Caste, Communalism, and Communism: Newars and the Nepalese State', in D.N. Gellner, J. Pfaff-Czarnecka, and J. Whelpton (eds.), *Nationalism and Ethnicity in a Hindu Kingdom: The Politics of Culture in Contemporary Nepal*, pp. 151-84. Amsterdam: Harwood Academic Publishers.

Gersony, R. 2003. *Sowing the Wind ... : History and Dynamics of the Maoist Revolt in Nepal's Rapti Hills.* Washington D.C.: Mercy Corps International, c/o Macfadden & Associates.

Gough, K. and H.P. Sharma (eds.). 1973. *Imperialism and Revolution in South Asia.* NY: Monthly Review Press.

Grierson, G.A. 1916. *Linguistic Survey of India.* Vol. 9, Part 4. Calcutta: Superintendent of Government Printing.

Griffin, D.M. 1988. *Innocents Abroad in the Forests of Nepal: An Account of Australian Aid to Nepalese Forestry.* Canberra: Anutech.

Guha, R. 1990. *The Unquiet Woods: Ecological Change and Peasant Resistance in the Himalaya.* Berkeley: University of California Press.

Gurung, G. 1993. 'Mail'. *Himal* (Sep./Oct.): 4-5.

Gurung, H. 1997. 'State and Society in Nepal', in D.N. Gellner, J. Pfaff-Czarnecka, and J. Whelpton (eds.), *Nationalism and Ethnicity in a Hindu Kingdom: The Politics of Culture in Contemporary Nepal*, pp. 495-532. Amsterdam: Harwood Academic Publishers.

Gurung, J.B. 1998. 'The Situation of Dalit and Matwali Groups Today'. *Tamu Dhi* (December): 61-3.

Hangen, S.I. 1999. 'Making Mongols: Identity Construction and Ethnic Politics in Ilam District, Nepal', in R.B. Chhetri and O.P. Gurung (eds.), *Anthropology and*

Sociology of Nepal: Cultures, Societies, Ecology and Development, pp. 69-80. Kathmandu: Sociological and Anthropological Society of Nepal.

Hoon, V. 1996. *Living on the Move: Bhotiyas of the Kumaon Himalaya.* Delhi and London: Sage.

Human Rights Watch. 1999. *Broken People: Caste Violence Against India's "Untouchables"*. NY: Human Rights Watch.

Hutt, M. (ed.). 2004. *Himalayan People's War: Nepal's Maoist Rebellion.* Bloomington: Indiana University Press.

Hyman, H.H. 1942. *The Psychology of Status.* NY: Archives of Psychology. No. 269.

ICIMOD. 1997. *Annual Report 1996.* Kathmandu: ICIMOD Nepal.

Ives, J.D. and B. Messerli. 1989. *The Himalayan Dilemma: Reconciling Development and Conservation.* The United Nations University. NY: Routledge.

Joshi, L.D. 1929. *The Khasa Family Law in the Himalayan Districts of the United Provinces of India.* Allahabad: Superintendent, Government Press, U.P.

Joshi, M.C. 1990. 'The Khasas in the History of Uttarakhand', in M.P. Joshi, A.C. Fanger and C.W. Brown (eds.), *Himalaya: Past and Present*, pp. 193-200. Almora: Shree Almora Book Depot.

Joshi, P.C. 2000. 'Some Observations on the Society and Culture in Uttarakhand'. India International Centre and Council for Social Development, New Delhi: Seminar on Uttaranchal. Unpublished Paper.

Kapoor, C. 1983. 'Quarrying: The Doon Doom'. *India Today* (Delhi) 15 June: 28-9.

Kapur, T. 1982. 'Religion and Ritual in Rural India: A Case Study in Kumaon'. Unpublished Ph.D. thesis, Department of Sociology, Delhi School of Economics, University of Delhi.

Kolenda, P. 1978. *Caste in Contemporary India: Beyond Organic Solidarity.* Menlo Park, California: Benjamin/Cummings Publishing Company.

Laine, J.W. 2003. Shivaji: Hindu King in Islamic India. NY: Oxford University Press.

Lecomte-Tilouine, M. 2004. 'Regicide and Maoist Revolutionary Warfare in Nepal'. *Anthropology Today* 20 (1): 13-19.

Lewis, T.T. and T. Riccardi Jr. 1995. *The Himalayas: A Syllabus of the Region's History, Anthropology, and Religion.* Ann Arbour, Michigan: Association for Asian Studies.

Majumdar, D.N. 1962. *Himalayan Polyandry: Structure, Functioning and Culture Change, a Field-Study of Jaunsar-Bawar.* NY: Asia Publishing House.

Mason, P. 1989. [See Woodruff, P. 1947.]

Merton, R.K. 1957. 'Contributions to the Theory of Reference Group Behavior' [with A.S. Rossi], and 'Continuities in the Theory of Reference Groups and Social Structure', in *Social Theory and Social Structure* (revised and enlarged edition), pp. 225-386. Glencoe, Illinois: The Free Press.

Metz, J.J. 1991. 'A Reassessment of the Causes and Severity of Nepal's Environmental Crisis'. *World Development* 19 (7): 805-20.

Mikesell, S.L. 1993. 'The Paradoxical Support of Nepal's Left for Comrade Gonzalo.' *Himal* 6 (2): 31-3.

——. 1994. 'Follow-Up: Comrade Gonzalo, Are You Still With Us?'. *Himal* 7 (1): 7.

——. 1999. *Class, State, and Struggle in Nepal: Writings 1989-1995*. Delhi: Manohar.

'Mountaineer' (ed.). 1860. *A Summer Ramble in the Himalayas*. London: Hurst & Blackett. [Reprinted as: 'Wilson, W. ('Mountaineer') (ed.). 1993. Gurgaon: Vintage Books.]

Munda, R.D. and S.B. Mullick (eds.). 2003. *The Jharkhand Movement: Indigenous Peoples' Struggle for Autonomy in India.* IWGIA Document 108. Copenhagen: International Work Group for Indigenous Affairs.

Naqvi, K.H. 1975. 'Furore over Parmar's book on Polyandry'. *News INDIA* (Air India International Publication) July: 10.

Negi, V.S. 1990. 'Tehri: A Dammed Shame'. *Himal* (May) 3: 24-36.

Nickson, R.A. 1992. 'Democratisation and the Growth of Communism in Nepal: A Peruvian Scenario in the Making'. *Journal of Commonwealth and Comparative Politics* 30 (3): 358-86.

Nitzberg, N. 1970. 'Land, Labour and Status: The Social Implications of Ecologic Adaptation in a Region of the Western Himalayas of India'. Unpublished Ph.D. thesis, Harvard University.

Ogura, K. 2001. *Kathmandu Spring: The People's Movement of 1990.* Kathmandu: Himal Books.

——. 2004 'Realities and Images of Nepal's Maoists after the Attack on Beni'. *European Bulletin of Himalayan Research* 27: 67-125. (ILCAA workshop paper.)

——. 2007 'Maoists, People and the State as Seen from Rolpa and Rukum', in H. Ishii, D.N. Gellner, and K. Nawa (ed.), *Social Dynamics in Northern South Asia*, Vol. 2: *Political and Social Transformations in North India and Nepal*, pp. 435-75. Delhi: Manohar.

Onesto, L. 1999-2000. 'Dispatches: Report from the People's War in Nepal'. *Revolutionary Worker.* In 22 parts: 21 (11) (18 July 1999) to 21 (40) (20 Feb. 2000), Nos. 1014-43.

——. 2005. *Dispatches: A Report from the People's War in Nepal*. London: Pluto Press & Chicago: Insight Press.

Overseas Hindustan Times. 1975. 'Feminine Wrath over CM's Book'. *The Overseas Hindustan Times* (May) 22: 3.

Pande, B.D. 1995. 'An Open and Shut Case for Uttarakhand'. *Himal* (March/April) 8 (2): 23-4.

Pandey, B. 1995. 'Because It Is There: Foreign Money, Foreign Advice and Arun III'. *Himal* (July/August) 8 (4): 29-35.

Pandey, B.K. and J. Bell 1993. 'Look Before You Leap'. *Himal* (March/April) 6 (2): 38-9.

Pant, S.D. 1935. *The Social Economy of the Himalayans*. London: George Allen and Unwin.

Parmar, Y.S. 1975. *Polyandry in the Himalayas*. Delhi: Vikas Publishing House.

Pradhan, R. 2002. 'Ethnicity, Caste and a Pluralist Society', in K.M. Dixit and S. Ramachandaran (eds.), *State of Nepal*, pp. 1-21. Lalitpur, Nepal: Himal Books.

Prasoon, K. 1979. '*Hindus of the Himalayas* and the Degree Furor'. *Ravivar* [*Sunday*] 9-15 September (in Hindi).

Ramachandaran, S. 2002. 'Nepal as Seen in India', in K.M. Dixit and S. Ramachandaran (eds.), *State of Nepal*, pp. 287-310. Lalitpur: Himal Books.

Saberwal, S. (ed.). 1968. 'Academic Colonialism: A Symposium on the Influences which Destroy Intellectual Independence'. *Seminar* No. 112, December, Delhi.

Said, E.W. 1978. *Orientalism*. NY: Random House.

Sarin, V.I.K. 1980. *India's North-East in Flames*. Delhi: Vikas Publishing House.

Sharma, L.T. and R. Sharma (eds.). 1981. *Major Dams – A Second Look: Development Without Destruction*. Delhi: Gandhi Peace Foundation.

Shrestha, S. 1997. 'Nepali Cart before Horse'. *Himal South Asia* 10 (5): 14-16.

Skar, H.O. 1994. 'Mail: No Shining Path in Nepal'. *Himal* 7 (3): 6-7.

Srinivas, M.N. 1962. *Caste in Modern India and Other Essays*. Bombay: Asia Publishing House.

——. 1966. 'Sanskritization', in *Social Change in Modern India*, pp. 1-45. Berkeley: University of California Press.

Thapa, D. 2002. 'The Maobadi of Nepal', in K.M. Dixit and S. Ramachandaran (eds.), *State of Nepal*, pp. 77-99. Lalitpur: Himal Books.

Thapa, D. and B. Sijapati. 2003. *A Kingdom under Siege: Nepal's Maoist Insurgency, 1996-2003*. Kathmandu: The Printhouse.

Toynbee, A.J. 1947. (Abridged by D.C. Somervell.) *A Study of History*. NY: Oxford University Press.

Upadhyay, H.C. 1990. *Harijans of Himalaya: With Special Reference to the Harijans of Kumaun Hills*. Nainital: Gyanodaya Prakashan.

Vatuk, V.P. 1979. 'Book on Garhwalis Called Honest Account'. *India Abroad* (29 June): 6 (NY: India Abroad Publications).

Vedantam, S. 2004. 'Wrath Over a Hindu God: US Scholars Writings Draw Threats from Faithful'. *The Washington Post* (10 April): A-1 and A-6.

Venable, V. 1945. *Human Nature: The Marxian View*. NY: Knopf.

Wilson, W. (ed.). 1993. [See 'Mountaineer' (ed.) 1860.]

Wiser, W.H. 1936. *The Hindu Jajmani System*. Lucknow: Lucknow Publishing House.

Wissler, C. 1950 (1917). *The American Indian*. NY: Peter Smith.

Wolf, E.R. 1982. *Europe and the People without History.* Berkeley: University of California Press.

Woodruff, P. 1947. *The Wild Sweet Witch.* London: Jonathan Cape. [Republished as: Mason, P. 1989. Delhi & London: Penguin Books.]

Yamanaka, K. 2000. 'Nepalese Labour Migration to Japan: From Global Warriors to Global Workers'. *Ethnic and Racial Studies* 23 (1): 62-93.

Abbreviations

Np Nepali
Nw Newari (Nepal Bhasha)
[Diacritical marks are omitted for editorial reasons.]

AIMA: All India Mangar Association (Akhil Bharatiya Mangar Sangha)
BACS: British Army Children's School.
BFBS: British Forces Broadcasting System
BMA: Bhutan Magar Association (Bhutan Magar Sangha)
CBS: Central Bureau of Statistics (Nepal)
CNRS: Centre National de la Recherche Scientifique, France
CVICT: Centre for Victims of Torture, Nepal
CWIN: Child Workers In Nepal Concern Centre, an advocacy organization to defend the rights of children in Nepal
CZOP: National Coalition for Children as Zones of Peace
DHPP: Department of Housing and Physical Planning, HMG
DIC: Drop-In Centre
DSP: Deputy Superintendent of Police
FGD: Focus Group Discussion
FM: Field Marshall
GAESO: Gurkha Army Ex-servicemen's Organisation
GCES: Gurkha Children's English School
GCO: Gurkha Commissioned Officer
GM: Gurkha Major
GONESA: Good Neighbour Service Association, a non-governmental organization established in Pokhara.
GTZ: Deutsche Gesellschaft für Technische Zusammenarbeit (German Agency for Technical Cooperation)
HMG: His Majesty's Government of Nepal
ICIMOD: International Centre for Integrated Mountain Development
ICRC: the International Committee of the Red Cross
INSEC: Informal Sector Service Centre. A Kathmandu-based human rights NGO

KYC/PJK: Kirant Yakthung Chumlung/Punarjiwan Kendra (Kirant Limbu Association/Rehabilitation Centre)
LACC: Legal Aid and Consultancy Centre. A Nepali NGO which offers free legal assistance to women in order to eradicate violence.
LUMANTI: an NGO active in providing help to *sukumbasi* families in the Kathmandu Valley. [lit. 'memory' (Nw)]
MAF: Medical Association for Foreigners. Established in the 1990s in Hamamatsu, Japan
MAHK: Magar Association Hong Kong (Magar Sangha Hong Kong)
MLRM: the Ministry of Land Reform and Management
MNO: Mongol National Organization founded in 1989 in eastern Nepal as an ethnic political party
MP: the Member of Parliament
MTCA: Ministry of Tourism and Civil Aviation, HMG
NC: Nepali Congress party, the biggest parliamentary party in post 1990 Nepal
NCA: Nepal Chantyal Association (Nepal Chantyal Sangha)
NCBL: the Nepal Campaign to Ban Landmines
NEFEN: Nepali Federation of Nationalities (Nepal Janajati Mahasangh). Changed its name to the Nepal Federation of Indigenous Nationalities (Nepal Janajati Adivasi Mahasangh, NEFIN) in 2003.
NEFIN: *see* NEFEN
NMA: Nepal Magar Association (Nepal Magar Sangha)
NPC: National Planning Commission, HMG Nepal
OBC: Other Backward Classes, official Indian grouping of disadvantaged castes, considered less disadvantaged than Scheduled Castes or Scheduled Tribes
1RGR: The First Battalion the Royal Gurkha Rifles
PABSON: Private and Boarding Schools' Organisation of Nepal
PLA: the Maoists' People's Liberation Army
PSMC: Pokhara Sub-Metropolitan City
QGO: Queen's Gurkha Officer
RNA: the Royal Nepalese Army
RUPP: Rural-Urban Partnership Development, established in September 1997 as a joint effort of HMG and the UN (UNDP and UNCHS)
Saathi: A Nepali NGO working to eliminate injustice and violence against women and children in Nepal and providing support to victims. [lit. 'friend' (Np)]
SAIR: South Asia Intelligence Review
SC: Scheduled Caste
SCE: Service Children's Education
Seria SCS: Seria Service Children's School

SLC: School Leaving Certificate, taken after finishing the tenth grade, usually around the age of sixteen
ST: Scheduled Tribe
TPA: Tripartite Agreement
2RGR: The Second Battalion the Royal Gurkha Rifles
UML: The Communist Party of Nepal (Unified Marxist-Leninist): the main parliamentary opposition party in post-1990 Nepal
UNAIDS: The Joint United Nations Programme on HIV/AIDS
UNCHS: United Nations Centre for Human Settlements (Habitat)
UNDCP: United Nations International Drug Control Programme
UNDP: United Nations Development Programme
UNHCR: United Nations High Commissioner for Refugees
VDC: Village Development Committee, the new name for Village Panchayats in Nepal after 1992 (Nepal)
v.s.: Vikram Samvat (Vikram Era)
WOCAS: Women and Community Awareness Society, a government-registered organization which aims to carry out advocacy work on behalf of, and otherwise help, exploited women in Nepal.

Glossary

G	Gurung
Np	Nepali
Nw	Newari (Nepal Bhasha)
Y	Yolmo

[Diacritical marks are omitted for editorial reasons.]

anna: a sixteenth of a *ropani*, about 32 square metres or 10 Japanese *tsubo* (Np)
arbajo: a string instrument played by Gaines, larger than *sarangi* (Np)
bali: annual payment by a *bista* [lit. standing crops] (Np)
bandh: general strike (Np)
bigha: = 13 *ropani* (Np)
biha: marriage (= *vivaha*). A conjugal union wherein the wife does not lose her caste status (Np)
biha darta: matrimonial registration (Np)
bista: one who employs service castes by paying an annual share of the harvest of principal crops (Np)
bivahita: a 'married' woman. A wife who has been brought with full wedding rites (Np)
bhupu-lahure: ex-Gurkha solders [*bhupu* < *bhutpurva* = former] (Np)
chöti: a wooden altar cum cupboard (Y)
chyang: distilled alcohol, usually made from millet (Y) [Note that the word is widely used for non-distilled alcohol in Himalayan regions outside Yolmo]
dhami: a medium (Np)
dhikur: rotating credit association (Np, Thakali) [also *dhigur*]
dhukuti: rotating credit, association for rotating credit [from *dhuku* = storeroom] (Nw)
dukha/duhkha: suffering, trouble, hardship, pain (Np)
had nata: lit. 'kin who share a bone', a term for incest in west Nepal
hat: one half arm's length of road frontage [lit. 'hand'] (Np)
hukumbasi: one who pretends to be a *sukumbasi* in order to obtain a *lal purja* (Np)

jamindar: local land revenue collector (Np)
Janajati: new term, popularized after 1990 in Nepal, to refer to 'tribal' minority groups (Np)
jar: a seducer (Np)
jari: adultery, an elopement leading to a conjugal union (Np)
jarimana: compensation (Np)
jat: caste/ethnic group (Nepal)
jati: caste (India); caste/ethnic group, ethnic group (Nepal)
jyami: non-skilled labourer (Np, originally Nw)
kanyadan: the gift of a virgin (Np)
kattha: = 1/20 *bigha*. 1/30 hectare in mid-west Nepal Tarai (Np)
kutumba: affines (in western Nepal), relatives, kin (Np)
lahure: Gurkha soldier, emigrant worker; serving in foreign armies or working abroad [lit. 'of Lahore'] (Np)
lal purja: land register title or certificates [lit. red card] (Np)
lami: a marriage go-between (Np and Nw)
lyaita: a 'brought' woman; a wife who has been brought by consent and without an elaborate wedding ritual (Np)
majuri (*majduri*): labour cost or wages (Np)
mama: mother's brother (Np)
mukhiya: village headman in the Rana period (Np)
Muluki Ain: (1) 1854 legal code (2) 1963 civil law code of Nepal
paju: mother's brother (Nw)
pancha: ad hoc council in villages in western Nepal; its member(s) (Np)
parma: labour exchange arrangement (Np)
Pradhan Panch: village head in the period 1962-92 (Np)
raba: 'street-wise', competent (G)
rithi-thiti: group-specific traditions (Np)
ropani: 1 *ropani* of land = 0.0509 hectare (Np)
Saathi: A Nepali NGO working to eliminate injustice and violence against women and children in Nepal and providing support to victims. [lit. 'friend'] (Np)
sai: a former husband, a cuckold (Np)
sai: 'heart-mind' (G)
saman: dowry [lit. belongings, baggage] (Np)
sarangi: a string instrument (instrumento da arco) played by Gaines (Np)
sauta: co-wife (Np)
Seria SCS: Seria Service Children's School
shyalgar: a bottle of chyang with three small pieces of butter placed at its mouth, offered as a token of goodwill or respect (Y)
stridan: dowry (Np)
sukumbasi: squatter (Np)

swayambar: a ritual in which the bride formally 'chooses' her bridegroom by garlanding him (Np)
tika: red paste dot placed in the centre of one's forehead as a blessing (Np)
tipne: abduction (Np)
varna: the four Hindu classical 'castes' ("caste categories" in the terminology of Berreman, this volume)

Personal Name Index

Subject Index